The **Rough Guide** to

Rome

written and researched by

Martin Dunford

with additional contributions from
Judy Edelhoff and Katie Parla

www.roughguides.com

Contents

Roman architecture colour section following p.144

Cucina romana colour section following p.240

Roman Forum Colosseum **Colour maps** following p.352

◄◄ Piazza San Pietro ◄ Rome street life

Introduction to

Rome

Is it the most monumental city in the world? The most historic? It's certainly one of the most visual. Whatever you think about Rome, it's a city which inspires superlatives. And yet there's an unpretentiousness to it and its inhabitants that belies its historical significance, and definitely marks it out from its rivals further north. It's as if it doesn't have to try too hard, aware that it is the most fascinating city in Italy – which arguably makes it the most fascinating city in the world.

 Evenly placed between Italy's North and South, Rome is perhaps the ideal capital for a country only fully united in 1870 and possessing no shortage of rival cities. Once the seat of the most powerful empire in history, and still the home of the papacy within the Vatican city state, Rome is seen as a place somewhat apart from the rest of the country, spending money made elsewhere on the bloated government machine.

For the traveller, all of this is much less evident than the sheer weight of **history** that the city supports. An ancient place, packed with the relics of well over two thousand years of inhabitation, you could spend a month here and still only scratch the surface. Beginning with the city's celebrated classical features, most visibly the Colosseum, and the Forum and Palatine Hill, Rome boasts an almost uninterrupted sequence of spectacular monuments – from early Christian basilicas, Romanesque churches and Renaissance palaces, right up to the fountains and churches of the Baroque period, which perhaps more than any other era has determined the look of the city today. The modern epoch has left its mark too, with the ponderous Neoclassical architecture of the post-Unification period and the self-aggrandizing edifices of the Mussolini years. All these various eras crowd in on one another to an almost overwhelming degree: there are medieval churches atop ancient basilicas above Roman palaces; houses and apartment blocks incorporate fragments of eroded Roman columns, carvings and inscriptions; roads and piazzas follow the lines of ancient amphitheatres and stadiums.

So much to see, so little time

As you'll see from our "20 things not to miss" (p.10), you can't take in everything on a first visit to Rome. The best approach is to enjoy the city: take in the attractions that interest you most at an easy pace, and look forward to the next time you're here when you can see what you missed. The following itineraries, mainly designed around the key sights, give you an idea of what's possible in a day, but don't be afraid to skip the galleries and monuments and just wander – one of the city's greatest pleasures.

Three days
1. Galleria Doria Pamphilj; Pantheon; centro storico (lunch at *Maccheroni*; see p.241); Piazza Navona; Palazzo Altemps; Campo de' Fiori.
2. Vittoriano; Capitoline Museums; Jewish Ghetto (lunch at *Piperno*; see p.244); Forum; Palatine; Colosseum.
3. Vatican Museums; Borgo/Prati (lunch at *Dal Toscano*; see p.255); St Peter's; Castel Sant'Angelo.

Five days
As above plus...
4. Galleria Barberini; Trevi Fountain; Piazza di Spagna (lunch at *Babette*; see p.245); Piazza del Popolo; Via del Corso; Ara Pacis.
5. Monti; Santa Maria Maggiore, Palazzo Massimo (lunch at *Open Colonna*; see p.249); Via Veneto; Galleria Borghese; Villa Borghese; Villa Giulia.

Eight days
As above plus...
6. Villa Farnesina; Galleria Corsini; Trastevere (lunch at *Da Lucia*; see p.253); Janiculum Hill.
7. Aventine Hill; Baths of Caracalla; Testaccio (lunch at *Da Felice*; see p.252); Ostia Antica.
8. San Clemente; San Giovanni in Laterano (lunch at *Valentini*; see p.250); Aurelian Wall; Via Appia Antica.

▼ Piazza del Popolo

All of which means the capital is not an easy place to absorb on one visit, and you need to take things slowly, even if you have only a few days here. Part of the city's allure is stumbling across things by accident, gradually piecing together the whole, rather than marching around

◄ The Campidoglio

to a timetable on a predetermined route. In any case, it's hard to get anywhere very fast. Despite regular pledges to ban motor vehicles from the city centre, the congestion can be awful. On foot, it's easy to lose a sense of direction winding about in the twisting old streets, but you're so likely to come upon something interesting it hardly makes any difference.

Rome doesn't have the nightlife of, say, Paris or London, or even of its Italian counterparts to the north – culturally it's relatively provincial – and its food, while delicious, is earthy rather than refined. But its **atmosphere** is like no other city – a monumental, busy capital and yet an appealingly relaxed place, with a centre that has yet to be taken over by chain stores and multi-national hotels. Indeed, there has perhaps never been a better time to visit the city, whose once notorious infrastructure is looking and functioning better than it has done for some time. This process began with the feverish activity that took place in the last months of the twentieth century to have the city centre looking its best for the Church's millennium jubilee – work that has been continued since, as the authorities do their best to haul Rome

► The Vatican Museums

into the twenty-first century. Plus, the city's **cultural life** has been enhanced, with frequent open-air concerts in the city's monuments and the opening of prestige new buildings like Zaha Hadid's cutting-edge MAXXI. Transport, too, is being tackled, with the long-awaited construction of a third metro line.

Whether all this will alter the character of the city remains to be seen: the enhanced crowds of visitors, spurred on by the growth of cheap flights, are certainly making their presence felt; and there's a sense that Rome has at last joined Europe's mainstream. But for now at least, there's definitely no place like Rome.

Orientation

Rome's city centre is divided neatly into distinct blocks. The warren of streets that makes up the **centro storico** occupies the hook of land on the left bank of the River Tiber, bordered to the east by Via del Corso and to the north and south by water. From here Rome's central core spreads east: across Via del Corso to the major shopping streets and alleys around the Spanish Steps – the **Tridente** – down to the main artery of Via Nazionale; to the major

Ancient Rome

Everyone who visits Rome wants to see the sites of the **ancient city**, and these are easy enough to find – they literally litter the city centre. There is, however, one concentrated sector that could keep you busy for a couple of days on its own: the **Forum**, the heart of the city during the Republic, and the adjacent **Palatine Hill**, where the ultra-rich lived – and where the city was founded, as legend has it, by Romulus and Remus. These two areas are surrounded by the columns and plinths of other fora built during Imperial times that are under continuous excavation, as well as the iconic bulk of the **Colosseum**, and some recently opened Roman houses up on the **Celian Hill**. Just beyond, the **Baths of Caracalla** and **Domus Aurea** both give a perfect impression of the gargantuan building tendencies of the late Empire and its despots (though the Domus Aurea is closed at the moment), while back in the city centre the giant dome of the **Pantheon** demonstrates the ingenuity of its architects.

A short trip outside the city, the ruins of **Ostia**, Rome's former port, are also strikingly well preserved, indeed one of the best examples of an ancient Roman city that you'll find. And the **Via Appia Antica**, to the south, is crammed with ancient Roman sights. Once you have seen what's left of the monuments and buildings of the Romans, take some time to visit the city's amazing Classical museums – the two main branches of the **Museo Nazionale Romano**, the Palazzo Altemps and Palazzo Massimo, plus the **Capitoline Museums** and their branch at the Centrale Montemartini. Together they house the most awesomely complete collection of Roman sculpture, frescoes and other relics that you'll find anywhere – all unmissable.

Modern Rome

Strolling in central Rome you could be forgiven for thinking that nothing new had been built for at least a century. But there are modern aspects of the city that are well worth searching out. Probably the most spectacular is the Mussolini-era EUR quarter on the southern edge of the city, where broad boulevards cut a rectangular grid between hulking white marble buildings designed to glorify the Roman legacy while at the same time looking to the future in an uncompromisingly modern way. It's a great example of the period, and has aged relatively well. More recently, the northern edge of the city centre, Flaminio, has become a focal point for development, home not only to Renzo Piano's multi-venue Auditorium, but also to the Zaha Hadid-designed MAXXI or Museum of Twenty-First Century Art, which opened in 2010 (see below). However, perhaps the best-known and most controversial new piece of architecture in Rome is Richard Meier's structure to house the Ara Pacis, which provides a suitably airy backdrop for the Augustan-period altar, as well as adding a welcome dose of modernism to the ancient centre; that said, the current mayor, Gianni Alemanno, claims it looks like a pizzeria and would like to pull it down.

sites of the **ancient city** to the south; and to the huge expanse of the **Villa Borghese** park to the north. The left bank of the river is distanced from the main hum of this part of the city, home to the **Vatican** and Saint Peter's, and, to the south, **Trastevere** – even in ancient times a distinct entity from the city proper and the focus of a good part of the city centre's nightlife.

To see most of this, you'd be mad to risk your blood pressure in any kind of vehicle – really the best way to get around the city centre is to walk. The same goes for the ancient sites, and the Vatican and Trastevere, too – although you might want to jump on a bus to cross the river. Keep public transport for the longer hops, down to **Testaccio**, **EUR** or the **catacombs** and, of course, for trips out of the city – to the excavations at **Ostia** and **Tivoli**, or one of the nearby **beaches**.

When to go

Visiting Rome at any **time of year** is a pleasure, though some months are better than others. If you can, you should avoid visiting in July and August, when the weather is hot and sticky, and those Romans who don't make their living exclusively from the tourist industry have left town;

Alfresco dining at Dar Filettaro a Santa Barbara

many businesses are closed, and in those places that are open most of the patrons will be fellow tourists. The weather is more comfortable in May, June and September, when most days will be warm but not unbearably so, and less humid, though you'll still find the city busy; April, outside Easter, and October, are quieter and the weather can still be clement – making this in many ways the ideal time to come. The winter months can be pleasant, with many of the city's more popular sights relatively uncrowded: you may have some rain but the temperatures are usually mild. Whenever you visit, you'd be well advised to book your accommodation in advance.

What to wear is almost as important as when to come. Sturdy, comfortable shoes are essential – you're going to be doing a lot of walking – and, if you're here during the summer, you should wear loose, cool clothes, and a sunhat. Bear in mind that some sights – the catacombs, even some churches – can be unlit and cold, even when it's warm outside, so dress in layers; and bear in mind also that even on the hottest days you are required to cover up to enter many churches.

Average monthly temperatures and rainfall

	Jan	Feb	Mar	Apr	May	Jun	Jul	Aug	Sep	Oct	Nov	Dec
Temperature												
max/min (°C)	12/3	13/4	15/5	18/8	23/11	23/15	30/17	30/18	27/15	22/11	16/7	13/4
max/min (°F)	53/37	55/38	59/41	65/46	73/52	81/58	87/63	87/64	80/59	71/51	61/44	55/39
Rainfall												
mm	103	98	68	65	48	34	23	33	68	94	130	111

things not to miss

*It's not possible to see everything that Rome has to offer in one trip –
and we don't suggest you try. What follows, in no particular order,
is a selective taste of the city's highlights, from outstanding museums
and ancient sites to Roman food and football. They're arranged in five
colour-coded categories to help you find the very best things to see, do,
eat and experience. All highlights have a page reference to take you
straight into the guide, where you can find out more.*

01 Ara Pacis Page **99** • Open again in a smart new purpose-built structure, this
ancient hunk of stone from the Augustan era gives us perhaps the greatest glimpse of
the Roman Imperial family.

02 Museo Nazionale Romano Pages **55** & **124** • Palazzo Altemps and Palazzo Massimo, the two main sites of the Museo Nazionale Romano, hold some of the city's finest ancient finds, such as these remarkably well preserved frescoes from the House of Livia.

03 Trevi Fountain Page **100** • Squeezed into the narrow streets of the city centre, this is Rome's flashiest and largest fountain – especially impressive if you stumble upon it by accident.

04 Football Page **290** • Roma-Lazio derbies at the Stadio Olimpico are extreme, passionate affairs: not to be missed if you're lucky enough to be here at the right time, and can get hold of a ticket.

05 San Clemente Page **131** •
The epitome of Rome – an ancient temple under an ancient basilica topped by an ancient church.

07 Capitoline Museums
Page **72** • Two amazing museums in one, situated at the heart of the ancient Roman Republic – one displaying Roman sculpture, the other Roman sculpture and Italian paintings.

06 Trastevere Page **154** •
Wandering through the cobbled streets and tiny piazzas of Trastevere is what a visit to Rome is all about.

08 Campo de' Fiori Page **61** •
The morning market here is one of Rome's oldest, while in the evening the square's bars and restaurants form one of the city centre's main nightlife hubs.

09 **Ostia Antica** Page **208** • This wonderfully preserved ancient site is within easy reach of Rome, and makes a fascinating day out.

10 **Villa Borghese** Page **164** • The city centre's largest open space has plenty to occupy you – a couple of superb galleries, a zoo and a boating lake – but also lots of quiet spaces to snooze if you just need to chill out.

11 **St Peter's** Page **184** • Set in one of Rome's most impressive squares, St. Peter's is not the most beautiful church you'll ever visit, but it overwhelms with its grandeur and significance.

12 **Pizza** Page **237** • There's nothing quite like Roman pizza – thin, crispy and utterly delicious.

13 **The Forum** Page **81** • The heart of the ancient world is almost unrecognizable now, but is no less evocative for that.

14 Piazza Navona Page **50** • If Rome has a centre, this is probably it. Strolling through the square and watching the world go by is the quintessential Roman experience.

15 Galleria Borghese Page **166** • A fantastic array of Bernini sculptures together with a fine collection of Renaissance paintings, in a beautifully restored seventeenth-century villa.

16 Keats-Shelley House Page **94** • An artist's garret that was occupied by Keats when he died, and which has been lovingly preserved as a shrine to the poet and his Romantic chums.

17 The Pantheon Page **45** • By far the most intact of Rome's – perhaps the world's – ancient Roman monuments.

18 Vatican Museums Page **189** • Highlights of this giant complex include the stunning Raphael Rooms and Michelangelo's magnificent Sistine Chapel.

20 Colosseum Page **89** • The most photographed of Rome's monuments, and deservedly so. The completeness and ingenuity of this forerunner of all arenas mean it doesn't disappoint.

19 Ice cream Page **239** • The best way to finish off an evening out in rome.

Basics

Basics

Getting there

The easiest way to get to Rome **from the UK and Ireland** is to fly, and the lowest-priced air tickets are generally cheaper than those for the long train or bus journey. **From the US and Canada** there are direct flights to Rome, although you could also consider flying via London or another European gateway and picking up a cheap onward flight from there. There are no direct flights to Italy **from Australia, New Zealand** or **South Africa**, but plenty of airlines fly to Rome via Asian or European cities, again including London.

There's no great need to take a **package tour** to Rome these days; it's easy to find flights online, and most websites offering cheap flights give plenty of hotel and other options too. Nonetheless, a plethora of operators sell short-break deals to Rome, including specialists offering small-group tours focusing on art, gastronomy or archeological sights (see p.22).

Flights from the UK and Ireland

There are plenty of flights from the **UK** and **Ireland** to Rome. Of the scheduled airlines, British Airways and Alitalia between them fly several times a day from London. Of the low-cost carriers, easyJet fly from London, Bristol and Newcastle; Ryanair fly from London, Dublin, East Midlands and Glasgow; bmibaby operate one flight a week from Edinburgh; Aer Lingus has daily nonstop flights from Dublin to Rome; while Alitalia covers the same route three to five times a week depending on the season. It is possible to find deals from Ireland if you book early, but prices are usually significantly higher and unless you're in a hurry it can sometimes make more sense to pick up an inexpensive flight to London or Birmingham and get a connecting flight from there. Alternatively, you could fly nonstop from Ireland to Brussels with Ryanair, who operate a cheap service from Brussels to Rome.

Fares depend more than ever on how far in advance you book, the time of year, and nowadays what days of the week you want to travel (and indeed what time of day). Travelling between June and August, when the weather is best, will cost more than in the depths of winter (excluding Christmas and New Year). As always the cheapest tickets come with restrictions: any changes incur additional fees, and tickets are rarely valid for longer than a month. Book far enough in advance with one of the low-cost airlines and you can pick up a ticket for under £100 return plus taxes, even in summer; book anything less than three weeks in advance and this could as much as triple. Scheduled airline fares, booked within a month of travel, will cost £100–160 during winter, spring and autumn, and £250–300 in summer.

Flights from the US and Canada

Alitalia fly the widest choice of direct routes between the **US** and Rome, with daily flights from New York, Newark, Chicago, Boston and Miami; Delta fly from New York and Atlanta nonstop. Flights from Chicago and LA have stopovers usually in New York or Atlanta. US Airways fly nonstop from Philadelphia and Charlotte; Continental fly from Newark and Miami; United fly nonstop from Washington/Dulles. In addition, many European carriers fly to Italy (via their capitals) from all major US and Canadian cities – for example British Airways (via London), Lufthansa (via Frankfurt), KLM (via Amsterdam), and so on.

The nonstop **scheduled fares** charged by each airline don't vary as much as you might think, and you'll often be basing your choice around flight timings, routes and gateway cities, ticket restrictions, and even the airline's reputation for comfort and service. It's a long flight, around nine hours from

New York, Boston and the eastern Canadian cities, twelve hours from Chicago, and fifteen hours from Los Angeles, so it's as well to be fairly comfortable and arrive at a reasonably sociable hour. The cheapest round-trip **fares** to Rome, travelling midweek in low season, start at around US$600 from New York or Boston, rising to US$750–1000 in spring and fall and US$1000–1200 during the summer. Add another US$100–200 for flights from LA, Miami and Chicago. Note that these prices do not include taxes.

Air Canada operate nonstop flights **from Toronto and Montréal** to Rome during the summer, and usually fly via Frankfurt during the rest of the year; fares are around Can$600 in low season, and around Can$1000 in summer, not including taxes.

Flights from Australia, New Zealand and South Africa

There are no nonstop flights to Italy **from Australia**. Round-trip fares to Rome from the main cities go for Aus$1500–1850 in low season, and around Aus$2000 in high season. You are likely to get most flexibility by travelling with Alitalia, Malaysian, Thai, British Airways or Qantas, which offer a range of discounted Italian tour packages and air passes, although you can sometimes find cheaper offers with Garuda and SriLankan Airlines. Round-trip fares to Rome **from New Zealand** cost from around NZ$2000 during low season to around NZ$3000 in high season. Of the national carriers, Air New Zealand flies in conjunction with KLM and Alitalia, with stops in Japan and Amsterdam; Alitalia with other carriers from Auckland via Sydney and Bangkok/ Singapore; British Airways from Auckland via Singapore/Bangkok or LA; Qantas from Auckland, Christchurch or Wellington via Sydney or Melbourne; JAL from Auckland (with an inclusive overnight stop in Tokyo/ Osaka); Malaysia and Thai from Auckland via Kuala Lumpur and Bangkok respectively. Finally, there are no direct flights **from South Africa** to Rome, and most flights make one European stop using one of the big carriers – Lufthansa, KLM, Olympic and South African Airways all offer decent deals. Reckon on paying around ZAR7000 return from Johannesburg, around ZAR8000 from Cape Town.

Trains

Travelling **by train** to Rome won't save much money, but it can be an enjoyable and leisurely (as well as environmentally friendly)

Four steps to a better kind of travel

At Rough Guides we are passionately committed to travel. We feel strongly that only through travelling do we truly come to understand the world we live in and the people we share it with – plus tourism has brought a great deal of **benefit** to developing economies around the world over the last few decades. But the extraordinary growth in tourism has also damaged some places irreparably, and of course **climate change** is exacerbated by most forms of transport, especially flying. This means that now more than ever it's important to **travel thoughtfully** and **responsibly**, with respect for the cultures you're visiting – not only to derive the most benefit from your trip but also to preserve the best bits of the planet for everyone to enjoy. At Rough Guides we feel there are four main areas in which you can make a difference:

• Travel with a purpose, not just to tick off experiences. Consider **spending longer** in a place, and getting to know it and its people.
• Give thought to how often you **fly**. Try to avoid short hops by air and more harmful night flights.
• Consider **alternatives to flying**, travelling instead by bus, train, boat and even by bike or on foot where possible.
• Make your trips "**climate neutral**" via a reputable carbon offset scheme. All Rough Guide flights are offset, and every year we donate money to a variety of charities devoted to combating the effects of climate change.

way of getting there, and you can stop off in other parts of Europe on the way. The choice of routes and fares is complex, but most trains from the UK pass through Paris and head down through France to northern Italy and then on to Rome. Advance booking is essential (and can often save you quite a lot of money; there are discounts for under-26s and special offers are common). Using slower trains won't cut the cost very significantly and neither will the cross-Channel ferry route, which is now barely used and accordingly badly timetabled. If you travel via Paris on Eurostar you will have to change stations, which means lugging your bags on the metro from the Gare du Nord to the Gare de Lyon.

The journey takes around 21 hours and the best way to do it is to leave London on the lunchtime Eurostar train, which arrives in Paris later that afternoon, and then leave Paris on the early evening train, travelling overnight to Rome. A return **fare** from London to Rome can be found for a total of £120–180 for the two legs (London–Paris from £60 return, Paris–Rome for £60–120 return). If you want to travel in style, take the **Palatino sleeper** from Paris to Rome, which costs £120–230 return depending on whether you travel in a six-berth couchette or a two-berth sleeper. The train has a decently priced restaurant car and is a wonderfully comfortable way to travel to Rome. If you want to dramatically increase the level of comfort, consider taking the **Orient Express**, which departs from London, stopping briefly in Paris. The train arrives in grand style the following day in Venice. In 2010 a few Venice–Rome trips were added; otherwise you can take the Eurostar Italian express service directly to Rome.

Details on all international rail tickets and passes are best obtained by calling personally at major train stations or by contacting the agents listed on p.22. Don't expect much help from travel agents on planning routes, however, or the Italian State Railways office to answer the phone. A good place to start looking, if you fancy the idea of getting to Paris in time for dinner before taking the evening sleeper to Rome, is the excellent ⓦ www.seat61.com.

Buses

It's difficult to see why anyone would want to travel to Rome by **bus** from the UK, unless they had a phobia of flying – and of trains. National Express Eurolines (see p.22) do, however, have occasional bargain offers, and regular tickets are in any case cheap – £69 to Rome if booked a week in advance, £98 for a fully refundable and flexible ticket. The service departs four times a week and takes around 30 hours.

Airlines, agents and operators

Airlines

Aer Lingus ⓦ www.aerlingus.com.
Air Canada ⓦ www.aircanada.com.
Air New Zealand ⓦ www.airnz.co.nz.
Alitalia ⓦ www.alitalia.com.
British Airways ⓦ www.ba.com.
bmibaby ⓦ www.bmibaby.com.
Continental Airlines ⓦ www.continental.com.
Delta ⓦ www.delta.com.
easyJet ⓦ www.easyjet.com.
Garuda Indonesia ⓦ www.garuda-indonesia .com.
JAL (Japan Airlines) ⓦ www.jal.com.
KLM (Royal Dutch Airlines) ⓦ www.klm.com.
Lufthansa ⓦ www.lufthansa.com.
Malaysia Airlines ⓦ www.malaysiaairlines.com.
Olympic Air ⓦ www.olympicair.com.
Qantas Airways ⓦ www.qantas.com.
Ryanair ⓦ www.ryanair.com.
South African Airways ⓦ www.flysaa.com.
SriLankan Airlines ⓦ www.srilankan.lk.
Thai Airways ⓦ www.thaiair.com.
United Airlines ⓦ www.united.com.
US Airways ⓦ www.usairways.com.

Travel agents

North South Travel UK ☏ 01245/608 291, ⓦ www .northsouthtravel.co.uk. Friendly, competitive travel agency, offering discounted fares worldwide. Profits are used to support projects in the developing world, especially the promotion of sustainable tourism.
STA Travel UK ☏ 0871/2300 040, US ☏ 1-800/781-4040, Australia ☏ 134 782, New Zealand ☏ 0800/474 400, South Africa ☏ 0861/781 781; ⓦ www.statravel.co.uk. Worldwide specialists in independent travel; also student IDs, travel insurance, car rental, rail passes, and more. Good discounts for students and under-26s.

Trailfinders UK ☎0845/058 5858, Ireland ☎01/677 7888, Australia ☎1300/780 212; ⓦwww.trailfinders.com. One of the best-informed and most efficient agents for independent travellers.
Travel CUTS Canada ☎1-866/246-9762, US ☎1-800/592-2887; ⓦwww.travelcuts.com. Canadian youth and student travel firm.
USIT Ireland ☎01/602 1906, Northern Ireland ☎028/9032 7111; ⓦwww.usit.ie. Ireland's main student and youth travel specialists.

Tour operators

There's no shortage of operators organizing **packages** to Rome, many of which offer specialist tours. For an ordinary city break, you can reckon on spending £600–800 for two staying for three nights in a 3–4-star hotel between April and October, including flights, though special offers can sometimes cut prices drastically, especially for late bookings. Specialist tours with guest lecturers tend to cost around £1500 for a week. Travelling **from the US**, you can expect to pay from around US$1500 for a week in a three-star hotel, which may not include flights, although tours limited to Rome can be hard to find – most take in Tuscany, or focus on the three cities of Rome, Florence and Venice.

UK

ACE Study Tours ☎01223/835 055, ⓦwww.acestudytours.co.uk.
Citalia ☎0870/909 7555, ⓦwww.citalia.co.uk.
Martin Randall Travel ☎020/8742 3355, ⓦwww.martinrandall.com.

US

Abercrombie & Kent ☎1-800/323-7308 or 630/954-2944, ⓦwww.abercrombiekent.com.
Central Holidays ☎1-800/935-5000, ⓦwww.centralholidays.com.
Cross Culture ☎1-800/491-1148 or 413/256-6303, ⓦwww.crosscultureinc.com.
Europe Through the Back Door ☎425/771-8303, ⓦwww.ricksteves.com.

Australia and New Zealand

Abercrombie and Kent Australia ☎03/9536 1800 or 1300/851 800, New Zealand ☎0800/441 638; ⓦwww.abercrombiekent.com.au.
CIT Australia ☎02/9267 1255, ⓦwww.cittravel.com.au.
Explore Holidays Australia ☎02/9857 6200 or 1300/731 000, ⓦwww.exploreholidays.com.au.

Rail contacts

European Rail UK ☎020/7619 1083, ⓦwww.europeanrail.com.
Eurostar UK ☎0843/218 6186, ⓦwww.eurostar.com.
Rail Europe UK ☎0844/848 4064, US ☎1-888/382-7245, Canada ☎1-800/361-7245, Australia ☎03/9642 8644, New Zealand 0937/7 5415; ⓦwww.raileurope.co.uk.
Venice Simplon Orient Express ⓦwww.orient-express.com.

Bus contacts

Eurolines UK ☎0871/781 8181, ⓦwww.eurolines.com.

Arrival

Reaching the centre of Rome is pretty straightforward for air and rail travellers. You'll most likely end up at **Termini** station – very close to the top attractions and the bulk of accommodation. If you take a **taxi** or **bus to the centre**, remember that Rome's notorious traffic can add significantly to your journey time (though not your fare as rates from the airport are fixed).

By air

Rome has two **airports**: Leonardo da Vinci, better known as Fiumicino, which handles the majority of scheduled flights, and Ciampino, where you may arrive if you're travelling with one of the low-cost airlines or on a charter flight.

Fiumicino airport

Fiumicino, or FCO (ⓦwww.adr.it; enquiries ⓣ06.65951) is Rome's largest airport, about 30km southwest of the city centre, near the coast. There are four terminals, T1, T2, T3 and the brand-new T4, and although they are all pretty close to each other it pays to know which one you are going to. The airport is connected to the centre of Rome by a direct train, the **Leonardo Express**, which takes thirty minutes to get to Termini and costs €11 from a *tabacchi* (or €12 from the official ticket office); services begin at 6.36am and then leave half-hourly until 11.36pm. Alternatively, there are slower trains every 15 minutes to Ostiense and Tiburtina stations, each on the edge of the city centre; tickets cost €5.50. Both stations are stops on Rome's metro (€1; see box, p.27), or you can catch city bus #175 from Ostiense, or #492 or #649 from Tiburtina, to the centre of town (again €1). **Trains to Fiumicino** leave Termini at 22 and 52 minutes past each hour; be aware that it is quite a schlep from the main part of the station to platform 25, where the train leaves from, and that taxis do stop close by if that's how you're getting to the station.

Two **buses** go from the airport to Termini. COTRAL have 7–8 services a day from 1.15am to 3.30pm (7pm at weekends) to Termini's Piazza dei Cinquecento (€4.50; ⓦwww.cotralspa.it), while SIT bus services run every half-hour from 7am to 11.45pm to Via Marsala (€8; ⓦwww.sitbusshuttle.it). Both take 40 minutes.

Taxis from Fiumicino to the city centre cost a flat-rate (*tariffa fissa*) €40 for up to four people and the journey time to the city centre is about 30 minutes.

Ciampino airport

The city's second airport, **Ciampino**, or CIA (ⓣ06.65951, ⓦwww.adr.it) is also pretty close to the city, only 15km southeast, but it's much smaller than Fiumicino and there are still no direct rail connections between the airport and city centre. Terravision (ⓦwww.terravision.eu) and SIT bus (ⓦwww.sitbusshuttle.it) run shuttle services to Termini, which leave roughly every 30 minutes and cost €8 return. They pull up on Via Marsala, right by the station (journey time around 45min). Otherwise ATRAL buses (ⓦwww.atral-lazio.com) run to Via Giolitti, on the south side of Termini, every 50 minutes to 1 hour (€1.50). If you don't want to get off at Termini, and are staying near a metro stop on the A line (near the Spanish Steps or Via Veneto areas, for example), you could take an ATRAL bus (€1.20) from the airport to Anagnina metro station at the end of metro line A, and take a metro from there to your destination (20min; €1).

Taxis cost a flat €30 and the journey time to the city centre is 30–40 minutes. However, be warned that many drivers don't like taking people into the city centre from Ciampino, especially for this fixed rate, and it can sometimes be hard to persuade someone to take you; stand your ground if no one seems to want to put their hand up, and don't pay more than €30 plus tip.

By train

Travelling by **train** from most places in Italy, or indeed Europe, you arrive at the central **Termini station**, the meeting point of the two metro lines and many bus routes. There are **left-luggage** facilities here, by platform 1 and platform 24 (both open daily 7am–11.30pm; €4 per piece for the first 5hr, then 60c per hr). Among other train stations in Rome, **Tiburtina** is a stop for some north–south intercity trains, and certain parts of Lazio and elsewhere, as are Trastevere, San Pietro, Ostiense and Tuscolana; if you're

Train enquiries

For general enquiries contact Trenitalia (ⓦwww.trenitalia.it, ☎06.892.021). For enquiries about schedules and prices, call ☎1478.88.088 (daily 7am–9pm). There are train information offices at Termini on the first concourse (daily 7am–9pm) and on the left side of the second concourse (daily 6am–midnight).

staying near any of these and travelling out of town it's always worth checking if you can pick up a train there and avoid Termini altogether. Selected routes **around Lazio** are also handled by Termini's Regionali platforms (near the Fiumicino platform, a further 5min walk beyond the end of the regular platforms); the Roma-Nord line station on Piazzale Flaminio runs to Viterbo and stations in between; and the Roma Lido/Porta San Paolo station next to Piramide Metro station serves stations down to Ostia Lido (including Ostia Antica).

By bus

Arriving by **bus** can leave you in any one of a number of places around the city. The main station for buses from outside the Rome region is **Tiburtina**, also the city's second railway station. Others include Ponte Mammolo (trains from Tivoli and Subiaco); Lepanto (Cerveteri, Civitavecchia, Bracciano area); EUR Fermi (Nettuno, Anzio, southern Lazio coast); Anagnina (Castelli Romani); Saxa Rubra (Viterbo and around). All of these stations are on a metro line, except Saxa Rubra, which is on the Roma-Nord line and connected by trains every fifteen minutes with the station at Piazzale Flaminio, on metro line A.

By car

Coming into the city **by car** can be quite confusing and isn't really advisable unless you're used to driving in Italy and know where you are going to park (see p.30). If you are on the A1 highway coming from the north take the exit "Roma Nord"; from the south, follow the exit "Roma Est". Both lead you to the Grande Raccordo Anulare (GRA), which circles the city and is connected with all of the major arteries into the city centre – the Via Cassia from the north, Via Salaria from the northeast, Via Tiburtina or Via Nomentana from the east, Via Appia Nuova and the Pontina from the south, Via Prenestina and Via Casilina or Via Cristoforo Colombo from the southeast, and Via Aurelia from the northwest.

From **Ciampino**, either follow Via Appia Nuova into the centre or join the GRA at junction 23 and follow the signs to the centre. From **Fiumicino**, just follow the A12 motorway into the city centre; it crosses the river just north of EUR, from where it's a short drive north up Via Cristoforo Colombo to the city walls and, beyond, to the Baths of Caracalla.

Getting around

As in most Italian cities, the best way to get around Rome is to **walk** – you'll see more and will better appreciate the city. Rome wasn't built for motor traffic, and it shows in the congestion, the pollution, and the bad tempers of its drivers. However, it's a big city and has good public transport on the whole – a largely efficient blend of buses, a few trams and a two-line metro – which you'll almost certainly need to use at some point if you want to see anything outside the immediate centre.

By bus, tram and metro

ATAC (*Agenzia del trasporto autoferrotranviario del Comune di Roma*) runs the city's bus, tram and metro service and on the whole is pretty efficient; it has an enquiries line (Mon–Sat 8am–8pm; ☎06.57.003) and its website (☻www.atac.roma.it) has plenty of information in English and an excellent route planner. There's also a sporadically open information booth in front of Termini on Piazza dei Cinquecento as well as basic transport information displayed outside, though while the works on metro line C are going on you may struggle to find much on-the-ground help around here.

Buses and trams

The city's **bus and tram** service is on the whole pretty good – cheap, reliable and as quick as the clogged streets of the city centre allow. Remember to board through the rear doors and punch your ticket as you enter. There is a also a small network of electric minibuses that negotiate the narrow backstreets of the old centre.

Around midnight a network of **nightbuses** clicks into service, accessing most parts of the city up to about 5am; it's worth keeping spare tickets handy as it can be difficult to buy one in the early hours. Nightbuses are easily identified by the letter N above the "bus notturno" schedule. For useful tram and bus **routes**, see the box on pp.28–29.

Metros

Rome's **metro** runs from 5.30am to 11.30pm daily, except on Saturdays, when it closes at 12.30am. The metro consists of two lines – A (red) and B (blue) – and they're working on line C, which should be finished

Tickets and passes

Flat-fare **tickets** cost €1 each and are good for any number of bus or tram rides and one metro ride within 75 minutes of validating them. You need to punch your ticket before you ride on the metro and as you get on a bus or tram; otherwise you can be fined. Tickets are available from tobacconists, or *tabacchi*, newsstands, some coffee bars, and ticket machines located in all metro stations and at major bus stops. You can also get a **day pass** (BIG), valid on all city transport until midnight of the day purchased, for €4, a **three-day pass** (BTI) for €11, or a **seven-day pass** (CIS) for €16. A **monthly pass** costs €30, and must be bought by the fifth day of each calendar month. Public transport is free with the Roma Pass (see p.40). BIRG tickets (**regional transport passes**) for COTRAL and ATAC services are well worth buying if you are going out of Rome for the day; see box, p.30. Finally, it's worth knowing that there are hefty spot fines of up to €100 for **fare-dodging**, and pleading a foreigner's ignorance will get you nowhere.

by 2012. It's mainly focused on ferrying commuters out to the suburbs, rather than transporting tourists around the city centre, but it can be useful for getting across the centre quickly: Termini is the hub of both lines, and useful stations include ones at the Colosseum, Piazza Barberini, Piazza del Popolo (the stop is called Flaminio), Piazza di Spagna and Ottaviano (for the Vatican).

The system also incorporates the major **overground trains** that head out to the suburbs – the Roma-Lido line, which connects the city to Ostia, and the Roma-Laziale and Roma-Nord lines, which run respectively east and north of the city centre.

Taxis

The easiest way to get a **taxi** is to find the nearest taxi stand (*fermata dei taxi*) – central ones are listed below. Alternatively, you can call a taxi (☏06.3570, 06.4994, 06.4157, 06.6645, 06.88177 or 06.5551), but these usually cost more, as the meter starts ticking the moment the taxi is dispatched to collect you. Meters start at €2.80 (€4 on Sundays and €5.80 between 10pm and 7am), plus a charge of about €1 per item of luggage; the meter clicks up at the rate of €1 or so every kilometre. A journey from one side of the city centre to the other should cost around €10, or around €15 on Sunday or at night. Pick-ups from Termini station incur a supplement of €2. Most taxis are white, and all carry a rate card in English giving the current tariff, and the extra charges for luggage, late-night, Sundays and holidays, and airport journeys.

The most centrally located **taxi ranks** are at Corso Rinascimento (Piazza Navona); Largo Argentina; Piazza Barberini; Piazza Belli (Trastevere); Piazza dei Cinquecento (Termini); Piazza del Popolo; Piazza San Silvestro; Piazza di Spagna; Piazza Venezia and Via Veneto (Porta Pinciana).

By bike and scooter

Renting a **bike, moped or scooter** can be a more efficient way of nipping around Rome's clogged streets than driving, and there are plenty of places offering this facility, although you'll need to have a full driving licence. Rates are around €3–4 an hour/€10 a day for bikes, and about €30 a day for mopeds, €40–50 a day for scooters. Some of the more central rental places are listed below; see also p.148 for renting bikes on the Via Appia Antica.

There's also a **bike-sharing** programme, Roma-Bike, where you pick up and drop off bicycles at around 20 designated points around the centre; purchase a prepaid card at metro stops Termini, Spagna, Ottaviano or any of the end-of-the-line stops for €10 – €5 for the card, and €5 to get you started; after that it costs €0.50 an hour (☏06.57003, ⊛www.atacbikesharing.com).

Barberini Via della Purificazione 84 ☏06.488.5485. Rents bicycles, mopeds and scooters. Bikes cost €10 per day, mopeds and scooters from €40.

Bici e Baci Via del Viminale 5 ☏06.482.8443. Bicycles for €4 an hour, €11 a day; scooters from €40. Daily 8am–7pm.

Useful transport routes

Buses

#23 Piazzale Clodio–Piazza Risorgimento–Ponte Vittorio Emanuele–Ponte Garibaldi–Via Marmorata–Piazzale Ostiense–Centrale Montemartini–Basilica di S. Paolo.

#30 Express (Mon–Sat only) Piazzale Clodio–Piazza Mazzini–Piazza Cavour–Corso Rinascimento–Largo Argentina–Piazza Venezia–Luntotevere Aventino–Via Marmorata–Piramide–Via C. Colombo–EUR.

#40 Express Termini–Via Nazionale–Piazza Venezia–Largo Argentina–Piazza Pia.

#60 Express Via Nomentana–Porta Pia–Via XX Settembre–Piazza della Repubblica–Via Nazionale–Piazza Venezia–Imperial Forums–Colosseum–Circus Maximus–Piramide.

#62 Piazza Bologna–Via Nomentana–Porta Pia–Piazza Barberini–Piazza San Silvestro–Via del Corso–Piazza Venezia–Corso V. Emanuele–Borgo Angelico–Piazza Pia.

#64 Termini–Piazza della Repubblica–Via Nazionale–Piazza Venezia–Largo Argentina–Corso V. Emanuele–Stazione S. Pietro.

#75 Via Poerio (Monteverde)–Via Induno–Porta Portese–Testaccio–Piramide–Circus Maximus–Colosseum–Via Cavour–Termini–Piazza Indipendenza.

#175 Termini–Piazza Barberini–Via del Corso–Piazza Venezia–Colosseum–Circus Maximus–Aventine–Stazione Ostiense.

#271 S. Paolo–Via Ostiense–Piramide–Viale Aventino–Circus Maximus–Colosseum–Piazza Venezia–Ponte Sisto–Castel Sant'Angelo–Via Vitelleschi–Piazza Risorgimento–Ottaviano–Foro Italico.

#492 Stazione Tiburtina–Piazzale Verano–Termini–Piazza Barberini–Via del Corso–Piazza Venezia–Largo Argentina–Corso del Rinascimento–Piazza Cavour–Piazza Risorgimento–Cipro (Vatican Museums).

#590 Same route as metro line A but with access for disabled; runs every 90 minutes.

#660 Largo Colli Albani–Via Appia Nuova–Via Appia Antica.

#714 Termini–Santa Maria Maggiore–Via Merulana–San Giovanni in Laterano–Terme di Caracalla–EUR.

#910 Termini–Piazza della Repubblica–Via Pinciana (Villa Borghese)–Piazza Euclide–Palazzetto dello Sport–Piazza Mancini.

Minibuses

These **small buses** negotiate ciricular routes through the narrow streets of Rome's centre.

#116 Porta Pinciana–Via Veneto–Via del Tritone–Piazza di Spagna–Piazza San Silvestro–Corso Rinascimento–Campo de' Fiori–Piazza Farnese–Lungotevere Sangallo–Terminal Gianicolo.

#117 San Giovanni in Laterano–Piazza Celimontana–Via dei Due Macelli–Via del Babuino–Piazza del Popolo–Via del Corso–Piazza Venezia–Via Nazionale–Via dei Serpenti–Colosseum–Via Labicana.

#119 Piazza del Popolo–Via del Corso–Piazza Venezia–Largo Argentina–Via del Tritone–Piazza Barberini–Via Veneto–Porta Pinciana–Piazza Barberini–Piazza di Spagna–Via del Babuino–Piazza del Popolo.

Trams

#2 Piazzale Flaminio–Via Flaminia–Viale Tiziano–MAXXI–Piazza Mancini.

#3 Stazione Trastevere–Via Marmorata–Piramide–Circus Maximus–Colosseum–San Giovanni–San Lorenzo–Via Nomentana–Parioli–Viale Belle Arti.

#8 Casaletto–Stazione Trastevere–Piazza Mastai–Viale Trastevere–Largo
Argentina.

#14 Termini–Piazza Vittorio Emanuele–Porta Maggiore–Via Prenestina (Pigneto).

#19 Porta Maggiore–San Lorenzo–Piazzale Verano–Viale Regina Margherita–Viale
Belle Arti–Via Flaminia–Ottaviano–Piazza Risorgimento.

Nightbuses

#N1 Same route as metro line A.

#N2 Same route as metro line B.

#N7 Piazzale Clodio–Piazzale Flaminio–Piazza Cavour–Largo Argentina–Piazza
Venezia–Via Nazionale–Termini.

#N8 Viale Trastevere–Piazza Venezia–Via Nazionale–Termini.

#N10 Piazzale Ostiense–Lungotevere De' Cenci–Via Crescenzio–Viale Belle
Arte–Viale Regina Margherita–Via Labicana.

Tourist buses

Three main **tourist buses** circle Rome and its major sights. They're in competition
with each other, but you can get combined tickets for two of them. See the box on
p.39 for more information on tours.

Bus #110 ☎800.281.281, ⓦwww.trambusopen.com. Good for general orientation
and a quick glance at the sights, this ATAC-run open-top bus has a guided
commentary. It leaves from Piazza dei Cinquecento outside Termini station and
stops at all the major sights, including Piazza di Spagna, Castel Sant'Angelo and the
Vatican. The whole round trip takes two hours, and in summer departures are every
twenty minutes from 8.30am until 8.30pm daily, including holidays and Sundays.
Tickets cost €20 and allow you to get on wherever you like and hop on and off
throughout the day. Combined tickets for the #110 and Archeobus (see below) cost
€30 and are valid for 48 hours. Tickets can be bought on board, before you get on
at Piazza del Cinquecento, or online (where there's a five percent discount). If you
have a Roma Pass (see p.40) discounts are higher.

Archeobus ☎800.281.281, ⓦwww.trambusopen.com. The Archeobus is another
hop-on-hop-off service that links some of the most compelling ancient sights, and
is much the best way of seeing some of the monuments on and around Via Appia
Antica. It starts at Piazza dei Cinquecento outside Termini, and heads down to the
southern edge of the city via Piazza Venezia, Piazza Bocca della Verità, Circo
Massimo, Terme di Caracalla and the Porta San Sebastiano. On Via Appia, there
are stops at Domine Quo Vadis, the catacombs of San Callisto and San Sebastiano, Cecilia Metella, Circus of Maxentius and the Villa dei Quintili. Buses run daily
every half-hour between 8.30am and 4.30pm. Tickets cost €15, and integrated
tickets are available, including the #110 bus and various museums, with different
lengths of validity. They can be bought on board, at Piazza dei Cinquecento, or
online (five percent discount).

Roma Cristiana ☎06.6989.6334, ⓦwww.josp.com. The Vatican's tourist bus
service with commentary links Rome's major basilicas and other Christian sights,
starting in front of Termini on Piazza dei Cinquecento, and also at St Peter's.
Services run daily every thirty minutes between 8.40am and 7pm, and tickets cost
€17 for 24 hours (€28 for 3 days); they can be bought on board, at Piazza dei
Cinquecento or at the PIT kiosks on Piazza Pio XII, next to St Peter's Square, and
San Giovanni in Laterano.

Travel around Lazio

The Lazio transport system is divided into six zones, which spread concentrically out from the city. If you're considering travelling outside Rome it's possible to buy season tickets – either by the day or week – to travel within them. The **BIRG** (Biglietto Integrato Regionale Giornaliero) is valid all day for unlimited travel on the state railway, COTRAL buses and the Rome metro, but not trains to the airport. Prices range from €2.50 to €10.50, depending on the zone. A €7 ticket, covering four zones, for example, ferries you between Rome and Viterbo. You can also buy three-day tourist tickets (BTR), which cost between €6.50 and €28.50 depending on the number of zones, and weekly passes – the **CIRS** (Carta Integrata Regionale Settimanale) – which cost from €9 to €41. Vendors – train and bus ticket offices, newspaper stands and tobacconists – can advise you on the required zone, or see ⓦ www.atac.roma.it.

Collalti Via del Pellegrino 80a–82 ☎ 06.6880.1084. Bike rental and repairs by the hour or day. Bikes cost €3.50 per hour, €12 per day, €16 from Sat–Mon. Mon–Sat 9am–7pm; closed 1–3.30pm.

Cyclo Via Cavour 80 ☎ 06.481.5669. Bikes from €12 a day, mopeds from €37, scooters from €47. Daily 9am–7pm.

Treno e Scooter Rent Piazza dei Cinquecento, Termini ☎ 06.4890.5823, ⓦ www.trenoescooter .com. On the right as you come out of the station. Bikes for hire for €4 an hour/€10 a day, mopeds/ scooters for €7–18 an hour and €34–70 a day. Daily 7am–7pm.

By car

Driving in central Rome can be a nightmare, and is something to be avoided at all costs. In any case much of the centro storico is within the ZTL (*zona di traffico limitato*), in which traffic is restricted during the day; if you're driving to a hotel in the centre, check if they are in the ZTL and if they can get you permission to enter. Only residents are allowed to **park** for free in central Rome, so you will always need to pay. You can park on the street for around €1.20 an hour (8am–8pm), and there are plentiful pay-and-display parking meters. There are garages in Villa Borghese (around €1.70/hr) in front of Termini station (€1.55/hr), at Terminal Gianicolo (€1.50/hr), which is a short walk to the Vatican, and next to each of the terminal metro stations, from where it's easy to get into the city centre.

In the event of a **breakdown**, call ☎ 116, or consult the Yellow Pages (Pagine Gialle) under "Autoriparazioni" for specialized repair shops.

If you are **renting a car**, all the usual suspects have desks at Fiumicino, Ciampino, Termini and elsewhere in the city, including the area on and around Via Veneto; the major operators are below.

Avis ⓦ www.avis.com.
Europcar ⓦ www.europcar.com.
Hertz ⓦ www.hertz.com.
Maggiore ⓦ www.maggiore.it.
Sixt ⓦ www.sixt.com.

Travel essentials

Crime and personal safety

Rome is a pretty safe city by any standards, but particularly when compared to its counterparts in the US and UK. The main thing is to make sure you're not too obvious a target for petty criminals by taking some common-sense **precautions**. Most of the crime you're likely to come across will be bag-snatching, where gangs of either street kids or *scippatori* or "snatchers" operate; *scippatori* work on foot or on scooters, disappearing before you've had time to react; the kids are more likely to crowd you in a group, trying to work their way into your bags or pockets while you're trying to shoo them away. As well as handbags, they whip wallets, tear off visible jewellery and, if they're really adroit, unstrap watches. You can minimize the risk of this happening by being discreet: don't flash anything of value, keep a firm hand on your camera, and carry shoulderbags, as Italian women do, slung across your body. It's also worth being vigilant when withdrawing money from ATMs. Be aware of anyone standing too close or trying to distract you – they may be trying to read your PIN or clone your card using a "skimmer" machine. Contact your bank or credit card provider immediately if you suspect you're a victim of card fraud.

There are not really any parts of town you should avoid, and although some of the areas around **Termini** can be a bit rough, the neighbourhood is changing and in any case it's more seedy than dangerous. Deserted stretches around **Ostiense** or **Testaccio** are probably worth avoiding at night, but again this is just to be on the safe side rather than because of any track record of violent crime in these areas.

If the worst happens, you may be forced to have some dealings with the **police**. In Italy this is principally divided between the Vigili Urbani, mainly concerned with directing traffic and issuing parking fines; the Polizia Statale, the main crime-fighting force; and the Carabinieri, with their military-style uniforms and white shoulder belts, who also deal with general crime, public order and drug control. The Polizia enjoy a fierce rivalry with the Carabinieri and are the ones you'll perhaps have most chance of coming into contact with, since thefts should be reported to them. Rome's main *questura* or police station is at Via San Vitale 15, off Via Nazionale (☎06.46861).

Note that all foreigners in Italy are required by law to carry **ID** with them at all times, so it's worth making a photocopy of your passport or other ID just in case.

Electricity

The supply is 220V, though anything requiring 240V will work. Most plugs have three round pins, though you'll find the older two-pin plug in some places: an adapter is very useful.

Entry requirements

British, Irish and other EU citizens can enter Italy and stay as long as they like on production of a valid **passport**. Citizens of the United States, Canada, Australia and New Zealand need only a valid passport, too, but are limited to stays of three months. South Africans require a schengen visa, which entitles you to travel through many of the countries in the Eurozone. All other nationals should consult the relevant embassy about **visa requirements**. Legally, you're required to register with the police within three days

Visiting Roman churches

Rome is very used to tourists, but the rules for visiting churches are much as they are all over Italy. **Dress modestly**, which usually means no shorts (not even Bermuda-length ones) and covered shoulders, and trying to avoid wandering around during a service.

Emergencies

For help in an emergency, call one of the following national telephone numbers:

Police or any emergency service, including ambulance (Soccorso Pubblico di Emergenza) ☎113.
Carabinieri ☎112.
Ambulance (Ambulanza) ☎118.
Fire (Vigili del Fuoco) ☎115.
Road assistance (Soccorso Stradale) ☎116.

of entering Italy, though if you're staying at a hotel this will be done for you.

Foreign embassies in Rome

Australia Via Bosio 5 ☎06.852.721.
Britain Via XX Settembre 80a ☎06.4220.0001.
Canada Via G.B. de Rossi 30 ☎06.445.981.
Ireland Piazza Campitelli 3 ☎06.697.9121.
New Zealand Via Zara 28 ☎06.441.7171.
US Via Veneto 119a ☎06.46.741.

Festivals and public holidays

Rome puts on a decent array of **festivals and events** throughout the year; see the calendar below. On **public holidays** (denoted by **PH** below), many sights and shops are closed, as well as some bars and restaurants.

Jan 1 New Year's Day. **PH**
Jan 6 Epiphany (La Befana; see box, p.298). **PH**
Mid-Feb Carnevale. For ten days Roman kids dress up and are paraded round the city by their proud parents, and clubs put on themed nights. Look out for the carnival delicacies sold throughout the city: *frappe* (deep-fried pastry strips) and *castagnole* (bite-sized pastries).
Mid-March Rome Marathon; see p.291.
Easter During Holy Week, Catholics from across the world descend on Rome to witness the pope's address. On Good Friday, a solemn procession makes its way from the Colosseum to the Capitoline Hill, while on Easter Sunday the main event is the pope's blessing in St Peter's Square.
Pasquetta (Easter Monday) Many Romans head out of town, traditionally for a picnic in the countryside. **PH**
April Settimana della Cultura (@www.beniculturali .it). For one week in April, you can enter all state-owned museums free of charge.
April Festa della Primavera. In late April, the Spanish Steps are lined with thousands of beautiful blooms.

April 21 Natale di Roma. A spectacular fireworks display set off from the Campidoglio marks Rome's birthday.
April 25 Liberation Day. **PH**
May 1 Labour Day. "Primo Maggio" is celebrated with a free rock concert in Piazza San Giovanni. **PH**
Late May Dissonanze (see box, p.264).
Late May to June Festival delle Letterature (Literature festival; see box, p.271).
Late May Piazza di Siena (@www.piazzadisiena .com). This swanky show-jumping event takes place in Villa Borghese.
June 2 Day of the Republic. The day is marked with a military parade along Via dei Fori Imperiali, and the gardens of the Quirinale Palace are open to the public (expect long queues). **PH**
June–Sept Estate Romana (see box, p.264).
June–Sept Villa Celimontana (see box, p.264).
June–Oct Concerti del Tempietto (@www .tempietto.org). Classical concerts with dramatic backdrops: the ancient Roman Teatro di Marcello and the Art Nouveau Casina delle Civette.
Mid-June to mid-Aug Roma Incontra il Mondo (@www.villaada.org). An eclectic programme of pop, rock and indie concerts takes place in Rome's largest park, Villa Ada. Tickets €8–22.
Mid-June to mid-Sept Fiesta (see box, p.264).
Late June to mid-Aug Teatro dell'Opera (@www .operaroma.it). The prestigious Teatro dell'Opera's summer season takes place in the spectacularly floodlit setting of the Baths of Caracalla.
Mid-July Festa di Noantri. Two weeks of street performances and events in Trastevere culminate in a huge fireworks display.
Aug 1 Festa delle Catene. The chains of St Peter are displayed during a special mass in the church of San Pietro in Vincoli.
Aug 5 Festa della Madonna della Neve. The miracle of a summer snowfall (see p.119) is remembered in the Basilica of Santa Maria Maggiore with a shower of white petals on the congregation.
Aug 15 Ferragosto. On the Feast of the Assumption, Rome empties as locals in search of cooling breezes head for the sea and mountains. **PH**

Late Sept to Dec RomaEuropa Festival (see box, p.271).

Mid-Oct Rome International Film Festival (see box, p.271).

Nov 1 Ognissanti. On All Souls' Day, Romans visit family graves in the Verano cemetery in San Lorenzo. **PH**

Nov Rome Jazz Festival (see p.264).

Dec 8 Immacolata Concezione. In honour of the Immaculate Conception of the Blessed Virgin Mary, a religious ceremony takes place in the Piazza di Spagna, often attended by the pope. **PH**

Dec 25 Christmas (Natale). **PH**

Dec 26 Boxing Day (Santo Stefano). **PH**

Health

As a member of the European Union, Italy has free reciprocal **health** agreements with other member states. EU citizens are entitled to free treatment within Italy's public health-care system on production of a **European Health Insurance Card** (EHIC), which you can obtain by picking up a form at the post office, calling ☏0845 606 2030, or applying online at ⓦwww.dh.gov.uk. Allow up to 21 days for delivery. The EHIC is free of charge and is valid for at least three years, and it basically entitles you to the same treatment as an insured person in Italy. The Australian Medicare system also has a reciprocal healthcare arrangement with Italy.

Vaccinations are not required, and Rome doesn't present any more health worries than anywhere else in Europe; the worst that's likely to happen to you is suffering from the extreme heat in summer or an upset stomach. The **water** that you'll see flowing from public fountains all over town is perfectly safe to drink, though look out for *acqua non potabile* signs, indicating that the water is unsafe to drink. It's worth taking insect repellent, too, as the countryside around Rome is rather prone to mosquitoes.

Staff in **pharmacies** (*farmacia*) are well qualified to give you advice on minor ailments and to dispense prescriptions. Central pharmacies open 24 hour include: Farmacia della Stazione at Piazza dei Cinquecento 49 (☏06.488.0019), Internazionale at Piazza Barberini 49 (☏06.6880.3278) and Piram at Via Nazionale 228 (☏06.488.0754).

If you need treatment, go to a **doctor** (*medico*); try AlphaMed at Via Zanardelli 36 (☏06.6830.9493; Mon–Fri 9am–8pm), a central medical practice with English-speaking doctors, or Tobias Wallbrecher at Via Domenico Silveri 30 (☏06.638.0569; Mon–Fri 9am–1pm & 3–6pm), an English-speaking family doctor close to the Vatican. If you need to see a **dentist**, try English-speaking Absolute Dentistry at Via G. Pisanelli 1–3 (☏06.3600.3837 or 339.250.7016), which has a 24-hour emergency service.

If you are seriously ill or involved in an accident, go straight to the **Pronto Soccorso** (casualty) of the nearest **hospital**, or phone ☏113 and ask for *ospedale* or *ambulanza*. The most central hospitals are Fatebenefratelli on the Isola Tiberina (☏06.683.7299), San Giovanni at Via A. Aradam 8 (☏06.49.971) and Santo Spirito, near the Vatican at Lungotevere in Sassia 1 (☏06.68.351).

Insurance

Even though EU healthcare privileges apply in Italy, you'd do well to take out an **insurance policy** before travelling to cover against theft, loss, illness or injury. A typical policy usually provides cover for the loss of

Rough Guides travel insurance

Rough Guides has teamed up with WorldNomads.com to offer great **travel insurance** deals. Policies are available to residents of over 150 countries, with cover for a wide range of **adventure sports**, 24-hour emergency assistance, high levels of medical and evacuation cover and a stream of **travel safety information**. Roughguides.com users can take advantage of their policies online 24/7, from anywhere in the world – even if you're already travelling. And since plans often change when you're on the road, you can extend your policy and even claim online. Roughguides.com users who buy travel insurance with WorldNomads.com can also leave a positive footprint and donate to a community development project. For more information go to ⓦ**www.roughguides.com/shop**.

baggage, tickets and – up to a certain limit – cash or cheques, as well as cancellation or curtailment of your journey. Most policies exclude so-called **dangerous sports** unless an extra premium is paid: in Italy this can mean scuba-diving, windsurfing and trekking. Many policies can be chopped and changed to exclude coverage you don't need – for example, sickness and accident benefits can often be excluded or included at will. If you do take medical coverage, ascertain whether benefits will be paid as treatment proceeds or only after your return home, and whether there is a 24-hour medical emergency number. When securing baggage cover, make sure that the per-article limit – typically under £500 – will cover your most valuable possession. If you need to make a claim, you should keep receipts for medicines and medical treatment, and in the event you have anything stolen, you must obtain an official statement from the police (see p.31).

Internet

Internet cafés are not as ubiquitous as they once were but you should never be stuck for a place to get online (reckon on paying around €3 an hour). Note that by law, internet cafés are required to check your ID, so be sure to carry this with you. There are also lots of wi-fi hotspots around the city centre, including many of the main piazzas; see ⓦwww.romawireless.com for details.
Bibli Via dei Fienaroli 28. Mon 5.30pm–midnight, Tues–Sun 11am–midnight.
Casa del Tazza d'Oro Via dei Pastini 4. Daily 10am–8pm.
Exto Café Piazza Firenze 25. Mon–Fri 8.30am–8.30pm, Sat & Sun 8.30am–6pm.
Museo del Corso Via del Corso 320. Tues–Sun 10am–8pm.
Yex Piazza Sant'Andrea delle Valle 1. Mon–Fri 10am–11pm, Sat 10am–8pm, Sun noon–8pm.

Laundries

You can usually get your **laundry** done in your hotel if you're staying at anywhere but the cheapest places but if you can't a laundry (*lavanderia*) is probably just a short walk from the hotel. Try self-service Onda Blu (Ⓣ 800.861.346, ⓦwww.ondablu.com) at Via Principe Amedeo 70 near Termini and

branches all over town; or Wash and Dry (Ⓣ800.231.172, ⓦwww.washedry.it), at Via Della Pelliccia 35 and Via della Chiesa Nuova 15/16 (both daily 8am–10pm). All offer a wash including soap and tumble-drying for around €10 for a 6kg (15lb) load.

Lost property

For property lost on a train call ⓉI06.4730.6682 (daily 7am–11pm); on a bus ⓉI06.581.6040 (Mon & Fri 8.30am–1pm, Tues–Thurs 2.30–6pm); on the metro ⓉI06.487.4309.

Mail

General information on Italian postal services is available on ⓉI803.160 or at ⓦwww.poste.it. Rome's main **post office** (*ufficio postale*), on Piazza San Silvestro, is open Monday to Saturday 8am to 7pm; other post offices can be found at Via Arenula 4, Via della Scrofa 61 and Corso V. Emanuele II 330. **Hours** vary, but tend to be Monday to Friday 8.30am to 2pm, Saturday 8.30am to 1pm.

Stamps (*francobolli*) are sold in *tabacchi* too, as well as in some gift shops; they will often also weigh your letter. The Italian postal system is one of the slowest in Europe, and if your letter is urgent make sure you send it "posta prioritaria", which has varying rates according to weight and destination. If you don't want to trust the Italian post at all, in Rome at least you have a choice: the Vatican postal system is quicker, loses less, and you get the benefit of an exotic postmark. However, not unreasonably, you have to use Vatican stamps and post your items from the Vatican itself. For this there are post offices and boxes in Piazza San Pietro and in the Vatican Museums.

Maps

For **walking around the city** you should find the maps in this book more than adequate for your needs. If you require something more detailed, then the best choice (though we would say this) is *Rome: The Rough Guide Map*, which is waterproof, rip-proof and includes the locations of most of the recommendations in this book. Another option is the 1:12,500 *TCI* map (€7), which includes more coverage of the outskirts and

Rome online

Ⓦ **www.comune.roma.it** The Italian-language website of the Rome's city council has some information in English, and is particularly useful if you're spending longer in the city.

Ⓦ **www.enjoyrome.com** Site of the helpful tourist organization, with information on accommodation and tours.

Ⓦ **www.eternallycool.net** Almost too cool for its own good, but certainly a useful mix of all that's hip and happening in the city.

Ⓦ **www.inromenow.com** Always up-to-date and very wide-ranging guide to the city.

Ⓦ **www.rome.angloinfo.com** Good current information directed at expats and English-speakers living in the city.

Ⓦ **www.romefile.com** Lots of information for both English-speaking visitors and expats.

Ⓦ **www.romeguide.it** Site of the "Il Sogno" cooperative, which aims to place young people in tourist industry jobs in Rome. A useful resource on sights and good for up-to-date information on concerts and events too.

suburban neighbourhoods. For **public transport**, metro maps are posted up in every station, and we've included one at the end of this book. If you're going to use the system a lot, especially the buses, it may be worth investing in the excellent and detailed *Lozzi* transport map (€6), available from most newsstands and bookshops.

Media

The city has three daily free (Italian-language) **newspapers** – *City*, *Metro* and the newer and slightly more highbrow *EPolis*, available in bars and cafés, and from street bins, all over town. All have weather reports, what's on info and useful phone numbers. If you want to get into things in a bit more depth, or to practise your Italian, you might want to dip into one of the Italian dailies – though be advised that however good your Italian is, most of the country's national newspapers offer a pretty turgid read. Of the big nationals, the posh paper is the right-of-centre *Corriere della Sera*, to which *La Repubblica* is the left-of-centre alternative – both have Rome news supplements daily. The Rome papers are the popular *Il Messaggero*, the right-leaning *Il Tempo*, and the Vatican daily *L'Osservatore Romano*, which also prints an English edition once a week. You'll notice that the sports coverage in all these papers is relatively thin. If you want in-depth football reporting you need to try one of three national sports dailies – either

the pink *Gazzetta dello Sport*, the Rome-based *Corriere dello Sport*, or *Tuttosport*.

If all you want is **what's on information**, the city's best source of listings is the weekly *Romac'è* (€1; out Wed), which has information on tours, clubs, restaurants, services and weekly events, and a decent website (Ⓦwww.romace.it). The twice-monthly English expat magazine, *Wanted in Rome* (€0.75) – Ⓦwww.wantedinrome.com – is also a useful source of information, especially if you're looking for an apartment or work. Both are available at central newsstands. For those with a bit of Italian, the daily arts pages of *Il Messaggero* list movies, plays and major musical events, and *La Repubblica* includes the "Trova Roma" supplement, another handy guide to current offerings, in its Thursday edition.

Finally, **English-language newspapers** are available the same day of publication, usually

Lost or stolen credit cards and travellers' cheques

Credit cards
American Express ☏01273.696.933.
Mastercard ☏800.870.866.
Visa ☏800.819.014.

Travellers' cheques
American Express ☏01273.571.600.
Visa ☏800.874.155.

B

BASICS | Travel essentials

after lunch, at newsstands all over town. *The International Herald Tribune*, available at most newsstands, is printed in Italy and includes an Italian news supplement.

Money

Italy's currency is the **euro** (€), split into 100 cents. There are seven euro **notes** – in denominations of 500, 200, 100, 50, 20, 10, and 5 euros, each a different colour and size – and eight different **coin** denominations, with 2 and 1 euros, then 50, 20, 10, 5, 2, and 1 cents. For the latest rates check Ⓦ www.oanda.com or www.xe.com.

If you're travelling from the UK it's a good idea to have some euros on you when you arrive; otherwise to get euros just use your **debit or credit card** in the local ATM machines (*Bancomats*); there's usually a charge but you won't spend more getting money this way than any other. As you might expect, credit cards are widely accepted in hotels and most shops, though some of the smaller restaurants are cash-only, so check first. Visitors from elsewhere, or on longer stays, may prefer to use **travellers' cheques**. American Express and the Thomas Cook and Visa alternatives are widely accepted. Buying online in advance usually works out cheapest. It's advisable to buy euro travellers' cheques rather than dollars or pounds sterling since you won't have to pay commission when you cash them.

Banking hours are normally Monday to Friday mornings from 8.30am until 1.30pm, and for an hour in the afternoon (usually between 2.30 & 4pm). Outside banking hours, the larger hotels will change money or travellers' cheques, or there are plenty of **exchange bureaux** – normally open evenings and weekends. Try American Express at Piazza di Spagna 38 (Ⓣ 06.67641; Mon–Fri 9am–5.30pm, Sat 9am–12.30pm) or Travelex at Piazza Barberini 21a (Mon–Sat 9am–8pm, Sun 9.30am–5pm) and Via della Conciliazione 23 (Mon–Sat 8.30am–7.30pm, Sun 9.30am–5pm). Post offices will exchange American Express travellers' cheques and cash commission-free. The last resort should be any of the many *Ufficio Cambio* kiosks, almost always offering the worst rates (despite "no commission" signs).

Opening hours

The city's **opening hours** are becoming more flexible, but much of Rome still follows a traditional Italian routine. Most shops and businesses in Italy open Monday to Saturday from around 8am until 1pm, and from about 4pm until 7 or 8pm, although many shops close on Saturday afternoons and Monday mornings; a few of the more international businesses follow a nine-to-five schedule. Traditionally, everything except bars and restaurants closes on Sunday, though there's usually a *pasticceria* (pastry shop) open in the mornings and in general Sunday opening is becoming more common.

Most **museums and galleries** are closed on Mondays. Opening hours for state-run museums are generally 9am to 7pm,

---

Rome's special churches

In the course of visiting and reading about Rome you may come across the concept of the city's four **patriarchal basilicas**: St Peter's, San Giovanni in Laterano, San Paolo fuori le Mura and Santa Maria Maggiore. These are the four most important churches in Rome, and therefore of the Catholic Church, and they symbolically represent the various parts of the world where the Catholic faith has reached. Apart from Santa Maria Maggiore, each one is technically part of the Vatican state (ie not Italian territory), and each has a Holy Door that is only opened – by the pope – every 25 years. San Giovanni in Laterano used to be the home of the pope and the Vatican, and is still technically the cathedral of Rome. Over the centuries pilgrims have always made a point of visiting these churches, plus the three other so-called **"pilgrimage" churches** – San Lorenzo fuori le Mura (occasionally included as a patriarchal basilica), Santa Croce in Gerusalemme and San Sebastiano fuori le Mura. It's a tradition that continues to this day, though Christian visitor numbers are these days swelled several-fold by tourists and other visitors.

Chiuso per restauro

Although the situation is much better than it used to be in Rome, you may find buildings of all kinds **closed for restoration** (*chiuso per restauro*), and it's usually pretty uncertain when they might reopen. The most notable casualty at the time of writing was the Domus Aurea, but openings change all the time, so ask at one of the tourist information kiosk for an update. If there's something you really want to see and you don't know when you might be back in Rome, it might be worth trying to persuade a workman or priest/curator to show you around.

Tuesday to Saturday, and 9am to 1pm on Sunday. Most other museums roughly follow this pattern, too, although they are more likely to close for a couple of hours in the afternoon, and have shorter opening hours in winter. Many large museums also run late-night openings in summer (till 10pm or later Tues–Sat, or 8pm on Sun). The opening times of **ancient sites** are more flexible: most sites open every day, often including Sunday, from 9am until late evening – frequently specified as one hour before sunset, and thus changing according to the time of year.

Most major **churches** open in the early morning, at around 7 or 8am, and close around noon or 1pm, opening up again at 4pm and closing at 6 or 7pm; hours may be shorter during the winter months. At any time of year some of the less-visited churches will open only for early-morning and evening services, and some are closed at all times except Sundays and on religious holidays; if you're determined to take a look, you may have to ask around for the key, or make an appointment with the custodian.

For the opening hours of **banks**, see "Money", opposite; for **post offices**, see "Mail" on p.34.

The other factors to be aware of are **public holidays** (see p.32) and the fact that in **August**, particularly during the weeks either side of Ferragosto (Aug 15), most of Rome flees to the coast, many shops, bars and restaurants close and the only people around are other tourists.

Phones

You can use your **mobile phone** – or *telefonino* – in Italy, and indeed you will hardly see an Italian without his or her mobile clasped to the ear. You are likely to be charged extra for incoming calls when abroad. If you want to retrieve messages while you're away, you might have to ask your provider for a new access code. For further information about using your phone abroad contact your network or check out ⓦ www.telecomsadvice.org.uk.

Public telephones, run by Telecom Italia, come in various forms, but they usually have clear instructions in English. Coin-operated

International calls

Calling home from Italy
Australia + 61 + city code.
Ireland + 353 + city code.
New Zealand + 64 + city code.
UK and Northern Ireland + 44 + city code.
US and Canada + 1 + area code.
South Africa + 27 + city code.

Calling Italy from abroad
To call Italy **from abroad**, dial the access code ☏ 00 from the UK, Ireland and New Zealand, ☏ 011 from the US and Canada, ☏ 0011 from Australia, followed by 39, then the area code **including the first zero** and finally the subscriber number.

machines are increasingly hard to find and you will probably have to buy a **telephone card** (*carta* or *scheda telefonica*), available from *tabacchi* and newsstands in denominations of €5 and €10. You always need to dial 06, the code for Rome, regardless of whether you are in the city.

All **telephone numbers** listed in this guide include the Rome code. Numbers beginning 800 are free, ☎170 will get you through to an English-speaking operator, ☎176 to international directory enquiries. Any numbers that start with the number 3 will be a mobile phone and consequently more expensive to call. Italian **phone tariffs** are expensive, especially if you're calling long-distance or internationally, and even Rome residents use **phone calling cards** if they're calling long-distance. You can buy these easily from *tabacchi* for upwards of €5. Common cards include the Columbus for calls to Western Europe and North America, the standard Scheda Telefonica Internazionale for the rest of the world, and the Europa Card for calls to Europe, the US and Canada only. To use one of these cards, you dial a central number and then enter a pin code given on the reverse of the card, before dialling the number you want to reach. Finally, you can make international reversed charge or collect calls (*chiamata con addebito destinatario*) by dialling ☎170 and following the recorded instructions.

Smoking

Smoking is banned in all public indoor spaces in Italy, including restaurants, bars and clubs. Some establishments have separate smoking rooms, though this is rare.

Study and libraries

The **American Academy** is at Via Angelo Masina 5, 00153 Rome (☎06.58.461, ⓦwww.aarome.org); the **British School at Rome** is at Via Gramsci 61, 00197 Rome (☎06.326.4939, ⓦwww.bsr.ac.uk).

The best **library** is the one at the American church of **Santa Susanna**, Via XX Settembre 14 (☎06.482.7510), which costs around €18 a year, and also has a good notice board for finding work, accommodation and so on (Tues 10am–1pm, Wed 3–6pm, Fri 1–4pm, Sat &

Sun 10am–12.30pm). Reference libraries include those of the **American Studies Center**, Via M. Caetani 32 (☎06.6880.1613) and the British School at Rome (see above; Mon–Thurs 9am–1pm & 2–6.30pm, Fri 9am–1pm & 2–5pm), although it can be hard to get access unless you're a scholar. The **British Council**, Via delle Quattro Fontane 20 (Mon–Tues & Thurs–Fri 10am–1pm, Wed 2–5pm; closed Aug & Christmas; ☎06.478.141), has a small video library.

Time

Rome is one hour ahead of GMT, six hours ahead of Eastern Standard Time, and nine hours ahead of Pacific Standard Time.

Toilets

Caught short? There are public lavatories on Piazza Zanardelli, just north of Piazza Navona, and on Piazza di Spagna, but these are something of a rarity in Rome. The only others, apart from the facilities in *McDonalds*, which are always worth trying if you're desperate, or in the lobbies of five-star hotels, are on Via Fori Imperiali, near the entrance to the Forum, in St Peter's Square, just to the left of the entrance to the basilica, in Piazza Vittorio Emanuele, and in Termini station and some city-centre metro stations.

Tourist information

There are official tourist information **booths** at Fiumicino in Terminal 2 (daily 9am–6.30pm) and in the Arrivals hall at Ciampino Airport (same hours), but no other main office in the city centre or at Termini. Instead there are green **information kiosks**, or PIT (daily 9am–6pm) in key locations around the city centre (see below) that are useful for free maps, directions (the staff usually speak English) and details about nearby sights – though they can be pretty clueless if you have anything other than an obvious need. The Rome tourist office website ⓦwww.turismoroma.it can help make up some of the slack, and has plenty of information in English. The council-run tourist information line ☎06.0608 is open daily 9am–9pm (calls charged at local rates), and the website ⓦwww.060608.it is another useful resource. You could also try the

Tours

A number of companies run organized trips around the city centre, though these are for the most part quite pricey; for general orientation and a glance at the main sights, the ATAC-run #110 Open bus (see p.29) is better value. The following offer the best of the more in-depth tours:

Context Travel Via Baccina 40 ⊕06.9762.5204. Context do excellent small-group walking tours of sights and neighbourhoods, led by engaging experts, and with subjects ranging from architecture to just a traditional Roman lunch with someone who knows their food; and of course they do all the major sights too. Tours from €55 per person.

Enjoy Rome see below. Walking tours of the city given by native English speakers in groups of no more than 25 people. Standard three-hour tours of places such as the Vatican, Ancient Rome, Trastevere or the old centre cost €35; tours of the Via Appia, Gastronomic Rome, or special themes like Caravaggio's or Bernini's Rome cost a bit more and have to be booked further in advance. Enjoy Rome also act as an agent for Vastours (see below).

Il Sogno Viale Regina Margherita 192 ⊕06.8530.1758, ⊛www.romeguide.it. This long-established cooperative runs a range of tours of individual sights and is perhaps the best option for a guided tour of a specific place.

Institute of Design and Culture ⊕940/202-4700, ⊛www.idcrome.org. US-based organization offering a great range of city courses with a cultural slant led by Rome experts. They mostly last half a day and are not cheap, but you get what you pay for; choose from anything from the Baroque to Ancient Rome to *Tosca* – or even a cooking class with visits to the city's markets.

International Wine Academy Vicolo del Bottino 8 ⊕06.699.0878, ⊛www.wine academyroma.com. Wine courses and occasional tours of Lazio's vineyards, right in the heart of Rome just off Piazza di Spagna.

Rome Revealed ⊕06.324.741, ⊛www.romerevealed.com. Informative and entertaining walking tours run by native English-speakers. Standard tours include the Vatican, the catacombs and the Fountains of Rome, but you can also attend a cookery workshop, or they can tailor tours to suit you. Standard group tours cost €29–41 plus museum admissions.

Through Eternity ⊕06.700.9336, ⊛www.througheternity.com. Everything from straightforward visits to the Vatican and Capitoline Museums for €35–40 to themed tours like Rome at Twilight (€29).

Vastours Via Piemonte 32 ⊕06.481.4246, ⊛www.vastours.it. This nationwide tour company operates a wide range of excursions by coach with English-speaking guides, for €35–40. They also do decent excursions to Ostia Antica and Tivoli for around €50–55 per person, as well as papal audience and Rome by Night tours (€39). Their Bus 'n' Boat tour (€13) allows you to hop on and off buses and boats that navigate six stops along the river and nine in the city centre every hour.

privately run **Enjoy Rome**, Via Marghera 8a (Mon–Fri 8.30am–5pm, Sat 8.30am–2pm; ⊕06.445.1843, ⊛www.enjoyrome.com), whose friendly, English-speaking staff hand out lots of free information; they also operate a free room-finding service, organize tours and run a shuttle service to Fiumicino and Ciampino.

Information kiosks

Castel Sant'Angelo Piazza Pia
Imperial Forums Piazza del Tempio della Pace
Piazza Navona Piazza delle Cinque Lune
San Giovanni Piazza San Giovanni in Laterano
Santa Maria Maggiore Via dell'Olmata
Termini station Piazza dei Cinquecento

Trastevere Piazza Sonnino
Trevi Fountain Via Minghetti
Via del Corso Largo Goldoni
Via Nazionale Palazzo delle Esposizioni

Tourist passes and discounts

There is no museum pass that will get you into all the main attractions in Rome. However, some sights are grouped together to make it easier and cheaper to visit them. The Colosseum and Palatine can be visited on a combined ticket, and you can buy an **Archeologia Card** for €23 (valid for 7 days) that gives free entry to the Colosseum, Palatine Hill, Baths of Caracalla, Villa dei Quintili, Tomba Cecilia Metella, Palazzo Altemps, Palazzo Massimo, Crypta Balbi and Terme di Diocleziano – perhaps the city's best bargain. Rome's ancient sculpture and other artefacts have been gathered together in the **Museo Nazionale Romano**, which operates on three main sites: Palazzo Massimo, the Terme di Diocleziano and the Palazzo Altemps. You can buy a ticket from each location that permits entry to all the others for just €7 and is valid for three days. Finally, the **Roma Pass**, available from all museums in the circuit and tourist information kiosks (☏060608, ⓦwww.romapass.it), costs €25 and is valid for three days. It entitles you to travel for free on buses, trams and the metro, gives free admission to two of some 44 museums or sights of your choice (the vast majority of places participate) and reduced entry to others – and, perhaps most importantly, the opportunity not to queue at the first two sights you visit (quite a lifesaver at the Colosseum).

Some sights and museums also give discounts or even free admission to **students and EU citizens under 18 or over 65** – but you need to make sure you

have the relevant ID. Many theatres and cinemas will offer discounts, as will the #110 tour bus and the Archeobus (15 percent and 20 percent respectively; see box, p.29).

Travel agents

For **discount tickets**, try the CTS offices at Via Genova 16 (☏06.462.0431) and Corso Vittorio Emanuele II 297 (☏06.687.2672), both open Saturday mornings, when other travel agents are closed. Another good place to try is Viaggiare, Via San Nicola da Tolentino 15 (☏06.421.171), which has some English-speaking staff.

Travellers with disabilities

Rome can be quite a challenge for those with disabilities: there are lots of steps, pavements are uneven, and Italy as a whole is just not as accessible as a lot of northern Europe and North America. Handy Turismo (☏06.350.75707, ⓦwww.handyturismo.it) makes things a bit easier, with a 9am–5pm information line. A disabled guide to the city, *Roma Accessible*, contains information on accessibility to major sights, museums, hotels and restaurants and is published occasionally. Only two stops on Metro line A are accessible for disabled persons (Cipro-Musei Vaticani and Valle Aurelia), but bus #591 does the same route and can accommodate those with disabilities. On line B, Circo Massimo, Colosseo and Cavour do not have accessibility, but bus #75 stops at those sights and new buses on this route can accommodate those with disabilities (although you may have to wait for a few of the older buses to go by). The buses on routes #81, #85, #90, #170, #490 and #H have also recently been furnished with elevator platforms.

The City

The City

The centro storico

The real heart of Rome is the **centro storico** or "historic centre", which makes up the greater part of the roughly triangular knob of land that bulges into a bend in the Tiber, above **Corso Vittorio Emanuele II** and to the west of **Via del Corso**, Rome's main street. In the days of ancient Rome, when it was known as the Campus Martius, this low-lying area lay outside the city centre and was mostly given over to barracks and sporting arenas, together with several temples – including the Pantheon. It became the heart of the Renaissance city, and today is the part of the town that is densest in interest, an unruly knot of narrow streets and alleys that holds some of the best of Rome's classical and Baroque heritage and its most vivacious **nightlife**.

It's here that most people find the Rome they have been looking for – the Rome of small crumbling piazzas, Renaissance churches and fountains, blind alleys and streets humming with scooters and foot-traffic. Whichever direction you wander in there's something to see; indeed it's part of the appeal of the centre of Rome that even the most aimless ambling leads you past some breathlessly beautiful and historic spots.

Palazzo and Galleria Doria Pamphilj

Walking north from Piazza Venezia, the first building on the left of Via del Corso, the **Palazzo Doria Pamphilj**, is among the city's finest Rococo palaces, with a facade added in 1734 to a building that was the product of years of construction and remodelling dating back to Roman times, when a storehouse stood on this site. The Doria Pamphilj family were (and are) one of Rome's most illustrious, and still own the building and live in part of it. They were also prodigious collectors of art, in particular Prince Camillo Pamphilj, who lived here in the mid-seventeenth century, and inside, the **Galleria Doria Pamphilj**, Via del Corso 305, is one of Rome's best late-Renaissance art collections (daily 10am–5pm; €9, including audioguide in English; ⓦwww.dopart.it/roma).

The picture gallery

The **picture gallery** extends around a lush courtyard, the paintings mounted in the style of the time, crammed in frame-to-frame, floor-to-ceiling. The information is better than it once was, but many paintings are not labelled, making the excellent audio tour, narrated by the urbane Jonathan Pamphilj, more or less essential. There are some marvellous and beautifully displayed classical statuary, busts, sarcophagi and figurines in the so-called Aldobrandini room, and just inside the courtyard a bust of Prince Camillo's wife Olimpia Aldobrandini Pamphilj, a formidable woman by all accounts and quite a collector in her own right. On the next corner of the courtyard, there's a badly cracked bust of Innocent X by **Bernini**, which the sculptor apparently

THE CENTRO STORICO

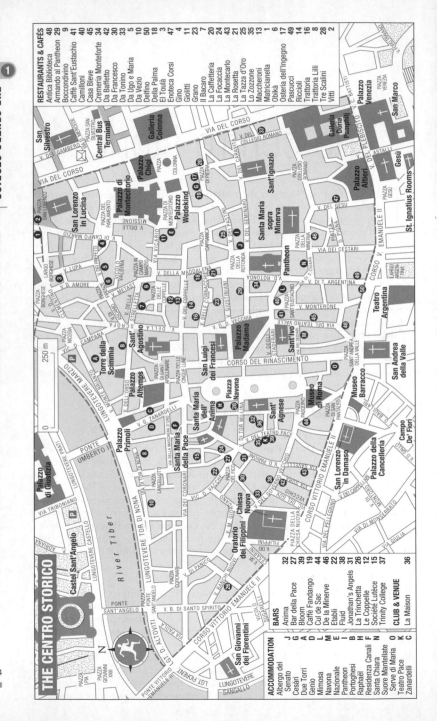

RESTAURANTS & CAFÉS	
Antica Biblioteca	48
Armando al Pantheon	29
Boccondivino	9
Caffè Sant'Eustachio	41
Camilloni	40
Casa Bleve	45
Cremeria Monteforte	34
Da Baffetto	42
Da Francesco	30
Da Tonino	33
Da Ugo e Maria	5
Da Vezio	10
Delfino	50
Della Palma	18
El Toulà	3
Enoteca Corsi	47
Gino	4
Giolitti	11
Grano	23
Il Bacaro	7
La Caffetteria	20
La Focaccia	24
La Montecarlo	43
La Rosetta	21
La Tazza d'Oro	25
Lo Zozzone	35
Maccheroni	13
Matricianella	1
Obikà	6
Osteria dell'Ingegno	17
Pascucci	49
Riccioli	14
Trattoria	16
Trattoria Lilli	8
Tre Scalini	28
Vitti	2

ACCOMMODATION	
Albergo del Senato	J
Cesàri	G
Due Torri	A
Genio	D
Mimosa	L
Nazionale	M
Navona	E
Pantheon	I
Portoghesi	B
Raphaël	H
Residenza Canali	F
Santa Chiara	N
Suore Mantellate	
Serve di Maria	
Teatro Pace	O
Zanardelli	K

BARS	
Anima	32
Bar della Pace	27
Bloom	39
Caffè Fandango	19
Cul de Sac	44
De la Minerve	46
Etabli	22
Fluid	38
Jonathan's Angels	31
La Trinchetta	26
Le Coppelle	12
Société Lutèce	15
Trinity College	37

CLUB & VENUE	
La Maison	36

0   250 m

replaced in a week with the more famous version down the hall, in a room off to the left, where he appears to have captured the pope about to erupt into laughter. In the same room, **Velázquez's** famous painting of the same man is quite different, depicting a rather irritable character regarding the viewer with impatience. "It's too real!", its subject is supposed to have exclaimed when he saw it.

The rest of the collection is just as rich in interest, and there are many works worth lingering over. These include perhaps Rome's best concentration of **Dutch** and **Flemish** paintings, among them a rare Italian work by Brueghel the Elder, showing a naval battle being fought outside Naples, complete with Vesuvius, Castel Nuovo and other familiar landmarks, along with a highly realistic portrait of two old men by Quentin Metsys, and a Hans Memling *Deposition*, in the furthest rooms, as well as a further Metsys painting – the fabulously ugly *Moneylenders and their Clients* – in the main gallery, close by Annibale Carracci's bucolic *Flight into Egypt*, painted shortly before the artist's death. Also in the rooms off the courtyard are three paintings by Caravaggio – *Repentant Magdalene* and *John the Baptist*, and his wonderful *Rest on the Flight into Egypt* – hanging near *Salome with the Head of St John*, by Titian. All in all, it's a fantastic collection of work, displayed in a wonderfully appropriate setting.

The private apartments

The second part of the gallery is made up of a series of **private apartments**, furnished in the style of the original palace. These take in the large and elegant reception hall of the original palace, crammed with landscape paintings by the seventeenth-century French artist, Dughet, off which there is a room where the Pamphilj pope, Innocent X, used to receive guests, complete with a portrait of the great man, and a couple of side salons filled with busts and portraits of the rest of the family. There's also a ballroom, complete with a corner terrace from which the band played, and a small private chapel, which contains the apparently incorruptible body of the Roman martyr St Theodora, swathed in robes, and the relics of St Justin under the altar. Be sure to also peek in at the former bedroom of Filippo Andrea and his wife Mary Talbot, the last Pamphilj art collectors, and the last to live in this part of the palace, whose nearby sitting room especially, with its overflowing bookcases, gives the apartments a relatively homely feel amid all the grandeur.

Sant'Ignazio

Via del Caravita, the next left off Via del Corso after the Palace, leads to **Piazza di Sant'Ignazio**, a lovely little square, laid out like a theatre set and dominated by the facade of the Jesuit church of **Sant'Ignazio** (daily 7.30am–12.30pm & 3–7.15pm). The saint isn't actually buried here; appropriately, for the founder of the Jesuit order, he's in the main Jesuit church, the Gesù, a little way south (see p.60). But it's a spacious structure, worth visiting for a marvellous Baroque ceiling, by Andrea Pozzo, showing the entry of St Ignatius into paradise. This spectacular work employs bold trompe l'oeil effects, notably in the mock cupola painted into the dome of the crossing. Stand on the disc in the centre of the nave, the focal point for the ingenious rendering of perspective: figures in various states of action and repose, conversation and silence, fix you with stares from their classical pediments.

The Pantheon and around

On the other side of Piazza di Sant'Ignazio lies **Piazza di Pietra**, a pleasant triangular open space dominated by the giant Corinthian columns of an ancient Roman temple, still supporting their frilled peristyle and incorporated in true Roman style into the building behind, now Rome's stock exchange. The temple was built by Antoninus Pius in 145 AD in memory of his father, Hadrian.

From here it's a short walk west, down Via dei Pastini, to **Piazza della Rotonda**, one of the city's most picturesque squares, and perhaps suffering because of it, invariably thronged as it is with sight-weary tourists, hawkers and street musicians, besieging the café tables that fringe the edge. The waters of the fountain in the middle, an eighteenth-century construction topped by yet another obelisk, are a soothing influence, but the main focus of interest is the **Pantheon** (Mon–Sat 8.30am–7.30pm, Sun 9am–6pm; free), which forms the square's southern edge, easily the most complete ancient Roman structure in the city and, along with the Colosseum, visually the most impressive.

Though originally a temple that formed part of Marcus Agrippa's redesign of the Campus Martius in around 27 BC – hence the inscription – it's since been proved that the building was entirely rebuilt by the Emperor Hadrian and finished around 125 AD. It remains a formidable architectural achievement, although like the city's other Roman monuments, it would have been much more sumptuous in its day. Consecrated as a Christian site in 609 AD, it was dedicated to Santa Maria ai Martiri in an allusion to the Christian bones that were found here; a thousand years later, the bronze roof was stripped from the ceiling of the portico by Pope Urban VIII, to be melted down for the baldachino in St Peter's and the cannons of the Castel Sant'Angelo. Interestingly, some of the "stolen" bronze later found its way back here when, after Unification, the cannons were in turn melted down to provide materials for the tombs of two Italian kings, which are housed in the right and left chapels.

Inside, you get the best impression of the engineering expertise of Hadrian: the diameter is precisely equal to its height (43m), the hole in the centre of the dome – from which shafts of sunlight descend to illuminate the musty interior – a full 9m across. Most impressively, there are no visible arches or vaults to hold the whole thing up; instead they're sunk into the concrete of the walls of the building. Again, it would have been richly decorated, the coffered ceiling heavily stuccoed and the niches filled with the statues of gods. Now, apart from the sheer size of the place, the main point of interest is the **tomb of Raphael**, between the second and third chapel on the left, with an inscription by the humanist cardinal Pietro Bembo: "Living, great Nature feared he might outvie Her works, and dying, fears herself may die." The same kind of sentiments might well have been reserved for the Pantheon itself.

Santa Maria sopra Minerva

There's more artistic splendour on view behind the Pantheon. Bernini's diminutive **Elephant Statue** is the Baroque artist's most endearing piece of work, if not his most characteristic, showing a cheery elephant trumpeting under the weight of the obelisk he carries on his back – a reference to Pope Alexander VII's reign and supposed to illustrate the fact that strength should support wisdom.

Behind it is the far grander **Santa Maria sopra Minerva** (Mon–Sat 7am–7pm, Sun 8am–7pm), modelled on the church of Santa Maria Novella in Florence. It is Rome's only Gothic church, and worth a look just for that, though its soaring lines have since been overburdened by marble and frescoes. Built in the late thirteenth century on the ruins of a temple to Minerva, it is also one of Rome's art-treasure churches, crammed with the tombs and self-indulgences of wealthy Roman families. Of these, the Carafa Chapel, in the south transept, is the best known, holding Filippino Lippi's late-fifteenth-century fresco of *The Assumption*, a bright, effervescent piece of work. Below, one painting shows a hopeful Carafa (the religious zealot who became Pope Paul IV) being presented to the Virgin Mary by Thomas Aquinas; another depicts Aquinas confounding a group of heretics in the sight of two beautiful young boys. The children, visible in the foreground on the right, are the future Medici popes Leo X and Clement VII; the equestrian statue of Marcus Aurelius, destined for the Capitoline Hill, is just visible in the background.

The lives of Leo and Clement come full circle in the church, where they are both buried, and remembered by two very grand tombs on either side of the high altar – Leo on the left, Clement on the right, and both of them proof, if any were needed, that beautiful boys don't always grow up to be beautiful men. You should look, too, at the figure of *Christ Bearing the Cross*, on the left-hand side of the altar, a serene work that Michelangelo completed for the church in 1521, and the tomb of Catherine of Siena underneath, who died in a convent here in 1380. The room where she died is viewable through the sacristy, though you may need to ask someone to open it for you.

You can leave the church by the passage to the left of the altar, taking in the tomb of Fra Angelico, who also died here in 1455, just in front of a chapel that contains a very soothing *Madonna and Child* by Benozzo Gozzoli, from 1449. You emerge on Via Sant'Ignazio, just around the corner from the church of the same name (see p.45).

Sant'Ivo alla Sapienza

Heading in the opposite direction from the Pantheon, on Corso del Rinascimento, the rather blank facade of the **Palazzo della Sapienza** cradles the church of **Sant'Ivo** (Sun 9am–noon) – from the outside at least, one of Rome's most impressive churches, with a playful facade designed by Borromini. Though originally built for the most famous Barberini pope, Urban VIII, the building actually spans the reign of three pontiffs. Each of the two small towers is topped with the weird, blancmange-like groupings that are the symbol of the Chigi family (representing the hills of Monti Paschi), and the central cupola spirals helter-skelter-fashion to its zenith, crowned with flames that are supposed to represent the sting of the Barberini bee, their family symbol. Inside, it's comparatively featureless but very cleverly designed – impressively light and spacious given the small space the church is squeezed into, rising to a tall parabolic cupola.

Palazzo Madama

Just north of Sant'Ivo, there's a constant police presence around the seventeenth-century **Palazzo Madama**, which owes its name to the "madame" Margaret of

Clerical fashions

Opposite the church of Santa Maria sopra Minerva, Via dei Cestari and Via Santa Chiara host Rome's **clerical fashion district**, long-time home to a number of shops selling liturgical garments to priests, monks and nuns. Oddly enough anyone is welcome to browse and even buy: should you be interested, a full set of cardinal's outfits, including a change of cassocks, a skullcap and something for special occasions, will set you back about €1500. Perhaps the most famous store of all is Gammarelli, Via Santa Chiara 34, in business since 1798 and apparently the personal favourite of John Paul II. Interestingly it's Gammarelli who are charged with delivering three sizes of white (or, strictly, ivory) garments to the Vatican during papal elections to ensure that, whoever is elected, there will be something ready in the new pope's size.

Parma, the illegitimate daughter of Charles V, who lived here in the sixteenth century, before its fancy Baroque facade was added. Nowadays it holds the offices and chamber of the Italian upper house or **Senate** (guided tours first Sat of each month 10am–6pm; free) – a rather ageist institution whose 315 representatives have to be at least 40 years old and elected every five years only by Italians over 25. Tours take in the main debating chamber and various public spaces but are only conducted in Italian but can form a good complement to the tours you can take of the lower house of the Italian parliament (see below).

San Luigi dei Francesi

Cutting back towards the Pantheon, on to the bottom end of **Via della Scrofa**, the French national church of **San Luigi dei Francesi** (daily except Thurs afternoon 8.30am–12.30pm & 4–7pm) is worth a look, mainly for the works by Caravaggio that have hung here since they were painted in the last years of the sixteenth century. In the last chapel on the left are three paintings: the *Calling of St Matthew*, in which Christ points to Matthew, who is illuminated by a shaft of sunlight; Matthew visited by an angel as he writes the Gospel; and the saint's martyrdom. Caravaggio's first public commission, these paintings were rejected at first, partly on grounds of indecorum, and it took considerable reworking by the artist before they were finally accepted. These days they are considered to be among the artist's greatest ever works, especially *The Calling of St Matthew*, which manifests the simple, taut drama, as well as the low-life subject matter, that Caravaggio became so well known for.

Sant'Agostino

Further north up Via della Scrofa, off to the left, the Renaissance facade of the church of **Sant'Agostino** (daily 7.45am–noon & 4–7.30pm) takes up one side of a drab piazza of the same name. It's not much to look at from the outside, but a handful of art treasures might draw you in: this was the church of Rome's creative community in the sixteenth century and as such drew wealthy patrons and well-connected artists. Just inside the door, the serene statue of the *Madonna del Parto*, by Sansovino, is traditionally invoked during pregnancy, and is accordingly surrounded by photos of newborn babes and their blissful parents. Further into the church, take a look at Raphael's vibrant fresco of *Isaiah*, on the third pillar on the left, beneath which is another work by Sansovino, a craggy *St Anne, Virgin and Child*. But the biggest crowds gather the first chapel on the left, where the *Madonna di Loreto*, painted in 1605 by Caravaggio, is a characteristic work of what was at the time almost revolutionary realism, showing two peasants praying at the feet of a sensuous *Mary and Child*, their dirty feet and scruffy clothes contrasting with the pale, delicate feet and skin of Mary.

Torre della Scimmia

Just beyond Sant'Agostino on Via dei Portoghesi, take a look at the **Torre della Scimmia** – literally the "Tower of the Monkey" – which grows almost organically out of a fork in the road above an ivy-covered *palazzo*. The story goes that in the seventeenth century a pet monkey kidnapped a child and carried it to the top of the tower; the father of the child called upon the Virgin for help and the monkey promptly clambered down, delivering the child to safety. By way of thanks, the man erected a shrine to the Virgin, which you can still see at the top of the tower, accompanied by a glowing lamp that is to this day kept constantly burning.

Piazza di Montecitorio

A couple of minutes' walk east from the Torre della Scimmia, the obelisk in the centre of **Piazza di Montecitorio** was brought to Rome by Augustus to celebrate his victory over Cleopatra and set up in the Campus Martius, where it formed the hand of a giant sundial. The square takes its name from the bulky **Palazzo di Montecitorio** on its northern side, a Bernini creation from 1650 and home since 1871 to the lower house of the Italian parliament (open the first Sun of each month 10am–6pm; free). You can only visit by guided tour (45min; Italian only), but for those who know Rome well, and have even the slightest interest in Italy's notoriously shaky parliamentary system, a visit can be very worthwhile.

The building is in fact two knocked into one: the original, Bernini-designed structure, and another incorporating the main Hall of Deputies. The main building is full of grand reception rooms around a large courtyard, of which the Sala della Lupa, used for press conferences and presidential meetings with foreign dignitaries, is so called for its frescoes glorifying Rome as the country's capital, and the she-wolf that stands centre stage – a Mussolini addition. On the other side of the courtyard, the first-floor Sala della Regina is a massive room lined with tapestries that contains the entrance to the presidential part of the Hall of Deputies next door.

The Hall itself is an impressive nineteenth-century space with seats for 635 deputies arranged in a semicircle under an Art Nouveau skylight; above the speaker's platform, a bronze representing the spirit of Italy, flanked by regal military groupings, does a great job of enhancing the solemnity the chamber tries hard to exude.

Piazza Colonna

Just east of here, by Via del Corso, **Piazza Colonna** is flanked on its north side by the late-sixteenth-century **Palazzo Chigi**, the official residence of the prime minister and as such not open to the public. The **Column of Marcus Aurelius**, which gives the square its name, was erected between 180 and 190 AD to commemorate military victories in northern Europe, and, like the column of Trajan which inspired it, is decorated with reliefs depicting scenes from the campaigns. The statue of St Paul on top was added by Sixtus V, made from bronze from the ancient doors of the church of Sant'Agnese fuori le Mura (see p.113). The square used to be the site of the city's principal coffee-roasters' market, so was always a busy spot, and it still has an elegant backdrop in the **Palazzo Wedekind**, home to the offices of Rome's *Il Tempo* newspaper, whose dozen or so Ionic columns, originally Roman, support a gracious balustraded terrace.

San Lorenzo in Lucina

A little further up Via del Corso, on the left, the wedge-shaped **Piazza San Lorenzo** is a surprisingly spacious and relatively peaceful escape from the bustle of the Corso. On its left side, the church of **San Lorenzo in Lucina** (daily 8am–noon & 5–8pm), with its manifestly ancient campanile and columned portico, stands out among the largely undistinguished buildings around; it originally dates from the fifth century but was rebuilt in the twelfth century. Inside, like so many Roman churches, it doesn't look or feel nearly so old – indeed much of it dates from the seventeenth century – but there are several features of interest, not least a section of the griddle on which St Lawrence was roasted (see p.127), in the first chapel on the right – though this is almost impossible to see. A little further down on the same side, the tomb of the French painter Nicolas Poussin is a delicate nineteenth-century marble affair by his compatriot Chateaubriand; Poussin spent much of his life in Rome, and died here in 1665. Beyond, take a look also at Bernini's bust of the doctor of Innocent X, Fonseca, in the next chapel but one, and the *Crucifixion* by Guido Reni in the apse.

Piazza Navona

The western half of the centro storico focuses on **Piazza Navona**, Rome's most famous square, and the surrounding area. This pedestrianized oval, as picturesque as any piazza in Italy, is lined with cafés and restaurants and often thronged with tourists, street artists and pigeons. The best time to come is at night, when the inevitably tourist-geared flavour of the place is at its most vibrant, with crowds hanging out around the fountains or people-watching while nursing a pricey drink at a table outside one of the bars, or watching the buskers and street artists entertain the throng.

Piazza Navona takes its name from the Greek word for "struggle", *agone* – due to the games that were traditionally held here – and its shape from the first-century AD Stadium of Domitian, the principal venue of the athletic events and later chariot races that took place in the Campus Martius (see p.43). Until the mid-fifteenth century the ruins of the arena were still here, overgrown and disused, but the square was given a facelift in the mid-seventeenth century by the Pamphilj Pope Innocent X, who built most of the grandiose palaces that surround it, including the largest, the **Palazzo Pamphilj**, which fills much of the southwestern side of the square. It's now home to the Brazilian embassy and is not open to the general public – which is a shame given the fact that one of its state rooms has a lavish frescoed ceiling by Pietro da Cortona, depicting the adventures of Aeneas, which you can glimpse at night if the lights are on in the embassy.

The Pamphilj pope also commissioned the church of **Sant'Agnese in Agone** next door to the palace (Mon–Sat 9.30am–12.30pm & 4–7pm, Sun 10am–1pm &

▲ Fountain of the Four Rivers, Piazza Navona

4–8pm), initially from Carlo Rainaldi and later from Carlo Borromini, who took over after Rainaldi was sacked for being too slow. The story goes that the 13-year-old St Agnes was stripped naked before the crowds in the stadium as punishment for refusing to marry, whereupon she miraculously grew hair to cover herself. She was later martyred by a sword blow to her throat; nowadays she is the patron saint of young girls. Her skull is encased in a reliquary in a chapel at the back of the church, which, typically squeezed into the tightest of spaces by Borromini, is supposedly built on the spot where it all happened.

Opposite, the **Fontana dei Quattro Fiumi** (Fountain of the Four Rivers), one of three that punctuate the square, is a masterpiece of 1651 by Bernini, Borromini's arch-rival. Each figure represents one of what were considered at the time to be the four great rivers of the world – the Nile, Danube, Ganges and Plate – though only the horse, symbolizing the Danube, was actually carved by Bernini himself. It's said that all the figures are shielding their eyes in horror from Borromini's church facade (Bernini was an arrogant man who never had time for the work of the less successful Borromini), but the fountain had actually been completed before the facade was begun. The grand complexity of rock is topped with an Egyptian obelisk, brought here by Pope Innocent X from the Circus of Maxentius.

Bernini also had a hand in the fountain at the southern end of the square, the so-called **Fontana del Moro**, designing the central figure of the Moor in what is another fantastically playful piece of work, surrounded by toothsome dolphins and other marine figures. The fountain at the opposite end of the square, the **Fontana del Nettuno**, is equally fanciful, depicting Neptune struggling with a sea monster, surrounded by briny creatures in a riot of fishing nets, nymphets, beards, breasts, scales and suckers.

Piazza Pasquino

Just south of Piazza Navona, immediately behind the Palazzo Braschi, it's easy to miss the battered torso of **Pasquino**, even in the small triangular space of **Piazza Pasquino**, in the corner of which it still stands. Pasquino is perhaps the best known of Rome's "talking statues" of the Middle Ages and Renaissance times, upon which anonymous comments on the affairs of the day would be attached – comments that had a serious as well as a humorous intent (see box, p.69). Pasquino gave us the word "pasquinade", meaning a satire or lampoon of a public figure, though whether the comments and photocopied poems that grace the statue these days live up to it or not is debatable.

Museo di Roma

Backing onto Piazza Navona, the eighteenth-century Palazzo Braschi is the home of the **Museo di Roma**, Piazza San Pantaleo 10 (Tues–Sun 9am–7pm; €6.50; Ⓦhttp://en.museodiroma.it, which has a permanent collection relating to the history of the city from the Middle Ages to the present day. To be honest, it's a large museum and is only sporadically interesting. Indeed the building – particularly the magnificent **Sala Nobile** where you go in, the main staircase, and one or two of the renovated rooms, not least the exotically painted Sala Cinese and Sala Egiziana – is probably the main event. But there's interest in some of the **paintings** too, which show the city during different eras – St Peter's Square before Bernini's colonnade was built; jousting in Piazza Navona and the Cortile Belvedere in the Vatican; big gatherings and processions in the Campidoglio and Piazza del Popolo – and **frescoes** from demolished palaces provide decent enough highlights. There are also portraits and busts of the most eminent Roman families, most of whom made pope at one time or another – not only Braschi, but also the Corsini, Chigi and Odelaschi. These names resonate around historic parts of the city, and their faces gaze out of the rooms here with deadly and penetrating self-importance.

Sant'Andrea della Valle

Across the road towards Largo Argentina, the church of **Sant'Andrea della Valle** (Mon–Sat 7.30am–noon & 4.30–7.30pm, Sun 7.30am–12.45pm & 4.30–7.45pm) has the distinction of sporting the city's second-tallest dome (after St Peter's), built by Carlo Maderno, and of being the location for the first scene of the opera *Tosca* by Puccini. Inside, it's one of the most Baroque of Rome's churches, a high, barn-like building whose dome is decorated with paintings of the *Glory of Paradise* by Giovanni Lanfranco. The marvellous set of frescoes in the apse illustrating the life of St Andrew are by his contemporary, Domenichino, and centre on the monumental scene of the saint's crucifixion on the characteristic transverse cross. In a side chapel on the right, you may recognize some good-looking copies of not only Michelangelo's *Pietà* (the original is in St Peter's), but also of his figures of Leah and Rachel from the tomb of his patron, Julius II, in the church of San Pietro in Vincoli (see p.117).

Museo Barracco

Immediately across the road from the Palazzo Braschi, at Piazza dei Baullari 1, is the so-called **Piccola Farnesina** palace, built by Antonio Sangallo the Younger. The palace itself actually never had anything to do with the Farnese family, and took the name "little Farnese" because of the lilies on the outside of the building, which were confused with the Farnese heraldic lilies. Recently thoroughly restored, it's home to the **Museo Barracco** on the first and second floors (Tues–Sun 9am–7pm, Sun 9am–1pm; €3), a small but extremely fine-quality collection of ancient sculpture that was donated to the city at the turn of the century by one Baron Barracco. There are ancient Egyptian pieces, including two sphinxes from the reigns of Hapsupset and Rameses II, an austere head of an Egyptian priest, a bust of a young Rameses II and statues and reliefs of the god Bes from various eras. Look out for ceramics and statuary from the Greek classical period – essentially the fourth and fifth centuries BC and Roman copies of the same period – which include a lovely, almost complete figurine of Hercules, a larger figure of an athlete copied from an original by Policlitus, a highly realistic bitch washing herself from the fourth century BC and a complete and very beautiful votive relief dedicated to Apollo. A small room at the front of the building contains later Roman pieces, most notably a small figure of Neptune from the first century BC and an odd, almost Giacometti-like column-sculpture of a hermaphrodite, along with beautifully realistic portrait busts of both anonymous and public figures like Sophocles and Euripides. The charming busts of two young Roman boys opposite date from the first century AD.

Palazzo della Cancelleria

Further west along Corso Vittorio Emanuele II is the grand **Palazzo della Cancelleria**, the seat of the papal government that once ran the city; Bramante is thought to have had a hand in its design, and this gorgeous edifice exudes a cool poise quite at odds with the rather grimy nature of its location. You can't get in to see the interior, but you can stroll into the marvellously proportioned, multi-tiered courtyard, which is a treat enough in itself, although the adjacent church of **San Lorenzo in Damaso** (daily 7.30am–12.30pm & 4.30–8pm) also forms part of the complex and is one of the oldest churches in Rome. It was rebuilt with the palace at the start of the sixteenth century and has since been greatly restored, the last time at the end of the nineteenth century, and has a painting by Federico Zuccaro over the altar, *The Coronation of the Virgin*, and a twelfth-century icon of the Virgin Mary in the chapel to the left of here.

Via del Governo Vecchio and around

Back in the heart of the old city, **Via del Governo Vecchio** leads west from Piazza Pasquino through one of Rome's liveliest quarters. The street was named for the Palazzo Nardini at no. 39, which was once the seat of the governors of Rome. It's currently being restored but normally you can wander in to look at its elegant courtyard. However, this part of Rome is best known for its cool independent shops and boutiques, and for the **nightlife** that fills the narrow streets and vigorous restaurants and bars.

A little way down on the left, the delightful small square of **Piazza del Orologio** is so called because of the quaint clocktower that is its main feature. The clock is part of the **Oratorio dei Filippini**, designed by Carlo Borromini, which backs onto the Chiesa Nuova (see below) and is part of the same complex: the followers of Filippo Neri (founder of the Chiesa Nuova) attended musical gatherings here as part of their worship, hence the musical term "oratorio". Nowadays it's given over to a library of nineteenth-century literature and hosts temporary exhibitions – take the time to sneak in and rest for five minutes in its elegant orange-tree-shaded courtyard. Just off the square, there's a scatter of antique and bric-a-brac shops, which signal that you're just around the corner from Rome's antiques quarter, Via dei Coronari (see p.54).

Chiesa Nuova and around

The **Chiesa Nuova** (Mon–Sat 7.30am–noon & 4.30–7.30pm, Sun 8am–1pm & 4.30–8pm) backs onto Via del Governo Vecchio and is another highly ornate Baroque church – which is strange, because its founder, **San Filippo Neri**, didn't want it decorated at all. Neri was an ascetic man, who tended the poor and sick in the streets around here for most of his life and commissioned this place of worship on the site of an earlier structure, Santa Maria in Valicella, which had been donated to him and his followers by Pope Gregory XIII in 1577. Neri died in 1595, and this large church, as well as being his last resting-place (he lies in the chapel to the left of the apse), is his principal memorial. Inside, three paintings by Rubens hang at the high altar, centring on the *Virgin with Angels*. Pietro da Cortona's ceiling paintings, meanwhile, show the *Ascension of the Virgin* in the apse, and, above the nave, the construction of the church and Neri's famous "vision of fire" of 1544, when a globe of fire entered his mouth and dilated his heart – a physical event which apparently affected his health thereafter.

San Giovanni dei Fiorentini

The architect Borromini is buried 300m to the west, in the church of **San Giovanni dei Fiorentini** (daily 8.30am–1pm & 4–7pm), set on its own small square, Piazza d'Oro, beyond which is the river. Its eighteenth-century facade is as monumental as any of Rome's churches, but inside it is a relatively plain affair, originally built by Sansovino on the orders of the Medici pope, Leo X, who wanted to see an expression of Florentine pride in what was then the heart of Rome. The church was finished in the early 1600s by Carlo Maderno, who added the dome, and is buried here, along with Borromini, who helped him, after finishing work on the nearby Palazzo Falconieri. Beneath here Raggi's flamboyant seventeenth-century altarpiece depicts *The Baptism of Christ*, and in the nearby south transept, Salvatore Rosa's *Martyrdom of Saints Cosma and Damian* – the patrons of the Medici – has a fleeing male nude figure in the foreground that Rosa challenged Michelangelo to better: "Let Michelangelo come and see if he can paint a better nude than this!" The chapel to the right of the high altar has a faded fresco by Filippino Lippi that is said to have miraculous powers. Look out, too, for the naive statue of a young John the Baptist in the south aisle, above the sacristy door, next to which there's a bust of another Florentine pope, Clement XII, carved by Bernini. San Giovanni extends a special welcome to pets, and you'll often see churchgoers wandering in with cat baskets and the like.

Via dei Coronari

Carlo Maderno lived across the road at Via Banchi Nuovi 4, and there's a plaque marking the house. Turn left from here and head north, and you find yourself at the end of narrow **Via dei Coronari**, which leads back through the centro storico to the top end of Piazza Navona. This is the fulcrum of Rome's antiques trade, and, although the prices are as high as you might expect in such a location, there are a huge number of shops (the street consists of virtually nothing else), selling a tremendous variety of stuff, and a browse along here makes for one of the city's absorbing bits of sightseeing.

Santa Maria dell'Anima

A few steps right off Via dei Coronari is Via dell'Anima, where the church of **Santa Maria dell'Anima** (daily 9am–12.45pm & 3–7pm) takes its name from the statue of the Virgin on its facade, between two pleading souls in purgatory. It's another darkly cosy Roman church, wide and squat and crammed into an impossibly small space. Nowadays it's the German national church in Rome, and a richly decorated affair, almost square in shape, with a protruding main sanctuary flanked by Renaissance tombs. The one on the right, a beautiful, rather sad concoction, is that of the last non-Italian pope before John Paul II, the Dutchman Hadrian VI, who died in 1523, while at the far end, above the altar, you can just about make out a dark and glowing *Virgin with Saints* by Giulio Romano.

Santa Maria della Pace

Just off to the left of Via dei Coronari, the church of **Santa Maria della Pace** (Mon, Wed & Sat 9am–noon) dates originally from the late fifteenth century but has a facade and portico that were added a couple of hundred years later by Pietro da Cortona. It's often closed when it shouldn't be, but if you're lucky enough to find it open, you can see Raphael's frescoes of various sibyls above the Chigi chapel (first on the right), executed in the early sixteenth century. But perhaps the most impressive part of the church is the attached **Chiostro del Bramante** (Ⓦwww.chiostrodelbramante.it), finished in 1504, a beautifully proportioned, two-tiered cloister that is given over to high-quality temporary art exhibitions and is at least the one part of the building you can be sure of seeing. It also has a good café and bookshop that you don't need an entrance ticket to visit.

Stadium of Domitian

At the far end of Via dei Coronari, just off the north side of Piazza Navona, there are some visible remains of the **Stadium of Domitian**, which used to occupy the whole of the piazza and which can help you to learn a little more about the stadium and its relationship with present-day Piazza Navona. Sadly they have been inaccessible for some time but you can get a reasonable view of them from the street, or from Piazza Navona 49, where there's a balcony built into the lobby.

Palazzo Altemps

Just across the street from the north end of Piazza Navona, **Piazza Sant'Apollinare** is the home of the beautifully restored **Palazzo Altemps** (Tues–Sun 9am–7pm; €7, includes Palazzo Massimo, Terme di Diocleziano, Crypta Balbi; valid 3 days). Begun in 1477 and completed just under a hundred years later, it now houses a branch of the Museo Nazionale Romano, a relatively new addition to the sights around Piazza Navona. It houses the cream of Museo Nazionale's collections of Roman statuary, and is well worth a visit. Divided between two storeys of the palace, in rooms which open off an elegant courtyard, most of what is on display derives from the collection of the seventeenth-century Roman cardinal, Ludovico Ludovisi. It's a mix of pieces he purchased to adorn his villa on the Quirinal Hill and found in the grounds of the villa itself, which occupied the site of a former residence of Julius Caesar.

The ground floor

First up, at the far end of the courtyard's loggia, is a statue of the emperor Antoninus Pius, who ruled from 138 to 161 AD, and, around the corner, a couple of marvellous heads of Zeus and Pluto, a large bronze bust of Marcus Aurelius, a bust of Julia, the disgraced daughter of Emperor Augustus, and a grave-looking likeness of the philosopher Demosthenes, from the second century AD. Further rooms hold more riches: there are two almost identical statues of *Apollo the Lyrist*, a magnificent statue of Athena taming a serpent, pieced together from fragments found near the church of Santa Maria sopra Minerva, an *Aphrodite* from an original by Praxiteles, a frieze from a third-century sarcophagus showing the labours of Hercules, and, in the far corner of the courtyard, a shameless *Dionysus* with a satyr and panther, found on the Quirinal Hill.

The first floor

Upstairs, you get a slightly better sense of the original sumptuousness of the building – some of the frescoes remain, and the north loggia retains its original late-sixteenth-century decoration, simulating a vine-laden pergola, heavy with fruit, leaves and gambolling cherubs and now home to a series of busts of Roman emperors. The objects on display are if anything even finer than those downstairs. The **Painted Views room**, so called for the bucolic scenes on its walls, has a fine statue of Hermes, restored in the seventeenth century in an oratorical pose according to the fashion of the time. The **Cupboard Room**, next door, with its fresco of a display of wedding gifts against a floral background, has a wonderful statue of a warrior at rest called the *Ludovisi Ares*, which may represent Achilles and was restored by Bernini in 1622, and, most engagingly, a charmingly sensitive portrayal of *Orestes and Electra*, from the first century AD by a sculptor called Menelaus – his name is carved at the base of one of the figures.

Beyond are even more treasures, and it is hard to know where to look first. One room retains a frieze telling the story of **Moses** as a cartoon strip, with each scene displayed by nude figures as if on an unfurled tapestry. In the room itself is a colossal head of **Hera**, now thought to be a head of Antonia (Mark Antony's daughter and mother of Caligula and Claudius), and – what some consider the highlight of the entire collection – the famous *Ludovisi Throne*: an original fifth-century BC Greek work embellished with a delicate relief portraying the birth of **Aphrodite**. She is shown being hauled from the sea, where she was formed from Uranus's genitals, while on each side reliefs show a flute player and a woman sprinkling incense over a flame – rituals associated with the worship of Aphrodite.

Further on, there is a depiction of **Aphrodite** after a bath, a first-century AD boy strangling a goose, and a relief of **Dionysos** in the former cardinal's bedroom, a bold, almost modern profile of a face in red marble. Beyond the bedroom is the **Fireplace Salon**, whose huge fireplace is embellished with caryatids and ibex – the symbol of the Altemps family – and holds the *Suicide of Galatian*, apparently commissioned by Julius Caesar to adorn his Quirinale estate. At the other end of the room, an incredible sarcophagus depicts a battle between the Romans and barbarians in graphic, almost visceral sculptural detail, while in the small room next door there are some quieter, more erotic pieces – a lovely *Pan and Daphne*, a *Satyr and Nymph*, and the muses *Calliope* and *Urania*. Once you've made it to here, you'll be ready for a quick peek at the **Altemps chapel**, off the opposite end of the fireplace room, and a skim back through your favourite pieces, before leaving what is one of Rome's best collections of classical art.

Palazzo Primoli

Around the corner from Palazzo Altemps, at the end of Via Zanardelli, the sixteenth-century **Palazzo Primoli** was the home of a descendant of Napoleon, Joseph Primoli. Newly restored, it houses two minor museums that may command your attention on the way to the Vatican, just across the Tiber from here. The first, the **Museo Mario Praz**, on the top floor (Tues–Sun 9am–1pm & 2.30–7.30pm, Mon 2.30–7.30pm; obligatory tours every hour on the hour in the morning, on the half-hour in the afternoon; free), was the home of one Mario Praz, a teacher of English literature, art historian and writer who lived here for fifteen or so years until his death in 1982. It is kept pretty much as the elegant and cultured Praz left it, its nine or so rooms stacked to the gills with books, magazines, paintings and ornate furniture; Praz lived in a larger apartment in the Palazzo Ricci on Via Giulia before moving here and amassed heaps of stuff – a period described in his signature book, *La Casa della Vita*. Tours of the apartment take around thirty minutes and give you a glimpse of the vanished way of life of a connoisseur.

Next door, the ground-floor **Museo Napoleonico** (Tues–Sat 9am–7pm; €3) is not that interesting unless you're an enthusiast for the great Frenchman and his dynasty, and their considerable influence on nineteenth-century Italy. Rome was home for the Bonapartes in the 1820s, after Pauline married Camillo Borghese; Napoleon's mother, Letizia, also lived nearby (on Via del Corso) – and this is a rather weighty assortment of their personal effects. There's a letter from Napoleon himself from his exile in St Helena, a room devoted to Pauline Bonaparte, another to Caroline Bonaparte, who married the French ruler of Naples at the time, Joachim Murat, busts and paintings, including a stirring depiction of Napoleon in battle and portraits of Napoleon's nieces, Carlotta and Zenaide, hung amongst a number of Carlotta's own quite adept paintings, and even a Napoleonic bike. You can even find a plaster cast of Pauline Borghese's right breast, done *in situ* by Canova, for his famous statue in the Galleria Borghese.

Campo de' Fiori and the Ghetto

This chapter is really Rome's old centre part two, covering the area which lies between Corso Vittorio Emanuele II – the main thoroughfare which bisects the historic city core – and the Tiber. As in the centro storico, cramped streets, ripe for wandering, open out onto small squares flanked by churches, although it's more of a working quarter – less monumental, with more functional buildings and shops, as seen in its main square, **Campo de' Fiori**, whose fruit and veg stalls and rough-and-ready bars form a marked contrast to the pavement artists and sleek cafés of Piazza Navona. Across the river to the west lies the Vatican and to the south Trastevere, both covered in separate chapters. To the east it merges into the gloomy streets and scrabbly Roman ruins of the old **Jewish Ghetto**, a small but atmospheric neighbourhood that nuzzles close to the city's giant central synagogue, while just north of here lies the major traffic intersection and ancient Roman site of **Largo di Torre Argentina**.

Largo di Torre Argentina

Largo di Torre Argentina is a good-sized square, frantic with traffic that circles around the ruins of four (Republican-era) temples and the channel of an ancient public lavatory, now home to a thriving colony of cats. It's more a place to catch a bus or tram than to linger deliberately. You can visit the **cat sanctuary** (daily noon–6pm; ⓦ www.romancats.com) down the steps on the southwestern corner, and if you wish donate money or buy a catty gift from their small shop, or even "adopt" a cat for a monthly fee. Around 300 cats live in the excavations here, most of them domestic creatures dumped by their owners, and the people who look after them are all volunteers and receive no support from the city. In fact, the helpers here care for all of the city centre's 4000 or so stray cats, whose colonies spread from the Forum to the ruins at Piazza Vittorio Emanuele. As for the **temples**, they are closed to the public for most of the year but there are occasional guided tours (details are sometimes posted at the site), but to be honest they don't add a lot to what you can see from the road.

On the western side of the square, the **Teatro Argentina** was the venue for the first performance of Rossini's *Barber of Seville*, in 1816. It was not a success: Rossini was apparently booed into taking refuge in a nearby pastry shop. Built in 1731,

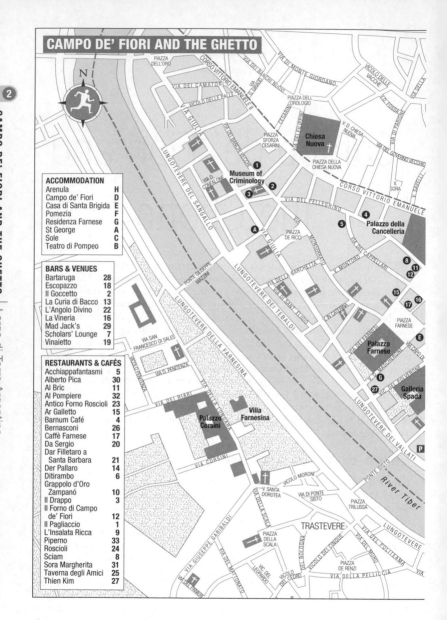

CAMPO DE' FIORI AND THE GHETTO

ACCOMMODATION

Arenula	H
Campo de' Fiori	D
Casa di Santa Brigida	E
Pomezia	F
Residenza Farnese	G
St George	A
Sole	C
Teatro di Pompeo	B

BARS & VENUES

Bartaruga	28
Escopazzo	18
Il Goccetto	2
La Curia di Bacco	13
L'Angolo Divino	22
La Vineria	16
Mad Jack's	29
Scholars' Lounge	7
Vinaietto	19

RESTAURANTS & CAFÉS

Acchiappafantasmi	5
Alberto Pica	30
Al Bric	11
Al Pompiere	32
Antico Forno Roscioli	23
Ar Galletto	15
Barnum Café	4
Bernasconi	26
Caffè Farnese	17
Da Sergio	20
Dar Filletaro a Santa Barbara	21
Der Pallaro	14
Ditirambo	6
Grappolo d'Oro Zampanó	10
Il Drappo	3
Il Forno di Campo de' Fiori	12
Il Pagliaccio	1
L'Insalata Ricca	9
Piperno	33
Roscioli	24
Sciam	8
Sora Margherita	31
Taverna degli Amici	25
Thien Kim	27

almost entirely of wood, by legend over the spot in Pompey's theatre (see p.61) where Julius Caesar was assassinated. Today it is one of the city's most important theatres and has a small museum that can be visited by appointment (℡06.06.08; €3), with displays on the history of the district, objects from the original building and relating to historic productions.

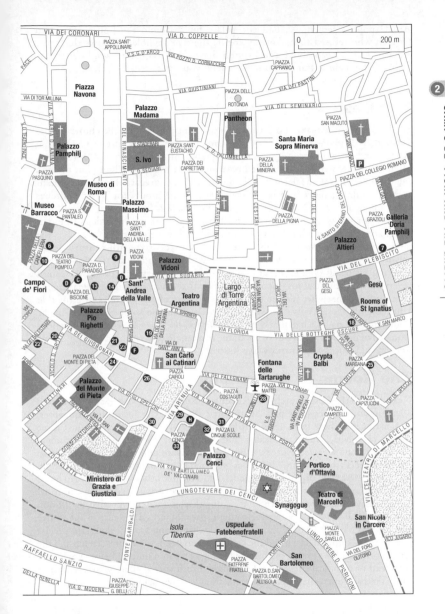

Via del Plebiscito

Via del Plebiscito, a dark, rather gloomy thoroughfare, links Largo Argentina with Piazza Venezia, 500m or so away. Halfway down on the left, flanking the north side of **Piazza del Gesù**, the grey decaying bulk of the **Palazzo Altieri** was a monster of a project in its time that – a contemporary satire posted on the Pasquino statue quipped – looked set to consume Rome by its very size. The

Altieri pope, Clement X, had the palace built around the house of an old woman who refused to make way for it: the two spyhole windows that were left can still be seen above the ground-floor windows, three windows to the right of the main entrance. Unfortunately, you can't visit the palace, which is now used as offices.

The Gesù

Lording it over the piazza (said to be the windiest in Rome) is the church of the **Gesù** (daily 6.45am–12.45pm & 4–7.30pm), the first Jesuit church to be built in Rome, and an appropriately dramatic symbol of the Counter-Reformation. High and wide, with a single-aisled nave and short transepts edging out under a huge dome, it was ideal for the large, fervent congregations the movement wanted to draw; indeed, it has since served as the model for Jesuit churches everywhere and is still well patronized. The facade is by Giacomo della Porta, the interior the work of Vignola, and the glitzy tomb of the order's founder, St Ignatius, in the north transept, is topped by a huge globe of lapis lazuli – the largest piece in existence. Opposite, the tomb of sixteenth-century Jesuit missionary St Francis Xavier, decorated with a painting by Carlo Maratta showing his death on a Chinese island, holds a reliquary containing the saint's severed arm; the rest of his (incorruptible) body remains a focus of pilgrimage in Goa, India. Otherwise, it's the staggering richness of the church's interior that you remember, especially the paintings by the Genoese painter Baciccia in the dome and the nave, particularly the *Triumph in the Name of Jesus*, an ingenious trompe l'oeil which oozes out of its frame in a tangle of writhing bodies, flowing drapery and stucco angels stuck like limpets.

The Rooms of St Ignatius

Next door to the Gesù church, the **Rooms of St Ignatius** (Mon–Sat 4–6pm, Sun 10am–noon; free) occupy part of the first floor of the **Jesuit headquarters**. St Ignatius lived here from 1544 until his death in 1556, and there are just three simple chambers, where the saint and founder of the Jesuit order studied, worshipped and received visitors. One was his **private chapel**, and the other two hold **artefacts** from his life – his shoes, vest and cloak, the robe he was buried in, his writing desks and original documents, and a bronze bust of the great man based on his death mask. But the true draw here is the **decorative corridor** just outside. Designed by Andrea Pozzo in 1680, it's a superb exercise in perspective, an illusion of a grand hall in what is a relatively small space. Stand on the rose in the centre and the room's architectural fancies, putti, garlands and scallop shells are precise and true; walk up and down and the ceiling beams bend, the figures stretch and the scrollwork buckles – giving the bizarre feeling of a room shifting before your eyes. It's a feast of technical trickery and grandiose brushwork – all in weird contrast to the basketball courts that occupy the quadrangle down below.

Crypta Balbi

Cutting back to Largo Argentina, following Via delle Botteghe Oscure, the **Crypta Balbi**, on the corner of Via Caetani (Tues–Sun 9am–7.45pm; €7, includes Palazzo Altemps, Palazzo Massimo, Terme di Diocleziano, valid 3 days), is the site of a Roman theatre, the remains of which later became incorporated in a number of medieval houses. There's a ground-floor exhibition which takes you through the evolution of the site in painstaking, sometimes excruciating, detail, with lots of

English explanation, along with bits of pottery, capitals and marble plaques. You have to take one of the hourly tours down into the site proper, where excavations are ongoing, and you can try to glean what you can from the various arches, latrines, column bases and supporting walls that make up the cellar of the current building. The real interest is in the close dissection of one city block over two thousand years – an exercise that could presumably be equally well applied to almost any city corner in Rome.

Campo de' Fiori

West of Largo Argentina a network of streets centres on the long oblong of **Piazza Campo de' Fiori** – in many ways Rome's most appealing square. Home to a lively fruit and vegetable **market** (Mon–Sat 8am–1pm), it's surrounded by restaurants and cafés, and is busy pretty much all day, although its function as heart of the area's nightlife, and the consequent glut of bars and outdoor drinkers has taken away much of its unique appeal, in the evenings at least.

No one really knows how the square came by its name, which means "field of flowers". One theory holds that it was derived from the Roman Campus Martius which used to cover most of this part of town. Another claims it is after Flora, the mistress of Pompey, whose theatre used to stand on what is now the northeast corner of the square – a huge complex by all accounts, which stretched right over to Largo Argentina, and where **Julius Caesar** was famously stabbed on the Ides of March, 44 BC. You can still see the foundations in the basement of the *Da Pancrazio* restaurant, on the tiny Piazza del Biscione, and the semicircular Via de' Grotta Pinta retains the rounded shape of the theatre. Later, Campo de' Fiori was an important point on papal processions between the Vatican and the major basilicas of Rome (notably San Giovanni in Laterano) and a site of public executions. The most notorious killing here is commemorated by the statue of **Giordano Bruno** in the middle of the square. Bruno was a late-sixteenth-century freethinker who followed the teachings of Copernicus and was denounced to the Inquisition; his trial lasted for years under a succession of different popes, and finally, when he refused to renounce his philosophical beliefs, he was burned at the stake.

Piazza Farnese

Just south of Campo de' Fiori, **Piazza Farnese** is a quite different square, with great fountains spurting out of carved lilies – the Farnese emblem – into marble tubs brought from the Baths of Caracalla, and the sober bulk of the **Palazzo Farnese** itself (Mon & Thurs visits in French or Italian at 3pm, 4pm & 5pm; free; book in advance at Via Giulia 250, on the river side of the palace, via ☏06.6889.2818 or at ✉visitefarnese@france-italia.it). Commissioned in 1514 by Alessandro Farnese – later Pope Paul III – from Antonio di Sangallo the Younger, the building was worked on after the architect's death by Michelangelo, who added the top tier of windows and cornice. It now houses the French Embassy, and access needs to be organized well in advance, but even from the outside it's a tremendously elegant and powerful building – indeed, of all the fabulous locations that Rome's embassies enjoy, this has to be the best.

If you're here for long enough, it is worth organizing a tour. The Farnese were great enthusiasts and collectors, and classical statuary litters the hallways and salons of the palace: on the first floor or *piano nobile*, the **Salone d'Ercole** has a copy of the so-called *Farnese Hercules* (the original of which used to stand here but is now in Naples), surrounded by busts of Roman emperors in a room decorated with the feats of Hercules by Federico Zuccari. Zuccari also had a hand in the room next door, the **Sala dei Fausti Farnesiani** or "Room of the Farnese Deeds", which is decorated with frescoes by Franceso Salinati illustrating the great acts of the family – though this is sadly not always open for tours because it's used for official functions. But the building's real treasure is at the back of the building – the Bolognese painter Annibale Carracci's **Loves of the Gods**, finished in 1603, and a work of such magnificent vitality, with complex and dramatically arranged figures, great swathes of naked flesh and vivid colours, that it is often seen as the **first great work of the Baroque era**. Commissioned by Odoardo Farnese, the main painting, centring on the *Marriage of Bacchus and Ariadne*, which is supposed to represent the binding of the Aldobrandini and Farnese families, leaps out of its frame in an erotic hotchpotch of cavorting, a fantastic, fleshy spectacle of virtuoso technique and perfect anatomy, surrounded by similarly fervent works illustrating various classical themes. Between and below them, nude figures peer out – amazing exercises in perspective that seem almost to be alongside you in the room. Carracci did the main plan and the central painting himself, but left the rest to his brother and cousin, Agostino and Ludovico, and assistants like Guido Reni and Guercino, who went on to become some of the most sought-after artists of the seventeenth century. It's a fantastic piece of work, perhaps only eclipsed in Rome by the Sistine Chapel itself, and it's sad to note that Carracci, disillusioned by the work, and bitter about the relative pittance that he was paid for it, didn't paint much afterwards, and died penniless a few years later.

Galleria Spada

If you can't get in to the Palazzo Farnese you'll have to make do with the **Palazzo Spada**, a couple of blocks east down Via Capo di Ferro. The **Galleria Spada** (Tues–Sun 8.30am–7.30pm; €5; Ⓦ www.galleriaborghese.it) is inside – walk right through the courtyard to the back of the building. Although its four rooms, decorated in the manner of a Roman noble family, aren't spectacularly interesting unless you're a connoisseur of seventeenth- and eighteenth-century Italian painting, it does have one or two items of interest. Highlights include two portraits of Cardinal Bernadino Spada by Reni and Guercino, alongside a *St Jerome*, also by Reni; works by Italian-influenced Dutch artists like Jan van Scorel; and, among bits and pieces of Roman statuary, a seated philosopher. The building itself is great: its facade is frilled with stucco adornments, and, left off the small courtyard, there's a crafty **trompe l'oeil** by Borromini – a tunnel whose actual length is multiplied about four times through the architect's tricks with perspective. To see this close up you have to wait for one of the guided tours (held every 45min), although you can peek at it from the courtyard. The **state apartments** on the first floor are also open, by appointment, on the first Sunday of each month, and contain, among many other things, some ancient Hellenistic reliefs, a series of seventeenth-century frescoes and a large statue of Pompey, at the feet of which it was for a long time believed that Julius Caesar died.

Ponte Sisto

Immediately behind the Palazzo Spada lies the river, and a pedestrian bridge across to Trastevere, the **Ponte Sisto**. Built by Pope Sixtus IV in 1479 on the site of a ruined structure, it was the first bridge to be built across the Tiber since Roman times. A relatively narrow structure, the inscriptions on each side of the entrance recall Sixtus IV's achievements, although they do not record the fact that the money to build it came from Cardinal Juan de Torquemada – uncle of the notoriously grisly tyrant of the Inquisition. One thing you can't see from the bridge itself is a large round hole in the middle, which functioned as an overflow in times of flood.

Via Giulia

Via Giulia runs parallel to the Tiber from the Ponte Sisto, and was laid out by Julius II to connect the bridge with the Vatican. The street was conceived as the centre of papal Rome, and Julius commissioned Bramante to line it with imposing palaces. Bramante didn't get very far with the plan, as Julius was shortly after succeeded by Leo X, but the street soon became a popular residence for wealthier Roman families. It is still packed full with stylish *palazzi* and antiques shops and as such makes for a nice wander, with features such as the playful **Fontana del Mascherone**, right behind the Farnese palace and topped with the Farnese emblem, to tickle your interest along the way. Just beyond the fountain, behind the high wall of the Palazzo Farnese, the ivy-draped **arch** across the street connects to more French diplomatic offices, the remnant of a Renaissance plan to connect the Farnese palace with the Villa Farnesina across the river, while further along still, the **Palazzo Falconieri**, recognizable by the quizzical falcons crowning each end of the building, now the home of the Hungarian Academy, was largely the work of Borromini, who enlarged it in 1646–49.

Museo Criminologico

On the corner of Via Gonfalone, the **Museo Criminologico** (Tues & Thurs 9am–1pm & 2.30–6.30pm, Wed, Fri & Sat 9am–1pm; €2; ⓦ www.museocrimino logico.it) offers a small but intriguing look at crime in general and Italy's under-world in particular. There are some gruesome early instruments of torture – manacles, lashes, head braces – a display on the unfortunate Beatrice Cenci (see p.65) and a selection of guillotines, nooses and various articles worn by the condemned, although inevitably the most interesting stuff – if you can read Italian – is that most pertinent to the world of **Italian crime**: the Mafia, the

Rome's Jews and the Ghetto

Across Via Arenula from the Campo de' Fiori area, the contrast with stately Via Giulia can be felt immediately: this crumbling area of narrow, confusing switchback streets and alleys with a lingering sense of age is one of Rome's most atmospheric. Rome's **Jewish population** stretches as far back as the second century BC, and, as the empire expanded into the Middle East, their numbers eventually swelled to around 40,000. Revolts in the colonies led to a small tax on Jews and a special census, but they were never an especially persecuted group, and were only effectively ghettoized in the mid-sixteenth century when Pope Paul IV issued a series of punitive laws that forced them into what was then one of Rome's most squalid districts: a wall was built around the area and all Jews, in a chilling omen of things to come, were made to wear yellow caps and shawls when they left the district. Later, after Unification, the ghetto was opened up.

By the late 1930s, Jews were again being victimized – barred from certain profes-sions and prohibited from marrying non-Jews under Mussolini's racial legislation. The subsequent **Nazi occupation** brought inevitable deportations but the majority of Rome's Jewish population survived, and currently numbers 16,000 (around half Italy's total). Nowadays, however, it is spread all over the city, and a handful of kosher restaurants, butchers and the like are pretty much all that remains to mark this out from any other quarter.

Brigate Rosse and Italian prison life. All in all, it is a perfect antidote to the more effete Renaissance splendours of Via Giulia and around, although it's worth knowing that Italy's Anti-Mafia Bureau has its headquarters at nearby Via Giulia 52, which explains the usually fairly robust police presence outside. You can continue to the end of Via Giulia for the church of **San Giovanni dei Fiorentini** (covered on p.53).

Via Portico d'Ottavia

The main artery of the Jewish area is **Via Portico d'Ottavia**, a short pedestrian street which leads southwest from Via Arenula to the **Portico d'Ottavia**, a not terribly well-preserved second-century BC gate, rebuilt by Augustus and dedicated to his sister in 23 BC, and then rebuilt again by Septimius Severus in 203 AD. It's next door to the **Teatro di Marcello**, and together (summer daily 9am–7pm; winter daily 9am–6pm; free) they form a site of mild interest and a short cut through to Via del Teatro di Marcello and the Capitoline Hill. The theatre has served many purposes over the years: begun by Julius Caesar and finished by Augustus, it was pillaged in the fourth century and not properly restored until the Middle Ages, after which it became a formidable fortified palace for a succession of different rulers, including the Orsini family. It has been recently restored and provides a grand backdrop for classical concerts in the summer (see p.270).

Piazza Mattei

On the north side of Via Portico d'Ottavia, narrow Via della Reginella leads to **Piazza Mattei**, whose **Fontana delle Tartarughe**, or "Turtle Fountain", is a delightful late-sixteenth-century creation, perhaps restored by Bernini, who apparently added the tortoises. The **Palazzo Mattei**, designed by Carlo Maderno, flanks one side of the square, and stretches down Via dei Funari ("Ropemakers' Street") to the corner of Via Caetani. The palace is now partly occupied by the Centro degli Studi Americani, but it's possible to wander into the courtyard,

Aldo Moro

Via Caetani is the site of a memorial to the former Italian prime minister **Aldo Moro**, whose dead body was left here in the boot of a car on the morning of May 9, 1978, 54 days after his kidnap by the **Brigate Rosse** or "Red Brigades". It was a carefully chosen spot, not only for the impudence it showed on the part of the terrorists in that it was right in the centre of Rome, but also for its position midway between the headquarters of the Communist and Christian Democrat parties. A plaque (and sometimes a wreath) marks the spot, and tells part of the story of how Moro, a reform-minded Christian Democrat, was the first right-wing politician to attempt to build an alliance with the then popular Italian Communists. Whether it was really left-wing terrorists who kidnapped him, darker, right-wing forces allied to the establishment, or perhaps a combination of the two, there's no doubt that Moro's attempt to alleviate the Right's postwar monopoly of power found very little favour with others in power at the time – though that didn't make his death any less of a shock.

During the **"Mani pulite"** years that followed, corruption in both politics and business was supposed to have been exposed and eliminated, but arguably little changed: the prime minister who took over after Moro's death was none other than the elder statesman of Italian politics **Giulio Andreotti**, whose alleged involvement with the Mafia saw him twice tried – and acquitted – for collusion, most recently in 2003. Political cynicism resurfaced in the 1990s and is still much in evidence today; as such, the tragedy of Moro's death still carries a lot of resonance for Romans.

whose antique friezes and statues still give some sense of the power and grandeur of this once-great Roman family.

Santa Maria in Campitelli

Via dei Funari continues towards Piazza Campitelli, where **Santa Maria in Campitelli** (daily 7am–7.30pm), opposite the Irish Embassy, is a heavy, ornate church built by Carlo Rainaldi in 1667 to house an ancient enamel image of the Virgin Mary, deemed to have miraculous powers following respite from a plague. It was originally housed in another church on Via Portico d'Ottavia but was moved here by Pope Alexander VII so as to be in more appropriately splendid surroundings. Everything in the church focuses on this small framed image, encased in an incredibly ornate golden altarpiece, which fills the entire space between the clustered columns of the transept. There's not much else to see, although the paintings, including a dramatic *Virgin with Saints* by Luca Giordano, in the second chapel on the right, represent Baroque at its most rampant, and in front a copy of the altar Virgin gives the opportunity for a close-up look at the miraculous image.

Piazza delle Cinque Scole

Just south of Via Portico d'Ottavia, **Piazza delle Cinque Scole**, named for the five religious schools that once stood here, is overlooked by one side of the **Palazzo Cenci**, which huddles into the dark streets here, a reminder of the untimely death of one **Beatrice Cenci**, who was executed, with her stepmother, on the Ponte Sant'Angelo in 1599 for the murder of her incestuous father – a story immortalized in verse by Shelley and in paint by an unknown artist whose portrait of the unfortunate Beatrice still hangs in the Palazzo Barberini.

The Synagogue

On the other side of the square is the area's principal Jewish sight: the huge **Synagogue** (June–Sept Mon–Thurs & Sun 10am–7pm, Fri 10am–4pm; Oct–May Mon–Thurs & Sun 10am–5pm, Fri 9am–2pm; closed Sat & Jewish hols; €7.50), built in 1904 and dominating all around with its bulk. Carabinieri stand guard 24 hours a day outside, ever since a PLO attack on the building in 1982 killed a 2-year-old girl and injured many others. The only way to see the building is on one of the short guided tours, which run regularly in English – just turn up – and take in the synagogue's **museum** afterwards. The impressive interior rises to a high, rainbow-hued dome, and the tours are excellent, giving good background on the building and Rome's Jewish community in general, and the recently revamped museum holds one of the most important collections of Judaica in Europe.

Isola Tiberina

Almost opposite the synagogue, the **Ponte Fabricio** crosses the Tiber to **Isola Tiberina**. Built in 62 BC, it's the only classical bridge to remain intact without help from the restorers (the Ponte Cestio, on the other side of the island, was partially rebuilt in the last century). As for the island, it's a calm respite from the city centre proper, and is mostly given over to Rome's oldest hospital, the **Fatebenefratelli**, founded in 1548 – appropriately, it would seem, as the island was originally home to a third-century BC temple of Aesclapius, the Roman god

▲ The Isola Tiberina

of healing. Opposite the hospital entrance, the church of **San Bartolomeo** (Mon–Sat 9am–12.30pm & 3.30–6pm, Sun 9am–1pm) stands on the temple's original site, and is worth a peep inside for its ancient columns, probably rescued from the temple, and an ancient wellhead on the altar steps, carved with figures relating to the founding of the church, including St Bartholomew himself. The saint also features in the painting above the altar, hands tied above his head, on the point of being skinned alive – his famous and gruesome mode of martyrdom. Beyond the island, you can see the remains of the **Ponte Rotto** (Broken Bridge) on the river, all that remains of the first stone bridge to span the Tiber. Built between 179 and 142 BC, it collapsed at the end of the sixteenth century.

Piazza Venezia and the Capitoline Hill

F or many people the modern centre of Rome is **Piazza Venezia**. It's not so much a square as a road junction, and a busy one at that, but it's a good place to start your wanderings, close to both the medieval and Renaissance centre of Rome and most of the city's ancient ruins. Flanked on all sides by imposing buildings, the piazza is a dignified focal point for the city in spite of the traffic, and a spot you'll find yourself returning to time and again – by some way the best landmarked open space in Rome, with the great white bulk of the Vittorio Emanuele Monument marking it out from almost anywhere in the city. Despite being a widely disliked building, the **Vittoriano**, as it's known, is one of the best sights in the city, both for its views and for the alternative route it gives to the Piazza del Campidoglio and the unmissable **Capitoline Museums** on the Capitoline Hill, the first-settled and most central of Rome's seven hills.

Piazza Venezia

There's not much need to linger on **Piazza Venezia** itself: it's more a place to catch a bus or pick up a taxi than soak up the atmosphere. A legacy of nineteenth-century Rome, it looked quite different a couple of hundred years ago, when it was the domain of the Venetian pope, Paul II, whose Palazzo Venezia dominated this part of the city, its gardens reaching around its south side, where the Vittoriano now stands. On the northern side, the canyon of Via del Corso, Rome's main street, begins its journey to the other side of the city centre at the Piazza del Popolo, its opening stretch flanked by the nineteenth-century **Palazzo Bonaparte** on the left, with its green-shuttered balcony. It was from here that Napoleon's mother Letizia Bonaparte, who lived here after he was deposed until her death in 1836, used to keep an eye on the comings-and-goings outside, though nowadays it's privately owned and the shutters are usually closed.

Palazzo Venezia

Forming the western side of the piazza, **Palazzo Venezia**, Via del Plebiscito 118 (Tues–Sun 9am–7.30pm; €4), was the first large Renaissance palace in the city, built

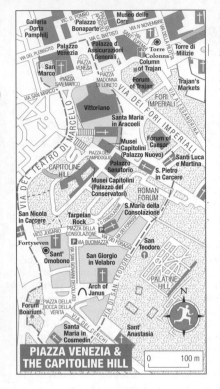

PIAZZA VENEZIA & THE CAPITOLINE HILL

0   100 m

in the mid-fifteenth century and for several centuries the embassy of the Venetian Republic. Famously, **Mussolini** moved in here while in power, occupying the vast Sala del Mappamondo (unfortunately only viewable if you're attending an exhibition) and making his declamatory speeches to the huge crowds below from the small balcony facing onto the piazza proper. In those days the palace lights would be left on to give the impression of constant activity in what was the centre of the Fascist government and war effort. Now it's a more peripheral building, a venue for good temporary exhibitions and home to a **museum of Renaissance arts and crafts** made up of the magpie-ish collection of Pope Paul II. The **paintings** include a lot of fifteenth-century devotional works from central and northern Italy. Among numerous Crucifixions and Madonnas, look out for an arresting double portrait of two young men by Giorgione in the first room; a late-sixteenth-century *Deposition of Christ* by Borgianni in room 6, in which Christ is viewed from the feet up by way of clever use of perspective (a copy, basically, of Mantegna's painting of the same subject); and, in a small anteroom, Algardi's 1650 bust of a severe-looking Innocent X. There are also a number of polychromatic wooden statues, notably two figures from a Magi group from the Marche and a lovely *Madonna and Child* from Lazio, both thirteenth-century. The ceiling paintings in room 7 are by Vasari, and depict Ceres, the Roman goddess of agriculture and the various months and seasons; they were in fact designed for another building and moved here in the late nineteenth century.

Beyond here, a corridor lined with ceramics skirts the courtyard to link with the *palazzetto* next door, where you can find a couple of rooms of beautifully displayed bronzes – a wide array of figures, animals and copies of ancient sculptures by Bernini and Giambologna among others. Around the corner are more sculptural pieces, including a tortured head of Seneca by Guido Reni and Algardi's representation of San Filippo Neri with an angel, a study of St Theresa for Bernini's statue in the church of Santa Maria Vittoria and some designs for the Trevi Fountain by Pietro Bracci; and finally some rooms full of weapons and ceramic jars from an ancient monastic pharmacy. You can walk out to the palace's upper **loggia** for a view over the palm-filled courtyard – the loggia is crammed full of ancient sculptural fragments and the gardens are some of the prettiest in Rome.

San Marco

Adjacent to the palace on its southern side, the church of **San Marco** (Mon 4–6.30pm, Tues–Sat 8am–noon & 4–6.30pm, Sun 9am–1pm & 4–8pm; closed

Rome's talking statues

As the home of the papacy, Rome has long been a political city, and its people have always enjoyed commenting on and arguing about the important issues of the day. In Renaissance times, the antics of the Church, in particular the pope and the powerful Roman families who vied to fill the post, were the subject of intense curiosity and scrutiny. A number of "**talking statues**" – usually ancient, unidentified pieces, among them Madam Lucretia outside the basilica of San Marco, Pasquino just off Piazza Navona, the "baboon" on Via del Babuino, and Marforio, now in the courtyard of the Palazzo Nuovo – were a focus for this, hung as they were with witty rhymes and notes commenting on the hubris and foolishness of the movers and shakers of the papal city: a kind of gossip column-cum-parliamentary sketch where people would gather to talk and laugh at their political masters.

third Thurs of the month), accessible from Piazza San Marco, is one of the oldest basilicas in Rome. This dark, cosy church was founded in 336 AD, on the spot where the apostle is supposed to have lived while in the city. It was rebuilt in 833 and added to by various Renaissance and eighteenth-century popes – Paul II restored it and added the graceful portico and gilded ceiling. It has a beautiful Cosmati-work floor and the apse mosaic dates from the ninth century and shows Pope Gregory IV offering his church to Christ, above a gracious semicircle of sheep that bear more than a passing resemblance to llamas. Back outside, tucked away in the corner, the statue of the busty harridan is "**Madam Lucretia**", actually an ancient depiction of Isis. Like Pasquino a few hundred metres away, she is one of Rome's so-called talking statues (see box above), commenting in a satirical fashion on the affairs of the day.

The Vittoriano

The rest of the buildings on Piazza Venezia pale into insignificance beside the marble monstrosity rearing up across the street from San Marco – the Vittorio Emanuele Monument or **Vittoriano** (daily 9.30am–6pm; free; lifts winter Mon–Thurs 9.30am–6.30pm, Fri–Sun 9.30am–7.30pm; summer Mon–Thurs 9am–7.30pm, Fri & Sat 9.30am–11.30pm, Sun 9.30am–8.30pm; €7), erected at the turn of the nineteenth century as the "Altar of the Nation" to commemorate Italian Unification. It has been variously likened to a typewriter (because of its shape), and, by American GIs, to a wedding cake (the white marble used will never mellow with age). King Vittorio Emanuele II, by all accounts a modest man, probably wouldn't have thought much of it. Indeed, the only person who seems to have benefited from the building is the prime minister at the time, who was a deputy for Brescia, from where (perhaps not entirely coincidentally) the marble was supplied.

There are things to see inside the monument (see p.70) but it's the outside of the structure that should command most of your attention, and it's great to clamber up and down the sweeping terraces and flights of steps which once upon a time you could only gaze at from the street. The structure is full of the weighty symbolism that was typical of the period. The figures either side of the entrance represent the two seas that surround Italy – the Tyrrhenian (on the right) and the Adriatic (on the left). At the top of the first lot of stairs is the Tomb of the Unknown Soldier, flanked by eternal flames and a permanent guard of honour, behind which a huge 1920s bas-relief represents the nation, focused on a figure of Minerva – for Rome – in the centre. Up another flight of stairs sits the figure of

▲ Piazza Venezia

Vittorio Emanuele II on horseback, at 10m x 12m one of the world's largest statues (his moustache alone is 3m long, and apparently twenty people once had lunch in the horse's belly) on a plinth friezed with figures representing the major cities of the Italian Republic. Above here, the huge, sweeping gallery stretches the width of the monument, with figures symbolizing the regions of Italy, while behind, glass lifts whisk you to the top of the monument for amazing views from between the massive *quadriglie* or chariots on each side. The whole thing is undeniably impressive, if only for the sheer audaciousness of its conception. Wherever you stand, though, the views of the city are the thing, perhaps because it's the one place in Rome from which you can't see the Vittoriano.

There's a **café** around the back, from where you can take a very useful short cut through to Piazza del Campidoglio behind. Inside the Vittoriano, the engaging **Museo di Risorgimento** (daily 9.30am–6pm; free) follows the long corridor that runs around the back of the building, full of busts, weaponry and mementoes of the Unification struggle and beyond. Temporary art and other exhibitions are held in the echoing chambers of the so-called **Complesso del Vittoriano**, which makes up the southeastern wing of the monument, accessible from Via di San Pietro in Carcere.

The Capitoline Hill and around

The real pity about the Vittoriano is that it obscures views of the **Capitoline Hill** behind – once, in the days of imperial Rome, the spiritual and political centre of the Roman Empire. The upside of this is that it gives a perfect route to the Capitoline, via the café right behind the Vittoriano and a passageway that delivers you right by the back entrance of Santa Maria in Aracoeli (see below), and just above the Piazza del Campidoglio.

The Capitoline's name derives from its position as the *caput mundi* or "head of the world", and its influence and importance resonate to this day, not least in language – "capitol" and "capital" originated here, as did "money", which comes from the temple to Juno Moneta that once stood on the hill and housed the Roman mint. The Capitoline also played a significant role in medieval and Renaissance times: the flamboyant fourteenth-century dictator, Cola di Rienzo, stood here in triumph in 1347, and was murdered here by an angry mob seven years later – a humble nineteenth-century statue marks the spot where he is said to have died. Michelangelo gave the hill's Piazza del Campidoglio its present form, redesigning it as a symbol of Rome's regeneration after the city was sacked by the troops of Holy Roman Emperor Charles V in 1527. These days the Capitoline forms a tight, self-contained group of essential attractions, with the focus on its pair of museums and the church of Santa Maria in Aracoeli.

Santa Maria in Aracoeli

The church of **Santa Maria in Aracoeli** (daily 9am–12.30pm & 3–6.30pm) crowns the highest point on the Capitoline Hill, and is built on the site of a temple to Jupiter where, according to legend, the Tiburtine Sibyl foretold the birth of Christ. It is reached by a flight of steps erected by Cola di Rienzo in 1348, the **Aracoeli Staircase**, although this is one of the city's steepest climbs and it's worth knowing that you can also access it from Piazza del Campidoglio, or direct from the Vittoriano. The church, one of Rome's most ancient basilicas, is worth the climb. Inside, in the first chapel on the right, there are some fine, humane frescoes by Pinturicchio recording the life of San Bernardino, with realistic tableaux of landscapes and bustling town scenes. The church is also known for its role as keeper of the so-called "Bambino", a small statue of the child Christ that was carved from the wood of a Gethsemane olive tree. Said to have healing powers, the statue was traditionally called out to the sickbeds of the ill and dying all over the city, its coach commanding instant right of way through the heavy Rome traffic. The Bambino was stolen in 1994, however, and a copy now stands in its place, in a small chapel to the left of the high altar.

Piazza del Campidoglio

Next door to the Aracoeli Staircase, the **Cordonata** is an elegant, smoothly rising ramp, and as such a much gentler climb. Topped with Roman statues of Castor and Pollux, it leads to **Piazza del Campidoglio**, one of Rome's most perfectly proportioned squares, designed by Michelangelo in the last years of his life for Pope Paul III, who was determined to hammer Rome back into shape for a visit by the Holy Roman Emperor, Charles V. In fact, Michelangelo died before his plan was completed (the square wasn't finished until the late seventeenth century), but his designs were faithfully executed, balancing the piazza, redesigning the facade of what is now Palazzo dei Conservatori and projecting an identical building across the way, known as Palazzo Nuovo. These buildings, which have been completely renovated in recent years, are home to the **Capitoline Museums** and feature some of the city's most important ancient sculpture. Both are angled slightly to focus on **Palazzo Senatorio**, Rome's town hall, with its double staircase and fountain, flanked by statues representing the Tiber and the Nile. In the centre of the square, Michelangelo placed an equestrian statue of Emperor Marcus Aurelius, which had previously stood unharmed for years outside San

Giovanni in Laterano; early Christians had refrained from melting it down because they believed it to be of the Emperor Constantine (the first Roman ruler to acknowledge and follow Christianity). The original is now beautifully displayed in the new wing of the Palazzo dei Conservatori, and a copy has taken its place at the centre of the piazza.

③ The Capitoline Museums

If you see no other museums of ancient sculpture in Rome, try at least to see the **Capitoline Museums** (Tues–Sun 9am–8pm; €6.50, €8.50 for joint ticket with Centrale Montemartini – see p.144, valid for one visit to each museum over seven days; ⓦ www.museicapitolini.org), perhaps the most venerable of all the city's collections. They're divided into two parts, one devoted only to sculpture, the other more extensive and wide-ranging with a gallery of paintings as well. You should if possible see both areas of the museum rather than choosing one, and tickets remain valid all day so you can easily take a break for a stroll around the other Capitoline sights in between.

Palazzo dei Conservatori

The **Palazzo dei Conservatori** on the right is perhaps the natural place to start, home as it is to the museums' ticket office and the larger, more varied collection, with ancient sculpture on the first floor and in the new wing at the back and paintings on the second floor. It has undergone quite a transformation in recent years with the incorporation of the Palazzo Caffarelli-Clementino into the museum, with its new wing housing some large ancient statuary and the newly discovered foundations of the Capitoline's original temple of Jupiter.

Ground and first floors

Some of the museum's ancient sculpture is littered around the ground-floor **courtyard** by the entrance – most impressively the feet, hand and other fragments of a gigantic statue, believed to be of the Emperor Constantine, and one of the most popular images of Rome. Upstairs, the first room you enter is the massive **Sala degli Orazi e Curiazi**, where the curators of the collections used to meet, appropriately decorated with giant late-sixteenth-century frescoes showing legendary tales from the early days of the city – *The Discovery of the She-wolf*, at the western end, faces the *Rape of the Sabine Women* at the opposite end, while presiding over all are colossal statues of Pope Urban XIII and his successor Innocent X, by Bernini and Algardi respectively. Appropriately, it was the venue for the signing of the Treaty of Rome in 1957, and for the presentation of the EU's ill-fated draft constitution nearly fifty years later.

The rooms that follow have more friezes and murals showing events from Roman history. Notably, the corner room contains the so-called *Spinario*, a Roman statue of a boy picking a thorn out of his foot, and a striking bronze head known as *Brutus* from the fourth century BC. The sacred symbol of Rome, the Etruscan bronze she-wolf nursing Romulus and Remus, the mythic founders of the city, gets a room to itself next door; the twins themselves are not Etruscan but were added by Pollaiuolo in the late fifteenth century, while on the walls the *Fasti* are an amazing record of magistrates and other political figures from the height of the Augustan age, rescued from the Forum. The next-door room is given over to two bronze Roman geese and a bust of Michelangelo, which Daniele da Volterra based on the artist's death mask, while further on there are more Roman bronzes – eagles this time – in a room with a Roman sculpture of the breast-laden Diana of Ephesus.

Retrace your steps slightly for the **Sala di Annibale**, covered in wonderfully vivid fifteenth-century paintings recording Rome's wars with Carthage, and so named for a rendering of Hannibal seated impressively on an elephant, before moving on to the airy **new wing**, where the original statue of Marcus Aurelius, formerly in the square outside, takes centre stage. Alongside it stand a giant bronze statue of Constantine – or at least its head, hand and orb – and a rippling bronze of Hercules, found near the Circus of Maxentius. Behind are part of the foundations and a retaining wall from the Capitoline's original temple of Jupiter, discovered when the work for the new wing was undertaken.

There are some great exhibits around the main hall here: some remnants from the Iron Age on the Capitoline, statuary rescued from ancient gardens on the Esquiline Hill, including a statue of the Emperor Commodus – the son of the decidedly more heroic Marcus Aurelius – as Hercules, the milk-white *Esquiline Venus*, and plenty more besides; and when museum fatigue sets in you can climb up to the second-floor **café**, whose terrace commands one of the best views in Rome.

Second floor

The second-floor picture gallery or **pinacoteca** holds Renaissance painting from the fourteenth to the late seventeenth century, with labels in Italian and English. The collection fills nine rooms; **highlights** include a couple of portraits by Van Dyck and a penetrating *Portrait of a Crossbowman* by Lorenzo Lotto; a pair of paintings from 1590 by Tintoretto – a *Baptism of Christ*, and a *Flagellation*; some nice small-scale work by Annibale Carracci; and a very fine early work by Ludovico Carracci, *Head of a Boy*. There are also several sugary pieces by Guido Reni, done at the end of his life, including *St Sebastian*. In one of two large galleries, there's a vast picture by Guercino depicting the *Burial of Santa Petronilla* (an early Roman martyr who was the supposed daughter of St Peter), which used to hang in St Peter's and arrived here via the Quirinale palace and the Louvre. It is displayed alongside several other works by the same artist, notably a lovely, contemplative Persian Sibyl and a wonderful picture of Cleopatra cowed before a young and victorious Octavius (later Augustus). In the same room, there are also two paintings by Caravaggio, one a replica of the young *John the Baptist* which hangs in the Palazzo Doria Pamphilj, the other a famous canvas known as *The Fortune-Teller* – an early work that's an adept study in deception. The large room at the back holds paintings from the Sacchetti collection, which includes a number of works by Pietro da Cortona, among them portraits of his patron Marchese Matteo Sacchetti and Pope Urban VIII, as well as a *Triumph of Bacchus*.

Palazzo Nuovo

The same ticket gets you into the **Palazzo Nuovo** across the square – also accessible by way of an underground **walkway** that takes in yet more sculpture, the remains of a Roman temple, and a terrace which has probably the best, and certainly the most close-up, views of the Roman Forum just below. The Palazzo Nuovo is the more manageable of the two museums, its first floor concentrating some of the best of the city's Roman sculpture into half a dozen or so rooms and a long gallery crammed with elegant statuary. There's the remarkable, controlled statue of the *Dying Gaul*, a Roman copy of a Greek original; a naturalistic *Boy with Goose* – another copy; an original, grappling *Eros and Psyche*; a *Satyr Resting*, after a piece by Praxiteles, that was the inspiration for Nathaniel Hawthorne's book *The Marble Faun*; and the red marble *Laughing Silenus*, another Roman copy of a Hellenistic original. In the main **Salone**, statues of an old and a young centaur face each other, and a naturalistic *Hunter* holds up a rabbit he has just killed. Walk through from here to the **Sala degli Imperatori**, with its busts of Roman emperors and other famous names, including a young Augustus, a cruel Caracalla, and, the centrepiece, a lifesize portrait of Helena, the mother of Constantine, reclining gracefully. Also, don't miss the *Capitoline Venus* – a coy, delicate piece, again based on a work by Praxiteles, housed in a room on its own. Finally, the **palace courtyard** is dominated by the large *Fountain of Marforio*, a bearded figure who was known as one of Rome's "talking statues" (see box, p.69), renowned in Renaissance times for speaking out in satirical verse against the authorities.

The Tarpeian Rock

After seeing the museums, walk around behind the Palazzo Senatorio for another great view down over the Forum, with the Colosseum in the background. There's a copy of the statue of Romulus and Remus suckling the she-wolf here, while on the right, Via del Monte Tarpeio follows the brink of the old **Tarpeian Rock** – named after Tarpeia, who betrayed the city to the Sabines – from which traitors were thrown in ancient times.

San Pietro in Carcere

Steps lead down from here to the little church of **San Pietro in Carcere** (April–Sept daily 9am–7pm; Oct–March daily 9am–5.30pm; donation expected for the prison). The low-vaulted church itself doesn't attract much interest; it's the ancient **Mamertine Prison** beneath that people come to see. Here spies, vanquished soldiers and other enemies of the Roman state, including St Peter and St Paul, were incarcerated. More steps lead down into the murky depths of the jail, where you can see the bars to which St Peter was chained, along with the spring the saint is said to have created to baptize other prisoners; there's an altar which shows these baptisms, and a cross – upside-down, because this was how Peter was crucified. At the top of the staircase, hollowed out of the honeycomb of stone, is an imprint claimed to be of St Peter's head as he tumbled down the stairs (though when the prison was in use, the only access was through a hole in the ceiling). It's an unappealing place even now, and you won't be sorry to leave – through an exit cunningly placed to lead you through the gift shop.

Santi Luca e Martina

Opposite San Pietro, the church of **Santi Luca e Martina** is two churches in one, an elegant building that has been here since the eighth century, when it was dedicated to the little-known Christian martyr Martina, who preached on this site back in the third century AD. Later, it was given by Sixtus V to the artists' group, Accademia San Luca, who dedicated it to St Luke, the patron saint of painters, as well, and had it rebuilt in the mid-seventeenth century by Pietro da Cortona, who in turn is buried in the church in a tomb of his own design. These days the upper church is dedicated to Santa Martina, with a statue of the saint on the altar, and the lower to St Luke, with an altar by Pietro da Cortona and two works by Alessandro Algardi: a newly restored bas-relief of the *Deposition of Christ* and a terracotta *Pietà*.

San Nicola in Carcere

On the other side of the Capitoline Hill, a little way down Via del Teatro di Marcello on the right, the church of **San Nicola in Carcere** (daily 10.30am–6pm; excavations €3) was built in the eighth century on the site of three Republican temples. It was later dedicated to St Nicholas, the patron saint of seafarers – this used to be the riverfront, and was the site of a lively fish market. The church is nice enough, but the real interest is in the ancient remnants it incorporates. The nave is formed by a wonderful mixture of ancient columns, both Ionic and Corinthian, while down below, informal guided tours of the excavations show how the church is supported by the central Temple of Juno and the columns of two temples either side. You can walk down the narrow Roman street that ran between the temples, squeezing between the massive blocks of the central temple and the column bases of the Temple of Janus that hold up one side of the church – columns that are clearly visible on the outside too.

Santa Maria della Consolazione

Cross the road and walk up, keeping the Capitoline Hill on your left, and you reach the church of **Santa Maria della Consolazione** (daily 6.30am–noon & 3–6pm), which was originally the chapel of a hospital that used to exist just behind. Inside, the Mattei chapel, immediately to the right of the entrance, has a wonderful series of frescoes by Zuccari depicting scenes from the life of Christ, including a naturalistic and dynamic flagellation scene on the left.

San Teodoro

A few steps from here, a little way down Via San Teodoro on the left, the round church of **San Teodoro** (Mon–Fri 9.30am–12.30pm) is Rome's Greek national church, an ancient structure though one that has been somewhat smoothed over inside by the paint and plaster of later years. St Theodore was martyred on this spot in the fourth century AD, and the church originally dates from the sixth century. The apse mosaics are contemporary with the original church, and show Christ with saints, including a bearded Theodore, next to St Peter on the right.

Piazza Bocca della Verità

Down towards the Tiber, Via di Teatro di Marcello meets the riverside main drag at the **Piazza della Bocca della Verità**, also known as the Forum Boarium due to its function as a cattle market in ancient times. There are two of the city's better-preserved Roman temples here, the **Temple of Portunus** and the **Temple of Hercules Victor** – the latter long known as the temple of Vesta because, like all vestal temples, it is circular. Both date from the end of the second century BC, and although you can't get inside, they're fine examples of Republican-era places of worship; the Temple of Hercules Victor is, for what it's worth, the oldest surviving marble structure in Rome.

Santa Maria in Cosmedin

Most people don't bother to enter the church of **Santa Maria in Cosmedin** (daily 10am–5pm), opposite, which is a shame because it's one of Rome's most beautiful – and typical – medieval basilicas, with a thirteenth-century baldachino over a pink ancient Roman bathtub that serves as the altar and a colourful and ingenious Cosmati mosaic floor – one of the city's finest. The sacristy acts as a rather dowdy gift shop, and also displays one of the church's greatest treasures – an eighth-century mosaic of the *Adoration of the Magi*. However, the church's fame rests on the so-called **Bocca della Verità** ("Mouth of Truth") in the portico outside, an ancient Roman drain cover in the shape of an enormous face that in medieval times would apparently swallow the hand of anyone who hadn't told the truth. It was particularly popular with husbands anxious to test the faithfulness of their wives; now it is one of the city's biggest tour-bus attractions, and there are queues most of the day of people having their photograph taken with their hand inside, though you'll rarely have to wait longer than ten minutes or so.

San Giorgio in Velabro

On its northern side, Piazza Bocca della Verità peters out peacefully at the stolid **Arch of Janus**, perhaps Rome's most weathered triumphal arch, beyond which the campanile of the church of **San Giorgio in Velabro** (daily 10am–12.30pm & 4–6.30pm) is a stunted echo of that of Santa Maria across the way. Inside is one of the city's barest and most beautiful ancient basilicas, an ancient-columned nave lit by bare stone windows carved with an intricate design. Only the late-twelfth-century fresco in the apse, the work of Pietro Cavallini, lightens the melancholy mood, showing Christ and the Virgin, and various saints, including St George on the left, to whom the church is dedicated – and whose cranial bones lie in the reliquary under the high altar canopy, placed here in 749 AD, shortly after the original basilica was built.

Immediately to the left of the church the building incorporates a small **arch**, erected by the Forum Boarium market traders in honour of Septimius Severus and his family – whose portraits you can see on the inside, apart from that of his son Geta which, like the version on Septimius Severus's arch in the main forum, was erased after his assassination by his brother Caracalla. Opposite the church, behind an iron gate, you can see the arches of the **Cloaca Maxima**, the ancient city's main sewer, which emerges on the Tiber just to the left of the nearby Ponte Palatino.

Ponte Palatino

The busy **Ponte Palatino**, which connects this side of the river to Trastevere on the opposite bank, is sometimes known as the "English Bridge" for the way the traffic flows across on it on the left (facilitating U-turns from the right to left bank of the river). Look close at the right bank of the river from the bridge itself and you should be able to spot the giant arch placed there to take the outflow of the ancient Cloaca Maxima sewer, now overgrown with trees and bushes.

Ancient Rome

There are remnants of the era of ancient Rome all over the city but the most concentrated and central grouping, which we've called **Ancient Rome**, is the area that stretches southeast from the Capitoline Hill. It's a reasonably traffic-free, self-contained part of the city. But it wasn't always like this: Mussolini ploughed **Via dei Fori Imperiali** through here in the 1930s with the idea of turning it into one massive archeological park. To an extent, of course, that's exactly what it is, and you can easily spend a day or more lazily picking your way through the rubble of what was once the heart of the ancient world. The most obvious place to start is with the original **Forum**, immediately below the Capitoline Hill, taking in the later **Imperial Forums** that lie nearby before heading up to the greener heights of the **Palatine Hill** or continuing straight on for the **Colosseum**.

The Forums and Trajan's Markets

Immediately beyond the Vittoriano, just south of Via dei Fori Imperiali, the original **Roman Forum** was the centre of Republican-era Rome. Even in ancient times Rome was a very large city, in many places stretching out as far as the Aurelian Wall (see p.146) in a sprawl of apartment blocks or *insulae*. The Forum was home to its political and religious institutions, its shops and market stalls, and a meeting-place for all – which it remained until the imperial era, when Rome's increased importance as a world power led to the building of the **Imperial Forums** nearby. Julius Caesar began the expansion in around 50 BC, building a new Senate building, and, beyond it to the northeast, a series of basilicas and temples. After his assassination, work was continued by his nephew and successor Augustus, and later by the Flavian emperors – Vespasian, Nerva and Trajan, who also built the arcade of **Trajan's Markets** behind.

Excavation work started in the mid-1990s and the markets and several of the **Imperial Forums** are now open to the public, and viewable by way of permanent walkways built through and alongside the main remains. The markets and Forum of Trajan and Forum of Augustus on the north side are the most impressive and accessible, but those of Nerva next door and Caesar on the south side might also detain you before you move on to the Forum proper.

The original **Forum** never really recovered from its downgrading, and it's odd to think that during the time when the empire was at its height, neglect had already set in. A fire in the third century AD destroyed many of the buildings, and although the damage was repaired, Rome was by this time in a general state of decay, the

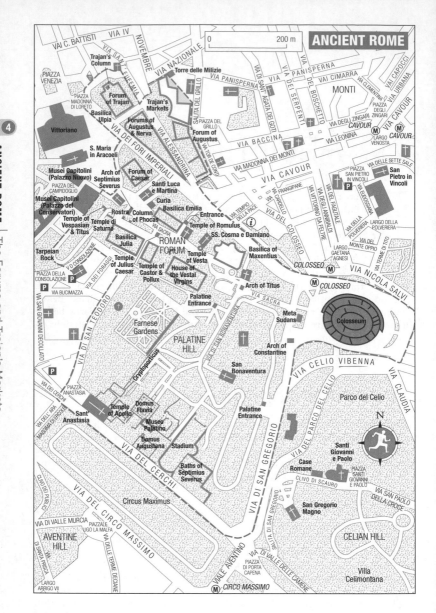

coming of **Christianity** only serving to accelerate the process, particularly for its pagan temples and institutions. After the fall of the city to barbarian invaders, the whole area was left in ruin, its relics quarried for the construction of other parts of Rome during medieval and Renaissance times; the odd church or tower was built *in situ* out of the more viable piles. Excavation of the site didn't start until the beginning of the nineteenth century, and has continued pretty much without stopping: you'll notice a fair part of the site, especially up on the Palatine Hill, closed off for further digs. Incidentally, a **Visitor Centre** (daily 9.30am–6.30pm) just beyond Via Cavour, opposite the church of Santi Cosma e Damiano, has information, a bookshop, toilets and a café to rest your aching feet, if you need to.

Via dei Fori Imperiali

From Piazza Venezia, **Via dei Fori Imperiali**, a soulless boulevard imposed on the area by Mussolini in 1932, cuts south through the heart of Rome's ancient sites. Before then this was a warren of medieval streets that wound around the ruins of the ancient city centre, but, as with the Via della Conciliazione up to St Peter's, the Duce preferred to build something to his own glory rather than preserve that of another era. A long-standing plan (previously championed by Mussolini) to make the entire ancient part of the city into a huge archeological park stretching right down to the catacombs on the Via Appia Antica is still mooted, but although excavations have been undertaken in recent years, they are continuing slowly. It's a dilemma for the city planners: Via dei Fori Imperiali is a major traffic artery, a function which must be preserved. One way around this would be to dig a tunnel under the road – an expensive option but one that is apparently being considered. For the moment, if you want a tranquil stroll between the major sights, you'll have to settle for coming on a Sunday, when a long stretch from Piazza Venezia to Via Appia Antica is closed to traffic and pedestrians take to the streets to stroll past the ruins of the ancient city.

Trajan's Markets

Built into the side of the Quirinale Hill that had been quarried in order to build the Forum, **Trajan's Markets** (Tues–Sun: April–Oct 10am–7pm; Nov–March 9am–5pm; €6.50, audioguide €3.50; ⓦwww.mercatiditraiano.it) are perhaps the

▲ Trajan's Markets

most exciting city-centre Roman ruins to be recently excavated and opened to the public, a perfectly preserved crescent of shops and arcades that don't leave as much to the imagination as many parts of the ancient city. The **great hall** in which you enter is an impressive two-storeyed space, flanked by rooms that house displays on each of the Imperial Forums – exhibits include a large head of Constantine, a torso of a warrior and a frieze from the temple of Venus Genetrix in the Forum of Caesar, the columns of which you can clearly see from the terrace upstairs. You can descend from the hall to the shop-lined **Via Biberatica**, which winds around the bottom of the arcade and side of the hall and afterwards come back up for a look at the fragments of masonry and statuary in the museum and climb up further to the belvedere for a view of the Forum of Trajan below. Take a look also at the **Torre delle Milizie**, behind the markets, which is fondly imagined to be the tower from which Nero watched Rome burn, although it's actually a twelfth-century fortification left over from days when Rome was divided into warring factions within the city walls. The top was destroyed by a blast of lightning in the fifteenth century and the tower is closed to visitors.

The Forum of Trajan

One of the major victims of Mussolini's plan for the area was the remains of the **Forum of Trajan** (Tues–Sun 9am–6pm; €3), a complex of basilicas, monuments, apartments and shops that was in its day the most sumptuous of the Imperial Forums, built at what was probably the very pinnacle of Roman power and prestige, after Trajan returned from conquering Dacia (modern Romania) in 112 AD. It's currently fairly unrecognizable, the main section no more than a sunken area of scattered columns to the left of the road, fronting the semicircle of **Trajan's Markets** (see above). Below the markets, the **Basilica Ulpia** was a central part of the Forum of Trajan, an immense structure, with five aisles and a huge apse at either end, that measured 176m long by 59m wide; the central nave is discernible from the large paved area in the centre, and the column stumps give an idea of its former dimensions. At the head of the basilica, enclosed in what was probably a small courtyard, the enormous **Trajan's Column** was erected to celebrate the emperor's victories in Dacia, and is covered top to bottom with reliefs commemorating the highlights of the campaign. The carving on the base shows the trophies brought back and bears an inscription saying that the column was dedicated to Trajan by the Senate and People of Rome in 113 AD. The statue on the top is of St Peter, placed here by Pope Sixtus V in the late sixteenth century, and made from the bronze doors of Sant'Agnese fuori le Mura on Via Nomentana (see p.113).

The Forum of Caesar

There's precious little to see at the **Forum of Caesar**, the first of the Imperial Forums to be built, and in any case you can only view it from the road. The site is dominated by the columns of the large temple dedicated to Venus Genetrix, the Roman goddess of motherhood and mother of Aeneas, from whom Caesar was said to be descended.

The Forum of Augustus

Back on Via dei Fori Imperiali, the round brick facade you can see to the left, across the field of ruins, now houses the Order of Malta but was once part of the **Forum of Augustus**. Just beyond, the monumental staircase and platform was Augustus's Temple of Mars the Avenger, put up by Augustus in memory of his uncle and adoptive father, Julius Caesar, after the last of his assassins had been killed. The temple is backed by a large wall of grey stone that was erected to prevent fire from spreading into the forums from the densely inhabited neighbourhood of Suburra up on the Esquiline Hill.

You can get up closer to the ruins here by way of a metal walkway, which also takes you through to the lower streets of the Monti district, or just continue on down past the various other Imperial Forums to the Visitor Centre and the church of Santi Cosma e Damiano opposite.

The Forum of Nerva

The **Forum of Nerva** is also known as the "transitional forum" for its role in connecting the Imperial Forums with each other and with the Suburra district behind. It was built by the crazed and cruel Emperor Domitian, but only finished after his murder by his successor, the elderly Emperor Nerva, who completed the temple of Minerva, and naturally dedicated the complex to himself; two columns supporting a gateway set in a stretch of wall are pretty much all that is left.

Santi Cosma e Damiano

Across the road from the Forum of Augustus, the vestibule of the church of **Santi Cosma e Damiano**, Via dei Fori Imperiali 1 (Fri–Sun 10am–1pm & 3–6pm) was originally created from the Temple of Romulus in the Forum, which you can look down into from the nave of the church. Turn around, and you'll see the mosaics in the apse, showing the naturalistically depicted figures of the two saints being presented to Christ by St Peter and St Paul, flanked by St Felix on the left and St Theodore on the right. Outside, the cloister is wonderfully peaceful compared to the busy roads around. For a €1 donation you can also visit the massive Neapolitan **presepio** or Christmas crib, displayed in a room in the corner here (Fri–Sun 10am–1pm & 3–6pm), a huge piece of work with literally hundreds of figures spread amongst the ruins of ancient Rome.

The Roman Forum

Not far from the church is the main entrance to the **Roman Forum** (Ⓦ www .capitolium.org) – not surprisingly one of the city's top attractions, but for many also one of its most disappointing, since you need a good imagination and some grasp of history to really appreciate the place. Certainly it holds some of the most ruined ruins you'll see: indeed it was abandoned (and looted) for so long that very little is anything like intact. But these five or so acres were once the heart of the Mediterranean world, and are a very real and potent testament to a power that held a large chunk of the earth in its thrall for close on five centuries, and whose influence reverberates right up to the present day – in language, in architecture, in political terms and systems, even in the romance that time has lent to its ruins.

Visiting the Forum and Palatine Hill

The **Forum**, **Palatine** and **Colosseum** are open every day at the following times: Jan to mid-Feb 8.30am–3.30pm, mid-Feb to mid-March 8.30am–4pm, mid- to end March 8.30am–4.30pm, April–Aug 8.30am–6.15pm, Sept 8.30am–6pm, Oct 8.30am–5.30pm, Nov & Dec 8.30am–3.30pm. Tickets cost €12 for all three sites and are valid for one day; 18- to 24-year-olds €7.50. There are guided tours of the Forum in English every day at 1pm, and of the Palatine at noon; both €4. Audioguides cost €4.50.

The decline and fall of the Forum

In 667 AD, Constans II, ruler of the Eastern empire, paid a state visit to Rome. He came to the Forum, and, seeing all the temples and basilicas held together with bronze and iron cramps, decided that the metal would serve better in his war against encroaching Islam and ordered all the metal to be transported back home and forged into spearpoints, arrowheads and armour for his forces. It took just twelve days to dismantle the metal props, but the result was a disaster: everything was captured en route to Constantinople by Saracen raiders, and the columns and arches supporting all the buildings in the Forum fell down with the next earth tremor. By the early ninth century hardly anything remained standing – ripe for the looters of later years, and one reason why so little is left today.

The Via Sacra

Immediately inside the main entrance, take some time to get orientated. You can sit down on the three long steps that flank the other side of the **Via Sacra**, which runs directly through the core of the Forum, from below the Capitoline Hill in the west to the far eastern extent of the site and the Arch of Titus (where there's a handy exit/entrance for the Colosseum). This was the best-known street of ancient Rome, along which victorious emperors and generals would ride in procession to give thanks at the Capitoline's Temple of Jupiter. It's possible, however, that the modern street isn't the original Via Sacra, and was in fact only given the name in the 1550s, when the Holy Roman Emperor, Charles V, visited Pope Paul III and the only triumphal arch they could find to march under was the Arch of Septimius Severus, a couple of hundred metres to your left.

The Regia and around

The steps you're sitting on are part of the **Regia**, or House of the Kings, an extremely ancient – and ruined – group of foundations that probably date from the reign of the second king of Rome, Numa, who ruled from 715 to 673 BC.

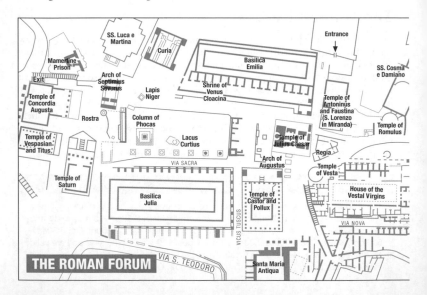

There was a shrine of Mars here, housing the shields and spears of the god of war, which generals embarking on a campaign rattled before setting off. If the shields and spears rattled of their own accord it was a bad omen, requiring purification and repentance rites. The Regia later became the residence of Julius Caesar, who moved in here in 45 BC – an imperious act which contributed to his downfall.

On the other side of the road from the Regia, the **Temple of Antoninus and Faustina** is the best-preserved temple in the Forum, mainly because of its existence since the seventh century as the church of **San Lorenzo in Miranda**. The six huge Corinthian columns across its front are still connected by an inscribed lintel, dedicating the temple by order of the Senate to the god Antoninus and the goddess Faustina, the parents of Marcus Aurelius – Roman emperors were always considered to be deities. Above the inscription was the roof architrave, along whose sides the original frieze of griffins, candelabra and acanthus scrolls can be seen. Otherwise, the brick stairs leading up to the floor of the temple are a modern reconstruction, while the facade of the church dates from 1602.

Next to the Regia, the pile of rubble immersed in cement with the little green roof is all that remains of the grandeur and magnificence that comprised the **Temple of Julius Caesar** – the round brick stump under the roof marks the spot where Caesar was cremated, and around which the temple was built. You may hear tour guides declaiming Mark Antony's "Friends, Romans, countrymen" speech from here; bear in mind that not only was the speech made up by Shakespeare, but also that apparently Mark Antony only read Caesar's will, and that he would have done it from the Rostra (see p.84).

The football pitch of broken columns across the street marks the site of the **Basilica Emilia**, built in the second century BC to house law courts, and, in the little booths and boutiques flanking it on the Via Sacra side, moneychangers. Close by, a little marble plaque dedicated to **Venus Cloacina** marks the site of a small shrine dedicated to Venus where the Cloaca Maxima canal drained the Forum, which was originally marshland. The Cloaca Maxima reaches all the way to the Tiber from here, and still keeps the area drained.

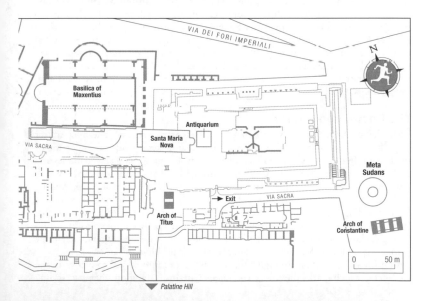

The Curia and around

A little way beyond, the large cube-shaped building on the right is the **Curia**, built on the orders of Julius Caesar as part of his programme for expanding the Forum – it connects with the Forum of Caesar outside – although what you see now is a third-century AD reconstruction built during the era of the Emperor Diocletian. The Senate met here during the Republican period, and augurs would come to announce the wishes of the gods. For centuries the Curia served as a church, reverting to its original form only earlier this century, when it was restored, and its bronze doors – which had been removed in the seventeenth century to San Giovanni in Laterano, where they remain – were replaced with reproductions.

Inside, three wide stairs rise left and right, on which about three hundred senators on folding chairs could be accommodated. In the centre is the speaker's platform, with a porphyry statue of a togaed figure. Otherwise, apart from the floor, elegantly patterned in red, yellow, green and white marble, there's not much left of its ancient decor, only the grey and white marble facing each side of the speaker's platform, which would once have covered the entire hall. The ceiling is a modern replacement, and in Roman times would have been gilded. The large marble reliefs here, the *Plutei of Trajan* – found outside and brought here for safekeeping – show Trajan in the midst of public-spirited acts, forgiving the public debt owed by citizens to the state (porters carry large register books and place them before the seated emperor, where they will be burnt) and, on the right giving a woman a sack of money, a representation of the emperor's welfare plan for widows and orphans. Look closely at the reliefs and you can see how parts of the Forum would have looked at the time: in one, a fig tree, the columns and arches of the Basilica Julia, the facade of the Temple of Saturn, a triumphal arch and the Temple of Vespasian and Titus; in the other, the columns and eaves of the Temple of Castor and Pollux, and the Arch of Augustus.

In front of the Curia, the black, fenced-off paving of the **Lapis Niger** marks the traditional site of the tomb of Romulus, the steps beneath (usually closed) leading down to a monument that was considered sacred ground during classical times. Across the travertine pavement from here, the **Column of Phocas** is one of a few commemorative columns here that retains its dedicatory inscription. To the right, the **Arch of Septimius Severus** was constructed in the early third century AD by his sons Caracalla and Geta to mark their father's victories in what is now Iran. The friezes on it recall Severus and in particular Caracalla, who ruled Rome with undisciplined terror for seven years. There's a space where Geta was commemorated – Caracalla, who had inherited the empire jointly, had him executed in 213 AD, and his name expediently removed from the arch altogether.

The Rostra and around

To the left of the arch, the low brown wall of the **Rostra** faces the wide-open scatter of paving, dumped stones and beached columns that makes up the central portion of the Forum. In its heyday it would have been crowded with politicians, tribunes and traders. Facing the central part of the Forum, the Rostra was the place where important speeches were made, and it was probably from here that Mark Antony spoke about Caesar after his death. Left of the Rostra are the long steps of the **Basilica Julia**, built by Julius Caesar in the 50s BC after he returned from the Gallic Wars. All that remain are a few column bases and one nearly complete column, and you can't climb the stairs – although you can still see the gameboards scratched in the marble steps where idlers in the Forum played their pebble-toss games.

A bit further along, on the right, the guardrails lead into a kind of alcove in the pavement, which marks the site of the **Lacus Curtius** – the spot where, according to legend, a chasm opened in the city's earliest days and the soothsayers determined that it would be closed only when Rome had sacrificed its most valuable possession into it. Marcus Curtius, a Roman soldier who declared that Rome's most valuable possession was a loyal citizen, hurled himself and his horse into the void and it duly shut. Further on, towards the Capitoline, you reach the **Temple of Saturn** – the oldest temple in the Forum, dating originally from 497 BC, although the base and eight columns you see today are the result of a series of restorations carried out between 42 BC and 380 AD. The temple was also the Roman treasury and mint. To the right of the temple, three columns still stand from the **Temple of Vespasian and Titus** of the 80s AD. Still further to the right, behind the Arch of Septimius Severus, the large pile of brick and cement rubble is all that remains of the **Temple of Concordia Augusta**, dedicated by Tiberius in 10 AD.

Santa Maria Antiqua and the Temple of Castor and Pollux

Retracing your steps past the Forum proper takes you to **Vicus Tuscus**, "Etruscan Street", at the end of which are public toilets and a water fountain, and the church of **Santa Maria Antiqua**, which formed the vestibule to the Emperor Domitian's palace on the Palatine Hill, and was the first ancient building to be converted for Christian worship – recently open again after many years. Back around the corner to the right, the enormous pile of rubble topped by three graceful Corinthinan columns is the **Temple of Castor and Pollux**, dedicated in 484 BC to the divine twins or Dioscuri, the offspring of Jupiter by Leda, who appeared miraculously to ensure victory for the Romans in a key battle. The story goes that a group of Roman citizens were gathered around a water fountain on this spot fretting about the war when Castor and Pollux appeared and reassured them that the battle was won – hence the temple, and their adoption as the special protectors of Rome.

House of the Vestal Virgins

Beyond here, the **House of the Vestal Virgins** is a second-century AD reconstruction of a building originally by Nero. Vesta was the Roman goddess of the hearth and home, and her cult was an important one in ancient Rome. Her temple was in the charge of the so-called **Vestal Virgins**, who had the responsibility of keeping the sacred flame of Vesta alight, and were obliged to remain chaste for the thirty years that they served (they usually started at around age 10). If the flame should go out, the woman responsible was scourged; if she should lose her chastity, she was buried alive (her male partner-in-crime was flogged to death in front of the Curia). Because of the importance of their office, they were accorded special privileges: a choice section in the Colosseum was reserved for them; only they and the empress could ride in a wheeled vehicle within the confines of the city; and they had the right to pardon any criminal who managed to get close enough to one of them to beseech their mercy. A vestal virgin could resign her post if she wished, but she had the benefit of residing in a very comfortable palace: four floors of rooms around a central courtyard, with the round **Temple of Vesta** at the near end. The rooms are mainly ruins now, though they're fairly recognizable on the Palatine side, and you can get a good sense of the shape of the place from the remains of the courtyard, still with its pool in the centre and fringed by the statues or inscribed pedestals of the women themselves.

The Basilica of Maxentius

Opposite the Vestals' house, the curved facade of the **Temple of Romulus** (the son of the Emperor Maxentius, not the founder of Rome), dating from 309 AD, has been sanctified and serves as vestibule for the church of **Santi Cosma e Damiano** behind (see p.81). Just past the temple, a shady walkway to the left leads up to the **Basilica of Maxentius**, sometimes called the Basilica of Constantine, which rises up towards the main road – in terms of size and ingenuity probably the Forum's most impressive remains. By the early fourth century, when this structure was built, Roman architects and engineers were expert at building with poured cement. Begun by Maxentius, it was continued by his co-emperor and rival, Constantine, after he had defeated him at the Battle of Ponte Milvio in 312 AD. It's said that Michelangelo studied the hexagonal coffered arches here when grappling with the dome of St Peter's and apparently Renaissance architects frequently used its apse and arches as a model.

The Antiquarium and Arch of Titus

Back on the Via Sacra, past the church of Santa Maria Nova, the **Antiquarium of the Forum** (free, but closed at the time of research) houses a collection of statue fragments, capitals, tiles, mosaics and other bits and pieces found around the Forum – none of it very interesting, apart from a number of skeletons and wooden coffins exhumed from an Iron Age necropolis found to the right of the Temple of Antoninus and Faustina.

From the basilica the Via Sacra climbs more steeply, past a grassy series of ruins that no one has been able to positively identify, to the **Arch of Titus**, which stands commandingly on a low arm of the Palatine Hill, looking one way down the remainder of the Via Sacra to the Colosseum, and back over the Forum proper. The arch was built by Titus's brother, Domitian, after the emperor's death in 81 AD, to commemorate his victories in Judaea in 70 AD and his triumphal return from that campaign, and it sets in stone the inauguration of the Vespasian dynasty and Rome's return to peace and stability following the disruption that ensued after Nero's death. It's a much-restored structure, and you can see, in reliefs on the inside, scenes of Titus riding in a chariot with Nike, goddess of Victory, being escorted by representatives of the Senate and Plebs, and, on the opposite side, spoils being removed from the Temple in Jerusalem.

The Colosseum and the Palatine Hill

Beyond the Forum, a lake lay where the **Colosseum** stands now, drained by a small stream that wove between the **Palatine** and **Celian hills**, curving to empty into the Tiber close by. The slopes of the Palatine and Celian hills were inhabited by people living in shanties and huts until the great fire of 64 AD, when Nero incorporated the area into his grand design for the city, building a gigantic nymphaeum or courtyard to support his planned gardens on the Celian Hill, part of his Domus Aurea (see p.115), and cleaning up the slopes of the two hills. Eventually a temple to the deified Claudius was built on the Celian Hill, and the Palatine became the residence of the emperors, fed by water brought by the arched span of the Aqua Claudia.

The Palatine Hill

Turning right at the Arch of Titus takes you up to the ticket booth and main entrance to the **Palatine Hill** (see box, p.81 for times and prices); there's another, usually quieter entrance five minutes' walk away on Via San Gregorio – the main

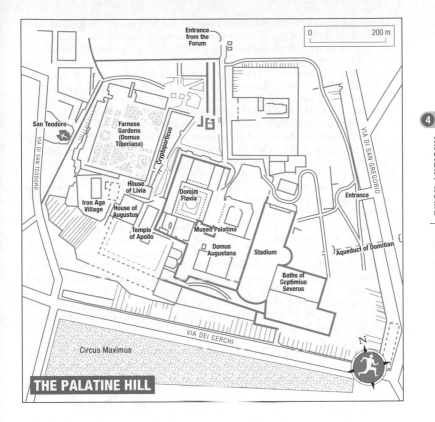

THE PALATINE HILL

road running up towards the Circus Maximus. The Palatine is supposedly where the city of Rome was founded, by Romulus and Remus, and holds some of its most ancient remnants. In a way it's a more pleasant site to tour than the Forum, larger, greener and more of a park – a good place to have a picnic and relax after the rigours of the ruins below. In the days of the Republic, the Palatine was the most desirable address in Rome (the word "palace" is derived from it), and the big names continued to colonize it during the imperial era, trying to outdo each other with ever larger and more magnificent dwellings.

Along the main path up from the Forum, the **Domus Flavia**, the work of the Emperor Domitian, was once one of the most splendid residences, and, although it's now almost completely ruined, the peristyle is easy enough to identify, with its fountain and hexagonal brick arrangement in the centre. To the left, the top level of the gargantuan **Domus Augustana** spreads to the far brink of the hill – not the home of Augustus as its name suggests, but the private house of any emperor (or "Augustus"). From here, you can look down onto its vast central courtyard with maze-like fountain and wander to the brink of the deep trench of the **Stadium**. On the far side of the stadium, the ruins of the Domus and **Baths of Septimius Severus** cling to the side of the hill, the terrace giving good views over the Colosseum and the churches of the Celian Hill opposite.

The large grey building nearby houses the **Museo Palatino** (daily 9am–6pm), which contains an assortment of statues, pottery and architectural fragments that have been excavated on the Palatine during the last 150 years. The ground floor has finds from the early years of Rome and reconstructions of the original Iron Age village. The upper floor leaps ahead to the imperial age, and highlights include three beautifully preserved black marble *herms*, statues of women that supposedly filled the niches in Augustus's Temple of Apollo (see below); a piece of terracotta frieze from the same temple showing Apollo and Hercules in dispute (a reference, perhaps, to Augustus's rivalry with Mark Antony, who frequently identified himself with Hercules); and busts of various emperors: two of Nero, one old, one young, Hadrian, Antoninus Pius and a very young Marcus Aurelius. There are nice details too – fragments of *intarsio*, a fragment of a relief showing Apollo playing the lyre; the bottom of a relief of a togaed figure carrying a brace of ducks – supposedly the personification of winter – from the fourth century AD.

In the opposite direction from the Domus Flavia is the **Cryptoporticus**, a long passage built by Nero to link the vestibule of his Domus Aurea (see p.115) with the Domus Augustana and other Palatine palaces, and decorated along with well-preserved Roman stucco-work at the far end, towards the **House of Livia**. This was originally believed to have been the residence of Livia, the wife of Augustus, but it's now been identified as part of the **House of Augustus** and recently restored – and its courtyard and some of the inner rooms are decorated with frescoes and tromple l'oeils in vivid colours. There's another set of ruins beyond, next to which are the scant remains of the Palatine **Temple of Apollo**, dedicated by Augustus himself in 28 BC.

Climb up the steps by the entrance to the Cryptoporticus and you're in the bottom corner of the **Farnese Gardens**, one of the first botanical gardens in Europe, laid out by Cardinal Alessandro Farnese in the mid-sixteenth century and now a tidily planted, shady retreat from the exposed heat of the ruins. The gardens occupy the ruins of a palace built by Tiberius, the **Domus Tiberiana**, the most extant remains of which form a terrace which looks back over the Forum. A terrace at the opposite end looks down on the church of San Teodoro, across to St Peter's, and down on the new excavations immediately below – the traces of an **Iron Age village** that perhaps marks the real centre of Rome's ancient beginnings.

Around the Colosseum

Leaving the Forum by way of the Via Sacra, under the Arch of Titus (see p.86), you see the huge **Arch of Constantine** to your right, placed here in the early decades of the fourth century AD after Constantine had consolidated his power as sole emperor. The deterioration of the arts during the late stages of the Roman Empire meant there were hardly any sculptors around who could produce original work, and most of the sculptural decoration here had to be removed from other monuments. The builders were probably quite ignorant of the significance of the pieces they borrowed: the round medallions are taken from a temple dedicated to the Emperor Hadrian's lover, Antinous, and show Antinous and Hadrian engaged in the hunt. The other pieces, removed from the Forum of Trajan, show Dacian prisoners captured in Trajan's war there. The large inscription in the centre was made for the arch, and dedicates the arch to Constantine for his wisdom – presumably in making Christianity the official religion of the empire, although no one really knows what this refers to.

Between the Arch of Constantine and the Colosseum, at a pivotal point in the Via Sacra, stood a monumental fountain or **Meta Sudans**, the outline of which can still be seen today in the form of a series of recently excavated low brick walls. A "Meta" was the marker in the centre of a racecourse, and was usually an obelisk or some other large, easily visible object. In this case it was a conical fountain that

Visiting the Colosseum

The **Colosseum** is open at the following times: Jan to mid-Feb 8.30am–3.30pm, mid-Feb to mid-March 8.30am–4pm, mid- to end March 8.30am–4.30pm, April–Aug 8.30am–6.15pm, Sept 8.30am–6pm, Oct 8.30am–5.30pm, Nov & Dec 8.30am–3.30pm. Entrance costs €12, which also includes the Forum and Palatine Hill and any temporary exhibitions; 18- to 24-year-olds €7.50. **Queues** can be a problem: while they do move quickly, they're rarely less than 100m long and often stretch through the arcade on the metro station side of the stadium and into the scrum of touts outside. To avoid them, try turning up before the Colosseum opens, or buy an Archeocard or RomaPass (see p.40), which allow you to use a different queue, or join a guided tour; or simply buy your ticket at the Palatine or Forum entrances which are usually quieter. There are **tours** in English roughly every 30 minutes from 9.15am (€4), or you can rent an audioguide (€4.50). If you'd rather not take the stairs, there's a lift in the northeastern corner – just keep walking from the ticket office.

Once inside, you're free to wander around most of the lower level, and all the way round the upper level, though even here you are still only about halfway up the original structure; all the higher parts of the stadium are closed these days. You can gaze down into the innards of the arena, but there's been no original arena floor since its excavation in the nineteenth century and as such it too is out of bounds to visitors. The upper floor on the northern side contains a decent bookshop and a space for temporary exhibitions; an area by the lifts is given over to a display of fragments of masonry and other finds from the Colosseum.

was probably dedicated to Apollo, and produced a slow supply of water that resembled sweat – hence its name the "Sweating Meta".

On the far side of the Colosseum, the ruins between Via di San Giovanni in Laterano and Via Labicana are what's left of the **Ludus Magnus**, a smaller arena that was surrounded by gladiators' barracks, and one of a number of buildings here that were connected to the main arena by tunnels – some of which still exist but are sadly not open to public view.

The Colosseum

Across the way from here, the **Colosseum** is perhaps Rome's most awe-inspiring ancient monument, and one which, unlike the Forum, needs little historical knowledge or imagination to deduce its function. This enormous structure was so solidly built that despite the depredations of nearly two thousand years – earthquakes, fires, riots, wars, and, not least, plundering for its seemingly inexhaustible supply of ready-cut travertine blocks (the Barberini and Cancelleria palaces, even St Peter's, all used stone from here) – it still stands relatively intact, a readily recognizable symbol not just of the city of Rome, but of the entire ancient world. It's not much more than a shell now, eaten away by pollution and cracked by the vibrations of cars and metro trains; around the outside, the arches would originally have held statues, and there are gaping holes where metal brackets linked the great blocks together. The basic structure of the place is easy to see, however, and has served as a model for stadiums around the world ever since: oddly enough, until Sydney 2000 it appeared on all winners' medals in the **Olympics**; and it still graces the (Italian) 5c coin. You'll not be alone in appreciating it, and during summer the combination of people and scaffolding can make a visit more like touring a modern building-site than an ancient monument. But visit late in the evening or early morning before the tour buses have arrived, go

Beastly happenings at the Colosseum

The Romans flocked to the Colosseum for many things, but **gladiatorial contests** were the big attraction. Gladiatorial combat as a Roman tradition was a direct import from the Etruscans, who thought it seemly to sacrifice a few prisoners of war or slaves at the funeral games of an important person. By the second century BC gladiatorial games had become so institutionalized in Rome that a gladiatorial school, or Ludus, was installed in the city – a rather grim affair, consisting of a barracks for gladiators and a ring in which they could practise with blunt weapons under supervision.

Gladiatorial combat was probably the greatest and cruellest of all bloodsports. At the start of the games the gladiators would enter through the monumental door at the eastern end of the arena. They would make a procession around the ring and halt in front of the emperor's box, where they would make their famous greeting, "Hail Caesar, we who are about to die salute you." Gladiators were divided into several classes, each performing different types of combat. There was the heavily armed "Samnite", named after the type of arms the Romans had captured on the defeat of that tribe in 310 BC, equipped with heavy armour, an oblong bronze shield, a visored helmet with crest and plumes, and a sword (*gladius*). Usually a Samnite would be pitted against a combatant without armour, equipped only with a cast net and a trident, whose main protection was that he was unencumbered and thereby could be fleet of foot. He had, however, only one cast of his net in which to entangle the Samnite and kill him with his trident. Neither man was allowed to flee from the arena, and, once captured or disarmed, the roaring mob would be asked whether the loser should be killed or be allowed to live. If he had put up a good fight he would usually be spared; if he had not fought as valiantly as he should, he would be slaughtered on the spot. The advent of Christianity brought a gradual end to the gladiatorial games (contrary to popular opinion, Christians were never fed to the lions here), and in 404 AD the Emperor Honorius abolished them altogether.

The other activities conducted in the Colosseum involved **animals**. In the hundred-day games that inaugurated the Colosseum, something like 9000 beasts were massacred – roughly twelve killings a minute – and during the 450 years of activity here several breeds of African elephant and lion were rendered extinct. There were also gladiatorial games which involved "hunting" wild animals, and sometimes creatures would be pitted against each other – bears would be tied to bulls and have to fight to the finish, lions would take on tigers, dogs would be set against wolves, and so on. The last games involving animals were conducted in the year 523 AD, after which the Colosseum gradually fell into disuse and disrepair.

up a level to get a real sense of the size of the building, and the arena can seem more like the marvel it really is.

Past and present

Originally known as the Flavian Amphitheatre (the name Colosseum is a much later invention), it was begun around 72 AD by the Emperor **Vespasian**, who was anxious to extinguish the memory of Nero, and so chose the site of Nero's outrageous Domus Aurea (see p.115) for the stadium. The gesture was meant to indicate that the days of Nero were over and the city was being given back to the people. The Colosseum is sited on a lake that lay in front of the vestibule of the palace, where Nero had erected a huge statue of himself as sun god. The lake was drained, and the Colosseum was – incredibly, given the size of the project – inaugurated by Vespasian's son Titus about eight years later, an event celebrated by a hundred days of continuous games; it was finally completed by Domitian, Titus's brother, the third of the Flavian emperors.

Up until this time gladiatorial and other bloody games had been conducted in a makeshift stadium in the Roman Forum, near the Curia. The stands were temporary and constructed of wood, and had to be erected and taken down every time there were games. It is said that seventy thousand Hebrew slaves did the heavy work at the Colosseum. Fifty thousand cartloads of pre-cut travertine stone was hauled from the quarries at Tivoli, a distance of 27km. In the depths of what must have been the muddy bottom of the lake, a **labyrinth** was laid out, walling in passages for the contestants and creating areas for assembling and storing sets, scenery and other requirements for gladiatorial contests.

The overall structure was tastefully designed, with close attention paid to decoration. On the outside, the arena's three **arcades** rose in strict classical fashion to a flat surface at the top punctuated only by windows, where there was a series of supports for masts that protruded at the upper limit. These masts, 240 in total, were used to array a canvas awning over the spectators inside the arena. Inside, beyond the corridors that led up to the seats, lavishly decorated with painted stuccoes, there was room for a total of around 60,000 people seated and 10,000 or so standing; the design was such that all 70,000 could enter and be seated in a matter of minutes – surely a lesson for designers of modern stadiums.

Seating was allocated according to social status, with the emperor and his attendants naturally occupying the best seats in the house, and the social class of the spectators diminishing further up the stands. There were no ticket sales as we conceive of them; rather, tickets were distributed through – and according to the social status of – Roman heads of households. These "tickets" were in fact wooden tags, with the entrance, row, aisle and seat number carved on them.

Inside the amphitheatre, the labyrinth below was covered over with a wooden floor, punctuated at various places for trapdoors and lifts to raise and lower the animals that were to take part in the games. The floor was covered with canvas to make it waterproof and the canvas was covered with several centimetres of sand to absorb blood; in fact, our word "arena" is derived from the Latin word for sand.

The Tridente and Trevi

The northern part of Rome's city centre is sometimes known as the **Tridente**, due to the trident shape of the roads leading down from the apex of Piazza del Popolo – Via del Corso in the centre, Via di Ripetta on the left and Via del Babuino on the right. The area around **Piazza di Spagna**, especially, is travellers' Rome. Historically it was the **artistic quarter** of the capital, and wealthy young men and women on eighteenth- and nineteenth-century grand tours would come here in search of the colourful and exotic. Keats and Giorgio de Chirico are just two of the many artists and writers who have lived on Piazza di Spagna, Goethe had lodgings along Via del Corso, and places such as *Caffè Greco* and *Babington's Tea Rooms* were the meeting-places of a local artistic and expat community for almost two centuries. Today these institutions have been supplemented by latter-day traps for the tourist dollar: American Express and McDonald's have settled into the area, and the local residents are more likely to be investment bankers than artists or poets – **Via Condotti** and the surrounding streets are these days strictly international designer territory, with some of Rome's fanciest stores. But the air of a Rome being discovered – even colonized – by foreigners persists, even if most of those hanging out on the **Spanish Steps** are flying-visit teenagers.

South of the Tridente, the area around the **Trevi Fountain** is similarly thronged by tourists, but not unpleasantly so. The knot of streets around the fountain – which itself is well worth seeing, however obvious a sight it may seem – holds a few less essential stops and are a logical prelude to the sights of the Quirinale immediately above (see Chapter 6).

Via del Corso

The central prong of the Tridente, **Via del Corso** is Rome's main thoroughfare, linking Piazza Venezia at its southern end with Piazza del Popolo to the north. You can follow it all the way up, dipping into the centro storico as and when you feel like it. The streets on this side of the centre focus on the ancient Roman dome of the **Pantheon** (see p.45) and further north on the offices of the **Italian parliament** and prime minister (see p.49), while on the opposite side it gives onto the swish shopping thoroughfares that lead up to Piazza di Spagna.

Named after the races that used to take place along here during Renaissance times, the street has had its fair share of **famous residents** during the years: Goethe lived at no. 18 for two years, close to the Piazza del Popolo end (see p.98); the Shelleys – Percy and Mary – lived for several years in the Palazzo Vesporio, at Via del Corso 375 (now a bank), during which time they lost their son William to a fever (see p.143). Since the middle of the last century, it has become Rome's principal **shopping** street, home to mid-range boutiques and

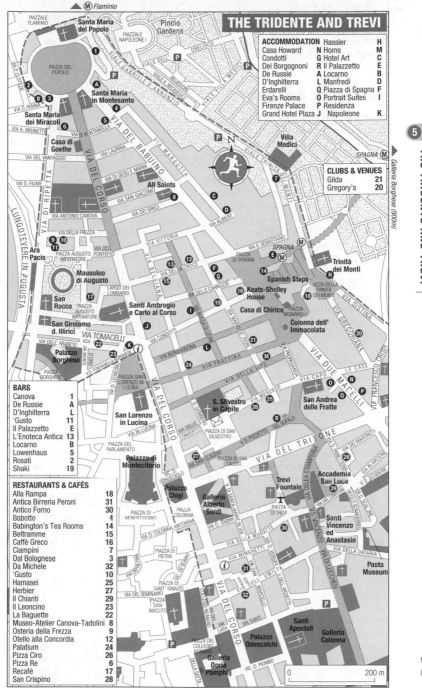

THE TRIDENTE AND TREVI

M Flaminio

PIAZZALE FLAMINIO
Santa Maria del Popolo
Pincio Gardens
PIAZZALE NAPOLEONE I
PIAZZA DEL POPOLO
Santa Maria in Montesanto
Santa Maria dei Miracoli
Casa di Goethe
Villa Medici
SPAGNA M
Galleria Borghese (900m)
All Saints
Ara Pacis
Mausoleo di Augusto
SPAGNA M
Trinità dei Monti
San Rocco
Santi Ambrogio e Carlo al Corso
PIAZZA DI SPAGNA
Spanish Steps
Keats-Shelley House
Casa di Chirico
San Girolamo d. Illirici
Colonna dell' Immacolata
Palazzo Borghese
San Lorenzo in Lucina
S. Silvestro in Capite
San Andrea delle Fratte
Palazzo di Montecitorio
Palazzo Chigi
Galleria Alberto Sordi
Trevi Fountain
Accademia San Luca
Santi Vincenzo ed Anastasio
Pasta Museum
Palazzo Odescalchi
Santi Apostoli
Galleria Colonna
Galleria Doria Pamphilj

ACCOMMODATION

Casa Howard	N	Hassler	H
Condotti	G	Homs	M
Dei Borgognoni	R	Hotel Art	C
De Russie	A	Il Palazzetto	E
D'Inghilterra	L	Locarno	B
Erdarelli	Q	Manfredi	F
Eva's Rooms	O	Piazza di Spagna	D
Firenze Palace	P	Portrait Suites	I
Grand Hotel Plaza	J	Residenza	
		Napoleone	K

CLUBS & VENUES

Gilda	21
Gregory's	20

BARS

Canova	1
De Russie	A
D'Inghilterra	L
'Gusto	11
Il Palazzetto	E
L'Enoteca Antica	13
Locarno	B
Lowenhaus	5
Rosati	2
Shaki	19

RESTAURANTS & CAFÉS

Alla Rampa	18
Antica Birreria Peroni	31
Antico Forno	30
Babotto	4
Babington's Tea Rooms	14
Beltramme	15
Caffè Greco	16
Ciampini	7
Dal Bolognese	3
Da Michele	32
'Gusto	10
Hamasei	25
Herbier	27
Il Chianti	29
Il Leoncino	23
La Baguette	22
Museo-Atelier Canova-Tadolini	8
Osteria della Frezza	9
Otello alla Concordia	12
Palatium	24
Pizza Ciro	26
Pizza Re	6
Recafé	17
San Crispino	28

0   200 m

chain stores that make it a busy stretch during the day, full of hurrying pedestrians and crammed buses, but a relatively dead one come the evening. The good news is that the top end, beyond Largo Goldoni, where the bulk of the shops are, is pedestrianized, making shopping and strolling much easier and more enjoyable.

Piazza di Spagna

Piazza di Spagna underlines the area's international credentials, taking its name from the Spanish Embassy which has stood here since the seventeenth century – though oddly enough part of the square was once known as Piazza di Francia for the French church of Trinità dei Monti at the top of the Spanish Steps (see opposite). It's a long, thin straggle of a square, almost entirely enclosed by buildings, and centring on the distinctive, boat-shaped **Fontana della Barcaccia**, the last work of Pietro Bernini, father of the more famous Gianlorenzo. It apparently commemorates the great flood of Christmas Day 1598, when a barge from the Tiber was washed up on the slopes of Pincio Hill close by. The square itself is fringed by high-end clothes and jewellery shops and is normally thronged with tourists, but for all that it's one of the city's most appealing open spaces. The large **Colonna dell'Immacolata** at the southern end commemorates Pius IX's official announcement, in 1854, of the dogma of the Immaculate Conception while, close by, hackles were raised when McDonald's unveiled plans to open a branch on the square in the early 1980s. Its presence here is proof that the American multinational won what turned out to be quite a battle. But it's to the city's credit that this is one of the most discreet examples you'll encounter, tucked into one end of the piazza, with thematically appropriate interior decor.

Keats-Shelley Memorial House

Facing directly onto the square, opposite the Barcaccia fountain at Piazza di Spagna 26, the house where the poet John Keats died in 1821 now serves as the **Keats–Shelley Memorial House** (Mon–Fri 10am–1pm & 2–6pm, Sat 11am–2pm & 3–6pm; €4; Ⓦwww.keats-shelley-house.org), an archive of English-language literary and historical works and a museum of manuscripts and literary mementoes relating to the Keats circle of the early nineteenth century – namely Keats himself, Shelley and Mary Shelley and Byron (who at one time lived across the square). Its four rooms contain manuscripts, letters and the like, and various personal effects of Keats, Shelley, Byron and associates, including an ancient silver scallop shell reliquary containing locks of Keats's, Shelley's, Milton's and Elizabeth Barrett Browning's hair – once owned by Pope Pius V – and an alabaster urn with Shelley's jawbone. Keats's death mask, stored in the corner room in which he died from tuberculosis, captures a resigned grimace, while the books that line the walls form the museum's library, which is devoted to the period and its literature.

Keats didn't really enjoy his time in Rome, referring to it as his "posthumous life": he came here only under pressure from doctors and friends when it was arguably already too late. He was also tormented by his love for Fanny Brawne, whom he had left behind in London, and he spent months in pain before he finally died, at the age of just 25, confined to the house with his artist friend Joseph Severn, to whom he remarked that he could already feel "the flowers growing over him". If you really want to get into the Romantic poet experience, there's an apartment on the third floor available to rent through the UK-based Landmark Trust (Ⓣ01628 825925, Ⓦwww.landmarktrust.org.uk). For more on Keats, see p.143.

Casa de Chirico

Almost next door to the Keats-Shelley House, the fourth-floor **Casa de Chirico** (Tues–Sat & the first Sun of every month 10am–1pm, tours every hour; €7) was the home of the Greek-Italian metaphysical artist Giorgio de Chirico for thirty years until his death in 1978 and is now a small, evocative museum. His wife, Isa, lived on here until 1990, when she too died, after which the apartment was donated to the city. It's kept pretty much as she left it, and gives a fantastic glimpse into how De Chirico lived, as well as having a great many of his paintings on display.

There are works from his classic period in the entrance hall and first living area, including portraits of himself, often dressed up, and others of his wife, who modelled for him until he died. The chair in which he used to watch TV (only with the sound turned down, apparently) sits by the door, while the next-door living room is filled with paintings from his last few years, all harking back to his proto-surrealist heyday. Upstairs, in keeping with the untouched nature of the house, De Chirico's cell-like bedroom is left with his books and rather uncomfortable-looking single bed, while across the hall the video player in Isa's bedroom is marked with stickers placed there to remind her how it worked. At the end of the corridor, De Chirico's studio, lit by a skylight in the terrace above, holds his brushes and canvases, more books and records, a portrait of his mother and a photo of his brother, Andrea, also a writer and artist.

The Spanish Steps

The **Spanish Steps** (or Scalinata di Spagna) sweep down in a cascade of balustrades and balconies beside De Chirico's house, the hangout, during the nineteenth century, of young hopefuls waiting to be chosen as artists' models. The scene has not changed much; it is still a venue for international posing and fast pick-ups late into the summer nights. It was, in fact, a largely French initiative to build them – before their construction the French church of Trinità dei Monti was accessible only by way of a rough path up the steep slope. After a few decades of haggling over the plans, the steps were finally laid in 1725, and now form one of the city's most distinctive attractions, built to a design, by one Francesco de Sanctis, that is deliberately showy, perfect for strollers to glide up and down while chatting and looking each other up and down. The steps also contain a religious message, the three flights and three landings an allusion to the Holy Trinity. If you don't think you can make it on foot, it's worth knowing that there's a lift in the entrance of the Spagna metro station – down Vicolo del Bottino.

Trinità dei Monti

At the top of the Spanish Steps is the **Trinità dei Monti** (daily 10am–noon & 4–6pm), a largely sixteenth-century church designed by Carlo Maderno and paid for by the French king. Its rose-coloured Baroque facade overlooks the rest of Rome from its hilltop site, and it's worth clambering up here just for the views. The church also has a couple of impressive works by Daniele da Volterra, notably a soft, beautifully composed fresco of *The Assumption* in the third chapel on the right, whose array of finely realized figures includes a portrait of his teacher Michelangelo (he's the greybeard on the far right), while a *Deposition*, across the nave in the second chapel on the left, has another ingenious arrangement, with Christ hauled down from the cross as his mother and other figures grieve below. The French seventeenth-century artist Poussin considered this work, which was probably painted from a series of cartoons by Michelangelo, as the world's third-greatest painting (Raphael's *Transfiguration* was, he thought, the best).

Villa Medici

Walking north from the top of the Spanish Steps, you reach the sixteenth-century **Villa Medici**. This was where Galileo was imprisoned in the 1630s by the Vatican's Holy Office for heretically claiming that the earth was not the centre of the universe but instead revolved around the sun. He was forced to recant his theory and say seven penitential psalms a week for his trouble. Nowadays, the villa is home to the French Academy, and although it's often open for exhibitions and concerts, for much of the year the only parts that are open to the public are its formal **gardens**, and then only on guided **tours** (daily at 10.30am, 11.45am in English, 2pm & 3.15pm; tours last 45min; ⓦ www.villamedici.it). As well as the gardens themselves, these take in the little **Studiolo** on the far side, decorated by Jacopo Zucchi in the mid-sixteenth century with frescoes of lush vegetation, birds and depictions of the villa itself, and the **Gipsoteca** just beyond, full of casts of classical sculpture, while the views of the city from the villa's terrace are among the best in Rome. During the summer you can also sometimes visit a selection of historic rooms inside the villa – the bedroom of Ferdinando de' Medici and a handful of other frescoed chambers – though tours are again compulsory and mainly in Italian and French. Finally, there's a very comfy **café**, with lots of sofas from which to enjoy the views.

Piazza del Popolo

At the far end of Via del Babuino, the oval-shaped expanse of **Piazza del Popolo** is a dignified meeting of roads laid out in 1538 by Pope Paul III (Alessandro Farnese) to make an impressive entrance to the city; it owes its present symmetry to Valadier, who added the central fountain in 1814. The monumental **Porta del Popolo** went up in 1655, the work of Bernini, whose patron Alexander VII's Chigi family symbol – the heap of hills surmounted by a star – can clearly be seen above the main gateway.

▲ Piazza del Popolo

During summer, the steps around the obelisk and fountain, and the cafés on either side of the square, are popular hangouts. But the piazza's real attraction is the unbroken view it gives all the way back down Via del Corso, between the perfectly paired churches of **Santa Maria dei Miracoli** and **Santa Maria in Montesanto**, to the central columns of the Vittorio Emanuele Monument. If you get to choose your first view of the centre of Rome, make it this one.

Santa Maria del Popolo

On the far side of the piazza, hard against the city walls, **Santa Maria del Popolo** (Mon–Sat 7am–noon & 4–7pm, Sun 8am–1.30pm & 4.30–7.30pm) holds some of the best Renaissance art of any Roman church, with works by Raphael, Bramante, Pinturicchio, Sansovino and Caravaggio. It was originally erected here in 1099 over the burial place of Nero, in order to sanctify what was believed to be an evil place (the emperor's ghost had appeared here several times), but took its present form in the fifteenth century. Inside, there are frescoes by Pinturicchio in the first chapel of the south aisle, including a lovely *Adoration of Christ*, full of tiny details receding into the distance. Pinturicchio also did some work in the next chapel but one – the altarpiece *Madonna and Child and Saints* – and in the Bramante-designed apse, which in turn boasts two fine tombs by Andrea Sansovino.

The **Chigi chapel**, the second from the entrance in the northern aisle, was designed by Raphael for Agostino Chigi in 1516 (he lies in the tomb on the right, his brother Sigismondo on the left), although most of the work was actually undertaken by other artists and not finished until the seventeenth century. The odd pyramid-shaped memorials on either side have come in for lots of recent speculation, due to Dan Brown's fictional conspiracy theories – in *Angels & Demons* its statues helped lead to the secretive Illuminati. Michelangelo's protégé, Sebastiano del Piombo, was responsible for the altarpiece; and two of the sculptures in the corner niches, of Daniel with the lions, on the left as you enter, and Habakkuk, diagonally opposite, are by Bernini.

But it's two pictures by **Caravaggio**, in the left-hand Cerasi chapel of the north transept, that attract the most attention. These are typically dramatic works: one, the *Conversion of St Paul*, shows Paul and horse bathed in a beatific radiance, while the other, the *Crucifixion of St Peter*, has Peter as an aged but strong figure, dominated by the musclebound figures hoisting him up. Like his paintings in the churches of San Luigi dei Francesi and Sant'Agostino (see p.48), both works were considered extremely risqué in their time, their heavy chiaroscuro and deliberate realism too much for the Church authorities; one contemporary critic referred to the *Conversion of St Paul*, a painting dominated by the exquisitely lit horse's hindquarters, as "an accident in a blacksmith's shop". In the middle, Carracci's boldly coloured altarpiece, with its golds and pinks, offers a massive contrast.

Via del Babuino

Leading south from Piazza del Popolo to Piazza di Spagna, **Via del Babuino** and the narrow **Via Margutta**, where the film-maker Federico Fellini once lived, set the tone for the area, which in the 1960s was the core of a thriving art community and home to the city's best galleries and a fair number of its artists. High rents forced out all but the most successful, and the neighbourhood now supports a prosperous trade in antiques and designer fashions. Via del Babuino – literally "Street of the Baboon" – gets its name from the statue of Silenus (Fontana del Babuino) which reclines outside the Tadolini studio about halfway down on the right. In ancient times the wall behind was a focus for satirical graffiti, although it is now coated with graffiti-proof paint. Inside the studio, the

Museo-Atelier Canova-Tadolini is really a café-restaurant, but a highly original one, littered as it is with the sculptural work of four generations of the Tadolini family. The nineteenth-century sculptor Canova donated the building to Adam Tadolini, his most promising student, in 1818, and the family occupied the building for the next 150 years. You can sip a drink outside, next to the baboon, or sit inside among the busts, friezes and disembodied limbs – an eccentric experience (see p.245 for more). A little further down on the right, the church of **All Saints** (daily 9am–1pm) is the official Anglican church of Rome, its solid steeple and brick construction, erected in the late nineteenth century, serving as a further reminder of the English connections in this part of town.

Casa di Goethe

A short way down Via del Corso from Piazza del Popolo, on the left at no. 18, the **Casa di Goethe** (Tues–Sun 10am–6pm; €3; ⓦ www.casadigoethe.it) is a genuinely engaging small museum. There seem to be houses all over Italy that Goethe stayed in, but he did spend over two years in this one, and wrote much of his classic travelogue *Italian Journey* here – indeed, each room is decorated with a quote from the book. Goethe had long dreamed of travelling to Italy, inspired by a journey his father made years earlier, and he came here – incognito, as Filippo Miller – in 1786, after touring the north of the country. His routine here was a bohemian one, associating with expat artists and writers, far removed from his life in Germany, where he was a celebrated writer.

The house has been restored as a modern exhibition space and holds books, letters, prints and drawings, plus a reconstruction of his study in Vienna. Among the objects on display are Piranesi prints of public spaces in Rome, watercolours by Goethe himself and drawings by the German artist **Tischbein**, with whom he shared the house, including a lovely one of Goethe leaning out of the window over Via del Corso and a more formal painting of him reclining in the foreground of an idealized Roman *campagna* landscape.

Santi Ambrogio e Carlo

The largest if not the most essential sight on the Corso, the church of **Santi Ambrogio e Carlo** is the Milanese church in Rome, dedicated to its most famous bishop – Ambrose, who died in 397 AD – and Carlo Borromeo, who was a humble and reforming archbishop of Milan around 1200 years later. The dome is one of the largest in the city and crowns a vast and highly decorative seventeenth-century church; the chapel at the back is home to a reliquary containing the heart of Carlo Borromeo.

Mausoleum of Augustus

Leading from Piazza del Popolo to Piazza del Augusto Imperatore, **Via di Ripetta** was laid out by Pope Leo X to provide a straight route out of the city centre from the old river port area here. **Piazza del Augusto Imperatore** is an odd square, made up of largely Mussolini-era buildings surrounding a peaceful ring of cypresses, circled by paths and flowering shrubs – what's left, basically, of the massive **Mausoleum of Augustus**, the burial place of the emperor and his family, currently under long-term restoration. Augustus died in 14 AD, giving way to his son Tiberius, who ruled until 37 AD (the last ten years from the island of Capri), when his nephew's son Caligula took over and effectively signalled the end of the Augustan age, and the order, prosperity and expansion that defined it. As Augustus himself had it, according to Suetonius: "I found Rome built simply out of bricks: I left her clad in marble." The mausoleum has been transformed into many buildings over the years, including a medieval fortress, and is currently under restoration, at the end of which you'll hopefully be able to get in to see the passageways and central crypt, where the ashes of the members of the Augustan dynasty were kept.

Ara Pacis

On the far side of the square, the **Ara Pacis** or "Altar of Augustan Peace" is now enclosed in a controversial purpose-built structure designed by the New York-based architect Richard Meier, its angular lines and sheer white surfaces dominating the river side of the square (daily 9am–7pm; €6.50, audioguide €3.50; Ⓦ www .arapacis.it). A marble block enclosed by sculpted walls, the altar was built in 13 BC, probably to celebrate Augustus's victory over Spain and Gaul and the peace it heralded. Much of it had been dug up piecemeal over the years, but the bulk was uncovered in the middle of the last century, in the heart of the Campus Martius, a few hundred yards south, where it had originally stood. Putting it back together was no easy task: excavation involved digging down to a depth of 10m and freezing the water table, after which many other parts had to be retrieved from museums the world over, or plaster copies made.

The result, on the surrounding walls especially, is a superb example of imperial Roman sculpture, particularly in the victory procession itself, on the mausoleum side of the altar. This is a picture of a family at the height of its power, with little inkling of the scandal and tragedy that would afflict it in years to come. The first part is almost completely gone, but the head of Augustus is complete, as are the figures that follow: the priests with their skullcap headgear, then, behind the figure carrying an axe, Augustus's great general, Marcus Agrippa, hooded, clutching a rolled piece of parchment, with his son Gaius pulling on his toga. Then, respectively, come Augustus's wife Livia, followed by her son (and Augustus's eventual successor) Tiberius and niece Antonia, the latter caught simply and realistically turning to her husband, Drusus, while holding the hand of her son Germanicus. Of the various other children clutching the togas of the elders, the last is said to be the young Claudius, while the old man towards the end may be Maecenas, Augustus's most trusted adviser during his heyday.

On the front of the altar is a frieze of Aeneas making a sacrifice, while on the back is a well-preserved representation of Mother Earth bestowing peace and prosperity on Rome, holding two babies in her arms – said by some to be Lucius and Gaius, Augustus's grandchildren and his planned successors. On the river side, the veiled figure is believed to be their mother, Julia, Augustus's daughter, with Lucius in front of her. Julia later married Tiberius and was constantly disgraced for her promiscuity about Rome, and both children died young, before they could take on the responsibility that Augustus had planned for them.

Via Sistina

Leading south from the top of the Spanish Steps to Piazza Barberini, **Via Sistina** was the first of Pope Sixtus V's planning improvements to sixteenth-century Rome, a dead-straight street designed to connect Santa Maria Maggiore to Trinità dei Monti, which it almost still does, under a variety of names, and in the other direction to Piazza del Popolo, which it never quite managed. Nowadays it's the quickest way of getting to the Via Veneto and Quirinale areas from the Spanish Steps.

Sant'Andrea delle Fratte

Just off Via Sistina to the right, **Sant'Andrea delle Fratte** is tucked into a tight spot – like so many churches by Borromini, who designed the characteristic campanile. This is another church in which the great men of the Baroque era came together: inside, the apse is flanked by two histrionic angels designed by Bernini, originally intended for the Ponte Sant'Angelo, the bridge which connects the centro storico and Prati. To the left of the north door, a plaque remembers Angelica Kauffmann, an accomplished late-eighteenth-century Swiss painter and great friend of the English artist Joshua Reynolds, who lived in Rome and was a good friend of Goethe (see p.98), while the door in the opposite aisle gives way to a very pleasant tree-filled cloister.

Piazza San Silvestro

Back on the eastern side of Via del Corso, off the busy bus terminus by **Piazza San Silvestro**, nowhere illustrates better how history sits cheek-by-jowl with the modern world in Rome than the church of **San Silvestro in Capite**. The peaceful, plant-filled terracotta courtyard that you walk through to get in feels a million miles away from the fume-drenched traffic outside. Inside, the blackened skull of John the Baptist that gives the church the second half of its name is displayed in a small chapel that doubles as a side entrance. The church itself was at one point the centre of the Franciscan movement in Rome, home to Margherita Colonna who espoused the then left-field beliefs of St Francis and whipped up a storm in the Catholic hierarchy. Nowadays its interior is classic over-stuffed Roman Baroque, although the dark, ancient feel suits its long and illustrious history well.

Galleria Alberto Sordi

On the other side of the square, and across Via del Tritone, the classic Y-shaped nineteenth-century shopping arcade of **Galleria Alberto Sordi** (daily 10am–10pm) has recently reopened after years of neglect. Renamed after an Italian film star (actors used to hang out here seeking work), it's as spruce and sleek as it was in its heyday, and provides a welcome escape from this ultra-busy part of central Rome, especially on a hot day.

The Trevi Fountain

The tight web of narrow, apparently aimless streets beyond open out on one of Rome's more surprising sights – the **Trevi Fountain**, or Fontana di Trevi, a huge, very Baroque gush of water over statues and rocks built onto the backside of a Renaissance palace; it's fed by the same source that surfaces at the Barcaccia fountain in Piazza di Spagna. The original Trevi Fountain, designed by Alberti, was around the corner in Via dei Crociferi, but Urban VIII decided to upgrade it in line with his other grandiose schemes of the time and employed Bernini, among others, to design an alternative. Work didn't begin until 1732, when Niccolò Salvi won a competition held by Clement XII to design the fountain, and even then it took thirty years to finish the project. Salvi died in the process, his lungs shot by the time spent in the dank waterworks of the fountain. The Trevi Fountain is now, of course, the place you come to chuck in a coin if you want to guarantee your return to Rome, though you might remember Anita Ekberg throwing herself into it in *La Dolce Vita* (there are police here to discourage you from doing the same thing). Recently restored, it's one of the city's most vigorous outdoor spots to hang out.

Accademia di San Luca

A short walk from the fountain, towards Via del Tritone, the **Accademia di San Luca** is Rome's school of art first and foremost, but it has a small permanent collection of pictures and hosts regular temporary exhibitions, although at time of writing its gallery was still under restoration. The building itself is worth visiting anyway for its Borromini ramp, which spirals up from the main lobby instead of a staircase. The collection includes a fresco by Raphael, a *Venus* by Guercino and a couple of pictures by Titian and Rubens, as well as lots of works by nineteenth-century Italian painters.

Santi Vincenzo ed Anastasio

Directly opposite the Trevi Fountain, the grubby little church of **Santi Vincenzo ed Anastasio** is the parish church of the Quirinal Palace, and, bizarrely, holds in marble urns the hearts and viscera of the 22 popes who used the palace as a **papal residence**. Two tablets – one either side of the high altar – record each of the popes whose bits and pieces lie downstairs, from Sixtus V, who died in 1590, to Leo XIII, who passed away in 1903.

Città dell'Acqua

Just around the corner from the Trevi Fountain, a small art-house cinema stands above a couple of recently opened ancient Roman excavations. The so-called **Città dell'Acqua** (Mon 4–7.30pm, Thurs–Sun 11am–5pm; €3) holds a couple of ancient Roman structures: one a palace of some kind, the other a building which was at some point converted to a series of cisterns, which still hold water today. Walkways weave about amongst the ruins, and take in a few finds from the site, but there's not a great deal to see.

Galleria Colonna

A short stroll south from the Trevi Fountain brings you to the **Galleria Colonna**, Via della Pilotta 17 (Sat 9am–1pm, closed Aug; free guided tours in English at 11.45am; €7), part of the Palazzo Colonna complex, whose gardens (not open to the public) stretch up the hill from here, linked to the palace by bridges over the narrow street. The gallery is outranked by many of Rome's other palatial collections, but it's worth visiting not only for its small but high-quality collection of art but also for the glimpse it gives you of the home of one of Rome's most powerful Renaissance families.

The so-called Battle Column room has two lascivious paintings of Venus and Cupid facing each other across the room – one by Bronzino on the far side, the other by Ghirlandaio – that were once considered so risqué that clothes were painted on in 1840 (they were removed during a restoration a few years ago). There are more fleshy creations by Ghirlandaio in the same room, while the ceiling paintings in the adjacent chandelier-decked Great Hall glorify the deeds of Marcantonio Colonna, notably his great victory against the Turks at the Battle of Lepanto in 1589. Of the paintings, the highlight is maybe the gallery's collection of landscapes by Dughet (Poussin's brother-in-law), housed in the next room, frescoed with more scenes of the Battle of Lepanto, while other rooms remember the Colonna pope, Martin V, not least the frescoes in the Room of the Apotheosis which show him being received into heaven, and Pisanello's pious portrait of him in the next room. Other paintings which stand out here include Annibale

Carracci's early and unusually spontaneous *Bean Eater* (though its attribution to him has since been questioned), a *Portrait of a Venetian Gentleman*, caught in a supremely confident pose by Veronese, *Narcissus* and a portrait of an old man by Tintoretto and Bronzino's lovely *Madonna with saints Elizabeth and John*.

Santi Apostoli

The back of Palazzo Colonna is taken up by the large church of **Santi Apostoli**, dedicated to the apostles Philip and James (daily 7am–noon & 4–7pm), a sixth-century basilica whose ancient origins are hard to detect now, encased as it is in an eighteenth-century shell and Napoleonic facade, and completely done up with Baroque finery inside. It too was part of the Colonna estate and is a Franciscan church, thanks to the family's early embrace of the movement, its wide, airy interior still looked after by the friars, who pad silently around while you take in its clash of Byzantine, Renaissance and Baroque architectural styles. The ceiling paintings are by the Genoese painter Baciccia, more famous for his work in the Gesù (see p.60), and the north aisle contains the nineteenth-century Italian sculptor Canova's first work in Rome, the very grand tomb of Clement XIV above the door to the sacristy. But the church's statue-encrusted portico is perhaps its most impressive feature, commissioned by Pope Julius II, who lived in the palace next door. It overlooks the equally grandiose **Palazzo Odelscalchi** opposite, which was renovated by none other than Bernini in the 1660s but is currently not open to the public.

Museo delle Cere

At the end of the street, the **Museo delle Cere** (daily 9am–8pm; €7) is a quirky first-floor museum of waxworks that hosts a diverse array of characters from history and Italian culture: not essential viewing by any means but certainly different from anything else you'll see in Rome. It starts with a room devoted to the Fascist Council of 1943, with Mussolini at its head, gloomily – and fairly spookily – giving up on the war. Off to the right are various titans of the war and postwar era: Hitler and Himmler, the Yalta conference threesome of Churchill, Stalin and Roosevelt, and Mao and Kruschev. Things lighten up a bit in other rooms, with footballers Totti – captain of AS Roma – and Nesta, the former Lazio captain, who subsequently moved to AC Milan. Deeper into the museum you're treated to various ancient musicians and artists, the usual chamber of horrors suspects – murderers, electric chairs and the like – and even some wax dinosaurs, although by far the most frightening exhibit shows a fairy-tale prince about to waken the sleeping princess; look at her long enough and you'll see that she's actually breathing.

The Quirinale and east

U p above the historic centre, and across Via Nazionale from the Esquiline Hill and Monti, the **Quirinale** is perhaps the most appealing of the hills that rise up on the eastern side of the centre of Rome, and the first to be properly developed, when, in the seventeenth century, those who could afford it moved up to the higher ground from the city centre, and the popes made their home here in the **Palazzo del Quirinale**. Nowadays this is the residence of the president of Italy, and is only open for viewing on Sundays, but the rest of the district holds some of the city's most compelling sights, not least the enormous **Palazzo Barberini**, home of some of the best of Rome's art, and a couple of its most ingenious Baroque churches. **Via XX Settembre** spears northeast from here to the edge of the city centre proper at the Porta Pia, beyond which **Via Nomentana** and the nineteenth-century neighbourhoods around are well worth the journey, not only for **Villa Torlonia**, the sumptuous former residence of Mussolini, and the nearby Casa di Pirandello, but also for the attractions at its far end – two of Rome's most ancient and sensual churches.

Piazza Barberini

At the junction of Via Sistina and the busy shopping street of Via del Tritone, **Piazza Barberini** centres on Bernini's **Fontana del Tritone**, a sea-god gushing a high jet of water from a conch shell in the centre of the square. The recently restored fountain lends a unity to the square in more ways than one: traditionally, this quarter of the city was associated with the Barberini, a family who were the greatest patrons of Bernini, and the sculptor's works in their honour are thick on the ground around here. He finished the Tritone fountain in 1644, before designing the **Fontana delle Api** ("Fountain of the Bees"), which you can see at the bottom end of Via Veneto. Unlike the Tritone fountain you could walk right past this, a smaller, quirkier work, its broad scallop shell studded with the bees that were the symbol of the Barberini.

Santa Maria della Concezione

A little way up Via Veneto on the right, the Capuchin church of **Santa Maria della Concezione** (daily 9am–noon & 3–6pm) was another sponsored creation of the Barberini (founded in 1626), though it's not a particularly significant building in itself, and its only real treasure is Guido Reni's androgynous *St Michael Trampling on*

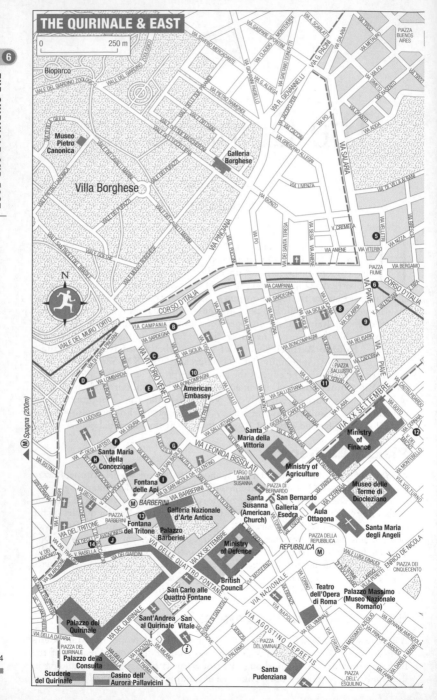

THE QUIRINALE & EAST

0 — 250 m

Bioparco

Museo Pietro Canonica

Galleria Borghese

Villa Borghese

N

M Spagna (200m)

VIA SALARIA

PIAZZA BUENOS AIRES

CORSO D'ITALIA

5

PIAZZA FIUME

6

CORSO D'ITALIA

VIA PIAVE

VIA CAMPANIA

VIA SARDEGNA

B

8

9

C

10

American Embassy

PIAZZA SALLUSTIO

11

VIA VITTORIO VENETO

D

E

F

G

Santa Maria della Vittoria

VIA XX SETTEMBRE

12

Ministry of Finance

Santa Maria della Concezione

H

Fontana delle Api

I

VIA LEONIDA BISSOLATI

LARGO DI SANTA SUSANNA

PIAZZA DI BERNARDO

Ministry of Agriculture

San Bernardo

Museo delle Terme di Diocleziano

M BARBERINI

13

Galleria Nazionale d'Arte Antica

Fontana del Tritone

Palazzo Barberini

PIAZZA BARBERINI

14

J

Santa Susanna (American Church)

Galleria Esedra

Aula Ottagona

Santa Maria degli Angeli

VIA DEL TRITONE

Ministry of Defence

REPUBBLICA

PIAZZA DELLA REPUBBLICA

M

British Council

San Carlo alle Quattro Fontane

Sant'Andrea al Quirinale

San Vitale

VIA NAZIONALE

Teatro dell'Opera di Roma

Palazzo Massimo (Museo Nazionale Romano)

PIAZZA DEI CINQUECENTO

Palazzo del Quirinale

PIAZZA DEL QUIRINALE

Palazzo della Consulta

i

VIA AGOSTINO DEPRETIS

Santa Pudenziana

PIAZZA DELL' ESQUILINO

Scuderie del Quirinale

Casino dell' Aurora Pallavicini

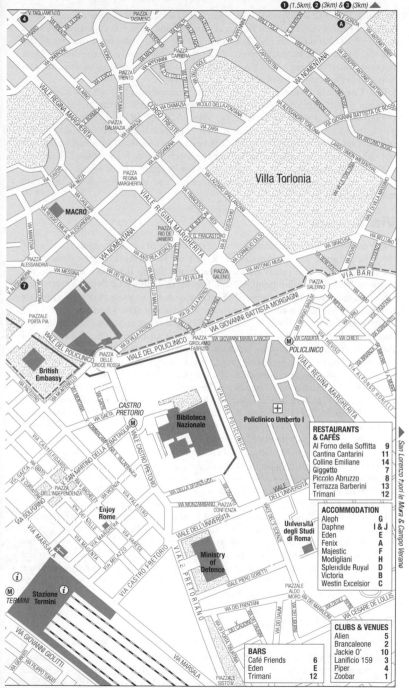

❶ (1.5km), **❷** (3km) & **❸** (3km) ▲

V. TAGLIAMENTO

Villa Torlonia

MACRO

British
Embassy

CASTRO
PRETORIO

Biblioteca
Nazionale

Policlinico Umberto I

Enjoy
Rome

Università
degli Studi
di Roma

Ministry
of
Defence

Stazione
Termini
TERMINI

San Lorenzo fuori le Mura & Campo Verano ▶

RESTAURANTS
& CAFÉS
Al Forno della Soffitta	9
Cantina Cantarini	11
Colline Emiliane	14
Giggetto	7
Piccolo Abruzzo	8
Terrazza Barberini	13
Trimani	12

ACCOMMODATION
Aleph	G
Daphne	I & J
Eden	E
Fenix	A
Majestic	F
Modigliani	H
Splendide Royal	D
Victoria	B
Westin Excelsior	C

CLUBS & VENUES
Alien	5
Brancaleone	2
Jackie O'	10
Lanificio 159	3
Piper	4
Zoobar	1

BARS
Café Friends	6
Eden	E
Trimani	12

San Lorenzo ▼

the Devil, in the first chapel on the right. The Devil in the picture is said to be a portrait of Innocent X, whom the artist despised and who was apparently a sworn enemy of the Barberini family. Take a look at the tomb slab of the founder of the church, Antonio Barberini, in front of the altar, which has an inscription – "Here lies dust, ashes, nothing" – that is quite at odds with the worldly, wealthy impression you get of the Barberini elsewhere in the city.

The **Capuchin cemetery** (same times; minimum €1 donation expected), attached to the right of the church, continues the deathly theme, home as it is to the bones of 4000 monks who died between 1528 and 1870, set into the walls of a series of six chapels – a monument to "Our Sister of Bodily Death", in the words of St Francis, that was erected in 1793. Some bones and skulls are simply piled up, but others appear in abstract or Christian patterns or as fully clothed skeletons, their faces peering out of their cowls in twisted expressions of agony. The effect lies somewhere between chilling and ludicrous, and makes for one of the more macabre and bizarre sights of Rome.

Via Veneto

Via Veneto, which bends north from Piazza Barberini up to the southern edge of the Villa Borghese, is a cool, materialistic antidote to the murky atmosphere of the Capuchin grotto. The pricey bars and restaurants lining the street were once the haunt of Rome's beautiful people, made famous by Fellini's *La Dolce Vita*, but they left a long time ago, and Via Veneto, despite being home to some of the city's fanciest hotels, has never quite recovered the cachet it had in the Sixties and Seventies.

The area is home to some of the city's best and most imposing Modernist and Fascist-era buildings and is worth a wander for just that. The **Grand Hotel Palace**, at Via Veneto 70, is the work of the Fascists' favourite architect, **Marcello Piacentini**. Its solid travertine elegance, punctuated by Art Deco lamps supported by sleek nymphettes, is reminiscent of a bygone age – a feel that is emphasized in the bar inside, frescoed with scenes of the wealthy and beautiful people of 1920s Rome. Just before here on the right, the **Ministry for Economic Development**, at Via Veneto 33, is a more brutal Fascist-era edifice, built of giant tufa blocks that set off well the bronze door panels of the main entrance, depicting musclebound scenes of industry, agriculture, commerce, transport and the like. Around the corner, at Via Bissolati 23, the giant **INA Building** was built in the 1920s, and the friezes of ships on either side of its main door are indicative of its original – and current – function. Across the road, the brick and travertine **BNL Building** is another Piacentini creation, and anchors the corner well, a dignified presence compared to the seemingly besieged **US Embassy** on the opposite corner.

Further up, Via Veneto takes on more of its classic air of pavement cafés, swanky stores and snooty hotels, whose uniformed hotel bellmen lend it an upscale European air that is quite unlike anywhere else in the city. There are any number of pricey café tables from which to soak up the atmosphere but be aware that the class here is only skin-deep and that some of these places have a reputation as being Mafia-run – the famous **Café de Paris**, halfway up on the left, was closed down in 2009 for its associations with the Mob.

Palazzo Barberini

On the other side of Piazza Barberini, the **Palazzo Barberini**, Via Barberini 18, is home to a series of apartments that were once occupied by the Barberini family and, more importantly, the **Galleria Nazionale d'Arte Antica** (Tues–Sun 8.30am–7.30pm; €5; apartment tours can be booked in advance on ☎06.481.4591,

@ www.galleriaborghese.it), a rich patchwork of mainly Italian art from the early Renaissance to late Baroque period. The gallery is still in the grip of a restoration that has been going on for several years, and which will be continuing for some time yet, not least because the military, who have shared the building for decades, have recently moved out, thus freeing up more gallery space. The result of the renovations is likely to be special, but it will be a while before you can safely predict what will be on display, and where.

Galleria Nazionale d'Arte Antica

It's an impressive collection: **highlights** – which are likely to be on display whatever changes take place – include works by Titian, El Greco and Caravaggio. But perhaps the most impressive feature of the gallery is the **building** itself, worked on at different times by the most favoured architects of the day – Bernini, Borromini, Maderno – and the epitome of Baroque grandeur. The **first-floor** Gran Salone, certainly, is guaranteed to impress, its ceiling frescoed by Pietro da Cortona in one of the best examples of exuberant Baroque trompe l'oeil work there is, a manic rendering of *The Triumph of Divine Providence* that almost crawls down the walls to meet you. Note the bees – the Barberini family symbol – flying towards the figure of Providence. What's more, like Bernini's Oval Room off to the right, it's effectively free, because the ticket office for the gallery lies in the room beyond.

Among the paintings that should be on display is Raphael's beguiling *Fornarina*, a painting of a Trasteveran baker's daughter thought to have been the artist's mistress (Raphael's name appears clearly on the woman's bracelet), although some experts claim the painting to be the work of a pupil. Nearby are a couple of Pietàs by Giacomo Francia, one of which, with St Paul, is one of the most overlooked works in the collection. Look out also for Piero di Cosimo's *St Mary Magdalene*, with lovely colour and detail, along with numerous Madonnas, including Fra' Filippo Lippi's warmly maternal *Madonna and Child*, painted in 1437 and introducing background details, notably architecture, into Italian religious painting for the first time. Next to it is a richly coloured and beautifully composed *Annunciation* by the same artist, and Sodoma's dark *Mystical Marriage of St Catherine* – a subject repeated in a later room by Lorenzo Lotto. In the same room are two works by Tintoretto – *Christ taken in Adultery* and *St Jerome* – as well as Titian's lively *Venus and Adonis*, while a further gallery brings together the collection's impressive array of portraiture: Bronzino's rendering of the marvellously erect *Stefano Colonna*, and a portrait of *Henry VIII* by Hans Holbein which feels almost as well known – probably because the painter produced so many of the monarch. Painted on the day of his marriage to his fourth wife, Anne of Cleves, he's depicted as a rather irritable but beautifully dressed middle-aged man – a stark contrast to the rather ascetic figure of *Erasmus of Rotterdam* by Quentin Matsys, which sometimes hangs nearby. Next door are two unusually small paintings by El Greco, *The Baptism of Christ* and *Adoration of the Shepherds* and Caravaggio's *Judith and Holofernes*, together with the seventeenth-century Neapolitan Ribera's controlled study of *St Gregory the Great*. Works by the Italians Guercino and Annibale Carracci may also feature, as well as Reni's haunting portrait of Beatrice Cenci (see p.65), canvases by the Dutch Mannerists, Terbrugghen and Van Bronckhorst, and later works by Boucher and Canaletto, among others.

The Barberini apartments

You can also take a pre-booked tour of the Barberini apartments on the **second floor**. This is worth doing not so much for the dusty, painted Rococo rooms themselves (though the so-called Room of the Battles, showing various members of the Barberini and Colonna families engaged in glorious strife, is impressive) as

▲ Palazzo Barberini

for the circular **staircase** you climb to get there: the work of Borromini, and in sharp contrast to the huge and stately Bernini staircase you take to reach the paintings on the other side.

San Carlo alle Quattro Fontane

Continue on down Via delle Quattro Fontane, which heads southeast over the Quirinale from Palazzo Barberini, and you're at a seventeenth-century landmark, the church of **San Carlo alle Quattro Fontane** (Mon–Sat 10am–1pm & 3–6pm, Sat noon–1pm). This was Borromini's first real design commission, and in it he displays all the ingenuity he later became known for, elegantly cramming the church into a tiny and awkwardly shaped site that apparently covers roughly the same surface area as one of the main columns inside St Peter's. Tucked in beside the church, the cloister is squeezed into a tight but elegant oblong, topped with a charming balustrade.

Outside the church are the **four fountains** that give the street and church their name, each cut into a niche in a corner of the crossroads that marks the highest point on the Quirinal Hill. They were put here in 1593, and represent the Tiber and Aniene rivers and *Strength* and *Fidelity*, and they make a fine if busy spot to look back down towards the Trinità dei Monti obelisk in one direction and the Santa Maria Maggiore obelisk in the other – all part of Sixtus V's grand city plan.

Via Rasella

More or less opposite Palazzo Barberini, **Via Rasella** was the scene of an ambush of a Nazi military patrol in 1944 that led to one of the worst Italian wartime atrocities – the reprisal massacre of 335 innocent Romans at the Ardeatine Caves outside the city walls (see p.149). A memorial now stands on the site of the executions, near the Via Appia Antica, and the event is commemorated there every March 24 with a solemn ceremony. Oddly enough, Mussolini had a flat on Via Rasella when he first came to Rome, in which he apparently entertained a string of mistresses.

Sant'Andrea al Quirinale

There's another piece of design ingenuity a few steps southwest of here, on Via del Quirinale, which is flanked on the left by public gardens and the domed church of **Sant'Andrea al Quirinale** (Mon–Sat 8.30am–noon & 3.30–7pm, Sun 9am–noon & 3.30–7.30pm), a flamboyant building that Bernini planned in a flat oval shape to fit into its wide but shallow site. Like San Carlo up the road, it's unusual and ingenious inside, and was apparently the church that Bernini himself was most pleased with, its wide, elliptical nave cleverly made into a grand space despite its relatively small size. Once you've taken this in, for a €1 fee you can visit the sacristry – whose frescoes are similarly artful, with cherubs pulling aside painted drapery to let in light from mock windows – and the upstairs rooms of one St Stanislaus Kostka, where the Polish saint lived (and died) in 1568. The rooms have changed quite a lot since then, with paintings by the Jesuit artist Andrea Pozzo illustrating the life of the saint and a chapel focused on a disturbingly lifelike painted statue of Stanislaus lying on his deathbed.

Palazzo del Quirinale

Opposite the church is the featureless wall – the so-called *manica lunga* or "long sleeve" – of the **Palazzo del Quirinale** (Sun 8.30am–noon; €5; Ⓦwww .quirinale.it), a sixteenth-century structure that was the official summer residence of the popes until Unification, when it became the royal palace. It's now the home of Italy's president (a largely ceremonial role), and it's worth braving the security for a glimpse of the style in which popes, despots, kings and now presidents like to live, with a fine set of state rooms and some very accomplished works of art – though note the limited opening hours.

The first and perhaps most impressive of the works here is Melozzo da Forlí's fifteenth-century fresco of Christ, on the staircase off the courtyard, a fragment of a work that was painted for the apse of Santi Apostoli – the rest is in the Vatican (see p.202). Once inside, the spectacular first room, the Salone dei Corazzieri, was partly decorated by Carlo Maderno and essentially intended to glorify the life of Paul V, with frescoes interspersing the life of Moses with scenes showing the pope greeting various foreign emissaries and ambassadors. In case you were in any doubt of Paul V's achievements, Maderno throws in monochrome representations of some of his big building projects, including the Acqua Paola at one end of the room and St Peter's and the Quirinale itself at the other end. You can't always enter Maderno's Cappella Paolina, through the next door, but it's no great loss: its dimensions are precisely the same as the Sistine Chapel but it couldn't be more different, studded with a tasteless decorative ceiling, its walls covered in colourless nineteenth-century representations of the Apostles.

More grand rooms follow: the Salone del Balcone was where Pius IX gave his blessing on his election as pope; the next room contains a copy of Raphael's *John the Baptist* by Giulio Romano; while the three rooms beyond used to be one enormously long space but were remodelled during Napoleon's occupation of the place. Even now they cut quite a dash, frescoed under the direction of Pietro da Cortona in 1656 to a commission by Pope Alexander VII, with big biblical events depicted in accomplished and naturalistic style by a variety of artists, culminating in a dazzling *Adoration of the Shepherds* by Carlo Maratta. The last rooms are largely decorated in the style of the Savoy kings, who took over the palace in the nineteenth century, but the last room you see, the Salone delle Feste – originally the Sala Regia, where Paul V received foreign dignitaries – still packs quite a punch, its ceiling massively higher than the others at 16m, and decorated with Agostino Tassi's pseudo-oriental perspectives.

6 Piazza del Quirinale

If the Palazzo is closed, you can make do with appreciating its exceptional setting in the **Piazza del Quirinale**, from which views stretch right across the centre of Rome. The main feature of the piazza is the huge statue of the **Dioscuri**, the name given to Castor and Pollux. These are massive five-metre-high Roman copies of classical Greek statues, showing the two godlike twins, the sons of Jupiter, who according to legend won victory for the Romans in an important battle (see also p.85). The statues originally stood at the entrance of the Baths of Constantine, the ruins of which lay nearby, and were brought here by Pope Sixtus V in the early sixteenth century to embellish the square – part of the pope's attempts to dignify and beautify the city with many large, vista-laden squares and long, straight avenues. Nowadays it forms an odd concoction with the obelisk, originally from the Mausoleum of Augustus, which tops the arrangement, and the vast shallow bowl in front, which was apparently once resident at the Roman Forum – all in all a classic example of how Rome has recycled most of its classical debris.

The Scuderie del Quirinale

The eighteenth-century **Scuderie del Quirinale** faces the palace from across the square, completing the triangle of buildings that make up the piazza. Originally the papal stables, it has been imaginatively restored as display space for some of the major travelling exhibitions that come to the city (opening times and prices vary; Ⓦ www.scuderiequirinale.it). It has an excellent art bookshop on the ground floor and the equestrian spiral staircase that winds up from here to the main exhibition rooms is impressive. There's also a decent restaurant and café, and the modern glass staircase added to the side of the building offers the best view over Rome from the Quirinale by far.

Casino dell'Aurora Pallavicini

Opposite the Scuderie, at Via XXIV Maggio 43, the **Palazzo Pallavicini-Rospigliosi** was originally commissioned by Cardinal Scipione Borghese in 1603 on the site of the Baths of Constantine, specifically to be near the papal action at the Quirinale Palace. There's a decent collection of Baroque painting in the gallery inside, but this can only be visited by appointment, and the only part you can turn up unannounced to see is the **Casino dell'Aurora Pallavicini** (open first day of every month 10am–noon & 3–5pm; free; Ⓦ www.casinoaurorapallavicini.it), attached to the gardens on the left, where you can admire the Roman sarcophagi that frieze the facade, which is wonderfully well preserved and full of tangled figures and exotic animals. It's a theme that is continued inside, with depictions of Roman triumphs at each end. However, the main focus is Guido Reni's ceiling fresco, *Aurora Scattering Flowers before the Sun* – a typically accomplished and smooth work, but somehow lacking in drama. In each corner, the poised and bucolic scenes of each season provide a nice counterpoint.

Via XX Settembre

Via XX Settembre spears out towards the Aurelian Wall from Via del Quirinale – not Rome's most appealing thoroughfare by any means, flanked by the deliberately faceless bureaucracies of the national government, erected after

Unification in anticipation of Rome's ascension as a new world capital. It was, however, the route by which Italian troops entered the city on September 20, 1870, after the French troops defending the city had withdrawn, and the place where they breached the wall is marked with a column.

Halfway up, just north of Piazza della Repubblica, the church of **Santa Susanna** (daily 9am–noon & 4–7pm) is one of an elegant cluster of facades, although behind its well-proportioned Carlo Maderno frontage it isn't an especially notable building, except for some bright and soothing frescoes. The headquarters of American Catholics in Rome, it looks across the busy junction to the **Fontana dell'Acqua Felice**, which is playfully fronted by four basking lions, and focuses on a massive, bearded figure of Moses, in the central one of three arches. Marking the end of the Acqua Felice aqueduct, the fountain forms part of Pope Sixtus V's late-sixteenth-century attempts to spruce up the city centre with large-scale public works.

Opposite the church and fountain, the church of **San Bernardo alle Terme** (daily 7am–7pm) is so named (from *terme* – baths or springs) for the fact that it was once part of the vast complex of Diocletian's baths, and with its coffered ceiling and roof light, it's like a mini pantheon inside – although it is of course highly restored.

Santa Maria della Vittoria

Immediately opposite the Acqua Felice fountain, the church of **Santa Maria della Vittoria** (daily 7am–noon & 3.30–7pm) was, like Santa Susanna, built by Carlo Maderno. Its interior is one of the most elaborate examples of Baroque decoration in Rome: almost shockingly excessive to modern eyes, its ceiling and walls are pitted with carving, and statues are crammed into remote corners as in an over-stuffed attic. The church's best-known feature, Bernini's carving of the *Ecstasy of St Teresa*, the centrepiece of the sepulchral chapel of Cardinal Cornaro, continues the histrionics; a deliberately melodramatic work, it features a theatrically posed St Teresa of Avila against a backdrop of theatre-boxes on each side of the chapel, from which the Cornaro cardinals murmur and nudge each other as they watch the spectacle. St Teresa is one of the Catholic Church's most enduring mystics, and Bernini records the moment when, in 1537, she had a vision of an angel piercing her heart with a dart. It is a very Baroque piece of work in the most populist sense: not only is the event quite literally staged, but St Teresa's ecstasy verges on the worldly as she lies back in groaning submission beneath a mass of dishevelled garments and drapery.

Porta Pia

At the end of Via XX Settembre, the **Porta Pia** was one of the last works of Michelangelo, erected under Pope Pius IV in 1561. It's famous as the spot at which Italian troops first entered Rome on the 20 September, 1870 – hence the name of the street. To the right of the gate is the low-slung modern home of the **British Embassy**, while the gate itself houses the small **Museo Storico dei Bersaglieri** (Tues & Thurs 9am–1pm; free), dedicated to a crack body of troops founded in 1836 (they're the ones with the large floppy feathers in their hats) and with displays on the founder, Alessandro La Marmora, along with sections on the Unification struggle, World War II and other conflicts.

MACRO

Across busy **Corso d'Italia** (in effect part of the central ring road that girdles the city centre), the wide boulevard of **Via Nomentana** leads northeast through a plush neighbourhood of large nineteeth-century villas and apartment blocks. The second turning on the left, Via Reggio Emilia, leads to the Museum of Contemporary Art in Rome, or **MACRO**, at no. 54 (Tues–Sun 9am–7pm; Ⓦwww.macro.roma.museum), a former brewery stables whose complex of buildings opened in 1999 as an arts and culture centre. There is a permanent collection of contemporary works here, mainly focusing on Italian artists since the 1960s, but its six large exhibition halls are mostly used to host temporary exhibitions, plus there's a library, bookstore and café.

Villa Torlonia

A few hundred metres further down Via Nomentana on the right is the large nineteenth-century estate of **Villa Torlonia** (April, May & Sept 7am–7.30pm; June–Aug 7am–8.30pm, Oct & March 7am–6pm, Nov–Feb 7.30am–5pm; access also possible from Via Siracusa and Via Spallanzani), which in the 1930s was given by the banker **Prince Giovanni Torlonia** to Mussolini to use as long as he needed it. Mussolini lived here from 1925 to 1943, occupying the central **Casino Nobile** (Tues–Sun: April–Sept 9am–7pm; March & Oct 9am–5.30pm; Nov–Feb 9am–4.30pm; €4.50, or €6.50 for all Villa Torlonia museums), all for the nominal rent of a lira a year. Designed by Valadier in the early nineteenth century, the house was a sumptuous place to live. Various rooms are decorated with cycles of frescoes whose unifying theme is frolicking and nakedness, alongside a general deference to bygone ages, with ancient Roman tableaux, including Antony and Cleopatra, hieroglyphics and portraits of great artists and thinkers. The Mussolinis didn't alter the house much, just installing a couple of en-suite bathrooms between their bedrooms on the first floor (since removed) and strengthening the basement to withstand an air raid; the gardens became a bit of a playground, with tennis courts and a riding track for Il Duce to show off – as evidenced by the photos on display here.

Close to the Casino Nobile, the smaller **Casino dei Principi** is now used for temporary exhibitions but was originally a farm building that was remodelled and used as an annexe to the main villa, to which it's connected by a tunnel. Its most impressive permanent feature is the room at the end, decorated in the mid-nineteenth century with views of the Bay of Naples.

Finally, don't miss the **Casina delle Civette** in the southeastern corner (same times as Casino Nobile; €3), the "small house of the owls". This is something unusual in Rome – a Liberty-style dwelling full of Art Nouveau features, such as stained glass, wood panelling and inlays, that contribute to the kind of complete design vision that was common at the turn of the nineteenth century. Though originally designed in 1840, it was transformed in 1917 by one Vincenzo Fasoli into a comfortable residence for a Roman aristocrat – in this case Prince Torlonia – in the fashionable style of the time. The house's name derives from the prince's love of owls, and their dominance in the decoration of the building (although much of this hasn't survived). Indeed, the prince was keen on all things of the night, as his upstairs bedroom shows, decorated as it is with a night sky and a bat-encrusted chandelier. The bird theme continues in the Room of the Swallows (with its stucco birds in each corner, and swallow-themed stained glass), and there are owls in the stained-glass windows at the front of the house and the relief above the back door.

The rest of the park remains in restoration, and there are plans to return its other features, including an outdoor theatre, to their original splendour too. They have recently finished the so-called **Casino Medievale**, which has been turned into the comfortable *La Limonaia* café-restaurant (Mon 7pm–midnight, Tues–Sun 10am–7pm), where you can sit outside in a lime-tree-filled garden, and a kids' attraction known as **Technotown** (in Italian only). But whether they will ever get around to restoring the third-century AD **Jewish catacombs**, which are said to extend under the gardens for some ten kilometres, remains to be seen.

Casa di Pirandello

Five minutes' walk from the Villa Torlonia, the building known as the **Casa di Pirandello**, Via Antonio Bosio 13 (Mon–Thurs 9am–2pm, Fri 9am–3pm; free), was the home of the Italian writer for twenty years, and he spent the last three years of his life, until his death in 1936, in the second-floor apartment here. This was more or less outside the city centre at that time, and he would have had a clear view of the Villa Torlonia from his bedroom balcony. The apartment is more or less untouched from that time, with his desk in the corner of the main sitting room left as if he had just got up to make a cup of coffee; the engraved cigar box was given to him by the Italian writer and politician Gabriele d'Annunzio, and the landscapes that hang behind were painted by Pirandello himself, and complement the portraits done by his son Fausto, who lived downstairs with his family.

Sant'Agnese fuori le Mura

Further up Via Nomentana is the church of **Sant'Agnese fuori le Mura** (Mon 9am–noon, Tues–Sat 9am–noon & 4–6pm, Sun 4–6pm), dedicated to the 13-year-old saint who was martyred in Domitian's Stadium in 303 AD (see p.50). It's part of a small complex of early Christian monuments that also includes the catacombs underneath and the neighbouring church of Santa Costanza. To get into the church, walk down the hill and through the courtyard to the narthex or entrance hall of the building which, apart from some very out-of-place later fixtures, is much as it was when it was built by Pope Honorius I in the seventh century, when he reworked Constantine's original structure – which had in turn been built over St Agnes's grave. Inside, the church proper has been updated in Baroque style, but the apse mosaic is contemporary with Honorius's building, showing Agnes next to the pope, who holds a model of his church, in typical Byzantine fashion.

Out of the narthex the custodian will lead you down into the **catacombs** (same hours; €5) that sprawl below the church, which are among the best preserved and most crowd-free of all the city's catacombs. Indeed, if you have time for only one set of catacombs during your stay in Rome (and they really are all very much alike), these are perhaps the best. The custodian also sells reasonably priced little terracotta lamps in the shape of fish, or Roman-style lamps with the "Chi-Rho" sign – probably the most ancient symbol of Christianity – which make a nice souvenir of the place.

Santa Costanza

After the catacombs the guide will show you the church of **Santa Costanza** (usually open the same hours as Sant'Agnese), whose decorative and architectural features illustrate the transition from the pagan to Christian city better than almost any other building in Rome. Built in 350 AD as a mausoleum for Constantia and Helena, the daughters of the Emperor Constantine, it's a round structure which follows the traditional shape of the great pagan tombs (consider those of Hadrian and Augustus elsewhere in the city), and the mosaics on the vaulting of its circular ambulatory – fourth-century depictions of vines, leaves and birds – would have been as at home on the floor of a Roman *domus* as they were in a Christian church. Unfortunately, the porphyry sarcophagus of Santa Costanza herself has been moved to the Vatican, and what you see in the church is a plaster copy.

The Esquiline, Monti and Termini

mmediately north of the Colosseum and east of Via Cavour, the **Esquiline Hill** is the highest and largest of the city's seven hills. Formerly a sparsely populated area, with vineyards, orchards and olive groves stretching out to the Aurelian Wall, its most easterly reaches formed one of the most fashionable residential quarters of ancient Rome. In fact it consists of four separate summits: the Oppian (the part nearest the Colosseum, now a small park); the Suburra, which was ancient Rome's most notorious inner-city suburb; the Fagutalis and – the highest (65m) and largest – the Cispius, which is the site of the basilica of Santa Maria Maggiore. Immediately to the west, stretching over as far as the shopping street of Via Nazionale, the **Viminale Hill** is less rich in interest, the smallest of Rome's hills and known as the home of Italy's interior ministry and not much else. Together, the central parts of the two hills form a district known as **Monti**, an appealing cobbled quarter with neighbourhood bars, restaurants, grocers and restorers' workshops. The nineteenth-century thoroughfare of **Via Cavour** is the spine of the area, a busy artery that ferries traffic from Termini down to the area around the Colosseum and the Roman Forums.

Overall this is a part of town that most travellers to Rome encounter at some point, partly because of key sights such as Nero's **Domus Aurea** (currently closed) and the basilica of **Santa Maria Maggiore**, but also because it's most likely where you'll arrive, at **Termini station**, and it's home to the lion's share of Rome's budget hotels, which populate the streets around. Right by Termini, the excellent **Palazzo Massimo** museum and the much less exciting **Museo delle Terme di Diocleziano** across the road, are where a good deal of the city's ancient treasure is on display, while on the far side of the station the district of **San Lorenzo** forms a hub for the city's students, and has some decent bars and restaurants.

Parco di Colle Oppio

Almost opposite the Colosseum, across Via Labicana, the **Parco di Colle Oppio** is a fairly undistinguished open space, and a slightly unsavoury spot after dark. But by day it's worth a wander, dotted as it is with remnants of the various Roman structures that once stood here: piles of rubble, the imposing fenced-off remains of **Trajan's Baths** on the far side, and a number of round brick stumps

– well-heads that led down into the Esquiline's other big sight, Nero's **Domus Aurea** or "Golden House".

Domus Aurea

Currently closed for restoration following flooding, and unlikely to be open any time soon, the **Domus Aurea** is nonetheless one of the city's most intriguing sights. The "house" was a vast undertaking built on the summit of the Oppian Hill and into its sides after a fire of 64 AD (allegedly started by Nero) devastated this part of Rome. It was not intended to be a residence at all; rather it was a series of banqueting rooms, nymphaeums, small baths, terraces and gardens, facing what at the time was a small lake fed by the underground springs and streams that drained from the surrounding hills. Rome was used to Nero's excesses, but it had never seen anything like the Golden House before. The facade was supposed to have been coated in solid gold, there was hot and cold running water in the baths, one of the dining rooms was rigged up to shower flower petals and natural scent on guests, and the grounds – which covered over two square kilometres – held vineyards and game. Nero didn't get to enjoy his palace for long – he died a couple of years after it was finished, and Vespasian tore a lot of the exposed facade down in disgust, draining its lake and building the Colosseum on top. Later, Trajan built his baths on top of the rest of the complex, and it was pretty much forgotten until its wall paintings were discovered by Renaissance artists, including Raphael. When these artists first visited these rooms, they had to descend ladders into what they first believed was some kind of mystical cave, or **grotto**; their attempts to imitate what they found here gave us the word "*grotesque*".

The interior

Inside, the temperature always hovers at around 10°C and this, and the almost 100 percent humidity, makes it necessary to wear a sweater or jacket even in the middle of the Roman summer. The house can at first be confusing – Trajan's attempts to obliterate the palace with his baths complex mean that the baths' foundations merge into parts of the palace, and vice versa.

There are various covered fountains, service corridors, terraces and, most spectacularly, the **Octagonal Room**, domed, with a hole in the middle, which is supposed to have rotated as the day progressed to emulate the passage of the sun. Most of the rooms are decorated in the so-called Third Pompeiian style, with garlands of flowers, fruit, vines and foliage, interspersed with mythical animals and fanciful depictions of people looking back through windows at the viewer. Perhaps the best preserved frescoes are in the **Room of Achilles at Skyros**, and illustrate Homer's story of Achilles being sent to the island of Skyros disguised as a woman to prevent him from being drawn into the Trojan Wars. In one fresco, Achilles is in drag at the Skyros court; another shows him putting his feminine clothes aside and picking up a shield, brought to him by Ulysses (in the crested helmet) to catch him out and betray his disguise.

Via Cavour and Monti

Via Cavour is one of Rome's busiest thoroughfares, slashed through the **Monti** neighbourhood in the 1890s to connect the station district to the river – although the last part was never completed. As you walk north, towards Santa Maria Maggiore, the streets off to the left are worth a wander and form Monti's most atmospheric quarter, focusing on Via dei Serpenti and Via del Boschetto, and the narrow streets between them.

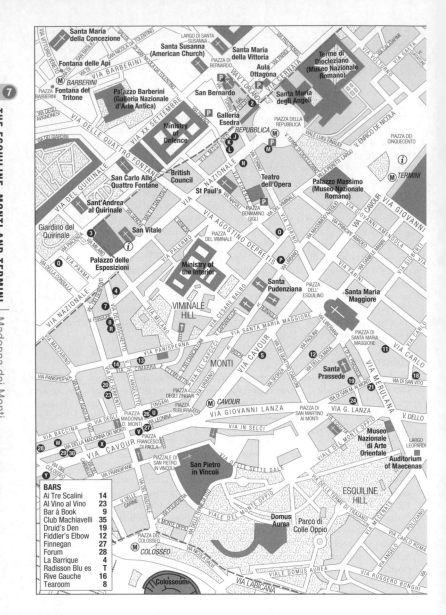

BARS

Ai Tre Scalini	14
Al Vino al Vino	23
Bar à Book	9
Club Machiavelli	35
Druid's Den	19
Fiddler's Elbow	12
Finnegan	27
Forum	28
La Barrique	4
Radisson Blu es	T
Rive Gauche	16
Tearoom	8

Madonna dei Monti

The large building at the bottom of Via dei Serpenti is the church of the **Madonna dei Monti (**daily 7am–noon & 5–7.30pm), built on the site of a convent where a miraculous image of the Virgin was found, and whose high dome and generous proportions make it well worth a peep. It was built in 1580 and is the work of Giacomo della Porta, who also contributed the fountains in the pleasant little

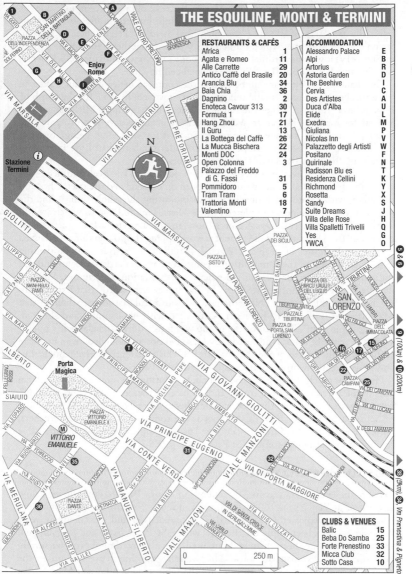

THE ESQUILINE, MONTI & TERMINI

RESTAURANTS & CAFÉS	
Africa	1
Agata e Romeo	11
Alle Carrette	29
Antico Caffè del Brasile	20
Arancia Blu	34
Baia Chia	36
Dagnino	2
Enoteca Cavour 313	30
Formula 1	17
Hang Zhou	21
Il Guru	13
La Bottega del Caffè	26
La Mucca Bischera	22
Monti DOC	24
Open Colonna	3
Palazzo del Freddo di G. Fassi	31
Pommidoro	5
Tram Tram	6
Trattoria Monti	18
Valentino	7

ACCOMMODATION	
Alessandro Palace	E
Alpi	B
Artorius	R
Astoria Garden	D
The Beehive	I
Cervia	C
Des Artistes	A
Duca d'Alba	U
Elide	L
Exedra	M
Giuliana	P
Nicolas Inn	V
Palazzetto degli Artisti	W
Positano	F
Quirinale	N
Radisson Blu es	T
Residenza Cellini	K
Richmond	Y
Rosetta	X
Sandy	S
Suite Dreams	J
Villa delle Rose	H
Villa Spalletti Trivelli	Q
Yes	G
YWCA	O

CLUBS & VENUES	
Balic	15
Beba Do Samba	25
Forte Prenestino	33
Micca Club	32
Sotto Casa	10

Ⓜ Manzoni (30m) & San Giovanni

piazza alongside, where – legend has it – heathen girls and boys were once brought to be baptized into the Catholic church.

San Pietro in Vincoli

On the other side of Via Cavour, steps lead up to the tranquil piazza in front of the recently restored church of **San Pietro in Vincoli** (daily: April–Sept

117

8am–12.30pm & 3.30–7pm; Oct–March 8am–12.30pm & 3–6pm), one of Rome's most delightfully plain places of worship, built to house an important relic, the two sets of chains ("vincoli") that held St Peter when he was in Jerusalem and in Rome, which miraculously joined together. During the papacy of Sixtus IV, it was the cardinal seat of the pope's nephew, Giuliano della Rovere, who became Pope Julius II, of Sistine Chapel ceiling fame.

The chains of St Peter can still be seen in the confessio beneath the high altar, in a beautiful gold and rock crystal reliquary, but most people come for the **tomb** of Pope Julius II at the far end of the southern aisle, which occupied Michelangelo on and off for much of his career. Michelangelo reluctantly gave it up to paint the Sistine Chapel, and was never able to return to it for very long, being always at the beck and call of successive popes, who understandably had little interest in promoting the glory of one of their predecessors.

No one knows how the tomb would have looked had it been finished – it's generally assumed that Moses would have been on one end and the risen Christ on the other, with a statue of Julius himself surmounting the whole thing – and the only statues Michelangelo completed are the *Moses*, *Leah* and *Rachel*, which are still in the church, and two *Dying Slaves*, now in the Louvre. *Moses*, pictured as descended from Sinai to find the Israelites worshipping the golden calf, and flanked by the gentle figures of Leah and Rachel, is one of the artist's most captivating works and the rest of the composition – completed by later artists – seems dull and static by comparison. Because of a medieval mistranslation of scripture, Moses is depicted with satyr's horns instead of the "radiance of the Lord" that Exodus tells us shone around his head. Nonetheless, this powerful statue is so lifelike that Michelangelo is alleged to have struck its knee with his hammer and shouted, "Speak, damn you!". The rest of the group was finished by Michelangelo's pupils, while the statue of Julius II at the top, by Maso del Bosco, modelled on an Etruscan coffin lid, sadly fails to evoke the character of this apparently active, courageous and violent man – who was in fact laid to rest in St Peter's.

There's not much else to see in the church, but during the summer months it can be a bit of a scrum to see the tomb, and it's nice to wander around the building's less congested areas. In the north aisle there's a seventh-century mosaic of St Sebastian and to the right of the door is the tomb of the Pollaioulo brothers, Antonio and Piero, the fifteenth-century Tuscan sculptors who were responsible for Sixtus IV's elaborate tomb in St Peter's (see p.188).

Santa Pudenziana

Left off the end of Via Cavour, the church of **Santa Pudenziana**, down below street level at Via Urbana 160 (daily 8.30am–noon & 3–6pm), has equally ancient origins. It was dedicated to St Prassede's supposed sister and was for many years believed to have been built on the site where St Peter lived and worshipped, though this has since been entirely discredited, and it's now thought to have simply been the site of a Roman bathhouse. The two relics the church used to house – the chair that St Peter used as his throne and the table at which he said Mass – have both long gone, to the Vatican and the Lateran, respectively. But the church still has one feature of ancient origin, the superb fifth-century apse mosaics – some of the oldest Christian figurative mosaics in Rome, though they've been tampered with and restored over the years. They're still fluid and beautiful works, centring on a golden enthroned Christ surrounded by the Apostles – not quite all of them, you'll notice, due to the fact that the mosaic was reduced in size when the church was restored in the sixteenth century and they cut off one from either side. Nonetheless, the mosaic is marvellous, not least the graphic arrangement of the

Apostles that remain, and the expressiveness of their faces, each one of which is purposefully different from the next.

Santa Maria Maggiore

Via Cavour opens out at Piazza Esquilino, behind the basilica of **Santa Maria Maggiore** (daily 7am–7pm). This is one of the city's five great basilicas, and has one of Rome's best-preserved Byzantine interiors – a fact belied by its dull eighteenth-century exterior. Unlike the other great places of pilgrimage in Rome, it was not built on any special Constantinian site, but instead went up during the fifth century after the Council of Ephesus recognized the **cult of the Virgin** and churches venerating Our Lady began to spring up all over the Christian world. According to legend, the Virgin Mary appeared to Pope Liberius in a dream on the night of August 4,352 AD, telling him to build a church on the Esquiline Hill, on a spot where he would find a patch of newly fallen **snow** the next morning. The snow would outline exactly the plan of the church that should be built there in her honour – which, of course, is exactly what happened, and the first church here was called Santa Maria della Neve ("of the snow"). The present structure dates from about 420 AD, and was completed under the reign of Sixtus III, who was pope between 432 AD and 440 AD.

Santa Maria Maggiore is noted for two special ceremonies. One, on August 5, celebrates the miraculous snowfall: at midday Mass white rose petals are showered on the congregation from the ceiling, and at night the fire department operates an artificial snow machine in the piazza in front and showers the area in snow that, naturally, melts immediately. The other takes place on Christmas morning, when the reliquary containing the crib is processed around the church and then displayed on the high altar.

The basilica

The **basilica** was encased in its eighteenth-century shell during the papacy of Benedict XIV, although the campanile, the highest in Rome, is older than this – built in 1377 under Pope Gregory XI. Inside, however, the original building survives intact, its broad nave fringed on both sides with strikingly well-kept mosaics (binoculars help), most of which date from the time of Pope Sixtus III and recount, in comic-strip form, incidents from the Old Testament. The ceiling, which shows the arms of the Spanish Borgia popes, Calixtus III and Alexander VI, was gilded in 1493 with gold sent by Queen Isabella as part payment of a loan from Innocent VIII to finance the voyage of Columbus to the New World.

The large chapel in the right transept holds the elaborate tomb of Sixtus V – another, less famous, **Sistine Chapel**, decorated with marble taken from the Roman Septizodium, and with frescoes and reliefs portraying events from his reign. In the middle, a bronze baldachino carried by four angels covers another small chapel. The chapel also contains the tomb of another zealous and reforming pope, Pius V, whose statue faces that of Sixtus; he's probably best known for excommunicating Queen Elizabeth I of England, in 1570.

Outside the Sistine Chapel is the modest tomb slab of the Bernini family, including Gian Lorenzo himself, to the right by the sanctuary steps, while opposite, the sumptuous **Pauline Chapel** is home to the tombs of the Borghese pope, Paul V, on the left, and his immediate predecessor Clement VIII, opposite. The floor is decorated with the Borghese arms, an eagle and dragon, and the magnificently gilded ceiling shows glimpses of heaven. The altar, of lapis lazuli and agate, contains a *Madonna and Child* dating from the twelfth or thirteenth century.

Between the two chapels, the **confessio** contains a kneeling statue of the dogmatic Pope Pius IX, the longest-serving pope in history, and the last one to hold real power – he was kicked out with Italian Unification in 1870, after 31 years. The reliquary here is said to contain fragments of the crib of Christ, in rock crystal and silver, while the high altar, above it, contains the relics of St Matthew, among other Christian martyrs. But it's the **mosaics** of the arch that really dazzle, a vivid representation of scenes from the life of Christ – *The Annunciation*, *The Adoration of the Magi* (in which Christ is depicted not as a child, unusually, but as a king himself) plus *The Massacre of the Innocents* on the left and *The Presentation in the Temple* and *Herod Receiving the Magi* on the right. The central apse mosaics are later, but are no less impressive, commissioned by the late-thirteenth-century pope, Nicholas IV, and showing *The Coronation of the Virgin*, with angels, saints and the pope himself.

The museum and loggia

There's a **museum** underneath the basilica (daily 9am–6.30pm; €4), which sports what even by Roman standards is a wide variety of relics – a hair of the Virgin and the arms of saints Luke and Matthew – as well as the usual liturgical garments and so on. The sporadically open nativity scene, or *Presepio*, the work of Arnolfo di Cambio, was originally created to decorate a chapel to hold the basilica's holy crib relics, and is well worth catching. You might prefer to save your money for the **loggia** above the main entrance (tours daily at 9am & 1pm, bookable in advance; ☏06.446.5836; €3), which has some magnificent mosaics showing Christ among various saints, sitting above four scenes that tell the story of the miracle of the snow: the one on the far left shows Mary appearing to Pope Liberius, the one on the far right shows the pope, and others trace the outline of the building in the miraculous snowfall.

Santa Prassede

Across the road from Santa Maria Maggiore, the ninth-century church of **Santa Prassede** at Via S. Prassede 9 (daily 7am–noon & 4–6.30pm) occupies an ancient site where it's claimed St Prassede harboured Christians on the run from persecution. She apparently collected the blood and remains of the martyrs and

Sixtus V

Although he reigned only five years, from 1585 to 1590, **Sixtus V**'s papacy was one of Rome's most memorable. He laid out several new streets, notably the long, straight thoroughfare that runs from the top of Trinità dei Monti to Santa Maria Maggiore (at various points Via Sistina, Via delle Quattro Fontane and Via de Pretis); he erected many of the present obelisks that dot the city, including those in Piazza San Pietro and Piazza San Giovanni; and he launched an attack on bandits in the surrounding countryside and criminal gangs in the city. As a priest at the time remarked: "I am in Rome after an absence of ten years, and do not recognize it, so new does all appear to me to be: monuments, streets, piazzas, fountains, aqueducts, obelisks and other wonders, all the works of Sixtus V." Sixtus was, like Julius II, a man of action and a Franciscan friar. He was perhaps most famously responsible for the execution of Beatrice Cenci (see p.65), although his reign was also notorious for his stripping the Roman Forum of its marbles and the Colosseum of its stone for St Peter's. He also demolished the so-called Septizodium, at the southeast end of the Palatine, marble from which decorated his tomb.

placed them in a well where she herself was later buried; a red marble disc in the floor of the nave marks the spot. In the southern aisle, the chapel of St Zeno was built by Pope Paschal I as a mausoleum for his mother, Theodora, and is decorated with marvellous ninth-century mosaics that make it glitter like a jewel-encrusted box. You'll need €0.50 to light them; Theodora is depicted on the left-hand arch. The chapel also contains a fragment of a column that Christ was supposedly tied to when he was scourged. In the apse are more ninth-century mosaics, showing Christ between saints Peter, Pudenziana and Zeno (on the right) and saints Paul, Praxedes and Paschal I (on the left). Note that Paschal's halo (like Theodora's) is in a rectangular form, indicating that he was alive when the mosaics were placed here.

San Martino ai Monti

Two minutes from Santa Prassede, the church of **San Martino ai Monti**, down the road of the same name, is another place of worship that dates back to the earliest days of Christianity. It was dedicated to saints Sylvester and Martin in the sixth century and incorporates an ancient Roman structure, but it was almost entirely rebuilt in the 1650s, and sports a ceiling from that time that is strangely modern in appearance, parts of it reminiscent of 1920s brushed stainless steel. The ceiling also shows the arms of the Medicis, specifically the family's last pope, Leo XI, who ruled briefly in 1605, and has a series of frescoes depicting scenes of the Roman countryside and the interiors of the old Roman basilicas of St Peter and San Giovanni before they were gussied up in their present Baroque splendour – St Peter's is at the far end of the north aisle, San Giovanni near the door.

Museo Nazionale di Arte Orientale

It's a short walk south from San Martino ai Monti to busy Largo Brancaccio, where the imposing Palazzo Brancaccio houses the **Museo Nazionale di Arte Orientale**, Via Merulana 248 (Mon, Wed, Fri & Sat 8.30am–2pm, Tues, Thurs & Sun 8.30am–7.30pm, closed first & third Mon of the month; €6) – a first-rate collection of oriental art (the best in Italy) that has recently been restored. Beginning with Marco Polo in the thirteenth century, the Italians have always had connections with the East, and the quality of this collection of Islamic, Chinese, Indian and Southeast Asian art reflects this fact – not to mention making a refreshing break from the multiple ages of Western art you are exposed to in Rome. There are finds dating back to 1500 BC from a necropolis in Pakistan; architectural fragments, artworks and jewellery from Tibet, Nepal and Pakistan; a solid collection from China, with predictable Buddhas and vases alongside curiosities such as Han dynasty figures and a large Wei dynasty Buddha with two bodhisattvas; and coins from twelfth-century Iran and northwest India.

Auditorium of Maecenas

Outside the Oriental Art museum, Largo Leopardi is home to the remains of the so-called **Auditorium of Maecenas**, the sole remnant of a villa that was home to the trusted friend and adviser of Augustus; the rest was swept up and incorporated into Nero's Domus Aurea (see p.115) long after Maecenas's death. Inside it's basically a large room with some seating arranged around an apse at one end, which is decorated with some badly damaged paintings. It is possible to visit, during the summer months at least, but opening times are very erratic.

Piazza Vittorio Emanuele II

A few metres from here, up Via Leopardi, **Piazza Vittorio Emanuele II** was the centre of a district which became known as the "quartiere piemontese" when the government located many of its major ministries here after Unification. The arcades of the square, certainly, recall central Turin, as do the solid palatial buildings that surround it. It's more recently become the immigrant quarter of Rome, with a heavy concentration of African, Asian and Middle Eastern shops and restaurants. You'll easily hear a dozen different languages spoken as you pass through, although sadly the open-air **market** that used to surround the piazza has moved a few blocks east to Via Giolitti, between Via Ricasoli and Via Lamarmora, where there are two covered halls, one selling clothes, the other food.

Close to the northern end of the piazza, an eighteen-metre-high pile of Roman bricks is all that is left of a monumental public fountain known as the **Nymphaeum of Alexander Severus** (emperor from 222 to 235 AD) – a distribution point for water arriving in the city by a branch of the Acqua Claudia aqueduct and now home to a prosperous colony of cats.

Santa Bibiana

A couple of blocks north of Piazza Vittorio, right up against the railway tracks at Via Giolitti 154, the church of **Santa Bibiana** (daily 7.30–11am & 5–7.30pm) is an inauspicious location for Bernini's first church in Rome. A rebuilding of a much older church, it incorporates a number of ancient columns, including the one at which the fifth-century martyr is supposed to have been tortured. The statue of the saint, however, in a niche on the high altar, is pure, theatrical Bernini, completed in 1626, and gives a hint of what was to come in his later work, most notably in the church of Santa Maria della Vittoria, just the other side of Termini station (see p.111).

The Viminale

Behind the church of Santa Pudenziana, the **Ministero dell'Interno** marks the top of the **Viminale** Hill. Piazza del Viminale, just in front, gives way to Via Viminale, and, on the left, Rome's **Teatro dell'Opera** (see p.272), an unassuming building, but one which until the completion of the new Auditorium, was the city's main music venue.

Via Nazionale

Following the dip between the Viminale and Quirinale hills, **Via Nazionale** connects Piazza Venezia and the centre of town with the area around Termini station and the eastern districts beyond. A focus for much development after Unification, its heavy, overbearing buildings were constructed to give Rome some semblance of modern sophistication when it became capital of the new country, but most are now occupied by hotels and mainstream shops and boutiques. At its bottom end, at the junction of Via XXIV Maggio, the palm-filled gardens of the **Villa Aldobrandini** are a pleasant respite from the traffic, high above the street and reached from the entrance on Via Mazzarino.

Palazzo delle Esposizioni

A little further up the road, the imposing **Palazzo delle Esposizioni** at Via Nazionale 194 (Tues–Thurs & Sun 10am–8pm, Fri & Sat 10am–10.30pm; ☎06.3996.7500, ⓦwww.palazzoesposizioni.it) was designed in 1883 by Pio

Piacentini (father of the more famous Marcello, favourite architect of Mussolini), and was until quite recently a bit of a white elephant, boarded-up and sad. But it reopened with much fanfare in 2008 after a five-year revamp and now hosts regular large-scale exhibitions and cultural events. It also houses a cinema, an excellent art and design bookshop and café in its basement, and up the steps on the left side of the building are lifts to the fancy *Open Colonna* restaurant (see p.249).

St Paul's within the Walls

At the corner of Via Nazionale and Via Napoli is the American Episcopal church of **St Paul's within the Walls** (daily 9am–1pm & 4–7pm), the first Protestant church to be built within the walls of the city after the Unification of Italy in 1870 and a peaceful and spiritual haven after the humdrum bustle of Via Nazionale. Dating from 1879, it was built in a neo-Gothic style by the British architect G.E. Street and is worth a quick peek inside for its works by English artists. The leaf-pattern ceramic tiles that line the walls of each side of the nave were designed by William Morris, and the apse mosaics, by the Pre-Raphaelite artist Edward Burne-Jones, depict one of the church's founders, the American financier J.P. Morgan as St Paul, alongside his family, Garibaldi, General Ulysses Grant, and Abraham Lincoln. The 1913 mosaics on the western wall are by George Breck, who was director of the American Academy at the time.

Piazza della Repubblica

At the top of Via Nazionale, **Piazza della Repubblica** (formerly Piazza Esedra) is typical of Rome's nineteenth-century regeneration, a stern and dignified semicircle of buildings that was until recently rather dilapidated but is now – with the help of the stylish *Hotel Exedra* – once again resurgent. The arcades make a fine place to stroll, despite the traffic, which roars ceaselessly around the **Fontana delle Naiadi**'s languishing nymphs and sea monsters.

Santa Maria degli Angeli

The piazza actually follows the semicircular outline of part of the Baths of Diocletian, built in 300 AD, the remains of which lie across the piazza and are partially contained in the church of **Santa Maria degli Angeli** (Mon–Sat 7am–6.30pm, Sun 7am–7.30pm). This is not Rome's most welcoming church by any means, but does give the best impression of the size and grandeur of Diocletian's bath complex, or at least of the tepidarium, whose structure it utilizes. It's a huge, open building, with an interior standardized by Vanvitelli into a rich eighteenth-century confection after a couple of centuries of piecemeal adaptation (started by an aged Michelangelo). The pink granite pillars, at three metres in diameter the largest in Rome, are original, and the main transept formed the main hall of the baths; only the crescent shape of the facade remains from the original caldarium (it had previously been hidden by a newer facing). The meridian that strikes diagonally across the floor in the south transept, flanked by representations of the twelve signs of the zodiac, was until 1846 the regulator of time for Romans (now a cannon shot fired daily at noon from the Janiculum Hill). Take the back exit through the sacristy and you'll find a small exhibition on the history of the baths and church.

The Aula Ottagona

The exit from the church of Santa Maria degli Angeli channels you through to Via Cernaia, behind another remnant of the baths, the **Aula Ottagona**

(Octagonal Hall), formerly a planetarium and now part of the **Museo delle Terme di Diocleziano** (same ticket, but currently closed for restoration). The large domed room contains marble statues taken from the Baths of Caracalla and Diocletian, and two remarkable statues of a boxer and athlete from the Quirinale Hill. Excavations underground – accessible by stairs – show the furnaces for heating water for the baths and the foundations of another building from the time of Diocletian.

Museo delle Terme di Diocleziano

The buildings that surround Santa Maria degli Angeli are also recycled parts of Diocletian's Baths – the complex was enormous, originally measuring 376m by 361m – and include the round church of San Bernardo alle Terme, off Via XX Settembre, and the round building in the other direction, at the corner of Via Viminale and Via delle Terme di Diocleziano. The rest of the baths – the huge halls and courtyards on the side towards Termini – have been renovated and, together with the Carthusian monastery attached to the church, now hold what is probably the least interesting part of the Museo Nazionale Romano (the better sections are across the street in Palazzo Massimo, see below, and in Palazzo Altemps, see p.55), the **Museo delle Terme di Diocleziano** (Tues–Sun 9am–7pm; €7, includes Palazzo Altemps, Palazzo Massimo, Crypta Balbi, valid 3 days).

Fronted by a fragrant garden, open to all, which centres on a large *krater* fountain with little cupids holding up its rim, the museum's most evocative part is the large cloister of the church whose sides are crammed with statuary, funerary monuments and sarcophagi and fragments from all over Rome. There's a lot to pick through, around three hundred bits and pieces in all, but standouts include the animal heads, found in the Forum of Trajan, a fine headless seated statue of Hercules from the second century AD, and a nice, if again damaged, statue of a husband and wife. There's also an upstairs gallery that wraps around the cloister and includes finds dating back to the seventh century BC, and a downstairs section with more items – busts, terracotta statues, armour and weapons found in Roman tombs – all effectively, if rather academically, presented, but hardly compulsory viewing.

Palazzo Massimo

Across from Santa Maria degli Angeli, the snazzily restored **Palazzo Massimo**, Largo di Villa Peretti 1, is home to one of the two principal parts of the Museo Nazionale Romano (the other is in the Palazzo Altemps) – a superb collection of Greek and Roman antiquities, second only to the Vatican's, which has been entirely reorganized and features many pieces that have remained undisplayed for decades (Tues–Sun 9am–7.45pm; €7, includes Palazzo Altemps, Terme Diocletian, Crypta Balbi, valid 3 days, €4 audioguide).

Basement

The basement has displays of exquisite gold **jewellery** from the second century AD – necklaces, rings, brooches, all in immaculate condition – and some fine gold imperial hairnets. There's also – startlingly – the mummified remains of an eight-year-old girl, along with a fantastic **coin collection**, from the first bronze coinage of the fourth century BC to the surprisingly sophisticated coins of the Republic and imperial times, right up to the lira and concluding with a display devoted to the euro. It's all shown in glass cases equipped with magnifying glasses on runners, controlled by the buttons mounted on the front of each case.

▲ Classical statuary at Palazzo Massimo

Ground floor

The ground floor of the museum is devoted to statues from the **early empire**, including a gallery on the right with an unparalleled selection of unidentified busts found all over Rome. Their lack of clear identity is no barrier to appreciating them; they are amazing pieces of portraiture, and as vivid a representation of patrician Roman life as you'll find. Look out for the so-called *Statue of the Tivoli General*, the face of an old man mounted on the body of a youthful athlete – sometimes believed to be a portrait of L. Munatius Plancus, the military officer who named Octavian "Augustus" (literally "Reverend") and so officially started the cult of the emperor. At the far end of the courtyard are more busts, this time identifiable as members of the imperial family: a bronze of Germanicus, a marvellous small bust of Caligula, several representations of Livia, Tiberius, Antonia and Drusus and a hooded statue of Augustus. You can find Greek sculpture on the far side of the courtyard, including bronzes of a Hellenistic prince holding a spear and a wounded pugilist at rest.

First floor

The museum really gets going on the first-floor gallery, with groupings of the various **imperial dynasties** in roughly chronological order set around the courtyard, starting with the Flavian emperors, deliberately realistic and unidealized. The craggy determination of Vespasian and the pinched nobility of Nerva are in complete contrast to the next room, where Trajan appears next to his wife Plotina as Hercules, next to a bust of his cousin Hadrian, who is in turn next to his lover Antinous. These were some of the most successful years of the empire, and they continued with the Antonine emperors in the next room, which features Antonius Pius in a heroic nude pose and in several busts, flanked by likenesses of his daughter Faustina Minor. Faustina was the wife of Antonius's successor, Marcus Aurelius, who appears in the corridor outside. Also here is Commodus, the last and perhaps least successful of the Antonine emperors. Further on, past a room full of sarcophagi, including one showing the muses conversing with philosophers, are the

Severans, with the fierce-looking Caracalla looking across past his father Septimius Severus to his brother Geta, whom he later murdered.

Just beyond the Severan emperors a hyper-realistic **sarcophagus** from 190 AD shows Roman victories over barbarians. Next door, at the back of the courtyard, there is an amazing sleeping hermaphrodite, an almost totally complete Dionysus that was fished out of the Tiber and bronzework from two imperial galleys found in southern Lazio, at Nemi, dating from the time of Caligula. A balustrade is studded with figures, each one different with a face on each side, handles are decorated with the faces of panthers, wolves and lions, and rudders come in the shape of forearms.

On the other side of the courtyard are more astonishing pieces, this time from various imperial villas outside Rome, many of them copies of **Greek originals**, including figures of Apollo and Dionysus, an Amazon and a barbarian, full of movement and vigour, as well as more dynastic busts discovered at Hadrian's villa in Tivoli, and a beautiful statue of a young girl holding a tray from Augustus's villa at Anzio.

Second floor

The second floor takes in some of the finest **Roman frescoes and mosaics** ever found and divides into three main parts. First there is a stunning set of **frescoes** from the Villa di Livia, depicting an orchard dense with fruit and flowers and patrolled by partridges, doves and other birds while beyond, on the same side of the courtyard, are floor **mosaics** showing naturalistic scenes – sea creatures, people boating – from the so-called Villa di Baccano on Via Cassia, a sumptuous mansion probably owned by the imperial Severi family. Four mosaic panels taken from a bedroom, featuring four chariot drivers and their horses, are so finely crafted that from a distance they look as if they've been painted, while in the adjoining room is a very rare example of *opus sectile*, a mosaic technique imported from the eastern provinces in the first century AD. Inlaid pieces of marble, mother-of-pearl, glass and hard stone are used instead of tesserae, the parts cut so as to enhance detail and give perspective depth.

More **mosaics** decorate the corridor outside, with floors showing Nile scenes, complete with crocodiles and hippos, while others come from Anzio, including one showing a reclining Hercules holding a cup and club while a wild boar emerges from a nearby cave.

The final section displays **wall paintings** rescued from what was believed to be the riverside villa of Augustus's daughter Julia and his trusted general Agrippa, built for their wedding. The villa wasn't lived in for long – Agrippa died of a fever nine years after their marriage – but the decoration was sumptuous in the extreme, including a room painted with garlands and an Egyptian-style frieze and two bedrooms painted deep red and covered with different figures.

Termini station

Across the street from the museum is the low white facade of **Termini station** (so named for its proximity to the Baths of Diocletian, nothing to do with being the terminus of Rome's rail lines) and the vast, bus-crammed hubbub that is Piazza dei Cinquecento in front. The station is a great building, an ambitious piece of modern architectural design that was completed in 1950 and still entirely dominates the streets around with its low, self-consciously futuristic lines – it's nicknamed "the dinosaur" for its curved front canopy. A few years back it received a huge and sleek renovation which converted part of its cavernous ticket hall to retail and restaurant space and upgraded the building in general, but to be honest it's still pretty seedy and full of pickpockets, although it does have a good bookshop, a branch of the UPIM department store, a supermarket open long hours, lots of other shops and even an exhibition space. **Piazza dei Cinquecento** is lined with a few stretches of Rome's original city wall, the Servian Wall, and is a good place to find buses and taxis. Like a lot of city railway stations, the streets around are low-life territory and, although not especially dangerous, are not a place to hang around for long.

San Lorenzo

Just east of Termini, and accessible on foot under the railway tracks from Via Giolitti, the neighbourhood of **SAN LORENZO** spreads from the railway tracks to the main campus of Rome's university, on the far side of Via Tiburtina – a working-class district, popular with students, that retains something of the air of a local neighbourhood, quite different from the rest of the city centre. It's home to some good and often inexpensive local restaurants (see pp.248–249), and is also the location of the enormous **Campo Verano cemetery** (daily 7am–6pm) – since 1830 the largest Catholic burial-place in Rome. It's worth a visit for the grandiose tombs, such as the she-wolf-topped stone of the poet, journalist and activist Goffredo Mameli, just inside on the left. A contemporary of Garibaldi, he wrote the lyrics to the Italian National Anthem, *Il Canto degli Italiani*, in 1847, and fought on the side of Unification forces, receiving the bayonet wound that killed him in 1849, at the age of just 22.

San Lorenzo fuori le Mura

The area takes its name from the church of **San Lorenzo fuori le Mura** on Via Tiburtina right by the cemetery (daily: summer 7.30am–12.30pm & 4–8pm; winter 7.30am–12.30pm & 3.30–7pm), one of the seven great pilgrimage churches of Rome. It is a beautiful plain basilica, in many ways the city's most atmospheric, and because of its relatively out-of-the-way location one of the most spiritual in feel, fronted by a columned portico and with a lovely twelfth-century cloister to its side. The original church here was built by Constantine over the site of St Lawrence's martyrdom – the saint was reputedly burned to death on a gridiron, halfway through his ordeal uttering the immortal words, "Turn me, I am done on this side." Where San Lorenzo differs is that it's actually a combination of three churches – one a sixth-century reconstruction of Constantine's church by Pope Pelagius II, which now forms the chancel, another a fifth-century church from the time of Sixtus III, with a basilica from the thirteenth century by Honorius II joining the two.

Because of its proximity to Rome's railyards, the church was bombed heavily during World War II, but it has been rebuilt with sensitivity, and remains much as it was originally. **Inside** there are features from all periods: a Cosmati floor, again perhaps the city's most impressive, a thirteenth-century pulpit and a paschal candle-stick with a twisted stem. The baldachino in the choir is dated 1147 and sits on its own colourful Cosmati floor, beyond which a thirteenth-century bishop's throne is perfectly placed to see the sixth-century mosaic on the inside of the triumphal arch – a sixth-century depiction of St Lawrence with Pelagius II offering his church to Christ; the underneath of the arch is decorated with fruit and flowers. There are more mosaics below here, nineteenth-century this time, adorning the tomb of Pope Pius IX. The body of the last papal ruler of Rome was carried here under cover of darkness in 1881, in a procession that was disrupted by a gang of Italian nationalists who attempted to throw his corpse into the river. Through the sacristy is the church's lovely small Romanesque **cloister**, one of Rome's simplest and most peaceful, with a well-tended garden and fish pond in the middle and a fragment of a bomb remembering the bombardment of the church in World War II. Downstairs, the **catacombs** (often closed) are where St Lawrence was apparently buried – a dank path leads to the pillars of Constantine's original structure.

The Celian Hill and San Giovanni

The area immediately behind the Colosseum, the **Celian Hill** is the most southerly of Rome's seven hills and one of its most peaceful, with few major roads and the park of Villa Celimontana at its heart, built on the site of an ancient zoo that was home to some of the animals that were to die in the nearby arena. The area immediately east of here is known as **San Giovanni**, after the basilica complex that lies at the end of the long narrow thoroughfare of Via San Giovanni in Laterano, which was, before the creation of the separate Vatican city state, the headquarters of the Catholic Church. It's a mixed area, mainly residential, but it has some compelling sights in the basilica of San Giovanni itself, the church of Santa Croce in Gerusalemme, and the amazing triple-layered church of San Clemente – all in all a worthy add-on to a morning spent at the Colosseum.

Santo Stefano Rotondo

Ten minutes' walk from the Colosseum down Via Claudia, and not on the Celian Hill proper, the round church of **Santo Stefano Rotondo** (Tues–Sat 9.30am–12.30pm & 2–5pm, Sun 9.30am–12.30pm) is a truly ancient structure, built in the 460s AD and consecrated by Pope Simplicius to commemorate Christianity's first martyr, St Stephen. Recently open again after a lengthy restoration, its four chapels form the shape of a cross in a circle, atmospherically lit by the 22 windows of the clerestory. The interior is a magnificent and moody circular space, made up of two concentric rings, but the feature that will really stick in your mind is the series of stomach-turning frescoes on the walls of the outer ring, showing various saints being martyred in different ways: impalings, drawings and quarterings, disembowelments, boilings in oil, hangings, beheadings – according to Charles Dickens, who visited in 1845, "such a panorama of horror and butchery no man could imagine in his sleep, though he were to eat a whole pig raw, for supper".

Santa Maria in Domnica

On the opposite side of the main road, Via Claudia opens out into Piazza della Navicella, named after the "navicella" or Roman stone boat that sits outside the church of **Santa Maria in Domnica** (daily 8.30am–12.30pm & 4.30–7pm), a sixth-century church at the bottom of the Celian Hill. Above its apse is a ninth-century mosaic of Christ with some wonderfully individualized apostles and angels, while in the apse itself another mosaic shows Pachal I, who restored the church, kneeling at the feet of the Virgin.

Villa Celimontana

The **Villa Celimontana** park can be accessed via **Piazza della Navicella**, next door to the church, or Piazza Giovanni e Paolo (see below). These shady public gardens make a nice spot for a picnic, with lots of leafy walkways and grassy slopes, and you could do worse than take a stroll through before moving on to the other sights of the Celian Hill. There are also pony rides, worth considering if you're with kids (€3), as well as a small playground, and outdoor concerts on summer evenings (see p.264).

Santi Giovanni e Paolo

On the other side of the park, at the Celian Hill's summit, the church of **Santi Giovanni e Paolo** (daily 8.30am–noon & 3.30–6.30pm), marked by its colourful campanile, is set in a peaceful **piazza** that makes it a popular location for weddings – despite the adolescent autograph hunters who occasionally throng outside the TV studios opposite. Originally founded by a Roman senator called Pammachius, the church acts as an unofficial memorial to conscientious objection, dedicated to two dignitaries in the court of Constantine who were beheaded here in 361 AD after refusing military service. The remnants of what is believed to be their house are now open to the public in the Case Romane (see below). Inside the church's dark interior, thronged with chandeliers, a railed-off tablet in mid-nave marks the shrine where the saints were martyred and buried, while outside in the far corner of the square, underneath the campanile, you can see the arches of part of a temple of Claudius, the remains of which extend far down the hill towards the Colosseum.

The Case Romane

The so-called **Case Romane** (daily except Tues & Wed 10am–1pm & 3–6pm; €6) are around the corner from – but actually situated underneath – Santi Giovanni e Paolo, on Clivo di Scauro, where the buttresses of the church arch over the street. It was believed to be the relatively lavish residence of Giovanni and Paolo – the two prominent citizens who were martyred during the third century AD and commemorated in the church (see above). The twenty or so rooms are in fact more likely to be a series of dwellings, separated by a narrow lane, rather than a single residence. Patchily frescoed with pagan and Christian subjects, most of the chambers are dark, poky affairs; you'll need some imagination to see them for the palatially appointed living quarters they must have been.

However, there are standouts, including the **Casa dei Genii**, frescoed with winged youths and cupids, and the **courtyard** or nymphaeum, which has a marvellous fresco of a goddess being waited on, sandwiched between cupids in boats, fishing and loading supplies. The **antiquarium**, too, beautifully pulls together finds from the site, among them a *Christ with Saints* fresco, and ceramics, amphorae and fascinating small domestic artefacts – an intact imperial-age spoon, a bronze reel, bone sewing needles and almost perfect oil lamps.

San Gregorio Magno

The road descends from the church and the Case Romane under a succession of brick arches to the originally medieval church of **San Gregorio Magno** on the left

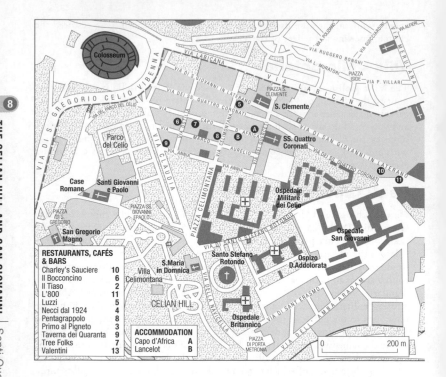

RESTAURANTS, CAFÉS & BARS

Charley's Sauciere	10
Il Bocconcino	6
Il Tiaso	2
L'800	11
Luzzi	5
Necci dal 1924	4
Pentagrappolo	8
Primo al Pigneto	3
Taverna dei Quaranta	9
Tree Folks	7
Valentini	13

ACCOMMODATION

Capo d'Africa	A
Lancelot	B

(daily 8.30am–12.30pm & 3–6.30pm; ring the bell marked "portinare" to gain admission), in a commanding position above the traffic drone of the road below, looking across to the lollipop pines of the Palatine Hill opposite. St Gregory founded a monastery here, and was a monk here before becoming pope in 590 AD. Stabilizing Rome after the fall of the empire, he effectively established the powerful papal role that would endure for the best part of the following 1500 years; he also dispatched St Augustine in the early seventh century to convert England to Christianity.

Today's rather ordinary Baroque **interior** doesn't really do justice to the historical importance of the church, but the lovely Cosmati floor remains intact, and the chapel of the saint at the end of the south aisle has a beautifully carved bath showing scenes from St Gregory's life along with his marble throne, a beaten-up specimen that actually predates the saint by 500 years. Just to the left of the church entrance, where the original monastery stood, there are three chapels surrounded by cypress trees, one of which, **Santa Barbara**, treasures the table at which St Gregory apparently fed twelve paupers daily with his own hands for years, while the chapels of **Santa Silvia** and **Sant'Andrea** contain frescoes by Guido Reni and Domenichino (Tues, Thurs, Sat & Sun 9.30am–12.30pm; call ☎06.7049.4966 to book an obligatory guided tour).

Santi Quattro Coronati

Between San Giovanni in Laterano and the Colosseum, the church of **Santi Quattro Coronati** (daily 6.15am–8pm; cloister and San Silvestro chapel Mon–Sat 9.30am–noon & 4.30–6pm, Sun 9–10.40am & 4–5.45pm: €1, handed over in the

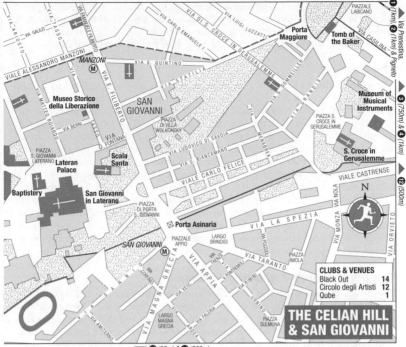

On the map:

PIAZZALE LABICANO

Porta Maggiore

Tomb of the Baker

Museum of Musical Instruments

MANZONI (M)

Museo Storico della Liberazione

SAN GIOVANNI

PIAZZA DI VILLA WOLKONSKY

PIAZZA S. CROCE IN GERUSALEMME

S. Croce in Gerusalemme

PIAZZA S. GIOVANNI LATERANO **Lateran Palace**

Scala Santa

VIALE CARLO FELICE

VIALE CASTRENSE

N

Baptistery

San Giovanni in Laterano

PIAZZA DI PORTA S. GIOVANNI

Porta Asinaria

VIA LA SPEZIA

SAN GIOVANNI (M)

PIAZZALE APPIO

LARGO BRINDISI

PIAZZA IMOLA

VIA TARANTO

CLUBS & VENUES

Black Out	14
Circolo degli Artisti	12
Qube	1

THE CELIAN HILL & SAN GIOVANNI

▼ 13 (50m) & 14 (300m)

old foundling wheel), up the steps off Via Santi Quattro Coronati, is dedicated to four soldier martyrs who died because they refused to worship a statue of Aesclapius during the persecutions of Diocletian. Originally built in 1110 by Pope Paschal II, it's a fortified, somewhat dishevelled building whose interior feels quiet and ancient, a world away from the crowds around the Colosseum below. The feel is intensified by the pretty cloister, accessed through a door in the north aisle, which is elegantly proportioned and contains a small, neat garden.

The church itself has an extra-wide apse and some very old frescoes on the south and west walls, as well as a giant series of apse paintings showing the martyrdom of the soldiers and a *matroneum*, or women's gallery – something rarely seen nowadays. A convent of Augustinian nuns lives here now, and it's they who administer entrance to the chapel of St Sylvester, which contains the oldest extant frescoes in Rome – painted in 1248, a beautifully preserved comic strip that tells the story of how the fourth-century pope cured the Emperor Constantine of leprosy (he's the one covered in spots) and then baptized him. A pox-free Constantine is also shown giving his crown to the pope in a symbolic transfer of power, and all of it takes place beneath an enthroned Christ surrounded by saints.

San Clemente

Back on Via San Giovanni in Laterano, the church of **San Clemente** (church daily 9am–7pm, free; lower church and temple Mon–Sat 9am–12.30pm & 3–6pm, Sun noon–6pm, €5) is a cream-coloured twelfth-century basilica that brilliantly encapsulates continuity of history in the city – it is in fact a conglomeration of three places of worship from three very different eras in the history of

Rome. Pope St Clement I, to whom the church is dedicated, was the third pope after St Peter (and is said to have been ordained by him), reigning from 90 AD until 99 AD, when he was exiled and martyred in the Crimea. His relics are kept in this church, and have been venerated here from the very earliest times.

The basilica

The **ground-floor church** is a superb example of a medieval basilica: its facade and courtyard face east in the archaic fashion, and there are some fine, warm mosaics in the apse. The choir is partitioned off with beautiful white marble slabs bearing the earliest papal insignia in the city, the monogram of Pope John II, who reigned from 533 to 535 AD. The gilded ceiling bears the arms of Pope Clement XI, from the early years of the eighteenth century, during whose papacy the church was remodelled. Perhaps the highlights of the main church, though, are the fifteenth-century **frescoes** in the chapel of St Catherine by Masolino, whose soft yet vivid colours show scenes from the life of St Catherine on the left: at the top, the saint – in the blue dress – attempts (in vain) to convert the Emperor Maxentius to Christianity, and in fact succeeds in converting his wife (in green), for which the wife is beheaded. In the centre St Catherine is shown being pulled apart by two wheels – hence the famous firework – until an angel intervenes and she too is beheaded (a scene shown in the far-right panel).

The early church and Mithraic temple

Downstairs there's the nave of an **earlier church**, dating back to 392 AD, with a frescoed narthex depicting, among other things, the *Miracle of San Clemente* and the transferral of his body from St Peter's to San Clemente. And at the western end of this church, steps lead down to the labyrinthine third level, which contains a dank **Mithraic temple** of the late second century, alongside several rooms of a Roman house built after the fire of 64 AD. In the temple is a statue of Mithras slaying the Bull and the seats upon which the worshippers sat during their ceremonies. The underground river that formerly fed the lake in front of the Domus Aurea can be heard rushing to its destination in the Tiber, behind the Circo Massimo, a reminder that Rome is built on very shaky foundations indeed.

Next door to the Roman house, across a narrow alleyway, are the ground-floor **rooms** of a first-century imperial building, all of which can be explored by the spooky light of fluorescent tubes set in the ceiling and along the mossy brick walls.

San Giovanni in Laterano

The basilica of **San Giovanni in Laterano** (daily 7am–6.30pm; call ☏06.6988.6392 for guided tours) is officially Rome's cathedral and the seat of the pope as bishop of Rome, and was for centuries the main papal residence. However, when the papacy returned from Avignon at the end of the fourteenth century, the Lateran palaces were in ruins and uninhabitable, and the pope moved across town to the Vatican, where he has remained ever since. The Lateran Treaty of 1929 accorded this and the other patriarchal basilicas extraterritorial status.

There has been a church on this site since the fourth century, the first established by Constantine, and the present building, reworked by Borromini in the mid-seventeenth century, evokes – like San Clemente or Santo Stefano – Rome's staggering wealth of history with a host of features from different periods; the statue of Constantine in the porch was found on the Quirinale Hill, while the doors of the church itself were taken from the Curia, or Senate House, of the Roman Forum. The obelisk that stands on the north side of the church is the oldest (and largest) in Rome, dating from the fifteenth century BC

▲ Mosaics, San Giovanni in Laterano

and brought here from Thebes by Constantine, originally for the Circus Maximus, but raised here by Sixtus V.

The basilica

The **interior** of San Giovanni has been extensively reworked over the centuries. Much of what you see today dates from the seventeenth century, when the Aldobrandini family pope, Clement VIII, had the church remodelled for Holy Year. The gilded ceiling of the nave has as its centrepiece the papal arms of Pope Pius VI, from the late 1700s, while the ceiling in the crossing bears, on the left, the Aldobrandini insignia, and on the right the tomb of Pope Innocent III, who died in 1216 and was buried here in the late 1800s at the behest of Pope Leo XIII, when he had this wing of the crossing remodelled. Leo XIII himself, who died in 1903, is buried opposite. The first pillar on the left of the right-hand aisle shows a fragment of Giotto's fresco of Boniface VIII, proclaiming the first Holy Year in 1300, a gentle work with gorgeous colours that is at odds with the immensity and grandeur of the rest of the building. On the next pillar along, a more recent monument commemorates Sylvester I – "the magician pope", bishop of Rome during much of Constantine's reign – and incorporates part of his original tomb, said to sweat and rattle its bones when a pope is about to die.

As for the **nave** itself, it's lined with eighteenth-century statues of the apostles in flashy and dramatic Rococo style, each one of which gives a clue as to their identity or manner of death: St Matthew, the tax collector, is shown with coins falling out of a sack; St Bartholomew holds a knife and his own skin (he was flayed alive); St Thomas holds a set square (he's the patron saint of architects) and St Simon a saw (he was, apparently, sawn to death). At the head of the nave, the heads of St Peter and St Paul, the church's prize relics, are kept secure behind the papal altar, while a museum holds assorted treasures through the bookshop (daily 9am–6pm; €1). The mosaics in the apse are undeniably impressive, but fake – they were added in the later nineteenth century to replace the lost originals; but the baldachino just in front is most definitely genuine, a splash of Gothic grandeur made by the Tuscan sculptor Giovanni di Stefano in the fourteenth century that shelters the glassed-over bronze tomb of Martin V – the Colonna pope who was responsible for returning the papacy to Rome from Avignon in 1419.

The cloisters

Outside the church, the **cloisters** (daily 9am–6pm; €2), reachable from a door by the north transept, are one of the most pleasing parts of the complex, decorated with early thirteenth-century Cosmati work and with fragments of the original basilica arranged around. Rooms off to the side form a small museum, with, in no particular order, the papal throne of Pius V and various papal artefacts (including the vestments of Boniface VIII).

The Lateran Palace

Adjoining the basilica is the **Lateran Palace**, home of the popes in the Middle Ages and also formally part of Vatican territory. Part of the palace is given over to the **Museo Storico Vaticano** (daily visits on the hour 9am–noon; €5), accessible from the portico of the basilica. Sixtus V destroyed the original building, which had fallen into disrepair, in the late 1500s, and raised the current structure in its place, and it retains most of the frescoes and other decoration from that time. One room, the so-called **Sala degli Imperatori**, is named for its frescoes of Christian-era Roman emperors, but most importantly is home to the Lateran Treaty, which ceded control of Rome and the papal territories to the Italian state and was signed at the large writing desk next door on February 11, 1929, in the well-named **Sala della Conciliazione**. This room is decorated with frescoes of those popes Sixtus V considered worthy of inclusion alongside the bust of himself, including above the desk St Peter, and on the left St Sylvester, who famously baptized Constantine, while around the main courtyard beyond are portraits of all the popes from the sixteenth century to the present day, along with ceremonial garb worn by the soldiers, courtiers and other officials of the Vatican through the centuries.

The Baptistry

Next door to the Lateran Palace, the **Baptistry** (daily 7.30am–12.30pm & 4–6.30pm; free) has been carefully restored, along with the side of the church itself, after a car bombing in 1993. It is the oldest surviving baptistry in the Christian world, an octagonal structure built during the fifth century that has been the model for many such buildings since. Oddly, it doesn't really feel its age, although the mosaics in the side chapels and the bronze doors to the chapel on the right, brought here from the Baths of Caracalla, quickly remind you where you are – as does the mosaic floor exposed under the large chapel opposite the entrance.

The Scala Santa and Sancta Sanctorum

There are more ancient remains on the other side of the church, on Piazza di Porta San Giovanni, foremost of which is the **Scala Santa** (daily: April–Sept 6.15am–noon & 3.30–6.45pm; Oct–March 6.15am–noon & 3–6.15pm), claimed to be the staircase from Pontius Pilate's house down which Christ walked after his trial. It was said to have been brought to Rome by St Helena and was placed here by Pope Sixtus V, who also moved the chapel here – it was formerly the pope's private place of worship. The 28 steps are protected by boards, and the only way you're allowed to climb them is on your knees, which pilgrims do regularly –

although there are staircases either side for the less penitent. At the top, the **Sancta Sanctorum**, or chapel of San Lorenzo, holds an ancient (sixth- or seventh-century) painting of Christ that is attributed to an angel, hence its name – *acheiropoeton*, or "not done by human hands". You can't enter the chapel, and, fittingly perhaps, you can only really get a view of it, with its beautiful thirteenth-century mosaic floor, by kneeling and peering through the grilles.

Museo Storico della Liberazione

Five minutes' walk from the San Giovanni basilica, the **Museo Storico della Liberazione**, Via Tasso 145 (Tues, Thurs & Fri 9.30am–12.30pm & 3.30–7.30pm, Wed, Sat & Sun 9.30am–12.30pm; free), is a very different sort of attraction, occupying two floors of the building in which Nazi prisoners were held and interrogated during the wartime Occupation. It's a moving place and deliberately low-key, with the original cells left as they were, including two isolation cells marked with the desperate notes and messages from the people held here. The other cells focus on different themes of the Occupation, one dedicated to the 335 victims of the Fosse Ardeatine massacre (see p.149), another to prisoners who died at Forte Bravetta on the outskirts of the city, and a former kitchen that was the cell of Colonel Giuseppe Montezemolo, who led the resistance and was executed at Ardeatine, complete with scraps of his clothing and other personal effects. Upstairs has German propaganda notices, pages from clandestine newspapers and anti-German media, as well as photos, lists of names and notices given to families during the deportation of the Jews from the Ghetto. Twenty minutes after receiving these they had to be ready to leave; most of them never returned.

Via Sannio and around

Across the far side of the square in front of San Giovanni in Laterano, the **Porta Asinaria**, one of the city's grander gateways, marks the Aurelian Wall (see p.146). If you're here in the morning, you could visit the regular morning market on **Via Sannio** just beyond (Mon Sat until about 1.30pm), with numerous stalls shadowing the wall touting cheap bags, jewellery, clothes and underwear, and then continue on for five minutes to **Piazzale Metronio**, from where you can follow the line of the **Aurelian Wall** as far as **Porta San Sebastiano** and the Aurelian Wall museum (see p.147) – a twenty-minute walk in total.

Santa Croce in Gerusalemme

Five minutes' away from the San Giovanni basilica, by way of Viale Carlo Felice, there's another key Roman church, **Santa Croce in Gerusalemme** (daily 7am–12.45pm & 2–7pm), one of the seven pilgrimage churches of Rome. Santa Croce, despite its Renaissance and Baroque adornments, feels a very ancient church – parts of it date from the fourth century AD. It is supposed to stand on the site of the palace of Constantine's mother St Helena, and houses the relics of the True Cross she had brought back from Jerusalem, stored in a Mussolini-era chapel up some steps at the end of the left aisle. The beautiful Renaissance apse frescoes are by Antoniazzo Romano, and show the discovery of the fragments, under a seated Christ – a marvellously technicolour, naturalistic scene showing trees and mountains and the saint at the centre, with the True Cross and a kneeling cardinal. Steps behind lead down to the original level of Helena's house – now a chapel dedicated to the saint and decorated with Renaissance mosaics; the tiles on the stairs down are an inscription relating to the True Cross discovery and were done at the same time as the apse frescoes. Finally, there's a lovely **vegetable garden** adjoining the church which is looked after by monks, with a gate designed by the Greek–Italian artist Jannis Kounellis in 2007. You need to make an appointment if you want to look around (☎06.701.4769, extension 103, or ⓔassamcroce@email.it), or you can just peek through the gate.

National Museum of Musical Instruments

The first floor of the palace next door to Santa Croce is the home of the **National Museum of Musical Instruments** (Tues–Sun 8.30am–7.30pm; €4), an interesting display of Italian and European instruments with good information, much of it in English. There are early Roman and Etruscan pieces, lots of stringed instruments, and others divided into mechanical instruments, instruments used by travelling musicans, church instruments and early pianofortes. Not what you came to Rome for, perhaps, but worth a look if you're in this part of town.

Porta Maggiore

North of here towards the rail tracks, the **Porta Maggiore** is probably the most impressive of all the city gates, built in the first century AD to carry water into Rome from the aqueducts outside, and incorporated into the Aurelian walls. The **aqueducts** that converge here are the **Acqua Claudia**, which dates from 45 AD, and the **Acqua Marcia**, from 200 BC. The Roman engineers built them one on top of the other to channel the water of the Acqua Claudia into the city in a way that did not interfere with the pre-existing Aqua Marcia – a feat recounted in the monumental tablet over the central arches.

The famous **Tomb of the Baker**, in white travertine, just outside the gate, is a monument from about 30 AD. The baker in question was a public contractor who made a fortune selling bread to the imperial government. The round holes in the tomb represent the openings of the baker's ovens – a style that strangely enough was picked up in the Mussolini era and can be seen time and again in Fascist architecture.

Pigneto

A ten-minute walk from the Porta Maggiore, **Pigneto** is an originally working-class district of apartment blocks, low-rise villas and cottages that grew up around the railway lines in the nineteenth century. It has always been slightly different – it was a favourite haunt of Pasolini, who shot some of his movies here – and is these days one of Rome's most up-and-coming neighbourhoods. The area hasn't been entirely gentrified, though, and retains a slight edge – although the completion of the Line C metro station that's being built on Via del Pigneto will surely hasten its upgrading. The pedestrianized strip of Via del Pigneto hosts a small **market** each morning (and a flea market on the last Sunday of every month) and it and the surrounding streets are home to an increasingly large handful of decent restaurants, cafés and bars (see p.251). Most are new, but *Necci dal 1924*, at Via Fanfulla da Lodi 68, with its pleasant garden, was a great favourite of Pasolini's and still serves good food and drink all day.

9

The Aventine Hill and south

The area south of the Forum and Palatine has some of the city's most atmospheric and compelling Christian and ancient sights, from the relatively central **Circus Maximus** and **Baths of Caracalla** – one of the city's grandest ruins, and the venue of inspirational summer opera performances – to the catacombs on the ancient Via Appia on the outskirts, with plenty worth seeing in between. Beyond the Circus Maximus you can scale the **Aventine Hill** – the heart of plebeian Rome in ancient times. These days the working-class quarters of the city are further south, and the Aventine is one of the city's more upscale residential areas, covered with villas with large gardens that lend a leafy, suburban feel, and make it one of the few places in the city centre where you can escape the traffic.

On the far side of the Aventine, **Testaccio** is a working-class enclave that has become increasingly gentrified over the past decade or so; it's home to the city's now defunct slaughterhouse and is known for its restaurants serving offal and traditional Roman meat dishes, as well as its good daily market and the nearby **Protestant Cemetery**, where the poets Keats and Shelley are buried. Close by lies the major traffic junction around Porta San Paolo, from which **Via Ostiense** spears off west, the ancient link between Rome to its port of Ostia and now the backbone of the industrial and lately rather hip district of **Ostiense**, whose regeneration is more recent than Testaccio's, spurred on by the conversion of the **Centrale Montemartini** electricity generating plant into an amazing new gallery. Beyond the vast derelict expanse of the Mercati Generali, **Garbatella** is one of the city's more interesting nineteenth-century residential developments, while further down lies the magnificent rebuilt basilica of **San Paolo fuori le Mura** and Rome's futuristic 1930s experiment in extra-urban town planning, **EUR**.

The Circus Maximus

The southern side of the Palatine Hill drops down to the **Circus Maximus**, a long green expanse bordered by heavily trafficked roads that was the ancient city's main venue for chariot races. At one time this arena had a capacity of up to 400,000 spectators, and if it were still intact it would no doubt match the Colosseum for grandeur. As it is, a litter of stones at the Viale Aventino end is all that remains, together with a little medieval tower built by the Frangipani family at the southern end, and, behind a chain-link fence traced out in marble blocks, the outline of the **Septizodium**, an imperial structure designed to show off the glories of the city and

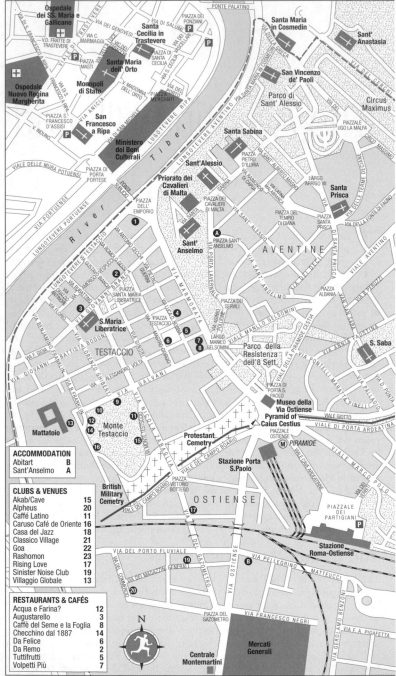

PONTE PALATINO

Ospedale dei SS. Maria e Gallicano

Santa Maria in Cosmedin

Sant' Anastasia

VIA DEI GENOVESI

VIA DEL CERCHI

VIA DI PONZIANI

P

PIAZZA DEI SALUMI

P

Santa Cecilia in Trastevere

V.D. FRATTE DI TRASTEVERE

VIA C. MARMAGGI

V.D. DEI SALUMI

VIA DEI GENOVESI

PIAZZA DI SANTA CECILIA

VIA DELLA GRECA

PIAZZA MASTI

P

San Vincenzo de' Paoli

VIA DI S. FRANCESCO A RIPA

Santa Maria dell' Orto

VIA ANICIA

VIA SAN FRANCESCO A RIPA

Monopoli di Stato

V. MADONNA DELL' ORTO

PIAZZA MERCANTI

Parco di Sant' Alessio

Circus Maximus

PIAZZALE UGO LA MALFA

CIRCO MASSIMO

Ospedale Nuovo Regina Margherita

San Francesco a Ripa

Ministero dei Beni Culturali

Santa Sabina

PIAZZA PIETRO D'ILLIRIA

PIAZZA S. FRANCESCO D'ASSISI

V. INDUNO

P

PIAZZA DI PORTA PORTESE

LUNGOTEVERE AVENTINO

Sant'Alessio

PIAZZA SANT' ALBERTO MAGNO

LARGO ARRIGO VII

Santa Prisca

VIALE DELLE MURA POTUENSI

Tiber

PONTE SUBLICIO

Priorato dei Cavalieri di Malta

PIAZZA DE' CAVALIERI DI MALTA

VIA RAIMONDO DA CAPUA

VIA DI SANTA SABINA

PIAZZA DEL TEMPIO DI DIANA

PIAZZA SANTA PRISCA

VIA DELLE TERME DECIANE

VIA DELLA FONTE DI FAUNO

VIA PORTUENSE

River Tiber

PIAZZA DELL' EMPORIO

①

Sant' Anselmo

Ⓐ

PIAZZA SANT' ANSELMO

AVENTINE

VIA SANTA

VIA DI PORTA LAVERNALE

VIA SANT' ALESSIO

VIA SANTA PRISCA

VIALE AVENTINO

VIA P. PERUZZI

LUNGOTEVERE VIA TESTACCIO

VIA ANTONIO CECCHI

②

VIA AMERIGO VESPUCCI

VIA GUSTAVO BIANCHI

VIA G.B. BRANCA

VIA LUCA DELLA ROBBIA

PIAZZA SANTA MARIA LIBERATRICE

VIA MARMORATA

PIAZZA DEI SERVILI

VIA ASINIO POLLIONE

PIAZZA ALBANIA

VIA S. SABA

LUNGOTEVERE PORTUENSE

③

VIA PIETRO QUERINI

VIA FLORIO

VIA GIOVANNI BRANCA

VIA BENIAMINO FRANKLIN

S.Maria Liberatrice

④

VIA LUIGI VANVITELLI

PIAZZA TESTACCIO

⑥ ⑤

VIA MASTRO GIORGIO

VIA SANT' ANSELMO

VIA DEI REMI

PIAZZALE DI SANTA SABA

VIA DELLA FONTE DI FAUNO

VIA L. DE SANCTIS

TESTACCIO

VIA G. NICOTERA

⑦ ⑧

Parco della Resistenza dell'8 Sett.

S. Saba

VIA A. BERTANI

VIA F. GIOIA

VIA LORENZO GHIBERTI

VIA GINORI

LARGO MANLIO GELSOMINI

VIA DELLA PIRAMIDE CESTIA

VIA L. VANNUCCI

VIA DI PORTA

VIA DANTE

VIA ALESSANDRO VOLTA

VIA MANLIO GELSOMINI

VIA L. FONTELLI MARATA

PINELLI

VIA GIOVANNI BATTISTA BODONI

VIA N. ZABAGLIA

VIA BEN FRANKLIN

GALVANI

⑨

PIAZZA DI PORTA S. PAOLO

Museo della Via Ostiense

VIALE GIOTTO

VIA DI PONTA

Mattatoio

⑬

⑩

⑫ ⑪

⑭

Monte Testaccio

⑮

⑯

Pyramid of Caius Cestius

PIAZZALE OSTIENSE

Ⓜ PIRAMIDE

VIALE DI PORTA ARDEATINA

VIA MARCO POLO

Protestant Cemetery

Stazione Porta S.Paolo

VIALE CAVE ARDEATINE

VIALE DEL CAMPO BOARIO

British Military Cemetery

PIAZZA VITTORIO BOTTEGO

OSTIENSE

PIAZZALE DEI PARTIGIANI

P

⑰

Stazione Roma-Ostiense

VIALE DEL CAMPO BOARIO

VIA DEL PORTO FLUVIALE

VIA DEL GAZOMETRO

VIA OSTIENSE

VIA PELLEGRINO MATTEUCCI

⑲

Ⓑ

VIALE DELLE COMMENDE

VIA DEI MAGAZZINI GENERALI

⑳

PIAZZA DEL GAZOMETRO

VIA FRANCESCO NEGRI

VIA GEROLAMO BENZONI

VIA F. A. PIGAFETTA

N

Centrale Montemartini

Mercati Generali

㉑ (400m), ㉒ (400m), ㉓ (400m) & San Paolo fuori le Mura (1km) ▼   ▼ Garbatella (500m)

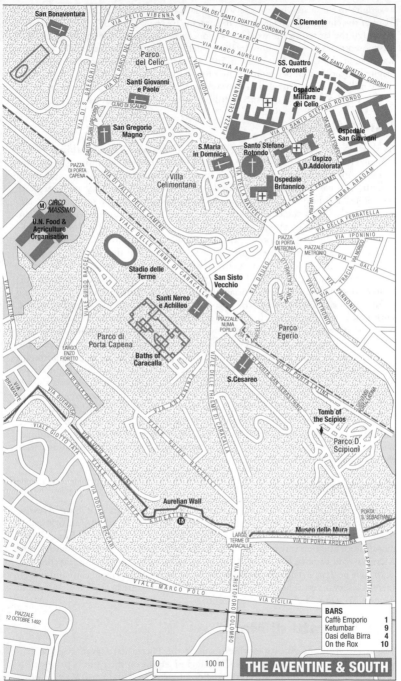

San Bonaventura

VIA DEI SANTI QUATTRO CORONATI

VIA CELIO VIBENNA

VIA CAPO D'AFRICA

S.Clemente

VIA MARCO AURELIO

VIA DI PARCO DEL CELIO

VIA ANNIA

Parco
del Celio

SS. Quattro
Coronati

VIA DEI SANTI QUATTRO CORONATI

VIA DI S. GREGORIO

Santi Giovanni
e Paolo

Ospedale
Militare
dei Celio

CLIVO DI SCAURO

PIAZZA CELIMONTIANA

San Gregorio
Magno

VIA DI SANTO STEFANO ROTONDO

Ospedale
San Giovanni

SALITA SAN GREGORIO

S.Maria
in Domnica

Santo Stefano
Rotondo

CLIVIO MELIO

Ospizo
D.Addolorata

PIAZZA
DI PORTA
CAPENA

Villa
Celimontana

VIA DELLA NAVICELLA

Ospedale
Britannico

VIA DI SANT'ERASMA

VIA ERASMA

VIA DELL' AMBA ARADAM

VIA DI VALLE DELLE CAMENE

VIA VALERIA

VIA DELLA FERRATELLA

M CIRCO
MASSIMO

U.N. Food &
Agriculture
Organisation

VIALE DELLE TERME DI CARACALLA

PIAZZA
DI PORTA
METRONIA

PIAZZALE
METRONIO

VIA IPONINIO

VIA GALLIA

VIA VANNIO

VIA TRAGIA

Stadio delle
Terme

VIA GUIDO BACCELLI

San Sisto
Vecchio

VIA DRUSO

VIALE METRONIO

VIA PANNONIA

VIA AVENTINA

Santi Nereo
e Achilleo

PIAZZALE
NUMA
POPILIO

Parco
Egerio

VIA M.MARCELLO

MONTE CAMNIO

Parco di
Porta Capena

LARGO
ENZO
FIORITTO

Baths of
Caracalla

VIALE DELLE TERME DI CARACALLA

VIA DI PORTA LATINA

VIA DI PORTA SAN SEBASTIANO

GIOVANNI
PORTA LATINA

VIA
BRAMANTE

VIA DI VILLA PEPOLI

S.Cesareo

VIALE AVENTINO

VIA GUERRIERI

Tomb of
the Scipios

VIALE GIOTTO TATA

VIA LUCIO FABIO CILONE

VIA DI PORTA ARDEATINA

Parco D.
Scipioni

VIA DI PORTA

VIA ODOARDO BECCARI

VIALE GUIDO BACCELLI

Aurelian Wall

PORTA
S. SEBASTIANO

VIA DI PORTA ARDEATINA

Museo delle Mura

ARDEATINA

VIA DI PORTA ARDEATINA

LARGO
TERME DI
CARACALLA

VIA CRISTOFORO COLOMBO

VIA APPIA ANTICA

PIAZZALE
12 OCTOBRE 1492

VIALE MARCO POLO

VIA CICILIA

BARS
Caffè Emporio   1
Ketumbar   9
Oasi della Birra 4
On the Rox   10

0   100 m

THE AVENTINE & SOUTH

Domine Quo Vadis (300m) & Catacombs of San Callisto (1km) ▼

its empire to those arriving on the Via Appia. The huge obelisk that now stands in front of the church of San Giovanni in Laterano (see p.132) – at 385 tonnes and over 30m high the largest in the world – was once the central marker of the arena, and it's known that the obelisk now in Piazza del Popolo stood here too. The last race was held at the Circus Maximus in 549 AD, but it still retains something of its original purpose as an occasional venue for festivals, concerts and large gatherings (three million people crowded in here when AS Roma won the Scudetto in 2001). Oddly, it's also the name of a successful Norwegian heavy metal band.

Santa Sabina

A short way southwest along Via Santa Sabina, **Santa Sabina** (daily 6.30am–12.45pm & 3–7pm) is the principal church of the Dominicans in Rome, and a strong contender for the city's most beautiful basilica, a high and wide structure, its nave and portico restored back to their fifth-century appearance in the 1930s. In the portico, look at the main doors at the far end, which are contemporary with the church and boast eighteen panels carved with Christian scenes, forming an illustrated Bible that includes (top left) one of the oldest representations of the Crucifixion in existence. Inside, the windows above the arches of the nave are among the most beautiful features of the church, each one different, letting in light by way of lacy patterns carved into the stone. The mosaic inscription on the wall above the doors heralds the achievements of Celestino I, flanked by two female figures representing converted Jews and pagans. Immediately below, in the corner, a smooth piece of black marble, pitted with holes, was apparently thrown by the Devil at St Dominic himself while at prayer, shattering the marble pavement but miraculously not harming the saint.

It's claimed that the orange trees in the garden behind the church (which you have to ask to see) are descendants of those planted by St Dominic himself. Whatever the truth of this, the views from the gardens are splendid – right across the Tiber to the centre of Rome and St Peter's – and beyond here you can also be taken up to see the room where the saint stayed: it's now a small, heavily decorated chapel, but the timbered far end hints at a more spartan authenticity. The cloister, accessible by way of a door off the portico, has been under restoration for some time. Take the time to wander into the **public gardens** next door to the church, which are a favourite with mothers and babies, and give wonderful views across the river towards the Vatican.

Sant'Alessio

A short walk beyond Santa Sabina on the right, the church of **Sant'Alessio** (daily 8am–noon & 4–7pm) is of less interest than its neighbour, an originally Romanesque structure but mostly eighteenth-century now, apart from a nice mosaic floor and two tiny mosaiced columns in the apse. A popular medieval saint, Alessio is said to have left his betrothed on their wedding night and travelled for years as a beggar, eventually returning to his father's house incognito and living there as a servant until he died – hence the wooden staircase in the left aisle, which denotes his secret "below stairs" existence.

The Priorato di Malta

The road across the Aventine widens out at the Piazza dei Cavalieri di Malta, where you'll find the **Priorato dei Cavalieri di Malta** on the right, a priory that is one of several buildings in the city belonging to the Knights of Malta – now known simply as the "Order of Malta", which has a celebrated view of the dome of St Peter's through the keyhole of its main gate. The little piazza has marble triumphal insignia designed and placed here by Piranesi to celebrate the Knights' dramatic history. Piranesi also designed the church of **Santa Maria del Priorato** inside, which you can see along with the lovely gardens, if you organize your visit in advance (call ✆06.6758.1234).

The **gardens** are quite formally planted, with roses and topiary, but lush too, with palms and subtropical plants that in combination with the high walls and entry restrictions give the feel of a secret, cloistered domain – in short, exactly what a city garden should be. They're beautifully tended, focusing on a small fountain and cage of doves in the centre, though to be honest the views are no better than the ones from the public gardens next to Santa Sabina. As for the **church**, it was rebuilt by Piranesi in 1765, the only structure the famous engraver built. Its elaborate decor is typical of Roman churches, but it differentiates itself with its monochromatic sculptural simplicity. Virtually all the decoration is in grey stone or marble, or covered in stucco, and the effect is impressively uniform – a fact that Piranesi, caught in thoughtful pose in a statue on the right, is no doubt contemplating.

Sant'Anselmo

Opposite the Priorato di Malta, spare five minutes or so for the church of **Sant'Anselmo** (daily 10am–noon & 4–7pm), a Benedictine complex containing a church and college, with pleasant gardens and a shop selling all manner of produce, Benedictine and otherwise: *limoncello*, *grappa*, *amaro*, as well as chocolate, beer, books, CDs and toiletries. The church is a plain basilica built in the last decade of the nineteenth century – not of much interest in itself, but known for its Gregorian chorus and reasonably regular concerts, usually held on Sunday evenings.

San Saba

Follow Via Sant'Anselmo through the leafy residential streets of the Aventine down to Piazza Albania, where there's a rare stretch of the so-called **Servian Wall** – the first wall to properly enclose Rome, built in the fourth century BC and named after the sixth-century Roman king Servius Tullius, who first planned it. Other stretches of the Servian Wall can be seen outside Termini. Cross the busy street and stroll up Via San Saba to the church of **San Saba** (daily 8am–noon & 4–7pm), built in the tenth century over a seventh-century structure constructed by monks who had fled here from the Middle East to escape the Arab advance. Topped with a fifteenth-century loggia and fronted by a pleasant if scruffy walled garden, it's worth visiting for its wonderful Cosmati-work door and floor, and an interior that feels very ancient, with a wonderful mixture of Roman pillars and thirteenth-century frescoes in a short additional left aisle and the beautifully proportioned apse.

The Baths of Caracalla

Southeast of the Aventine, beyond the large UN Food and Agriculture building, the **Baths of Caracalla**, at Viale delle Terme di Caracalla 52 (Mon 9am–2pm, Tues–Sun 9am–1hr before sunset; €7.50, includes the Tomb of Cecilia Metella and the Villa dei Quintili, valid 7 days), give a far better sense of the monumental scale of Roman architecture than most of the extant ruins in the city – so much so that Shelley was moved to write his Romantic play *Prometheus Unbound* here in 1819. The baths are no more than a shell now, but the walls still rise to very nearly their original height. There are many fragments of mosaics – none spectacular, but quite a few bright and well preserved – and it's easy to discern a floor plan. Set in extensive walled gardens, with numerous outbuildings, the baths were built around the long spine of the central hall, or frigidarium, at each end of which are vast courtyards – palestrae – which were used for sports before bathing. Off to the right of the frigidarium was the tepidarium – now hard to make out – and beyond this the domed chamber of the circular caldarium, which is easier to see outside the baths themselves. On the other side of the frigidarium was the piscina or swimming pool, a huge open space which would have been accessed by way of the apodyteria, or changing rooms, on either side – you can get the best sense of this by following the route from the palestra at the far end.

As for Caracalla, he was one of Rome's most brutal and shortest-lived rulers, and it's no wonder there's nothing else in the city built by him. The baths are the summer venue of the Teatro dell'Opera (one of Mussolini's better ideas), and attending an **opera performance** here is a thrilling way to see the baths at their most atmospheric.

Santi Nereo ed Achilleo

Just outside the baths, the church of **Santi Nereo ed Achilleo** (daily except Tues 10am–noon & 4–6pm) makes for a peaceful spot after the crowds at the baths, and is of interest for the ninth-century mosaic on the arch above its apse, which depicts Christ and three prostrate apostles, between a scene of the Annunciation on the left and a Virgin and Child on the right. The beautiful Cosmati work on the marble choir screen and the altar itself is also worth a look, as is the ornate throne sitting on two lions in the apse, said to have been preached from by Gregory the Great (see p.132) – a fact emphasized by the apse fresco showing St Gregory preaching to various cardinals. This is full of charming detail: you'll notice one of the cardinals – second from the right – has trouble hearing, while others confer as to what the great pope might be saying.

Back outside the church, on the far side of the Piazzale Numa Pompilio roundabout, Via di Porta San Sebastiano leads onto the **Via Appia Antica** which heads towards the catacombs and other archeological delights, a few kilometres south (see p.117).

Testaccio

Back towards the Tiber, across Via Marmorata, the working-class neighbourhood of **Testaccio** groups around a couple of main squares – Piazza Testaccio and Piazza Santa Maria Liberatrice. For many years this tight-knit community was synonymous with the slaughterhouse that sprawls down to the Tiber just beyond. In the last couple of decades the area has become a trendy place to live, property prices have soared, and some unlikely juxtapositions have emerged, with vegetarian restaurants opening their doors in an area still known for the offal dishes served in its traditional trattorias, and gay and alternative clubs standing cheek-by-jowl with the car-repair shops gouged into Monte Testaccio.

The Mattatoio

The slaughterhouse, or **Mattatoio**, once the area's main employer, is now home to the *centro sociale* "Villaggio Globale", a space used for concerts and offbeat events, along with stabling for the city's horse-and-carriage drivers and a gym. For years there has been talk of sprucing it up into a chichi affair of shops and restaurants, but so far nothing has happened, and it's likely to remain as it is for some time to come. It also houses a branch of the **Museum of Contemporary Art of Rome**,

MACRO Future, Piazza Orazio Giustiniani 4 (Tues–Sun 4pm–midnight), just inside the main gate, where a couple of large pavilions stage adventurous temporary exhibitions (for MACRO's main branch, see p.111).

Monte Testaccio

Opposite the slaughterhouse, **Monte Testaccio**, a 50-metre-high mound of historic landfill, gives the area its name. The ancient Romans broke terracotta amphorae up into small shards and laid them down in an orderly manner over several centuries, sprinkling quicklime on them to dissolve the residual wine or oil. It's estimated that there are around 53 million amphorae here and it makes for an odd sight, the ceramic curls clearly visible through the tufts of grass that crown its higher reaches, the bottom layers hollowed out by the workshops of car and bike mechanics – and, now, clubs and bars.

The Protestant Cemetery

On the far side of Monte Testaccio, off Via Marmorata, on Via Caio Cestio X, the **Protestant Cemetery** (Mon–Sat 9am–5pm, Sun 9am–1pm; donation expected; ⓦwww.protestantcemetery.it) isn't in fact a Protestant cemetery at all, but is reserved for non-Roman Catholics of all nationalities, so you'll also find famous Italian atheists, Christians of the Orthodox persuasion, and the odd Jew or Muslim, buried here. It is nonetheless one of the shrines to the English in Rome, and a fitting conclusion to a visit to the Keats-Shelley Memorial House on Piazza di Spagna (see p.94).

Most visitors come to see the grave of **Keats**, who lies next to his friend, the painter Joseph Severn, in the furthest corner of the less crowded, older part of the cemetery (turn left from the entrance), his stone inscribed as he wished with the words "here lies one whose name was writ in water". Severn died much later than Keats but asked to be laid here nonetheless, together with his brushes and palette. Just behind Severn and Keats lies Severn's one-year-old son; behind, a plaque on the wall remembers the Swedish doctor and writer Axel Munthe, his wife Hilda and their two sons.

As for **Shelley**, his ashes were brought here at Mary Shelley's request and interred, after much obstruction by the papal authorities, in the newer part of the cemetery, at the top against the back wall – the Shelleys had visited several years earlier, the poet praising it as "the most beautiful and solemn cemetery I ever beheld". It had been intended that Shelley should rest with his young son, William, who died while they were in Rome and was also buried here, but his remains couldn't be found (although his small grave is nearby). Mary Shelley was so broken-hearted by the deaths of her son and husband that it was twenty years before she could bring herself to visit their graves.

Shelley's great friend, the writer and adventurer Edward Trelawny, lies next to him, while in front of Shelley's grave is a slab marking the final resting-spot of the American Beat poet Gregory Corso, who died in 2001 but was buried here, at his request, next to his hero Shelley. To the right, a headless torso marked simply "Belinda" marks the grave of Belinda Lee – a little-known Hollywood starlet, who died in her mid-twenties in a car crash in Hollywood in 1961, just as her career was beginning to take off – and after a scandalous affair with one of the Orsini princes, hence her burial here. Among other famous internees, the political writer and activist Antonio Gramsci lies on the far right-hand side of the cemetery in the middle, and the Italian novelist Carlo Emilio Gadda is nearby. If you're at all interested in star-spotting you should either borrow or buy the booklet available at the entrance.

The Pyramid of Caius Cestius

Overlooking the cemetery, the most distinctive landmark in this part of town is the **Pyramid of Caius Cestius**, who died in 12 BC. Cestius had spent some time in Egypt, and part of his will decreed that all his slaves should be freed. The white pyramid you see today was thrown up by them in only 330 days of what must have been joyful building. It's open to the public on the second and fourth Saturday of each month, though you can visit the cats who live here, and the volunteers who care for them, any afternoon between 2 and 4pm.

Museo della Via Ostiense

Right by the pyramid, the **Museo della Via Ostiense** (Tues & Thurs 9.30am–1.30pm & 2.30–4.30pm, Wed, Fri, Sat & first & third Sun of each month 9.30am–1.30pm; free), housed in the old Porta San Paolo, is a museum devoted to the road that spears off on the far side of the intersection, originally built to join Rome to Ostia and its port. There's not a huge amount of interest here but if you have half an hour to kill on your way to catch a train to Ostia Antica from the Porta San Paolo station opposite, the model of Ostia is worth studying, as is that of the old port of Trajan. There are sepulchral monuments and other items that used to line the old road, and you can stand on top of the gate to contemplate the traffic chaos outside.

Ostiense

Immediately south of Testaccio, the industrial neighbourhood of **Ostiense** is one of the city's most up-and-coming areas, home to those who can no longer afford to live in already-gentrified Testaccio. There was until a few years ago no real reason to come here at all, unless you were on your way down the basilica of San Paolo (see opposite), but nowadays the Capitoline collections at the **Centrale Montemartini** alone make it worth the trip, as well as the clubs, bars and restaurants that are beginning to spring up to serve the media types and companies that are moving in. There was a project afoot to redevelop the large and long-disused site of the **Mercati Generali**, Rome's vast former wholesale food market, on the left-hand side of Via Ostiense as you travel south, but this seems to have stalled and at the moment it's a huge derelict area between Ostiense and the district of Garbatella (see opposite).

Centrale Montemartini

For the moment it's the **Centrale Montemartini**, Via Ostiense 106 (Tues–Sun 9am–7pm; €4.50, €8.50 for joint ticket with Capitoline Museums, valid 7 days) that has done the most to put Ostiense on the map. A former electricity generating station, it was requisitioned to display the cream of the Capitoline Museums' sculpture while the main buildings were being renovated, and was so popular that it has become a permanent outpost of the venerable institution. Ten minutes' walk from Piramide metro station, or reachable Monday to Friday by bus #271 from Piazza Venezia, the huge rooms of the power station are ideally suited to showing off ancient sculpture, although checking out the massive turbines and furnaces has a fascination of its own.

The size of the building is the thing, most obviously in the **Machine Hall**, where there's the head, feet and an arm from a colossal statue, once 8m high, found in Largo di Torre Argentina. Elsewhere in the chamber are various heads, some of emperors (Claudius, Tiberius, Domitian), a large Roman *Athena*, and a fine statue of a Roman soldier from the Esquiline Hill, tucked away in a corner. In the adjacent **Furnace Hall**, the most obvious features are the furnace itself at the far end and a fragmented mosaic of hunting scenes that occupies half the floor; a

Roman architecture

Rome is an open-air museum, with its architecture as the main exhibit. The city's organic growth is often plain to see, with periods and styles crowded together and sometimes even built one on top of the other. It's this sense of the city as a living organism, the notion that each generation has made use of what has gone before and then left its own mark, that makes Rome so endlessly fascinating. What is perhaps missing is a contemporary sense: the last big building boom was over a hundred years ago and apart from Mussolini's EUR experiment and a few notable recent examples, you sometimes long to see a distinguished twentieth-century building sprouting in its pristinely preserved centre.

The Classical era

Just as much of ancient Rome's architecture was based on Greek models, the buildings of the Imperial city formed the blueprint for more or less everything that has followed, right up to the present day. The Romans were keen and innovative architects, and their legacy is everywhere you look: they invented concrete, brickwork, the dome, and of course the column-and-pediment designs of ancient Roman temples that have been recycled countless times over the years.

Most of ancient Rome lies in ruins, but the dome of the **Pantheon** is still the second largest in the city; the design of the Colosseum is as impressive today as it ever was; the recently restored **Trajan's Markets** are a model for modern shopping centres; and the ruins of **Ostia Antica** give us a glimpse of ancient urban life. But perhaps the most enduring structure of ancient Rome is the imposing **Aurelian Wall**, built by the eponymous emperor in the late third century AD to keep the barbarians at bay.

The Pantheon ▲

Castel Sant'Angelo ▼

The Middle Ages

The Aurelian Wall may continue to stand but it was breached many times, and the city was more pillaged than developed in the centuries that followed the collapse of Rome. Despite this, in the early seventh century Pope Gregory I reinvigorated the city as the headquarters of the church, building many of its great basilicas and presciently preserving Hadrian's tomb as the **Castel Sant'Angelo** to withstand invaders – a purpose that was much needed in the centuries that followed; indeed it's indicative that most of the medieval structures that remain in Rome are military buildings and watchtowers.

The Renaissance

Rome flourished during the Renaissance, drawing Italy's best artists and architects, who contributed to its transformation from a papal city to a more worldly one. Michelangelo was active in the city, not just in the **Sistine Chapel**, but laying out the **Piazza del Campidoglio**, finishing off **Palazzo Farnese** and overseeing the rebuilding of **St Peter's**, though this would continue well into the **Baroque period** – an era of flamboyance in art and architecture that grew out of the Catholic Church's bid to reassert itself during the Reformation. More than anything, Rome is a Baroque city: the facade of the **Gesù** (1575), designed by Giacomo della Porta, became a model for Roman churches for the next century, and the curvy and playful buildings, fountains and sculptures of the style's main protagonists – Maderno, Bernini and Borromini – are everywhere you look in Rome today.

▲ The Gesù

▼ Via Nazionale

The nineteenth century

Rome changed hugely during the nineteenth century, particularly after becoming capital of Italy in 1870, when the Italian royals were desperate to turn the city into a worthy showpiece. The city expanded outwards into the new suburbs of Prati and Salaria, among others, with their stately apartment blocks and rigid grid plans. New thoroughfares were ploughed through the city centre – **Via Cavour**, **Via Nazionale** and **Piazza Vittorio Emanuele** – and plodding Neoclassical palaces built to house the newly formed departments of state, although their most memorable legacy to Rome's skyline is without doubt the still hideously inappropriate **Vittoriano** in Piazza Venezia.

The Ara Pacis ▲

MAXXI ▼

Modern times

Rome is dominated by its past, and that's nowhere more true than in its architecture, which in the city centre at least, is relentlessly pre-twentieth century. There are exceptions, most famously in the southern suburb of EUR, which was planned as a futuristic city extension in the 1930s and still feels quite contemporary today, but for the most part the only example of architecture of the last hundred years is in the concrete tower blocks of the city's sprawling suburbs and housing estates.

However, the revitalization of the city in recent years has led to some prestige architectural projects overseen by internationally renowned architects – most notably, Richard Meier's Ara Pacis, the Auditorium by Renzo Piano and Zaha Hadid's futuristic new MAXXI arts complex north of the city centre. Finally, it seems, Rome is joining the modern world, and doing so with some degree of style and success.

walkway gives a good view of the latter's deer and boar, and figures on horseback or crouching to trap their prey in nets. Among the sculptures on display is an amazing third-century BC statue of a girl seated on a stool with legs crossed. Hercules stands next to the soft *Muse Polymnia*, the former braced for activity, the latter leaning on a rock and staring thoughtfully into the distance. Look out, too, for a wonderful pair of magistrates, one old, one young, but both holding the handkerchief they would use to herald the start of competitions and circuses.

Garbatella

Just to the east of Via Ostiense, the neighbourhood of **Garbatella** was planned as new residential housing for the growing city in the 1920s. Originally known as the Borgata Giardino, it was – and to some extent still is – a solid, left-leaning, working-class district. An odd mixture of undistinguished postwar apartment blocks and low-rise cottages set in leafy gardens that evoke a peaceful, suburban feel, it makes quite a change from the industrial grittiness that pervades so much of this part of the city. If Garbatella has a centre, it's Piazza Damiano Sauli, whose shabby civic buildings centre on a trio of brick arches, through which you can walk to wander the area's shady lanes. It's becoming rather gentrified, as you might expect, but the district as a whole remains fairly close to its old roots, with a solid base of support for AS Roma and some decent, long-established restaurants that are alone worth the metro ride.

San Paolo fuori le Mura

Some 2km south of the Porta San Paolo, the basilica of **San Paolo fuori le Mura** or "St Paul's Outside the Walls" (summer daily 7am 6.30pm; winter 7am 6pm) is one of the four patriarchal basilicas of Rome (and thus not technically Italian

▲ Basilica of San Paolo fuori le Mura

territory), occupying the supposed site of St Paul's tomb, where he was laid to rest after being beheaded at Tre Fontane (see p.153). St Paul is joint patron saint of Rome, with St Peter. Of the four basilicas, this has probably fared the least well over the years. It was apparently once the grandest, connected to the Aurelian Wall by a colonnade over a kilometre in length, made up of eight hundred marble columns, but a ninth-century sacking by the Saracens and a devastating fire in 1823 (a couple of cack-handed roofers spilt burning tar, almost entirely destroying the church) means that the building you see now is largely a nineteenth-century reconstruction. You can reach the basilica by taking metro line B to San Paolo and walking two minutes to the eastern entrance, or bus #271 from Piazza Venezia – it stops outside the west entrance – though it doesn't run at weekends.

The church is a very successful – if somewhat clinical – rehash of the former building. Perhaps even more than St Peter's, it impresses with sheer size and grandeur, and whether you enter by way of the cloisters or the west door, it's impossible not to be awed by the space of the building inside, its crowds of columns topped by round-arched arcading, and the medallions of all the **popes** fringing the nave and transepts above, starting with St Peter to the right of the apse and ending with Benedict XVI at the top of the south aisle. Of all the basilicas of Rome, this gives you the feel of what an ancient Roman basilica must have been like: the huge, barn-like structure, with its clerestory windows and roof beams supported by enormous columns, has a powerful and authentic sense of occasion.

Some parts of the building did survive the fire. In the south transept, the **paschal candlestick** at the head of the nave, behind two large statues of St Peter (on the left) and St Paul (on the right) is a remarkable piece of Romanesque carving, supported by half-human beasts and rising through entwined tendrils and strangely human limbs and bodies to scenes from Christ's life, the figures crowding in together as if for a photocall; it's inscribed by its makers, Nicola d'Angelo and Pietro Vassalletto. The bronze, eleventh-century **doors** at the end of the south aisle were also rescued from the old basilica, as was the thirteenth-century tabernacle by Arnolfo di Cambio, under which a slab from the time of Constantine, inscribed "Paolo Apostolo Mart", is supposed to lie – although it's hard to get a look at this. The arch across the apse is original, too, embellished with **mosaics** (donated by the Byzantine queen Galla Placidia in the sixth century) that show angels, saints Peter and Paul, the symbols of the Gospels, and Christ giving a blessing. The mosaics in the apse date from 1220 and show Luke, Paul, Peter and Andrew and the kneeling figure of Honorius III kissing the feet of Christ. The **cloister**, through the shop, is probably Rome's finest piece of Cosmati work, its spiralling, mosaic-encrusted columns enclosing a peaceful rose garden. Just off here, the **Relics Chapel** houses a dustily kept set of artefacts, and the **Pinacoteca** shows engravings depicting San Paolo before and after the fire.

The Aurelian Wall

From Piazza di Porta San Paolo, you can make a long detour back into the city centre following the **Aurelian Wall**, built by the Emperor Aurelian (and his successor Probus) in 275 AD to enclose Rome's seven hills and protect the city from invasion. The Aurelian Wall surrounds the city and, if you really are an enthusiast, you can walk its seventeen-kilometre circumference in an eight-hour day with a pause for lunch. However, for a taster, one of the best-preserved stretches runs between Porta San Paolo and Porta San Sebastiano, following Via di Porta Ardeatina: cross the road from Piramide metro station, turn right and follow the walls, keeping them always on your left.

It is around two kilometres from Porta San Paolo to **Porta San Sebastiano**, built in the fifth century, where the **Museo delle Mura**, Via di Porta San Sebastiano 18 (Tues–Sat 9am–2pm; €3), occupying a couple of floors of the gate, has displays of Aurelian's original plans and lots of photos of the past and present walls that are helpful in showing what is original and what medieval additions and how different structures have been incorporated into the walls over the years. The museum tells you more about the walls and the various gates than you really need to know, but you can climb up to the top of the gate for great views over the Roman country-side beyond, and walk a few hundred metres along the walls themselves – towards the east – before having to return to the museum.

From Porta San Sebastiano it is only a short walk up Via di Porta San Sebastiano to the Baths of Caracalla, past the **Tomb of the Scipios**. This stretch of the Via Appia was once lined with the tombs of rich families, and the Scipios were one of the great Republican dynasties, generals in the Punic Wars against Carthage. This family tomb was discovered in 1780 and its Etruscan-style sarcophagus transported to the Vatican, where it is on display. These days the tomb is a rather sad sight, and you have to make do with peeking into the small entrance or looking down from the scruffy park just above.

Failing that, continue following the walls by walking along Via delle Mura Latine to Piazzale Metronio, from where you're just a short walk from San Giovanni in Laterano (see p.132).

Via Appia Antica and the catacombs

Starting at the Porta San Sebastiano, the **Via Appia Antica** (or "Appian Way") is the most famous of the consular roads that used to strike out in each direction from the ancient city. The road, built by the censor Appio Claudio in 312 BC, is the only Roman landmark mentioned in the Bible. During classical times it was the most important of all the Roman trade routes, the so-called "Queen of Roads", carrying supplies right down through Campania to the port of Brindisi, some 500km southeast. It's no longer the main route south out of the city – that's Via Appia Nuova from nearby Porta San Giovanni – but it was an important part of early Christian Rome, its verges lined with numerous pagan and Christian sites, most famously the underground burial cemeteries or **catacombs** of the first Christians. Laws in ancient Rome forbade burial within the city walls, and most Romans were cremated. There are catacombs in other parts of the city – those attached to the church of Sant'Agnese on Via Nomentana (see p.113) are some of the best – but this is by far the largest concentration.

There are five complexes in all, dating from the first century to the fourth century, almost entirely emptied of bodies now but still decorated with the primitive signs and frescoes that were the hallmark of the then burgeoning Christian movement. Despite much speculation, no one really knows why the Christians decided to bury their dead in these tunnels: the rock here, tufa, is soft and easy to hollow out, but the digging involved must still have been phenomenal, and there is no real reason to suppose that the burial places had to be secret – they continued to bury their dead like this long after Christianity became the established religion. Whatever the reasons, they make intriguing viewing now. The three principal complexes are within walking distance of each other, though it's not really worth trying to see them all – the layers of shelves and drawers lose their fascination after a while. If you only go for one, you'd do best to focus on San Sebastiano (and maybe San Callisto) and explore the other attractions nearby. For further information, see ⓦ www.catacombe.roma.it.

Domine Quo Vadis

About 500m from Porta San Sebastiano, where the road forks, the church of **Domine Quo Vadis** is the first obvious sight, and signals the start of the catacomb stretch of road. Legend has this as the place where St Peter saw Christ while fleeing from certain death in Rome and asked, "Where goest thou, Lord?", to which Christ replied that he was going to be crucified once more, leading Peter to turn around and accept his fate. The small church is ordinary enough inside, except for its replica of a piece of marble that is said to be marked with the footprints of Christ (the original is in the church of San Sebastiano).

Catacombs of San Callisto

A kilometre or so further on, down a walled and often traffic-choked stretch of road, you reach the **Catacombs of San Callisto** at Via Appia Antica 110 (daily except Wed 9am–noon & 2–5pm; €6; bus #118 or #218), also accessible from Via Ardeatina, the largest of Rome's catacombs. The regular tours in English (around 45min) are usually run by priests, and take in a bit of preliminary explanation before heading into the high-vaulted passages, which stretch for some twenty miles and hold around half a million bodies. The catacombs were founded in the second century AD, and many of the early popes are buried here in the papal crypt,

Visiting the Via Appia Antica

If you want to see a lot of the area, including the Villa dei Quintili and Parco degli Acquedotti, the **Archeobus** (Ⓦ www.trambusopen.com) is probably the best choice: buses run from Termini and Piazza Venezia, among other city-centre locations, roughly every hour; tickets cost €15 for a return trip that lasts all day and you can hop on and off as you wish; it also gives discounts on entry prices to the catacombs and on bike rental charges.

If you're concentrating on Via Appia Antica proper – that is just the catacombs and the attractions close by – you might be better off saving your money and taking **public transport**: buses run south along Via Appia Antica and conveniently stop at or near to most of the main attractions. Bus #118 runs from Piazzale Ostiense almost as far as San Sebastiano; you can also take bus #218, which goes down Via Ardeatina, or bus #660, which runs from Colli Albani metro station to beyond the Tomb of Cecilia Metella. The top part of Via Appia Antica isn't particularly picturesque (and has no real pavement for much of the way) until you get down to San Sebastiano (where you can also rent bikes), and a good option is to take a bus to San Callisto or San Sebastiano and double back or walk on further for the attractions you want to see.

You could also walk from Porta San Sebastiano and take everything in on foot; this takes about fifteen minutes to Domine Quo Vadis and allows you to stop off at the **Parco Regionale dell'Appia Antica information office** for the area – which is actually classified as a national park – at Via Appia Antica 58/60, on the right just before you get to Domine Quo Vadis (daily: summer 9.30am–5.30pm; winter 9.30am–4.30pm; Ⓣ 06.513.5316, Ⓦ www.parcoappiaantica.org), where you can pick up a good map and other information on the various Appia Antica sights. Their website has lots of good information in English, including recommended walking tours and places to go horseriding in the area. The park information office also rents **bikes** (Mon–Sat 9.30am–1.30pm & 2–5.30pm; Ⓣ 06.513.5316; €3 an hour or €10 a day), as do the San Sebastiano catacombs (Mon–Sat 9am–5pm; Ⓣ 06.785.0350; €3 an hour, €9 a day).

Finally, there are a couple of handy – and decent – **restaurants** down by San Sebastiano too: *L'Archeologica*, just past the church at Via Appia Antica 125 (closed Tues), and *Cecilia Metella*, right opposite at Via Appia Antica 139 (closed Mon); neither is especially cheap but both have nice gardens for alfresco eating in summer.

including Callisto himself. St Callisto was in fact the guardian of the cemetery before he became pope; he was later killed in a riot and buried here in 222 AD, along with Sixtus II and seven other early popes. The numerous passages and burial vaults are as atmospheric as you would expect and also feature some well-preserved seventh- and eighth-century frescoes, and the **crypt of Santa Cecilia**, who was buried here after her martyrdom, before being shifted to the church dedicated to her in Trastevere (see p.155) – a copy of Carlo Maderno's famous statue marks the spot.

Mausoleo delle Fosse Ardeatine

Close by the alternative entrance to the San Callisto catacombs, there's a catacomb of a different kind at the **Mausoleo delle Fosse Ardeatine**, Via Ardeatine 174 (daily 8.30am–4.45pm; free; bus #218 or #714), where a site remembers the massacre of over 300 civilians during the Nazi occupation of Rome, after the resistance had ambushed and killed 32 soldiers on Via Rasella in the centre of the city (see p.108). The Nazis killed ten civilians for every dead German, burying the bodies here and then exploding mines to cover up their crime. The bodies were dug up after the war and reinterred in the mausoleum. Chapels have been installed in the so-called Grotta dell'Eccidio, where the bodies were found, all of which have been interred in a nearby area under serried rows of stone slabs, itself under one huge stone slab. Just up from here there's a small museum with newspaper cuttings telling the story of the event, and various other artefacts relating to the tragedy.

Catacombs of Santa Domitilla

In the opposite direction from the San Callisto exit, up Via delle Sette Chiese on the left at no. 282, the **Catacombs of Santa Domitilla** (daily except Tues 8.30am–noon & 2.30–5pm; €6) are quieter than those of San Callisto; again you can take bus #218, or #714 down Via Cristoforo Colombo at the other end of Via delle Sette Chiese.

The catacombs adjoin the remains of a fourth-century basilica erected here to the martyrs Achilleus and Nereus, the servants of Domitilla, niece of Domitian. They fled south of Rome with her to escape the persecutions of Hadrian, but were killed and eventually buried here. The network itself is huge, stretching for around 17km in all, and contains more frescoes and early wall etchings, as well as the tombs of Nereus and Achilleus and a relief showing their martyrdom.

Catacombs of San Sebastiano

The **Catacombs of San Sebastiano** (Mon–Sat 8.30am–noon & 2.30–5.30pm; €6), 500m further on from San Callisto on the right side of Via Appia Antica, are situated under a much-renovated basilica that was originally built by Constantine on the spot where the bodies of the Apostles Peter and Paul are said to have been laid for a time. In the church, the first chapel on the left holds a statue of the saint as he lay dying, built above his original tomb, while opposite is the original slab of marble imprinted with the feet of Christ that you may have seen in the church of Domine Quo Vadis. Downstairs, half-hour tours wind around the catacombs, dark corridors showing signs of early Christian worship – paintings of doves and fish, a contemporary carved oil lamp and inscriptions dating the tombs themselves. The most striking features, however, are not Christian at all, but three **pagan tombs** (one painted, two stuccoed), discovered when archeologists were burrowing beneath the floor of the basilica upstairs. Just above here, Constantine is said to have raised his chapel to Peter and Paul, and although St Peter was later removed to the Vatican, and St Paul to San Paolo fuori le Mura, the graffiti above records the fact that this was indeed, albeit temporarily, where the two Apostles rested.

The Circus of Maxentius and Tomb of Romulus

A couple of hundred metres further on from the San Sebastiano catacombs, the group of brick ruins trailing off into the fields to the left are the remains of the **Villa and Circus of Maxentius** (Tues–Sat 9am–1pm; €3), a large complex built by the emperor in the early fourth century AD before his defeat by Constantine. It's a clear, long oval of grass, similar to the Circus Maximus (see p.137) back in town, but slightly better preserved and in a rather more bucolic location – making it a fantastic place to eat a picnic, lolling around in the grass or perching on the ruins. Clambering about in the remains, you can make out the twelve starting gates to the circus, or racetrack, the enormous towers that contained the mechanism for lifting the gates at the beginning of the races and the remains of a basilica. Other structures surround it, including, closer to the road, the ruins of what was once a magnificent mausoleum of an unknown person or persons, the so-called **Tomb of Romulus**, in the middle of a huge quadrangle of walls.

The Tomb of Cecilia Metella and beyond

Further along the Via Appia is the circular **Tomb of Cecilia Metella** (daily 9am–4.30pm; €2, or €7.50 including Terme di Caracalla and Villa dei Quintili) from the Augustan period, converted into a castle in the fourteenth century. Known as "Capo di Bove" for the bulls on the frieze around it, the tomb itself, a huge brick-built drum, is little more than a large pigeon coop these days; various fragments and finds are littered around the adjacent later courtyards, and down below you can see what's left of a lava flow from thousands of years earlier.

Beyond Cecilia Metella the **Via Appia Antica** hits proper countryside, and the road heads straight south, its verges littered with ancient rubble, including tombs, shrines, gateposts and watchtowers, most of them excavated during the nineteenth century. There's no bus out here (although the Archeobus comes part of the way), but it's by far the most atmospheric stretch of the ancient Via Appia, and you should walk at least as far as the circular tomb of the **Casale Rotondo** – the largest of Via Appia's monuments, dating from the last decades of the first century BC – if you get the chance. Just past here, the road turns left towards the main entrance of the Villa dei Quintili.

Villa dei Quintili

The **Villa dei Quintili**, at Via Appia Nuova 1092 (daily: March 9am–4.30pm; April–Aug 9am–6.30pm; Sept 9am–6pm; Oct 9am–5.30pm; Nov–Feb 9am–3.30pm; €4, or €7.50 including Cecilia Metella and Caracalla; metro to Colli Albani and then a #663 or #664 bus), crowns the crest of a hill not far from the main road out to Ciampino. It's one of the largest and most complete suburban villas close to Rome, and dates from the mid-second century AD. As you might expect from the position of the place, the Quintili were an influential Roman family; two brothers were consuls under Commodus, and subsequently executed by him in 182 AD.

The main building has a one-room **museum** with finds from the villa and surrounding area: a large statue of Zeus and three heads of Hermes, a lovely head of a woman and another of a man from the residential section of the villa, a fragment of a relief of Mithras slaying the Bull from the villa's baths, and three almost perfect wall designs of male nude figures in *opus sectile*.

The villa itself is up a track on the mound of the hill, enjoying panoramic views of the Roman countryside on all sides. On the northern side, the baths complex rears up, with steps leading down to its well-preserved caldarium, in which a rectangular pool is overlooked by massive windows designed to keep the temperature inside comfortably warm. A few rooms over, the frigidarium is perhaps the best-preserved room in the complex, with considerable traces of its mosaic floor and two columns at the far end. Retracing your steps, you can also walk the corridors of the residential part of the villa, though sadly many of the rooms and steps are closed off, while on the far side of the complex you wander into what must have been a hugely impressive main reception hall, whose large windows would have made the most of the countryside views.

Parco degli Acquedotti

A few minutes from the Villa dei Quintili on the Archeobus, or a few minutes' walk from Subaugusta metro station, the **Parco degli Acquedotti** is a lovely spot, where two aqueducts snake between the pines of suburban Rome. Of the pair, the **Acqua Claudia** is unusually intact, its arches leading off south into the far distance. Looking north, along its more ruinous stretches, you can see central Rome, marked by the dome of St Peter's. The other, more sunken aqueduct is the **Acqua Felice**, which is supplemented by a modern pipe. Eleven major aqueducts supplied ancient Rome with water, built between the fourth century BC and third century AD. At its height the population of the city was around a million, and between them the aqueducts ensured that each member of the Roman populace had access to around 75 litres a day – more, in fact, than the people of many modern countries use. Designed to allow water to flow freely towards the city, they mostly consisted of tunnels bored underground, and it was only when they got closer to the city that the water would run along a conduit raised on arches, to help the water pressure when it got to the city itself. They're still an impressive sight, and make a nice place for a picnic.

EUR

From Piazza di Porta San Paolo and the Piramide metro station, Via Ostiense leads south to join up with Via Cristoforo Colombo, which in turn runs down to **EUR** (pronounced "eh-oor") – the acronym for the district built for the "Esposizione Universale Roma". This was laid out to the designs of Marcello Piacentini for Mussolini and the aborted 1942 World's Fair, though it was not finished until well after the war. Reachable by bus #714 from Termini or taking metro line B, this is not so much a neighbourhood as a statement in stone, a rather soulless grid of square buildings, long vistas and wide processional boulevards linked tenuously to the rest of Rome by metro but light years away from the city in feel. Come here for its numerous museums, some of which – notably the exhaustive Museo della Civiltà – are worth the trip, or if you have a yen for modern city architecture and planning.

Exploring EUR

The great flaw in EUR is that it's not really built for people: the streets are wide thoroughfares designed for easy traffic flow and the shops and cafés are easily outnumbered by offices, although the columned buildings provide shade in numerous arcades. Of the main structures, it's the prewar, Fascist-style constructions that are of most interest; the postwar development of the area threw up bland office blocks for the most part.

Piazza Marconi is the nominal centre of EUR, where the wide, classically inspired boulevards intersect to swerve around a friezed obelisk in the centre. A few minutes' walk from here, in the northwest corner of EUR, the **Palazzo della Civiltà del Lavoro** is a visual highlight – Mussolini-inspired architecture at its most assured, and chauvinistic: the inscription around the top reads "One Nation, of Poets, Artists, Heroes, Saints, Thinkers, Scientists, Navigators and Travellers." With a heroic statue on each corner, it's a successful and imposing structure, and

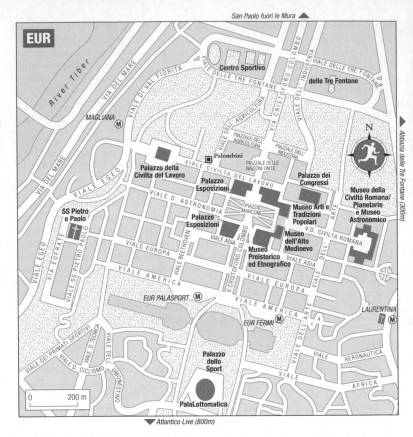

Atlantico Live (800m) ▼

far and away the best piece of architecture in EUR. Some have called it the "square Colosseum", which sums up its mixing of modern and classical styles perfectly. It's been undergoing a much-needed restoration for several years now, but when finished it is due to reopen as Rome's new audiovisual museum.

All of EUR's other museums are within easy reach of here. On Piazza Marconi itself, the **Museo Nazionale delle Arti e delle Tradizioni Popolari** (Tues–Sat 9am–6pm; €4) is a run-through of applied arts, costumes and religious artefacts from the Italian regions, though everything is labelled in Italian; bring a dictionary. The **Museo Nazionale Preistorico ed Etnografico Luigi Pigorini**, Viale Lincoln 1 (Tues–Sat 10am–6pm; €6), is arranged in manageable and easily comprehensible order, but its prehistoric section is mind-numbingly exhaustive; the ethnographic collection does something to relieve things, however, with artefacts from South America, the Pacific and Africa. In the same building, further down the colonnade, the **Museo dell'Alto Medioevo**, Viale Lincoln 3 (Tues–Sat 9am–1.30pm; €2), concentrates on artefacts from the fifth to the tenth centuries – local finds mainly, including some beautiful jewellery from the seventh century and a delicate fifth-century gold *fibula* found on the Palatine Hill.

But of all the museums, the most interesting is the **Museo della Civiltà Romana**, Piazza Agnelli 10 (Tues–Fri 9am–2pm, Sat & Sun 9am–7pm; €6.50, or

€8.50 including astronomy museum & planetarium). It's a very large museum, and amid the reconstructed statuary, tablets and inscriptions, the ordinary stuff impresses most – small bronze lamps, medical instruments, carved zodiac charts, musical instruments and the like. Among many reconstructions, the long corridor housing large casts of the reliefs from Trajan's Column is instructive, to say the least. The pièce de résistance is a room-filling model of Rome during the time of Constantine to a 1:250 scale that you can look down on from above – perfect for setting the rest of the city in context.

Part of the same complex, the city's **Planetario e Museo Astronomico** (July & Aug Tues–Fri 8.30–11.30pm, Sat & Sun 4.30–11.30pm; Sept–June Tues–Fri 9am–2pm, Sat & Sun 9am–7pm; €6.50, or €8.50 including the Museo della Civiltà Romana) has a small exhibition of astronomy and the planets and regular programmes in its domed planetarium, but they're in Italian only, and frankly not the most spectacular planetarium shows you'll see.

The Abbazia delle Tre Fontane

The perfect antidote to EUR is just a ten-minute walk from the Museo della Civiltà Romana. The **Abbazia delle Tre Fontane**, Via di Acque Salvie 1 (daily 6am–9pm), is a complex of churches founded on the spot where St Paul was martyred; it's said that when the saint was beheaded his head bounced and three springs erupted where it touched the ground. In those days this was a malarial area, and it was all but abandoned during the Middle Ages, but in the second half of the nineteenth century Trappist monks drained the swamp and planted eucalyptus trees in the vicinity; they still distil a eucalyptus-based chest remedy here, as well as an exquisite liqueur, chocolate bars, wine, toiletries and all manner of other monastic products – all sold at the small **shop and bar** by the entrance. Bus #761 from the Basilica di San Paolo goes right past, or it's a ten-minute walk from Laurentina metro on line B.

The abbey churches

The churches were rebuilt in the sixteenth century and restored by the Trappists. They're not particularly outstanding buildings, appealing more for their peaceful location, which is relatively undisturbed by visitors, than any architectural distinction.

The first and largest church, originally built in 625 and rebuilt and finally restored by the Trappists, is **Santi Vincenzo e Anastasio**. Its gloomy atmosphere is exacerbated by the fact that most of the windows are of a thick marble that admits little light – although the stained-glass ones, dating from the Renaissance with papal heraldry from that period, are beautiful. The three fountains in the floor, supposedly formed by the saint's bouncing head, have long since run dry.

To the right, the church of **Santa Maria Scala Coeli** owes its name to a vision St Bernard had here in which he saw the soul he was praying for ascend to heaven; the Cosmatesque altar where this is supposed to have happened is down the cramped stairs, in the crypt, where St Paul was allegedly kept prior to his beheading. Beyond, the church of **San Paolo alle Tre Fontane** (daily 8am–1pm & 3–6pm) holds the pillar to which St Paul was tied in the right transept and a couple of very well-preserved mosaic pavements from Ostia Antica. Try to be here, if you can, in the early morning or evening, when the monks come in to sing Mass in Gregorian chant – a moving experience.

On the way out, the **gatehouse** contains ceiling frescoes from the thirteenth century that show the possessions of the abbey at the time. They're in a pretty bad state, but the ones that remain have been restored and are still very interesting, showing a kind of picture map of Italy in the thirteenth century.

10

Trastevere and the Janiculum Hill

cross the river from the centre of town, on the right bank of the Tiber, **Trastevere** is a smallish district, sheltered under the heights of the Janiculum Hill. It was the artisan area of the city in classical times, neatly placed for the trade that came upriver from Ostia and was unloaded nearby. Located outside the city walls, Trastevere (the name means literally "across the Tiber") was for centuries heavily populated by immigrants, and this uniqueness and separation lent the neighbourhood a strong identity that lasted well into this century. The separate identity remains, and it's one of the city's nicest neighbourhoods, no question. But Trastevere's working-class origins are long gone, and it's nowadays mainly a hub for eating out and nightlife, with a host of **bars and restaurants** that in summer are thronged with tourists, lured by the charm of its narrow streets and closeted squares. However, even if the local Festa de' Noantri ("celebration of we others"), held every July, seems to symbolize the slow decline of local spirit rather than celebrate its existence, there are plenty of reasons to come to Trastevere. It's the home of one or two of the city's most compelling sights – the **Villa Farnesina** on one side of Viale Traste-vere, the church of **Santa Cecilia** on the other. It's also one of the most pleasant places to stroll in Rome, peaceful in the morning, lively come the evening, as dozens of trattorias set out tables along the cobblestone streets, and still buzzing late at night, when its bars and clubs provide a focus for one of Rome's most dyanamic night-time scenes (see chapters 15–17 for details). While you're in the area, don't forget to visit the **Janiculum Hill**, up above Trastevere, for some of the best views in Rome.

East of Viale Trastevere

The quietest part of Trastevere lies on the southeastern side of **Viale Trastevere**, the wide boulevard that cuts through the centre of the district. Just the other side of the Tiber from the Aventine Hill and Testaccio, it feels oddly cut off from the city centre, a small knot of peeling streets and echoing squares that are a peaceful contrast to the relatively spruced-up Trastevere proper. You can get here either by walking across the Ponte Garibaldi and turning left off Viale Trastevere, by way of

Isola Tiberina or Ponte Palatino, or from Testaccio, from where a short stroll over the Ponte Sublicio leaves you right by the Porta Portese.

Porta Portese

Trastevere at its most disreputable but also at its traditional best can be witnessed on Sunday mornings, when the **Porta Portese** flea market stretches from the Porta Portese gate down Via Portuense to Trastevere train station in a congested medley of antiques, old motor spares, cheap clothing, trendy clothing, cheap *and* trendy clothing, household goods, bric-a-brac and assorted junk. Haggling is the rule, and keep a good hold of your wallet or purse. It starts around 7am, and you should come early if you want to buy, or even move – most of the bargains, not to mention the stolen goods, have gone by 10am, by which time the crush of people can be intense. It's pretty much all over by lunchtime.

San Francesco a Ripa

Not far from Piazza di Porta Portese, the church of **San Francesco a Ripa** on Piazza di San Francesco d'Assisi (daily 7am–noon & 4–7pm), is best known for the fact that St Francis himself once stayed here. You can see the actual room he slept in (through the sacristy and up some steep stairs), which includes the rock he used as a pillow and embroidery that is apparently the work of Santa Chiara. It's also the burial place of the twentieth-century Italian artist Giorgio de Chirico (see p.95), who lived in Rome until his death in the 1970s and is buried behind the first chapel on the left, in a simple white room named after the painter. But perhaps the most visually memorable item in the church is the writhing, orgasmic statue of a minor saint, the Blessed Ludovica Albertoni, that Bernini sculpted towards the end of his career. As a work of Baroque sauciness, it bears comparison with his more famous *Ecstasy of St Teresa* in the church of Santa Maria in Vittoria; indeed it's perhaps even more shameless in its depiction of an earthily realized divine ecstasy – the woman is actually kneading her breasts.

Santa Cecilia in Trastevere

Five minutes north of San Francesco, on its own quiet piazza off Via dei Genovesi, is the church of **Santa Cecilia in Trastevere** (daily 9.30am–12.30pm & 4–6.30pm), a cream, rather sterile church – apart from a pretty front courtyard – whose antiseptic eighteenth-century appearance belies its historical associations. A church was originally built here over the site of the second-century home of St Cecilia, whose husband Valerian was executed for refusing to worship Roman gods and who herself was subsequently persecuted for her Christian beliefs. The story has it that Cecilia was locked in the caldarium (hot room) of her own baths for several days but refused to die, singing her way through the ordeal (Cecilia is the patron saint of music). Her head was finally half hacked off with an axe, though it took several blows before she finally succumbed. Below the high altar, under a Gothic baldachino, Stefano Maderno's limp, almost modern statue of the saint shows her incorruptible body as it was found when exhumed in 1599, with three deep cuts in her neck – a fragile, intensely human piece of work that has helped make Cecilia one of the most revered Roman saints. Behind all this presides an apse mosaic from the ninth century showing Paschal I, who founded the current church, being presented to Christ by St Cecilia flanked by various saints.

The excavations of the baths and the rest of the Roman house are on view in the **crypt** below (€2.50) – a series of dank rooms with some fragments of mosaic and

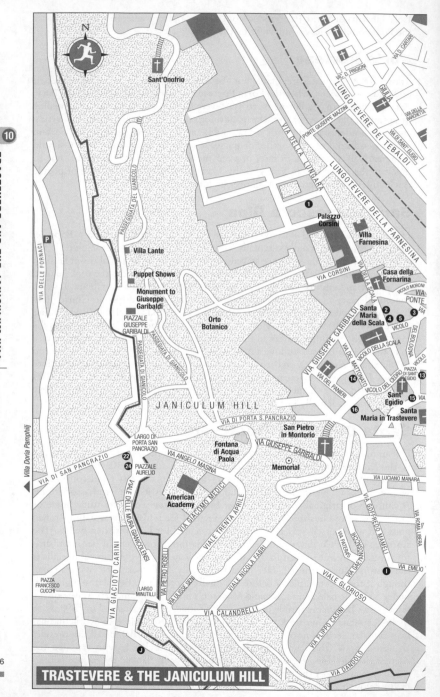

Sant'Onofrio

N

Villa Lante

Puppet Shows

Monument to
Giuseppe
Garibaldi

PIAZZALE
GIUSEPPE
GARIBALDI

Orto
Botanico

PASSEGGIATA DEL GIANICOLO

PASSEGGIATA DI GIANICOLO

PASSEGGIATA DI GIANICOLO

VIA DELLE FORNACI

P

JANICULUM HILL

Largo di
Porta San
Pancrazio

LARGO DI
PORTA SAN
PANCRAZIO

PIAZZALE
AURELIO

22

24

American
Academy

VIA ANGELO MASINA

Fontana
di Acqua
Paola

VIA DI PORTA S.PANCRAZIO

San Pietro
in Montorio

VIA GIUSEPPE GARIBALDI

Memorial

VIA DI SAN PANCRAZIO

VIA GIACIOTO CARINI

VIALE DELLE MURA GIANICOLENSI

VIA PIETRO ROSELLI

VIA GIACOMO MEDICI

VIALE TRENTA APRILE

VIALE NICOLA FABRI

VIA ULISSE SENI

PIAZZA
FRANCESCO
CUCCHI

LARGO
MINUTILLI

VIA CALANDRELLI

J

VIA LUCIANO MANARA

VIA GOFFREDO MAMELI

VIA ROMA LIBERA

VIA PATERAS

VIA DIOSCURI

VIA GALLIA

VIALE GLORIOSO

VIA EMILIO

I

VIA FILIPPO CASINI

VIA DANDOLO

Palazzo
Corsini

1

Villa
Farnesina

Casa della
Fornarina

Santa
Maria
della Scala

2

4   5

3

13

VIA DELLA LUNGARA

PONTE GIUSEPPE MAZZINI

LUNGOTEVERE DEI TEBALDI

LUNGOTEVERE DELLA FARNESINA

VIC. D. PRIGIONI

GIULIA

VIA D. CARTARI

VIA DELLA
BARCHETTA

VALO SANT'ELIGIO

VIA CORSINI

VIA DELLA SCALA

VICOLO MORONI

VIA
PONTE

VICOLO
DEI BOLOGNA

VIA DEI BOLOGNA

PIAZZA
DI SANT'
EGIDIO

VIA GIUSEPPE GARIBALDI

VIA DI MATTONATO

VICOLO DELLA SCALA

VIA DEL PANIERI

14

VICOLO DEL CEDRO

16

Sant'
Egidio

15

VIA

Santa
Maria in Trastevere

Villa Doria Pamphilj

Villa Doria Pamphilj

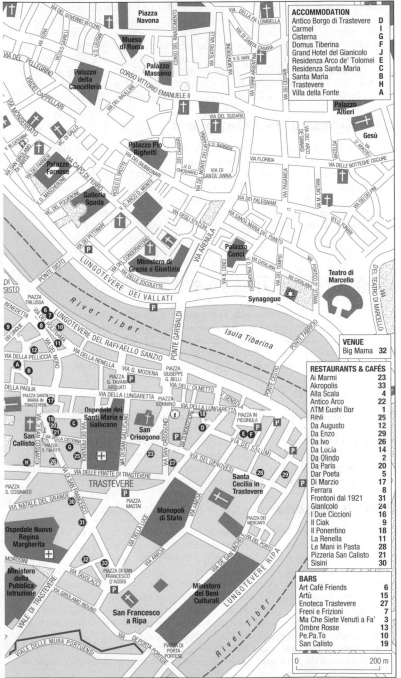

ACCOMMODATION
Antico Borgo di Trastevere	D
Carmel	I
Cisterna	G
Domus Tiberina	F
Grand Hotel del Gianicolo	J
Residenza Arco de' Tolomei	E
Residenza Santa Maria	C
Santa Maria	B
Trastevere	H
Villa della Fonte	A

VENUE
Big Mama	32

RESTAURANTS & CAFÉS
Ai Marmi	23
Akropolis	33
Alla Scala	4
Antico Arco	22
ATM Sushi Bar	1
Bibli	25
Da Augusto	12
Da Enzo	29
Da Ivo	26
Da Lucia	14
Da Olindo	2
Da Paris	20
Dar Poeta	5
Di Marzio	17
Ferrara	8
Frontoni dal 1921	31
Gianicolo	24
I Due Ciccioni	16
Il Ciak	9
Il Ponentino	18
La Renella	11
Le Mani in Pasta	28
Pizzeria San Calisto	21
Sisini	30

BARS
Art Café Friends	6
Artù	15
Enoteca Trastevere	27
Freni e Frizioni	7
Ma Che Siete Venuti a Fa'	3
Ombre Rosse	13
Pe.Pa.To	10
San Calisto	19

▼ Via Portuense & Stazione Trastevere (1.5km)

a gaudily decorated chapel at the far end. More alluring by far is the singing gallery above the nave of the church (Mon–Sat 10.15am–12.15pm, Sun 11.15am–12.15pm; €2.50; ring the bell to the left of the church door to get in), where Pietro Cavallini's late-thirteenth-century **fresco of the Last Judgement** is all that remains of the decoration that once covered the entire church. It's a powerful painting, an amazingly fluid, naturalistic piece of work for the time, with each of the Apostles, ranked six each side of Christ, captured as an individual portrait, while Christ sits in quiet, meditative majesty in the centre, flanked by angels.

San Giovanni dei Genovesi

Following Via dei Genovesi towards Viale Trastevere, you pass the church and ancient hospital of **San Giovanni dei Genovesi** on the left at Via Anicia 12, set up to care for sailors from Genova in the fifteenth century, from which the street takes its name. This in itself isn't of much interest and in any case is rarely open. But just past the church on the right its **cloister** (Tues, Fri & Sun 3–6pm; closed Aug; ring the bell marked "sposi magnanti") is a lovely and very peaceful spot, a two-tiered quadrangle filled with orange and lime trees.

West of Viale Trastevere

The most obvious way to approach Trastevere is to cross over from Isola Tiberina or from the pedestrian Ponte Sisto at the end of Via Giulia, both of which leave you five minutes from the heart of the neighbourhood. There's a bit more life on this west side of Viale Trastevere, centred on the **Piazza Santa Maria in Trastevere**, the heart of old Trastevere, named after the church in its northwest corner.

Piazza Belli

Right by the river, the traffic junction of **Piazza Belli** marks the beginning of Viale Trastevere. The brick building with the crenellations and tower is known as the **Casa di Dante**, although it's doubtful that the poet ever stayed here, and the top-hatted statue opposite is of the Roman poet Giuseppe Gioacchino Belli – "the poet of the people of Rome", according to the inscription – who in the nineteenth century produced thousands of sonnets recording life in the city in dialect.

San Crisogono

Piazza Belli gives way to Piazza Sonnino, where the church of **San Crisogono** (daily 7.30–11.30am & 4–7pm; excavations €2) is a large, typically Roman basilica, with a nave lined with ancient columns and one of the city's finest Cosmati mosaic floors. The church itself is relatively featureless apart from a beautiful thirteenth-century apse mosaic showing the church's saint and St James; it's the remains of the earlier buildings below that mark the church out – two buildings really, an early Christian structure from the third century AD and a later fifth-century basilica whose substantial remnants cover almost the entire footprint of the main church. There are some very worn frescoes – San Crisogono himself in the centre of the apse, and a saint healing a sick man (covered in spots) in the north aisle, as well as various bits of Roman stonework, including a couple of impressively carved sarcophagi.

▲ Piazza di Santa Maria in Trastevere

Santa Maria in Trastevere

The church of **Santa Maria in Trastevere** (daily 7am–9pm) is held to be the first Christian place of worship in Rome, built on a site where a fountain of oil is said to have sprung on the day of Christ's birth. The greater part of the structure now dates from 1140, after a rebuilding by Innocent II, a pope from Trastevere. These days many people come here for the church's **mosaics**, which are among the city's most impressive: those on the cornice were completed a century or so after the rebuilding and show the Madonna surrounded by ten female figures with lamps – once thought to represent *The Wise and Foolish Virgins*. Inside, there's a nineteenth-century copy of a Cosmatesque pavement of spirals and circles, and more twelfth-century mosaics in the apse, Byzantine-inspired works which depict a solemn yet sensitive parade of saints thronged around Christ and Mary, while underneath a series of panels shows scenes from the life of the Virgin by the painter Pietro Cavallini. Beneath the high altar on the right, an inscription – "FONS OLEI" – marks the spot where the oil is supposed to have sprung up, to the right of which there is a chapel crowned with the crest of the British monarchy – placed here by Henry, Cardinal of York, when he and his family, the Stuarts, lived in exile in Rome.

Museo di Roma in Trastevere

A short walk from Santa Maria in Trastevere, the long triangle of Piazza di Sant'Egidio is home to the small **Museo di Roma in Trastevere** (Tues–Sun 10am–8pm; €3), a small collection of artefacts illustrating Roman folklore – paintings of nineteenth-century life, models of popular Roman sights, and, best of all, life-sized tableaux showing scenes of nineteenth-century Roman life – an *osteria*, a pharmacy, a *saltarello* dance and the like. There is also a permanent display of the watercolours of one Ettore Roesler Franz, which capture a rustic Rome –

when the countryside started beyond the Aurelian Wall – that almost entirely disappeared with the turn-of-the-century developments of the city centre. All in all, the museum is much more accessible and engaging than the displays of its counterpart in the centre (see p.51), and it has decent temporary exhibitions too.

Piazza Trilussa

Facing the pedestrian Ponte Sisto (see p.62), **Piazza Trilussa** is a busy open space that focuses on the steps up to its grand 1613 fountain, where the waters of the **Acqua Paola** emerge. On the other side, the upper torso of the poet **Trilussa**, after whom the square is named, casually leans on a marble plinth as if declaiming his poems – one of which is printed beneath him. Trilussa is actually the pen-name (and an anagram) of Carlo Alberto Salustri, who, like the nineteenth-century Roman poet Belli (see p.158), wrote in dialect – often for humorous effect.

Palazzo Corsini

Cutting northwest through the backstreets towards the Tiber, you'll come across the **Palazzo Corsini**, Via della Lungara 10, built originally for Cardinal Riario in the fifteenth century, and totally renovated between 1732 and 1736 by Ferdinando Fuga for the cardinal and art collector Neri Maria Corsini. He collected most of the paintings on display in the **Galleria Nazionale d'Arte di Palazzo Corsini** (Tues–Sun 8.30am–7.30pm; €4), a relatively small collection that only takes up a few rooms of the giant palace. This sets out to dwarf everything with its size – a fitting final home for Queen Christina of Sweden, who renounced Protestantism and with it the Swedish throne in 1655, bringing her library and fortune to Rome, to the delight of the Chigi pope, Alexander VII. She lived first in Palazzo Farnese and then here for a number of years, dying in the palace in 1689. She is one of only three women to be buried in St Peter's, notwithstanding the fact that her life left quite a lot to be desired by the papal standards of the time: she was an affirmed lesbian, murdered one of her own servants, and enjoyed a notoriously wild lifestyle.

It's not hard to imagine the queen roaming the lofty rooms and drafty corridors of the palace – such is its haunting grandeur – and there are echoes of northern Europe in the first room of the gallery, where a number of Netherlandish **paintings** introduce the collection – a *Village Fete* by Maarten van Cleve, *Butcher's Shop* by David Teniers and Rubens' *St Sebastian Tended by Angels*. There is also a depiction of *St George and the Dragon* by Francesco Raibolini, a *Madonna and Child* by Murillo and the sensitive *Straw Madonna* by Van Dyck, and in the next room a *St John the Baptist* by Caravaggio and *Madonna and Child* by Gentileschi. Beyond here there's a room full of landscapes, including lush scenes by Dughet and a depiction of the Pantheon by Charles-Louis Clérisseau, when there was a market held in the piazza outside – though it's a rather fanciful interpretation, squeezing the Pyramid of Cestius and Arch of Janus into the background.

Queen Christina's **bedchamber** is decorated with frescoes by an unknown artist – grotesques with scenes of the miracles of Moses as well as the Riario coat of arms, and on the wall a portrait of the queen by Justus van Egmont. Next door, look out for the curious **Corsini Throne**, thought to be a Roman copy of an Etruscan throne from the second or first century BC. Cut out of marble, its back is carved with warriors in armour and helmets, below which wild boars the size of horses are pursued by hunters. The base is decorated with scenes of a sacrifice, notably the minotaur devouring a human being – only discernible by the kicking legs that protrude from the feasting beast. The final rooms are chock-full of more paintings from the seventeeth and eighteenth centuries, best of which are a famous portrayal of *Salome with the Head of St John the Baptist* by Guido Reni, and *Ecce Homo* by Guercino. Following the corridor back to the entrance takes you past a painting of *Prometheus* by Salvatore Rosa – one of the most vivid and detailed expositions of human internal anatomy you'll see – and Luca Giordano's *Entry of Christ into Jerusalem*.

The Orto Botanico

The grounds of the Palazzo Corsini are now the site of the **Orto Botanico** (Mon–Sat 9am–6.30pm; €4), which, after Padua's botanical gardens, are the most important in Italy – and a good example of eighteenth-century garden design. It's a pleasantly neglected expanse these days, a low-key bucolic retreat clasping the side of the Janiculum Hill. You can clamber up to high stands of bamboo and ferns cut by rivulets of water and stroll through a wood of century-old oaks, cedars and conifers. A grove of acclimatized palm trees stands in front of the so-called Fountain of the Tritons, a rather grand name for the relatively small-scale fountain that forms the centrepiece of the lower part of the gardens. There's a herbal garden with medicinal plants, greenhouses holding succulents and cacti and a collection of orchids that bloom in springtime and early summer – and, a nice touch, a garden of aromatic herbs put together for the blind; the plants can be identified by their smell or touch, and are accompanied by signs in Braille. The garden also has the distinction of being home to one of the oldest plane trees in Rome, between 350 and 400 years old, situated by the recently restored monumental staircase.

Villa Farnesina

The **Villa Farnesina** (Mon–Sat and first Sun of the month 9am–1pm; €5), across the road from the Palazzo Corsini at Via della Lungara 230, is more interesting than its larger neighbour. Built during the early sixteenth century by Baldassare Peruzzi for the Renaissance banker Agostino Chigi, it is a unique building, known for its Renaissance frescoes and contributed to by some of the masters of the Renaissance. Chigi situated his villa here to be close to the papal court and away from his business cronies.

Most people come to view the Raphael-designed painting of **Cupid and Psyche** in the now glassed-in loggia (at the original front of the building, which is now at the back), completed in 1517 by the artist's assistants, Giulio Romano, Francesco Penni and Giovanni da Udine. The painter and art historian Vasari claims Raphael didn't complete the work because his infatuation with his mistress – "La Fornarina", whose father's bakery was situated nearby – was making it difficult to concentrate, and says that Chigi arranged for her to live with the painter in the palace while he worked on the loggia. More likely he was simply so overloaded with commissions that he couldn't possibly finish them all.

Whoever was responsible, it's mightily impressive, a flowing, animated work bursting with muscular men and bare-bosomed women. Actually it would have made even more of an impact if completed as planned because the blue would have been much brighter – what you see is just the preparatory colour. The only part Raphael is said to have completed is the female figure with her back turned on the lunette to the right of the door leading out to the east. He did, however, apparently manage to finish the **Galatea** in the room next door, which he fitted in between his Vatican commissions for Julius II. Kenneth Clark called it "the greatest evocation of paganism of the Renaissance", although Vasari claims that Michelangelo, passing by one day while Raphael was canoodling with La Fornarina, finished the painting for him. It's more of a mixed bag thematically, with bucolic country scenes interspersed with Galatea on her scallop-shell chariot and a giant head once said to have been painted by Michelangelo in one of the lunettes – which otherwise feature scenes from Ovid's *Metamorphoses* by Sebastiano del Piombo. The ceiling shows Chigi's horoscope constellations, frescoed by the architect of the building, Peruzzi, who also decorated the upstairs **Salone delle Prospettive**, where trompe l'oeil balconies give views onto contemporary Rome – one of the earliest examples of the technique. This room leads through to Chigi's bedroom, decorated with Sodoma's bold and colourful scenes from the life of Alexander the Great.

The Janiculum Hill

It's about a fifteen-minute walk up Via Giuseppe Garibaldi to the summit of the **Janiculum Hill** – not one of the original seven hills of Rome, but the one with the best and most accessible views of the centre. If you don't want to take the main road, follow Vicolo del Cedro from Via della Scala and take the steps up from the end, cross the main road, and continue on the steps that lead up to San Pietro in Montorio. Failing that, bus #115 crosses the hill from Viale Trastevere to the Gianicolo terminal on the Vatican side, although the walk from Piazzale Garibaldi down to the Vatican only takes a further twenty minutes or so.

San Pietro in Montorio

Now part of a complex that includes the Spanish Academy and Spanish ambassa-dor's residence, the church of **San Pietro in Montorio**, on the piazza of the same name (Mon–Fri 8.30am–noon & 3–4pm, Sat & Sun 8.30am–noon), was built on a site once believed to have been the place of the saint's crucifixion. The compact interior is particularly intimate – it's a favourite for weddings – and features some first-rate paintings, among them Sebastiano del Piombo's graceful *Flagellation*. Don't miss Bramante's little **Tempietto** (same times) in the courtyard on the right, one of the seminal works of the Renaissance, built on what was supposed to have been the precise spot of St Peter's martyrdom. The small circular building is like a classical temple in miniature, perfectly proportioned and neatly executed.

Fontana dell'Acqua Paola

The Janiculum was the scene of a fierce 1849 set-to between Garibaldi's troops and the French, and the white marble **memorial** around the corner from the church is dedicated to all those who died in the battle. A little further on, the **Fontana dell'Acqua Paola** – constructed for Paul V in 1612 with marble from the Roman Forum – gushes water at a bend in the road, a recently restored and very grandiose affair whose ancient water supply is provided by Lake Bracciano way to the north of Rome, and in turn goes on to feed the fountain down below on Piazza Trilussa, as well as those on Piazza Farnese across the river.

Porta San Pancrazio

At the top of the hill, the city gate of **Porta San Pancrazio** was built during the reign of Urban VIII, destroyed by the French in 1849, and rebuilt by Pope Pius IX five years later. It has recently been restored and will house the new **Museum of** the **Roman Republic 1848–49** (yet to open at the time of writing). On the far side is Piazzale Aurelio, the start of the old Roman Via Aurelia, and close by the numerous buildings of the American Academy in Rome. By the time you get up here you might also be ready for a drink, in which case the American Academy's local bar, *Gianicolo*, on the square, is the perfect spot for a drink and a bite to eat.

Villa Doria Pamphilj

Just beyond the Porta, down Via di San Pancrazio, is the rather grand entrance to the grounds of the **Villa Doria Pamphilj**, the largest and most recent of Rome's parks, laid out in the mid-seventeenth century for Prince Camillo Pamphilj and acquired for the city in the 1970s. The stately white Baroque villa is not open to the public, but the sprawling greenery that surrounds it is an enchanting mix of formal parterres and shady lawns and glades, dotted with fountains and statues, and wilder, more bucolic tracts. From the main gate, a path leads downhill and round to the right for around 250m, emerging at the villa. From here, follow the path southwest past the house for around 500m to reach the tree-fringed lake, fed at its northern end by a once-grand cascade of tiny waterfalls and grottoes, and inhabited by scores of turtles that bask photogenically on its banks. It all makes for a delightful wander (beware, signposting is minimal), though it's best to bring a picnic as there's no café.

Passeggiata del Gianicolo

Most people turn right before they reach the crest of the hill, however, following the **Passeggiata del Gianicolo** along the ridge to **Piazzale Giuseppe Garibaldi**, where there's an equestrian monument to Garibaldi – an ostentatious work from 1895. Just below is the spot from which a cannon is fired at noon each day for Romans to check their watches, leaving a whiff of powder in the air and setting all the car alarms off, although most people bring their kids up here for the weekend puppet shows or the nearby carousel.

Further on, the statue of **Anita Garibaldi** is a fiery, melodramatic work (she cradles a baby in one arm, brandishes a pistol with the other, and is galloping full speed on a horse) that recalls the important part she played in the 1849 battle and also marks her grave – she died later in the campaign. Spread out before her are some of the best views over the city. Immediately opposite, the Renaissance **Villa Lante** is a jewel of a place that is now the home of the Finnish Academy in Rome and gives a panoramic view of the city, although you can only visit on official business or for an exhibition or performance. Descending from here towards the Vatican and St Peter's, follow some steps off to the right and, next to a small amphitheatre, you'll find the gnarled old oak tree where the sixteenth-century Italian poet **Torquato Tasso**, friend of Mannerist sculptor Benvenuto Cellini and author of *La Gerusalemme Deliverata* ("Jerusalem Delivered"), is said to have whiled away his last days. Further down the hill, next to the Jesuit children's hospital, the church of **Sant'Onofrio** (Sun 10am–noon) sits on the road's bend, with an L-shaped portico and one of the city's most delightful small cloisters, to the right. Tasso moved into the church in the last weeks of his life and died while living here; if you're lucky and it's open you can visit the poet's cell, which holds some manuscripts, his chair, his death mask and personal effects.

11

Villa Borghese and north

The area outside the Aurelian walls, to the north and northeast of the city, was once a district of market gardens, olive groves and patrician villas, trailing off into open country. During the Renaissance, these vast tracts of land were appropriated as summer estates by the city's wealthy, particularly those affiliated in some way to the papal court. One of the most notable estates, the **Villa Borghese**, was the summer playground of the Borghese family and is now a public park, home to the city's most significant concentration of museums, including the **Galleria Borghese**, which houses the resplendent art collection of the aristocratic family – a Roman must-see in anyone's book – and the **Villa Giulia**, built by Pope Julius III for his summer repose and now the National Etruscan Museum. North of Villa Borghese, **Flaminio** and other post-Unification residential districts, were until recently not of much interest in themselves, except perhaps for the **Foro Italico** across the river – worth visiting either to see Roma or Lazio play at the Olympic Stadium, or simply to admire Mussolini's stylish, of-its-time sports complex. But recently – as a neat coda to the Foro Italico – Renzo Piano's **Auditorium** complex and Zaha Hadid's **MAXXI** have reinvented Flaminio as a hotbed of modern architecture. It's still a sleepy neighbourhood, but definitely worth visiting for these attractions, and for food and fun there are restaurants and increasingly lively nightlife across the river in the **Ponte Milvio** area, or posher fare just to the east in **Parioli**.

Villa Borghese

Immediately above Piazza del Popolo, the hill known as the **Pincio** marks the edge of the city's core and the beginning of a collection of parks and gardens that forms Rome's largest central open space – **Villa Borghese**. Made up of the grounds of the seventeenth-century palace of Scipione Borghese, which were bought by the city at the turn of the twentieth century, it's a huge area, and its woods, lake and grass, crisscrossed by roads, are about as near as you can get to peace in the city

(11)

Villa Borghese vehicle rentals

You can **rent** bikes, go-karts, rollerblades, segways and – the most popular option – a *risciò* (a sort of pedal-driven chariot with a small electric motor) from various places in the park, and all make getting around much easier.

Bikes, *risciò*, etc are available from two places in the Pincio Gardens (one on the corner of Viale Obelisco and Viale Orologio, and a second by the waterclock); outside the Casa del Cinema; and outside the zoo. Segways are available from a booth on the Piazza del Popolo side of the Pincio Gardens.

Prices are as follows: bikes from €4/hr, €10/3hr, €12/day; mountain bikes from €5/hr, €12/3hr, €15/day; tandems from €8/hr, €20/3hr, €25/day; go-karts from €5/hr; rollerblades from €5/hr; 2-person *risciò* from €10/hr, 4-person from €20/hr; segways from €8/30min, €15/hr, €60/day.

---

centre. There are any number of attractions for those who want to do more than just stroll or sunbathe: a tiny boating lake, a zoo – renamed the "Bioparco" in an attempt to re-brand a previously poor image (see p.295) – and some of the city's finest museums.

The Pincio Gardens

Further along, on the edge of the Villa Borghese, the **Pincio Gardens**, laid out by Valadier in the early nineteenth century and fringed with dilapidated busts of classical and Italian heroes, give fine views over the roofs, domes and TV antennae of central Rome, right across to St Peter's and the Janiculum Hill. The view is the

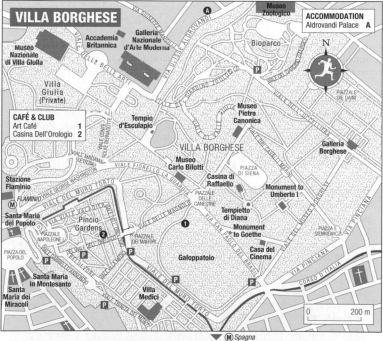

main event here, but the benches are pleasantly shaded and a good place to take some weight off your feet, and the nineteenth-century **waterclock** at the back is a quirky attraction.

Galleria Borghese

The best place to make for first, if you want some focus to your wanderings, is the Casino Borghese itself, on the far eastern side, which was built in the early seventeenth century and turned over to the state when the gardens became city property in 1902 as the **Galleria Borghese**, Piazza Scipione Borghese 5 (Tues–Sun 8.30am–7.30pm; €10.50, 18- to 25-year-olds €7.25; pre-booked visits obligatory at ⓣ06.32.810 or online at ⓦwww.ticketeria.it). Reopened several years ago after a lengthy restoration, Galleria Borghese has taken its place as one of Rome's great treasure houses and should not be missed.

Some history

When Camillo Borghese was elected pope and took the papal name Paul V in 1605, he elevated his favourite nephew, **Scipione Caffarelli Borghese**, to the cardinalate and put him in charge of diplomatic, ceremonial and cultural matters at the papal court. Scipione possessed an infallible instinct for recognizing artistic quality, and, driven by ruthless passion, used fair means or foul to acquire prized works of art. He was also shrewd enough to patronize outstanding talents such as Gian Lorenzo Bernini, Caravaggio, Domenichino, Guido Reni and Peter Paul Rubens. To house the works of these artists, as well as his collection of antique sculpture and other pieces, he built the Casino, or summerhouse, predictably sparing no expense. The palace, which was built in the early 1600s, is a celebration of the ancient splendour of the Roman Empire: over the years its art collection has been added to, and its rooms redecorated – most notably during the last quarter of the eighteenth century, when the ceilings were re-done to match the artworks in each room. The recent restoration of the sumptuous interior seemed to go on forever, but now the gallery's Roman-era mosaics, rich stucco decorations and trompe l'oeil ceilings provide the perfect surroundings in which to enjoy the artworks that Cardinal Scipione Borghese collected so voraciously.

The porch and entrance hall

Entrance is through a **porch**, which displays classical sculpture, notably several large statues of Dacian prisoners from the time of the Emperor Trajan. Inside, the **entrance hall** has a splendid ceiling by Marino Rossi, painted in 1775–78, depicting the foundation and early history of Rome – Jupiter is in the centre, surrounded by various moral and spiritual attributes and historical and mythological characters such

Pauline Borghese

Pauline Borghese, the sister of Napoleon and married (reluctantly) to the reigning Prince Borghese, was a shocking woman in her day, with grand habits. There are tales of jewels and clothes, of the Negro who used to carry her from her bath, of the servants she used as footstools, and, of course, of her long line of lovers. The statue of her in the Villa Borghese was considered outrageous by everyone but herself: when asked how she could have posed almost naked, she simply replied, "Oh, there was a stove in the studio." Interestingly, the couch on which she reposes originally had a kind of clockwork mechanism inside, which allowed the statue to rotate while the viewer remained stationary.

as Romulus, Remus and the she-wolf. On the floor, a series of Roman mosaics from about 320 AD depict gladiators fighting and killing various animals and each other – a circle with a line drawn through it next to the name indicates the deceased, and blood gushes gruesomely from the pierced throats and hearts of the animals. Among a number of notable statues, there's a *Bacchus* from the second century AD, a *Fighting Satyr*, and, on the wall facing the entrance door, a melodramatic piece in marble of Marcus Curtius flinging himself into the chasm (see p.84) – his horse is a Roman sculpture and the figure is by Bernini's father. There are also colossal heads of the emperors Hadrian and Antoninus Pius on the right, and a female head of the Antonine period, with a lotus flower to represent Isis, on the left.

The ground floor

The **ground floor** beyond the entrance hall contains sculpture, a mixture of ancient Roman items and seventeenth-century works, roughly linked together with late-eighteenth-century ceiling paintings showing scenes from the Trojan War. The first room off the entrance hall, whose paintings depict the *Judgement of Paris*, has as its centrepiece Canova's famous statue of *Pauline Borghese* posed as Venus (see box opposite), with flimsy drapery that leaves little to the imagination.

The second ground-floor room, the **Room of the Sun**, has a marvellous statue of *David* by Bernini, finished in 1624, when the sculptor was just 25. The face is a self-portrait, said to have been carved with the help of a mirror held for him by Scipione Borghese himself, and its expression of grim determination is perfect. There's more work by Bernini in the next room, where his statue of *Apollo and Daphne* is a dramatic, poised work that captures the split second when Daphne is transformed into a laurel tree, with her fingers becoming leaves and her legs tree trunks. Mocked by Apollo, Cupid had taken revenge by firing a golden arrow which infected the god with immediate and ardent love, and shooting Daphne with a leaden one designed to hasten the rejection of amorous advances. Daphne, the daughter of a river god, called on her father to help her avoid being trapped by Apollo, who was in hot pursuit; her father changed her into a laurel tree just as Apollo took her into his arms – a desperately sad piece of drama to which Bernini's statue does full justice. This statue also caused a great scandal when it was unveiled. The poet and playwright, Maffeo Barberini, who later became Pope Urban VIII, wrote a couplet in Latin, which is inscribed on the base, claiming that all who pursue fleshly lusts are doomed to end up holding only ashes and dust.

Next door, the walls of the large **Room of the Emperors** are flanked by red porphyry seventeenth- and eighteenth-century busts of Roman emperors, facing another Bernini sculpture, *The Rape of Proserpine*, dating from 1622, a coolly virtuosic work that shows the story of the carrying off to the underworld of the beautiful nymph Proserpine, daughter of Gaia, goddess of the earth. The brutal Pluto grasps the girl in his arms, his fingers digging into the flesh of her thigh as she fights off his advances, while the three-headed form of Cerberus snaps at their feet.

In the small room next door, there's a marvellous statue of a sleeping hermaphrodite, from the first century AD, and a large porphyry Roman bathtub whose feline feet are almost modern in style. But it's back to the Berninis in the following **Aeneas Room**, where a larger-than-life statue of Aeneas, carrying his father, Anchises, out of the burning city of Troy, was sculpted by both father Pietro and his then 15-year-old son Gian Lorenzo in 1613. The statue portrays a crucial event in Roman myth when, after the defeat of the Trojans, Aeneas escaped with his family and went on a long voyage that ended up on the shores of what became Latium – his descendants eventually founding the city of Rome. The old man carries the statues representing their family household gods; the small boy carrying a flaming pot with what became the Vestal Fire is Aeneas's son Ascanius. Also here, in the far corner, is a late, in fact unfinished work by Bernini, *Truth Revealed in Time*, done late in his career when he had been accused of faulty architectural work in part of St Peter's. Truth, with a sappy look on her face, clutches the sun, representing time, to her breast.

The **Egyptian Room**, beyond, contains artefacts, friezes and paintings with an Egyptian theme, Roman floor mosaics, and a statue of a satyr on a dolphin dating from the first century AD. Further on, the **Room of Silenus** contains a variety of paintings by Cardinal Scipione's protégé **Caravaggio**, including the *Madonna of the Grooms* from 1605 on the right wall, a painting that at the time was considered to have depicted Christ far too realistically to hang in a central Rome church – Cardinal Scipione happily bought it for his collection. Take note also of Caravaggio's self-portrait as Bacchus as you enter, gazing lasciviously at the coy boy with the basket of fruit opposite. *St Jerome* on the far wall is captured writing at a table illuminated only by a source of light that streams in from the upper left of the picture, while *David Holding the Head of Goliath* on the right wall, sent by Caravaggio to Cardinal Scipione from exile in Malta, where he had fled to escape capital punishment for various crimes, is perhaps the last painting he ever did; the head of Goliath is believed to be a self-portrait. The cardinal managed to get the artist off, but Caravaggio died of malaria after landing in Italy at Porto Ercole, north of Rome, in 1610.

The first floor

Upstairs – reachable by a spiral staircase out of the Room of the Emperors – houses one of the richest small collections of paintings in the world. Turn left for a room with several important works by **Raphael**, his teacher Perugino and other

▲ Villa Borghese

masters of the Umbrian School from the late fifteenth and early sixteenth centuries, not least Raphael's *Deposition* over the fireplace, produced in 1507 for a noble of Perugia in memory of her son, and pillaged from Perugia cathedral by associates of Cardinal Scipione. Look also for the *Lady with a Unicorn* and *Portrait of a Man*, by Perugino, and, over the door, a copy of the artist's portrait of a tired-out Julius II, painted in the last year of the pope's life, 1513. The room also contains a beautiful, sensitive *Virgin with Child* by Giuliano Romano, while nearby Andrea del Sarto tackles the same subject with slightly more gusto. The next room contains more early-sixteenth-century paintings, prominent among which are Cranach's *Venus and Cupid with a Honeycomb*, from 1531, and Brescianino's *Venus and Two Cupids*, from about 1520 – both remarkable at the time for their departure from classical models in their treatment of their subjects. The Cranach *Venus*, dressed in a diaphanous robe, shows Cupid carrying a honeycomb, demonstrating the dangers of carnal love. Opposite, they are complemented perfectly by Correggio's saucy *Danae*.

Retracing your steps, look out for two early-sixteenth-century copies of Leonardo's *Leda and the Swan* (the original has been lost), Lorenzo Lotto's touching *Portrait of a Man*, a soulful study that hints at grief over a wife lost in childbirth, symbolized by the tiny skull and rose petals under the subject's right hand, and, in the large **Gallery of Lanfranco** at the back of the building, a series of self-portraits done by Bernini at various stages of his long life. Next to these are a lifelike bust of Cardinal Scipione executed by Bernini in 1632, accurately portraying him as a worldly connoisseur of fine art and fine living, and a smaller bust of Pope Paul V, also by Bernini. Next door's *Young Man and Faun* is the sculptor's earliest-known work, from 1615.

Beyond here a small room has Dosso Dossi's *SS Cosma e Damiano* and Jacopo Bassano's lively and naturalistic *Last Supper*, while further on there are two paintings by Domenichino: the *Cuman Sibyl* and a large *Diana*, the latter showing the goddess and her attendants celebrating and doing a bit of target practice – one of them has just shot a pheasant through the head and everybody else is jumping with enthusiasm; in the foreground a young nymph, lasciviously bathing, looks out with a lustful expression. Scipione was so keen on the work that he apparently imprisoned the artist until he agreed to sell it. Next, the **Room of Psyche** has, along with works by Bellini and the other Venetians of the early 1500s, Titian's *Sacred and Profane Love*, painted in 1514 when he was about 25 years old, to celebrate the marriage of the Venetian noble Nicolò Aurelio (whose coat of arms is on the sarcophagus). It shows his bride, Laura Bagarotto, dressed in white representing Sacred Love, and Venus, representing Profane Love, carrying a lamp symbolizing the eternal Love of God. The bride cradles a bowl of jewels that refer to the fleeting happiness of life on earth.

Museo Carlo Bilotti

Recently opened in the orangery of the Villa Borghese, the **Museo Carlo Bilotti** (Tues–Sun 9am–7pm; €6) is, like the Galleria Borghese, made up of a family bequest, this time of Carlo Bilotti – a perfume and cosmetics baron who, until his death in 2006, collected art and hobnobbed with the brightest and best in the international art world. Portraits of him by Larry Rivers, and of his wife and daughter by Andy Warhol, open the exhibition and add to the slightly self-congratulatory air of the place. However, the paintings are beautifully displayed, and act as a nice adjunct to the Modern Art Museum ten minutes' walk away, since most of the 22 works exhibited here are by the great modern Italian painter **Giorgio de Chirico**. It's a small but varied collection of his work, and you get a good sense of de Chirico's versatility, from the Impressionistic *Nude Woman from Behind* to his almost perversely traditional *Self-Portrait with the Head of Minerva* and the pastiche Canaletto scene that hangs next to it. The weird stuff with which he made his name is here too, including *Metaphysics with Biscuits* and *Melancholy of a Street*, and plays on the *Archeologists* theme you might have seen in the Modern Art Museum, although these are 1960s copies of canvases he produced during his earlier "metaphysical" period. If you're a fan, the Casa de Chirico (see p.95) is a kilometre or so southwest of here, near the Spanish Steps.

Museo Pietro Canonica

Across the road from the large oval of the Piazza di Siena, the **Museo Pietro Canonica** occupies the house and studio of the nineteenth-century Italian sculptor (Tues–Sun 9am–7pm; €3). Canonica was an establishment artist and as such not only did the city bequeath him this impressive, castellated bolt hole to live in, but the museum devoted to him is virtually a roll call of European historical names. Canonica seemingly knew everyone and sculpted everybody, and one room alone contains busts of a king of England (Edward VII), the man who took Turkey to independence (Mustafa Kemal Atatürk), numerous Italian royals and nineteenth-century dignitaries, and Pope Benedict XV (a supplement to the artist's memorial to him in St Peter's). Other rooms document nineteenth-century world history – Simón Bolívar astride a stallion (1954), Atatürk again, this time leading the Turkish charge, and an equestrian statue of King Faisal of Iraq (1933) – to name only the most prominent examples of an epic collection.

The museum also includes Canonica's **studio** on the ground floor, still with his tools and the piece he was working on when he died in 1959, along with a couple of portraits of the great man and some of his own botched attempts at landscapes – which show that he was probably right to stick to sculpture. Upstairs are the **apartments** he occupied with his wife, who continued to live here until she died in 1987. The rooms are left much as they were then, with original furniture, the living room with a piano and a score of music on it (Canonica was also an accomplished musician and composer) and family photographs. Oddly, there is only one that shows Canonica himself, a holiday snap taken in the mountains, on the right side of the dining room.

Galleria Nazionale d'Arte Moderna

Villa Borghese's two other major museums are situated on the northwestern side of the park, along the Viale delle Belle Arti, in the so-called "Academy Ghetto" – the Romanian, British, Dutch, Danish, Egyptian and other cultural academies are all situated here. The **Galleria Nazionale d'Arte Moderna**, Via delle Belle Arti 131 (Tues–Sun 8.30am–7.30pm; €8; ⓦ www.gnam.arti.beniculturali.it), is probably the least obviously appealing building here, a huge, lumbering, Neoclassical construction housing a wide selection of nineteenth- and twentieth-century Italian (and a few foreign) names. However, the museum's compact and surprisingly engaging collection is beautifully displayed – and can make a refreshing change after several days of having the senses bombarded with Etruscan, Roman and Renaissance art. There is also a reasonably priced **café**, the *Caffè delle Arti*, out the back door at Via Gramsci 73, which is part of the gallery complex and is the best place to grab something to eat and drink if you're wilting.

The **ground floor** is given over to nineteenth-century works, with the left side concentrating on works up to 1883, including early pieces by the so-called Macchiaioli School of Tuscany – Fattori, Lega, Cecioni, Nino Costa – with a giant

The Etruscans

The **Etruscans** remain something of a historical mystery. We know that they lived in central Italy – in Etruria – from around 900 BC until their incorporation into the Roman world in 88 BC. However, whether they were native to the region, or whether they had originally migrated here from overseas, specifically from Asia Minor, remains a matter of debate. The Romans borrowed heavily from their civilization, and thus in many ways the influence of the Etruscans is still felt today: our alphabet, for example, is based on the Etruscan system, and bishops' crooks and the "fasces" symbol (a bundle of rods with an axe that is found, among other places, behind the speaker's rostrum in the US House of Representatives) are just two other Etruscan symbols that endure. The Etruscans were also masters of working in terracotta, gold and bronze, and accomplished carvers in stone, and it is these skills – together with their obvious sensuality and the ease with which they appeared to enjoy life – that make a visit to the Villa Giulia so beguiling.

statue of Hercules by Canova in the large central hall. Rooms on the right side are devoted to later nineteenth-century paintings, including more work from Fattori and other like-minded Italian Impressionists, while the large hall is dominated by Ettore Ferrari's 1886 model for his statue of Bruno Giordano in Campo de' Fiori (see p.61) and some mighty battle scenes promoting the glory and sacrifice of the Italian Unification, including Fattori's *Battle of Custoza*. The rooms beyond contain a handful of paintings by Courbet, Degas, Van Gogh and Cézanne, as well as the Dutchman Mesdag, amongst Italian works of the same period, although the peculiar mystic paintings of the "Divisionist" Gaetano Previati stand out – indeed they're so odd they get an entire room to themselves.

The museum's twentieth-century collection on the **upper level** has sculptural works by Rodin and the Croatian Ivan Meštrović, but the most significant parts of the collections are Italian. These include early works by Giacomo Balla, with a view of the Villa Borghese, divided into fifteen different panels, and some painterly portraits from everyday life – *La Pazza* and *Il Mendicante*. The swirling, Futurist abstract works he painted five years later hang in the next room, alongside paintings by his student Boccioni. There are also pieces by Carlo Carrà and Giorgio Morandi, while Giorgio de Chirico (see p.95) dominates one room. Later rooms focus on the art of the 1930s, some of it – like Libero Andreotti's *Affrico e Mensola* and Sironi's *The Constructor* – iconic and fascistic in look and intent, before leading on to the totally abstract paintings of Jackson Pollock, Mark Rothko and Cy Twombly, Rome's own American artist, who has lived in the city for most of his life.

Museo Nazionale Etrusco di Villa Giulia

Villa Giulia, five minutes' walk away towards Via Flaminia, is a harmonious collection of courtyards, loggias, gardens and temples put together in a playful Mannerist style for Pope Julius III in the mid-sixteenth century, and arguably a more essential stop than the Modern Art Museum. It's home to the **Museo Nazionale Etrusco di Villa Giulia**, Piazzale Villa Giulia 9 (Tues–Sun 8.30am– 7.30pm; €4), which, along with the Etruscan collection in the Vatican, is the world's primary collection of Etruscan treasures, and a good introduction – or conclusion – to the Etruscan sites in Lazio, which between them contributed most of the artefacts on display here. It's not an especially large museum, but it's worth taking the trouble to see the whole collection.

The east wing

The entrance room of the **east wing** houses two pieces of Etruscan sculpture, one showing a man astride a seahorse, a recurring theme in ancient Mediterranean art, and an oddly amateurish centaur – basically a man pasted to the hindquarters of a horse – both from Vulci and dating from the sixth century BC. The next rooms contain bronze objects from the seventh and sixth centuries BC – urns used to contain the ashes of cremated persons, among which a beautiful bronze example, in the shape of a finely detailed dwelling hut, stands out – and a number of terracotta votive offerings of anatomical parts of the human body, their detail alluding to the Etruscans' accomplishments in medicine. A gold dental bridge shows their skill at dentistry too.

The next room displays items found in Veio – among them Hercules and Apollo disputing over the sacred hind which Apollo had shot and Hercules claimed. Next door, in the octagonal room, the remarkable *Sarcophagus of the Married Couple* (dating from the sixth century BC, and actually containing the ashes of the deceased rather than the bodies), is from Cerveteri, and is one of the most famous pieces in the museum – a touchingly lifelike portrayal of a husband and wife lying on a couch. He has his right arm around her; she is offering him something from her right hand, probably an egg – a recurring theme in Etruscan art. Their clothes are modelled down to the finest detail, including the laces and soles of their shoes, and the pleats of the linen and lacy pillowcases. In case you're wondering, the holes in the backs of their heads, and at other spots, are ventilation holes to prevent the terracotta from exploding when the hollow piece was fired. Beyond are more finds from Cerveteri: hundreds of vases, pots, drinking vessels and other items, and, among a number of busts and images, clearly portraits of real people, a depiction of a man, complete with cauliflower right ear, and a finely stitched cut to the right of his mouth – clearly a tough customer.

Upstairs, in the balcony over the married couple sarcophagus, there are displays on the Etruscan language, and the *cistae* recovered from tombs around Praeneste – drum-like objects, engraved and adorned with figures, that were supposed to hold everything the body needed after death – including a special area devoted to the beautiful and justifiably famous *Ficorini Cista*, made by an Etruscan craftsman named Novios Plautios for a lady named Dindia Malconia and probably a wedding present. In the same room, marvellously intricate pieces of gold jewellery have been worked into tiny horses, birds, camels and other animals. Further on you'll find mostly bronzes, mirrors, candelabra, religious statues and tools used in everyday life. Notice, particularly, the elongated statues of priests and priestesses, some of whom hold eels in their hands and are engaged in some kind of rite. There is also a realistic bronze statuette of a ploughman at work, plodding along behind his oxen.

After this hall you are at the bottom of the "U" curve that forms the building's outline, and holds an enormous collection of **jewellery** – all of it fascinating. Branching off are items and reconstructions from the enormous temple excavated at Pyrgi, Cerveteri's seaport, in the 1960s, including replicas of gold foil plates thought at one time to offer a Rosetta Stone-like key to the Etruscan language – the plates are in three different languages, Etruscan, Punic and Greek, and represent some of the oldest pre-Roman inscriptions ever found. The rooms to the west of here hold items from the very earliest Etruscan collections, together with the story of how everything was brought together, a model of the villa, and original architectural drawings by, among others, Michelangelo.

The atrium and beyond

Exiting the U-shaped room you will find several hundred examples of Etruscan pottery, terracotta and bronze items, including charcoal braziers and pieces of armour, and, remarkably, a trumpet that has not sounded for two thousand years. This gallery will lead you to the steps down to the upper floor of the west wing, which is devoted to the **Faliscians**, a people from northeast Lazio who spoke a dialect of Latin but were culturally Etruscans. This part of the museum was reorganized relatively recently and is clearly labelled in English, with good information in each room from the excavations at Narce, Falerii Nuovi, Civita Castellana and other sites in the Faliscian area. The displays include a drinking horn in the shape of a dog's head that is so lifelike you almost expect it to bark; a *holmos*, or small table, to which the maker attached 24 little pendants; and a bronze disc breastplate from the seventh century BC decorated with a weird, almost modern abstract pattern of galloping creatures.

In the **atrium**, two storeys high, are finds from the temples at Sassi Caduti and the Sanctuary of Apollo in Civita Castellana – Etruscan artistry at its best, with gaudily coloured terracotta figures that leer, run, jump and climb; a beautiful, lifelike torso of Apollo, dating from around the turn of the fourth century BC; and a bust of Juno which has the air of a dignified matron, the flower pattern on her dress still visible, as are her earrings, necklace and crown.

The west wing ground floor

The ground floor of the **west wing** displays more artefacts with obvious connections to the Etruscans, including North African ostrich eggs, an Etruscan symbol of resurrection and rebirth, and mirrors, some of which have mythological events etched on their backs. The next series of galleries has items from Lake Nemi and the Alban Hills in southern Lazio, with an oak log that was used as a coffin and cases of terracotta votive offerings – anatomical parts, babies in swaddling clothes and models of temples and houses. There are also more *cistae*, gold breastplates and belt buckles, bronze pots with griffins' heads looking in to see what's cooking, and a wonderful bronze throne with elaborately worked scenes of hunting, military parades and horse racing.

Museo Hendrik Christian Andersen

Around ten minutes' walk north from Piazzale Flaminio, the **Museo Hendrik Christian Andersen**, Via PS Mancini 18 (Tues–Sun 9am 7.30pm; free), is a delightful small collection – and one of the best of Rome's lesser-known free attractions. Affiliated to the Modern Art Museum, it's devoted to the work of the eponymous Norwegian–American sculptor and painter, who was a friend and contemporary of Henry James and lived in Rome for almost half his long life, producing the giant Neoclassical pieces in grand and heroic poses now in his old **studio**; it's hard to imagine a room more crammed full of elegantly shaped buttocks and penises. Don't miss the cast for his tomb in the Protestant Cemetery (p.143), where he is buried with other members of his family.

Andersen wasn't just a sculptor: in the **gallery** next door are his 1912 plans for a utopian world city, a planned centre of civilization on so epic a scale that not surprisingly it was never built, although Mussolini later got behind it and it's conceivable that his EUR (see p.151) was based at least in part on Andersen's ideas. **Upstairs**, where the artist lived, is more restrained, now given over to his modest paintings of landscapes around Lazio and Campania, as well as a handful of family holiday snaps and scribbled postcards – personal insights into Andersen's full and creative life in Italy.

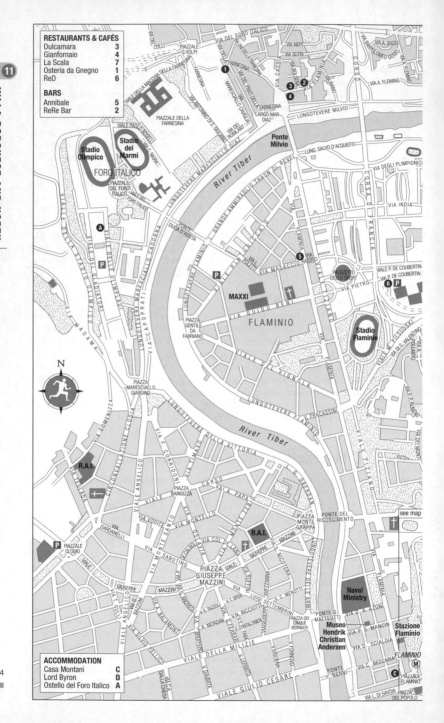

RESTAURANTS & CAFÉS

Dulcamara	3
Gianfornaio	4
La Scala	7
Osteria da Gnegno	1
ReD	6

BARS

Annibale	5
ReRe Bar	2

ACCOMMODATION

Casa Montani	C
Lord Byron	D
Ostello del Foro Italico	A

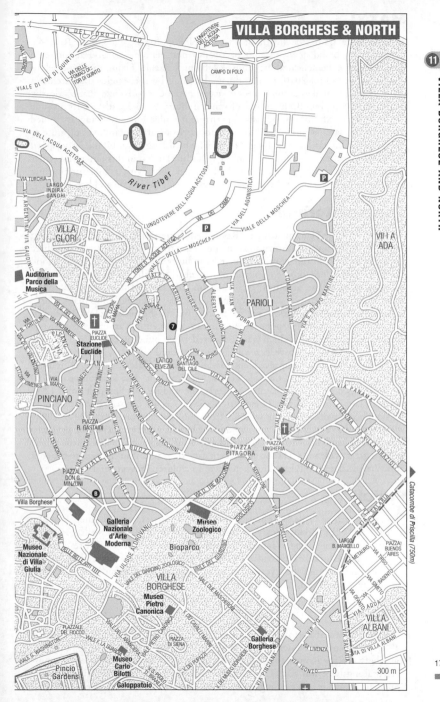

VIA DEL FORO ITALICO

VIA DELLE FORNACI DI TOR DI QUINTO

VIALE DI TOR DI QUINTO

VIA DELLE FORNACI DI TOR DI QUINTO

CAMPO DI POLO

LUNGOTEVERE DELL'ACQUA ACETOSA

VIA DELL'ACQUA ACETOSA

VIA TURCHIA

LARGO INDIRA GANDHI

River Tiber

VIA DELLA MOSCHEA

VIALE DELLA MOSCHEA

VIA DEL CAMP

VIA DELL'AGONISTICA

VIA TIBERIA

VIA ARGENTINA

VIA GAUDINI

P

P

VILLA GLORI

VIA PONTE DELL'ACQUA ACETOSA

VIALE DELLA MOSCHEA

VIA DELLA MOSCHEA

VILLA ADA

Auditorium Parco della Musica

VIALE DEI PARIOLI

VIA RUGGERO

VIA GIAN G. PORRO

VIA S. FILIPPO MARTIRE

VIA TOMASO SALVINI

VIA TS. DEL MONTE

VIA ARCHIMEDE

VIA B. TORTOLINI

V. PISANO

VIA N. MARTELLI

VIA S. VALENTINO

VIA TORQUATO

V. VITTORE DI CAMIA

VIA BARNABA

VIA BERNABA

Stazione Euclide

PIAZZA EUCLIDE

❼

VIA C. PLANA

VIA TUCCIMEI

VIA PIETRO ANTONIO MICHELI

VIA FRANCESCO DENZA

VIA DOMENICO CHELINI

VIA E. MANFRED

LARGO ELVEZIA

PIAZZA SANTIAGO DEL CILE

VIA ALBERTO CADLOLO

VIA FAURO

VIA G. BORSI

VIALE DEI PARIOLI

VIA G. CASTELLINI

PARIOLI

VIA PANAMA

PINCIANO

VIA ETTORE XIMENES

VIA ARCHIMEDE

VIA FILIPPO CIVININI

VIA LUIGI LUCIANI

VIA P. SACCHINI

PIAZZA R. GASTALDI

VIALE ROMANIA

VIA G. ANTONELLI

VIA LISBONA

VIA VILLA GRAZIOLI

VIALE BRUNO BUOZZI

VIA MICHELE

VIA TRE MADONNE

PIAZZA PITAGORA

PIAZZA UNGHERIA

VIALE LIEGI

VIA SEBENICO

VIALE TIMONT

PIAZZALE DON G. MINZONI

Ⓑ

"Villa Borghese"

VIALE DEL GIARDINO ZOOLOGICO

VIA U. ENRISCO

VIA CASSALIA

VIA TAGLIAMENTO

VIA SALARIA

LARGO B. MARCELLO

PIAZZA BUENOS AIRES

VIA METAURO

VIA TIRSO

Galleria Nazionale d'Arte Moderna

VIALE DELLE BELLE ARTI

VIA ULISSE ALDROVANDI

Museo Zoologico

Bioparco

VIALE DEL GIARDINO

VIALE DEL GIARDINO ZOOLOGICO

VIA BASENTO

VIA SINELLO

VIA QUINTO ADDA

Museo Nazionale di Villa Giulia

VILLA BORGHESE

Museo Pietro Canonica

VIALE DEI CAVALLI MARINI

VIA DEL MASCHERON

VILLA ALBANI

VIA DI VILLA ALBANI

PIAZZALE DEL FIOCCO

VIALE DEL ARMERI

VIALE PIETRO CANONICA

VIALE F. LA GUARDIA

PIAZZA DI SIENA

IL BRUGLIO

VIA DEI CAVALLI MARINI

VIA LIVENZA

Galleria Borghese

VIALE G. WASHINGTON

Museo Carlo Bilotti

VIA S. PIA V

VIALE PIETRO

VIA PINCIANA

VIA ISONZO

Pincio Gardens

Galoppatoio

▶ Catacombe di Priscilla (750m)

0   300 m

MAXXI

A ten-minute tram ride north of Piazza del Popolo, at Via Guido Reni 4a, **MAXXI** is a brand-new museum of twenty-first-century art and architecture (Ⓦwww.maxxi.beniculturali.it; tram #2 from Piazzale Flaminio). Opened to much fanfare in mid-2010, in a landmark building by the Anglo–Iraqi architect **Zaha Hadid**, it makes a great modern accompaniment to Renzo Piano's nearby Auditorium complex. Built around a former military barracks, it's mainly a venue for temporary exhibitions, but small permanent collections are being assembled from scratch: late-twentieth-century Italian works of art and archives of influential Italian architects like Pier Luigi Nervi. The **building**, a simultaneously jagged and curvy concrete spaceship that looks like it's just landed in this otherwise rather ordinary part of the city, is worth a visit in its own right, with its long, unravelling galleries and a towering lobby encompassing the inevitable café and bookstore.

The Auditorium

In the heart of the Flaminio district, Rome's **Auditorium** (daily 10am–6pm; free; Ⓣ06.80.242, Ⓦwww.auditorium.com; bus #M from Termini) is in fact three auditoriums built in one complex, their large bulbous shapes making them look like three giant, lead-skinned armadillos crouched together. Designed by everyone's favourite Italian architect, Renzo Piano, and opened in spring 2006, it's a clever building: the foyers all join up and, above, the three buildings make a large amphitheatre, used for outdoor performances given in the piazza below. It's clever, too, in the way it has incorporated the remains of a Republican-era villa between two of the concert halls, which was discovered when building began, and actually halted the project for two years while it was excavated.

Each concert hall is conceived and designed for a different kind of musical performance: the smallest, the Sala Petrassi on the right side, accommodates 700 people and is designed for chamber concerts, the middle Sala Sinopoli holds 1200, while the largest of the three, the eastern Sala Santa Cecilia, can seat 2700 listening to big symphonic works, and is now home to Rome's flagship orchestra, the Academy of Santa Cecilia. You can walk right around the building outside, exploring the Parco della Musica, as it's known. The main entrance is on Via Pietro de Coubertin, where there's a great book and CD shop and decent café, or you can cut through to the park from Viale Maresciallo Pilsudski, where there's a children's playground.

Parioli

The area north of Villa Borghese is the **Parioli** district, whose quiet, winding streets, large villas and lush, leafy gardens make up one of Rome's wealthier neighbourhoods. Its main drag, **Viale dei Parioli**, is home to some decent restaurants, and the **Villa Glori** park provides a splash of green on its northern edge, but the main reason you might find yourself here is before or after attending a concert at the nearby Auditorium.

Villa Ada

Immediately east of Parioli, the enormous expanse of **Villa Ada** is Rome's largest public park, connected with Villa Borghese by Via Salaria – the old trading route between the Romans and Sabines, so called because the main product transported along here was salt. The Villa Ada was once the estate of King Vittorio Emanuele III and is a nice enough place in which to while away an afternoon, with a bucolic atmosphere that is a world away from the busy streets of the city centre; the lake on the Via Salaria side is full of turtles, and you can rent bicycles, canoes or ponies from the southerly reaches of the park, where there is also a children's playground. The original royal villa is now the site of the Egyptian Embassy, but you can also visit the catacombs of Priscilla just outside the park walls (see below), and the "Roma Incontra il Mondo" **world music festival** has been held here every June since 1994, at which – who knows? – you may get to hear the rap-reggae sounds of local band Villa Ada Posse.

The Catacombe di Priscilla

Just outside Villa Ada, and reachable on bus #63 or #92, the **Catacombe di Priscilla** (Tues–Sun 8.30am–noon & 2.30–5pm; €6) are among Rome's most extensive, a frescoed labyrinth of tunnels on three levels that can be visited on regular (obligatory) guided tours. No one quite knows why these catacombs are here, or whether they are Christian or pagan in origin, but some of the city's most recognized martyrs ended up here, a roll call of names that echoes from some of the city centre's most prominent churches – Prassede and Pudenziana, among others. Tours last half an hour and take in a number of locations, best of which is the so-called Greek Chapel whose frescoes, painted between the second and fourth centuries AD, are probably more impressive than you'll see in any of Rome's catacombs, showing the Adoration of the Magi, Daniel in the lions' den, the resurrection of Lazarus, Noah, the sacrifice of Isaac, and other biblical events. There is also the earliest known depiction of the Virgin and Child, though this could simply be a picture of a mother and child, both of whom were probably buried here.

Ponte Milvio

To the west of the Parioli district the Tiber sweeps around in a wide hook-shaped bend. These northern outskirts of Rome aren't particularly enticing, though the **Ponte Milvio**, the old, originally Roman, footbridge where the Emperor Constantine defeated Maxentius in 312 AD, still stands and provides wonderful views of the meandering Tiber, with the city springing up green on the hills to both sides and the silty river running fast below. Inside a **guardhouse** on the right (northern) bank of the Tiber, a marble plaque bears the arms of the Borgia family – including the papal badge in the centre, the shield of Callisto III – featuring a bull – on the right and the arms of Rodrigio Borgia, who later became Pope Alexander VI but was at the time his father's secretary of state, on the left.

But the main thing you'll notice about the bridge is its collection of **padlocks**, placed here by lovers who then throw the keys into the river – an enactment of a ritual popularized by Federico Moccia's best-selling novel, *Ho Voglia di Te* (*I Want You*), published in 2006. The lampposts the padlocks were attached to eventually started to collapse beneath the weight, which was when the council installed the posts you can see here now; but if you can't be bothered to bring your own padlock, there's a website – ⓦ www.lucchettipontemilvio.com – where you can attach a virtual padlock as a symbol of your undying love.

Like the bridge, the area on the northern side of the river, around **Piazzale di Ponte Milvio**, attracts a youthful crowd these days, who increasingly flock here for the cool bars and restaurants that have sprung up in the neighbourhood. There's a cheap and cheerful **market** and a number of good places to eat and drink if you want to break for lunch or just take the weight off for a while – see p.254.

▲ The Foro Italico

Foro Italico

It's just ten minutes' walk from Ponte Milvio – past the huge Italian Foreign Ministry building – to the **Foro Italico** sports centre, one of the few parts of Rome to survive intact pretty much the way Mussolini planned it. This is still used as a sports centre, but it's worth visiting as much for its period feel and architecture as anything else. Its centrepiece is the **Ponte Duca d'Aosta**, which connects the Foro Italico to the town side of the river, and is headed by a white marble obelisk capped with a gold pyramid that is engraved MUSSOLINI DUX in beautiful 1930s calligraphy. The marble finials at the side of each end of the bridge show soldiers in various heroic acts, loading machine guns and cannons, charging into the face of enemy fire, carrying the wounded and so forth, each bearing the face of Mussolini himself – a very eerie sight indeed.

Beyond the bridge, an avenue patched with more mosaics revering "Il Duce" leads up to a fountain surrounded by images of muscle-bound figures revelling in sporting activities. Either side of the fountain are the two main stadiums: the larger of the two, the **Stadio Olimpico** on the left, was used for the Olympic Games in 1960 and is still the venue for Rome's two football teams on alternate Sundays (see p.290). The smaller **Stadio dei Marmi** ("stadium of marbles") is ringed by sixty great male statues, groins modestly hidden by fig leaves, in a variety of elegantly macho poses – each representing both a sport and a province of Italy. It's a typically Fascist monument in many ways, but a rather ironic choice for what was a notoriously homophobic government.

The Vatican

O n the west bank of the Tiber, directly across from Rome's historic centre, the **Vatican City** was established as an independent sovereign state in 1929. It's a tiny territory, with a population of around a thousand, surrounded by high walls on its western side, while its eastern side opens its doors to the rest of the city in the form of St Peter's and its colonnaded piazza.

The Latin name Mons Vaticanus (Vatican Hill) is a corruption of an Etruscan term, indicating a good place for observing the flights of birds and lightning on the horizon – believed to prophesy the future. It's believed that later **St Peter** himself was buried in a pagan cemetery nearby, giving rise to the building of a basilica to venerate his name and the later siting of the headquarters of the Roman Catholic Church here. The Vatican ruled Rome until 1870, when Italian Unification led to an impasse, and a period of over fifty years when the pope didn't leave the Vatican. After reaching an uneasy agreement with Mussolini, the Vatican became a sovereign state in 1929, and nowadays has its own radio station, daily newspaper (*L'Osservatore Romano*), its own version of the euro complete with the pope's head

Vatican practicalities

The **Vatican Museums** (see p.189) and the **Basilica di San Pietro** or **St Peter's** (see p.184) are both open to visitors (knees and shoulders must be covered for St Peter's). For opening times and prices, see the individual attractions below.

It's also possible to visit the lovely **Vatican Gardens**, which offer great views of St Peter's. You can only visit on a guided tour (daily except Wed & Sun; 2hr; book in advance on ☎06.6988.3145 or 06.6988.4676, ⓦwww.vatican.va; €31 per person, payable on the day). Tickets include entry to the Vatican Museums so you'll probably want to make a day of it; the dress code is as for St Peter's.

You can also, if you wish, attend a **papal audience**: these happen once a week, on Wednesdays at 10.30am in the Audiences Hall of Paul VI on the south side of St Peter's, and are by no means one-to-one affairs – you'll be with hundreds of others. During the summer months they are occasionally held in the square or at the pope's country residence in Castel Gandolfo (see p.215). They're free, you don't have to be a Catholic to attend and it's often possible to get a place on one if you apply in advance: either in person, to the office of the Prefettura della Casa Pontificia, 00120 Città del Vaticano (Mon & Tues 9am–1pm; ☎06.6988.3114, ⓕ06.6988.5378), on the right-hand side of St Peter's Square, or by sending a letter or fax with your name, your home address, your Rome address, and your preferred date of audience. Bear in mind that the pope also appears each Sunday at noon to bless the crowds on St Peter's Square – or, in late July and throughout August, in Castel Gandolfo.

Finally, if you want to send a postcard with a Vatican postmark, there are Vatican **post offices** on the north side of Piazza San Pietro and inside the Vatican Museums.

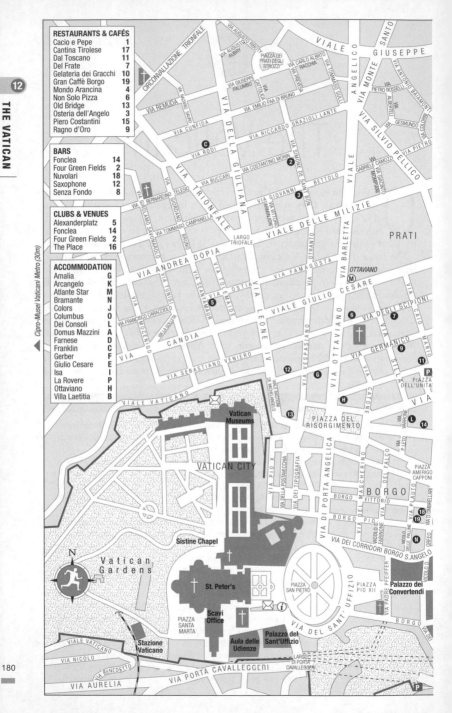

RESTAURANTS & CAFÉS

Cacio e Pepe	1
Cantina Tirolese	17
Dal Toscano	11
Del Frate	7
Gelateria dei Gracchi	10
Gran Caffè Borgo	19
Mondo Arancina	4
Non Solo Pizza	6
Old Bridge	13
Osteria dell'Angelo	3
Piero Costantini	15
Ragno d'Oro	9

BARS

Fonclea	14
Four Green Fields	2
Nuvolari	18
Saxophone	12
Senza Fondo	8

CLUBS & VENUES

Alexanderplatz	5
Fonclea	14
Four Green Fields	2
The Place	16

ACCOMMODATION

Amalia	G
Arcangelo	K
Atlante Star	M
Bramante	N
Colors	J
Columbus	O
Dei Consoli	L
Domus Mazzini	A
Farnese	D
Franklin	C
Gerber	F
Giulio Cesare	E
Isa	I
La Rovere	P
Ottaviano	H
Villa Laetitia	B

Cipro–Musei Vaticani Metro (30m)

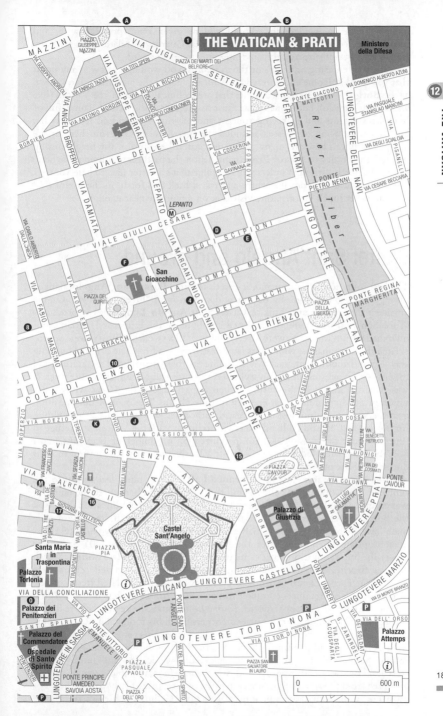

THE VATICAN & PRATI

Ministero della Difesa

PIAZZA GIUSEPPE MAZZINI

VIA LUIGI

PIAZZA DEI MARITI DEI BELFIORE

LUNGOTEVERE DELLE ARMI

River

LUNGOTEVERE DELLE NAVI

PONTE GIACOMO MATTEOTTI

VIA DOMENICO ALBERTO AZUNI

VIA PASQUALE STANISLAO MANCINI

VIA DEGLI SCIALOIA

VIA CESARE BECCARIA

MAZZINI

VIA GIUSEPPE ANDREOLI

VIA GIUSEPPE FERRARI

VIA ENRICO TAZOLI

VIA TITO SPERI

SETTEMBRINI

VIA NICOLA RICCIOTTI

VIA EDOARDO FEDERICO FABBRI

VIA FEDERICO CONFALONIERI

VIA GIUSEPPE AVEZZANA

VIALE DELLE MILIZIE

VIA ANTONIO MORDINI

VIA ANGELO BROFFERIO

BORSIERI

VIA COSSERIA

VIA FORNOVO

VIA GAVINANA

VIA VIGLIENA

PONTE PIETRO NENNI

Tiber

VIA DAMIATA

VIA CARLO ALBERTO DALLA CHIESA

VIA LEPANTO

LEPANTO M

VIALE GIULIO CESARE

VIA MARCANTONIO COLONNA

VIA DEGLI SCIPIONI

VIA POMPEO MAGNO

PIAZZA DELLA LIBERTÀ

LUNGOTEVERE

PONTE REGINA MARGHERITA

San Gioacchino

VIA PAOLO EMILIO

PIAZZA DEL QUIRITI

VIA EZIO

VIA DEI GRACCHI

VIA COLA DI RIENZO

MICHELANGELO

VIA FABIO

VIA MASSIMO

VIA DEI GRACCHI

VIA COLA DI RIENZO

VIA VALADIER

COLA DI RIENZO

VIA VIRGILIO

VIA PLINIO

VIA ORAZIO

VIA TACITO

VIA CICERONE

VIA ENNIO QUIRINO VISCONTI

CESI

VIA FEDERICO CESI

VIA GIOACCHINO BELLI

PONTE REGINA MARGHERITA

VIA PROPERZIO

VIA CATULLO

VIA BOEZIO

VIA HOEZIO

VIA TERENZIO

VIA OVIDIO

VIA CASSIODORO

VIA PIETRO COSSA

VIA UGO BASSI

VIA PALESTRINA

VIA MUZIO CLEMENTI

VIA BENEDETTI PISTRUCCI

VIA CRESCENZIO

VIA MARIANNA DIONIGI

VIA PIETRO CAVALLINI

VIA PER

VIA FRANCESCO ZANCCELLIER

VIA SFORZA PALLAVICINI

VIA DELLA VALE

VIA COLONNA

VIA UGO CALAMATTA

VIA LUIGI CALAMATTA

VIA ULPIANO

VIA DEI COSMATI

VIA ALRCRICO II

VIA BASTIONI

VIA DEL TRE PUPAZZI

VIA GIOVANNI VITELLESCHI

VIA DELLA PORTA CASTELLO

PIAZZA ADRIANA

VIA TRIBONIANO

PIAZZA CAVOUR

PONTE CAVOUR

PONTE UMBERTO I

PIAZZA PIA

Castel Sant'Angelo

Palazzo di Giustizia

LUNGOTEVERE PRATI

VIA TRASPONTINA

Santa Maria in Traspontina

Palazzo Torlonia

VIA DELLA CONCILIAZIONE

Palazzo dei Penitenzieri

LUNGOTEVERE VATICANO

LUNGOTEVERE CASTELLO

PONTE SANT'ANGELO

LUNGOTEVERE UMBERTO I

LUNGOTEVERE MARZIO

VIA DI MONTE BRIANZO

SANTO SPIRITO

Palazzo del Commendatore

Ospedale di Santo Spirito

VIA PIO X

PONTE VITTORIO EMANUELE II

LUNGOTEVERE TOR DI NONA

VIA DI TOR DI NONA

VIA DELL'ORSO

VIA DEI SOLDATI

Palazzo Attemps

PONTE PRINCIPE AMEDEO SAVOIA AOSTA

PIAZZA PASQUALE PAOLI

PIAZZA SAN SALVATORE IN LAURO

VIA DEGLI ACQUASPARTA

VIA G. ZANARDELLI

VIA DI BANCO DI SPIRITO

PIAZZA DELL'ORO

0   600 m

(collector's items, incidentally, should you be given one), postal service, and security service in the colourfully dressed Swiss Guards. Its relationship with the Italian state is, not surprisingly, anything but straightforward.

Apart from entering St Peter's or the museums, you wouldn't know at any point that you had left Rome and entered the Vatican; indeed the area around it, known as the **Borgo**, holds one or two sights that are technically part of the Vatican (like Castel Sant'Angelo), but is one of the most cosmopolitan districts of Rome, full of hotels, restaurants and scurrying tourists and pilgrims – as indeed it always has been since the King of Wessex founded the first hotel for pilgrims here in the eighth century. There are many mid-range hotels here and in the neighbouring nineteenth-century district of **Prati** (named after the pastures that used to lie here) just to the north, although unless you're a pilgrim it's a better idea to base yourself in the more atmospheric city centre and travel back and forth on the useful #64 bus. However much you try, one visit is never anywhere near enough.

Castel Sant'Angelo and around

The best route to the Vatican and St Peter's is across **Ponte Sant'Angelo**, flanked by angels carved to designs by Bernini and known as his "breezy maniacs". On the far side is the great circular hulk of **Castel Sant'Angelo**, Lungotevere Castello 50 (Tues–Sun 9am–7pm; €8.50), designed and built by the Emperor Hadrian as his own mausoleum (his ashes were interred here until a twelfth-century pope appropriated the sarcophagus, which was later destroyed in a fire). The original building was a grand monument, faced with white marble, surrounded by statues and topped with cypresses, similar in style to Augustus's mausoleum across the river. It was renamed in the sixth century, when Pope Gregory the Great witnessed a vision of St Michael here that ended a terrible plague. The mausoleum's position near the Vatican was not lost on the papal authorities, who converted the building for use as a fortress and built a passageway to link it with the Vatican as a refuge in times of siege or invasion – a route utilized on a number of occasions, most notably when the Medici pope, Clement VII, sheltered here for several months during the Sack of Rome in 1527.

Inside, from the monumental **entrance hall**, a spiral ramp leads up into the centre of the mausoleum itself, passing through the chamber where the emperor was entombed and over a drawbridge, one of the defensive modifications made by the Borgia pope, Alexander VI, in the late fifteenth century. It continues to the main level at the top, where a small palace was built to house the papal residents in appropriate splendour. After the Sack of Rome, Pope Paul III had some especially fine renovations made, including the beautiful **Sala Paolina**, which features frescoes by Pierno del Vaga, among others. The gilded ceiling here displays the Farnese family arms, and on the wall is a trompe-l'oeil fresco of one of the family's old retainers coming through a door from a darkened room. You'll also notice Paul III's personal motto, *Festina Lente* ("make haste slowly"), scattered throughout the ceilings and in various corners of all his rooms. Elsewhere, some rooms hold swords, armour, guns and the like, while others are lavishly decorated with grotesques and paintings (don't miss the bathroom of Clement VII on the second floor, with its prototype hot and cold water taps and mildly erotic frescoes). Below are **dungeons** and storerooms (not visitable), which can be glimpsed from the spiralling ramp, testament to the castle's grisly past as the city's most notorious Renaissance prison – Benvenuto Cellini and Cesare Borgia are just two of its more famous detainees. The quiet **café** upstairs offers one of the best views of Rome and excellent coffee.

Ospedale di Santo Spirito

One of the cornerstones of the Borgo neighbourhood is the **Ospedale di Santo Spirito**, Borgo Santo Spirito 2 (tours all year except Aug; Mon 10am & 3.30pm; €7.50), the oldest hospital in Rome, founded in the eighth century by Pope Innocent III, who, as legend has it, was moved after dreaming of dead and unwanted babies being tossed into the Tiber. It was later developed by Sixtus IV as a hospital for pilgrims; the oldest buildings date from this time and have recently been opened to the public. These two giant halls, each 60 metres long and joined by an octagonal hall that used to serve as the main entrance, served as wards until 2000. **Frescoes** illustrating the lives and deeds of Innocent III and Sixtus IV, twelve of whose building projects around Rome are illustrated, line the main walls, while outside the main door a window contains a **barrel** in which *proietti* or abandoned babies were left anonymously – alongside a slot for donations. Behind the two wards the hospital still functions, and tours take in two cloisters – one originally designated for nuns, the other for monks – and the main courtyard of the later Palazzo del Commendatore; you can in fact peek into the latter – an elegant courtyard that's now used as car parking space by the hospital officials – without going on a tour.

If you're in the mood for more hospital history, walk around the corner to the river side of the complex, where, just before the modern entrance, the **Museo Storico dell'Arte Sanitaria**, Lungotevere in Sassia 3 (Mon, Wed & Fri 10am–noon; €4) is currently under restoration but usually houses a rather macabre jumble of ancient medical artefacts. There's a model of the original hospital, anatomical models of body parts and casts, horrible pickled babies in jars, vile-looking scalpels, forceps and syringes as well as the inevitable old-style pharmacy – not for the squeamish.

Piazza San Pietro

The approach to St Peter's from Castel Sant'Angelo is disappointing, and has been so since Mussolini created the approach of **Via della Conciliazione**, when he realized the earlier plan of Pope Nicholas V and swept away the houses of the previously narrow streets and replaced them with this wide, sweeping avenue. Nowadays St Peter's somehow looms too near as you get closer, and the vastness of Bernini's **Piazza San Pietro** is not really apparent until you're right on top of it. In fact, in tune with the spirit of the Baroque, the church was supposed to be even better hidden than it is now: Bernini planned to complete its colonnade with a triumphal arch linking the two arms, so obscuring the view until you were well inside the square, but this was never carried out and the arms of the piazza remain open, symbolically welcoming the world into the lap of the Catholic Church. The **obelisk** in the centre was brought to Rome by Caligula in 36 AD, and it stood for many years in the centre of Nero's Circus on the Vatican Hill (to the left of the church); according to legend, it marked the site of St Peter's martyrdom. It was moved here in 1586, when Sixtus V ordered that it be erected in front of the basilica, a task that took four months and was apparently carried out in silence, on pain of death.

▲ Nuns in Piazza San Pietro

The matching **fountains** on either side are the work of Carlo Maderno (on the right) and Bernini (on the left). In between the obelisk and each fountain, a circular stone set into the pavement marks the focal points of an ellipse, from which the four rows of columns on the perimeter of the piazza line up perfectly, so that the colonnade appears to be supported by a single line of columns.

St Peter's

The piazza is so grand that you can't help but feel a little let down by the sight of **St Peter's**, or to give it its full name, the **Basilica di San Pietro** (daily: April–Sept 7am–7pm; Oct–March 7am–6pm; Ⓦ www.stpetersbasilica.org). From here, its facade – by no means the church's best feature – obscures the dome that signals the building from just about everywhere else in the city. Amid a controversy similar to that surrounding the restoration of the Sistine Chapel a few years ago, the facade has also recently been restored, leaving the previously sober travertine facade a decidedly yellowish grey.

The experience of visiting St Peter's has changed quite a bit over recent years. Not so long ago you could freely stroll around the piazza and wander into the basilica when you felt like it. Now much of the square is fenced off, and you can only enter St Peter's from the right-hand side (exiting to the left); you also have to go through security first, and the queues can be horrendous unless you get here early in the morning. Once you get close to the basilica, you're channelled through various entrances depending on what you want to see first – all of which is strictly enforced by the unsmiling suited functionaries that appear at every turn. A carefree experience it is not.

Some history

Built to a plan initially conceived at the turn of the fifteenth century by **Bramante** and finished off, heavily modified, over a century later by **Carlo**

Maderno, St Peter's is a strange hotchpotch of styles, bridging the gap between the Renaissance and Baroque eras with varying levels of success. It is, however, the principal shrine of the Catholic Church, built as a replacement for the run-down structure erected here by Constantine in the early fourth century on the site of St Peter's tomb. As such it cannot fail to impress: worked on by the greatest Italian architects of the sixteenth and seventeenth centuries, it occupies a site rich with historical significance. In size, meanwhile, St Peter's beats most other churches hands down (although it's not officially the largest in terms of area – that honour belongs to the Basilica of Our Lady of Peace, Côte d'Ivoire).

Bramante had originally conceived a Greek cross plan rising to a high central dome, but this design was altered after his death and revived only with the elderly Michelangelo's accession as chief architect. Michelangelo was largely responsible for the dome, but he too died (in 1564) before its completion. He was succeeded by Vignola, and the dome was eventually finished in 1590 by Giacomo della Porta. Carlo Maderno, under orders from the Borghese Pope Paul V, took over in 1605, and stretched the church into a Latin cross plan, which had the practical advantage of accommodating more people and followed more directly the plan of Constantine's original basilica. But in so doing he completely unbalanced all the previous designs, not least by obscuring the dome (which he also modified) from view in the piazza. The inside, too, is very much of the Baroque era, largely the work of Bernini, who created many of the most important fixtures. The church was finally completed and reconsecrated on November 18, 1626, exactly 1300 years to the day after the original basilica was first consecrated. At least the inscription on the facade leaves no doubt as to who was responsible for getting the job finished: as Pasquino commented at the time, "I thought it was dedicated to St Peter!"

Inside St Peter's

One of the channels on the right side of the piazza funnels you into the basilica, with the other two leading to the underground grottoes (see p.188) and the ascent to the dome (see p.188) – both of the latter have exits into the main church, allowing you to visit the three sights in an order of your choice. Bear in mind that whichever you opt for first, you need to observe the **dress code** to enter, which means no bare knees or shoulders – a rule that is very strictly enforced.

Entering the basilica, to the left of the **Holy Door**, which is only opened every fifty years and was last kept open during the jubilee year 2000 by John Paul II, the first thing you see on the right is Michelangelo's **Pietà**, completed when he was just 24. Following an attack by a vandal a few years back, it sits behind glass, strangely remote from the life of the rest of the building. When you look at the piece, its fame comes as no surprise: it's a sensitive and individual work, and an adept one too, draping the limp body of a grown man across the legs of a woman with grace and ease. Though you're much too far away to read it, etched into the strap across Mary's chest are words proclaiming the work as Michelangelo's – the only piece ever signed by the sculptor and apparently done after he heard his work, which had been placed in Constantine's basilica, had been misattributed by onlookers. You can see the inscription properly on the plaster cast of the statue in the Pinacoteca of the Vatican Museums.

Women dominate the north aisle. Just after the *Pietà*, on a pillar, is a monument to the controversial **Queen Christina of Sweden** (see p.160), in the shape of a huge medallion (she's buried in the grottoes downstairs), while on the next pier along is Bernini's statue of **Countess Mathilda of Tuscany**. At the end of the aisle, the remains of **John XXIII** lie under a wax effigy, and get a lot of attention from pilgrims. It's a suitably humble memorial to a humble pope.

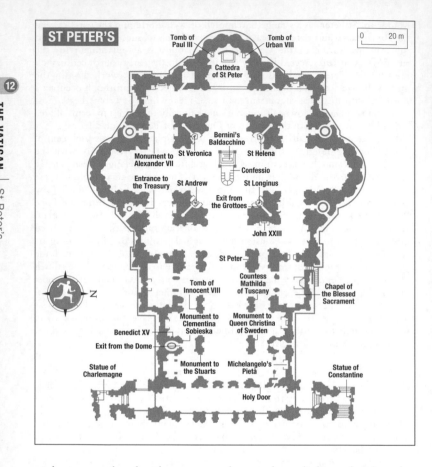

ST PETER'S

Tomb of
Paul III

Tomb of
Urban VIII

Cattedra
of St Peter

0   20 m

Bernini's
Baldacchino

Monument to
Alexander VII

St Veronica

St Helena

Entrance to
the Treasury

St Andrew

Confessio

St Longinus

Exit from
the Grottoes

John XXIII

St Peter

Countess
Mathilda
of Tuscany

Chapel of
the Blessed
Sacrament

Tomb of
Innocent VIII

Monument to
Clementina
Sobieska

Monument to
Queen Christina
of Sweden

Benedict XV

Exit from the Dome

Statue of
Charlemagne

Monument to
the Stuarts

Michelangelo's
Pietà

Statue of
Constantine

Holy Door

John is remembered with more pomp by a modern relief in a chapel on the other side of the basilica in the south aisle, opposite a kneeling rendering of an equally pious pope, **Benedict XV**, the work of Pietro Canonica (see p.170). On a pillar to the right of here is Antonio Pollaiuolo's tomb of the late-fifteenth-century pope, **Innocent VIII** – banker to Queen Isabella of Spain and the financier of Columbus's voyage to the New World – the only tomb to survive from the Constantinian basilica. In the upper statue of the monument the pope holds what looks like a mason's trowel – in fact the spearpoint of Longinus, given to him by the Ottoman sultan Bajazet II to persuade him to keep the sultan's brother and rival in exile in Rome. On the last pillar of the south transept is an austere monument by Canova depicting the last of the **Stuart** pretenders to the English throne, while opposite, over the exit from the dome, is a monument to **Clementina Sobieska**, the wife of the Stuart James III – the third of the three women buried in St Peter's.

As you walk down the **nave**, the size of the building becomes more apparent – and not just because of the bronze plaques set in the floor that make comparisons with the sizes of other churches. For the record, the length of the nave is 186m from the door to the back of the apse, while the width at the crossing is 137m;

even at its narrowest part, the nave is 60m wide. Off the north transept, the wonderful gilded Baroque **Chapel of the Blessed Sacrament** was designed by Borromini, with work by Pietro da Cortona, Domenichino and Bernini. It's not open to the casual sightseer, but it is worthy of a visit, which can be managed if you go there to pray along with the clergy, who maintain a vigil there during the time the basilica is open.

The **dome** is breathtakingly imposing, rising high above the supposed site of St Peter's tomb. With a diameter of 44m, it is only 1.5m smaller than the Pantheon, and the letters of the inscription inside its lower level are nearly 2m high. It's supported by four enormous piers, decorated with reliefs depicting the basilica's "**major relics**": St Veronica's handkerchief, which was used to wipe the face of Christ and is adorned with his miraculous image; the lance of St Longinus, which pierced Christ's side; and a piece of the True Cross, in the pier of St Helen (the head of St Andrew, which was returned to the Eastern Church by Pope Paul VI in 1966, was also formerly kept here). On the right side of the nave, near the pier of St Longinus, the bronze statue of **St Peter** is another of the basilica's most venerated monuments, carved in the thirteenth century by Arnolfo di Cambio; its right foot has been polished smooth by the attentions of pilgrims. On holy days the statue is dressed in papal tiara and vestments.

Bronze was also used in Bernini's **baldachino**, the centrepiece of the sculptor's Baroque embellishment of the interior, a massive 26m high (the height, apparently, of Palazzo Farnese), cast out of 927 tonnes of metal removed from the Pantheon roof in 1633. To modern eyes, it's an almost grotesque piece of work, with its wild spiralling columns copied from columns in the Constantine basilica. But it has the odd personal touch, with female faces expressing the agony of childbirth on each corner except the front right one, where there's a beaming baby – said to have been commissioned by a niece of Bernini's patron (Urban VIII), who gave birth at the same time as the sculptor was finishing the piece. You'll also notice the bees that adorn just about anything to do with the Barberini family – in this case Bernini's patron Urban VIII.

Bernini's feverish sculpture decorates the apse, too, his bronze **Cattedra** enclosing the supposed chair of St Peter in a curvy marble and stucco throne, surrounded by the doctors of the Church (the two with bishops' mitres are St Augustine of Hippo and St Ambrose, representing the Western Church; the two to the rear are portraits of St John Chrysostom and St Athanasius of the Eastern Church). Puffs of cloud surrounding the alabaster window displaying the dove of the Holy Spirit (whose wingspan, incidentally, is 2m) burst through brilliant gilded sunbeams. On the right, the **tomb of Urban VIII**, also by Bernini, is less grand but more dignified, while on the left, the **tomb of Paul III**, by Giacomo della Porta, was moved up and down the nave of the church before it was finally placed here to balance that of Urban. More interesting is Bernini's **monument to Alexander VII** in the south transept, its winged skeleton struggling underneath the heavy marble drapes, upon which the Chigi pope is kneeling in prayer. The Grim Reaper clutches an hourglass: the Baroque at its most melodramatic, and symbolic. On the left sits *Charity*, on the right, *Truth Revealed in Time*; to the rear are *Hope* and *Faith*.

The Treasury

An entrance off the south aisle, under a giant monument to Pius VIII, leads to the steeply priced **Treasury** (daily: summer 9am–6pm; winter 9am–5pm; €6), where a wall tablet records the names of all the popes buried in St Peter's. Along with more recent additions, this holds artefacts from the earlier church: a spiral marble

The Vatican necropolis

The baldachino and confessio just in front are supposed to mark the exact spot of the **tomb of St Peter**, and excavations in the 1940s under Pius XII did indeed turn up – directly beneath the baldachino and the remains of Constantine's basilica – a row of Roman family tombs with inscriptions confirming that the Vatican Hill was a well-known burial ground in classical times. The tombs are decorated with frescoes, mosaic floors and stucco figures, and surround an ancient tomb that is believed to be that of the apostle. You can see what's left of the canopy that used to cover it, a graffitied wall, and behind it a transparent plastic box that may contain his remains – one of 19 such boxes – or at least those of an elderly man who died in the first century AD, though whether or not they are the remains of St Peter will forever be open to question. It is possible to take an English-language **tour** of the Vatican necropolis but you need to book well in advance. The Scavi office is through the arch to the left of St Peter's (Mon–Sat 9am–3.30pm; ☎06.6988.5318, ℻06.6987.3017; ℮scavi@fsp.va; tours cost €12 per person).

column (the other survivors form part of the colonnade around the interior of the dome), once thought to be from the old temple of Jerusalem; a wall-mounted tabernacle by Donatello showing the dead Christ being revealed by angels (the latter carved by Michelozzo); a rich blue-and-gold dalmatic that is said once to have belonged to Charlemagne (though this has since been called into question); the vestments and tiara for the bronze statue of St Peter in the nave of the basilica; and the massive though fairly ghastly late-fifteenth-century bronze tomb of Sixtus IV by Pollaiuolo, viewable from above – said to be a very accurate portrait.

The Grottoes

The middle channel outside leads to the Vatican **Grottoes** (daily: summer 8am–6pm; winter 7am–5pm), which extend right under the main footprint of the main church and hold some column bases from Constantine's original basilica, as well as a number of beautiful mosaics. The majority of the popes are buried here, with the more significant honoured by monuments. Canova's statue of Pius VI hogs the central aisle, while the tombs in the south aisle include a plain slab commemorating Paul VI, John Paul I, who reigned for just 33 days and whose death has been clouded by numerous (mostly disproved) conspiracy theories, and a little further down on the left, John Paul II – whose plain tomb perhaps unsurprisingly receives by far the most attention. The last pope specifically requested that he should rest down here, and perhaps not entirely accidentally he lies in the space previously occupied by the revered John XXIII. Across the aisle the supposed tomb of St Peter sits immediately beneath Bernini's baldachino and is marked by two lions. Leaving, you emerge in the main basilica, by Bernini's statue of St Longinus.

Ascending to the roof and dome

You can make the **ascent to the roof and dome** (daily: May–Sept 8am–6pm; Oct–April 8am–5pm; €7 via lift, €4 using the stairs) by taking the furthest right of the three entrances to the basilica complex, through the northern courtyard between the church and the Vatican Palace. You'll probably need to queue when you get here, and, even with the lift (which takes care of 200 steps), there's a long climb via a slender stairway that spirals up the dome – another 300 or so steps that grow increasingly narrow as you get higher. The views from the gallery around the interior of the dome give you a fantastic sense of the enormity of the church, and the roof has views all around, though sadly you can't get right up behind the statues of the apostles any longer. There's a small **café** serving coffee and soft drinks, along with a souvenir shop, and from here you make the final ascent to the lantern at the top of the dome, from which the **views** over the city are as glorious as you'd expect – pretty much the best in the city. Remember, though, that it is a fairly claustrophobic climb through the double shell of the dome to reach the lantern; you should give it a miss if you're either in ill health or uneasy with heights or confined spaces. The exit leads you back into the south aisle of the church itself.

The Vatican Museums

A fifteen-minute walk out of the northern side of the piazza takes you up to the only part of the Vatican Palace you can visit independently, the **Vatican Museums**, at Viale Vaticano 13 – quite simply, the largest, richest, most compelling and perhaps most exhausting museum complex in the world (Mon–Sat 9am–6pm, last entrance at 4pm; last Sun of each month 9am–2pm, last entrance at 12.30pm; closed public and religious holidays; €15, €8 under-18s and under-26s with student ID, €4 extra for all tickets pre-booked online, last Sun of the month free; audioguides €6; ⓦwww.vatican.va). If you have found any of Rome's other museums disappointing, the Vatican is probably the reason why: so much booty from the city's history has ended up here, and so many of the Renaissance's finest artists were in the employ of the pope, that not surprisingly the result is a set of museums so stuffed with antiquities as to put most other European collections to shame.

As its name suggests, the complex actually holds a collection of museums on very diverse subjects, with displays of classical statuary, Renaissance painting, Etruscan relics and Egyptian artefacts, not to mention the furnishings and decoration of the palace itself. There's no point in trying to see everything in one visit.

Once inside, you have a choice of routes, but the only features you really shouldn't miss are the Raphael Rooms and the Sistine Chapel – and there are plenty of signs to make sure you don't. Above all, decide how long you want to spend here, and what you want to see, before you start; you could spend anything from an hour to the better part of a day inside, and it's easy to collapse from museum fatigue before you've even got to your most important target of interest. Be conservative – the distances between different sections alone can be vast and very tiring.

Finally, bear in mind that in high season at least there may be a **queue** to get into the museums, and even getting here before opening may mean you have to stand in line for a while. It's always a good idea to avoid Mondays, when the rest of the city's museums are closed and everyone flocks to the Vatican and St Peter's, and getting to the museums late morning or after lunch can often mean a shorter wait. But really the best thing to do is to pay a little extra and book online and thereby jump the queues altogether.

The other thing you may want to do is take a **tour**: Enjoy Rome's are popular (see p.39), but you will be in a large group and tours take in St Peter's as well – they cost €30 per person for a three-hour tour; Context (☎06.9762.5204, ⓦwww .contexttravel.com) are very good, and their tours focus just on the Vatican Museums. They charge a pricey €60 a head for a four-hour tour, although groups are no larger than six.

The Vatican Palace and the Museums' layout

The **Vatican Palace** complex was built piecemeal over the years, and in fact the two long corridors that make up most of the "museum" space were built to join the original palace next to St Peter's, constructed around 1450, with a newer building, the Belvedere, built on the higher ground to the north by Innocent VIII in 1490 as a summer casino. Bramante oversaw the connection of the two buildings in the 1500s, creating a vast courtyard that during the early sixteenth century was used for festivals and banquets, until Sixtus V divided it into separate quadrangles. It was divided again by the construction of the nineteenth-century Braccio Nuovo, resulting in its current form.

The museums occupy four principal structures: the **original Palace** at the end nearest St Peter's; the **Belvedere Palace** to the north, and the two long **galleries**. In the middle of all are the three **courtyards**: the **Cortile del Belvedere** at the southern end, the small **Cortile della Biblioteca** in the middle, created by the construction of the Vatican Library and Braccio Nuovo, and, the northernmost of the three, the **Cortile della Pigna** – named after the huge bronze pine cone mounted in the niche at the end, an ancient Roman artefact that was found close to the Pantheon. In classical times this was a fountain with water pouring out of each of its points. Also in this courtyard is a large modern bronze sculpture of a sphere within a sphere, which occasionally rotates – though to an erratic schedule. If you're on a guided tour, you'll stop here to be talked through the Sistine Chapel paintings before going in, as it's forbidden to speak inside. Even if you're not, it can be worth listening in if there's one being given in English, but be discreet.

The old main entrance to the museums was created by Pope Pius XI, in 1932, and its huge bronze spiral staircase, the work of one Giuseppe Momo, provides a dignified exit to the museums. On it are displayed the heraldic arms of all the popes from 1447 (Nicholas II) to Pius XI's predecessor (Benedict XV), while the staircase is in the form of a double helix, one half ascending, the other descending – an idea that Frank Lloyd Wright copied when designing the Guggenheim in New York. The museum entrance has since been modernized, and you now enter through a door in the bastion wall to the left of the monumental entrance, through a large hall and a new monumental marble staircase. An escalator carries you up to the actual museum.

Finally, bear in mind that the collections of the Vatican Museums are in a constant state of restoration, and are often closed and shifted around with little or no notice, though the most important departments are usually open; check ⓦwww.vatican.va for up-to-date details.

Museo Pio-Clementino

To the left of the entrance, the small **Museo Pio–Clementino** is home to some of the Vatican's best classical statuary, including the fourth-century BC statue of *Apoxmenos* in the **vestibule**, in which an athlete is shown scraping dirt from his body. The adjoining **Octagonal Courtyard** holds two statues that proved a huge influence on Renaissance artists: the serene *Apollo Belvedere*, in the left corner as you go in, a Roman copy of a fourth-century BC original, and the first-century BC **Laocoön** in the far left corner. The latter was discovered near Nero's Domus Aurea in 1506 by a ploughman who had inadvertently dug through the roof of a buried part of Trajan's Baths, and depicts the prophetic Trojan priest with his sons being crushed by serpents sent by the gods to punish him for warning his fellow citizens of the danger of the Trojan horse. It is perhaps the most famous classical statue ever, referred to by Pliny who thought it carved from a single piece of marble, and written about by Byron – who described its contorted realism as "dignifying pain". Some scholars theorize that the statue is in fact a sixteenth-century fake by Michelangelo, which isn't as mad is it sounds – Michelangelo did design a substitute arm for the statue, and this was found to be an almost exact match for the "original". Diagonally opposite the *Apollo Belvedere* is a statue of Hermes that Poussin thought the greatest male nude he'd ever seen, while diagonally opposite the *Laocoön* is a group of nineteenth-century classical figures by Canova. In between the two stands a statue of Venus from the second century AD, said to be a portrait of Marcus Aurelius's wife Faustina.

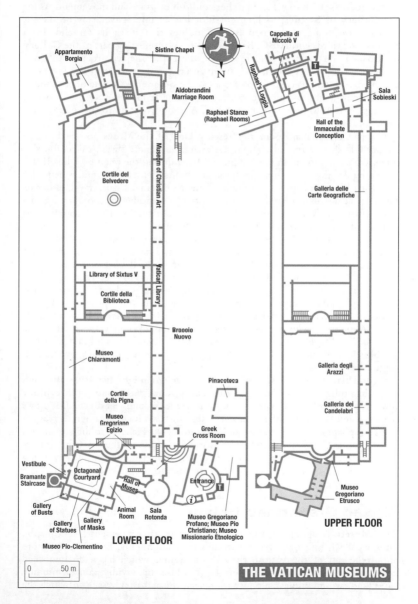

THE VATICAN MUSEUMS

Leave the courtyard between the two howling dogs and you're in the **Animal Room**, named for its animal sculptures, although only a few are of ancient provenance and perhaps the most impressive features are the floor and wall mosaics, all from Hadrian's villa at Tivoli. There are more mosaics from Hadrian's villa through the Gallery of Statues in the small **Gallery of Masks**. This room is often closed but you can still peer in to see these, an ancient Roman toilet, and the statue of *Venus of Cnidos*, the first known representation of the goddess, with towel and pitcher, and full of grace and movement. As for the **Gallery of Statues**, its long corridor has an impressive array of ancient statuary, including two seated Roman nobles that mark its far end, from the first and third century BC. Beyond, the most interesting part of the **Gallery of Busts** is on your immediate right, where the shelves groan with great emperors, from Julius Caesar and Augustus (as a young man and also as a God, crowned with wheat) right up to Trajan at the other end. On the upper shelves you'll see how in subsequent centuries it became fashionable to sport a beard, starting with Antoninus Pius and Marcus Aurelius right up to the intense gaze of Caracalla.

Back past the Animal Room, the frescoed **Hall of the Muses**, so called for the statues that line its central section, has as its centrepiece the so-called *Belvedere Torso*, which was found in the Campo de' Fiori during the reign of Julius II. It's signed by Apollonius, a Greek sculptor of the first century BC, and is generally thought to be a near-perfect example of male anatomy. Its portrayal, either of Hercules sitting on his lion skin or Ajax resting, was studied by most key Renaissance artists, including Michelangelo, who incorporated its turning pose into his portrait of Christ in the *Last Judgement* in the Sistine Chapel.

A short corridor leads to the **Sala Rotonda**, centring on a vast bowl from the Domus Aurea and with a floor paved with a second-century AD Roman mosaic from the town of Otricoli, north of Rome, depicting battles between men and sea monsters. There is more classical statuary around the room, notably a huge gilded bronze statue of a rather dim-witted-looking Hercules, also from the second century AD and the only surviving gilded bronze statue on display in the Vatican Museums. On each side of the statue are busts of the Emperor Hadrian and his lover, Antinous – who is also depicted in the same room, to the right of the entrance, as a huge statue dressed as Bacchus. Opposite this is a beautiful white marble statue of Claudius, in the guise of Jupiter, with his oak-leaf crown and an eagle at his feet.

Beyond here, the **Greek Cross Room** is decorated in Egyptian style, although the pharaonic statues flanking the entry door are nineteenth-century imitations. Another Roman mosaic, from the second century AD, shows Minerva and the phases of the moon, while the two huge porphyry boxes are the sarcophagi of queens Helen and Costanza. On Helen's, soldiers vanquish their enemies, a reference to the fact that she was the mother of Constantine, while that of Costanza, the daughter of the emperor, shows putti carrying grapes, loaves of bread and lambs – a reference to the Eucharist, as she was a devout Christian.

Museo Gregoriano Egizio

The **Museo Gregoriano Egizio**, founded in the nineteenth century by Gregory XVI, isn't one of the Vatican's main highlights. But this says more about the rest of the Vatican than the museum, which has a distinguished collection of ancient Egyptian artefacts. It holds some vividly painted mummy cases (and two mummies), along with *canopi*, the alabaster vessels in which the entrails of the deceased were placed. There is also a partial reconstruction of the Temple of Serapis from Hadrian's Villa near Tivoli, along with another statue of his lover Antinous, who drowned close to the original temple in Egypt and so inspired Hadrian to build his replica – dressed here as Osiris. The Egyptian-style statues in shiny black basalt next door are also Roman imitations, as is the reclining figure of the Nile river god, complete with crocodile, next door. Hadrian collected some original Egyptian bits and pieces, too, some of which are housed in the room which curves around the niche containing the pine cone, including various Egyptian deities – look out for the laughing dwarf god Bes. The next rooms contain Egyptian bronzes from the late pharaonic period and early days of the Roman Empire, including a group of items from the cult of Isis, which became popular in Rome itself. Beyond are a couple of rooms with clay tablets inscribed in cuneiform writing from Mesopotamia; Assyrian, Sumerian and Persian bas-reliefs on stone tablets; and, in the last room, a lovely relief of a kneeling winged god from 850 BC.

Museo Gregoriano Etrusco

Past the entrance to the Egyptian Museum a grand staircase, the Simonetti Stairs, leads up to the **Museo Gregoriano Etrusco**, which holds sculpture, funerary art and applied art from the sites of southern Etruria – a good complement to Rome's specialist Etruscan collection in the Villa Giulia, although you have to be keen on the Etruscans to visit both.

The first exhibits on display are finds from the seventh-century BC **Regolini-Galassi tomb**, which was discovered near Cerveteri, and contained the remains of three Etruscan nobles, two men and a woman; the breastplate of the woman and her huge *fibula* (clasp) are of gold. Take a look at the small ducks and lions with which they are decorated, fashioned in the almost microscopic beadwork for which Etruscan goldsmiths were famous. There's also armour, a bronze bedstead, a funeral chariot and a wagon, as well as a great number of enormous storage jars, in which food, oil and wine were contained for use in the afterlife.

Beyond here are **Etruscan bronzes**, including weapons, candelabra, barbecue sets (skewers and braziers); beautiful make-up cases known as *cistae* and, most notably, the so called *Mars of Todi*, a three-quarter size votive statue found in the Umbrian town of Todi. On a flap of the figure's armour an inscription gives the name of the donor. Further on, there is a large collection of Etruscan sarcophagi and stone statuary from Vulci, Tarquinia and Tuscania in northern Lazio. Particularly interesting here are the finely carved horses' heads from Vulci and the sarcophagus of a magistrate from Tarquinia which still bears traces of the paint its reliefs were coloured with. There is also Etruscan jewellery, with exquisite goldsmith work, crowns of golden oak and laurel leaves, necklaces, earrings and rings set with semiprecious stones and a *fibula* complete with the owner's name etched on it in such small writing that a magnifying glass is provided for you to read it.

Heading up some stairs from this room you come to a series of large rooms which look out from the north side of the Belvedere Palace and offer stunning **views** of the hill of Monte Mario. Inside, you'll find lots of vases, assorted weapons and items of everyday household use, as well as a magnificent terracotta statue of Adonis lying on a lacy couch, found near the town of Tuscania in the 1950s. Finally, don't miss the Greek *krater*, among a lot of Greek pottery found in Etruscan tombs, which shows Menelaus and Ulysses asking the Trojans for the return of Helen. It's housed in a special display case and can be rotated by pressing the electrical switch on the bottom of the case.

Galleria dei Candelabri and Galleria degli Arazzi

Outside the Etruscan Museum, the staircase leads back down to the main – and consequently crowded – Sistine route, taking you first through the **Galleria dei Candelabri**, the niches of which are adorned with huge candelabra taken from imperial Roman villas. This gallery is also stuffed with ancient sculpture, its most memorable piece a copy of the famous statue of *Diana of Ephesus*, on the right, whose multiple breasts are, according to the Vatican official line, bees' eggs. Beyond here the deliberately darkened **Galleria degli Arazzi** has, on the left, Belgian tapestries to designs by the school of Raphael which show scenes from the life of Christ and, on the right, tapestries made in Rome at the Barberini workshops during the 1600s, showing scenes from the life of Maffeo Barberini, who became Pope Urban VIII.

Galleria delle Carte Geografiche and Hall of the Immaculate Conception

Next, the **Galleria delle Carte Geografiche** (Gallery of the Maps), which is as long (175m) as the previous two galleries put together, was decorated in the late sixteenth century at the behest of Pope Gregory XIII, the reformer of the calendar, to show all of Italy, the major islands in the Mediterranean and the papal possessions in France, as well as large-scale maps of the maritime republics of Venice and Genoa. The maps are fantastic, illustrative yet precise, and this gallery, with its ceiling frescoes, illustrating scenes that took place in the area depicted in each adjacent map, is considered by many to be the most beautiful in the entire museum complex.

After the Gallery of the Maps, there is a hall with more tapestries and, to the left, after one more room, the **Hall of the Immaculate Conception**, which sports nineteenth-century frescoes of Pope Pius IX declaring the Doctrine of the Immaculate Conception of the Blessed Virgin Mary on December 8, 1854. From here all visitors are directed to a covered walkway suspended over the palace courtyard of the Belvedere, which leads through to the Raphael Rooms.

The Raphael Rooms

The **Raphael Rooms** or **Stanze di Raffaello** are, apart perhaps from the Sistine Chapel, the Vatican's greatest work of art. This set of rooms formed the private apartments of Pope Julius II, and when he moved in here he commissioned Raphael to redecorate them in a style more in tune with the times. Raphael died before the scheme was complete, but the two rooms that were completed by him, as well as others completed by pupils, are among the highlights of the Renaissance.

Stanza di Costantino

The first of the Raphael Rooms that you come to, the **Stanza di Costantino**, was not in fact done by Raphael at all, but painted partly to his designs about five years after he died by his pupils Giulio Romano, Francesco Penni and Raffaello del Colle, between 1525 and 1531. It shows scenes from the life of the Emperor Constantine, who made Christianity the official religion of the Roman Empire. The enormous painting on the wall opposite the entrance is the *Battle of the Milvian Bridge* by Giulio Romano and Francesco Penni – a depiction of a decisive battle in 312 AD between the warring co-emperors of the West, Constantine and Maxentius. With due regard to the laws of propaganda, the victorious emperor is in the centre of the painting mounted on his white horse while the vanquished Maxentius drowns in the river to the right, clinging to his black horse. The painting to your left as you enter, the *Vision of Constantine* by Giulio Romano, shows Constantine telling his troops of his dream-vision of the Holy Cross inscribed with the legend "In this sign you will conquer". Opposite, the *Baptism of Constantine*, by Francesco Penni, is a flight of fancy – Constantine was baptized on his deathbed about thirty years after the battle of the Milvian Bridge.

Sala dei Chiaroscuri and Cappella di Niccolò V

Beyond the Stanza di Constantino, the **Sala dei Chiaroscuri** was originally painted by Raphael, but curiously Pope Gregory XIII had his paintings removed and the room repainted in the rather gloomy style you see today – although there is a magnificent gilded and painted ceiling which bears the arms of the Medici. Through the windows you can glimpse a covered balcony known as **Raphael's Loggia**, which was built by Bramante in 1513 and decorated by Raphael and his pupils, but there's usually no entry to it. A small door on the other side of the room leads into the little **Cappella di Niccolò V**, with wonderful frescoes by Fra Angelico painted between 1448 and 1450, showing scenes in the lives of saints Stephen and Lawrence.

Stanza di Eliodoro

From here head straight through the souvenir shop to the **Stanza di Eliodoro**, the first of the Raphael rooms proper. The fresco on the right of the entrance, *The Expulsion of Heliodorus from the Temple*, tells the story of Heliodorus, the agent of the Eastern king Seleucus IV, who was slain by a mysterious rider on a white horse while trying to steal the treasure of Jerusalem's Temple. It's an exciting piece of work, painted in the years 1512–14 for Pope Julius II, and the figures of Heliodorus, the horseman and the fleeing men are adeptly done, the figures almost jumping out of the painting into the room. The group of figures on the left, however, is more interesting – Pope Julius II, in his papal robes, Giulio Romano, the pupil of Raphael, and, to his left, Raphael himself in a self-portrait.

On the left wall as you enter, the *Mass of Bolsena* is a bit of anti-Lutheran propaganda, and relates a miracle that occurred in the town in northern Lazio in the 1260s, when a German priest who doubted the transubstantiation of Christ found the wafer bleeding when he broke it during a service – the napkin onto which it bled can be seen in the cathedral at Orvieto, 90km north of Rome. The pope facing the priest is another portrait of Julius II. The composition is a neat affair, the colouring rich, the onlookers kneeling, turning and gasping as the miracle is realized. On the window wall opposite, the *Deliverance of St Peter* shows the saint being assisted in a jail-break by the Angel of the Lord – a night scene, whose clever chiaroscuro predates Caravaggio by nearly one hundred years. It was painted by order of Pope Leo X, as an allegory of his imprisonment after a battle that took place in Ravenna a few years earlier. Finally, on the large wall opposite *The Expulsion of Heliodorus from the Temple*, *Leo I Repulsing Attila the Hun* is an allegory of the difficulties the papacy was going through in the early 1500s and shows the chubby cardinal Giovanni de' Medici, who succeeded Julius II and became Leo X in 1513. Leo later had Raphael's pupils paint a portrait of himself as Leo I, so, confusingly, he appears twice in this fresco, as pope and as the equally portly Medici cardinal just behind.

Stanza della Segnatura

The next room, the **Stanza della Segnatura**, or Pope's Study, is probably the best known – and with good reason. Painted in the years 1508–11, when Raphael first came to Rome, the subjects were again the choice of Julius II, and, composed with careful balance and harmony, it comes close to the peak of the painter's art.

The School of Athens, on the near wall as you come in, steals the show, a representation of the triumph of scientific truth in which all the great minds of antiquity are represented. Plato and Aristotle discuss philosophy at the centre of the painting: Aristotle, the father of scientific method, motions downwards; Plato, pointing upward, indicating his philosophy of otherworldly spirituality, is believed to be a portrait of Leonardo da Vinci. On the far right, the crowned figure holding a globe was meant to represent the Egyptian geographer, Ptolemy; to his right the young man in the black beret is Raphael, while in front, demonstrating a theorem to his pupils on a slate, the figure of Euclid is a portrait of Bramante. Spread across the steps is Diogenes, lazily ignorant of all that is happening around him, while to the left Raphael added a solitary, sullen portrait of Michelangelo as Heraclitus writing – a homage to the artist, apparently painted after Raphael saw the first stage of the Sistine Chapel almost next door. Other identifiable figures include the beautiful youth with blonde hair on the left looking out of the painting, Francesco Maria della Rovere, placed here by order of Julius II. Della Rovere, the Duke of Urbino, also appears as the good-looking young man to the left of the seated dignitaries, in the painting opposite, the *Disputation over the Sacrament*, an allegory of the Christian religion and the main element of the Mass, the Blessed Sacrament – which stands at the centre of the painting being discussed by all manner of popes, cardinals, bishops, doctors, even the poet Dante.

Stanza dell'Incendio

The last room, the **Stanza dell'Incendio**, was the last to be decorated, to the orders (and the general glorification) of Pope Leo X, and in a sense it brings together three generations of work. The ceiling was painted by Perugino, Raphael's teacher, and the frescoes completed to Raphael's designs by his pupils (notably Giulio Romano). The most striking of them is the **Fire in the Borgo**, facing the main window – an oblique reference to Leo X restoring peace to Italy after Julius II's reign but in fact describing an event that took place during the reign of Leo IV, when the pope stood in the loggia of the old St Peter's and made the sign of the cross to extinguish a fire. As with so many of these paintings, the chronology is deliberately crazy: Leo IV is in fact a portrait of Leo X, while on the left, Aeneas carries his aged father Anchises out of the burning city of Troy, two thousand years earlier. This last Raphael Room is connected to the **Sala Sobieski**, with its nineteenth-century painting of the Polish king driving Turks out of Europe, by the small **Chapel of Urban VI**, with frescoes and stuccoes by Pietro da Cortona.

Appartamento Borgia

Outside the Raphael Rooms, you can either proceed direct to the Sistine Chapel, or take the stairs down to the **Appartamento Borgia**, which was inhabited by Julius II's hated predecessor, Alexander VI – a fact which persuaded Julius to move into the new set of rooms he called upon Raphael to decorate. Nowadays host to a large collection of **modern religious art**, the Borgia rooms were almost exclusively decorated by Pinturicchio in the years 1492–95, on the orders of Alexander VI, though sadly the lighting is poor – more focused on the modern art than it is on the ceilings. The first room is named after its ceiling decorations of the twelve Sibyls, and the next shows Euclid kneeling at Geometry's throne above the fireplace, but it's the frescoes in the third, the **Sala dei Santi**, that are especially worth seeing, typically rich in colour and detail and depicting the legend of Osiris and the Apis bull – a reference to the Borgia family symbol. Among other images is a scene showing St Catherine of Alexandria disputing with the Emperor Maximilian, in which Pinturicchio has placed his self-portrait behind the emperor. The Arch of Constantine is clearly visible in the background. The figure of St Catherine is said to be a portrait of Lucrezia Borgia, and the room was reputedly the scene of a decidedly un-papal party to celebrate the first of Lucrezia's three marriages, which ended up with men tossing sweets down the fronts of the women's dresses.

The religious collection is spread throughout the main apartments and the forty or so rooms include works by some of the most famous names in the **modern art** world: a typically tortured Van Gogh *Pietà*; an exquisite pastel drawing of Joan of Arc by Redon; liturgical vestments designed by Matisse; a fascinating *Landscape with Angels* by Salvador Dalí, donated by King Juan Carlos of Spain; and one of Francis Bacon's studies of Innocent X after Velázquez.

The Sistine Chapel

Steps lead up from the Appartamento Borgia to the **Sistine Chapel** (Cappella Sistina), a huge, barn-like structure built for Pope Sixtus IV between 1473 and 1481. It serves as the pope's official private chapel and the scene of the conclaves of cardinals for the election of each new pontiff. The ceiling paintings here, and the *Last Judgement* on the wall behind the altar, together make up arguably the greatest masterpiece in Western art, and the largest body of painting ever planned and executed by one man – Michelangelo. They are also probably the most viewed paintings in the world: it's estimated that on an average day about 15,000 people trudge through here to take a look, and during the summer and on special occasions the number of visitors can exceed 20,000. It's useful to carry a pair of binoculars with you in order to see the paintings better, but bear in mind that it is strictly forbidden to take pictures of any kind in the chapel, including video, and it is also officially forbidden to speak – although this is something that is rampantly ignored.

The wall paintings

Upon completion of the structure, Sixtus brought in several prominent painters of the Renaissance to decorate the walls. The overall project was under the management of Pinturicchio and comprised a series of paintings showing (on the left as you face the altar) scenes from the life of **Moses** and, on the right, scenes from the life of **Christ**. There are paintings by, among others, Perugino, who painted the marvellously composed cityscape of *Jesus Giving St Peter the Keys to Heaven*; Botticelli, with *The Trials of Moses* and *Cleansing of the Leper*; and Ghirlandaio, whose *Calling of St Peter and St Andrew* shows Christ calling the two fishermen to be disciples, surrounded by onlookers, against a fictitious medieval landscape of boats, birds, turrets and mountains. Some of the paintings were in fact collaborative efforts, and it's known that Ghirlandaio and Botticelli in particular contributed to each other's work. Anywhere else they would be pored over very closely indeed. As it is, they are entirely overshadowed by Michelangelo's more famous work.

The ceiling paintings

Michelangelo's **frescoes** depict scenes from the Old Testament, from the *Creation of Light* at the altar end to the *Drunkenness of Noah* over the door. The sides are decorated with prophets and sibyls and the ancestors of Jesus. Julius II lived only a few months after the Sistine Chapel ceiling was finished, but the fame of the

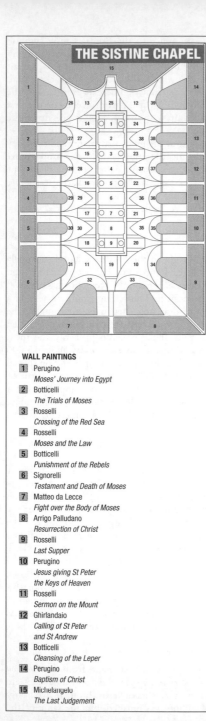

THE SISTINE CHAPEL

WALL PAINTINGS

1 Perugino
Moses' Journey into Egypt
2 Botticelli
The Trials of Moses
3 Rosselli
Crossing of the Red Sea
4 Rosselli
Moses and the Law
5 Botticelli
Punishment of the Rebels
6 Signorelli
Testament and Death of Moses
7 Matteo da Lecce
Fight over the Body of Moses
8 Arrigo Palludano
Resurrection of Christ
9 Rosselli
Last Supper
10 Perugino
*Jesus giving St Peter
the Keys of Heaven*
11 Rosselli
Sermon on the Mount
12 Ghirlandaio
*Calling of St Peter
and St Andrew*
13 Botticelli
Cleansing of the Leper
14 Perugino
Baptism of Christ
15 Michelangelo
The Last Judgement

CEILING PAINTINGS

1 The Creation of Light
2 The Creation of the Sun and the Moon
3 The Separation of Land and Water
4 The Creation of Adam
5 The Creation of Eve
6 The Temptation and Expulsion from
the Garden of Eden
7 The Sacrifice of Noah
8 The Story of the Flood
9 The Drunkenness of Noah
10 David and Goliath
11 Judith and Holofernes
12 The Punishment of Haman
13 The Brazen Serpent
14 The Libyan Sibyl
15 Daniel
16 The Cumaean Sibyl
17 Isaiah
18 The Delphic Sibyl
19 Zachariah
20 Joel
21 The Erythraean Sibyl
22 Ezekiel
23 The Persian Sibyl
24 Jeremiah
25 Jonah and the Whale
26 Aminadab
27 Salmon, Booz, Obed
28 Roboam, Abia
29 Ozias, Joatham, Achaz
30 Zorobabel, Abiud, Elichiam
31 Achim, Eliud
32 Jacob, Joseph
33 Eleazar, Matthan
34 Azor, Sadoch
35 Josias, Jechonias, Salathiel
36 Ezekias, Manasses, Amon
37 Asa, Josophat, Joram
38 Jesse, David, Solomon
39 Naasson

work he had commissioned soon spread far and wide. Certainly, it's staggeringly impressive, all the more so for its recent restoration (financed by a Japanese TV company to the tune of $3 million in return for three years' world TV rights), which has lifted centuries of accumulated soot and candle grime off the ceilings to reveal a much brighter, more vivid painting than anyone thought existed. The restorers have also been able to chart the progress of Michelangelo as he moved across the vault. Images on fresco were completed before the plaster dried, and each day a fresh layer of plaster would have been laid, on which Michelangelo would have had around eight hours or so before having to finish for the day. Comparing the different areas of plaster, it seems the figure of Adam, in the key *Creation of Adam* scene, took four days; God, in the same fresco, took three. You can also see the development of Michelangelo as a painter when you look at the paintings in reverse order. The first painting, over the door, the *Drunkenness of Noah*, is done in a stiff and formal style, and is vastly different from the last painting, the *Creation of Light*, over the altar, which shows the artist at his best, the perfect master of the technique of fresco painting.

Entering from behind the altar, you are supposed, as you look up, to imagine that you are peering into heaven through the arches of the imaginary architecture that springs from the sides of the chapel, supported by little putti caryatids and *ignudi* or nudes, bearing shields and the oak-leaf garlands of the Della Rovere family of Julius II. Look at the pagan sibyls and biblical prophets which Michelangelo also incorporated in his scheme – some of the most dramatic figures in the entire work, and all clearly labelled by the painter, from the sensitive figure of the Delphic Sibyl to the hag-like Cumaean Sibyl, whose biceps would put a Bulgarian shot-putter to

Julius II and the origins of the Sistine Chapel frescoes

When construction was completed in 1483 during the reign of Pope Sixtus IV, the Sistine Chapel ceiling was painted as a blue background with gold stars to resemble the night sky. Over the altar there were two additional paintings by Perugino and a large picture of the Virgin Mary. Sixtus IV was succeeded by Innocent VIII, who was followed by Alexander VI, the Borgia pope who, after the brief reign of Pius III, was succeeded in 1503 by Giuliano della Rovere, who took the name Julius II. Though a Franciscan friar, he was a violent man with a short temper; his immediate objective as pope was to try to regain the lands that had been taken away from the papacy during the reigns of Innocent VIII and Alexander VI by the French, Germans and Spanish. For this purpose he started a series of wars and secret alliances.

Julius II was also an avid collector and patron of the arts, and he summoned to Rome the best artists and architects of the day. Among these was **Michelangelo**, who, through a series of political intrigues orchestrated by Bramante and Raphael, was assigned the task of decorating the Sistine Chapel. Work commenced in 1508. Oddly enough, Michelangelo hadn't wanted to do the work at all: he considered himself a sculptor, not a painter, and was more eager to get on with carving Julius II's tomb (now in San Pietro in Vincoli, see p.117) than the ceiling, which he regarded as a chore. Pope Julius II, however, had other plans, drawing up a design of the twelve Apostles for the vault and hiring Bramante to design a scaffold for the artist to work from. Michelangelo was apparently an awkward, solitary character: he had barely begun painting when he rejected Bramante's scaffold as unusable, fired all his staff, and dumped the pope's scheme for the ceiling in favour of his own. But the pope was easily his match, and there are tales of the two men clashing while the work was going on – Michelangelo would lock the doors at crucial points, ignoring the pope's demands to see how it was progressing, and legend has the two men at loggerheads at the top of the scaffold one day, resulting in the pope striking the artist in frustration.

shame. Look out, too, for the figure of the prophet Jeremiah – a brooding self-portrait of an exhausted-looking Michelangelo.

We've detailed the paintings of the central panels in the chart (see p.198), but, specifically, they start with a large portrait of **Jonah and the Whale** and move on, consecutively, to **The Creation of Light** – God's arms bowed, beard flowing, as he separates light from darkness; **The Creation of the Sun and the Moon**, in which Michelangelo has painted God twice, once with his back to us hurling the moon into existence and simultaneously displaying another moon to the audience; **The Separation of Land and Water**; and, in the fourth panel, probably most famous of all these paintings, **The Creation of Adam**, in which God sparks Adam into life with the touch of his finger. God's cape billows behind him, where a number of figures stand – representatives of all the unborn generations to come after Adam. The startled young woman looking at Adam is either Eve or the Virgin Mary, here as a witness to the first events in human history.

The fifth panel from the altar shows **The Creation of Eve**, in which Adam is knocked out under the stump of a Della Rovere oak tree and God summons Eve from his side as he sleeps. She comes out in a half-crouch position with her hands clasped in a prayer of thanksgiving and awe. The sixth panel is the powerful **Temptation and Expulsion from the Garden of Eden**, with an evil spirit, depicted as a serpent, leaning out from the tree of knowledge and handing the fruit to Adam. On the right of this painting the Angel of the Lord, in swirling red robes, is brandishing his sword of original sin at the nape of Adam's neck as he tries to fend the angel off, motioning with both hands. The eighth panel continues the story, with **The Story of the Flood**, the unrighteous bulk of mankind taking shelter under tents from the rain while Noah and his kin make off for the Ark in the distance. Panel seven shows the **Sacrifice of Noah** as he and his family make a sacrifice of thanksgiving to the Lord for their safe arrival after the flood; one of Noah's sons kneels to blow on the fire to make it hotter, while his wife brings armloads of wood. Lastly, there's **The Drunkenness of Noah**, in which Noah is shown getting drunk after harvesting the vines and exposing his genitals to his sons – it is strictly prohibited in the Hebrew canon for a father to show his reproductive organs to his children. Oddly enough, Noah's sons are naked too.

The Last Judgement

The Last Judgement, on the altar wall of the chapel, was painted by Michelangelo more than twenty years later, between 1535 and 1541. Michelangelo wasn't especially keen to work on this either – he was still engaged on Julius II's tomb, under threat of legal action from the late pope's family – but Pope Paul III, an old acquaintance of the artist, was keen to complete the decoration of the chapel. Michelangelo tried to delay by making demands that were likely to cause the pope to give up entirely, insisting on the removal of two paintings by Perugino and the closing of a window that pierced the end of the chapel. Furthermore, he insisted that the wall be replastered, with the top 15cm out of the perpendicular to prevent the accumulation of soot and dust. Surprisingly, the pope agreed.

The painting took five years, again single-handed, and is probably the most inspired and most homogeneous large-scale painting you'll ever see, Michelangelo's technical virtuosity taking a back seat to the sheer exuberance of the work. The human body is fashioned into a finely captured set of exquisite poses, in which even the damned can be seen as a celebration of the human form. Perhaps unsurprisingly, the painting offended some, and even before it was complete Rome was divided as to its merits, especially regarding the etiquette of introducing a display of nudity into the pope's private chapel. But Michelangelo's response to this was unequivocal, lampooning one of his fiercer critics, the pope's master of ceremonies at the time,

Biagio di Cesena, as Minos, the doorkeeper of hell, with ass's ears and an entwined serpent in the bottom right-hand corner of the picture. Later the pope's zealous successor, Pius IV, objected to the painting and would have had it removed entirely had not Michelangelo's pupil, Daniele da Volterra, appeased him by carefully – and selectively – adding coverings to some of the more obviously naked figures, forever earning himself the nickname of the "breeches-maker". During the recent work, most of the remaining breeches have been discreetly removed, restoring the painting to its former glory.

Briefly, the painting shows the **last day of existence**, when the bodily resurrection of the dead takes place and the human race is brought before Christ to be either sent to eternity in Paradise or condemned to suffer in Hell. The centre is occupied by Christ, turning angrily as he gestures the condemned to the underworld. St Peter, carrying his gold and silver keys, looks on in astonishment at his Lord filled with rage, while Mary averts her eyes from the scene. Below Christ a group of angels blasts their trumpets to summon the dead from their sleep. Somewhat amusingly, one angel holds a large book, the book of the damned, while another carries a much smaller one, the book of the saved. On the left, the dead awaken from their graves, tombs and sarcophagi (one apparently has the likeness of Martin Luther) and levitate into the heavens or are pulled by ropes and the napes of their necks by angels who take them before Christ. At the bottom right, Charon, keeper of the underworld, swings his oar at the damned souls as they fall off the boat into the waiting gates of Hell. Among other characters portrayed are many martyred saints, the Apostles, Adam, and, peeking out between the legs of the saint on the left of Christ, Julius II, with a look of fear and astonishment.

Museum of Christian Art and the Vatican Library

After the Sistine Chapel, you're channelled all the way to the exit by way of the **Museum of Christian Art,** which is not of great interest in itself, but does give access to a small room off to the left that contains a number of ancient Roman frescoes and mosaics, among them the celebrated *Aldobrandini Wedding*, a first-century BC Roman fresco that shows the preparations for a wedding in touching detail. Other items in a room that is extremely rich in interest include frescoes showing scenes from the *Odyssey*, and another, later piece from Ostia depicting a ship being loaded with grain, as well as some fantastic mosaics of wild beasts.

Back down the main corridor, the **Vatican Library**, home to around a million books and manuscripts (you can't touch any of them) is decorated with scenes of Rome and the Vatican as it was during his reign. Over one of the doors of the corridor you can see the facade of St Peter's as it was in the late 1500s, before Maderno's extension of the nave; over the facing door you can see the erection of the obelisk outside in the Piazza San Pietro, showing the men, ropes, animals and a primitive derrick, with the obelisk being drawn forward on a sled, while beyond the corridor opens out into the dramatic **Library of Sixtus V** on the right, a vast hall built across the courtyard in the late sixteenth century to glorify literature – and of course Sixtus V himself.

Braccio Nuovo and Museo Chiaramonti

Off the Cortile della Pigna, the **Braccio Nuovo** and **Museo Chiaramonti** both hold classical sculpture, although be warned that they are the Vatican at its most overwhelming – close on a thousand statues crammed into two long galleries – and you need a keen eye and much perseverance to make any sense of it all. The **Braccio Nuovo** was built in the early 1800s to display classical statuary that was particularly prized, and it contains, among other things, probably the most famous extant image of Augustus addressing the army, hand outstretched, found on the Via Flaminia, near the Villa di Livia (the cupid riding the dolphin is a reference to the imperial family's descent from Venus and her son Aeneas). There's also a nice statue of Silenus clutching an infant Dionysos nearby, and a bizarre-looking statue depicting the Nile, whose yearly flooding was essential to the fertility of the Egyptian soil. It is this aspect of the river that is represented here: crawling over the hefty river god are sixteen babies, thought to allude to the number of cubits the river needed to rise to fertilize the land.

The 300-metre-long **Chiaramonti gallery** is especially unnerving, lined with the chill marble busts of hundreds of nameless, blank-eyed ancient Romans, along with the odd deity (such as a colossal head of Neptune from Hadrian's villa). It pays to have a leisurely wander, for there are some real characters here: sour, thin-lipped matrons with their hair tortured into pleats, curls and spirals; kids, caught in a sulk or mid-chortle; and ancient old men with flesh sagging and wrinkling to reveal the skull beneath. Many of these heads are ancestral portraits, kept by the Romans in special shrines in their houses to venerate their familial predecessors, and in some cases family resemblances can be picked out. The fine head of Athena, on the right, has kept her glass eyes, a reminder that most of these statues were originally painted to resemble life, with eyeballs where now a blank space stares out.

The Pinacoteca

The **Pinacoteca**, housed in a separate building on the far side of the Vatican's main spine, ranks possibly as Rome's best picture gallery, with works from the early primitives right up to the nineteenth century.

The display is chronological, and starts with a beautiful collection of works from the **Gothic period**, among them an amazing, almost mosaic-like *Last Judgement* by Nicolò and Giovanni from the second half of the twelfth century in the first room, and the stunning Simoneschi triptych by Giotto in the next room, depicting the *Martyrdom of Sts Peter and Paul* and painted in the early 1300s for the old St Peter's, where it remained until 1506 when it was removed for the rebuilding of the new church. In the rooms that follow are lovely pieces by Masolino, Fra Angelico and Filippo Lippi, while the next room has the naturalistic works of Marco Palmezzano and Melozzo da Forlì's musical angels – fragments of a fresco commissioned for the family church of Santi Apostoli by Giuliano della Rovere, the future Pope Julius II. Another part of the same fresco resides in the Palazzo Quirinale (see p.109). Julius II also makes an appearance in da Forlì's *Sixtus IV opening the Vatican Library* in the same room – he's the large figure in red, and the painting is as much a family scene as anything, also showing the pope's brother Raffaele Riario (Giuliano's father) behind him (in blue), another nephew, Girolamo, also in blue, and on the far left Giuliano's brother Giovanni, then the prefect of Rome.

The next room holds Carlo Crivelli's magnificently angst-ridden *Pietà*, while beyond here lie the rich backdrops and elegantly clad figures of the **Umbrian School painters**, Perugino and Pinturicchio. Raphael has a room to himself, with three very important oil paintings, and, in climate-controlled glass cases, the tapestries that were made to his designs to be hung in the Sistine Chapel during conclave. The cartoons from which these tapestries were made are now in the Victoria and Albert Museum in London. Of the three paintings, the *Coronation of the Virgin*, on the right, was done when he was only 19 years old; the *Transfiguration*, in the middle, was interrupted by his death in 1520 and finished by his pupils; and the *Madonna of Foligno*, on the left, shows saints John the Baptist, Francis of Assisi and Jerome, and was painted as an offering after a cannonball (in the centre of the painting) struck his house.

Leonardo's *St Jerome*, in the next room, is unfinished, too, but it's a remarkable piece of work, with Jerome a rake-like ascetic torn between suffering and a good meal. Look closely at this painting and you can see that a 25-centimetre square, the saint's head, has been re-glued to the canvas after the painting was used as upholstery for a stool in a cobbler's shop in Rome for a number of years. Caravaggio's *Descent from the Cross*, two rooms on, however, gets more attention, a warts 'n' all canvas that unusually shows the **Virgin Mary** as a middle-aged mother grieving over her dead son, while the men placing Christ's body on the bier are models that the artist recruited from the city streets – a realism that is imitated successfully in Reni's *Crucifixion of St Peter* in the same room: the Baroque at full throttle. Take a look, too, at the most gruesome painting in the collection, Poussin's *Martyrdom of St Erasmus*, which shows the saint stretched out on a table with his hands bound above his head in the process of having his small intestine wound onto a drum – basically being "drawn" prior to "quartering". The views over the Vatican Gardens nearby, with the dome of St Peter's in the background, provides a suitable antidote if you need it.

Musei Gregoriano Profano, Pio Cristiano and Missionario Etnologico

Outside the Pinacoteca, you're well placed for the further grouping of museums in the modern building next door – and their lack of popularity can be something of a relief from the crowds in the rest of the museum. The **Museo Gregoriano Profano** holds more classical sculpture, mounted on scaffolds for all-round viewing, including mosaics of athletes from the Baths of Caracalla and Roman funerary work, notably the Haterii tomb friezes, which show backdrops of ancient Rome and realistic portrayals of contemporary life. It's thought the Haterii were a family of construction workers and that they grabbed the opportunity to advertise their services by incorporating reliefs of the buildings they had worked on (including the Colosseum), along with a natty little crane, on the funeral monument of one of their female members. The adjacent **Museo Pio Cristiano** has intricate early Christian sarcophagi and, most famously, an expressive late-third-century AD statue of the *Good Shepherd* – a subject you'll see on many of the other fourth-century sarcophagi nearby. One of the best is the "Two Brothers" sarcophagus from 325 AD, swathed in biblical scenes and meditations on the deceased.

The **Museo Filatelico e Numismatico**, below, is unsurprisingly quiet, displaying stamps and coins from the Vatican through the ages, while below that the **Museo Missionario Etnologico** has art and artefacts from China, Japan and the rest of the Far East collected by Catholic missionaries. It's quite enlightened in its way, at pains to explain the principles of Taoism, Buddhism, Shintoism and the rest, and keen to point out that missionary work is not about conquest, but there's no getting away from the fact that this is the darkest and most neglected part of the entire museum complex.

Day-trips from Rome

Y ou may find there's quite enough of interest in Rome to keep you
occupied during your stay. But it can be a hot, oppressive city, its surfeit
of churches and museums sometimes wearying, and if you're around
long enough you really shouldn't feel any guilt about seeing something
of the countryside around. Two of the main attractions visitable on a day-trip
are admittedly ancient Roman sites (Ostia Antica and Hadrian's Villa at Tivoli),
but just the process of getting to them can be energizing. About an hour by bus
east of Rome, **Tivoli** is a small town famous for its nearby travertine quarries,
and has lots to lure you there: two Renaissance villas with landscaped gardens
in the town itself, and the glorious remains of the Villa Adriana just outside.
Ostia, southwest of the city near the sea, and similarly easy to reach on public
transport, is the city's main seaside resort. But it was also the site of the port of
ancient Rome, the ruins of which – **Ostia Antica** – are well preserved and
definitely worth seeing: the equal, more or less, of any ancient site in the
country. North of Rome, the Etruscan sites of **Cerveteri** and **Tarquinia** are
atmospheric alternatives to Roman archeology, while **Bracciano** has the airy
location on its lake and the appeal of an Italian provincial town. South of
Rome, the **Castelli Romani** provide the most appealing stretch of countryside
close to Rome; and the coastal towns of **Anzio** and **Nettuno** some of its most
accessible **beach resorts**, although there are many choices if all you want to do
is flop (see box, pp.216–217).

Tivoli and around

Perched high on a hill and looking back over the plain, **TIVOLI** has always
been something of a retreat from the city, due to its fresh mountain air and
pleasant position on the Aniene River. In classical days it was a retirement town
for wealthy Romans; later, during the Renaissance, it again became the
playground of the moneyed classes, attracting some of the city's most well-to-
do families out here to build villas. Nowadays the leisured classes have mostly
gone, but Tivoli does very nicely on the fruits of its still-thriving travertine
business, exporting the precious stone worldwide (the quarries line the main
road into town from Rome), and supports a small airy centre that preserves a
number of relics from its ritzier days. To do justice to its celebrated villas, **Villa
d'Este**, **Villa Gregoriana** and **Villa Adriana** – especially if the latter is on
your list – you'll need most of the day; set out early, and try to be in Tivoli by
mid-morning at the latest.

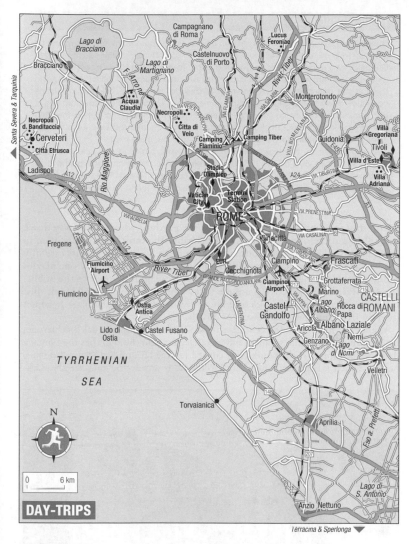

Terracina & Sperlonga ▼

Villa d'Este

Tivoli's major sight is the **Villa d'Este**, across the main square of Largo Garibaldi (daily: May–Aug 8.30am–6.45pm, Sept 8.30am–6.15pm, Oct 8.30am–5.30pm, Jan, Nov & Dec 8.30am–4pm, Feb 8.30am–4pm, March 8.30am–5.15pm, April 8.30am–6.30pm; €6.50; Ⓦ www.villadestetivoli.info). Once a convent, it was transformed into a country villa by Pirro Ligorio in 1550 for Cardinal Ippolito d'Este, and is now often thronged with visitors even outside peak season. The **villa** itself is worth a visit. It has been recently restored to its original state, with beautiful Mannerist frescoes in its seven ground-floor rooms showing scenes from the history of the d'Este family in

Tivoli practicalities

Buses leave Rome for Tivoli every 10min from outside Ponte Mammolo metro station (line B; journey time 30–45min), dropping off on Tivoli's main square, Piazza Garibaldi, two minutes' walk from **Villa d'Este**. To get to the **Villa Gregoriana** from here, make a right off Piazza Garibaldi to Piazza Santa Croce and follow Via del Trivio through the pedestrianized old town to Piazza del Plebiscito, where Via Palatina continues down to the bridge over the gorge. Cross over, and the back entrance is just around the corner on the left – a ten-minute walk in all. To get to the **Villa Adriana**, ask the Rome–Tivoli bus to drop you off, or take the CAT #4 bus from Tivoli's Piazza Garibaldi; it's a ten-minute walk from the main road.

As regards lunch, overlooking the Villa Gregoriana park, right by the entrance, *Sibilla*, Via Sibilla 50 (☎0774.335.281), is the most obvious and one of the best **restaurants** in Tivoli, while *I Portici*, right in the centre of town at Piazza Garibaldi 5, is a good place to get a piece of *baccalà* or slice of pizza, and has tables outside.

Tivoli. But most people come here to see the **garden**, which peels away down the hill in a succession of terraces. It's probably the most contrived garden in Italy, but also the most ingenious, almost completely symmetrical, its carefully tended lawns, shrubs and hedges interrupted at decent intervals by one playful fountain after another. Newly restored and once again fully open to the public, the **fountains** are collectively unique and a must-see if you're in Tivoli; just make sure that you don't *touch or drink* the water in the fountains – it comes directly from the operating sewers of Tivoli.

Among the highlights, the central, almost Gaudí-like Fontana del Bicchierone, by Bernini, is one of the simplest and most elegant. On the right lies the Fontana dell'Ovato, topped with statues on a curved terrace around artificial mountains, behind which is a rather dank – and accessible – arcade; beyond are the dark,

▲ Fountains in the gardens of Villa d'Este

gushing Grottoes of the Sibyls. Behind this the Fontana dell'Organo is a giant and very elaborate water organ, whose air pipes are forced by water valves, and play every couple of hours; right in front, the similarly large Fontana del Nettuno ejects a massive torrent down into a set of central fish ponds, while at the far end the many pendulous breasts of the somewhat denuded fountain of Diana of Ephesus gush yet more water. Finish up on the far side of the garden, where the Rometta or "Little Rome" has reproductions of the city's major buildings and a boat holding an obelisk.

Villa Gregoriana

Tivoli's other main attraction, the **Villa Gregoriana** (April to mid-Oct Tues–Sun 10am–6.30pm, March & mid-Oct to end Nov Tues–Sat 10am–2.30pm, Sun 10am–4pm; €5), recently reopened after restoration, isn't actually a villa at all, but an impressively wild set of landscaped gardens, created when Pope Gregory XVI diverted the flow of the river here to ease the periodic flooding of the town in 1831. At least as interesting and beautiful as the d'Este estate, it remains less well known and less visited, and has none of the latter's conceits – its vegetation is lush and overgrown, descending into a **gorge** over 60m deep. It's harder work than the Villa d'Este – if you blithely saunter down to the bottom of the gorge, you'll find that it's a long way back up the other side – but it is in many ways more rewarding.

There are two main **waterfalls** – the larger Grande Cascata on the far side, and a small Bernini-designed one at the neck of the gorge. The best thing to do is walk the main path in reverse, starting at the back entrance, over the river, and winding down to the bottom of the canyon. The ruins of a Republican-era villa cling to the far side of the gorge, and you can peek into them and then catch your breath down by the so-called Grotto of the Mermaid, before scaling the other side to the Grotto of Neptune, reached by a tunnelled-out passage through the rock, where you can sit right by the roaring falls, the dark, torn shapes of the rock glowering overhead. The path leads up from here to an exit and the substantial remains of an ancient **Temple of Vesta**, which you'll have seen perched on the side of the hill, and which marks the main entrance to the villa. You can take a breather at the small café here, and the view is probably Tivoli's best – down into the chasm and across to the high green hills that ring the town.

Villa Adriana

Once you've seen these two sights you've really seen Tivoli – the rest of the town is nice enough but there's not much to it. But just outside town, at the bottom of the hill, the **Villa Adriana** (Hadrian's Villa; daily 9am–1hr before sunset; €10; Ⓦwww .villa-adriana.net) puts the achievements of the Tivoli popes and cardinals very much into the shade. This was probably the largest and most sumptuous villa in the Roman Empire, the retirement home of the Emperor Hadrian between 135 AD and his death three years later, and it occupies an enormous site. You need time to see it all; there's no point in doing it at a gallop and, taken with the rest of Tivoli, it makes for a long day's sightseeing. It's worth knowing, incidentally, that the Auditorium in Rome organizes a series of open-air music and dance events (festiVAl) here on summer evenings (mid-June to mid-July), so this is another way to see the site; see Ⓦwww.auditorium.com/villaadriana for details.

The site is one of the most soothing spots around Rome, its stones almost the epitome of romantic, civilized ruins. The imperial palace buildings proper are in fact one of the least well-preserved parts of the complex, but much else is clearly recognizable. Hadrian was a great traveller and a keen architect, and parts of the villa were inspired by buildings he had seen around the world. The massive **Pecile**, for instance, through which you enter, is a reproduction of a building in Athens. The **Canopus**, on the opposite side of the site, is a liberal copy of the sanctuary of Serapis near Alexandria, its long, elegant channel of water fringed by sporadic columns and statues leading up to a temple of Serapis at the far end.

Near the Canopus a **museum** displays the latest finds from the ongoing excavations, though most of the extensive original discoveries have found their way back to Rome and many museums in Europe. Walking back towards the entrance, make your way across the upper storey of the so-called **Pretorio**, a former warehouse, and down to the remains of two **bath complexes**. Beyond is a fish pond with a **cryptoporticus** (underground passageway) winding around underneath. It's enjoyable to walk through the cryptoporticus and look up at its ceiling, picking out the names of the seventeenth- and eighteenth-century artists (Bernini, for one) who visited and wrote their signatures here using a smoking candle. Behind this are the relics of the emperor's imperial apartments. The **Teatro Marittimo**, adjacent, with its island in the middle of a circular pond, is the place to which it's believed Hadrian would retire at siesta time to be sure of being alone.

Ostia

There are two Ostias. One is the over-visited seaside resort of **Lido di Ostia**; the other, one of the finest ancient Roman sites you'll find anywhere, the excavations of the port of **Ostia Antica**, which are on a par with anything you'll see in Rome itself and easily merit a half-day out.

Ostia Antica

The site of **Ostia Antica** marked the coastline in classical times, and the town which grew up here was the port of ancient Rome, a thriving place whose commercial activities were vital to the city further upstream – until they were curtailed by the silting up of the harbour. The **excavations** (April–Oct Tues–Sun 8.30am–6pm; March 8.30am–5pm; Nov–Feb 8.30am–4pm; €6.50) remain relatively unvisited; indeed until the 1970s the site was only open one day a week and few people realized how well the port had been preserved by the Tiber's mud. Still relatively free of the bustle of tourists, it's an evocative site, and it's much easier to reconstruct a Roman town from this than from any amount of pottering around the Forum – or even Pompeii. It's very spread out, so be prepared for a fair amount of walking; and carry some water, to avoid the rather pricey snack bar at the back of the museum.

Ostia practicalities

Ostia Antica is easily reachable by regular trains from Roma–Porta San Paolo (next door to Piramide metro station, on line B; journey time 30min). All you need is a regular €1 ATAC ticket. During summer you can also get to Ostia on the river. **Boats** leave from Ponte Marconi, in Ostiense near the Basilica San Paolo, and take two hours to reach Ostia; see ⓦ www.battellidiroma.it for details.

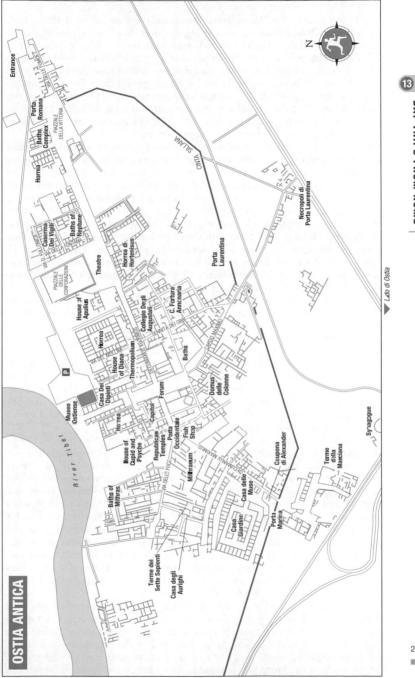

OSTIA ANTICA

River Tibet

Entrance

Porta Romana

Baths Complex

Horrea

PIAZZALE DELLA VITTORIA

Caserma Dei Vigili

Baths of Neptune

VIA D. FULLONICA
VIA DELLA FONTANA

Horrea

Theatre

House of Apulius

PIAZZALE DELLE CORPORAZIONI

Horrea di Hortensius

Collegio Degli Augustali

C. Fortura Annonaria

Museo Ostiense

P

Casa Dei Dipinti

House of Diana

Thermopolium

VIA DEI MOLINI

DECUMANUS MAXIMUS

SEMITA DEI CEHI

Baths

Porta Laurentina

Horrea

Capitol

Forum

Domus delle Colonne

CARDO MAXIMO

House of Cupid and Psyche

Republican Temples

Porta Occidentale

Fish Shop

Mithraeum

VIA DELLE FOCE

Baths of Mithras

Casa delle Muse

Caupona di Alexander

Terme dalla Marciana

DECUMANUS MAXIMUS

Syapgague

Casa Giardino

Porta Marina

Terme dei Sette Sapienti

Casa degli Aurighi

SILLANA

CINTA

Necropoli di Porta Laurentina

N

Lido di Ostia

Fiumicino Airport

From the entrance, the **Decumanus Maximus**, the main street of Ostia, leads west, past the **Baths Complex** on the right, where there's an interesting mosaic of seahorses and other creatures. A little way down on the right, at the corner of **Via della Fontana**, a pavement inscription of a cup marks what would have been a bar. Via della Fontana itself is a wonderfully preserved street, and gives a good idea of a typical Roman urban layout, with its ground-floor shops and upper-floor apartments. The fountain that gives the street its name is on the right, a long coffin-shaped thing that would have been a source of fresh water for the homes and businesses nearby. Right past here takes you to **Caserma dei Vigili**, whose courtyard focuses on a shrine to the cult of Fortuna.

The Decumanus Maximus continues to the town's commercial centre, **Piazzale delle Corporazioni**, where the remains of shops and trading offices still fringe the central square. These represented commercial enterprises from all over the ancient world, and the mosaics of boats and fish and suchlike just in front denote their trade (grain merchants, ship fitters, rope-makers and so on) as well as their origin (Carthage, for example). Flanking the southern side of the square, the **theatre**, with its comic and tragic masks, has been much restored but is nonetheless impressive, enlarged by Septimius Severus in the second century AD to hold up to four thousand people; it sometimes hosts performances of classical drama during the summer. On the left of the square, the **House of Apulius** preserves mosaic floors and, beyond, a dark-aisled **mithraeum** with more mosaiced benches illustrating the practices of the cult of Mithras.

Behind here – past the substantial remains of the *horrea* or warehouses that once stood all over the city – the **House of Diana** is probably the best-preserved private house in Ostia, with a dark, mysterious set of rooms around a central courtyard, and again with a mithraeum at the back. Across the road, the **Thermopolium** is an ancient Roman café, complete with seats outside, a high counter, display shelves and even wall paintings of parts of the menu. At the back is a marble wall slab which once held hooks for hanging coats, beyond which is what would have been a peaceful small courtyard with a fountain. Opposite the Thermopolium, steps lead to the top of the **Casa dei Dipinti**, giving a fine view over the site. The house itself is sometimes locked but if you can get in you'll be rewarded with a wonderful mosaic fragment showing birds and people.

North of here, the half a dozen rooms of the **Museo Ostiense** are full of sculptural finds from the site and well worth seeing. In a room to the left as you enter is a wall painting of *Mithras Slaying the Bull* from one of Ostia's mithraeums. The central room has a fine headless male figure in repose, his foot resting on a column base, and a figure of Trajan in full battle dress, between two busts of him and another of Hadrian, along with a likeness of Commodus as a young boy. The room beyond has a statue of Septimius Severius next to his wife, Julia Donna, as the goddess Ceres, while opposite a beautifully preserved figure of Maxentius and his sister Fausta look on. In a room off here are various carved sarcophagi found on Via Ostiense, all amazingly well preserved, including one of a young boy, decorated with cupids, while off to the other side are various representations of Venus and a wall painting of the Three Graces from the second century AD.

Left from here, the **Forum** centres on the **Capitol** building, reached by a wide flight of steps, and is fringed by the remains of baths and a basilica. Continuing on down the main street, more **horrea**, superbly preserved and complete with pediment over the entrance and names inscribed on the marble, merit a detour off to the right (although you can't enter, you can peer into the courtyard), before reaching the **Porta Occidentale** or western gate a few yards further on.

On the left here is what may have been a **fish shop**, judging by its floor mosaics, still with its shelves and marble table, across from which Via delle Foce leads off right. To the left of here a long alley leads to another **mithraeum**, this time painted with scenes of mithraic rites. On the other side of Via delle Foce is a complex of **Republican temples**, possibly dating back to the time of Sulla, behind which is the **House of Cupid and Psyche**. The house has a courtyard you can walk into and holds a copy of the statue of Cupid and Psyche that you can see in the museum, its rooms clearly discernible on one side, a colourful marbled floor at the top, and a columned nymphaeum, with marble niches, on the right.

Keep on down Via delle Foce from here and you soon reach the **Terme dei Sette Sapienti** on the left, with its round arcaded courtyard and wonderfully intact floor mosaic. Steps lead up to the roof for good views over this part of the site and the fragments of wall paintings below. The atmospheric arcaded passageways of the complex lead to the **Casa degli Aurighi**, which you can ascend for more excellent views, beyond which Via degli Aurighi takes you back to the main Decumanus Maximus. A right turn takes you down to the **Porta Marina**, or sea gate. This is marked by the **Caupona di Alexander** on the left, a wine shop with flower mosaics identifying the owner and showing various forms of combat. Beyond here the road continues on for a little way to what was once the sea – but is now just the main road.

Cerveteri

Cerveteri provides the most accessible Etruscan taster from Rome. The settlement here dates back to the tenth century BC and was once a trading heavyweight, one of the Mediterranean's largest centres. Cerveteri, also known as Caere, ranked among the top three cities in the twelve-strong Etruscan federation, its wealth derived largely from the mineral-rich **Tolfa hills** to the northeast – a gentle range that gives the plain a much-needed touch of scenic colour. In its heyday, the town spread over 8km (something like thirty times its present size), controlling territory 50km up the coast. Rot set in from 351 BC, when the Romans assumed control without granting full citizenship rights.

The site
The present town is a thirteenth-century creation, dismissed by D.H. Lawrence – and you really can't blame him – as "forlorn beyond words". On arrival, make straight for the Etruscan **necropolis** (Tues–Sun: May–Sept 8.30am–7pm;

Cerveteri practicalities

You can get to Cerveteri from Rome's Cornelia station on line A by COTRAL **bus** (every 30min; 1hr); buses drop off in Piazza Aldo Moro. The same Rome–Cerverteri bus also links to the train station 7km away at **Ladispoli**, which you can reach from Termini station in about 45 minutes (2 trains an hour). The site is just over 1km away in Banditaccia and is well signposted from the town.

You can quench your appetite at the little **trattoria**, *Tukulcha*, on the necropolis road, which serves hearty country-style food and crisp Cerveteri white wines (no credit cards; closed Mon).

Oct–April 8.30am–4pm; €6). It's the largest extant necropolis; from the seventh to first century BC, the Etruscans constructed a literal city of the dead here, weird and fantastically well preserved, with complete streets and homes. Some tombs are strange round pillboxes carved from cliffs; others are covered in earth to create the barrows that ripple the surrounding plateau. Archeologists speculate that women were buried in separate small chambers within each "house" – easy to distinguish – while the men were laid on deathbeds (occasionally in sarcophagi) hewn directly from the stone. Indeed archeological evidence suggests that the position of women in Etruscan society was roughly on a par with that of men. Cremated slaves lie in urns alongside their masters – civilized by comparison with the Romans, who simply threw them into mass burial pits. The twelve or so show-tombs, lying between the two main roads, open and close in random rotation. If possible, don't miss the **Tomba Bella** (Tomb of the Bas-Reliefs), **Tomba dei Letti Funebri** (Tomb of the Funeral Beds) and the **Tomb of the Capitals**.

The Town

You could spend several hours wandering about, but you might be better off heading back into town to the **Museo Nazionale Cerite**, at the top of the old quarter in the sixteenth-century **Castello Ruspoli** (Tues–Sun 8.30am–7.30pm; €4). This has two large rooms containing a fraction of the huge wealth that was buried with the Etruscan dead – vases, terracottas and a run of miscellaneous day-to-day objects; most of the best stuff has been whisked away to Villa Giulia in Rome (see p.171).

Tarquinia

Second only to Cerveteri among northern Lazio's Etruscan sites, Tarquinia is both an evocative site and pleasant town, its partial walls and crop of medieval towers making it a good place to pass an afternoon after seeing the ruins. Its **museum** is also the region's finest outside Rome.

Tarquinia practicalities

Trains run roughly hourly to Tarquinia from Rome's Termini and Ostiense stations; journey time is around an hour and twenty minutes from Termini, just under an hour from Ostiense. The train station is 2km below the town centre, connected with the central Barriera San Giusto by regular local shuttles. There are also around eight **buses** a day from Rome's Lepanto station on Metro line A that take around two hours.

To **get to the Necropolis of Monterozzi**, take one of the regular buses from the central Barriera San Giusto, or it's a twenty-minute walk: take Via Umberto I from Piazza Cavour, pass through the Porta Romana, cross Piazza Europa, follow Via IV Novembre/Via delle Croci up the hill, and the site is on the left.

Perhaps the most atmospheric place to **eat** is *Re Tarquinio*, at Via Alberata Dante Alighieri 10, which serves meals in tufa caves tastefully made up like tombs (℡0766.842.125; closed Tues). Otherwise, try *La Cantina dell'Etrusco* on Via Menotti Garibaldi 13, which offers rustic local fare in a converted fourteenth-century *cantina* (℡0766.858.418; closed Tues).

The site

Once the artistic, cultural and probably political capital of Etruria, the wooden city has now all but vanished and all that is left is the **Necropolis of Monterozzi** (Tues–Sun: summer 8.30am–7.30pm; winter 8.30am–2pm; €6, €8 including museum). Founded in the tenth century BC, the city's population peaked around 100,000, but the Roman juggernaut triggered its decline six hundred years later and only a warren of graves remains. Since the eighteenth century, six thousand tombs have been uncovered (900 in 1958 alone), with many more to go. Grave-robbing is common (thieves are known as *tombaroli*). Fresh air and humidity have also damaged the **wall paintings** and attempts at conservation mean tombs are open on a rotating basis.

Some frescoes depict the inhabitants' expectations of the afterlife: scenes of banqueting, hunting and even a *ménage à trois*. The famed Tomba dei Caronti makes a darker prediction with demons greeting the deceased. The earliest paintings emphasize mythical and ritualistic scenes, but the sixth- to fourth-century works – in the dell'Orco, degli Auguri, and della Caccia e Pesca tombs – show greater social realism. This style is a mixture of Greek, indigenous Etruscan and eastern influences: the ease and fluidity points to a civilization at its peak. Later efforts grow increasingly morbid with purely necromantic drawings – enough to discourage picnic lunches on the pleasant, grassy site.

Museo Nazionale Tarquiniense

Back in town, the **Museo Nazionale Tarquiniense** on the Piazza Cavour (Tues–Sun 8.30am–7.30pm; €6, €8 including necropolis), has a choice collection of Etruscan finds, sensitively housed in an attractive Gothic-Renaissance *palazzo*. The ground floor exhibits superb sculpted sarcophagi, many decorated with warm and human portraits of the deceased. Upstairs are displays of exquisite Etruscan gold jewellery, painted ceramics, bronzes, candlesticks, heads and figures. The impressive top floor houses the collection's finest piece – the renowned winged horses (fourth century BC), probably from a temple frieze. The Sala delle Armi boasts panoramic views of the countryside and sea.

Bracciano and around

The closest of northern Lazio's lakes to Rome, the smooth, roughly circular expanse of **Lago di Bracciano** fills an enormous volcanic crater. Though nothing spectacular, with few real sights and a landscape of rather plain, rolling countryside, it's popular with Romans escaping the heat of the city. The lake's shores are fairly peaceful even on summer Sundays, however, and you can eat excellent lake fish in its restaurants.

The lake's main settlement is **Bracciano**, on the western shore, a small town that was catapulted into the news when Tom Cruise and Katie Holmes got married there in 2006. The couple tied the knot at the imposing **Castello Orsini-Odescalchi** at Piazza Mazzini 14 (April–Sept Tues–Sat 10am–12.30pm & 3–6pm, Sun 9am–12.30pm & 3–6.30pm; Oct–March Tues–Sat 10am–noon & 3–5pm, Sun 9am–noon & 3–5.30pm; tours every 30min; 1hr; €7) which dominates the town, a late-fifteenth-century structure privately owned by the Odescalchi family. The outer walls, now mostly disappeared, contained the rectangular piazza of the medieval town; nowadays the castle is a little run-down, its interior home to rusting suits of armour and faded frescoes, but the view from the ramparts, over the broad blue oval of the lake, is worth the admission price alone.

Trains run to Bracciano from Roma Ostiense every half an hour (direction Viterbo), and take just over an hour (less from Trastevere and San Pietro, where they also stop). There are also hourly **buses** from Saxa Rubra station on the Roma Nord line, which also take around an hour. Bracciano's train station is reasonably central, just ten minutes' walk from the castle and centre of town. Trains run on from Bracciano to Anguillara, from where there are regular buses to Trevignano.

If you're after a bite to eat, Lungolago Argenti, below the town, has some good, inexpensive **trattorias** – try *Da Tonino* at no. 18, which serves tasty pasta and fish right on the water's edge. Trevignano and Anguillara also have good restaurants; one of the best is Trevignano's *Casina Bianca*, Via della Rena 100 (☎06.999.7231; closed Fri), which serves fresh fish on a terrace overlooking the lake.

The best place to **swim** in the lake is from the beach at Lungolago Argenti, below Bracciano town, where you can rent a boat and enjoy a picnic. The shore between Trevignano and Anguillara also boasts fine swimming spots, as well as some good restaurants (see box above).

The Castelli Romani

Just free of the sprawling southern suburbs of Rome, sixteen towns that make up the **Castelli Romani** date back to medieval times. The surrounding hills – the **Colli Albani** – have long cooled rich and powerful urbanites, and their fertile volcanic soil produces some extraordinary white wines. The region is now pretty heavily built-up, with most of the historic centres ringed by unprepossessing suburbs, and summer weekends see traffic jams of Romans trooping out to local trattorias. But off-peak, it's worth the journey, either as an excursion from Rome or a stop on the way south. By car, there are two obvious routes, both starting with Frascati and Grottaferrata and then spearing off at Marino along either the eastern or western side of Lago Albano.

Frascati and around

Just 20km away from Rome, **Frascati** is the nearest of the Castelli towns and also the most striking, dominated by the majestic **Villa Aldobrandini**, designed by Giacomo della Porta at the turn of the sixteenth century (1598–1603). The Baroque *palazzo* is off-limits, but the **gardens** are open (Mon–Fri: summer 9am–1pm & 3–6pm; winter 9am–1pm & 3–5pm; €2). Sadly the elaborate water theatre, where statues once played flutes, no longer spouts as well as it used to, but the view from the front terrace is superb, with Rome visible on a clear day.

Frascati's main square, **Piazza Marconi**, is right beneath Villa Aldobrandini, and home to a **tourist office** (Tues–Fri 8am–2pm & 4–7pm, Sat 8am–2pm;

COTRAL **buses** serve the area roughly every half an hour from Rome's Anagnina metro station (line A) and it takes 45 minutes to an hour to reach most of the Castelli Romani towns.

Ⓣ06.942.0331). Just beyond here is the pedestrianized old centre, which revolves around the two squares of **Piazza San Pietro** and **Piazza del Mercato** just beyond. Frascati is also about the most famous of the Colli Albani **wine** towns: ask at the tourist office for details of winery tours and tastings, or simply indulge at one of the many trattorias in town. Better yet, pick up a *porchetta* (roast pork) sandwich from one of the stands on Piazza del Mercato and take the greasy bundle into a *cantina*, where wine is sold from giant wooden barrels for just 50c a glass; try the *Antica Osteria di Castello*, just off Piazza del Mercato, or *Grappolo d'Oro*, just off Piazza del Gesù. If you want to sit down and eat, the restaurant of the *Hotel Pinocchio*, Piazza del Mercato 21 (Ⓣ06.941.7883), specializes in porcini mushrooms and duck.

Grottaferrata

Some 3km down the road, **Grottaferrata** is known for its wine and its eleventh-century **abbey** – a fortified Basilian (Greek Orthodox) monastery surrounded by high defensive walls and a now-empty moat (daily: summer 6am–12.30pm & 3.30–7pm; winter 6am–12.30pm & 3.30pm–sunset; free). It's a timeless spot; the little **church of Santa Maria** inside has a Byzantine-style interior decorated with thirteenth-century mosaics and the **chapel of St Nilo** off the right aisle has frescoes by Domenichino. If you're lucky, the small museum through the inner courtyard may be open again after its lengthy restoration.

Marino

Marino, 4km further on, is a pleasant little town set around a pretty main square, Piazza Matteotti, and its **wine** is perhaps the region's best after Frascati. On Piazza Matteotti, the Fontana dei Mori has mermaids and manacled Moors commemorating the Battle of Lepanto, and spouts *vino* on special occasions such as the first Sunday of October during its **Sagra dell'Uva festival**, while at other times of the year you can sample the local wine in the *For de Porta vineria* in the corner of the square or the food at the *Rotonda* restaurant in the opposite corner.

Rocca di Papa

On the far side of Monte Cavo, the road bears right for **Rocca di Papa**, at 680m the loftiest Castelli Romani town. It's also one of the most picturesque, with a medieval quarter that tumbles down the hill in haphazard terraces, and motor traffic kept to a strictly enforced minimum. Make for the small Piazza Garibaldi, a lively place in summer, with a bar and restaurant, and soak up the views. Among other things, the town is famous for its roast chestnuts, and has a **chestnut festival** every year during the third weekend in October.

Castel Gandolfo

Leaving Marino, the road joins up with the ancient Roman Via Appia, which travels straight as an arrow down the west side of Lago Albano. **Castel Gandolfo** is the first significant stop, best known as the pope's summer retreat. Set four hundred metres above the lake, it's a pleasantly airy place, and enjoys great views over the entire lake from its terraces close by the main Piazza della Libertà, a bustling oblong of cafés and papal souvenir shops, at the end of which is the imposing bulk of the **Papal Palace** itself. Inevitably Vatican business predominates, especially on Sundays between July and September when the pope traditionally gives a midday address from the palace. If it's hot, you can take good advantage of the **lake** here: there's a pleasant lido just below town, with lots of restaurants and pizzerias and a small stretch of grey beach from where you can stroll the whole shoreline in about two hours. The road leads down from the main road, just north of Castel Gandolfo's old centre.

Albano Laziale and around

From Castel Gandolfo a panoramic road leads to **Albano Laziale**, one of the larger towns along the ancient Via Appia, and with a strategic position that has left it with lots of **Roman remains**: a crumbled old amphitheatre, once with room for 15,000 spectators, fragments of a gate right in the town centre, and the foundations of the Roman garrison's baths behind the church of San Pietro, on the main street, Corso Matteotti. In one direction on Corso Matteotti, busy

Where to flop: the best beaches near Rome

There are plenty of places to head near Rome if you fancy a day at the **beach** – and on a hot summer's day in the city there's sometimes nothing else for it but to get out of town. Some of the best seaside spots are below.

Lido di Ostia

Lido di Ostia has for years been the number one or at any rate the closest and most accessible seaside resort for Romans. The beaches are fine, and much cleaner than they used to be, but you have to pay to use them and the town doesn't have a great deal to recommend it apart from its thumping nightlife in summer. Ostia is, however, easy to get to, just 30 minutes by train from Porta San Paolo station, next door to Piramide mero on line B; get off at Lido Centro or the last stop, Cristoforo Colombo, where the crowds might be thinner.

Torvaianica

South of Ostia, towards **Torvaianica**, the water is cleaner and the crowds not so thick, plus there are gay and nudist sections of the beach, and not a lot of development. Buses run from Cristoforo Colombo station in Ostia; take #07 or #061. The beaches along this stretch are known as the **cancelli**, after the numbered gates to the beach; the higher the number, the better the beach so it's worth staying on the bus for a bit.

Fregene

Like Ostia, **Fregene**, a little way north, is one of the busier resorts of the Rome area but posher and more family-orientated than Ostia; its beaches are equally crowded and expensive though. Take a train to Maccarese from Termini or Ostiense, a roughly thirty-minute journey; it's a short local bus ride from there to Fregene.

Ladispoli

Ladispoli is one of the best of the resorts to the north of the capital. There are swimming spots about ten minutes' walk from the town's station, although the best are further north, a twenty-minute walk away around the **Torre Flavia** – a medieval construction restored in 1565 by an Orsini cardinal, now collapsing elegantly into the water in four equal parts. Trains run twice an hour from Termini to Ladispoli-Cerveteri station and take about forty minutes.

Santa Severa

Further north from Rome, there's not much to sleepy **Santa Severa**, but it's easy to get to and has everything you need for a day at the beach, with long stretches of sand – some free, the rest given over to the usual *letti* and *ombrelloni* – and a decent *tavola calda* right on the seafront; there's also a **castle** at the southern end of the beach, home to a small municipal museum. The only drawback is the fact that the train station is a twenty-minute walk from the town and beach, with erratic connecting buses and no alternative transport. But trains are regular and quick: hourly from Termini station, and the journey takes just under an hour.

Piazza Mazzini looks south over the Villa Comunale park, where there are sketchy remains of a villa that once belonged to Pompey, while in the other direction, off to the right down Via della Stella, the **Tomb of the Horatii and Curiatii**, whose strange "chimneys" – giant truncated cones resembling Etruscan funerary urns – date from the Republican era. You can get the lowdown on all this in the nearby **Museo Civico**, Viale Risorgimento 3 (Mon–Sun 9am–1pm, also Wed & Thurs 4–7pm; €2.50), which also has a small but high-quality archeological collection.

If you're looking for a bite to **eat**, *Sesto*, a bar and *tavola calda* on the main street at no. 40, is a good place for either a snack or full lunch, with outdoor seating out the back.

Capalbio

Far to the north of Rome and almost in Tuscany, **Capalbio** feels a long way from the capital and its satellite towns; and it's an upscale resort by comparison, with fine beaches, clean water and good restaurants. It's not too hard to reach either: about five trains a day run from Termini station and journey time is roughly an hour and forty minutes. The beaches are about 2km from the station; if you don't fancy the walk, there are infrequent buses.

Anzio and Nettuno

About 40km south of Rome, and fairly free of the pull of the capital, **Anzio** is worth visiting both for its beaches and its history – much of the town was damaged during a difficult Allied landing here on January 22, 1944, to which two military cemeteries (one British, another, at nearby Nettuno, American), as well as a small museum, bear testimony; and it was also a favoured spot of the Roman Emperor Nero, the ruins of whose villa spread along the cliffs above and even down onto the beach. Anzio is a good place to eat lunch: it hosts a thriving fishing fleet and some great restaurants down on the harbour; *La Cicala*, right by the water at Riviera Zanardelli 11 (☏06.984.6747; closed Wed), is as good as any, with outside seating and decent food and service; or try *Fiaschetta del Mare* on the harbour, where they will bring you an endless supply of fishy specialities depending on the day's catch, for a fixed price of €16 a head. The town is easy to get to, with trains every hour from Termini; the journey takes an hour and it's just a ten-minute walk from the station down to the main square and harbour, with the beaches stretching out north of the centre.

Nettuno, a couple of kilometres down the coast, and walkable by the shoreline road, offers more of the same, but with slightly smaller beaches, and less clear and calm water. Again, it's a mostly modern town, but there's a well-preserved old quarter, still walled, with a couple of decent trattorias on the main square.

Terracina and Sperlonga

The resorts of Terracina and Sperlonga are a bit of a schlep; they are doable as a day-trip, though you might want to consider staying overnight. **Terracina** boasts lovely sandy beaches and a welcoming small-town feel, as well as a couple of good restaurants. A little further south, little **Sperlonga** is a more chichi resort, with equally good beaches and an attractive old quarter piled up on the headland just beyond. The ruins of the so-called **Grotto of Tiberius** lie just to the south of the town, a sea cave once filled with sculptures that have found their way into a purpose-built museum nearby.

You can get to both Terracina and Sperlonga by train from Termini to Fondi (hourly), which takes just over an hour, and a local bus from there. There are direct trains to Terracina, which take around an hour and a half, but the first doesn't leave till after lunch so they're not much use unless you're staying the night.

Ariccia

The Via Appia continues on to **Ariccia**, across the nineteenth-century **Ponte di Ariccia** – whose Roman viaduct arches are visible below – into the town's central piazza, a well-proportioned square embellished with Bernini's round church of **Santa Maria dell'Assunzione**. Ariccia, incidentally, is famous for **porchetta** – roast pork – as well as being the site of the **Palazzo Chigi** at Piazza di Corte 14 (Tues–Fri guided tours at 11am, 4pm & 5.30pm, Sat & Sun hourly 10.30am–7pm; €7), built by Bernini for Pope Alexander VII.

Genzano

Just beyond Ariccia, **Genzano** was once the seat of the Sforzas, an aristocratic Renaissance family, and is still dominated by the **Castello Sforza-Cesarini** at the top of the town, a decrepit building whose grounds now form the pleasantly bucolic **Parco Sforza** (daily 10am–1pm & 3–8pm; free), with wooded paths and ponds giving wonderful views over the Lago di Nemi. There's a great **restaurant** here, *La Scuderia*, right opposite the castle at Piazza Sforza Cesarini 1 (℡06.939.0521; closed Mon), whose impeccable service and superb, moderately priced local food is worth stopping for. If you're lucky you may get to sample Genzano's highly prized local **bread**, which is famous for keeping its freshness and aroma for days. The town is also famous for its spectacular flower festival, the **Infiorata**, which takes place every year in June.

Nemi

A detour east will take you to **Nemi**, built high above the tiny crater lake of the same name. The village itself isn't much to write home about, but a cobbled road leads down to fields of strawberries that lie between the steep walls of the crater and the shores of the lake and make a good place to picnic. The town is known for its **strawberry harvest**, and celebrates this on the first Sunday in June in the Sagra delle Fragole.

On the northern shore of the lake, the large, hangar-like local **museum** (daily 9am–6pm; €2) contains the scanty remains of two Roman pleasure boats said to have been built by Caligula, which caught fire and sank in ancient times. They were raised in the 1930s by the Mussolini government and placed in the specially constructed hangars, prime examples of reinforced concrete engineering and Fascist architecture. In the last days of the German occupation in 1944 they were set on fire again, so what you see are the ruins of a ruin. Many of the bronze fittings of these boats have been transferred to Palazzo Massimo in Rome but there are always interesting exhibitions of recent local archeological finds on display.

Listings

Listings

Accommodation

A s you might expect, there is no shortage of accommodation in Rome, and for much of the year you can usually find something without too much trouble. However, it's always worth **booking in advance** if you want to snag a bargain, especially in **high season** – from Easter to July and September to the end of October, and during the Christmas and New Year period. In recent years, the amount of accommodation has increased significantly at all levels, although boutique hotels have been the most significant trend, with many of the centro storico's *palazzi* being given designer makeovers.

Overall, **hotel rates** have held fairly steady over the last few years, or in some cases even dropped, and it's always worth seeing if there is a deal to be had; there are often excellent but unpredictable last-minute **online discounts**, making some of the more upscale options accessible to those on more modest budgets. You're most likely to pick up a bargain in low season, particularly during the heat of August, when many places, especially the higher-grade hotels, drop their prices by up to fifty percent. Rates vary hugely, but as a very rough guide, you'll pay €70–100 for a basic en-suite room, though don't expect much in the way of decor; €100–180 will get you a few homely touches and a more central location; for boutique elegance, budget for €150–250, with the price rising the closer you are to the centre; €250–600 (and beyond) is the price of grand, five-star luxury or the most exclusive of the boutique hotels.

As for **services**, nearly all hotels have computer facilities and **internet** hook-ups of some kind and many now also have **wi-fi** coverage too. Most also offer satellite **TV** with English-language news stations. Few hotels in the centro storico have their own **parking**, but many have a contract with local garages, which charge €35–50 per day; for more on driving and parking restrictions in the centre, see p.30. Unsurprisingly, **swimming pools** and spas are confined to the five-star hotels, but they are open to all – at a price (see box, p.292). Some of the top hotels have on-site **bars and restaurants** (see boxes, p.260 & p.250), with fantastic food, great patios or terraces, or stupendous views – and sometimes all three.

Renting an **apartment** (see box, p.222) or staying in a **bed and breakfast** can be cheaper alternatives; www.b-b.rm.it, www.romaclick.com and The Tourist Friend (06.6821.0410, www.bandbinrome.com) have a good range all over the city. Prices start relatively low – around €50–60 for a double – with the more upscale options going for up to €140. Alternatively, many of the city's **convents** open their doors to paying guests (see box, p.231), though this is not now the bargain it used to be. **Hostels** and **campsites** are listed separately on pp.233–234.

The Italian hotel booking site www.venere.com is a good **last-minute** option (you can also call them on 00800.8363.7300; Mon–Sat 10am–8pm), but bear in mind that you can often get better rates by booking directly with the hotel. If you arrive in Rome without booking, Enjoy Rome (see p.39) may be able to help you, or try Hotel Reservation (☎06.699.1000, ⓦ www.hotelreservation.it), which has desks at both airports and at Termini station. The rooms offered by the touts at Termini are rarely a good deal, and should only be a last resort; if you do take the bait, be sure to establish the (full) price beforehand, in writing if possible.

Where to stay

You'll enjoy Rome the most if you stay right in the heart of things – in the **centro storico** or around **Campo de' Fiori**. There are plenty of hotels in these areas, and plenty too that aren't all that expensive, but they fill quickly so book well in advance if you can. The **Tridente** and the area east of Via del Corso, towards **Via Veneto** and around the **Spanish Steps**, is the city's prime hunting-ground for more upscale accommodation, but there are more affordable options here too. Consider also staying across the river: in **Prati**, the pleasant nineteenth-century neighbourhood close to the **Vatican** and nicely distanced from the hubbub of the city centre, or in lively **Trastevere**, which boasts some relatively new options, all located within easy walking distance of the centre of town and the sights, and lots of places to eat. The area around **Villa Borghese**, including neighbourhoods north of the centre such as Parioli, are further away from the action but offer a glimpse of upscale Roman life.

Many of the city's hostels and cheaper hotels are located close to **Termini** – convenient if you have to catch an early train or flight, but not the city's most atmospheric quarter, and a bus ride away from the centro storico. Despite attempts

---

Short-term apartment rentals

Renting an **apartment** in Rome has many advantages: for families with children or small groups, it can be a cheaper option than a hotel, and much more flexible. Short-term rentals are becoming very popular, however, so book well in advance. All of the agencies listed below have accommodation ranging from small city-centre apartments to grand villas outside the city. You can also find a good array of freelance options in the magazine **Wanted in Rome**, which also has an online edition (ⓦ www.wantedinrome.com). Hotels *Campo de' Fiori* (see p.224), *The Beehive* (see p.228) and *Colors* (see p.232) also have central apartments.

If you really want to do things in style, you can rent one of two apartments in the Keats-Shelley House on Piazza di Spagna, either through the museum itself or the UK's **Landmark Trust** (see p.94), or stay on the coast north of Rome in Palo Laziale near Ladispoli where you can live like an oil baron-art collector at J. Paul Getty's former villa, *La Posta Vecchia* (see p.225).

Apartment agencies

Home Via Margutta 13 ☎06.3212.0102, ⓦ www.at-home-italy.com. Katia and Sabrina have perhaps the city's best choice of short-let apartments, and the best service too. If you're considering renting an apartment for anything from a week to six months, they should be the first people you call.

City Apartments Viale Opita Oppio 78 ☎06.7698.3140, ⓦ www.roma.cityapartments .it. A great selection of apartments all over the city, from around €140 a night, and very flexible on length of stay, especially out of season.

The Tourist Friend see p.221.

Welcome in Rome Via Ottaviano 73 Rome 00192 ☎06.3975.1474, ⓦ www.homesin rome.com. Fairly upscale apartments in the city centre, with prices starting at around €150 a night for a one-bedroom to several times that for 3–4 bedrooms. A good selection of larger options.

Hotel rates

The rates given in our listings are for the **cheapest double room in high season**; at other times, hotels may drop prices by up to 50 percent. A simple **breakfast** is usually included in the rate, except in five-star places, where you can expect to pay upwards of €30 per person.

to regenerate the area, some streets are persistently seedy, especially those south of the station. For those on a tight budget, however, this is where the choice is: the streets both sides of the station are stacked full of bargain hotels and hostels, and some buildings have several pensions to choose from.

Centro storico

See the **map** on p.44.

Albergo del Senato Piazza della Rotonda 73 ℡06.678.4343, Ⓦwww.albergodelsenato.it. A classy choice next door to the Pantheon, with friendly service and magnificent views of the Pantheon from some rooms and the city from the roof. Huge discounts in low season. Doubles €335.

Cesàri Via di Pietra 89a ℡06.674.9701, Ⓦwww .albergocesari.il. In a perfect position close to the Pantheon, this has been a hotel since 1787 – as they will be sure to tell you – with the new addition of the Stendhal room named for their most famous former guest. The quiet, comfortable rooms are elegant and modern, and you can enjoy the roof terrace at breakfast and for drinks on summer evenings. Doubles €130–240.

Due Torri Vicolo del Leonetto 23 ℡06.6880.6956, 06.607.0983 or 00.087.5765, Ⓦwww.hotelduetorriroma.com. Tucked away down a quiet side street just north of Piazza Navona, this little hotel was once a residence for cardinals, after which it served as a brothel. It's been completely remodelled since then, but retains a homely feel, with cosy rooms, some of which have small terraces with rooftop views. Doubles €170–230.

Genio Via G. Zanardelli 28 ℡06.683.3781, Ⓦwww.hotelgenioroma.it. Perfectly located for Piazza Navona and the rest of the centro storico, as well as for the Vatican sights, this comfortable, recently refurbished hotel draws tour groups as well as individual travellers. The view from the rooftop terrace is superb; a few rooms also have the same view, and each comes with a desk. Doubles €240.

Mimosa Via Santa Chiara 61 ℡06.6880.1753, Ⓦwww.hotelmimosa.net. Clean, if slightly scruffy rooms, most without bathroom. In a good position, though, on a quiet street, close to Santa Maria sopra Minerva and the Pantheon, and popular with groups of visiting students. The lobby has a computer with internet. No credit cards. Doubles without bath €75, with bath €95–110.

Navona Via dei Sediari 8 ℡06.686.4203, Ⓦwww.hotelnavona.com. Completely renovated *pensione*-turned-hotel in a building that dates back to the first century AD, built on the ancient Roman baths of Agrippa. A great location, very close to Piazza Navona, and rooms and service are excellent. They also have a sister hotel, the *Zanardelli* (see p.224). The lobby and breakfast area have free wi-fi and there's a free laptop at reception for brief internet use. Doubles €130–160.

Nazionale Piazza Montecitorio 131 ℡06.695.001, Ⓦwww.nazionaleroma.it. This luxury hotel is housed in a sixteenth-century *palazzo* in peaceful Piazza Montecitorio, perfectly located halfway between Piazza Navona and Piazza di Spagna. Inevitably, given its position next door to the Italian parliament, it's popular with visiting politicians and dignitaries, and the rooms are accordingly well fitted out, with every modern convenience. Doubles €270–350.

Pantheon Via Pastini 131 ℡06.678.7746, Ⓦwww.hotelpantheon.com. This comfortable four-star is, as you might expect, a stone's throw from the Pantheon. The well-equipped rooms range from the functional, with beamed wooden ceilings, to deluxe suites on two levels with skylighted sitting rooms. Doubles €190–290.

Portoghesi Via dei Portoghesi 1 ℡06.686.4231, Ⓦwww.hotelportoghesiroma.com. Decent, modern rooms, five minutes from the heart

223

of the centro storico. Breakfast is served on the roof terrace. Doubles €190.

Raphaël Largo Febo 2 ☎06.682.831, ⓦwww .raphaelhotel.com. Set on a quiet, picturesque piazza just off Piazza Navona, the *Raphaël* is a mix of plush traditional style – antiques and rich colours – and sleek contemporary furnishings by American architect Richard Meier (of Ara Pacis fame) on the second and third floors. Diners need to book well ahead in the summer0 to enjoy *La Terrazza Bramante*'s Mediterranean cuisine on the lovely rooftop terrace, so close to the church dome that you can see its rivets. There's also a bar, a library, free wi-fi in all rooms and two free internet points, an exercise room with sauna and steam bath, and free street parking (limited). Doubles €250–800.

Residenza Canali Via dei Tre Archi 13 ☎06.4543.9416, ⓦwww.residenzacanali.com. Tucked away on a side street just a three-minute walk from Piazza Navona, this family-run hotel is hard to beat for location and service. The bright rooms, with wood-beamed ceilings and modern en-suite bathrooms, are great value too, especially rooms 1 and 2, each with its own terrace. Note that there are several flights of stairs – and no lift. The lobby has a free internet terminal. Doubles €210.

Santa Chiara Via Santa Chiara 21 ☎06.687.2979, ⓦwww.albergosantachiara .com. A friendly, family-run hotel in a great location, on a quiet piazza behind the Pantheon. Nice rooms too, some of which overlook the church of Santa Maria sopra Minerva. Doubles €200–250.

🏃 **Teatro Pace** Via del Teatro Pace 33 ☎06.687.9075, ⓦwww.hotelteatropace .com. This beautifully restored *palazzo*, a few paces from Piazza Navona, was once home to one of the Vatican's most prominent cardinals. Leading off an impressive Baroque spiral staircase (no lift) are four floors of elegant, mostly spacious rooms with original wood beams, floor-sweeping drapes and luxurious bathrooms. Doubles €210.

🏃 **Zanardelli** Via G. Zanardelli 7 ☎06.6821.1392, ⓦwww.hotelnavona .com. Just north of Piazza Navona, this is a slightly more lavish alternative to its sister hotel, the *Navona* (see p.223). The building used to be a papal residence and retains many original fixtures and furnishings. The rooms are elegant, with antique iron beds,

silk-lined walls and modern amenities, but are still decently priced considering the location. The lobby and breakfast areas have free wi-fi, and there's a free laptop for brief internet use. Doubles €150–180.

Campo de' Fiori and the Ghetto

Unless marked otherwise, see the **map** on pp.58–59.

Arenula Via S. Maria de' Calderari 47 ☎06.687.9454, ⓦwww.hotelarenula.com. Simple, clean rooms, each with its own bathroom, plus free wi-fi or keypad to use with room TV. No lift, and top-floor rooms are quite a climb, but a good location near Largo Argentina and the bridge that leads to Trastevere. Doubles €100–133.

Campo de' Fiori Via del Biscione 6 ☎06.6880.6865, ⓦwww.hotelcampodefiori .com. A friendly hotel with clean and pleasant rooms that come in all shapes and colours. The large roof terrace offers great views, and the hotel also owns a number of small apartments nearby (around €180 a night for two people). Doubles vary quite a lot in price, but you should be able to find something for around €150.

Fortyseven Via Petroselli 47 ☎06.678.7816, ⓦwww.fortysevenhotel.com. See map, p.68. Tasteful, elegant rooms above the ancient cattle market near the Bocca della Verità and within striking distance of the Forum, Trastevere and the Ghetto. There's a fitness centre and a rooftop bar and restaurant too. Doubles €300.

Pomezia Via dei Chiavari 13 ☎06.686.1371, ⓦwww.hotelpomezia.it. Slightly more upscale than its budget neighbours, but still a low-priced choice. A small bar occupies half of the reception area, and Maurizio, the owner, keeps it open all night for those who want it. Doubles €80–150.

Residenza Farnese Via del Mascherone 59 ☎06.6889.1388, ⓦwww.residenzafarneseroma .it. On a quiet side street right by Palazzo Farnese, rooms here are large, tastefully appointed and some overlook the French Embassy gardens. The staff are very helpful, and the location can't be bettered – great for both the centro storico and Trastevere, just across the bridge. Parking is available in the courtyard, but only by advance request. Doubles €180.

St George Via Giulia 62 ☎06.686.611, ⓦwww .stgeorgehotel.it. Situated on one of Rome's

Historic hotels

If Rome's unique historical pedigree inspires you to seek out a hotel with similar credentials, the places below won't disappoint.

La Posta Vecchia Palo Laziale, Ladispoli ☏06.994.9501, ⓦwww.lapostavecchia .com. If you don't mind being way out of town, this seaside hotel – the former home of oil baron John Paul Getty – is a luxurious and romantic choice. It was Getty's base for collecting art; the lower floor is now a museum with second-century BC artefacts unearthed during renovation. There's a tennis court, a spa and a pool overlooking the sea. To rent Getty's private apartment, reckon on €1200 a night; otherwise, doubles cost from €320.

Residenza Napoleone III Largo Goldoni 56 ☏06.6880.8083, ⓦwww.residenza napoleone.com. See map, p.93. In the opulent setting of the sixteenth-century Palazzo Ruspoli, two rooms are sumptuously furnished with priceless antiques and vast oil paintings – a level of luxury of which one-time resident Napoleon obviously approved. Doubles from €620.

Torre Colonna Via delle Tre Cannelle 18 ☏06.6228.9543, ⓦwww.torrecolonna.com. See map, p.68. Occupying a defensive tower built by the noble Colonna family in 1247, this new 5-room guesthouse has been decorated in fresh, contemporary style – there's modern art on the walls, as well as a rooftop jacuzzi with panoramic views over neighbouring Piazza Venezia. Doubles from €207.

Villa Laetitia Lungotevere delle Armi 22 ☏06.322.6776, ⓦwww.villalaetitia.com. See map, pp.180–181. Once a decrepit riverside villa, this 14-room residence has been restored to its former Art Nouveau glory by Anna Fendi Venturini of the Italian fashion dynasty. Furnishings sourced from antiques fairs around the world turn rooms into mini-museums, and the marble pillars and ornate ceilings create a sophisticated, old-world feel. Doubles from €190.

Villa Spalletti Trivelli Via Piacenza 4 ☏06.4890.7934, ⓦwww.villaspalletti.it. See map, pp.116–117. In a great location – a five-minute walk from Piazza Venezia – this aristo-cratic villa with a fascinating history is one of Rome's most luxurious accommodation options. The twelve rooms are impeccably furnished with antiques, and the common areas – including a lovely garden – exude an aura of exclusivity. Doubles from €462.

most beautiful streets, this is a stylish and contemporary five-star done out with touches of neo-Baroque whimsy. There's an on-site spa and fitness centre, as well as a chic restaurant, *I Sofà di Via Giulia*, and an inviting bar. Doubles €260–350.
Sole Via del Biscione 76 ☏06.6880.6873, ⓦwww.solealbiscione.it. This place enjoys one of the best locations in the centre, and has reasonable rooms with televisions and phones, and several roof terraces with spectacular views of the nearby domes. No breakfast; no credit cards. Doubles with bath €130–160; with shared bath €100.
Teatro di Pompeo Largo del Pallaro 8 ☏06.687.2812, ⓦwww.hotelteatrodipompeo.it. Built above the remains of Pompey's ancient Roman theatre, the rooms here are comfort-able, with high-beamed wooden ceilings, marble-topped furniture, and (in some) great views. Doubles €180–210.

The Tridente and Trevi

See the **map** on p.93.

Casa Howard Via Capo le Case 18 and Via Sistina 149 ☏06.6992.4555, ⓦwww .casahoward.com. This boutique hotel offers a series of themed rooms in two locations, one close to Piazza di Spagna, the other just off Piazza Barberini. Rooms are on the small side, but elegantly and stylishly furnished; service is very personal and welcoming and there's free wi-fi in each room. Breakfast is served in your room. Doubles €200–300.
Condotti Via Mario de' Fiori 37 ☏06.679.4661, ⓦwww.hotelcondotti.com. The *Condotti* is cosy and inviting, with rooms that are comfortable, if a little lacking in personality. The staff are cheerful and welcoming, though, and there's a free internet point in the lobby and wi-fi in the rooms. Not a bad price for the location: doubles from €175.

Dei Borgognoni Via del Bufalo 126
☎06.6994.1505, ⓦ www.hotelborgognoni.it.
A surprisingly big hotel, considering its
location down a side street not far from
Piazza di Spagna, this four-star hotel has
pleasant, nicely renovated large rooms. You
pay for wi-fi, but the lobby has an internet
terminal. The bar serves light meals, and in
2010 a cosy library with fireplace was
added. Doubles from €280.

De Russie Via del Babuino 9
☎06.328.881, ⓦ www.roccofortehotels
.com. Since opening in 2000, the *De Russie*
has quickly become the abode of choice for
visiting movie stars and hip travellers
spending someone else's money, with
rooms that are among the city's most
expensive. It still has a buzz about it, and
if you can't afford the €9000 Nijinsky
Suite or even one of the standard stylishly
modern double rooms, just pop in for a
drink in the *Stravinskj Bar* or dine in the
lovely terraced garden that rises to the
Pincio. The beautifully designed spa – one
of Rome's best – has an enticing array of
treatments. Doubles from €680.

D'Inghilterra Via Bocca di Leone 14
☎06.699.811, ⓦ www.royaldemeure.com. Billing
itself as one of the world's finest hotels, this
old favourite, formerly the apartments of the
princes of Torlonia, does not disappoint, and
is pretty good value compared to the cost of
a similar level of pampering elsewhere in the
city. Intimacy, opulence, exquisite antiques,
frescoed rooms, and all the delights of the
ancient city centre on your doorstep.
Doubles from €400.

Erdarelli Via dei Due Macelli 28 ☎06.679.1265,
ⓦ www.erdarelliromehotel.com. A rather plain
hotel with no-frills rooms and services (no
internet access, TV only in the lobby, and
a/c only in some rooms), but it's welcoming
enough and for its location, just around the
corner from the Spanish Steps, the prices
can't be beaten: doubles without bath
€70–80, with bath €90–130.

Eva's Rooms Via dei Due Macelli 31
☎06.6919.0078, ⓦ www.evasrooms.com.
A great location – just a two-minute walk
from the Spanish Steps – is this B&B's
main draw, but that's not all: rooms are
large and cosily furnished, there's free wi-fi
and the soaring ceiling of the junior suite is
decorated with frescoes. If you don't mind
sacrificing a few frills – breakfast is far from
sumptuous, and the decor is a little tired –

this is a bargain, with doubles as low
as €110 in the off season, though
normally €150.

Firenze Palace Via dei Due Macelli 106
☎06.678 0038, ⓦ www.hoteldogerome.it.
A combination of the hotels *Doge* and
Firenze, this has a bit more character than
its neighbours, and large double rooms
with TV that are good value for money at
around €200.

Grand Hotel Plaza Via del Corso 126
☎06.6992.1111, ⓦ www.grandhotelplaza
.com. One of the most sumptuous hotels in
Rome, and a fitting backdrop to films like
Angels and Demons and *Ocean's 12*. The
fantastic lobby is worth dropping into even if
you're not staying here: plush velvets,
sumptuous brocades, fine wall textiles,
grand chandeliers, a stained-glass ceiling
and a fabulous bar – all meticulously
maintained. The huge rooms have been
updated and now have wi-fi. Rates are high,
but not bad considering the atmosphere
and location. Doubles around €360.

Hassler Trinità dei Monti 6 ☎06.699.340,
ⓦ www.hotelhasslerroma.com. Location,
location, location – at the top of the
Spanish Steps, you can't get a much more
commanding position above Rome than
this. A luxury hotel with simple, elegant
rooms and every convenience a guest
could possibly require, including a spa, but
what you are paying for is the reputation
and – of course – the view. The "classic"
rooms – the cheapest – will set you back
€550–700.

Homs Via della Vite 71–72 ☎06.679.2976,
ⓦ www.hotelhoms.it. In the heart of the
Spanish Steps neighbourhood, this small
four-star has a very friendly atmosphere –
something that's not always guaranteed in
the hotels of this ritzy area. The rooms have
been recently refurbished, and there's also a
two-bedroom rooftop apartment for around
€250 a night. Doubles from €180.

Hotel Art Via Margutta 56 ☎06.328.711,
ⓦ www.hotelart.it. Tucked away on Via
Margutta, this luxury hotel – converted in
part from a convent – features contemporary art and innovative design. It has a wide
range of amenities, including a Turkish bath,
gym, spa, and a bar that once was a
chapel. Doubles €250–320.

Il Palazzetto Vicolo del Bottino 8 ☎06.699.0878,
ⓦ www.wineacademyroma.com. The International Wine Academy is a project of the

owners of the *Hassler* hotel (see p.226), and as well as running courses on wine and hosting a distinguished restaurant and rooftop bar (Aug & Sept 7.30pm–1am), it rents out four of its sumptuously decorated rooms. Not especially quiet (three of the rooms open onto the Steps), but the location is great, and guests can use the *Hassler*'s spa and have breakfast there. Doubles €200–300.

Locarno Via della Penna, 22 ☎06.361.0841, ⓦ www.hotellocarno.com. The *Locarno* has devoted regulars who are most content when nothing changes. No two rooms are alike, filled with antiques of various periods, and the hotel's atmospheric bar on some nights can attract a cast of hundreds, which is heaven if you are into the somewhat decadent scene; otherwise request a room away from the bar (or the roof terrace, which the bar occupies, too, in summer). Literati, the film world, artists and those that could afford to pay much more relish the *Locarno*'s quirkiness and genteel nature. Doubles from around €200.

Manfredi Via Margutta 61 ☎06.320.7676, ⓦ www.hotelmanfredi.com. This sixteenth-century building once housed a theatre, renamed Teatro delle Dame because for the first time women were allowed to perform. On picturesque, artsy Via Margutta, the hotel is moments from the Spanish Steps. Rooms were given a makeover in 2008 and are fairly fancy for the price. The wine bar under a triple-domed ceiling makes a pleasant spot for a drink. Doubles €160–240.

Piazza di Spagna Via Mario de' Fiori 61 ☎06.679.3061, ⓦ www.hotelpiazzadispagna.it. This small hotel just a few minutes' walk from the Spanish Steps is a good alternative to the sumptuous palaces that characterize this area. Family-owned and run, its rooms are comfortable, all have a/c and TV, and some have jacuzzis. Friendly staff, too. Doubles around €200.

Portrait Suites Via di Bocca di Leone 23 ☎06.6938.0742, ⓦ www.lungarnohotels .com. A relative newcomer to the boutique hotel circuit, this converted townhouse with 14 suites, owned and designed by fashion designer Salvatore Ferragamo, is a bastion of luxury and comfort. Prices are high, but the suites are superbly appointed, and there's a lovely rooftop bar. Wi-fi or the loan of a laptop is free, and service is second to none. Doubles €400.

The Quirinale, Via Veneto and east

See the **map** on pp.104–105.

Aleph Via di San Basilio 15 ☎06.422.901, ⓦ www.boscolohotels.com. One of the city's slickest hotels, with ultra-cool, contemporary rooms and every facility, including a health club housed in a former bank vault, and a quirky lobby with whose Las Vegas take on Egyptian–Roman history is an appropriate prelude to the very red *Sin Restaurant*. Doubles from €350.

Daphne Via di San Basilio 55 and Via degli Avignonesi 20 ☎06.8745.0086, ⓦ www .daphne-rome.com. A welcoming place in two locations either side of Piazza Barberini, run by an American woman and her Roman husband. Most of the rooms are bright, modern and spacious (though a few are not), and you can choose between shared bathrooms and en suite. Doubles €150–220.

Eden Via Ludovisi 49 ☎06.478.121, ⓦ www .hotel-eden.it. Just off Via Veneto, this former private residence, on a quiet tree-lined street, is one of Rome's most enchanting hotels, with an inviting lobby and a fireplace that blazes in winter. Its recent renovation has spruced up the rooms and public spaces while retaining their elegance. Rooms on the fifth floor are a bit more special, with balconies offering spectacular views of the city. Even if you can't get one of these, you can take in the views in the rooftop restaurant, *La Terrazza dell'Eden*, where Federico Fellini had a regular table and conducted most of his interviews. Good rates out of season. Doubles from around €480.

Fenix Viale Gorizia 5–7 ☎06.854.0741, ⓦ www .fenixhotel.it. Just off Via Nomentana, and an easy walk to Villa Torlonia or Santa Costanza, the drab modern exterior of this hotel belies the bright silks, carpets and antique furniture within. It's very comfortable, with magazines everywhere, an eclectic library, free internet terminal and wi-fi, and there's a cheery little restaurant that is very reasonably priced, much favoured by the business travellers that stay here. The small garden with gauzy gazebo and comfy divans makes a good place for an *aperitivo*. Doubles from about €140.

Majestic Via Veneto 50 ☎06.421.441, ⓦ www .hotelmajestic.com. Opened in 1889, this is Via Veneto's oldest hotel, and with its precious antiques and sumptuous furnishings, it set the standard for those that followed. Ceiling frescoes, silk hangings, and big, elaborate furniture are reminders of its Victorian origins, but colours have been brightened for a more contemporary feel. Rooms are elegant and roomy, with huge marble bathrooms, and wi-fi and internet points are free. In 2009 the upstairs terrace was transformed into *Filippo La Mantia* (see p.250), a Sicilian restaurant, bright with antique mirrors and natural light. Doubles from around €350.

Modigliani Via della Purificazione 42 ☏06.4281.5226, ⓦ www.hotelmodigliani.com. A young artist couple run this tastefully modern hotel on a quiet street just off Piazza Barberini. Rooms are comfortable, and all have a/c. Splash out on a superior room if you can – they're larger and have views of St Peter's. There's a small garden courtyard too, and one of the common rooms has free wi-fi. Doubles €197.

Splendide Royal Via di Porta Pinciana 14 ☏06.421.689, ⓦ www.splendideroyal.com. No room for minimalism in the *Splendide Royal's* decor: this nineteenth-century former convent is splashed in neo-Baroque energy. The spacious, light bedrooms are decorated in rich gold, cream and red; those that face the Aurelian Wall have magical views of the umbrella pines below. Film buffs should check out the lobby chandelier, which once glittered above Burt Lancaster and Claudia Cardinale in *The Leopard*, and don't miss the rooftop bar, whose views are enhanced by mirrors. Doubles from €230.

Victoria Via Campania 41 ☏06.473.701, ⓦ www.hotelvictoriaroma.com. Newly remodelled in imperial Roman style, this Swiss-managed hotel is situated between the super-deluxe grandeur of Via Veneto and the verdant freedom of Villa Borghese. Many rooms enjoy views of the ancient walls and beyond. Doubles around €300.

Westin Excelsior Via Veneto 125 ☏06.47.081, ⓦ www.starwoodhotels.com. This grand white palace on Via Veneto was recently renovated to its original turn-of-the-century Empire style and is once again the choice of royalty when they visit Rome. Rooms are crammed with antiques, crystal chandeliers and tapestries and the extravagant Villa La Cupola suite is the priciest night in town. There's also an indoor pool and spa. Doubles around €380–550.

The Esquiline, Monti and Termini

See the **map** on pp.116–117.

Alpi Via Castelfidardo 84 ☏06.444.1235, ⓦ www.hotelalpi.com. One of the more peaceful yet convenient options close to Termini, recently renovated, with pleasant if somewhat small en-suite doubles – better than you would normally expect in a hotel of this category. Doubles around €150.

Artorius Via del Boschetto 13 ☏06.482.1196, ⓦ www.hotelartoriusrome.com. On a cobbled Monti street and with just ten rooms, decorated in classic style, this family-run hotel is an appealing mid-range option. The attractive courtyard makes a pleasant spot for breakfast in fine weather, and for drinks after dark. No wi-fi but rooms have free internet access via cable. Doubles €185.

Astoria Garden Via Bachelet 8 ☏06.446.9908, ⓦ www.hotelastoriagarden.it. In a peaceful area east of Termini near Piazza Indipendenza, this renovated 1904 *palazzo* was once the home of an Italian count. Rooms are pleasant and quiet and some have balconies that look onto the Mediterranean plants and orange trees in the large garden. Guests are entitled to an hour's free wi-fi. There's a bar in the lobby too. Doubles €80–260.

The Beehive Via Marghera 8 ☏06.4470.4553, ⓦ www.the-beehive.com. "Hotel, Café, Art" is the slogan of this ecological – and economical – bright yellow hotel run by an American couple. The doubles – all of which share bathrooms – are basic but very well decorated; more spartan dorms go for €25 a head, and they also manage a number of apartments nearby (ⓦ www.cross-pollinate .com). Wi-fi and internet are free. There is free internet access, and a restaurant that serves vegetarian breakfast, lunch and dinner daily. Doubles €80.

Cervia Via Palestro 55 ☏06.491.057, ⓦ www .hotelcerviaroma.com. Pleasant rooms in a lively and very friendly *pensione*. If you don't mind lugging your bags a few more steps, ask for the discounted rooms on the third floor. Basic but clean rooms – Great value. Doubles €60–90.

Des Artistes Via Villafranca 20 ☏06.445.4365, ⓦ www.hoteldesartistes.com. One of the better hotels in the Termini area – exceptionally good value, spotlessly clean, and with a wide range of rooms, including dorm beds for around €25. Rooms with bathrooms have wi-fi, and you can eat breakfast or recover from a long day of sightseeing on the breezy roof terrace. En-suite doubles around €150.

Duca d'Alba Via Leonina 14 ⊤06.484.471, ⓦwww.hotelducadalba.com. A reliable three-star in the heart of Monti, just steps from the district's best restaurants and nightlife, with stylish, recently renovated rooms, with free wi-fi and a/c; some also have balconies. Rooms are heavily discounted in low season, otherwise doubles cost €250–280.

Elide Via Firenze 50 ⊤06.488.3977, ⓦwww .hotelelide.com. A *pensione* for over fifty years, this has clean, simple rooms and friendly staff. Several of the rooms are right on a busy street, though; if noise bothers you, ask for a room at the back. Free wi-fi in rooms and in lobby. Doubles from €80.

Exedra Piazza della Repubblica 47 ⊤06.489.381, ⓦwww.boscolohotels.com. Opened in 2003 in a Neoclassical *palazzo* that curves around a segment of the piazza, the *Exedra* breathed new life into the Termini area, with elegantly furnished rooms, a champagne bar and a lovely spa, including a small pool (see p.292). Wi-fi available in the lobby and on the fifth-floor terrace. Doubles around €300.

Giuliana Via A. Depretis 70 ⊤06.488.0795, ⓦwww.hotelgiuliana.com. This newly renovated Termini area hotel has a loyal following, and a friendly and helpful owner. Very simple rooms, but the hotel is excellently maintained. A rudimentary breakfast is included. Doubles €90–165.

Nicolas Inn Via Cavour 295 ⊤06.9761.8483, ⓦwww.nicolasinn.com. A brief stroll from the Colosseum, this B&B is run by a friendly American–Italian couple, who are keen to make guests feel at home. The rooms are a good size, spotless and elegant, and have free wi-fi. Breakfast is included but is served in a nearby bar. Doubles €180.

Palazzetto degli Artisti Via della Madonna dei Monti 108 ⊤06.6992.4931, ⓦwww.palazzetto degliartisti.com. These mini-apartments, on the edge of the Monti district, are an exercise in sophisticated minimalism, but they're practical too: attached kitchens with all mod cons make this a good choice for those who want the option of self-catering, with the comfort and services of a four-star hotel, although TVs offer no English-language channels. Wi-fi is free. The suites are pricey, but offer knockout views of the Roman Forum. Doubles €200.

Positano Via Palestro 49 ⊤06.490.360, ⓦwww .hotelpositano.it. Not glamorous, but reasonably priced and convenient, with comfortable rooms two minutes' walk from Termini. The helpful management is adding wi-fi in 2010. Doubles €55–100.

Quirinale Via Nazionale 7 ⊤06.470.7804 or 06.4707, ⓦwww.hotelquirinale.it. About as convenient for the nearby Teatro dell'Opera as it gets (Giuseppe Verdi greeted the crowds here after the 1893 Rome premiere of *Falstaff*), this pleasantly old-fashioned stalwart has a fireplace and free internet point in its lobby. A secret passageway leads directly to the opera house without going onto the street (open to hotel or dinner guests with a performance ticket), and despite being situated on one of Rome's busiest streets its large, antique-filled rooms are surprisingly quiet and have elegant, spacious marble bathrooms and (for a fee) wi-fi. Parking €15. Doubles €130–214.

Radisson Blu es Via F. Turati 171 ⊤06.444.841, ⓦwww.radissonblu.com/eshotel-rome. One of the first hotels to spark the renaissance of the Termini area, with starkly aesthetic rooms and a state-of-the-art rooftop bar and pool. Within walking distance of Termini, although it could be better illuminated at night. Rates aren't bad, but breakfast is extra and service can be patchy. Wi-fi is free. Doubles €140–210.

Residenza Cellini Via Modena 5 ⊤06.4782.5204, ⓦwww.residenzacellini.it. The rooms here are comfortable and large with a slightly old-fashioned feel; you may feel it's worth paying the extra for a spacious junior suite (€280), with hydromassage bath. Staff are extremely friendly and wi-fi is free, as is the lobby's internet point. Doubles €240.

Richmond Largo Corrado Ricci 36 ⊤06.6994.1256, ⓦwww.hotelrichmondroma .com. For devotees of Rome's most ancient splendours, this is the perfect choice; right across the way from the Forums and the Colosseum, and with a roof terrace for taking in the views of the ancient city. Rooms are small, but well planned and newly freshened. Doubles €175–214.

Rosetta Via Cavour 295 ⊤06.4782.3069, ⓦwww.rosettahotel.com. Family-run *pensione* in a nice location very close to the Colosseum. The small rooms are a bit shabby and lacking in frills – TV has no English-language channels – but they're comfortable enough, and have private baths. Wi-fi in the lobby only. No breakfast. Doubles from €90.

Suite Dreams Via Modena 5 ☎06.4891.3907, ⊛www.suitedreams.it. The owner of this recently opened hotel has years of experience in the industry behind him – and it shows. The rooms are simple but stylish, with generous bathrooms, but it's the attention to detail and friendly service that really stand out. Services such as a DVD library for guests' use and free wi-fi are an unexpected bonus in this price bracket. Doubles €180.

Villa delle Rose Via Vicenza 5 ☎06.445.1788, ⊛www.villadellerose.it. This centuries-old aristocratic villa sits amidst its own tranquil gardens, belying the fact that it's only a block from Termini station. Newly done up, it's quiet, pleasant and appealingly decorated, with very friendly staff. The lobby has a free internet point and wi-fi. Limited parking is free, on a first-come, first-served basis. Doubles €70–150.

Yes Via Magenta 15 ☎06.4436.3836, ⊛www.yeshotelrome.com. The location – just down the road from Termini – is probably not what you dreamt of for your Roman holiday, but *Yes* is a huge step up from the grotty options that litter the area, and you'll pay considerably less here than for a similar room in the centre. Tailored to the needs of Termini's business travellers – rather than its backpackers – the rooms are comfortable but bland. Doubles around €150.

The Celian Hill and San Giovanni

See the **map** on pp.130–131.
Capo d'Africa Via Capo d'Africa 54 ☎06.772.801, ⊛www.hotelcapodafrica.com. A former nineteenth-century convent, this sleek hotel has a brightly modern interior accented with contemporary art and furniture, though TV has no English-language channels. The bar forms part of the lively lobby, while the roof terrace breakfast room has a good view of Colle Oppio and the Colosseum. Doubles from about €350.

🏃 **Lancelot Via Capo d'Africa 47** ☎06.7045.0615, ⊛www.lancelothotel .com. Just two minutes from the Colosseum, this friendly family-run hotel has rooms with oriental carpets on wood or terrazzo floors, and an attractive bar. Dinner is good too, served at intimate round tables with other

guests for €25 a head. The terrace and some rooms have a view of the Colosseum and the staff are well informed and helpful. Wi-fi is free, as is the lobby internet point. They also have limited parking for €10. Doubles €150–190.

The Aventine Hill and south

See the **map** on pp.138–139.
Abitart Via P. Matteucci 10–20 ☎06.454.3191, ⊛www.abitarthotel.com. This hotel's main attraction is its eight quirky art-themed suites – Metaphysical, Pop Art, Deconstructionist, and so on. It's just off Via Ostiense – a neighbourhood that has a bit more grit to it than the refined piazzas of the centro storico, but getting to the centre as well as the coast is easy (it's a 5min walk from Piramide metro station), and it's well placed for clubbing in Testaccio. Free wi-fi and internet, generous breakfasts, and garage parking for €18. It's targeted at business customers so weekend room rates are usually lower. Doubles €149–199.

🏃 **Sant'Anselmo Piazza Sant'Anselmo 2** ☎06.570.057, ⊛www.aventinohotels .com. One of the most peaceful places you could stay and yet still be in the city centre. One of several hotels on the Aventine Hill that make up a small chain, the *Sant'Anselmo* has beautifully furnished rooms (each with a different theme) that have been fairly recently renovated. Breakfast is good, there's a nice lounge and garden, and parking is free. Deals available outside high season. Doubles €180.

Trastevere and the Janiculum Hill

See the **map** on pp.156–157.
Antico Borgo di Trastevere Vicolo del Buco 7 ☎06.588.3774, ⊛www.trasteverehouse.it. This small seventeenth-century palace has been neatly done up, although some of the rooms can be a bit cramped, and TVs have no English-language channels. It's located in a quiet corner of this bustling district, but is just seconds away from all the action. Guests can go to its sister hotel, *Domus Tiberina* (see below), to use free wi-fi. Doubles around €120.

Carmel Via G. Mameli 11 ☎06.580.9921, ⊛www .hotelcarmel.it. Pleasant, simply furnished en-suite rooms, two with their own terrace, on the western side of Trastevere. There's also a leafy roof terrace for all guests. Free wi-fi in lobby; TV has no English-language channels. Doubles €80–105.

Cisterna Via della Cisterna 7–9 ⊤06.581.7212, ⓦwww.cisternahotel.it. Friendly two-star with a homely feel, bang in the middle of Trastevere. Twenty rooms, some with colourful tiled floors and wood-beamed ceilings, and all with private bathrooms. The peaceful terrace garden out the back is a treat in fine weather. Free internet point and wi-fi. Doubles from €100.

Domus Tiberina Via in Piscinula 37 ⊤06.580.3033, ⓦwww.hoteldomustiberina.it. Located on the quieter side of Trastevere, this small hotel nevertheless lies within a few minutes' walk of everything you might want to see. Rooms are small, but newly refurbished. Free wi-fi in the lobby; TVs have no English-language channels. Doubles €65–150.

Grand Hotel del Gianicolo Viale delle Mura Gianicolensi 107 ⊤06.5833.3405, ⓦwww .grandhotelgianicolo.it. Commanding the heights of the Janiculum Hill, and with views over the entire city, this former convent is a block from the American Academy and the joys of Villa Pamphilj. The rooms are elegant and understated and there's a large, mosaic-tiled swimming pool set in subtropical gardens. A wonderful choice if you want somewhere that feels far from the hubbub of the city centre. There are easy bus connections, though it's a good twenty-minute bus ride to the centre of town. On-site parking. Doubles €120–270.

Residenza Arco de' Tolomei Via Arco de' Tolomei 27 ⊤06.5832.0819, ⓦwww.bbarcodeitolomei .com. In an attractively crumbling *palazzo* on Trastevere's quieter, eastern side, this old-world B&B is full of antiques passed

down from generation to generation of the Italian owners' family, but the atmosphere is anything but stuffy. The generous breakfast is served in the conservatory. Doubles €220.

Residenza Santa Maria Via dell'Arco di San Calisto 20 ⊤06.5833.5103, ⓦwww.residenza santamaria.com. Opened in 2007 by the owners of the ever-popular *Santa Maria* (see below), this small hotel has a more intimate feel. The eighteenth-century building – which once housed craftsmen's workshops – has been attractively restored, with features such as brick arches, wood-beamed ceilings and an internal courtyard giving it a welcoming feel. It's especially recommended for families: four of the six rooms are triples or quads. Free internet point in lobby and wi-fi. Parking €15–25. Doubles €230.

Santa Maria Vicolo del Piede 2 ⊤06.589.4626, ⓦwww.hotelsantamaria.info. A few metres off Piazza Santa Maria in the heart of Trastevere, the rooms of this small three-star surround an orange-tree-filled garden, giving the feel of a place far removed from the noise of the city. The hotel recently added several more rooms, has free bikes for guests to use, free wi-fi and internet, and serves *aperitivi* in the afternoon. Parking €15–25. Doubles €150–230.

Trastevere Via Luciano Manara 24–25 ⊤06.581.4713, ⓦwww.hoteltrastevere.net. A good place to stay if you want to be in the heart of Trastevere, with nicely renovated doubles, and apartments for up to five people. Simply furnished yet homely. Ground-floor windows are double-glazed and wi-fi is free. Doubles €90–150.

Villa della Fonte Via della Fonte d'Olio 8 ⊤06.580.3797, ⓦwww.villafonte.com. This

Convents

Rome also has lots of accommodation run by **religious organizations**. Many are no longer as cheap as they used to be and hotel websites often have the better bargains, but they can often be found in central locations (see ⓦwww.monasterystays.com for more). Bear in mind that most have strict rules about curfews and often a single-gender policy. The **Casa di Santa Brigida**, Piazza Farnese 96 (⊤06.6889.2596, ⓦwww .brigidine.org; see map, pp.58–59), has a location that is hard to beat, and its rooms are clean and comfortable, with private bathroom and no curfew, and breakfast is included, but it's not cheap at €190 a room. They also have a sister residence that costs less, north of the centre at Via delle Isole 34 (⊤06.814.393; doubles around €140), near Via Nomentana and Santa Costanza. Otherwise try the **Suore Mantellate Serve di Maria**, bang in the centre near Piazza Navona on Via S. Giuseppe Calasanzio (⊤06.6880.3344; see map, p.44), which has double rooms for around €80.

attractive place has a hidden-away, almost secret feel to it, yet is just a few steps from Piazza Santa Maria in Trastevere. Rooms are cosy and done up in traditional medieval style, with free wi-fi. Doubles €120–160.

Villa Borghese and north

See the **maps** on p.165 & pp.174–175.

Aldrovandi Palace Via Ulisse Aldrovandi 15 ☎06.322.3993, ⓦwww.aldrovandi.com. Just north of Villa Borghese, this luxurious hotel reveals a bright, quiet interior that looks out over a lovely landscaped garden with swimming pool, and the Michelin-starred restaurant, *baby*, is superb. It is way outside the centre (a long walk to the other side of the Villa Borghese), but a free car service will whisk you to Via Veneto and the Spanish Steps in no time. Parking is free. Doubles around €200.

Casa Montani Piazzale Flaminio 9 ☎06.3260.0421, ⓦwww.casamontani.com. Just outside the Porta del Popolo, this self-styled "luxury town house", opened in 2007, is a boutique hotel with a personal feel. The rooms – all designed by the owners, a friendly French–Italian couple – are decked out in a chic palette of neutrals, with touches of luxury: designer bathrooms, widescreen TVs, free internet point and wi-fi, and breakfast served on fine porcelain. The five rooms are rightly popular – book well ahead. Doubles around €220.

Lord Byron Via Giuseppe De Notaris 5 ☎06.322.0404, ⓦwww.lordbyronhotel.com. Hidden in a residential neighbourhood of Parioli, the guest rooms here combine modern and Art Deco furnishings, and come with writing desks, and luxurious baths with heated towels. Doubles from €340.

The Vatican and Prati

See the **map** on pp.180–181.

Amalia Via Germanico 66 ☎06.3972.2356, ⓦwww.hotelamalia.com. Located on an attractive corner of a busy shopping area close to the Vatican, this place provides four-star amenities at three-star prices, including double-glazing on all windows for maximum peace and security, and nicely renovated double rooms. Don't be misled by the claims of its website, though – it's nowhere near the Spanish Steps! Doubles from €150.

Arcangelo Via Boezio 15 ☎06.687.4143, ⓦwww.hotelarcangeloroma.com. This clean and reliable hotel on a quiet street not far from the Vatican was renovated in 2009 and has maintained an emphasis on comfort and elegance in its rooms and public spaces, which have a warm, clubby feel. Free wi-fi. Parking free but space is limited. Doubles €150–210.

Atlante Star Via Vitelleschi 34 ☎06.687.3233, ⓦwww.atlantehotels.com. Just a five-minute walk from the Vatican, this is perhaps Prati's most luxurious option, with lovely, antique-filled rooms and marble bathrooms. Its most impressive feature is the rooftop terrace, which offers a 360-degree view of Rome, and the popular *Les Etoiles* restaurant. There are free airport pick-ups, and a nearby annexe, the *Atlante Garden* (Via Crescenzio 78; ☎06.687.2361), offers similar luxury at slightly lower rates. Doubles €100–250.

Bramante Vicolo delle Palline 24 ☎06.6880.6426, ⓦwww.hotelbramante.com. Small and welcoming hotel that has a great location on this peaceful Borgo street and nicely furnished en-suite rooms with large bathrooms. Doubles €180–200.

Colors Via Boezio 31 ☎06.687.4030, ⓦwww.colorshotel.com. All rooms at this hostel/hotel in a quiet neighbourhood near the Vatican were renovated in Spring 2010. There are kitchen facilities, free wi-fi in the lobby, TV in guest rooms, and a small terrace, and the same management rents out self-catering apartments for €80–120 a night with two people sharing. Dorm beds from €25 a night, doubles without bath from €80, with bath from €100.

Columbus Via della Conciliazione 33 ☎06.686.5435, ⓦwww.hotelcolumbus.net. Though situated on the main route to St Peter's, the *Columbus* is discreetly set in Palazzo della Rovere, once a cardinal's palace that now belongs to the Order of the Holy Sepulchre. Rooms are plainly furnished with tasteful antiques, while the public areas have an interesting collection of paintings, and the *Colonne* bar on the ground floor is a tranquil oasis from the world outside. The *Veranda* restaurant, with its fifteenth-century frescoed ceiling, is lovely by candlelight, or you can dine on the patio in warm weather. Free parking. Doubles from €200.

Dei Consoli Via Varrone 2d ☎06.6889.2972, ⓦwww.hoteldelconsoli.com. From the location, just around the corner from the

Vatican, to the thoughtfully designed rooms, this is an excellent choice. The decor on each floor is inspired by Old Masters; the top floor, curiously adorned with battle scenes, is where honeymooners are usually lodged. Parking €20. Doubles from €260.

Domus Mazzini Via Monte Zebio 9 T 06.4542.1592, W www.bbdomusmazzini.it. Small *pensione* with just four nicely decorated double rooms. A bit of a hike from the Vatican and St Peter's, but the neighbourhood is pleasant, and the place has the feel of staying in someone's home. Free internet. Doubles €80–120.

Farnese Via Alessandro Farnese 30 T 06.321.1953, W www.farnese.hotelinroma .com. Another grand aristocratic residence that has been turned into an upscale hotel. The rooms have handmade walnut furniture, marble bathrooms and soundproof windows and doors. Some have private balconies, and the rooftop terrace now boasts a breakfast room to make the most of its great view of the Vatican. Free wi-fi. Limited free parking (first-come, first-served). Doubles €100–225.

Franklin Via Rodi 29 T 06.3903.0165, W www .franklinhotelrome.it. The central theme here is music – everywhere: don't be surprised to find a snare drum for a night table or a disco ball in the bathroom. Rooms come equipped with Bang & Olufsen stereos and you can choose from a library of hundreds of Cds. The quirkiness of it all might lift sagging spirits. Free wi-fi. Doubles €159–229.

Gerber Via degli Scipioni 241 T 06.321.9986, W www.hotelgerber.it. Great value for its convenient location on a quiet street not far from the Vatican, with elegant, comfortable rooms which come with free wi-fi. Ten percent discount for *Rough Guide* readers. Doubles around €170.

Giulio Cesare Via degli Scipioni 287 T 06.321.0751, W www.hotelgiuliocesare.com. This charming hotel is no longer the Villa Patricia, home of an Italian countess, but you may feel like royalty once you step into the foyer, with its glistening golden ceiling. Attentive staff lead you down mirror-lined hallways to elegant rooms with marble bathrooms – all very handsome. Doubles €180.

Isa Via Cicerone 39 T 06.321.2610, W www .hotelisa.com. Ten minutes' walk from the Vatican, the grim exterior of this hotel is deceptive, hiding moderately large rooms, renovated in 2008, which have warm wooden panelling, bright bed linen and shiny marble fittings in the bathrooms. Free wi-fi and internet in the lobby, and a great roof garden bar. Excellent value. Doubles €180–240.

La Rovere Vicolo Sant'Onofrio 4–5 T 06.6880.6739, W www.hotellarovere.com. Just round the corner from St Peter's and across the bridge from Piazza Navona, this attractive small hotel is tucked quietly away from all the bustle and offers a terrace garden and antique-filled common areas for its guests to relax in. Rooms are simply furnished but nice enough. Free internet point and wi-fi. Doubles upwards of €140.

Hostels

Rome has plenty of **hostels**, although they can get pretty crowded during peak season. Some places separate guests by gender, but most have private rooms as well as dorms. As well as the options below, *Colors* (see p.232), *Des Artistes* (see p.228) and *The Beehive* (see p.228) have dorm accommodation and budget private rooms. These and the hostels below offer breakfast, and with the exception of the *YWCA*, none of them has a curfew.

Alessandro Palace Via Vicenza 42 T 06.446.1958, W www.hostelsalessandro.com. See map, pp.116–117. This place has been voted one of the top hostels in Europe, and it sparkles with creative style. Pluses include no lock-out or curfew, a good bar with free pizza every night, internet access and satellite TV. Dorm beds €15–21, doubles €65, with bath €90. A few blocks away, on the city-centre side of Termini (Via C. Cattaneo 23; T 06.4434.0147), is *Alessandro Downtown*, with dorm beds for €23.

Ostello del Foro Italico Viale delle Olimpiadi 61 T 06.323.6267, W www.ostellodiroma.it. See map, pp.174–175. Rome's official HI hostel is not particularly central or easy to get to – take bus #32, #69, #224 or #280 from

Camping

For those determined to sleep outdoors, there are a few **campsites** – unsurprisingly some way out of the city. However they are easy enough to get to, and also offer bungalows. Bear in mind that they are only open from spring to early autumn. The closest site is **Camping Flaminio**, 8km north of the centre at Via Flaminia Nuova 821 (March–Oct; ☎06.333.2604, ⊛www.villageflaminio.it), where you can camp for €10 a head, plus €6 for a tent. It also has bungalows (double €52–72 or for 5 €155–170) and a swimming pool and restaurant. To get there from the city centre, either take the Roma-Nord train from Piazzale Flaminio to Due Ponti, or take bus #910 to Piazza Mancini and transfer to bus #200 (ask the driver to drop you at the *fermata più vicino al campeggio*). **Camping Tiber**, on Via Tiberina at Km1400 (March–Oct; ☎06.3361.0733, ⊛www.campingtiber.com), is right beside the Tiber, quiet, spacious and friendly, with a supermarket, bar/pizzeria, swimming pool and really hot showers; and it has some 100 bungalows (double with bath €42) as well as three camping areas, where you can camp for €11 per person and €5 a tent. It has a free shuttle service (8am–11pm every 30min) to and from the nearby Prima Porta station, where you can catch the Roma-Nord train service to Piazzale Flaminio (about 20min).

Termini and ask the driver for the "ostello". You can join here if you're not already an HI member. Facilities include a bar, restaurant, laundry and free unattended parking. Wi-fi and internet available for a fee. You can call ahead to check out availability, and you can book online but they won't take phone bookings. Dorm beds €19.

Ottaviano Via Ottaviano 6 ☎06.3973.8138, ⊛www.pensioneottaviano.com. See map, pp.180–181. This simple hostel near the Vatican is very popular with backpackers; book well in advance. Facilities are a bit sparse: no wi-fi, one internet connection and no TV in the rooms, though the communal TV does play DVDs. Fluent English spoken. Dorm beds (4–8 per room) cost €28–37.

Sandy Via Cavour 136 ☎06.488.4585, ⊛www.sandyhostel.com. See map, pp.116–117. Run by the same management as the *Ottaviano*, with free internet. Dorm beds €21–27, double room €90.

YWCA Via C. Balbo 4 ☎06.488.0460, ⊛www.ywca-ucdg.it. See map, pp.116–117. Opera, ballet and music fans on a budget can stay right by the Teatro dell'Opera. Open to women and men, and just ten minutes' walk from Termini, although the market outside may wake you up earlier than you might want. Midnight curfew. Common room with TV. No wi-fi, but there is an internet point. Singles from €50, doubles with bath from €80, triples and quads without bath €26 per person.

Eating

R ome is undeniably a major-league cultural and historic city, but it just doesn't compare to London or Paris for cutting-edge sophistication and trendiness: in many ways it's like an overgrown village. This can be bad news for nightlife, but it's great news for **food**. Romans, as a group, are still very much in touch with the land – many even have small farms of their own in the countryside nearby, or they return to their home villages regularly. So the city's denizens know a good deal about freshness and authenticity, and can be very demanding when it comes to the quality of the dishes they are served. Having said that, Rome is changing. That wonderful, cheap trattoria serving high-quality authentic Roman cuisine has become a bit harder to find in the last decade or so, and eating out has become pricier. But food remains one of the highlights of any trip to Rome; eating out is a major, often hours-long, activity, with dishes ranging from the good to the truly remarkable.

Most city-centre restaurants offer standard Italian dishes, and many specialize purely in **Roman fare** (see box, p.237), but there have been a few more adventurous places cropping up of late. At the geographical centre of the country, the capital also has numerous establishments dedicated to a variety of **regional cuisines** (see box, p.241), and a reasonable number of excellent **ethnic restaurants** (see box, p.248). The city is also blessed with an abundance of good, honest **pizzerias**, churning out thin, crispy-baked pizza from wood-fired ovens, plus there are plenty

Breakfast and snacks

Most Italians start their day in a bar, their **breakfast** consisting of a cappuccino and a *cornetto* – a jam-, custard- or chocolate-filled croissant, sweeter than the French variety. At other times of the day, **sandwiches** (panini) can be pretty substantial, and cost €2–3; bars also offer *tramezzini*, ready-made sliced white bread with mixed fillings – less appetizing than the average *panino* but still tasty and slightly cheaper at around €1.50 a time. Don't forget that **bakeries and delis** are also great places to pick up a spot of lunch; see p.283 for the best of these. For **food markets**, see the box on p.287; for city-centre **supermarkets**, see the box on p.285.

If you want hot **takeaway food, pizza** by the slice (*pizza rustica* or *pizza al taglio*) is sold pretty much everywhere. Expect to pay €3–4 for a decent-sized slice. A *rosticceria* or **tavola calda** is a good bet for Roman specialities – *supplì* or *arancini* (deep-fried rice balls), *baccalà* (pieces of battered cod) and other deep-fried delights, as well as roast chicken and potatoes, and even green vegetables. A complete meal for two at one of these places can cost less than €10, and although they're usually standing-room only, some have a counter and a few chairs. Finally, **wine bars** always serve some sort of snacky food, usually cold cuts and cheeses.

of good **snack food** options, and scores of **gelaterias**, selling top-quality ice cream and fruit shakes (see box, p.239).

One final caveat: generally speaking it's hard to find truly bad food and rip-off prices in Rome. However, it may be wise to **avoid places** that are adjacent to some major monuments, such as the Pantheon, Piazza Navona, or the Vatican. The food in these places can be poor, and the prices truly outlandish, sometimes as much as three times the going rate. Note also that many places are closed during **August**.

Cafés and bars

There isn't a big difference between cafés and bars in Rome. Italian bars are typically open from 7am for breakfast, and remain open for coffee, tea and snacks throughout the day, closing at around midnight. Bars do serve alcohol, but are rarely a place to linger over a drink. A place calling itself a café is more likely to have seating and be a little less functional than the standard Roman bar.

It's important to be aware of the procedure when you enter an Italian bar. It's cheapest to drink standing at the counter (there's often nowhere to sit anyway), in which case you pay first at the cash desk (*cassa*), present your receipt (*scontrino*) to the barperson and give your order. It's customary to leave an extra 10c or 20c coin on the counter as a tip, although no one will object if you don't. If there's waiter service, just sit where you like, though bear in mind that this will cost perhaps twice as much, especially if you sit outside (*fuori*) – the difference is usually shown on the price list as *tavola* (table) or *terrazzo* (any outside seating area).

Coffee and tea

Coffee is always excellent, drunk small and black (espresso, or just *caffè*), which costs around €0.80 a cup, or as a cappuccino (€1–1.50). If you want your espresso watered down ask for a *caffè americano* or *caffè lungo*. Coffee with a shot of alcohol is *caffè corretto*; with a drop of milk it's *caffè macchiato*; a full small cup of the same is *caffè macchiato lungo*. Many places also now sell decaffeinated coffee (ask for "Café Hag", even when it isn't), while in summer you might want to have your coffee cold (*caffè freddo*). For a real treat ask for *granita di caffè* – cold coffee with crushed ice, usually topped with cream. In summer you can drink iced **tea** (*tè freddo*) – excellent for taking the heat off; hot tea (*tè caldo*) comes with lemon (*con limone*) unless you ask for milk (*con latte*). Milk itself is drunk hot as often as cold, or you can get it with a dash of coffee (*latte macchiato* or *caffè latte*) and sometimes as milk shakes – *frappe* or *frullati*.

Other drinks

Among the **soft drinks**, a *spremuta* is a fresh fruit juice, squeezed at the bar, usually orange, lemon or grapefruit. There are also crushed-ice *granitas*, offered in several flavours, and available with or without whipped cream (*panna*) on top. Otherwise there's the usual range of fizzy drinks and concentrated juices; the home-grown Italian version of Coca Cola, Chinotto, is less sweet – good with a slice of lemon. **Tap water** (*acqua del rubinetto*) is quite drinkable, and you won't pay for it in a bar. **Mineral water** (*acqua minerale*) is a more common choice, either still (*senza gas* or *naturale*) or sparkling (*con gas* or *frizzante*) – about €1 for a small bottle.

For **alcoholic drinks**, see p.256.

Restaurants and pizzerias

There are numerous good restaurants in the **centro storico**, and it's still surprisingly easy to find places that are not tourist traps – **prices** in all but the really swanky places remain pretty uniform throughout the city, as do menus, especially in traditional Roman-cuisine restaurants. In an average trattoria, a substantial meal – an antipasto or a pasta dish, plus main course, dessert and house wine, will set you back around €30 a head. The **Tridente** and around **Campo de' Fiori** are similarly well served, and the neighbouring **Ghetto** is full of appealing Jewish restaurants. The area around **Termini** is packed with cheap places to eat, although some of them are of dubious reliability, and you might do better heading up to the nearby student area of **San Lorenzo**, where you can often eat far better for the same money. South of the centre, **Testaccio** is well endowed with good, inexpensive trattorias, a few of the most traditional serving the best of Rome's offal specialities, while, across the river, **Trastevere** is Rome's traditional restaurant enclave and is accordingly thronged with eating options – and people. The number of authentic "Trastè" trattorias has declined over recent years, but you'll still easily find good to great meals here, at all price levels.

The menu

An Italian meal traditionally starts with the **antipasto** (literally "before the meal"), consisting of various cold cuts of meat, seafood and vegetable dishes. A plateful of antipasti from a self-service buffet will set you back €5–10 a head, an item chosen from the menu slightly less. Bear in mind that if you're moving onto pasta, let alone a main course, you may need quite an appetite to tackle this. The next course, **il primo**, consists of a soup or pasta dish, and it's fine to eat just this and nothing else; pasta dishes go for around €8–12. This is followed by **il secondo** – the meat or fish course, usually served alone, except for perhaps a wedge of lemon or tomato, a garnish of salad, or a potato or two. Watch out when ordering **fish**, which will either be served whole or by weight: 250g is usually plenty for one person, or ask to have a look at the fish before it's cooked. Main fish or meat courses will normally be €10–20 (more only in truly gourmet restaurants). **Vegetarians** will find plenty of options: many pasta dishes and pizzas, of course, are made entirely without meat; lentils and other beans and pulses are a part of traditional cookery; and wonderful fresh vegetables and cheeses are always available.

Side dishes – **contorni** – are ordered and served separately, and sometimes there won't be much choice: potatoes

Traditional Roman restaurants

You can eat Roman cuisine all over the city centre, but there are some places that do the **classics** – such as the pasta dishes *cacio e pepe*, carbonara and *alla gricia* – better than anywhere else. Other places specialize in **Roman–Jewish specialities** like *carciofi alla giudia*, or the **meat and offal** dishes typical of Testaccio, such as *coda alla vaccinara* and *pajata*. And some places excel at all three. Below is our top ten of places at which you can't go wrong.

Al Pompiere p.243
Augustarello p.251
Checchino dal 1887 p.252
Da Felice p.252
Da Paris p.253

Gino p.241
Matricianella p.241
Piperno p.244
Sora Margherita p.244
Trattoria Lilli p.242

For a glossary of **food and drink terms**, see p.329.

will often come as chips (*patatine fritte*); salads are either green (*verde*) or mixed (*mista*). Afterwards you nearly always get a choice of **frutta** (fresh fruit) and a selection of **dolci** (desserts) – sometimes just ice cream, but often more elaborate items, such as *zuppa inglese* (sponge cake or trifle).

Many Italians wouldn't dream of going out to eat and not ordering a full five-course meal, plus wine, mineral water, coffee and a *digestivo*, such as an *amaro* (home-made herb liqueur) – but don't feel you have to follow suit; you can order as little or as much as you want, and no one will raise an eyebrow.

For tips on what to **drink**, see the box on p.256.

Opening hours and the bill

Roman restaurants keep pretty rigid **opening hours**, generally from noon to 3pm and from 7.30 to 11pm, although some stay open later, especially in summer. Early in the week tends to be quieter, and many places are closed in August. It's always a good idea to **book a table**, particularly towards the weekend. Getting the **bill** (*il conto*) can sometimes be a struggle – nothing moves fast in Rome when it comes to mealtimes – but, when you do, service of 10–15 percent will occasionally be included, and if so it will be clearly indicated. Otherwise a small **tip** is fine, rounding the bill up €2–3 or so, as waiters in Italy are paid well. Almost everywhere they add a cover charge of around €2 a head; on your bill it will either be labelled as "**coperto**" or "pane", as it is technically for the bread, which they bring automatically.

Centro storico

See the **map** on p.44.

Cafés and bars

Caffè Sant'Eustachio Piazza Sant'Eustachio 82. No phone. Mon–Thurs 8.30am–1am, Fri 8.30am–1.30am, Sat 8.30am–2am. Just behind the Pantheon you'll find what many believe is Rome's best coffee, usually served Neapolitan style – that is, very, very sweet. You can ask for it without sugar, but they'll think you're weird. They also do a good line in coffee-based sweets and cakes.

Camilloni Piazza Sant'Eustachio 54 ☎06.686.4995. Tues–Sun 8.30am–midnight. A contender for Rome's best coffee, larger than its rival *Sant'Eustachio* across the square, with inside seating and great cakes.

Delfino Corso V. Emanuele 67 ☎06.686.4053. Daily 8am–9pm. A fairly ordinary but very central and busy cafeteria right on Largo Argentina, with a huge choice of snacks and full meals. Good for a fast fill-up between sights.

La Tazza d'Oro Via degli Orfani 84/86 ☎06.679.2768. Just a few paces from the Pantheon, this place is well named, since it is by common consent the home of one of Rome's best cups of coffee, plus decent iced coffee and sinfully rich *granita di caffè*, with double dollops of whipped cream. Good pastries and sandwiches too.

Da Vezio Via Tor di Nona 37 ☎06.678.6036. Mon–Sat 7.30am–9pm. Visible from the flags outside, this tiny bar, tucked away by the river, is a shrine to the Italian Left, Castro and all aspects of the workers' struggle. Not the most welcoming bar in town, but it's worth lingering over a coffee to study the memorabilia that coats the walls.

La Caffetteria Piazza di Pietra 65 ☎06.678.8147. Tues–Sun 8.30am–midnight. Bureaucrats flock to this Neapolitan café from the nearby Parliament: the pastries are imported from Naples daily, and the espresso is among Rome's best. Good for lunch too.

Lo Zozzone Via del Teatro Pace 32 ☎06.6880.8575. Mon–Fri 9am–9pm, Sat 10am–11pm. This Roman legend, just

Italian **ice cream** (*gelato*) is justifiably famous; reckon on paying upwards of €2 for a cone (*un cono*) with one scoop (*gusto*), with the price rising with each scoop you have. Most bars have a fairly good selection, but for real choice go to a *gelateria*, where the range is a tribute to the Italian imagination and flair for display; our favourites are below.

Alberto Pica Via della Seggiola 12 ⊤06.6880.6153. Mon–Sat 8.30am–2am, April–Sept & Dec also open Sun 4.30pm–2am. See map, pp.58–59. Long-running and award-winning Ghetto area favourite with lots of unusual flavours. The place to try rice-pudding ice cream if you've ever fancied it.

Alla Scala Via della Scala 51 ⊤06.581.3174. Mon–Fri 1pm–midnight, Sat & Sun 1pm–1am. See map, pp.156–157. This Sicilian-owned place in Trastevere has some of the very best ice cream in town. Sublime consistency and unusual flavours such as cinnamon and cassata. The cherry and coconut are also great.

Cremeria Monteforte Via della Rotonda 22 ⊤06.686.7720. Tues–Sun 11am–11pm. See map, p.44. There's no better place to eat ice cream than sitting on one of the walls that surround the Pantheon, and this award-winning *gelateria* has lots of flavours.

Della Palma Via della Maddalena 20 ⊤06.6880.6752. Daily 8am–1am. See map, p.44. Not necessarily the city's best ice cream, but certainly its largest selection by some way, with over 100 flavours to choose from.

Gelateria dei Gracchi Via dei Gracchi 272. Daily 11am–1am. See map, pp.180–181. This unassuming, almost spartan place is the most popular *gelateria* for miles around, with a small but perfectly realized range of flavours.

Giolitti Via Uffici del Vicario 40 ⊤06.699.1243. Tues–Sun 7am–2am. See map, p.44. An Italian institution that once had a reputation – now lost – for the country's top ice cream. Still pretty good, however, and always very busy, with a choice of seventy flavours.

Old Bridge Via Bastioni di Michelangelo 5. Daily 10am–2am. See map, pp.180–181. Generous helpings at this long-standing Vatican area favourite, It's famous for its chocolate, coffee and nutella flavours, but most of all for the size of its portions.

Palazzo del Freddo di Giovanni Fassi Via Principe Eugenio 65/7 ⊤06.446.4740. Tues–Sun noon–midnight, Sat noon–12.30am. See map, pp.116–117. Known as "Fassi", this wonderful, huge and airy 1920s ice-cream parlour does brilliant fruit ice creams and good milk shakes.

Pascucci Via di Torre Argentina 20 ⊤06.686.4816. Mon–Fri 6.30am–midnight, Sat 6.30am–12.30am, Sun 10am–midnight. See map, p.44. This tiny stand-up bar is *frullati* central: your choice of fresh fruit whipped up with ice and milk – the ultimate Roman refreshment on a hot day.

San Crispino Via della Panetteria 42 ⊤06.7045.0412. Mon–Thurs & Sun noon–12.30am, Fri & Sat noon–1.30am; closed Tues in autumn and winter. See map, p.93. Near the Trevi Fountain, this is considered by many to make the best ice cream in Rome. They do interesting flavours like ginger and cinnamon, but you may not find common-or-garden strawberry and it's a bit more expensive than your average ice-cream joint. However, it will make the other *gelato* you've tried pale by comparison. Other branches in the centro storico at Piazza Maddalena 3, right by the Pantheon, and at Via Acaia 56 in San Giovanni.

Tre Scalini Piazza Navona 30 ⊤06.6880.1996. Thurs–Tues 8am–1.30am. This Piazza Navona institution is renowned for its famous *tartufo* – dark chocolate truffle – a pricey affair which you can enjoy at one of its outside tables on the square or more cheaply by buying from its takeaway counter and sitting by one of the fountains. See map, p.44.

⑮

EATING

around the corner from Piazza Navona and with outside seating, serves the best *pizza bianca* in town, filled with whatever you want, as well as lots of delicious *pizza al taglio* choices.

Vitti Piazza San Lorenzo in Lucina 3. A Roman institution, serving a wide selection of pastries and sandwiches, along with delicious coffee; there are a few tables inside and lots on the square. A short lunch menu, too, served from 12.30pm.

Restaurants

Antica Biblioteca Largo del Teatro Valle 9 ☎06.6813.6830. Formerly a nightclub, and in a previous existence one of the hotspots of the sixties, this artfully cool restaurant and wine bar still exudes some *Dolce Vita*-era glamour. The food is pretty good as well – Roman and Italian, and usually well presented with an inventive twist. It's moderately priced too, despite the sleek surroundings.

Armando al Pantheon Salita de' Crescenzi 30 ☎06.6880.3034. Mon–Fri 12.30–3pm & 7–11pm, Sat 12.30–3pm. Surprisingly unpretentious surroundings and moderately priced hearty food in this long-standing staple close by the Pantheon (open since 1961).

Boccondivino Piazza in Campo Marzio 6 ☎06.6830.8626. Mon–Sat 12.30–3pm & 7.30–11pm. A nice setting with outdoor seating, a short walk from the Pantheon. *Boccondivino*'s aspirations for a chicer brand of diner is matched by the slightly higher prices, but not always by the food, which – like the service – can be a bit hit and miss. When it's good, though, it's excellent.

Casa Bleve Via del Teatro Valle 49 ☎06.686.5970. Tues–Sat 12.30–3pm & 7.30–10.30pm. This atmospheric, echoing hall in the heart of the centro storico is where Rome's beautiful folk come to enjoy great wine and the food to go with it. As befits the restaurant of an old-established Ghetto wine shop, there's a huge wine list, and a menu of six or so hot dishes, plus cheese and salami plates. It's not cheap – most dishes go for €20–25, and there are no wines under €25 – but the food is great and the service attentive and knowledge-able. There's also a wine shop out front.

Da Baffetto Via del Governo Vecchio 114 ☎06.686.1617. Daily 6.30pm–1am. A tiny, highly authentic pizzeria that has long been a

Rome institution, though it now tends to be swamped by tourists. Amazingly it's still good value, and has tables outside in summer, though you will always have to queue. The *bruschette* are especially good. Another branch – *Baffetto 2* – is on Piazza del Teatro del Pompeo near Campo de' Fiori.

Da Francesco Piazza del Fico 29 ☎06.686.4009. Mon & Wed–Sun 7pm–1am. Not just delectable pizzas in this full-on pizzeria in the heart of the centro storico, but good antipasti, *primi* and *secondi* too. The service can be slapdash, but the food and atmosphere are second to none.

Da Tonino Via del Governo Vecchio 18–19. Mon–Sat noon–3.30pm & 7pm–midnight. Basic Roman food, always freshly cooked, and always delicious, is the order of the day at this unmarked centro storico favourite. The simple pasta dishes start at €6, while the *straccetti* (strips of beef with rocket) are a steal at €7. The few tables fill up quickly, so come early or be prepared to queue. No credit cards.

Da Ugo e Maria Via dei Prefetti 19 ☎06.687.3752. Daily 1–3pm & 8–10pm. Just four starters and four mains to choose from at this basic, family-run restaurant around the corner from the Italian parliament – usually gnocchi and a couple of classic Roman pasta dishes, followed by meat *secondi*, usually a choice between rabbit, chicken, veal and lamb. There's no real ambience, unless you count the blaring radio, but that's really the point: the food is hearty and home-cooked, not expensive (mains around €10), and served in an environment that feels like it hasn't changed in years.

El Toulà Via della Lupa 29b ☎06.687.3570. Mon–Fri 1–3pm & 8–11pm, Sat 8–11pm. Once upon a time all posh restaurants looked like this, and this is certainly one of Rome's most beautiful places to eat, with a lovely old-fashioned interior and a menu of food from the Veneto region – it has a sister restaurant in Treviso. Pretty expensive, with *primi* at €20–30 and *secondi* from €30, but it does good fixed-price menus for upwards of €50.

Enoteca Corsi Via del Gesù 87–88 ☎06.679.0821. Mon–Sat noon–3pm. Tucked away between Piazza Venezia and the Pantheon, this is an old-fashioned Roman trattoria and wine shop where you eat what they happen to have cooked that morning. The menu changes each day, and it gets

Cucina romana

Rome is rightly proud of its own cuisine, and has numerous restaurants serving local specialities to a clientele that would be satisfied with nothing less. Roman cooking is dominated by the earthy preferences of the working classes, with a little influence from the city's millennia-old Jewish population thrown in. Pasta is a staple, and sauces are hearty and satisfying, while meat dishes famously lean towards various unspeakable parts of cows and lambs.

Pasta

The most popular varieties of pasta are **tonnarelli** or **bucatini** – thick, hollow spaghetti, basically – which stand up well to the coarse, gutsy sauces the Romans prefer: **cacio e pepe** (pecorino and ground black pepper), **alla carbonara** (with beaten eggs, cubes of pan-fried *guanciale* – cured pork jowl – or pancetta, and pecorino cheese), **alla gricia** (with pecorino and *guanciale*) and **all'amatriciana** (with tomato and *guanciale*). Spaghetti **alle vongole** (with baby clams) is also common, best when a little *peperoncino* is added to give it an extra kick, and **maccheroni alla ciociara**, with slices of sausage, prosciutto and tomato is another favourite. Pasta **alla pajata** (with calf's intestines) is an old Roman standard, as are **gnocchi**, in Rome usually served with a meat sauce and traditionally eaten on Thursdays.

Rigatoni al pomodoro ▲

Coda alla vaccinara ▼

Main courses

The classic Roman meat dish is **abbacchio**, milk-fed lamb roasted to melting tenderness with rosemary, sage and garlic; you'll also find it *allo scottadito* – grilled and eaten with the fingers. **Saltimbocca alla romana**, thin slices of veal cooked with a slice of prosciutto and sage on top, is ever popular. Otherwise Roman meat dishes are defined by the so-called *quinto quarto* (or fifth quarter) of the animal: basically **offal**, which you'll still find on the menus of traditional places, especially those in the old slaughterhouse district of Testaccio. One of the most palatable dishes is **coda alla vaccinara**, oxtail stewed in a rich sauce of tomato and celery. You'll also come across *pajata* (see above), as well as *lingua* (tongue), *rognone* (kidney), *milza* (spleen – delicious as a pâté on toasted bread) and *trippa* (tripe).

Look out too for *testerelle d'abbacchio*, lamb's head baked in the oven with herbs and oil; and *coratella*, lamb's heart, liver, lungs and spleen cooked in olive oil with lots of black pepper and onions.

More conventionally, fish also features, usually as cod or *baccalà* and best eaten Jewish-style, deep-fried in batter: like British fish and chips without the chips.

Pizza, snacks and fritti

Rome is surpassed only by Naples in the quality of its **pizzas**, and even this is arguable if you prefer the thin and crispy Roman variety, best when baked in a wood-burning oven (*forno a legna*). Other Roman street food includes various deep-fried specialities, or **fritti**, like *supplì* (fried rice balls with mozzarella) and *arancini* (*supplì* with added tomato), as well as spit-roast chicken and **porchetta** – pork stuffed with herbs and roasted on a spit; you'll find the latter most commonly in the Castelli Romani, where it's munched between thick hunks of rustic bread.

▲ *Da Remo* pizzeria

▼ Courgette flowers

Vegetables

Artichokes (*carciofi*) are the quintessential Roman vegetable, best in late winter and early spring, either served *alla romana* (stuffed with garlic and roman mint and stewed) or *alla giudea*, flattened and deep fried in olive oil. Another not-to-be-missed side dish is batter-fried **courgette blossoms** (*fiori di zucca*), stuffed with mozzarella and a sliver of anchovy. Among other vegetables, you can find heavenly **roast potatoes**, cooked with rosemary and served with lamb or chicken; great fresh **asparagus** in spring; **puntarelle** or chicory salad, and various broccoli-like greens, in winter; and haricot and borlotti bean dishes year-round.

A Roman *gelateria* ▲

List of wines at *Enoteca Cavour 313* ▲

Wine time at *L'Enoteca Antica* ▼

Cheese and desserts

The king of Roman cheeses is **pecorino romano**, sharp, salty and crumbly and used in cooking instead of Parmesan. The very best **buffalo mozzarella** from Campania has also become more common in Rome, which is close enough to Naples for it to be rushed up here and eaten fresh.

As for desserts, you may want to try a **tartufo** – chocolate ice cream covered in chocolate, basically – or just have an **ice cream**: the city centre's *gelaterie* are among the country's best, and there's nothing like enjoying your dessert Italian-style, strolling through the streets after the sun has gone down; see the box on p.239 for our pick of the best.

Vintage Rome

Much of the wine served in Rome comes from the **Castelli Romani** just south of the city. The best known is **Frascati**, a light, easy-drinking white made from a blend of Malvasia and Trebbiano grapes – like many Italian wines it's much better than the exported varieties would have you believe. The small town of **Marino** (see p.215) has a great wine festival on the first Sunday of October, at which you can sample Castelli Romani wines to your heart's content. Elsewhere in Lazio, the big wine is called Est! Est! Est!, another drinkable white that hails from Montefiascone. The story goes that in the twelfth century a bishop's servant was sent to find the best wines of the region, and to indicate the ones he liked by daubing the word "Est" on the door of the producer. He liked the wines of Montefiascone so much he daubed the word three times for emphasis. Hopefully you'll feel the same.

very busy at lunchtimes – you may have to wait for a table. Very cheap – €5 for a pasta dish, €8 or so for a main course.

Gino Vicolo Rosini 4 ☎06.687.3434. Mon–Sat 1–3pm & 8–10.30pm. Down a small alley right by the parliament building, *Gino* presides over his constantly bustling restaurant with unhurried authority, serving a determinedly trad Roman menu at keen prices – pasta dishes €5–8, mains €9–10. Try the house speciality – *tonnarelli ciociara*, with peas, mushrooms and ham – and top it off with the excellent *saltimbocca alla romana*. It's been very much discovered by tourists, but at heart it remains a locals' joint.

Grano Piazza Rondanini 53 ☎06.6819.2096. Daily noon–midnight. This great centro storico restaurant has changed hands several times in recent years but this latest incarnation is the best for a while: simple, unfussy Italian food – particularly the fish and seafood – made with the freshest ingredients, and at fairly keen prices too. Let's hope it lasts.

Il Bacaro Via degli Spagnoli 27 ☎06.686.4110. Mon–Fri 12.30–3pm & 7.15–11pm, Sat 7.15–11pm. This tiny restaurant tucked away down a small side street has a small, focused menu featuring an interesting selection of antipasti and *primi*, and mostly meaty mains, particularly beef. The feel of the place is rather romantic but it's really too cramped for a truly private liaison.

La Focaccia Via della Pace 11 ☎06.6880.3312. Daily noon–3.30pm & 7.30pm–1am. In a great location, just off Piazza Navona, this dependable restaurant does tasty Neapolitan pizzas and has a decent choice of pastas and mains too. Tables outside in summer.

La Montecarlo Vicolo Savelli 12 ☎06.686 1877. Daily noon–3pm & 6.30pm–1am. This hectic pizzeria not far from Piazza Navona is owned by the daughter of the owner of *Da Baffetto* (see p.240) and serves similar crisp, blistered pizza, along with good pasta dishes. Tables outside in summer, but be prepared to queue.

La Rosetta Via della Rosetta 9 ☎06.686.1002. Mon–Sat 12.45–2.45pm & 7.30–11pm, Sun 7.30–11pm. One of Rome's premier fish restaurants, and certainly among its most expensive, although the quality of the food and service can't be beaten. A block from the Pantheon, it's an elegant dining experience, and well worth the prices. Pasta dishes around €25, mains €30–50.

Maccheroni Piazza delle Coppelle 44 ☎06.6830.7895. Mon–Sat 12.30–3pm & 8pm–midnight. This friendly restaurant enjoys a wonderful location right in the heart of the centro storico. Inside is spartan yet comfortable, with basic furniture, marble-topped counters and the kitchen in view, while the outside tables make the most of the pretty square. The food is good, basic Italian fare, affordably priced and cheerfully served.

Matricianella Via del Leone 4 ☎06.683.2100. Mon–Sat 12.30–3pm & 7.30–11pm. Handily placed just off Via del Corso, this old favourite is perhaps the best place to try real Roman food in the city centre, with classic deep-fried dishes like *baccalà* and various vegetable *fritti*, classic Roman pasta dishes such as *cacio e pepe*, and a great wine list – all of which you can consume in the bustling main dining room or on the outside terrace.

Obikà Via dei Prefetti 26 ☎06.683.2630. Daily 10am–midnight. On secluded Piazza Firenze, this was the world's first restaurant specializing in mozzarella from Campania, served with everything from tomatoes to salami to anchovies and much more, and has since expanded to include branches in London

Italian regional cuisine

Rome offers a good sampling of the varied **cucina** of Italy's many distinct regions; below is our pick of the city's best.

Acchiappafantasmi (Calabrian; p.242)
Baia Chia (Sardinian; p.248)
Cantina Cantarini (Le Marche; p.247)
Colline Emiliane (Emilian; p.247)
Dal Bolognese (Emilian; see p.246)
Dal Toscano (Tuscan; p.255)
El Toulà (Venetian; p.240)
Ferrara (multi-regional; p.253)

Il Chianti (Tuscan; p.246)
Il Ciak (Tuscan; p.254)
Il Drappo (Sardinian; p.244)
Palatium (Lazio; p.246)
Piccolo Abruzzo (Abruzzese; p.247)
Tram Tram (Pugliese; p.249)
Trattoria Monti (Le Marche; p.249)

and Manhattan. There are a few salads and pasta dishes on offer too, but cheese is the main thing here, making it a great place for lunch. Dishes start at €8. There's another branch on Campo de' Fiori (☎06.6880.2366; daily 8am–2am).

Osteria dell'Ingegno Piazza di Pietra 45 ☎06.678.0662. **Daily 12.30–3pm & 7pm–midnight.** A relaxed newbie on a happening square, with tables outside and plenty of room in. There's an inventive menu that breaks free from the Roman specialities you'll find elsewhere, with dishes inspired by most of the country's regions. There are variations on traditional classics like pumpkin gnocchi and *cacio e pepe* with "square" pasta, and buffalo steaks and seafood with couscous – all to a background of cool jazz. A good choice of wine too. *Aperitivo* buffet every evening 5–8pm.

Riccioli Piazza della Coppelle 13 ☎06.6821.0313. **Mon–Sat 9am–2am, kitchen open noon–2am.** This swish modern restaurant, on a busy square in the heart of old Rome, does great sushi, oysters and other seafood, and its funky bar is open till late.

Trattoria Via Pozzo delle Cornacchie 25 ☎06.6830.1427. **Mon–Fri 12.30–3.30pm & 7.30–11.30pm, Sat 7.30–11.30pm.** You feel a million miles away from the centro storico in the cool, contemporary upstairs room of this Sicilian restaurant. Service is really good, as is the food, and the sleek modern interior artfully done, with the kitchen behind glass and two well-lit dining rooms. There are *amuse bouches* to start, and complimentary chocs to finish, between which you can feast on excellent Sicilian-influenced starters and mains – *caponata*, *bucatini con sarde*, and meatballs and grilled king prawns. Pasta dishes around €16, mains €23–28, and well worth it.

Trattoria Lilli Via di Tor di Nona 23 ☎06.686.1916. **Mon–Sat 12.30–2.30pm & 8–10pm.** One of the city centre's best and most untouristy old-style trattorias. Great selection of classic Roman staples, well prepared and served with gritty Roman directness.

Campo de' Fiori and the Ghetto

See the **map** on pp.58–59.

Cafés and bars

Antico Forno Roscioli Via dei Chiavari 34 ☎06.686.4045. **Mon–Fri 6am–8pm, Sat 6am–2pm.** Old bakery that's associated with the swanky restaurant and deli around the corner and does great bread, lots of different kinds of pizza and other savoury and sweet delights to take out.

Barnum Café Via del Pellegrino 87. ☎06.6476.0483. **Mon–Fri 8.30am–midnight, Sat & Sun 8.30am–2am.** A welcome addition to the area, this friendly circus-themed café with free wi-fi is great for breakfast, coffee and cake or a light lunch. After dark, it's a relaxing bar with great cocktails, and there's a popular *aperitivo* buffet with Dj set on Sunday evenings.

Bernasconi Piazza Cairoli 16 ☎06.6880.6264. **Tues–Sun 7am–8.30pm; closed Aug.** A great family-run *pasticceria*, with *sfogliatelle* to die for and a host of other goodies including great one-bite panini. Good coffee, too, though it's standing-room only.

Caffè Farnese Piazza Farnese 106 ☎06.6880.2125. **Daily 7am–2am.** Popular with business types and beautiful young things, but actually not expensive, and a pleasant place to come for breakfast or lunch as well as evening drinks. Good cappuccino and *cornetti*, and excellent pizza and sandwiches. There's free seating at the window bar, but you might want to pay to sit outside on a warm evening for the view of Palazzo Farnese.

Il Forno di Campo de' Fiori Campo de' Fiori 22 ☎06.6880.6662. **Mon–Sat 7am–1.30pm & 5.30–8pm; closed Sat evening in summer, Thurs evening in winter.** Great Campo bakery that is always busy with devotees. The *pizza bianca* here (just drizzled with olive oil on top) is a Roman legend and their *pizza rossa* (with a smear of tomato sauce) follows close behind. Get it hot from the oven.

Restaurants

Acchiappafantasmi Via dei Cappellari 66 ☎06.687.3462. **Tues–Sun 8pm–2am.** Fine "ghost-shaped" pizzas – the name of the place is Italian for "Ghostbusters" – appetizers, *bruschette* and antipasti from

Calabria. Always busy, with a very lively atmosphere, and service can suffer as a result.

Al Bric Via del Pellegrino 51 ℡06.687.9533. **Daily 7.30–11.30pm.** A refined alternative to the generally more down-at-heel and touristy hangouts around the Campo, *Al Bric* takes its wine and food very seriously – as evidenced by the hushed atmosphere, gigantic wine list and frankly high prices. But the food is good and varied, with influences from all over Italy, and there are some interesting starters and pasta dishes, and excellent steaks. The wine list has quite a few options at good prices, too. Pastas €10–15, mains €20–25.

Al Pompiere Via Santa Maria dei Calderari 38 ℡06.686.8377. **Mon–Sat noon–3pm & 7pm–midnight.** Housed in a frescoed old *palazzo* in the heart of the Ghetto, this fusty, old-fashioned restaurant exudes tradition and serves up some of the best Roman–Jewish food you'll find at decent prices in its busy warren of high-ceilinged rooms.

Ar Galletto Piazza Farnese 102 ℡06.686.1714. **Mon–Sat 12.30–3pm & 7.30–11pm.** This place is situated on one of Rome's stateliest piazzas, and just off one of its trendiest, too, and yet retains the feel of a provincial trattoria. It's been a local favourite for at least a quarter of a century and specializes in traditional Roman cookery with a homely touch. In winter, the atmospheric indoor setting is old Rome at its best; in warmer months, you can sit outside and enjoy the magnificent Renaissance square. Reasonable prices too.

Da Sergio Via delle Grotte 27 ℡06.606.4293. **Mon–Sat 11.30am–3.30pm & 7pm–midnight.** Towards the river from Campo de' Fiori, this is an out-of-the-way, cosy trattoria with a traditional, limited menu and the deeply authentic feel of old Rome. Inexpensive, and with limited outdoor seating in summer.

Dar Filettaro a Santa Barbara Largo dei Librari 88 ℡06.686.4018. **Mon–Sat 6–10.30pm; closed Aug.** A fish-and-chip shop without the chips, with paper-covered Formica tables (outdoors in summer), cheap wine, beer and fried cod. Located a short walk from Campo de' Fiori, off busy Via dei Giubbonari, this is a great place to sample this timeless Roman speciality, though service can be offhand, to say the least.

Der Pallaro Largo del Pallaro 15 ℡06.6880.1488. **Tues–Sun noon–3pm &**

7pm–midnight. It's not everyone's cup of tea but this old-fashioned trattoria serves a set four-course daily menu for around €20, including wine (whether you want it or not), on a quiet piazza between Campo de' Fiori and Largo Argentina. It's a good option when you're starving, but service can be haphazard and the food is definitely more rustic rather than refined. No credit cards.

Ditirambo Via della Cancelleria 74 ℡06.687.1626. **Mon 7.30–11.30pm, Tues–Sun 1–3pm & 7.30–11.30pm.** In a fantastic location around the corner from the Campo de' Fiori, you might expect this to be no more than a typical tourist haven – but it offers much more. A few tables outside, and lots of room in, its dishes are inventive takes on traditional Italian dishes and ingredients – often successful, occasionally not. Service is breezy and bright, and if you don't want to sample their more complex offerings you can always go for their *tonnarelli cacio e pepe*, which is as good as anywhere in the city centre.

Grappolo d'Oro Zampanó Piazza della Cancelleria 80 ℡06.689.7080. **Mon & Fri–Sun 1–3pm & 7.30–11.15pm, Tues–Thurs 7.30–11.15pm; closed Aug.** This place has had a bit of a facelift recently but still remains relatively unscathed by the hordes in nearby Campo de' Fiori, and serves imaginative Roman cuisine in a traditional trattoria atmosphere at moderate prices.

▲ *Grappolo d'Oro Zampanó*

Il Drappo Vicolo del Malpasso 9 ☎06.687.7365. Mon–Sat 1–3pm & 7–11.30pm. This cosy, family-run Sardinian restaurant just off Via Giulia has been going for years, and attracts large crowds of loyal regulars to sample its fish, seafood, rabbit stew and suckling pig, along with wafer-thin flat Sardinian "sheet music" bread. Great Sardo desserts, too.

Il Pagliaccio Via dei Banchi Vecchi 130 ☎06.6880.9595. Mon & Tues 8–10pm, Wed–Sat 1–3pm & 8–10pm. Where do Rome's top chefs and hoteliers go on their night off? In *Il Pagliaccio,* chef Anthony Genovese has set the standard of creativity high. It's pricey, but worth it for the inventiveness of the dishes, which take familiar ingredients and mix them to the point of bizarre: ever thought of serving chicken with lychees and red roses, or cooking pancetta with rhubarb? Tasting menus range from €135 to €155 a head.

L'Insalata Ricca Largo dei Chiavari 85–86 ☎06.6880.3656. Daily noon–3.30pm & 7pm–1am. Part of a small Roman chain, this is a good choice for vegetarians, with inter-esting big salads, as the name suggests, wholefood options and reasonably priced Italian fare, including pizzas. The setting is pleasant too, next to the church of Sant'Andrea della Valle, between Piazza Navona and Campo de' Fiori. There's another branch nearby on Piazza Pasquino, one on Piazza del Risorgimento – very handy for the Vatican Museums – and one in Trastevere, on Via Santini, just off Viale Trastevere.

Piperno Monte de' Cenci 9 ☎06.6880.6629. Tues–Sat 12.45–2.30pm & 7.45–10.30pm, Sun 12.45–2.30pm. Tucked away on this tiny piazza, there's perhaps no better place to sample Roman food. Not cheap, and the service can be a bit snooty, but it's a lovely space, there's outside seating on the square in the summer, and the food is great. All the trad Roman starters – *carciofi alla giudia, baccalà, fiori di zucca* – for around €14, pasta dishes for about the same and mains for €25. A good wine list too, with lots of decent alternatives for €15 a bottle or less.

Roscioli Via dei Giubbonari 21–22 ☎06.687.5287. Mon–Sat 12.30–4pm & 6pm–midnight. Is it a deli, a wine bar, or fully fledged restaurant? Actually it's all three, and you can either just have a glass of wine and some cheese or go for the full menu, which has great pasta dishes and *secondi.* Nothing is cheap here, and the service can be a bit high-handed, but the food is good – stand-outs include the buffalo mozzarella and the carbonara. See p.284 for more on the deli, and p.242 for the bakery around the corner.

Sciam Via del Pellegrino 55 ☎06.6830.8957. Daily 4pm–1am. Lovely, authentically Middle Eastern café and restaurant with lots of good, mainly Lebanese and Syrian food – a choice of meze dishes for €18, which can easily feed two – and hookahs to finish off for €6 for two. No alcohol.

Sora Margherita Piazza delle Cinque Scole 30 ☎06.686.4002. Tues–Sun 12.30–3pm, Sat & Sun also 12.30–3pm & 8.30–11pm. A tiny and famous trattoria in the heart of the Jewish quarter serving reasonably priced home-made pasta, gnocchi and desserts. Great Jewish-style artichokes and *fiori di zucca.* For something rare and delicious, try *aliciotti,* a casserole of fresh anchovies and curly endive. There's no sign outside – look for the doorway on the northern side of the square.

Taverna degli Amici Piazza Margana 36 ☎06.6992.0637. Tues–Sun 12.30–3pm & 7.30–11pm. There are lots of tables outside at this long-established restaurant on the fringes of the Ghetto – a great place for lunch after the rigours of the Forum and an atmospheric spot for dinner too, with a lovely location on this quiet square. The menu is relatively unadventurous, but there are lots of Roman classics, as well as less obvious options. Prices are moderate – pasta dishes €12, mains €15–20.

Thien Kim Via Giulia 201 ☎06.6830.7832. Mon–Sat 7.30–11pm. Perhaps Rome's only Vietnamese restaurant, but it's been here since the 1970s so it must be doing something right. Not expensive, and good if you want something different, but it's very small so it's a good idea to book.

The Tridente

See the **map** on p.93 and Trevi.

Cafés and bars

Antico Forno Via delle Muratte 8 ⊕06.679.2866. **Daily 7am–9pm.** The last thing you'd expect just by the Trevi Fountain: freshly cooked pizza, a sandwich bar, fresh fruits and salads, a bakery and grocery store, all rolled into one – and open on Sundays!

Babington's Tea Rooms Piazza di Spagna 23 ⊕06.678.6027. **Daily 9am–8.15pm.** In business for over a hundred years, *Babington's* serves light lunches and English tea-time delicacies such as scones with jam. It is extremely expensive – €9 for a pot of tea for one, €13.50 for poached eggs on toast – but very handy, and it has a great selection of teas and does a great Sunday brunch too.

Caffè Greco Via Condotti 86 ⊕06.678.5474. **Mon–Sat 8am–9pm.** Founded in 1742, and patronized by, among others, Casanova, Byron, Goethe and Stendhal. Nowadays, it's a rather dubious tourist joint, but Romans still use the stand-up area in the front. For curiosity value only, although the *granita di caffè* (iced coffee) is a hit on a hot summer's day.

Da Michele Via dell'Umiltà 31 ⊕349.252.5347. **Mon–Thurs & Sun 9am–7.30pm, Fri 9am–2pm.** This classic Roman snack joint used to be in the Jewish Ghetto but was replaced by a burger bar, and the Ghetto's loss is very much the Trevi area's gain. It still does kosher pizza to go – the house speciality is with fresh anchovies and *indivia* (endives) – roast chicken and *supplì*.

Herbier Via San Claudio 87 ⊕06.678.5847. **Mon–Sat 8am–8pm.** Well-located bar, just off Piazza San Silvestro in a small arcade and thus a real oasis of calm away from the hectic and fumy traffic. Offers snacks or even a full lunch.

La Baguette Via Tomacelli 22–25 ⊕06.6880.7727. **Tues–Sun 9am–midnight.** *La Baguette*'s wonderful organic breads, French cheeses and hearty soups, served to diners along communal dining banquettes, have quickly found their way into Roman hearts. The weekend brunches for €20 are popular.

Museo-Atelier Canova-Tadolini Via del Babuino 150a. It's a bit odd eating amongst the grand sculptures of this café-cum-museum, and certainly not cheap. But it provides one of the few places to sit down along this busy street, and serves decent sandwiches, salads and simple pasta dishes. There are a few outside tables, too, to watch the designer bags bustle by.

Restaurants

Alla Rampa Piazza Mignanelli 18 ⊕06.678.2621. **Closed Sun.** An unashamedly touristy joint, but with one of the best antipasti buffets in town – a snip for €10 a head – excellent service and pretty decent food. And the outside terrace, just off Piazza di Spagna, is large and undeniably appealing, even if you are surrounded by all the languages under the sun – except, perhaps, Italian. Moderately priced; no credit cards.

Antica Birreria Peroni Via di San Marcello 19 ⊕06.679.5310. **Mon–Sat noon–midnight, Fri & Sat noon–12.30am.** Big, bustling *birreria* with an excellent and cheap Italian–German fusion menu of simple food that's meant to soak up the beer. There are the usual starters and pasta dishes, plus a good selection of meat dishes, *scamorza* cheese and wurstel specialities. Its walls are decorated with photos of old Rome and a frieze adorned by cherubs and slogans urging you to drink more beer – something that's very hard to resist in this lovely old wood-panelled space.

Babette Via Margutta 1–3 ⊕06.321.1559. **Daily 1–3pm & 8–11.15pm.** Yes, the name is derived from the Danish foodie film, *Babette's Feast*, but food here is Italian with a few twists rather than Danish, with a great-value lunch buffet on weekdays (€15) and a lovely courtyard to eat it in. Dinner is good value too.

Beltramme Via della Croce 39. No phone. Daily noon–3pm & 7–11pm. Originally this place sold only wine. Now, a few blocks from the Spanish Steps, it is a full-blown restaurant and just about always packed, and consequently service can be a bit slow. But if you want authentic Roman food and atmosphere at affordable prices – €10 for a *primo*, €15 for a *secondo* – then this is the place. No credit cards.

Ciampini Viale Trinità dei Monti ⊕06.678.5678. **Daily 8am–midnight.** Across the road from the French Academy, this is a café, good for coffee and snacks in the morning and at lunchtime, but a restaurant too, with a great setting in an enclosed garden overlooking the roofs and domes below. There's a good selection of pasta dishes and salads for €10–12, and fish, steaks and chicken from the grill for main courses. A good place for kids, who can watch the turtles playing in the fountain between courses.

Dal Bolognese Piazza del Popolo 1 ☎06.361.1426. Tues–Sun 12.45–3pm & 8.15–11pm. This elegant – and expensive – restaurant is the place to go if you want to treat yourself to good Emilian cuisine; *tortellini in brodo* is a must if you like chicken soup. Reservations are recommended, especially if you'd rather eat outside and watch the passers-by in the piazza.

'Gusto Piazza Augusto Imperatore 9 ☎06.322.6273. Daily 12.45–3pm & 7.45pm–1am. This swish establishment is more like something you might find in San Francisco or Sydney. However, the food is unique and the steaks and chicken from the grill often wonderful, and the atmosphere very chic. The downstairs pizzeria is excellent and there's also a popular Mediterranean buffet lunch – great value at €8 a head, €13 at weekends – and a restaurant upstairs that offers more upscale and imaginative food at higher prices, including unusual, well-executed desserts, and an extensive wine list. See also below for *Osteria della Frezza*, and p.286 for details of the 'Gusto shop.

Hamasei Via della Mercede 35–36 ☎06.679.2134. Tues–Sun noon–2.30pm & 7pm–10.30pm. A medium-priced and elegant Japanese restaurant right in the centre of town. There's a tranquil, refined atmosphere and a full range of Japanese dishes, including a sushi bar. A la carte prices are high, but there are cheaper lunch specials.

Il Chianti Via del Lavatore 81–82a ☎06.678.7550. Mon–Sat 12.30–3.30pm & 7.30–11.30pm. Just metres from the Trevi Fountain, this Tuscan specialist, both in wine and food, is a good find in a part of town not generally known for its good-value food and drink. There are spreads of cheese and cold meats, a good selection of beef and other meat dishes, the usual pastas and decent pizzas, but if you don't fancy a full meal you can just stop by for a drink. Sit outside in summer if you can bear the travelling musicians who congregate to entertain the tourists.

Il Leoncino Via del Leoncino 28 ☎06.687.6306. Mon–Fri 1–2.30pm & 7pm–midnight, Sat & Sun 7pm–midnight; closed during Aug. Cheap, hectic and genuine pizzeria, little known to out-of-towners, and one of the very best for lovers of crispy Roman-style pizza, baked in wood ovens. Just off Via del Corso, and quite a boon in this neighbourhood. No credit cards.

Osteria della Frezza Via della Frezza 16 ☎06.322.6273. Daily noon–3.30pm & 7pm–12.30am. Part of the super-cool – and ultra-successful-'*Gusto* empire (see above), this place is good for snacks such as cheese or salami plates or for full meals – the pasta is great, and service is excellent. There's a large wine list, and the whole thing is carried with the usual '*Gusto* panache.

Otello alla Concordia Via della Croce 81 ☎06.679.1178. Mon–Sat 12.30–3pm & 7.30–11pm. This place used to be one of Fellini's favourites – he lived just a few blocks away on Via Margutta – and it remains an elegant yet affordable choice in the heart of Rome. A complete offering of Roman and Italian dishes, but ask for "spaghetti Otello" for a taste of tradition – fresh tomatoes and basil with garlic.

Palatium Via Frattina 94 ☎06.6920.2132. Mon–Sat 11am–11pm. Cool and sleek, this wine bar-cum-restaurant celebrates the produce of the Lazio region and Rome, with a short menu of regional specialities and a long list of Lazio wines. You can settle for just a plate of salami and cheese for €5–7 or go for dishes like the classic *tonnarelli cacio e pepe*, Viterbese vegetable soup or mains such as sausages or rabbit from the hills to the north and south of the city. A nice location near Piazza di Spagna, and very good value for money.

Pizza Ciro Via della Mercede 43–45 ☎06.678.6015. Daily noon–3pm & 7pm–midnight. Just up from Piazza San Silvestro, this is a big, friendly pizza place that also has *primi* and *secondi*. The pizzas are great, but you should also try the *linguine al Ciro,* which comes with seafood.

Pizza Re Via di Ripetta 14 ☎06.321.1468. Mon–Sat 12.30–3pm & 7pm–midnight, Sun 7pm–midnight. Just up from Piazza del Popolo, this place serves up authentic Neapolitan pizza (thicker than Roman) made in a wood-stoked oven. It's busy, so book. Another, larger branch is in Prati, at Via Oslavia 39 ☎06.372.1173, just north of Piazza Mazzini.

Recafé Piazza Augusto Imperatore 9
⊤06.6813.4730. Daily 12.45pm & 7.30pm–1am.
The entrance on Via del Corso is a
Neapolitan café, while on the Piazza
Augusta Imperatore side you can enjoy
proper Neapolitan pizzas, good pasta and
salad dishes and excellent grilled *secondi*
for moderate prices – €10 or so for a *primo*,
€15–18 for a *secondo*. There are Neapolitan
desserts and *fritti* too. The ambience is
deliberately chic and the large outside
terrace always has a buzz about it.

The Quirinale and east

See the **map** on pp.104–105.

Cafés and bars

Terrazza Barberini Via Barberini 16/a
⊤06.4201.4596. Mon–Sat 7.30am–1am.
Fashioned out of the stables of the Palazzo
Barberini, this is a favourite haunt of the
area's office workers, with panini and pizzas
inside and on the terrace outside, while
upstairs is a more formal restaurant and
pizzeria. Nothing fancy, but open long hours
and handily placed.
Trimani Via Cernaia 37b ⊤06.446.9630.
Mon–Sat noon–midnight. This classy wine bar
(with Rome's biggest selection of regional
Italian vintages) is good for a lunchtime tipple
and an indulgent snack. You'll spend around
€15 to sample a range of good-quality
cheeses and cured pork meat, or a soup and
salad, including a glass of wine. It also has a
wine shop around the corner (see p.285).

▲ *Trimani*

Restaurants

Al Forno della Soffitta Via Piave 62
⊤06.4201.1164. Mon–Fri noon–midnight, Sat
& Sun 7pm–midnight. Popular restaurant
and pizzeria that does excellent *fritti* and
thick-crusted Neapolitan-style pizzas, as
well as pasta and grilled meat dishes.
Excellent Neapolitan cakes and desserts
too. Always busy.
Cantina Cantarini Piazza Sallustio 12
⊤06.485.5281 Mon–Sat 12.30–3.30pm &
7.30–11pm. This old-style trattoria just off Via
XX Settembre serves a very simple menu of
food from the Marche region. There's rabbit,
good fish and seafood at the end of the
week, and a reassuringly unprepossessing
interior, though there are tables outside for
much of the year.
Colline Emiliane Via degli Avignonesi 22
⊤06.481.7538. Tues–Sat 12.45am–
2.45pm & 7.30–10.45pm, Sun 12.45am–2.45pm.
Many Italians consider the cuisine of the
Emilia Romagna region to be the country's
best. Try it for yourself, lovingly prepared by
a family, oddly enough, from the Marche
region. Located just down from Piazza
Barberini, on a quiet backstreet parallel to
Via del Tritone. Moderate prices.
Giggetto Via Alessandria 43–49 ⊤06.841.2157.
Namesake of the more famous Jewish
Ghetto restaurant, this big and bustling
pizzeria that proclaims itself "king of pizza",
and who can blame them? Great, crispy-
thin Roman pizzas, for just €6–8; lots of *fritti*
and main dishes too.
Piccolo Abruzzo Via Sicilia 237
⊤06.4282.0176. Daily noon–4pm &
7pm–1.30am. A five-minute stroll up unprepossessing Via Sicilia from Via Veneto, this is
a great alternative to the glitzy, mob-run
places on the *Dolce Vita* street, with no
menu, just a seemingly endless parade of

International cuisine

Chinese restaurants – most of them pretty average – abound in Rome, and there's a slowly growing list of **international options** in and around the centre. Below is our pick of the best.

Africa (Eritrean; p.248)
Akropolis (Greek; p.253)
ATM Sushi Bar (Japanese; p.253)
Charley's Sauciere (French; p.250)
Il Guru (Indian; p.249)

Hamasei (Japanese; p.246)
Hang Zhou (Chinese; p.249)
Sciam (Middle Eastern; p.244)
Thien Kim (Vietnamese; p.244)

Abruzzese and other goodies plonked on your table at regular intervals. What you get will depend on what they have that day, but there's a fair chance it will include mozzarella and/or ricotta, a vegetable course, a couple of pasta dishes, a meat course and a dessert – plus as much wine as you can manage from the barrel. All for around €35 a head.

The Esquiline, Monti and Termini

See the **map** on pp.116–117.

Cafés and bars

Antico Caffè del Brasile Via dei Serpenti 23 ☎06.488.2319. Mon–Sat 6am–8.30pm, Sun 7am–2pm. Reliable old Monti stand-by that has been selling great coffee, snacks and cakes for around a century, and with a handful of seats and tables at the back should you want to take the weight off.

Dagnino Galleria Esedra, Via E. Orlando 75 ☎06.481.8660. Daily 7.30am–10.30pm. Good for both a coffee and snack or light lunch, this long-established Sicilian bakery, *gelateria* and café-restaurant is a peaceful retreat in the Termini area, with tables outside in this small shopping arcade.

La Bottega del Caffè Piazza Madonna dei Monti 5 ☎06.474.1578. Daily 8am–2am. Bang in the heart of the best bit of Monti, this is a good place for a lunchtime snack and an early-evening drink, with tables outside on this peaceful square. Excellent value and service, just a short walk from the Colosseum.

Restaurants

Africa Via Gaeta 26 ☎06.494.1077. Tues–Sun noon–3.30pm & 7.30–11pm. Arguably the city's most interesting ethnic food – Eritrean – and the first culinary sign of Rome's mostly recently arrived Ethiopian and Somalian population. Mains are very reasonable, at €9–12.

Agata e Romeo Via Carlo Alberto 45 ☎06.446.6115. Mon–Fri 12.30–2.30pm & 7.30–10.30pm. Much-lauded chef Agata Parisella takes traditional Roman cuisine to more refined heights, in dishes such as her *baccalà* (salt cod) cooked five ways. Unusually pricey for this part of town, but a great place for a blow-the-budget feast. Booking essential.

Alle Carrette Via Madonna dei Monti 95 ☎06.679.2770. Daily 8pm–midnight. Inexpensive and large pizzeria just up Via Cavour from the Imperial Forums. It's always crowded – expect to wait for the exceptional pizza here. There are great home-made desserts too.

Arancia Blu Via Prenestina 396 ☎06.445.4105. Mon–Fri 8pm–midnight, Sat & Sun noon–midnight. This long-standing vegetarian restaurant recently relocated way out along Via Prenestina but still reckons itself a cut above the rest – and with some justification, although in a city with very few vegetarians it doesn't have to try too hard. It prides itself on serving good food using fresh ingredients in an imaginative fashion, and decent salads.

Baia Chia Via Machiavelli 5 ☎06.7045.3452. Mon–Sat 12.30–3.30pm & 7.30–11.30pm. This moderate Sardinian restaurant has lots of good fish starters and tasty first courses, and the fish baked in salt is spectacular. For dessert, try the *sebadas* (hot pastries stuffed with cheese and topped with Sardinian honey).

Enoteca Cavour 313 Via Cavour 313 ⊤06.678.5496. Mon–Sat 12.30–2.45pm & 7.30pm–12.30am. This lovely, wood-panelled old wine bar has long stood out amongst the pizza joints at this end of Via Cavour, just a stone's throw from the Forum. You can enjoy mixed plates of salami and cheese on wooden benches for around €10 or a daily selection of different hot dishes, from couscous to lasagne, as well as a selection of veggie alternatives. Excellent and enthusiastic service too, and a great choice of wine.

Formula 1 Via degli Equi 13 ⊤06.445.3866. Mon–Sat 7.30pm–midnight. Cheap and justifiably popular San Lorenzo pizzeria, with tables outside in summer. Delicious *pizza all'ortolana* (with courgettes, aubergines and peppers), and good courgette-flower fritters.

Hang Zhou Via di San Martino ai Monti 33 ⊤06.487.2732. Daily noon–3pm & 7pm–midnight. Rome isn't the best place to eat Chinese food – in fact, it's one of the worst – but this Monti favourite, plastered with photos of the sociable owner, is arguably the only place in the centre of town to eat authentic Chinese food, and cheaply too.

Il Guru Via Cimarra 4/6 ⊤06.474.4110. Daily 7.30pm–midnight. Rome has a few decent Indian restaurants if you're dying for a curry, and this is one of them, with an elegant, inviting atmosphere and good northern Indian cuisine. The location is great too, just above the Imperial Forums in Monti. Fixed menus from €16.

La Mucca Bischera Via degli Equi 56 ⊤06.446.9349. Mon–Fri 7.30pm–1am, Sat & Sun 1–3pm & 7.30pm–1am. This cheap-and-cheerful San Lorenzo restaurant is packed with locals every night. The decor is kitsch – plastic vines, twinkling fairy lights and stuffed cows – but the food is good, and hearty: Tuscan steaks and grilled meats from about €12, and generous pizzas from €6. And if you overindulge, there's a rickshaw outside to take you back to Termini free of charge.

Monti DOC Via G. Lanza 93 ⊤06.487.2696. Tues–Fri 1–3.30pm & 7pm–1am, Sat & Sun 7pm–1am. Comfortable Santa Maria Maggiore neighbourhood wine bar, with a good wine list and decent food: cold cuts and cheese, soups, quiches, salads and pastas, including some good veggie dishes, chalked on the blackboard daily.

Open Colonna Palazzo delle Esposizioni, Via Milano 9a ⊤06.4782.2641. Tues–Sat noon–midnight, Sun 8pm–midnight. The top floor of the newly refurbished Palazzo delle Esposizioni (see p.122) is the domain of big-shot Italian chef Antonello Colonna, who presides over this impressively light-drenched modern space given over to eating, drinking – and looking cool. The €15 weekday lunch buffet is already an institution, as is the €28 weekend brunch. A modern Rome experience.

Pommidoro Piazza dei Sanniti 44 ⊤06.445.2692. Mon–Sat noon–3pm & 7.30–11pm. Family-run Roman trattoria on San Lorenzo that's been around forever and serves great Roman home-cooking, very seasonal, with an emphasis on grilled lamb and game, cooked on a big open grill. All the pasta classics too, with a great carbonara among other things. Once the favourite haunt of Pasolini, it has a breezy open veranda outside on the square in summer.

Tram Tram Via dei Reti 44–46 ⊤06.490.416. Tues–Sun noon–3pm & 7.30pm–midnight. A grungy location but a cosy spot, this trendy, animated San Lorenzo restaurant serves good Pugliese pasta dishes, fish and seafood and unusual salads, with mains at €15–18. Reservations are recommended. There's also a bar if you want to carry on drinking after dinner.

Trattoria Monti Via di San Vito 13a ⊤06.446.6573. Tues–Sat noon–3pm & 7.30–11pm, Sun noon–3pm. Small, family-run restaurant that specializes in the cuisine of the Marche region, which means hearty food from a short menu – great pasta and interesting cabbage-wrapped *torte* as starters, and mainly meaty *secondi*, with beef, lamb and rabbit predominating. Close enough to Termini to be convenient, but this is as homely and friendly a restaurant as you could want – something places in this neighbourhood often aren't.

Valentino Via del Boschetto 37 ⊤06.488.0643. Mon–Sat 12.45–2.45pm & 7.30–11.30pm. With only a faded Peroni sign above the door, this trattoria on one of Monti's most atmospheric streets is easy to miss. Inside, it's always buzzing, with waiters zipping between the closely packed tables. You'll find lots of grilled meat options, plus a *scamorza* (grilled cheese) menu – great for vegetarians.

The Celian Hill and San Giovanni

See the **map** on pp.130–131.

Cafés and bars

L'800 Via di San Giovanni in Laterano 278 ⊤06.7045.1306. Right across from the basilica of San Giovanni, this bar is a handy place for a bite between sights, with good sandwiches, a *tavola calda* with hot food and plenty of inside seating, and an outside terrace.

Valentini Piazza Tuscolo 2 ⊤06.7720.7427. Café, pastry shop and *tavola calda*, just five minutes from San Giovanni and a great spot for lunch, with outside seating too.

Restaurants

Charley's Sauciere Via di San Giovanni in Laterano 270 ⊤06.7049.5666. Mon–Sat 12.30–3pm & 7.30–11pm. If the background chansons don't make you think you're in France – albeit a mythical one from the 1930s – the menu certainly will, with lots of French classics – coq au vin, onion soup and

Cutting-edge cuisine in Rome's hotel restaurants

In the past decade or so some of Italy's best chefs have exited and entered the revolving doors of Rome's major hotels, and their cuisine is at the cutting edge of Italy's food trends, with fresh local ingredients, some exotic touches and fantastic presentation. Eating at any of these places can be pricey, but the atmosphere in these restaurants is usually special, and sometimes accompanied by breathtaking views.

The undisputed pioneer of Rome's fine restaurant dining is Heinz Beck, chef at **La Pergola** atop the *Cavalieri Hilton* (Via A. Cadlolo 1; book via ⓔlapergolareservations .rome@hilton.com). Often voted by Italian food critics as Italy's best chef, he put hotel restaurants on the map for quality and creativity – and high prices. The food is superb too at **La Terrazza dell'Eden** at the *Hotel Eden* (see p.227); their stuffed courgette flowers are amazing, as are the gnocchi, grilled fish and meats, and desserts like tarte tatin or crème brûlée – and the *Eden*'s dove-grey-and-cream rooftop perch is wonderful. Nearby, at the **Hotel Majestic** (see p.227), chef Filippo La Mantia's food is Sicilian-with-a-twist; the French pastry chef here makes desserts worthy of Palermo, but also produces a colourful array of delicate French sweets that burst with flavour. The *Splendide Royal* (see p.228), just off Via Veneto on Porta Pinciana, serves beautifully presented creative dishes at its **Mirabelle** restaurant – and a view looking toward Villa Borghese and beyond – while the restaurant at the *Aleph* (see p.227), **Sin**, might just have the best seafood ravioli in Rome.

If you can nab a table that overlooks the Spanish Steps at **Il Palazzetto** (see p.226), you'll have as much fun people-watching as enjoying delightfully fresh food – good value, too, with a nice selection of wines by the glass, and prices a notch below most of the other places here. Their parent hotel, the *Hassler* (see p.226), at the top of the Steps, has **Imágo**, a formal restaurant open only for dinner, with a famous view matched by flawless service and refined Italian cuisine. The **Jardin de Russie** restaurant at the nearby *De Russie* (see p.226) has a secret feel enhanced by its enclosed terraced garden (the buffet at lunch attracts a well-heeled business crowd), while across town the picturesque secluded piazza and ivy-covered facade of the *Raphaël* (see p.224) exude romance, which the restaurant – **La Terrazza Bramante** – delivers too, filled with flowers and with a view across the domes to make you swoon. The food is good too: variations on tradition like pasta *all'amatriciana* made with seafood and lobster lasagne. Finally, on the northern edge of Villa Borghese, **baby** at the *Aldrovandi Palace* (see p.224) has a tasteful, tranquil atmosphere and is run by Alfonso Iaccarino – of the legendary *Don Alfonso 1890* restaurant on the Sorrentine peninsula, reckoned to be one of the best restaurants in Italy. Their pasta with lobster and cherry tomatoes is sublime.

excellent steaks. This French–Swiss old-timer does fondues too. Moderate prices – soups and starters €8–10, mains €18, and it's just a five-minute walk from the Colosseum.

Il Bocconcino Via Ostilia 23 ☎06.7707.9175. Mon, Tues & Thurs–Sun noon–3pm & 7–11pm. Not the greatest service, but a cut above most of the other places within sight of the Colosseum, with high-quality Roman food served in an old-fashioned environment.

Il Primo Via del Pigneto 46 ☎06.701.3827. Tues–Sun noon–3pm & 8–11pm. This place epitomizes the cool vibe of modern-day Pigneto, with its clean, contemporary interior and short menu of well-chosen seasonal dishes, most of which are examples of simple yet modern cooking and usually delicious. *Primi* go for around €10, *secondi* €15–28. You may need to book for dinner.

Luzzi Via di San Giovanni in Laterano 88 ☎06.709.6332. Mon, Tues & Thurs–Sun noon–3pm & 7pm–midnight. Midway between San Giovanni in Laterano and the Colosseum, this bustling restaurant is a good choice amid the tourist joints of the neighbourhood. The

food is hearty and simple, if unspectacular, there's outside seating and it's extremely cheap – *secondi* go for €6–9. There's pizza too, but only in the evening.

Necci dal 1924 Via Fanfulla da Lodi 68 ☎06.9760.1552. Daily 8am–1am. Pasolini shot some of his films in the Pigneto district, and this bar-restaurant was apparently one of his favourite places to eat and drink. Five minutes' walk from the busy stretch of Via del Pigneto, it has a lovely shady garden where you can have a drink, sandwich or a full meal from its short menu, chalked afresh on the blackboard each day.

Taverna dei Quaranta Via Claudia 24 ☎06.700.0550. Very relaxed locals' joint with chequered tablecloths and good, very reasonably priced home cooking. The dishes are Roman with a twist: classics such as roast lamb and courgette flowers, but polenta too, and some interesting pasta dishes, on a menu that changes regularly. *Primi* €7–8, *secondi* €8–10. Only in Rome could this sort of place exist, five minutes from the tourist scrum at the Colosseum.

The Aventine and south

Unless marked otherwise, see the **map** on pp.138–139.

Cafés and bars

Caffè del Seme e la Foglia Via Galvani 18 ☎06.574.3008. Mon–Sat 8am–1.30am, Sun 6pm–1.30am. Pleasantly low-key café popular with Testaccio trendies and students from the nearby music school. During the day it's good for sandwiches and big salad lunches – with fairly exotic options such as avocado with shrimp or crab, and curried turkey sandwiches – and in the evenings a mellow place to relax before visiting the area's more energetic offerings.

Palombini Piazzale Adenauer 12 ☎06.591.1700. Mon–Thurs 7am–10pm, Fri & Sat 7am–1am, Sun 8am–10pm. See map, p.152. Great EUR café whose outside terrace and large interior are a haven amidst the brutal boulevards. Appropriately housed on the ground floor of EUR's official "restaurant building", it's a café, *tabacchi* and wine shop all rolled into one, and serves excellent cakes and sandwiches.

Volpetti Più Via A. Volta 8. No phone. Mon–Sat 11am–9pm. *Tavola calda* that's attached to

the famous deli a few doors down (see p.285). Great pizza, *supplì*, chicken, deep-fried veg and much more.

Restaurants

Acqua e Farina? Piazza O. Giustiniani 2 ☎06.574.1382. Daily noon–3pm & 8pm–midnight. This very reasonable Testaccio restaurant serves dishes that are unique: everything, from starters to desserts, is a variation on the theme of pastry – hence the name, "Water & Flour?". Ideal for a light meal, lunch or dinner, for as little as €10 a head. A very busy place in the middle of an area bustling with streetlife, especially in summer.

Augustarello Via G. Branca 98 ☎06.574.6585. Mon–Sat noon–3.30pm & 7.30–11.30pm. Moderately priced Testaccio standard serving genuine Roman cuisine in an old-fashioned atmosphere. A good place to come if you appreciate oxtail and sweetbreads, although, as with all Italian restaurants, even strict vegetarians can find good choices.

Checchino dal 1887 Via di Monte Testaccio 30
⊕06.574.6318. Tues–Sat noon–3pm &
8–11.30pm. Right in the heart of Monte
Testaccio's bars and clubs, this is a historic –
and expensive – symbol of Testaccio cookery,
and one of the best places to sample the
stalwarts of Rome's offal-based cuisine –
appropriately as it's right opposite the old
slaughterhouse. An excellent wine cellar too.
Da Felice Via Mastro Giorgio 29 ⊕06.574.6800.
Mon–Sat 12.30–2.45pm & 8–11.30pm. Always
crowded, this isn't quite the rough-and-
ready establishment it was, and some feel
it's not as good as when Felice used to
choose his customers from a line outside.
But in reality it still serves honest, seasonal
Roman cooking – *bucatini cacio e pepe*,
lamb, and artichokes in winter: all the
classics, well cooked and served. Listen for
the daily specials, usually just half a dozen
primi (€8–10) and *secondi* (€12–15).
**Da Remo Piazza Santa Maria Liberatrice
44** ⊕06.574.6270. Mon–Sat 7.30pm–1am.
Da Remo is the best kind of pizzeria: usually
crowded with locals, very basic, and serving
the thinnest, crispiest Roman pizza you'll

▲ *Da Remo*

find. Try also the heavenly *bruschette* and
other snacks like *supplì* and *fiori di zucca*.
Almost worth travelling out to Testaccio for
– and very cheap.
Tuttifrutti Via Luca della Robbia 3a
⊕06.575.7902. Tues–Sun 7.30–11.55pm.
This Testaccio favourite is pretty much the
perfect restaurant – family-run, with good
food, decent prices and lots of customers.
The menu changes daily, and offers interesting variations on traditional Roman
dishes. Recommended.

Trastevere

See the **map** on pp.156–157.

Cafés and bars

Bibli Via dei Fienaroli 28 ⊕06.588.4097.
Tues–Sun 11am–midnight; Mon
5.30pm–midnight. This café and bookshop
does a good American brunch at the
weekend, and decent food – lunch and
dinner – the rest of the time. There's
internet access too (€3.50/hour).
Di Marzio Piazza di Santa Maria in Trastevere 15
⊕06.581.6095. Daily 7am–1am. This bar isn't
much on the inside, but it's a friendly place
whose terrace right on Piazza Santa Maria
makes it one of the best people-watching
spots in Trastevere.
Frontoni dal 1921 Viale Trastevere 52
⊕06.581.2436. Great *fritti* and focaccia
sandwiches among many other snacks at
this bustling Trastevere bar-*birreria*, which is
busy at all hours of the day and night.
Gianicolo Piazzale Aurelia 5 ⊕06.580.6275.
Tues–Sun 7am–2am. Quite an ordinary bar,
but in a nice location and a bit of a hangout
for Italian media stars, writers and

academics from the nearby Spanish and
American academies. Good sandwiches too.
La Renella Via del Moro 15 ⊕06.581.7265.
Daily 9am–9pm. Arguably the best
bakery in Rome, right in the heart of Trastevere, with great focaccia and superb *pizza al
taglio*. Take a number and be prepared to
wait at busy times. You can take away or
eat on the premises at its long counter.
Sisini Via San Francesco a Ripa 137
⊕06.589.7110. Mon–Sat 11am–11pm. Just half
a block from Viale Trastevere, there's no
sign outside this *pizza al taglio* hole-in-the-
wall, which is ironic as it may well have the
best pizza by the slice in Rome. Also roast
chicken and potatoes, *supplì* and all the
usual *rosticceria* fare. Try their unique
chopped spicy green olive pizza.

Restaurants

Ai Marmi Viale Trastevere 53–59
⊕06.580.0919. Thurs–Tues 6.30pm–2.30am.
Nicknamed "the mortuary" because of its

Città del Gusto

This industrial building by the river in the southern reaches of Trastevere (Via Enrico Fermi 161; ☎06.551.1221, ⓦwww.gamberorosso.it) is a six-floor testimony to the success of the **Gambero Rosso** food empire, which has grown from a food and wine supplement in the communist newspaper *Il Manifesto* to Italy's most successful gourmet publisher, with a bestselling magazine, TV show and a series of restaurant guides. At their headquarters they run **food and wine tastings**, host a wine bar (Tues–Sat 7.30pm–midnight) and restaurant (Mon 9am–4.30pm, Tues–Fri 7.30pm–midnight; ☎06.5511.2251), a shop selling cookbooks and kitchen equipment (Mon–Fri 9am–7pm), and a theatre and TV studio.

stark interior and marble tables, this place serves unique "*supplì al telefono*" (so named because of the string of mozzarella it forms when you take a bite), fantastic fresh *baccalà* and the best pizza in Trastevere. Nice house red wine, too, and service is quick, despite the crowds. A lively, inexpensive feel of the real Rome.
Akropolis Via S. Francesco a Ripa 103 ☎06.5833.2600. Mon & Sat 7.30–11.30pm, Tues–Fri noon–2.30pm & 7.30–11.30pm. Small Greek restaurant and takeaway with good *souvlaki* and all the usual snacks and honeyed sweets. Good prices too.
Antico Arco Piazzale Aurelio 7 ☎06.581.5274. Mon–Sat 7.30pm–midnight. Located above Trastevere, next to the Janiculum Hill, this is one of Rome's finest restaurants, serving superb, exquisitely presented dishes, plus an enormous fine wine list. It's always good, and reservations are definitely required.
ATM Sushi Bar Via della Penitenza 7 ☎06.6830.7053. Tues–Sun 7pm–midnight. Tucked away in Trastevere, this cool yet cosy place comes as a real – and affordable – surprise, serving delicious sushi and sashimi, as well as lacy, perfect tempura. The sashimi salad is very special. Start off with a flawless miso soup and finish with home-made green tea ice cream, and a lime cocktail. There's a great wine list, too.
Da Augusto Piazza de' Renzi 15 ☎06.580.3798. Mon–Sat noon–3pm & 8–11pm. Diner-style Trastevere stand-by serving Roman basics in an unpretentious, bustling atmosphere. Good pasta and soup starters, and daily meat and fish specials – not haute cuisine, but decent, hearty Roman cooking.
Da Enzo Via dei Vascellari 29 ☎06.581.8355. Mon–Sat noon–3pm & 7.30–11pm. Tiny restaurant close to the river in Trastevere that does good basic Roman food at good prices – a million miles away from some of the glitzy new places that have opened up over in the district's busier quarter.
Da Ivo Via di San Francesco a Ripa 158 ☎06.581.7082. Wed–Mon 7.30pm–1am. *The* Trastevere pizzeria, almost in danger of becoming a caricature, but still good and very reasonable. A nice assortment of desserts, too – try the *monte bianco* for the ultimate chestnut cream and meringue confection. Arrive early to avoid a chaotic queue.
Da Lucia Vicolo del Mattonato 2 ☎06.580.3601. Tues–Sun noon–3pm & 7.30–11.30pm. Outdoor Trastevere dining in summer is at its best at this wonderful old Roman trattoria. Spaghetti *cacio e pepe* is the speciality here – arrive early to nab a table outside.
Da Olindo Vicolo della Scala 8 ☎06.581.8835. Mon–Sat noon–3pm & 8–11pm. Great, family-run Trastevere trattoria with traditional Roman fare. There's a small menu of staples, and prices are cheap and easy to remember: *primi* cost €7, *secondi* €9.
Da Paris Piazza San Calisto 7a ☎06.581.5378. Tues–Sat noon–3pm & 8–11.30pm, Sun noon–3pm. Fine Roman–Jewish cookery in one of Trastevere's most atmospheric piazzas, with tables outside in summer and a whole host of excellent traditional dishes. Moderate prices.
Dar Poeta Vicolo del Bologna 45 ☎06.588.0516. Tues–Sun noon–1am. Without any doubt, one of the top ten pizzerias in Rome. Don't expect the typical crusty Roman pizza here; the margherita (ask for it *con basilico* – with basil) comes out of the oven soft and with plenty of good mozzarella on top. They have good imported *birra rossa* – a rarity outside a pub – as well as a few outside tables.
Ferrara Via del Moro 1a ☎06.5833.3920. Daily 7.30pm–1am. Just off Piazza Trilussa, this used to be just a wine bar and shop but has

grown to encompass an exciting, if pricey restaurant housing an inviting series of rooms elegantly stripped back to their medieval walls. The vegetarian antipasto selection is a great choice, and different every time, depending on the season and the chef's inspiration, and the sommelier really knows the perfect wine to accompany the regional Italian dishes. Reservations are a must. Expect to spend at least €60 a head, including wine.

I Due Ciccioni Vicolo del Cedro 3b ☎06.589.4880. Tues–Sat 7.30–10.30 pm. The closest you can get to eating in someone's kitchen, this tiny restaurant has no sign and no waiters – but if you're bold enough to walk in they'll bring you four courses and a bottle of wine for €25 a head. The food isn't bad, and cooked right in front of you on the stove – lovely antipasti, a choice of pastas, and whatever *secondo* they're making that day – all washed down with as much *grappa* or *limoncello* as you can drink. Don't go if you hate smoking though – most of the regulars puff away like mad.

Il Ciak Vicolo del Cinque 21 ☎06.589.0774. Closed Sun. Honest, no-frills Tuscan grill with

chops, chicken and of course steaks, as well as more arcane meats and pasta dishes with gamey sauces. A simple trattoria that's a refreshing change on this touristy stretch.

Il Ponentino Piazza del Drago 10 ☎06.588.0680. This restaurant serves all the usual suspects – decent pasta, a full complement of pizzas, good *secondi* – and does them all fairly well. But its main attraction is its location on peaceful Piazza del Drago and its pleasant outside terrace.

Le Mani in Pasta Via dei Genovesi 37 ☎06.581.6017. Tues–Sat 12.20–3pm & 7.30–11pm. This small and very comfy restaurant with an open kitchen cooks up great pasta and fish dishes for €10–12 (*primi*) and €20 or so (*secondi*). Often very crowded, and it's worth reserving to be sure of getting in. Excellent service and fantastic food.

Pizzeria San Calisto Piazza di San Calisto 9a ☎06.581.8256. Tues–Sun 7.30pm–1am. Large pizzas at small prices. Friendly, fast service and a vibrant, welcoming atmosphere, whether you sit inside or out on the piazza.

Villa Borghese and north

Unless marked otherwise, see the **map** on pp.174–175.

Cafés

Casina dell'Orologio Pincio Gardens. See map, p.165. Handy Pincio bar with sandwiches and cakes and a shady garden to eat them in, as well as a full-service restaurant with pasta dishes for €10 or so. A much better place for a snack or even a meal than the much pricier and rather full-of-itself *Casina Valadier* across the way.

Gianfornaio Piazzale Ponte Milvio 35–37. Mon–Sat noon–11pm. Great bakery with pizza and other goodies, and lots of seating inside and out.

Restaurants

Dulcamara Via Flaminia Vecchia 449 ☎06.333.2108. Daily 12.15pm–2am; closed Mon evening. Busy place up in the increasingly hip neighbourhood across the

Ponte Milvio. A varied menu of good pasta dishes, soups and salads.

La Scala Via dei Parioli 79d ☎06.808.4463. Closed Wed. One of Parioli's posh choices, but sedate rather than pretentious, and always busy. It serves excellent food in its cosy inside rooms and outdoor terrace, with great fish and seafood risotto.

Osteria da Gnegno Via Prati della Farnesina 10 ☎06.333.6166. Daily 12.30–3pm & 7–11.30pm. A classic old Roman trattoria, tucked away behind Piazzale Ponte Milvio. Good food and well priced.

ReD Via Pietro de Coubertin 30 ☎06.8069.1630. Part of the Auditorium complex (see p.176), this sleek designer bar-restaurant is good for a drink or something to eat before or after a performance. During the day you might like to stop by for its €15 buffet lunch if you're in the area, but it's not worth a special trip.

The Vatican and Prati

See the **map** on pp.180–181.

Cafés and bars

Gran Caffè Borgo Borgo Pio 170–171. There are plenty of places to get something quick to eat on Borgo Pio, but this family-run café is a cut above the rest, with an excellent selection of sandwiches, panini and cakes, and a few inside – as well as outside – seats.

Mondo Arancina Via Marcantonio Colonna 38 ℡06.9761.9213. Great *pizza al taglio* at this Sicilian takeaway in Prati, but the real treats are the *arancini* (deep-fried rice balls), of which there are any number of varieties – tomato and mozzarella, ham and cheese, bolognese – all delicious and just €2 a throw. There's a second branch at Via Flaminia 42.

Non Solo Pizza Via degli Scipioni 95–97 ℡06.372.5820. Tues–Sun 8.30am–10pm. Pizza by the slice, Roman *fritti suppli, olive ascolane, fiori di zucca, crocchette* – and a complete selection of hot dishes *tavola calda*-style; plus from 7pm they offer made-to-order round pizzas, too. No extra charge to sit, inside or out.

Restaurants

Cacio e Pepe Via Avezzana 11 ℡06.321.7268. Mon–Fri 12.30–3pm & 7.30–11.30pm, Sat 12.30–3pm. Rough-and-ready Prati cheapie with a menu taped to the wall and great pasta staples like *cacio e pepe, carbonara* and one of the best *pasta alla gricias* in town for around €7; mains go for €9–10 and are equally good. With mostly outside tables and a small inside space, it's always busy. No credit cards.

Cantina Tirolese Via G. Vitelleschi 23 ℡06.6813.5297. Tues–Fri noon–3pm & 7.30–11pm, Sat & Sun noon–3pm & 7.30pm–midnight. This rustic Prati restaurant was reputedly the current pope's favourite lunch spot while he was still a cardinal, and no wonder – the hearty and wholesome Austrian and German fare served here is excellent, and there's lots of it. Choose from dumplings and goulash soup to start for around €8 and various meaty

mittel-European meat specialities for your main course; fondue for around €26 for two is about the only vegetarian option you'll find. The lunchtime buffet (noon–3pm) is excellent value at €9.50 a head.

Dal Toscano Via Germanico 58–60 ℡06.3972.5717. Tues–Sun 12.30–3pm & 8–11.15pm. Don't come here for a salad. This restaurant specializes in *fiorentine* (the famous thick Tuscan T-bone steaks), perfectly grilled on charcoal, delicious *pici* (thick home-made spaghetti) and *ribollita* (veg and bread soup) – all at honest prices: *primi* around €10, mains for €12–15. Not far from the Vatican, it's tremendously popular with Roman families, so reservations are recommended for dinner.

Del Frate Via degli Scipioni 118–124 ℡06.323.6437. Mon–Sat 1–3pm & 7.30pm–midnight. This large wine and spirits shop is a wine bar, too, with a great selection of cheeses and cold meats as well as regular pasta dishes. Very handy for the Vatican, for lunch or at the end of the day.

Osteria dell'Angelo Via G. Bettolo 24 ℡06.372.9470. Mon, Wed, Thurs & Sat 8–11.15pm, Tues & Fri 12.45–2.30pm & 8–11.15pm. Above-average traditional Roman food, at extremely reasonable prices, in a highly popular restaurant run by an ex-rugby player. Booking is advisable, as it's often heaving with locals.

Piero Costantini Piazza Cavour 16 ℡06.321.1502. Mon–Sat 12.30–2.30pm & 7.30–11pm. On the corner of Piazza Cavour, right behind Castel Sant'Angelo, this old-fashioned wine bar and restaurant has a fine and authentic Art Nouveau feel. Look for the wrought-iron grapes on the doors and windows. The food is good, but pricey. See also p.284 for details of its wine shop.

Ragno d'Oro Via Silla 26 ℡06.321.2362. Daily 12.30–2.30pm & 7.30–11.30pm. This family-run restaurant not only has great Roman cooking and good service, but it's also just five minutes' walk from the Vatican. Good antipasti and pizzas, and moderate prices too.

Drinking

Drinking is not something Romans do a lot of, at least almost never to drunken excess. Despite that, you'll find plenty of bars in Rome – although, as with the rest of Italy, many are functional daytime haunts and not at all the kinds of places you'd want to spend an evening (see Chapter 15 for the best of these). However, partly due to the considerable presence of Brits and Americans in Rome, there are nowadays plenty of bars and pubs conducive to an evening's drinking, from spit-and-sawdust wine bars to sleek cocktail lounges to Irish pubs. Our listings are divided into **neighbourhoods**; Campo de' Fiori and the centro storico around Piazza Navona, plus Monti, Trastevere and Testaccio, are the densest and most happening areas.

There can be considerable crossover between Rome's bars, restaurants and clubs: for the most part, the places listed in this chapter are drinking spots, but you can eat, sometimes quite substantially, at many of them, and several could be classed

---

What to drink

Beer (*birra*) is always a lager-type brew which usually comes in one-third or two-third litre bottles, or on draught (*alla spina*), measure for measure more expensive than the bottled variety. A small beer is a *piccola* (20cl or 25cl), a larger one (usually 40cl) a *media* (pronounced "maydia"). If you want Italian beer, or lager, ask for *birra chiara*. You may also come across darker beers (*birra nera* or *birra rossa*). Prices start at €4–5 for a *media*, but anywhere remotely fancy won't charge any less than €6–7.

All the usual **spirits** are on sale and known mostly by their generic names. There are also Italian brands of the main varieties: the best Italian brandies are Stock and Vecchia Romagna. A generous shot of these costs about €3, imported stuff much more. The home-grown Italian firewater is **grappa**, available just about everywhere. It's made from the leftovers from the winemaking process (skins, stalks and the like) and is something of an acquired taste; should you acquire it, it's probably the cheapest way of getting plastered. You'll also find **fortified wines** such as Campari; ask for a Campari-soda and you'll get a ready-mixed version from a bottle; a slice of lemon is a *spicchio di limone*, ice is *ghiaccio*. You might also try Cynar – believe it or not, an artichoke-based sherry often drunk as an aperitif.

There's also a daunting selection of **liqueurs**. *Amaro* is a bitter after-dinner drink: it has a base of pure alcohol in which various herbs are steeped, according to various family traditions. It's highly regarded as a digestive aid to cap a substantial meal. *Amaretto* is much sweeter with a strong taste of almond; Sambuca, a sticky-sweet aniseed concoction, traditionally served with a coffee bean in it and set on fire (though, increasingly, this is something put on to impress tourists); Strega – yellow, herb-and-saffron-based stuff in tall, elongated bottles – is about as sweet as it looks but not unpleasant.

just as easily as clubs, with loud music and occasionally even an entrance charge; places that are more club than bar are listed in Chapter 17.

Many bars are slick and expensive excuses for people to sit and pose, but most have the advantage of late **opening hours**, sometimes until 4am in summer, and almost always until 1am – though note that many places are **closed during August**. One relatively new phenomenon worth noting: a lot of bars are now laying on an early-evening buffet to tempt drinkers in for a **pre-dinner aperitivo**, with a choice of food free with the price of a drink, and it's become a popular way to kick off an evening. We've noted where places offer free buffets in the reviews.

Centro storico

See the **map** on p.44.

Anima Via Santa Maria dell' Anima 57
℡06.6889.2806. Tues–Sun 10pm–3am. This late-night bar-club is one of the most popular spots in town, tricked out in post-modern-meets-*The Flintstones* chic and offering an assortment of elegant snacks to go with your cocktails. Music tends towards chill-out, lounge and softer soul.

Bar della Pace Via della Pace 5 ℡06.686.1216.
Daily 10am–2am. Just off Piazza Navona, this is *the* summer bar, with outside tables full of Rome's self-consciously beautiful people. It's at its quietest during the day, when you can enjoy the nineteenth century interior marble, mirrors, mahogany and plants – in peace.

Bloom Via del Teatro Pace 30 ℡06.6880.2029.
Wed–Mon 11.30pm–5am. Perhaps the most self-consciously cool bar in the centre of Rome, It serves food, too, but you'd do better to fill up elsewhere and come on here afterwards, saving your money for one of *Bloom*'s cocktails.

Caffè Fandango Piazza di Pietra 32–33
①06.4547.2913. Tues–Sun 4pm–2am. Cool bar that does an excellent early-evening buffet and hosts Djs and live music later, when you can feast on panini for €5 and a cold buffet for €10.

Cul de Sac Piazza Pasquino 73
℡06.6880.1094. Daily noon–4pm & 7pm–12.30am. Busy, long-running wine bar with an excellent wine list, a great city-centre location with outside seating, and decent wine-bar food – cold meats, cheeses, salads and soups. One of the best centro storico locations for a snack.

Etabli Vicolo delle Vacche 9a ℡06.9761.6694.
Daily 12.30–3pm & 7pm–2am. Lounge-style bar and restaurant in the heart of the centro storico's drinking triangle. Comfy sofas, free wi-fi, and a pleasant, not-too-cool vibe.

Fluid Via del Governo Vecchio 46
℡06.683.2361. Daily 6pm–2am. With its sleek decor attracting a well-dressed crowd, this is perhaps the coolest bar on one of central Rome's coolest streets.

Jonathan's Angels Via della Fossa 18
℡06.689.3426. Daily 1pm–2am. This quirky bar, just behind Piazza Navona, certainly wins the "most decorated" award. Every inch (even the toilet, which is worth a visit in its own right) is plastered, painted or tricked out in outlandish style by the artist/ proprietor.

La Trinchetta Via dei Banchi Nuovi 4
℡06.6830.0133. Daily 12.30–3pm & 8pm–2am.
This wine bar is tucked away in the warren of streets between Piazza Navona and the Tiber and is well worth seeking out. There's not only a great selection of wines, but also what may be Rome's most extensive list of *grappa* labels.

Le Coppelle Piazza delle Coppelle 52
℡06.683.2410. Mon–Sat 6pm–2am. Snazzy bar decked out in 1970s disco style that very much functions outdoors during the warm months, when there's a nice array of sofas and pillows on the usually heaving small piazza to sink into.

Société Lutèce Piazza di Montevecchio 17
℡06.6830.1472. Tues–Sat 6pm–2am. Tucked away on this tiny square, this is one of the city centre's most self-consciously cool bars, where patrons sip cocktails late into the night in a dark interior hung with abstract art. There's an early-evening *aperitivo* buffet (from 7pm) – free for the price of a drink.

Trinity College Via del Collegio Romano 6
℡06.678.6472. Daily noon–3am. A warm and inviting establishment offering international beers and food, though its two levels can get quite loud and crowded. Food includes a bit of everything – pasta, burgers, salads, TexMex – and is served until 1am, plus there's a brunch menu for around €12.

Wine bars

One of Rome's more traditional types of drinking establishment is the **wine bar**, known as an *enoteca* or *vineria*. The old ones have gained new cachet in recent years, and newer ones, with wine lists the size of unabridged dictionaries, are weighing in, too, often with gourmet menus to go with the superb wines they offer. There's also been a recent proliferation of wine-tastings (*degustazioni*), which offer a chance to sample some interesting vintages, often at no cost.

Wine bars that also feature great **food**, or in which food is the major activity, have been listed in Chapter 15, either under "Cafés" or "Restaurants"; we've listed the best of those that still concentrate on the fruit of the vine in this chapter. Our five favourite places are below.

Ai Tre Scalini see p.259
Cul de Sac see p.257
Il Goccetto see p.258

La Barrique see p.260
L'Angolo Divino see p.258
La Trinchetta see p.257

Campo de' Fiori and the Ghetto

See the **map** on pp.58–59.
Bartaruga Piazza Mattei 7 ☎06.689.2299.
Mon–Sat 3pm–2am. This very theatrical bar attracts members of the city's entertainment demimonde, and even provides costumes for clients who feel like a change of persona. The setting is wonderfully camp, eclectically furnished with all sorts of eighteenth-century bits and pieces; nothing really matches and the feel is sumptuously comfortable.
Il Goccetto Via dei Banchi Vecchi 14
☎06.686.4268. **Mon–Sat noon–2pm & 6pm–midnight.** A short walk from Campo de' Fiori, this is one of the city centre's nicest wine bars, with lots of options by the glass and good plates of cheese and salami to go with it.
La Curia di Bacco Via del Biscione 79
☎06.689.3893. **Daily 4pm–2am.** This long, thin, bustling wine bar was hollowed out of the ruins of Pompey's Theatre, near Campo de' Fiori. A very young crowd, some good wines, pricey beer and interesting snacks – *crostini*, *bruschette*, cheese plates and the like.
L'Angolo Divino Via dei Balestrari 12
☎06.686.4413. **Tues–Sun 11am–2.30pm & 5.30pm–2am.** Quite a peaceful haven after the furore of Campo de' Fiori, this wine bar has a large selection of wine, and simple, typical wine-bar fare – bread, cheese, cold cuts and the like, as well a selection of hot meals.
La Vineria Campo de' Fiori 15 ☎06.6880.3268.
Mon–Sat 8.30am–2am. This long-established bar/wine shop right on the Campo, patronized by devoted regulars, has more recently started making concessions to comfort, and

offering light meals. Much cheaper if you sit or stand inside.
Mad Jack's Via Arenula 20 ☎06.6880.8223.
Daily 11am–2am. One of many Irish pubs, but one of the nicest and most authentic, as well as one of the easiest to find, right across from Piazza Cairoli. Guinness is a speciality, and there are light snacks, burgers and the like, too. Frequented by Italians as well as tourists and expats.
Scholars' Lounge Via del Plebiscito 101b
☎06.6920.2208. **Daily 11am–3am.** One of the better city-centre Irish pubs, with regular live music and giant screens showing premier league football and other sports. Monday's quiz night can be fun too, as can the karaoke night on Tuesday.
Vinaietto Via Monti della Farina 38. **Mon–Sat 10.30am–3pm & 6.30–10pm.** This hole-in-the-wall *enoteca* has just a handful of tables, so most of its regulars drink their wine outside on the cobbles. Though mainly a wine shop, the enthusiastic owners offer a range of wines to drink by the glass – and it's far less expensive than nearby Campo de' Fiori.

The Tridente and Trevi

See the **map** on p.93.
Canova Piazza del Popolo 16 ☎06.361.2231.
Daily 8am–midnight. Once the haunt of the monied classes, *Canova* is not really the place it was. Still, it does all sorts of cocktails and reasonable food, and is a fine place to sit and take the air and watch the world go by on Piazza del Popolo. Politically, *Canova*'s clientele was traditionally a right-wing one, while dyed-in-the-wool lefties patronized *Rosati* across the square (see below).

'Gusto **Piazza Augusto Imperatore 9**
⊤06.322.6273. **Daily 10am–2am.** This stylish
modern bar is part of the 'Gusto foodie
empire that occupies this corner (see also
p.246) and serves drinks, sandwiches and
Catalan one-bite tapas to Rome's chattering
classes. Entrance to the bar is around the
corner on Via della Frezza.
L'Enoteca Antica **Via della Croce 76b**
⊤06.679.0896. **Daily 11am–1am.** An old
Spanish Steps-area wine bar with a
selection of hot and cold dishes, including
soups and attractive desserts. Intriguing
trompe l'oeil decorations inside, majolica-
topped tables outside.
Lowenhaus **Via della Fontanella 16d**
⊤06.323.0410. **Daily 11am–2am.** Just off
Piazza del Popolo, this is a Bavarian-style
drinking establishment with beer and snacks
– and full meals too – to match. A handy
place to get a beer in this location.
Rosati **Piazza del Popolo 5** ⊤06.322.5859. **Daily
8am–midnight.** This was the bar that hosted
left-wingers, bohemians and writers in years
gone by, though now it's cocktails and food
that draw the crowds to its outside terrace.
Shaki **Via Maria de' Fiori 29** ⊤06.679.1694.
Daily 11am–11pm. Wine bar of the nearby
gourmet store, and serving salads, soups,
light lunches and snacks at outside tables,
footsteps from Piazza di Spagna. Good
wine, and very handy, if a little too self-
consciously chic.

The Quirinale and east

See the **map** on pp.104–105.
Café Friends **Via Flavia 48. Daily 7.30am–2am.**
Bright, modern cafe – part of a small chain
– fashioned out of a stretch of Roman wall.
Good for breakfast and lunch, but also
cocktails in the evening, when there's a
decent buffet early on.
Trimani **Via Goito 20** ⊤06.446.9661. **Mon–Sat
11am–midnight.** This fine enoteca has a truly
vast wine list and has also lately received
accolades for its interesting dining options.
Mediterranean specialities such as octopus
salad and black rice are hits, as well as
some unusual cheeses.

The Esquiline, Monti and Termini

See the **map** on pp.116–117.
Ai Tre Scalini **Via Panisperna 251**
⊤06.4890.7495. **Mon–Fri noon–1am, Sat
& Sun 6pm–1am.** Great, easy-to-miss little

▲ L'Enoteca Antica

Monti bar, cosy and comfortable, with a
good wine list, but beer on tap too, and
decent food – cheese and salami plates
plus porchetta, lasagne parmigiana and
other simple staples.
Al Vino al Vino **Via dei Serpenti 19**
⊤06.485.803. **Daily 11.30am–1.30pm &
5pm–12.30am.** The Monti district's most
happening street offers this seriously good
wine bar with a choice of over 500 labels,
many by the glass. Snacks are generally
Sicilian specialities.
Bar à Book **Via dei Piceni 23** ⊤06.9604.3014,
Ⓦwww.barabook.it. **Tues–Sun 4pm–2am.** A
welcome addition to studenty San Lorenzo,
this friendly bookshop and wine bar makes
a very laidback place for a drink. They
also organize events, from poetry readings
to Dj sets.
Club Machiavelli **Via Machiavelli 49**
⊤06.9761.4348. **Wed–Sat 8pm–1am.** Located
in a historic palace, which accounts for the
beautiful vaulted ceilings, in up-and-coming
Piazza Vittorio, this place serves wines and
cocktails, plus home-made desserts and
other treats. There are piano-bar-style
evenings too, with occasional live jazz
combos and other cultural events.
Druid's Den **Via San Martino ai Monti 28**
⊤06.4890.4781. **Mon–Thurs & Sun
6pm–1.30am, Fri & Sat 6pm–3am.** Appealing
Irish pub near Santa Maria Maggiore with a
genuine Celtic feel (and owners). It has a
mixed expat/Italian clientele, and is not just

Rome's best hotel bars

Every great city has its great bars, and in Rome many of them are in **hotels**, and not just the most expensive ones either: some have fantastic or historic spaces, court-yards or gardens, an unusual and alluring clientele, or just great views over the city. Whatever the reason, they are great places for sipping an early-evening aperitif and realizing that you couldn't be anywhere else in the world. Here are our favourites.

D'Inghilterra Via Bocca di Leone 14 ⓣ06.699.811. See map, p.93. The folk at Gambero Rosso (see box, p.253) reckon this to be one of the best bars in Italy, and its clubby interior a perfect place to enjoy one of its excellent cocktails.

De la Minerve Piazza de la Minerva 69 ⓣ06.695.201. See map, p.44. Right behind the Pantheon, the outdoor roof garden bar here gives about the best view you can get over the rooftops and domes of the old centre – a perfect place to wind up after you've been trudging around at street level all day.

De Russie Via del Babuino 9 ⓣ06.328.881. See map, p.93. A haven for chic drinkers, plus the odd celebrity, this bar always has a buzz about it. The minimalist neutral bar, with a generous selection of champagnes and wines by the glass, as well as cocktails, opens to a tiered "secret" garden.

Eden Via Ludovisi 49 ⓣ06.478.121. See map, pp.104–105. Expansive views of Rome across the Spanish Steps, the umbrella pines of Villa Borghese, and more rooftops and domes than you could count, made this terrace perch a favourite spot for film director Federico Fellini.

Forum Via Tor de' Conti 25–30 ⓣ06.679.2446. See map, pp.116–117. The American bar at this Monti four-star commands magical views over the Forum and Colosseum – great for a drink just as the sun is setting.

Il Palazzetto/International Wine Academy Vicolo del Bottino 8 ⓣ06.699.0878. See map, p.93. Two bars in one: situated in the same building, the *Wine Academy* bar has a wonderful clubby feel that in warm weather expands to the stone terrace that overlooks the Spanish Steps, while *Il Palazzetto*'s bar sits atop the Steps – both perfect to watch the action below. A good selection of international wines by the glass or bottle at both.

Locarno Via della Penna, 22 ⓣ06.361.0841. See map, p.93. The slightly decadent atmosphere graced with hip, modern cocktail-sippers and a clubby back room with cosy fireplace make the *Locarno* Rome's most egalitarian hotel bar. It's frequented by literati, artists, princes, near-paupers, poseurs, fashionistas and just ordinary folk, and the warm weather adds a roof terrace to the mix.

Radisson Blu Es Via Turati 171 ⓣ06.444.841. See map, pp.116–117. Rome's sleek Radisson-Blu Es hotel also sports one of the city's most elegant cocktail bars. Poolside drinks give top-floor views over Termini's train tracks below.

for the homesick. Cheap and lively, with occasional impromptu Celtic music.

Fiddler's Elbow Via dell'Olmata 43 ⓣ06.487.2110. Mon–Sat 5pm–1.15am, Sun 3pm–1.30am. One of the two original Irish bars in Rome, one block closer to Santa Maria Maggiore than its rival, the *Druid's Den*, and roomier, with a decidedly more Latin feel.

Finnegan Via Leonina 66 ⓣ06.474.7026. Mon–Fri 1pm–12.30am, Sat & Sun noon–12.30am. Another of the area's crop of Irish pubs, with live football on TV, pool, and a friendly expat

crowd. There's seating outside, too, on this bustling Monti street.

La Barrique Via del Boschetto 41/b ⓣ06.4782.5953. Mon–Fri 1–3.30pm & 6pm–2am, Sat 6pm–2am. This labyrinthine wine bar in the heart of Monti is a great spot for an *aperitivo*. French and Italian wines are the main attraction here – champagne is a speciality – and platters of meats and cheeses keep pre-dinner hunger pangs at bay.

Rive Gauche Via dei Sabelli 43 ⓣ06.445.6722. Daily 7pm–3am. The San Lorenzo district's smoky, noisy, cavernous evocation of intellectual Left Bank Paris – more or less. Lots of Irish beer and snacks. *Aperitivo* hour with buffet till 9pm.

Tearoom Via del Boschetto 34 ☎347.009.5009. **Daily 6pm–2am.** This tiny, dimly lit space with an old-world, decadent feel has become hugely popular with the area's discerning trendies. It serves tea and biscuits from 6pm, and there's a Dj from 8pm, when its comfy, overstuffed sofas are in high demand. You have to be a member to enter, but membership is free.

The Celian Hill and San Giovanni

See the **map** on pp.130–131.
Il Tiaso Via Ascoli Piceno 20 ☎333.284.5283. **Daily 6pm–2am.** This relaxed wine bar with free wi-fi has book-lined shelves and lots of wines to try by the glass, accompanied by cheese and salami platters, as well as some more substantial meals. There are often live acoustic sets, too – a great place to kick off an evening out.

Pentagrappolo Via Celimontana 21b ☎06.709.6301. **Tues–Fri noon–3pm & 6pm–1am, Sat & Sun 6pm–1am.** Celio wine bar with lots of good wines by the glass, cheese plates and the usual cold cuts, and live piano music several nights a week.

Tree Folks Via Capo d'Africa 29. **Daily 6pm–2am.** Lots of Belgian and German brews, as well as food – plates of cold cuts, burgers and chips, salads – and their other speciality is whisky, with a selection of single malts that must be one of the city's best.

The Aventine and south

See the **map** on pp.138–139.
Caffè Emporio Piazza dell'Emporio 1 ☎06.575.4532. **Daily 8.30pm–2am.** Cool, sparsely furnished café-wine bar on the trendy Testaccio side of the Porta Portese (Trastevere) bridge, a good venue for a midday snack or evening drinks.

Ketumbar Via Galvani 24 ☎06.5730.5338. **Daily 8–11.30pm; bar open till 2am; closed Aug.** Convenient for all the district's clubs, this ultra-cool Testaccio venue plays laidback world music, and has very attitude-free service, despite its chic clientele. It's also one of Rome's few fusion restaurants, where Mediterranean tradition meets Oriental pizzazz.

Oasi della Birra Piazza Testaccio 41 ☎06.574.6122. **Mon–Sat 7.30pm–1am.**

Unassumingly situated under an *enoteca* on Piazza Testaccio, the cosy basement rooms here house an international selection of beers that rivals anywhere in the world – 500 in all, and plenty of wine to choose from as well. On the menu are generous plates of cheese and salami, and a great selection of bruschetta and polenta dishes. It's not particularly Roman, but it's a very alluring place to get hammered and eat good food nonetheless.

On the Rox Via Galvani 54 ☎06.574.6013. **Tues–Sat 8pm–4am, Sun 7pm–2am.** Around the corner from the clubs of Via di Monte Testaccio, and bang in the heart of the Via Galvani nightlife strip, this is as convivial a bar as you could imagine, run by a couple of Danes.

Trastevere

See the **map** on pp.156–157.
Art Café Friends Piazza Trilussa 34 ☎06.581.6111. **Mon–Sat 6am–2am, Sun 5pm–2am.** This fashionable bar on busy Piazza Trilussa serves salads and light lunches, as well as being a pleasant place to drink.

Artù Largo F. Biondi 5 ☎06.588.0398. **Tues–Sun 6pm–2am.** This bar and pub is on one of the district's busiest corners, and its terrace is great for watching the world go by, plus there's a full menu if you're peckish.

Enoteca Trastevere Via della Lungaretta 86 ☎06.588.6650. **Mon, Tues & Thurs–Sat 5pm–2am, Sun 11am–1am.** The district's largest *enoteca* is also a local favourite, with lots of mostly Italian wines to choose from, including some organic labels. Good choices, too, if you're into *grappa* and *amaro*.

Freni and Frezioni Via del Politeama 4 ☎06.5833.4210. **Daily 6pm–2am.** Just off Piazza Trilussa, this former auto workshop – the name means "brakes and clutches" – is now home to this bustling bar with good cocktails. There's a long table piled high with buffet fare between 7 and 10pm, after which everyone gathers on the terrace by the river and the Djs take over.

Ma Che Siete Venuti A Fa' Via Benedetta 25 ☎06.9727.5218. **Daily 3pm–2am.** There's an amazing choice of artisanal beers from all over the world in this tiny Trastevere bar. Most of them can't be found anywhere else in the city, or even Italy, and this is a cosy place to work your way through them.

Ombre Rosse Piazza di Sant'Egidio 12 ☎06.588.4155. Mon–Sat 7am–2.30am, Sun 5pm–2.30am. Pubby yet very Italian café with a shady outside terrace and clubby interior that hosts live jazz and blues. Something of a Trastevere institution, and serving decent wine-bar-style snacks and light meals. Along with *San Calisto* (see below), perhaps the neighbourhood's nicest bar.

Pe.Pa.To Via del Politeama 8 ☎06.5833.5254. Daily 7pm–2am. There are plenty of places to hide at this sleek, cavernous bar, one block back from the river.

San Calisto Piazza San Calisto 4 ☎06.583.5869.Mon–Sat 6am–2am. An old-guard Trastevere bar which attracts a huge crowd of just about everybody on late summer nights; the booze is cheap, and you can sit at outside tables for no extra cost. Things are slightly less demimonde-ish during the day, when it's simply a great spot to sip a cappuccino, read and enjoy the sun.

Villa Borghese and north

See the **map** on pp.174–175.

Annibale Piazza dei Carracci 4 ☎06.322.3835. **Closed Sun.** Right around the corner from the MAXXI, and not far from the Auditorium, this wine bar looks set to benefit from the resurgence of the area, and deservedly so. Its cool white interior is a nice place to sip a glass of wine, and there's an outdoor terrace in summer.

ReRe Bar Via Flaminia Vecchia 475 ☎06.334.0483. Daily 6pm–2am. Just off Piazzale Ponte Milvio, this bar is all dressed up in a kitschy bordello style that draws folk from far and wide. It also serves food and hosts resident Djs.

The Vatican and Prati

See the **map** on pp.180–181.

Fonclea Via Crescenzio 82a ☎06.689.6302. Daily 7pm–2am. This historic basement joint is loaded with devoted regulars and those who have happily discovered that there is life in the Vatican's sometimes somnolent Borgo and Prati areas. Live music adds to the fun (see p.265 for more info).

Four Green Fields Via C. Morin 42 ☎06.372.5091. Daily 2pm–2am. This large Irish pub, decked out in wood and terracotta, stretches over two floors, with live music downstairs every evening (see p.265 for more). Draught Guinness and Kilkenny complement the scene, along with decent pub grub.

Nuvolari Via degli Ombrellari 10 ☎06.6880.3018. Mon–Sat 6pm–2am. A welcoming Borgo bar that serves a full menu next door but also has a free buffet between 6.30 and 8.30pm every night during the week. A good choice of wines, and a pleasant local vibe – not at all what you expect in this part of town.

Saxophone Via Germanico 26 ☎06.3972.3039. Daily 4pm–2am. A welcoming pub in the shadow of the Vatican walls that does a good line in international beers, and has Italian football on TV and occasional live music.

Senza Fondo Via Germanico 168 ☎06.321.1415. Daily 9pm–3am. Convivial Prati basement pub with a good choice of beers and decent food. There's sometimes live music, too.

Clubs and live music

Roman **nightlife** retains some of the smart ethos satirized in Fellini's film *La Dolce Vita*, and designer-dressing-up is still very much a part of the mainstream scene. Entrance prices to the big **clubs** tend to be high, but there are a few smaller, more alternative places, where your travel-crumpled clothes will be perfectly acceptable. To get around the licensing laws, some of Rome's night haunts are run as private clubs – usually known as **centri sociali** or *associazioni culturali*, a device that means you may be stung for a membership fee, particularly where there's music, but entry will be free – although as a one-off visitor some places will let you in without formalities, and others charge no fee at all to be a member. In recent decades these sorts of places have sprung up all over the city, particularly in the suburbs, and are becoming the focus of political activity and the more avant-garde elements of the music and arts scene. **Entrance prices** vary hugely: sometimes entry is free, but mostly you won't pay more than €10 for "membership".

If you're after **live music**, there are regular summer festivals (see box, p.264), with venues all over town, including free events featuring major rock acts in Circo Massimo, Piazza del Popolo or in front of the Colosseum. However, the chances of catching big names elsewhere are low, due to the lack of suitable venues; promoters book the cities up north, especially Milan and Bologna, and traditionally leave Rome entirely out of the loop. However, it's worth looking out for up-and-coming US and UK indie bands playing in some of the city's more alternative venues.

Roman nightlife can be found all over the city, including neighbourhoods on the very edge of town. However, in the centre the **best areas** tend to be Ostiense and Testaccio (especially in summer), Trastevere, and the centro storico from the Jewish Ghetto to the Pantheon. For what's-on information, *Romac'è* (€1; out Wed; ⓦ www.romace.it); the newspaper *Il Messaggero* lists major musical events, and *TrovaRoma* in Thursday's edition of *La Repubblica* is another handy guide to current offerings.

Live music

Rome's **rock and pop** scene is a relatively limp affair, especially compared to the cities of the north, focusing mainly on foreign bands and the big venues like the Stadio Olimpico. Summer sees local bands giving occasional free concerts in

---

See the next chapter, "Culture and entertainment", for details of Rome's more **highbrow entertainment** – classical music, opera, dance – and film.

Live music festivals

Rome hosts a variety of **music festivals**, especially during the summer. The first big music event of the year is the **Dissonanze** festival of electronica, avant-garde and indie music, held in May at the Palazzo dei Congressi in EUR (ⓦ www.dissonanze.it). There are regular jazz concerts in the **Villa Celimontana** park, with evening performances between early June and the end of September (ⓣ 06.5833.5781, ⓦ www.villacelimontanajazz.com) – a great venue, with some big names. Kiosks selling food and drink set up shop, so you can make a night of it. Later in the year, the **Rome Jazz Festival** (ⓦ www.romajazzfestival.it) is held in November at the Auditorium.

There's a big Latin music scene, too, particularly Brazilian, which includes the **Fiesta** event in summer, held from mid-June to mid-September at the Ippodromo delle Capannelle at Via Appia Nuova 1245 (tickets €10; ⓣ 333.775.1851, ⓦ www.fiesta.it; bus #664 from Metro A Colli Albani). The other main cultural focus of the summer is the **Estate Romana** (ⓣ 06.0608, ⓦ www.estateromana.comune.roma.it), a series of mainly outdoor events that last all summer, including theatrical and musical performances, film projections, art exhibits, and events for children staged in venues throughout the city, including the Pincio terrace, Centrale Montemartini and the Villa Medici. The festival also includes the concerts and performances of **Testaccio Village**, which offer a different artist every night during the warm months, followed by three outdoor discos, all for free on production of a low-priced weekly pass – available at the ticket booth near the entrance or from Rome's tourist offices. Check *Romac'è* or *TrovaRoma* for details (see p.35).

the piazzas, but the city is much more in its element with jazz, with lots of venues and a healthy array of local talent.

Big venues

For information about events at any of these three **venues** – really the city's only options for big, internationally renowned visiting bands and solo acts – call the Orbis agency (see p.270).
Atlantico Live Viale dell'Oceano Atlantico 271d ⓣ 06.4807.8220, ⓦ www.atlanticoroma.it. Metro B EUR Fermi or bus #714 from Termini. See map, p.152. A giant tent-like structure 400m from PalaLottomatica, this is one of two sports arenas where major acts tend to end up. It holds about 1500 people and hosts everything from sporting events to club nights.
PalaLottomatica Piazzale dello Sport ⓣ 199.128.800, ⓦ www.forumnet.it. Metro B EUR Palasport or bus #714 from Termini. See map, p.152. This circular hall has recently undergone a total overhaul, including work on its acoustics, and hosts major Italian and a handful of foreign acts.
Stadio Olimpico Viale dei Gladiatori ⓣ 06.36851. Bus #32 or tram #2 from Metro A Ottaviano. See map, pp.174–175. When the likes of U2 and Madonna come to town, they play in this 82,000-spectator stadium in the northern part of the city between Monte Mario and the Tiber.

Rock and pop

Akab/Cave Via Monte Testaccio 69 ⓣ 06.5725.0585, ⓦ www.akabcave.com. Metro B Piramide or bus #30 or #60 from Piazza Venezia, #75 from Termini, #95 from Metro A Barberini, or #280 from Metro A Lepanto. See map, pp.138–139. Tues & Thurs–Sat 10pm–4am. Two venues in one. *Akab* is at ground level and usually plays house music. *Cave* is below-ground and features r'n'b. Concerts are generally once or twice a week.
Alpheus Via del Commercio 36 ⓣ 06.574.7826, ⓦ www.alpheus.it. Metro B Piramide or bus #30 or #60 from Piazza Venezia, #75 from Termini, #95 from Metro A Barberini, or #280 from Metro A Lepanto. See map, pp.138–139. Daily 10pm–4am. Housed in an ex-factory off Via Ostiense, a little way beyond Testaccio, the Alpheus has space for three simultaneous events – usually a disco, concert and exhibition or piece of theatre. Sat is "Gorgeous" – gay night.
Circolo degli Artisti Via Casilina Vecchia 42 ⓣ 06.7030.5684, ⓦ www.circoloartisti.it. Metro

A San Giovanni, or bus #105 from Termini, or #810 from Piazza Venezia. See map, pp.130–131. Daily 7pm–4am. This very large venue with several bars, dancefloors and exhibition spaces is located beyond Porta Maggiore. A good range of bands, with frequent discos and theme nights – hip-hop, electronica, house, ska, revival, etc. On Fri it hosts "Omogenic" – gay night. In summer, their pool is open to the public.

Fonclea Via Crescenzio 82a ☎06.689.6302, 🌐www.fonclea.it. Metro A Ottaviano or bus #81 from Piazza Venezia, #492 from Largo Argentina or #590 from Termini. See map, pp.180–181. Daily 7pm–2am. Busy and happening basement bar in the Vatican area that hosts regular live music – usually jazz, soul and funk. Happy Hour 7–8pm. Free Mon–Fri and Sun. See also p.262.

Forte Prenestino Via F. Delpino 100 ☎06.2180.7855, 🌐www.forteprenestino.net. Tram #5 from Termini or bus #542 or #544 from Metro B Monti Tiburtini. See map, pp.116–117. This early-twentieth-century fortress, and giant squat since 1986, is home to one of Rome's most active *centri sociali*, with regular live music, film screenings and other events held both inside and out in the castle courtyards. It also boasts a bookstore, various studios, and a very inexpensive restaurant (Mon–Fri). Its May Day "non-lavoro" events, held to celebrate the anniversary of the occupation of the building, are popular.

Four Green Fields Via C. Morin 42 ☎06.372.5091, 🌐www.fourgreenfields.it. Metro A Ottaviano or bus #81 from Piazza Venezia, #492 from Largo Argentina or #590 from Termini. See map, pp.180–181. Daily 2pm–2am. Mixed crowds visit this long-running, versatile Vatican-area pub, which also has a cocktail bar. Live music in the basement every night starting at 9.30pm. Free admission.

Rising Love Via delle Conce 14 ☎333.308.2245, 🌐www.risinglove.it. Metro Piramide, or bus #30 or #60 from Piazza Venezia, #75 from Termini, #95 from Metro A Barberini, or #280 from Metro A Lepanto. See map, pp.138–139. This Ostiense club's Thursday "I Love Rock" nights host indie bands and DJs. Other evenings see reggae, funk, hip-hop and jam sessions.

Sotto Casa Via dei Reti 25 ☎347.814.6544, 🌐www.sottocasa.org. Bus #71 from Via del Tritone, #492 from Largo Argentina or tram #3 from the Colosseum. See map, pp.116–117.

Tues–Sun 9pm–3am. Multi-room multi-venue in the San Lorenzo district, featuring live rock, reggae and jazz, plus performance art, theatre and cabaret in the main hall. Elsewhere you can dine and chat. Admission/annual membership fee €5.50.

The Place Via Alberico II 27–29 ☎06.6830.7137, 🌐www.theplace.it. Metro A Ottaviano or bus #40 from Termini, #62 from Largo Argentina, or #87 from Piazza Venezia. See map, pp.180–181. Tues–Sun 8pm–2am. Singer-songwriters, jazz, Latin and r'n'b and – later – DJs at this Prati live music club. The restaurant serves up interesting fusion cuisine, and admission is free with a drink.

Villaggio Globale Lungotevere Testaccio 22 ☎347.413.1205, 🌐www.vglobale.biz. Metro B Piramide or bus #95 from Metro A Barberini, #170 from Termini, or #781 from Piazza Venezia. See map, pp.138–139. Winter months only; opening hours depend on events. Situated in the old slaughterhouse along the river, the "global village" has something on almost every night, whether it's world music, indie rock or avant-garde performance art, in its Spazio Boario.

Jazz, Latin and blues

Alexanderplatz Via Ostia 9 ☎06.5833.5781, 🌐www.alexanderplatz.it. Metro A Ottaviano or tram #19 from Viale Regina Margherita. See map, pp.180–181. Daily 8.30pm–2am. Rome's top live jazz club/restaurant with reasonable membership (€10) and free entry, except when there's star-billing. Reservations recommended. Doors open at 8pm, concerts at 10pm.

Big Mama Vicolo San Francesco a Ripa 18 ☎06.581.2551, 🌐www.bigmama.it. Bus #75 or #170 from Termini, or tram #8 from Largo Argentina. See map, pp.156–157. Tues–Sat 9pm–2am. Trastevere jazz/blues club of long standing, hosting acts five nights a week. Membership €8, and free entry except for star attractions (when it's important to book ahead). Doors open 9pm.

Beba Do Samba Via dei Messapi 8 ☎339.878.5214, 🌐www.bebadosamba.it. Tram #3 from the Colosseum or #14 from Termini. See map, pp.116–117. Daily 9pm–2.30am. Brazil Central in Rome, and each night they highlight a new group, with the focus on Latin sounds, while the chill-out room is replete with comfortable cushions and divans.

Caffé Latino Via Monte Testaccio 96 ⓣ06.5728.8556, ⓦwww.caffelatinodiroma.com. Metro B Piramide or bus #30 from Piazza Venezia, #75 or #170 from Termini, #95 from Metro A Barberini, or #280 from Metro A Lepanto. See map, pp.138–139. Daily 10.30pm–4am. Multi-event Testaccio club with varied live music almost every night, as well as cartoons, films and cabaret. There's also a disco playing a selection of funk, acid jazz and r'n'b. Best at weekends when it gets more crowded.

Caruso Café de Oriente Via Monte Testaccio 36 ⓣ06.574.5019, ⓦwww.carusocafe.com. Metro B Piramide or bus #30 from Piazza Venezia, #75 or #170 from Termini, #95 from Metro A Barberini, or #280 from Metro A Lepanto. See map, pp.138–139. Tues–Sun 10pm–4am. Three rooms – and a roof terrace in the warm months – host Latin music most of the week, with soul, r'n'b and occasional live cover groups. Monthly membership €8.

Casa del Jazz Viale di Porta Ardeatina 55 ⓣ06.704.731, ⓦwww.casajazz.it. Metro B Piramide, or bus #714 from Termini. See map, pp.138–139. Sponsored by the city, and very much the project of Rome's previous mayor, jazz-loving Walter Veltroni. This converted villa in leafy surroundings is the ultimate jazz-lovers' complex, with a book and CD store and restaurant, recording studios and a 150-seat auditorium that hosts jazz names most nights of the week. Admission €10.

Escopazzo Via d'Aracoeli 41 ⓣ389.683.5618, ⓦwww.escopazzo.it. Bus #40, #64 or #H from Termini, #280 from Metro A Lepanto, #492 or #630 from Metro A Barberini. See map, pp.58–59. Daily 10pm–5am. Halfway between Piazza Venezia and Largo Argentina, this friendly bar attracts a crowd of thirty-somethings and offers food and wine along with live concerts or jam sessions most nights.

Gregory's Via Gregoriana 54a ⓣ06.679.6386, ⓦwww.gregorysjazz.com. Metro A Spagna or bus #117 from Via Nazionale. See map, p.93. Tues–Sun 8pm–3am. Just up the Spanish Steps and to the right, this elegant nightspot pulls in the crowds with its live jazz, improvised by Roman and international musicians.

Clubs

Rome's clubs run the gamut. There are vast glitter palaces with stunning lights and sound systems, predictable dance music and an over-dressed, over-made-up clientele – good if you can afford it and just want to dance (and observe a good proportion of Romans in their natural Saturday-night element). But there are also places that are not much more than ritzy bars with music, and other, more down-to-earth places to dance, playing a more interesting selection of music to a younger, more cautious-spending crowd (we've listed some of these in Chapter 16 as well). There is also a small group of places catering specifically to gay or lesbian clubbers (see p.277).

All clubs tend to open and close late, and **entrance fees** vary from €10 to €25, though they often include a drink. During the hot summer months, many clubs close down or move to outdoor locations like EUR's parks or the beaches of Ostia and Fregene.

Alien Via Velletri 13 ⓣ06.841.2212. Bus #38 from Termini, or #63 from Metro A Barberini. See map, pp.104–105. Tues–Sun 11pm–4am. The two halls here feature starkly contrasting decor, one redolent of maharajah plushness, the other done up in Modernistic monochrome. Music is a mixture of house and techno.

Art Café Via del Galoppatoio 33 ⓣ06.3600.6578. Metro A Spagna. See map, p.165. Tues–Sat 9pm–6am. Housed in the underground car park at Villa Borghese, this is one of Rome's trendiest clubs. Expect to queue, and dress up – otherwise you might not get in.

Balic Via degli Aurunci 35 ⓣ06.9761.2428, ⓦwww.balic.it. Tram #3 from Termini or #19 from Metro A Ottaviano. See map, pp.116–117. Tues–Sun 10pm–3am. This cool lounge bar and club in San Lorenzo has modern ethnic decor and hosts occasional live music and dance music on Fri and Sat. There's a restaurant too.

Black Out Via Casilina 713 ⓣ06.241.5047, ⓦwww.blackoutrockclub.com. Metro A San Giovanni or Re di Roma or bus #85 from Metro B

Colosseo or #105 from Termini. See map, pp.130–131. Thurs–Sat 11pm–4am; closed in summer. Murky industrial San Giovanni club that plays punk, heavy metal and Goth music, with occasional gigs by US and UK bands.

Brancaleone Via Levanna 13 ℗06.8200.4382, ⓦwww.brancaleone.eu. Bus #60 from Piazza Venezia or #84 from Termini. See map, pp.104–105. Tues–Sat 11pm–4am. Minimalist spaces with the feel of a Berlin squat, this *centro sociale* off the Via Nomentana hosts live acts and DJ sets. Thursday nights see reggae, while Fridays are given over to techno and Saturdays to house.

Classico Village Via Libetta 3 ℗06.5728.8857, ⓦwww.classico.it. Metro B Garbatella. See map, pp.138–139. Wed–Sun 9pm–2am. Industrial Ostiense location with a big dancefloor, a venue for live music, often jazz, and a restaurant.

Gilda Via Mario de' Fiori 97 ℗06.678.4838, ⓦwww.gildabar.it. Metro A Spagna or bus #85 or #850 from Metro B Colosseo, #95 or #116 from Metro A Barberini, or #119 from Piazza Venezia. See map, p.93. Thurs–Sun 11pm–5am. A few blocks from the Spanish Steps, this slick, stylish and expensive club is the focus for the city's minor celebs and wannabes, mainly of the middle-aged variety. Dress smart to get in. Their summer venue, *Gilda on the Beach*, is in Fregene, at Lungomare di Ponente 11 (℗06.6656.0649).

Goa Via Libetta 13 ℗06.574.8277. Metro B Garbatella. See map, pp.138–139. Tues–Sat 11pm–5am. This long-running Ostiense club near the Basilica di San Paolo was opened by famous local DJ Giancarlino and is still playing techno, house, and jungle. *Goa* has an ethnic feel – a shop sells handmade crafts, there's incense burning, and sofas to help you recover after high-energy dancing. This is where all the biggest DJs that come to Rome spin.

Jackie O' Via Boncompagni 11 ℗06.4288.5457. Bus #52, #53, #61 or #116 from Metro A Barberini, #492 from Largo Argentina, #95 or #119 from Piazza Venezia, or #175 from Termini. See map, pp.104–105. Daily 8pm–4.30am; closed Mon in winter. Amazingly, this 1960s Via Veneto jet-set glitter palace is still going strong, even attracting its share of celebs from time to time. Long on attitude, it can actually be fun if you enjoy its rather retro notion of a night out, including a preponderance of mainstream Italian pop.

La Maison Vicolo dei Granari 3 ℗06.683.3312, ⓦwww.lamaisonroma.it. Bus #40, #64 or #175 from Termini. See map, p.44. Tues–Sun 11pm–3am, until 5am on Fri & Sat. Ritzy club whose chandeliers and glossy decor attracts Rome's gilded youth.

Lanificio 159 Via di Pietralata 159a ℗06.372.5091, ⓦwww.lanificio159.com. Bus #60 from Piazza Venezia or #84 from Termini. See map, pp.104–105. Thurs–Sun 11pm–4am. Set in the restored remains of an industrial textile complex, *Lanificio* hosts concerts, art installations and DJ sets. Admission €10.

Micca Club Via Pietro Micca 7a ℗06.8744.0079, ⓦwww.miccaclub.com. Bus #105 from Termini, tram #5 or #14 from Termini, or #19 from Metro A Ottaviano. See map, pp.116–117. Mon, Tues & Thurs–Sat 10pm–4am, Sun 6pm–2am; closed late May to mid-Sept. This cavernous underground club, with brick walls and plenty of cosy booths, has a hugely varied programme, with popular themed nights – from swing to funk

▲ *Micca Club*

to burlesque. It also hosts a vintage market every Sunday from 6pm. Admission €10 Mon, Tues, Thurs & Sun, or free after 10pm; €10–15 Fri & Sat.

Piper Via Tagliamento 9 ℗06.855.5398, ⓦwww.piperclub.it. Bus #63 from Via Torre Argentina, #86, #92, #217 or #360 from Termini, tram #3

17

CLUBS AND LIVE MUSIC | Clubs

from Metro A Manzoni or #19 from Metro A Ottaviano. See map, pp.104–105. Tues–Sun 11pm–4am. Established back in the 1970s, but still going strong, *Piper* has nightly events (fashion shows, art shows, gigs), and a wide variety of music, having survived by under-going a reincarnation every season. There are two levels, a smart-but-casual mixed-aged crowd, and a heavy pick-up scene.

Qube Via di Portonaccio 212 ℡ 06.438.5445, ⓦ www.qubedisco.com. Metro B Tiburtina, or tram #5 or #14 from Termini, or #19 from Metro A Ottaviano. See map, pp.130–131. Thurs–Sat 10.30pm–4am. Big Tiburtina club hosting a variety of nights each week, including live music. Not the most original for music but its Friday gay and drag night – Muccassassina ("Killer Cow") – draws a big crowd.

Rashomon Via degli Argonauti 16 ℡ 347.340.5710, ⓦ www.myspace.com /rashomonclub. Metro B Garbatella. See map, pp.138–139. Wed & Thurs 10pm–2am, Fri & Sat 11pm–4am. This live music, performance

space and electronic music venue walks the line between underground club and trendy point of reference for Roman indie musicians, artists and DJs. Thursday night's "Loaded" party draws the biggest crowds.

Sinister Noise Club Via dei Magazzini Generali 4b ℡ 347.33.10.648, ⓦ www.myspace.com /sinisternoiseclub. Metro B Piramide. See map, pp.138–139. Tues–Sun 7pm–2am. This venue has a more intimate feel than the mega-clubs along this stretch, with a lively bar on the ground floor and a small dancefloor upstairs, where the music tends to be garage, alternative and experimental rock. Admission €5–10.

Zoobar Via Bencivenga 1 ℡ 339.27.27.995, ⓦ www.zoobar.roma.it. Bus #84 or #90 from Termini, or #60 from Metro B Colosseo. See map, pp.104–105. Thurs–Sat 11pm–3.30am. This club out near Nomentana station plays a wide range of different music – oldies, ska, funk, r'n'b and much more.

Culture and entertainment

t has to be said: Rome is a bit of a backwater for the **performing arts**. Northern Italy is where creativity in theatre and dance – and, of course, opera – flourishes, and relatively few international-class performers put in an appearance here. The current mayor has made significant cutbacks in the city's cultural funds, playing down the Rome Film Festival and eliminating several of his predecessor's cultural initiatives altogether. Nevertheless, the city does have a cultural life, and its quality is sometimes better than you might expect, helped by the continued success of the Auditorium, north of the city centre (see p.176). In any case, what the arts scene may lack in professionalism has always been made up for in the charm of the city's settings. Rome's **summer festival**, or "Estate Romana", for example, means that there's a good range of classical music, opera, theatre and cinema running throughout the warmer months, often in picturesque locations – amid ancient ruins with soaring columns, or perched on hills with brilliant panoramas of Rome by night – although obviously some of what's on may only be of interest if you speak Italian.

▲ The Auditorium

Information and ticket agencies

For current **information** about what's on where in English, consult **Romac'è** (€1; out Wed; ⓦ www.romace.it) or English-language bi-weekly **Wanted in Rome** (€2.50, out every other Wed; ⓦ www.wantedinrome.com), which you can pick up at almost any newsstand in the centre. Otherwise, in Italian, the "TrovaRoma" booklet inserted in *La Repubblica*'s Thursday edition is your best bet.

Ticket agencies

HelloTicket ⓣ 800.907.080, ⓦ www.helloticket.it. Online and telephone sales.

La Feltrinelli Largo Argentina 5a ⓣ 06.6830.8596; Viale Giulio Cesare 88 (Prati) ⓣ 06.377.2411.

Messaggerie Musicali Via del Corso 472 ⓣ 06.6819.2349.

Orbis Piazza Esquilino 37 (Santa Maria Maggiore) ⓣ 06.474.4776.

During the winter, you'll find a regular programme of **classical music** mounted by the city's principal orchestra, the Accademia Nazionale di Santa Cecilia, and other sporadic musical offerings of mixed quality, sometimes in beautiful churches or palatial halls, and on occasions free. **Opera** is well established in Rome and now and again approaches world-class levels, though perhaps not often enough. High-quality **dance** performances are a rarity in Rome, although international companies do show up from time to time, usually at the Teatro Olimpico and the Teatro Argentina (see p.57). Unfortunately, **cinema-lovers** will find few films in the original language, as Italy clings as strongly as ever to its historic dubbing tradition, but we've listed a few places where you might be able to find films in their unadulterated forms.

Classical music and opera

Under new directors, Rome's own **orchestras** of late are approaching international standards, and although the city attracts far fewer prestigious artists than you might expect of a capital, it is becoming more and more a magnet for contemporary works – a sea-change that has been inspired by the completion of Renzo Piano's **Auditorium/Parco della Musica**. Critics say that beauty has been sacrificed for acoustics here, but the three halls of various sizes certainly do deliver on sound quality, while the outdoor space can be used for anything from rock to opera, and even as a skating rink in the winter. See p.176 for more on the building, and p.271 for details on booking.

Listings magazines (see p.35) and posters around town advertise little-known **concerts** – a wide range of choral, chamber and organ recitals – in churches like Sant'Agnese in Agone and Sant'Ignazio or other spectacular venues, including the private halls and courtyards of Renaissance or Baroque palaces. Otherwise, the many national academies and cultural institutes (Belgian, Austrian, Hungarian, British, American, French, et al) frequently offer free concerts as well. In the summer, concerts are staged in cloisters, in the Teatro di Marcello, just off Piazza Venezia, and in the ancient Roman theatre at Ostia Antica and at Villa Adriana. It may be that you'll just stumble across a concert-in-progress while out on an evening stroll, passing by some ancient church with all its lights on (a rarity not to be missed); Rome is a city where such magical musical moments can still happen.

The city's **opera scene** has long been overshadowed by that of Milan, Parma, and even Naples, grand opera's acknowledged birthplace, but it is improving. In summer, opera moves outdoors and ticket prices come down. Summer performances are held in the stunning setting of the ancient **Baths of Caracalla**, as well as in the courtyard of the San Clemente basilica and in other churches and venues all around Rome, in the context of the various summer music festivals which have multiplied remarkably in recent years.

Classical music and opera venues

Accademia d'Opera Italiana All Saints' Church, Via del Babuino 153 ☏ 06.784.2702, Ⓦ www.accademiadoperaitaliana.it. Metro A Spagna or bus #117 from Via Nazionale or #119 from Piazza Venezia. Performances generally include popular standards such as *La Traviata*, *Tosca* and *The Barber of Seville*, as well as Mozart's *Requiem* and *Carmina Burana*. Tickets €30.

Auditorium/Parco della Musica Via P. de Coubertin 30 ☏ 06.802.41281, 892.982, Ⓦ www.auditorium .com. Bus #53 from Piazza San Silvestro, #217, #910 or line "M" from Termini station, or tram #2 from Piazzale Flaminio. This relatively new landmark musical complex is Rome's most prestigious venue. It is home to the city's premier orchestra, the Accademia Nazionale di Santa Cecilia, who are resident part of the year in its largest hall, while two smaller venues host smaller chamber, choral, recital and experimental works. The complex also hosts major rock and jazz names when they come to town, as well as Rome's international film festival in October. Daily 11am–6pm to visit; guided tours €9. Box office Mon–Sat 11am–6pm & Sun 10am–6pm.

Aula Magna dell'Università La Sapienza Piazzale Aldo Moro 5 ☏ 06.361.0051, Ⓦ www .concertiiuc.it. Metro B Policlinico or bus #61 from Piazza San Silvestro, #490 or #495 from Piazzale Flaminio, or tram #19 from Viale Regina Margherita. La Sapienza University's Istituzione Universitaria dei Concerti is deliberately experimental and eclectic, with musical offerings ranging from Bach to Miles Davis, and from Chopin to Kurt Weill. The season runs from October to May, and performances are usually held on Tuesday evenings and weekends. Tickets €16.50–33.

Oratorio del Gonfalone Via del Gonfalone 32a ☏ 06.8530.1758, Ⓦ www.romeguide.it/oratorio gonfalone/oratoriogonfalone.htm. Bus #64 or #40 from Termini, or #116 from Piazza Barberini. This lovely theatre stages performances of chamber music, with an emphasis on the Baroque every Thursday at 9pm, with the season running from November to early June. Tickets cost €15; telephone reservations are strongly recommended. You can visit the Oratorio, or pick up tickets in advance, by appointment only (Mon–Fri 10am–4pm); the entrance is at Vicolo della Scimmia 1b.

Teatro Ghione Via delle Fornaci 37 ☏ 06.637.2294, Ⓦ www.teatroghione.it. Bus #46,

Cultural festivals

Festival delle Letterature ☏ 06.0608, Ⓦ www.festivaldelleletterature.it. Metro B Colosseo or bus #75 from Termini, #81 from Largo Argentina, or #87 from Piazza Venezia. A summertime international literature festival set in the spectacular ruins of the Basilica of Maxentius in the Roman Forum. Celebrated authors like Roberto Saviano (of *Gomorrah* fame) and John Grisham lecture or read their works, collaborating with actors and musicians.

Festival Internazionale del Film di Roma Via P. de Coubertin ☏ 06.4040.1900, Ⓦ www.romacinemafest.it. Bus #53 from Piazza San Silvestro, #217, #910 or line "M" from Termini station, or tram #2 from Piazzale Flaminio. This festival of film is held over nine days in late October at the Auditorium and a variety of other venues around town. Tickets cost €5–20 and can be purchased from the Auditorium box office (see above) or from Lottomatica Italia Servizi (Ⓦ www.listicket.it). Screenings cost from €5.50 to €20.

Roma Europa Festival ☏ 06.4229.6300, Ⓦ www.romaeuropa.net. This cultural festival has gathered pace in recent years, and is now a pretty big deal, with dance, drama and highbrow music events at the Auditorium and other venues around town from September until early December.

#64 or #916 from Corso Vittorio Emanuele. This traditional little theatre offers chamber music and recitals, often by well-known musical lights. Tickets €16–28. Box office daily 10am–1pm & 4–7pm.

Teatro Olimpico Piazza Gentile da Fabriano 17 ☎06.326.5991, ✆www.teatroolimpico.it. Bus #53 from Piazza Barberini, #910 from Termini, tram #2 from Metro A Lepanto, or tram #19 from Viale Regina Margherita. Classical standards, chamber music and ballet are performed here, by resident orchestra Accademia Filarmonica Romana (✆www.filarmonica romana.org), as well as other companies. The theatre also hosts the occasional contemporary work. Performances are on Tuesdays, Thursdays and weekends, and run from November to early May. Tickets (€15–37) are relatively easy to come by.

Teatro dell'Opera di Roma Piazza Beniamino Gigli 1 ☎06.481.60255, ✆www.operaroma.it. Metro A Repubblica or bus #40, #64 or #70 from Corso Vittorio Emanuele, or #170 from Piazza Venezia. Nobody compares it to La Scala, but cheap tickets are a lot easier to come by at Rome's opera and ballet venue – they start at €23 for opera, less for ballet – and important artists do sometimes perform here. If you buy the very cheapest tickets, bring some high-powered binoculars, as you'll need them in order to see anything at all. Don't miss the summer opera season, which is set in the Baths of Caracalla. Box office Mon–Sat 9am–5pm, Sun 9am–1.30pm.

Theatre and dance

There is a great deal of **theatre** in Rome, but it's virtually all in Italian, or even Roman dialect. Very occasional English-language musicals, usually put together by some travelling American company, come to town during the winter season. The venue for such rare events is almost always either the Teatro Olimpico or the Teatro Sistina, sometimes Teatro Argentina. Check the listings magazines (see p.35) for current programmes; incidentally, virtually all Roman theatres close on Mondays.

As for **dance**, apart from the very occasional international company, it's generally home-grown troupes doing their thing on the city's stages, and it is rarely an inspiring sight. Though the origins of ballet can be traced back to eighteenth-century Italy, there are at present few Italian companies that rise above amateurish levels. See also Teatro dell'Opera (see above) for ballet.

Mainstream and English theatres

English Theatre of Rome Teatro L'Arciliuto, Piazza Montevecchio 5 ☎06.444.1375, ✆www .rometheatre.com. Bus #40 or #64 from Termini, or #87 from Piazza Venezia. Rome's longest established English-language theatre group perform five plays each season between November and June in this tiny theatre off Piazza Navona. Tickets €15.

Miracle Players ✆www.miracleplayers.org, ✆info@miracleplayers.org. One of Rome's two English-language theatre companies, performing light-hearted renderings of the classics and lots of material with an ancient Rome theme, often in authentic venues – for example the Forum of Julius Caesar in summer. Tickets are usually free, though donations are welcomed.

Teatro di Argentina Largo Argentina 52 ☎06.6840.00311, ✆www.teatrodiroma.net /index_argentina.html. Bus #40 or #64 from Termini, #62 or #492 from Piazza Barberini, #87 or #628 from Piazza Venezia, or tram #8 from Viale Trastevere. One of the city's most important theatres for dramatic works in Italian, as well as the occasional production in English, and for dance. Tickets €12–27. Box office daily 10am–2pm & 3–7pm.

Teatro Greco Via R. Leoncavallo 10–16 ☎06.860.7513, ✆www.teatrogreco.it. Bus #63 or #630 from Piazza Barberini, or #342 from Via Nomentana. Located well out of the centre, on the far side of Villa Ada, this theatre generally offers some of the best Italian dance and even has its own company, with tickets starting at €15.

Teatro Sistina Via Sistina 129 ☎06.420.0711, ✆www.ilsistina.com. Metro A Spagna or Barberini or bus #52 or #116 from Villa Borghese, #71 from Via Giolitti (Termini), #95, #119, #160 or #630 from Piazza Venezia. Every now and then an English-language (American, very off-Broadway) musical revue blows into town and it generally ends up here, just up from Piazza di Spagna.

272

Gershwin seems to be a perennial favourite, along with other jazzy-bluesy musical confections.

Teatro Valle Via del Teatro Valle 21 ☎06.6880.3794, ⊛www.teatrovalle.it. Bus #40 or #64 from Termini, #62, #63 or #492 from Piazza Barberini, #46, #70 or #916 from Corso Vittorio Emanuele, #87 or #628 from Piazza Venezia. Between Piazza Navona and the Pantheon, this theatre sometimes offers special works in English by visiting actors and companies.

Teatro Vittoria Piazza Santa Maria Liberatrice 8–11 ☎06.574.0170, ⊛www.teatrovittoria.it. Bus #30 from Piazza Venezia, #75 from Metro B Colosseo, #95 from Metro A Barberini, or #170 from Termini. In Testaccio's main square, this large theatre sometimes books cabaret-like acts or dance-theatre companies that need no translation.

Other theatres

Teatro Brancaccio Via Merulana 244 ☎06.9826.4500, ⊛www.teatrobrancaccio.it. Metro A Vittorio Emanuele or Manzoni, or bus #16 from Termini, or #71 from Via Nazionale. Musicals and comedies, sometimes featuring major Italian players, are generally the focus here. Not a top choice for good acoustics, so your Italian has to be excellent to follow the action, if not to enjoy the songs.

Teatro Eliseo Via Nazionale 183 ☎06.4887.2222, ⊛www.teatroeliseo.it. Metro A Repubblica, or bus #40, #64 or #70 from Corso Vittorio Emanuele, or #170 from Piazza Venezia. One of Rome's main theatres, hosting plays by Italian playwrights, and adaptations into Italian of foreign works, and featuring some

of the top dramatic talent Italy has to offer. Tickets start at €12.

Teatro Prati Via degli Scipione 98 ☎06.3972.7242, ⊛www.teatroprati.it. Metro A Ottaviano or bus #81 from Largo Argentina, #492 from Piazza Barberini, #590 from Termini. A few blocks away from St Peter's, this is another small space that often features Italian comic classics. Tickets start at €16.

Teatro Romano di Ostia Antica Ostia Antica ☎06.6880.4601; Lido train from Metro B Piramide to Ostia Antica. Box office daily 10am–2pm & 3–6pm. In July specially scheduled performances of all kinds are offered in the restored ancient Roman theatre – a spectacular, unforgettable setting, even if you don't speak Italian. Performances begin at 8.45pm, but go early for a chance to visit the ruins. It's a thirty-minute train ride to Ostia Antica, then a short walk over the footbridge into the ruins. A great Roman summer experience.

Teatro Rossini Piazza Santa Chiara 14 ☎06.6821.6852. Bus #40 or #64 from Termini, #46, #70 or #916 from Corso Vittorio Emanuele, #62 or #492 from Piazza Barberini, #87 or #628 from Piazza Venezia. Traditional Roman-dialect productions are one of the main focuses in this atmospheric old theatre that runs a handful of productions annually.

Salone Margherita Via Due Macelli 75 ☎06.679.1439, ⊛www.salonemargherita.com. Metro A Spagna or Barberini or bus #52 or #116 from Villa Borghese, #71 from Via Giolitti (Termini), #95, #119, #160 or #630 from Piazza Venezia. Traditional Roman political satire and cabaret – worth it for the atmosphere, even if you don't understand the admittedly difficult verbal sallies.

Film

There tends to be limited **English-language cinema** on offer in Rome these days, partly due to lack of foreign demand, partly due to the Italian penchant for dubbing. If your Italian is up to it, you'll naturally find current Italian-language productions available all over town. Look out for the words *versione originale* (abbreviated "VO" in print listings) if you want to be sure it's not dubbed. You'll find usually accurate **listings** in *Romac'è* (see p.35) and in all the newspapers, which also include a section on "film clubs" or "cinema d'essai", a euphemism for stifling rooms where two or three aficionados sit on hard wooden chairs in front of a tiny, blurred screen watching films in their original language. **Tickets** at all cinemas cost €5–10.

For details on Rome's **film festival**, see p.271.

Cinemas

Alcazar Via Merry del Val 14 ☎06.588.0099.
Bus #75 from Metro B Colosseo, #780 from
Piazza Venezia, H from Termini or tram #8 from
Largo Argentina. Trastevere cinema featuring
mainstream American and English films,
with the occasional weird one slipping in, on
Mondays.

Barberini Piazza Barberini 26 ☎06.482.1082,
🌐www.multisalabarberini.it. Metro A Barberini
or bus #63 from Via del Corso, #71 from Via
Giolitti (Termini), #95, #119, #160 or #630 from
Piazza Venezia. Mainstream films and block-
busters with matinees in the original version
on at least one screen.

Casa del Cinema Largo Marcello Mastroianni 1
☎06.423.601, 🌐www.casadelcinema.it. Bus
#116 from Metro A Barberini. Right by the
Porta Pinciana entrance to the Villa
Borghese, this building epitomizes Rome's
cultural renaissance under former mayor
Walter Veltroni, opened in 2004 as a venue
for re-runs and retrospectives and dedicated
to Italy's most famous international film
actor, Marcello Mastroianni.

Filmstudio Via degli Orti d'Alibert 1c
☎334.178.0632, 🌐www.filmstudioroma.com.
Bus #23 from Via Arenula, or #40 or #64 from
Termini. Arty films and themed retrospectives
in this renovated old cinema in the nether
reaches of Trastevere.

Metropolitan Via del Corso 7 ☎06.320.0933.
Metro A Flaminio or bus #95, #119 or #628 from
Piazza Venezia, or #117 from Via Nazionale.
Lots of mainstream films and the occasional

quirky choice, with at least one of the four
screens showing the undubbed version.

Nuovo Olimpia Via in Lucina 16 ☎06.686.1068.
Metro A Spagna, or bus #63 from Via Veneto,
#117 from Via Nazionale or #492 from Largo
Argentina. Very central, just off Via del Corso,
with two screens, and they regularly feature
foreign films in the original language.

Nuovo Sacher Largo Ascianghi 1 ☎06.581.8116.
Bus #75 from Metro B Colosseo, #780 from
Piazza Venezia, H from Termini or tram #8 from
Largo Argentina. This Trastevere film theatre,
oddly enough housed in the old Fascist
youth HQ, shows current films in their
original version on Mon and Tues. Their
choices tend toward independent, Left-
leaning works from around the world – as
you might expect from film director and
owner Nanni Moretti, staunch communist
and scourge of Berlusconi.

Quattro Fontane Via Quattro Fontane 23
☎06.474.1515. Metro A Barberini or bus #40 or
#64 from Termini, #70 from Corso Vittorio
Emanuele, or #170 from Piazza Venezia. Lots of
mainstream and the occasional art-house
choice, with at least one of the four screens
showing the undubbed version.

**Warner Village Moderno Piazza della Repubblica
45–46** ☎06.4777.9202, 🌐www.warnervillage.it.
Metro A Repubblica or bus #40 or #64 from
Corso Vittorio Emanuele, #170 from Piazza
Venezia. This American-style multiplex
sometimes shows a Hollywood blockbuster
in the original undubbed version on one of
its five screens.

Gay and lesbian Rome

E ver since "World Pride 2000" broke down the closet door, **gay and lesbian Rome** seems to have come into its own. Italy has never had any laws prohibiting same-sex couplings, but until recently the overwhelming pressure was enough to keep everyone suitably zipped up, and even now Italy has quite a bit of catching up to do before it is quite as laidback about gay sex as much of the rest of Europe. Nonetheless, these days Rome has not just generic gay clubs, but specialist bars, restaurants and hotels, and all sorts of regular clubs are organizing gay nights to cater for the growing scene (see box, p.277). There's also the tremendously successful **Gay Village** (Ⓦ www.gayvillage .it), which holds events throughout the summer at an open-air venue in Testaccio, and the ever-popular **Gay Pride** in June (Ⓦ www.romapride.it).

Still, discretion is important in the community at large; Rome remains a city where eyebrows may still be raised at men holding hands in the street and the city is certainly not quite ready for kissing in public. Apart from a short stretch

▲ Gay Pride parade through Piazza Venezia

of **Via di San Giovanni in Laterano**, dubbed "Gay Street" for its nightlife scene, there's no specifically gay area, and most other bars and clubs are spread far and wide. Choices exclusively for women remain very few, although most places welcome both gay men and lesbians.

Contacts, shops and services

ARCI-Gay Ora Via Zabaglia 14 ☎06.6450.1102, ⓦwww.arcigayroma.it. Mon–Fri 4–8pm. Rome branch of the Italian gay organization that runs a gay helpline on (☎800.713.713; Mon, Wed, Thurs and Sat 4–8pm); has gatherings for those new to the city on Thurs (6.15–9pm); and social events every Fri (6–9pm). Annual membership costs €15 and can be useful for getting into clubs and bars (there's also a cheaper monthly version available).
Casa Internazionale delle Donne Via della Lungara 19 ☎06.6840.1720, ⓦwww .casainternazionaledelledonne.org. Not a gay organization but rather a group of facilities for women only, including a bookstore, library, restaurant and café, housed, appropriately enough, in an old convent. It also has accommodation in its *Orsa Maggiore* hostel (☎06.689.3753, ⓦwww .foresteriaorsa.altervista.org).
Circolo di Cultura Omosessuale Mario Mieli di Cultura Via Efeso 2a ☎06.541.3985,

ⓦwww.mariomieli.org. Rome's most important gay activist organization offers a broad range of social and health services, including counselling and a helpline. Weekly welcome group, political group and volunteer group meetings; call for details. Their magazine, *Aut*, features interesting articles, as well as listings, and is free at many gay spots.
Libreria Gabi International Via Gabi 30a/b/c, ☎06.687.6628, ⓦwww.libreriababeleroma.it. Mon 4–7.30pm, Tues–Sat 10am–2pm & 4–7.30pm. Just west of Piazza Re di Roma, this gay- and lesbian-friendly bookshop has gay-themed books, some in English, plus videos, guides and postcards.
Zipper Via dei Gracchi 17 ☎06.4436.2281, ⓦwww.zippertravel.it. Mon–Sat 9.30am–1pm & 2–6.30pm. Gay travel agent, located near Termini, brokering round-the-world or round-Italy travel for gay and lesbian groups and individuals.

Bars and clubs

L'Alibi Via Monte Testaccio 44 ☎06.574.3448, ⓦwww.lalibi.it. Thurs–Sun midnight–5am. This predominantly – but by no means exclusively – male venue is one of Rome's oldest gay clubs, situated in the heart of the city's alternative night scene in Testaccio. It's no longer quite cutting edge, but is a good, all-round venue, with a multi-room cellar disco and an upstairs open-air bar and big terrace to enjoy in the warm months.
Coming Out Via di San Giovanni in Laterano 8 ☎06.700.9871. Daily noon–3am. If any area is developing as Rome's gay zone, it is the stretch between the Colosseum and San Clemente. This little pub is the epicentre of the scene, frequented mostly by a younger clientele.

Frutta e Verdura Via di Monte Testaccio 94 ☎347.244.6721, ⓦwww.fruttaeverdura.roma.it. This after-hours bar in Testaccio is open Sundays from 4.30am onwards – though it's open to ARCI-Gay members only (see above).
Gay Village Mattatoio, Testaccio ⓦwww .gayvillage.it. July and Aug see gay performers and events take over Testaccio in the annual Gay Village festival. See the website and flyers for what's on.
Garbo Vicolo di Santa Margherita 1a ☎06.581.6700. Wed–Mon 9pm–2am. Friendly Trastevere bar, just behind Piazza di Santa Maria in Trastevere, with a relaxed atmosphere and a nice setting.
Hangar Via in Selci 69 ☎06.488.1397, ⓦwww .hangaronline.it. About halfway between

Gay nights

Many Rome clubs have a dedicated **gay night**, plus there are specifically gay nights that move around from venue to venue. For up-to-date details of specific gay nights, check out the relevant websites.

Gloss Thurs & Sun at *L'Alibi* (see p.276)
Gorgeous Sat at *Alpheus* (see p.264)
Muccassassina Fri at *Qube* (see p.268)
Omogenic Fri at *Circolo degli Artisti* (see p.264)
Tommy Sat at *L'Alibi* (see p.276)
Venus Rising Lesbian night, last Sun of the month at *Goa* (see p.267)

Termini and the Roman Forum, just off Via Cavour, this is one of Rome's oldest and least expensive gay spots, always crammed with young people. No charge with an ARCI-Gay card; without a card, you have to pay for at least one drink.

Il Giardino dei Ciliegi Via dei Fienaroli 4 ℡06.580.3423, ⓦwww.ilgiardinodeiciliegi.net. Mon–Sat 5pm–2am & Sun 1pm–2am. A gay-friendly café, bar and tea house in lively Trastevere.

Max's Bar Via A. Grandi 7a ℡06.7030.1599. Tues Sun 10.30pm–3am. A very friendly bar with dancefloor in the Esquiline/San Giovanni area, popular with a broad cross section of gay Romans.

Qube Via di Portonaccio 212 ℡06.438.5445, ⓦwww.qubedisco.com. Thurs–Sat 10.30pm–4am. This club plays host to the extremely successful Muccassassina ("Killer Cow") gay night every Friday. See also p.268.

Skyline Via Pontremoli 36 ℡06.700.9431, ⓦwww.skylineclub.it. Daily 10.30pm–4am. Gay male strippers, dark zones and a decidedly macho decor make this San Giovanni club a magnet for various creatures of the night, possibly drawn by the heavy cruising along the balcony. Various regular theme nights, including "Naked Party" Mondays.

Restaurants

Asinocotto Via dei Vascellari 48 ℡06.589.8985, ⓦwww.asinocotto.com. Mon–Fri noon–2.30pm & 7.30–11pm, Sat & Sun 7.30–11pm. One of the first restaurants to hang the rainbow flag above its door, this Trastevere restaurant is run by a gay couple and has a great, Proust-inspired menu of moderately priced pasta, meat and fish dishes. Worth a visit whatever your non-culinary preferences.

La Taverna di Edoardo II Vicolo Margana 14 ℡06.6994.2419, ⓦwww.edoardosecondo.com. Daily except Tues 7pm–12.30am. In the Jewish Ghetto, just off Piazza Venezia, this place used to be a medieval torture chamber theme bar, and was named after the infamously gay English king. It's now a gay restaurant and still attracts the same young and cruisy crowd. Membership is required, but it's free.

Luna e l'Altra Via della Lungara 19 ℡06.6889.2465. Mon–Sat 12.30–3pm & 7.30–11pm. This Trastevere bar and restaurant, serving Italian and international cuisine, is the only exclusively lesbian place in town. Buffet lunch, table service at dinner.

Saunas

Europa Multiclub Via Aureliana 40 ℡06.482.3650, ⓦwww.europamulticlub .com. Mon–Thurs 1pm–midnight, Fri 1pm until Sun at midnight. Near Termini, this has pleasantly stylish, clean facilities and a snack bar. €15 per visit, €12 after 11pm.

Mediterraneo Via Pasquale Villari 3, ℡06.7720.5934, ⓦwww.saunamediterraneo.it. Daily 1pm–midnight. Close to Piazza Vittorio

Emanuele, this is a sauna on three levels, with all the usual choices, including a snack bar. Notably clean and attracts all ages. ARCi-Gay membership required. €15.

Accommodation

58 Le Real De Luxe Via Cavour 58 T 06.482.3566, W www.bed-and-breakfast -rome.com. Double rooms from around €85 in this small gay-friendly Via Cavour *pensione*. **Ares Rooms Via Domenichino 7** T 06.474.4525, W www.aresrooms.com. Gay-friendly B&B near Termini station. Not all rooms are en suite. Doubles from €50.

Gayopen Via dello Statuto 44 T 06.482.0013, W www.gayopen.com. Centrally situated gay B&B right on Piazza Vittorio Emanuele, with doubles for around €100.

Shops and markets

A t first glance, you may wonder where to start when it comes to **shopping** in a big, chaotic city like Rome. In fact the city promises a more appealing shopping experience than you might think, abounding with pleasant shopping streets and colourful markets, most of which are in the city centre. Many shopping areas have been pedestrianized, and best of all, the city hasn't yet been entirely overrun by department stores and shopping malls, or by the international chain stores that characterize most European city centres. One-stop shopping opportunities are rare, but you will find corners of the city that have been colonized by stores featuring the same sort of merchandise – fashion, antiques, food – making it easy for you to check out the competition's products and prices. You will also find true artisans in central Rome, who take great pride in their crafts.

You can find the best of Italy in Rome. **Fashion** straight from the catwalk is well represented on the fashionable streets close to the Spanish Steps – Via Condotti, Via Borgognona, Via Frattina and Via del Babuino – where you'll find all the major A-list designers (see box, p.282) as well as lots of alluring one-off boutiques. You can find more mainstream fashions and all the chains on Via Cola di Rienzo, near the Vatican, and also along Via Nazionale, near to which the streets of the Monti district are home to an increasing number of stylish independent stores. Bang in the centre of town, Via del Corso is the home of mainstream young fashion stores and various chains, while Via dei Giubbonari, near Campo de' Fiori, is a good place to shop for affordably priced yet stylish clothes and shoes, and Via del Governo Vecchio is probably the city centre's best stretch of funky, stylish independent fashion boutiques and vintage stores.

Among other specialities, **antiques** shops – a huge selection – line Via dei Coronari and neighbouring Via dell'Orso and Via dei Soldati, just north of Piazza Navona; Via Giulia, southwest of Campo de' Fiori, as well as Via del Babuino and Via Margutta, between Piazza del Popolo and the Spanish Steps, are also good sources of art and antiques.

Opening hours

These days quite a few shops in the centre of Rome stay open all day and are open on Sunday too. However, many still observe the city's traditional **opening hours** – roughly Monday 3.30–7.30pm, Tuesday–Saturday 9.30am–1.30pm & 3.30–7.30pm, and closed on Sunday. Food shops are also often closed on Thursday afternoon in the winter and Saturday afternoon during the summer. Most places accept all major **credit cards.**

Markets tend to open early – around 7am – and close up by 2pm. **Supermarkets** are generally open all day from 8am until 8pm. Bear in mind that a lot of stores close down during **August** for their annual holiday.

For **food**, we've listed a number of the city's best *gastronomie* should you want to take home a bottle of extra virgin olive oil or some vacuum-packed porcini mushrooms. Finally, the city's many **markets** offer a change of pace from Rome's busy shopping streets. Many of these are bustling local food markets and, even in the centre, are still very much part of Roman life. The market in Campo de' Fiori is probably the most central, but we've listed others on p.287 and p.288. Otherwise, there's Trastevere's **Porta Portese** flea market, selling heaps of antiques, clothing, books, and indeed virtually anything else, every Sunday morning.

Shops

Antiques

Antichità Archeologia Largo della Fontanella di Borghese 76 ⊤06.686.4054. **Mon 3.30–7pm, Tues–Sat 9am–1pm & 3.30–7.30pm.** If you want to take home your own piece of ancient Rome, this is the place for you. Genuine, certified Greek, Etruscan and Roman antiquities, such as terracotta oil lamps, figurines and incised jewels, start at about €100.

Antique Trade Via del Boschetto 4 ⊤06.4782.5539. **Mon 3.30–7pm, Tues–Sat 9am–1pm & 3.30–7.30pm.** Antiques of all kinds and eras can turn up here. However, the speciality is fine old prints. A satisfying place to browse through Rome's history.

Arabesco Via del Panico 14 ⊤06.686.9659. **Mon–Sat 9.30am–8pm.** One of a couple of such stores on this street, around the corner from Via dei Coronari, this has old Turkish carpets and kilims, oriental glassware and other bits and pieces from the East.

Oasi Antiquariato Via del Babuino 83 ⊤06.320.7585. **Mon–Sat 9.30am–7.30pm.** One of several fine antiques stores in the area, with a large collection of stunning Italian furnishings from the 1700s. There is also an entrance on Via Margutta.

Papadato Antichità Piazza di Pietra 41 ⊤06.679.6199. **Tues–Sat 10.30am–7pm.** Friendly store that has both Italian and English antiques. The store is mostly known for its large selection of European fans from the sixteenth and seventeenth centuries.

Valerio Turchi Via Margutta, 91a ⊤06.323.5047. **Mon 3.30–7pm, Tues–Sat 10.30am–7pm.** A bit different from the other antiques shops on Via Margutta, with exquisite pieces from Rome's past – various pieces of Roman statues and sarcophagi dating from as early as 300 AD.

▲ Antiques for sale on Via dei Coronari

Books

The Almost Corner Bookshop Via del Moro 45 ⊤06.583.6942. **Mon–Sat 10am–1.30pm & 3.30–8pm, Sun 11am–1.30pm & 3.30–8pm; closed Sun in Aug.** Of all Rome's English bookshops, this is the best bet for having the very latest titles on your list of must-reads.

Anglo-American Bookshop Via della Vite 102 ⊤06.679.5222. **Mon 3.30–7.30pm, Tues–Sat 10.30am–7.30pm.** Excellent city-centre English-language bookstore, with one of the best selections of new English books in Rome. Especially good on history and academic books, but lots of mainstream and literary fiction too.

Feltrinelli International Via Emanuele Orlando 84 ⊤06.482.7878. **Mon–Sat 9am–8pm, Sun 10.30am–1.30pm & 4–8pm.** Just off Piazza della Repubblica, this international branch of the nationwide chain has a great stock of books in English, as well as French, German, Spanish and Portuguese.

Giunti al Punto A great kids' bookstore; see p.298.

Libreria del Cinema Via dei Fienaroli 31d ☎06.581.7724, ⓦwww.libreriadelcinema.roma .it. Mon–Fri & Sun 10am–9pm, Sat 11am–11pm. Books, DVDs, magazines on film and everything related to it – many in English. There's a small café too, where you can browse your purchases with other film buffs.

Libreria del Viaggiatore Via del Pellegrino 78 ☎06.6880.1048. Mon 4–8pm, Tues–Sat 10am–2pm & 4–8pm. A small store, but with central Rome's best stock of guides and travel books, many of which are in English.

Lion Bookshop Via dei Greci 33 ☎06.3265.4007. Mon 3.30–7.30pm, Tues–Sun 10am–7.30pm. The comfortable location of this veteran English bookshop has a lounge area where you can enjoy a coffee or tea. One of Rome's longest-established outlets for books in English.

Open Door Bookshop Via della Lungaretta 23 ☎06.589.6478, ⓦwww.books-in-italy.com. Mon 4.30–8.30pm,Tues–Fri 10.30am–8.30pm, Sat 10.30am–midnight, Sun noon–6pm; afternoons and evenings only in summer. Although they do have some new titles, especially on Rome and Roman history, used books dominate the shelves at this friendly Trastevere bookshop, where you never know what treasures you might turn up. They also have a selection of books in Italian, German, French and Spanish.

Clothes

Arsenale Via del Governo Vecchio 64 ☎06.686.1380. Mon 3.30–7.30pm, Tues–Sat 10am–7.30pm. This large store is one of the main boutiques along this funky stretch, with great dresses by the owner Patrizia Pieroni and lots of other stuff by small independent designers.

Aspesi Via del Babuino 144 ☎06.323.0376. Flagship Rome store of the contemporary Italian designer, with cool designs for both men and women in this very sleek store in the heart of the Piazza di Spagna-area designer shopping mecca.

Cinzia Via del Governo Vecchio 45 ☎06.686.1791. Mon 3.30–7.30pm, Tues–Sat 10am–2pm & 3.30–7.30pm. The best of

several used clothing shops along this street, where you can find anything from an elegant raincoat to black leather biker jeans, and much more.

Davide Cenci Via di Campo Marzio 1–7 ☎06.699.0681. Mon 3.30–7.30pm, Tues–Fri 9.30am–1.30pm & 3.30–7.30pm, Sat 10am–2pm & 3.30–7.30pm. Flagship store of this long-established purveyor of elegant and refined clothing, offering conservative high-quality fashion to men, women and children for the past 75 years.

Diesel Via del Corso 186 ☎06.678.3933. Mon–Sat 9.30am–7.30pm. The largest and most central branch of this Italian manufacturer of trendy styles for studiously disaffected youth. Other branches at Via del Babuino 94–95 (☎06.6938.0053) and Via Cola di Rienzo 245–249 (☎06.324.1895).

Dress Agency Donna Via del Vantaggio 1b ☎06.321.0898. Mon 4–7.30pm, Tues–Sat 10am–1pm & 4–7.30pm. Used women's clothing and accessories from Versace, Armani and all the big-name Italian designers. Not as cheap as you might expect, but still worth a rummage.

Emporio Armani Via del Babuino 140 ☎06.3600.2197. The city-centre branch of the designer's chain of more affordable yet still very stylish stores.

Energie Via del Corso 179 & 486 ☎06.322.7046. Mon–Sun 10am–8pm. One of Rome's most popular clothing stores, mainly aimed at teenagers, with trendy clothes, loud music and an omnipresent group of kids hanging out around the 00. Definitely the place to be seen if you're loaded and under 21. Another branch at Via Cola di Rienzo 143–147.

Fiorucci Via Nazionale 236 ☎06.488.3175. The bright and funky clothes of this icon of 1980s Italian fashion still shine as brightly in this flagship Rome store. Particularly good for jeans and tops, and also stocks other like-minded young and sexy brands.

Intimissimi Via del Corso 167. There are several city-centre branches of this stylish yet affordable Italian lingerie chain, but this is the most central.

La Perla Via Condotti 79 ☎06.6994.1934. The flagship store of this international designer lingerie and beachwear chain is the last word in underwear.

Le Gallinelle Via del Boschetto 76 ☎06.488.1017. Mon 4–8pm, Tues–Sat 10am–1pm & 4–8pm. Vintage clothing, stage

The big designers

Bulgari Via Condotti 10 ☎06.679.3876.
Dolce & Gabbana Via Condotti 51/52 ☎06.6992.4999.
Fendi Largo Goldoni ☎06.334.501.
Ferre Via Borgognona 7 ☎06.6920.0815.
Giorgio Armani Via Condotti 77 ☎06.699.1460.
Gucci Via Condotti 8 ☎06.6994.0667.
Krizia Piazza di Spagna 87 ☎06.679.3772.
MaxMara Via Condotti 17–19 ☎06. 6992.2104.
Missoni Piazza di Spagna 78 ☎06.679.2555.
Moschino Via Borgognona 32 ☎06.678.1144.
Prada Via Condotti 88/95 ☎06.679.0897.
Roberto Cavalli Via Borgognona 25 ☎06.6992.5469.
Salvatore Ferragamo Via Condotti 65 & 73–74 ☎06.678.1130/679.1565.
Valentino Via Condotti 13 ☎06.679.0479.
Versace Via Bocca di Leone 26 ☎06.678.0521.

costumes and stylish own-brand designs at this cool Monti store.
Maga Morgana Via del Governo Vecchio 27 & 98 ☎06.687.9995. Mon–Sat 9.30am–7.30pm. Two shops selling attractive, original women's tops, skirts and knitwear, and great dresses.
Max & Co Via Condotti 46 ☎06.678.7946. Mon–Sat 10am–7.30pm, Sun 11am–7.30pm. Central Rome branch of MaxMara's more accessible and more youthful chain.

Shoes and accessories

Borsalino Piazza del Popolo 20 ☎06.3265.0838. Mon 3–7.30pm, Tues–Sat 9.30am–1.30pm & 3–7.30pm. Home of the classic fedora as sported by Jean-Paul Belmondo and others, as well as a whole host of other kinds of hats.
Bozart Via Bocca di Leone 4 ☎06.6929.2163. Mon 4–8pm Tues–Sat 9.30am–8pm. These fakes are truly fabulous, each necklace or bracelet making its own statement. Semiprecious stones, as well as Swarovski crystal pieces and resin and wooden elements are freely used to create dazzlingly alluring costume jewellery, ranging in price from €25 to €300.
Fabio Piccioni Via del Boschetto 148 ☎06.474.1697. Mon–Sat 10.30am–8pm; closed Mon morning. Vintage jewellery store with original Art Nouveau and especially Art Deco pieces, along with exquisite reproductions and inspired one-of-a-kind adornments made in the workshop.

Giorgio Sermoneta Piazza di Spagna 61 ☎06.679.960. Mon–Sat 9am–8pm, Sun 10am–7pm. This long-standing glove specialist has a large collection of Italian gloves in every price range, and has catered to celebrities, politicians and tourists for 35 years.
Ibiz Via dei Chiavari 39 ☎06.6830.7297. Mon–Sat 10am–7.30pm. Great leather bags, purses and rucksacks in exciting contemporary designs made on the premises.
Il Gancio Via del Seminario 82–83 ☎06.679.6646. Mon 3.30–7.30pm, Tues–Sat 10am–1pm and 3.30–7.30pm. High-quality leather bags, purses and shoes, all made in the workshop on the premises.
La Cravatta su Misura Via di Santa Cecilia 12 ☎06.8901.6941. Tues–Sat 10am–2pm & 3.30–7.30pm, June & July closed Sat afternoon. Ezio Pellicano sells only one thing: ties, made by Ezio himself or his daughter. You can buy any of the hundreds of ties you see on display, or you can choose from one of the hundreds of rolls of material and have your own made up in about a week.
Lefevre Via del Pellegrino 99 ☎06.687.1763. Mon 4–8pm Tues–Sat 10am–1pm & 4–8pm. Exclusive designs here include seed pearl ropes hung with cut crystals of ruby, emerald and sapphire matrix, for under €100. There are silver frames too, as well as fine porcelains.
Loco Via dei Baullari ☎06.6880.8216. Mon 3.30–8.30pm, Tues–Sat 10.30am–8.30pm.

Cool shoe store just off Campo de' Fiori with plenty of styles for men and women. **Mandarina Duck Via dei Due Macelli 59** ☎06.678.6414. Mon 3.30–7.30pm, Tues–Sat 10am–7.30pm. The main branch of the trendy Bologna bag company is a two-tier homage to how to be both practical and stylish at the same time.
NuYorica Piazza Pollarola 36/37 ☎06.6889.1243. Mon–Sat 10.30am–7.30pm. Just a few steps from Campo de' Fiori, this stylish shop specializes in shoes and bags by contemporary designers – though nothing here comes cheap.
Zannetti Via Monte d'Oro 18–23 ☎06.6819.2566. Flagship store of the distinctive Italian handmade watch specialist and jeweller.

Department stores and malls

COIN Via Cola di Rienzo ☎06.3600.4298. Mon–Sat 10am–8pm, Sun 10.30am–8pm. Inexpensive clothes and accessories, and a great place to find stylish kitchenware at bargain prices. Other branches around town, including a very large one at Piazzale Appio 7 by San Giovanni metro station (☎06.708.0020; Mon–Fri 9.30am–8pm, Sat 9.30am–8pm, Sun 10.30am–8.30pm).
La Rinascente Via del Corso 190 ☎06.678.4209. Daily 10am–9pm. The first department store in Rome, and now part of a national chain, this is the closest the city gets to an upscale department store, with several floors of high-quality merchandise displayed in an architecturally interesting setting. There's another central Rome branch on Piazza Fiume (☎06.884.1231; Mon–Sat 9.30am–9.30pm, Sun 10am–9pm).
M.A.S. Piazza Vittorio Emanuele 138 ☎06.446.8078. Mon–Sat 9am–1pm & 3.45–7.45pm. It doesn't get any cheaper than this. The "Magazzini allo Statuto" (Statutory Warehouses) are like one vast, multi-level rummage sale, but take your time

and you'll find something you want. There's everything from clothing to housewares.
TAD Via del Babuino 155a ☎06.369.5131. Mon noon–8pm, Tues–Sat 10am–8pm. This stylish store looks tiny from the outside, but in fact its one level houses departments selling clothes, perfume and cosmetics, flowers and home furnishings, as well as having a hairdressing salon and ultra-cool café. It's as sleek and expensive as it gets for the most part, but it does have some clothes and accessories at prices most people can afford – unlike most of the other shops on this street – and the café is a nice spot for a designer lunch.
UPIM Via del Tritone 172 ☎06.678.3336. Mon 3.30–7.30pm, Tues–Sat 10am–7.30pm. Central Rome branch of the nationwide chain of reasonably priced family department stores, selling everything from clothes to toiletries to housewares. There are other branches on Piazza Santa Maggiore and in Termini station.

Food and wine

Antica Norcineria Via della Scrofa 100 ☎06.3549.6806. Mon–Sat 9am–8pm. Very central and long-running butcher's shop and deli, which cures its own *guanciale* and sells great fresh mozzarella, *pecorino romano* and other cheeses. Lots of canned and dry goods too.
Buccone Via di Ripetta 19 ☎06.361.2154. Mon–Thurs 9am–8.30pm, Fri & Sat 9am–midnight, Sun 10am–5pm. Every alcoholic beverage you could dream of, with a large selection of wines from all over the world, plus spirits, and even ten-litre bottles of *grappa*.
Castroni Via Cola di Rienzo 196 ☎06.687.4383. Mon–Sat 8am–8pm. Huge, labyrinthine food store with a large selection of Italian treats including chocolates, pastas, sauces, and olive oils, as well as hard-to-find international favourites such as plum pudding

Termini: a shopping centre with train station attached?

Time was when the Mussolini-era masterwork was looking way past its best, but **Termini station** has been updated massively over the past decade and is now almost as much a place to shop as take a train, with one of the city's best bookshops in Borri Books, a branch of the department store UPIM and two supermarkets, plus the Sephora perfumery and branches of several of the big Italian chains. It's still not a place for a relaxing shopping experience, though – watch out for pickpockets.

and Mexican specialities – plus a café with coffee, cakes and sandwiches. There's another branch nearby at Via Ottaviano 55 and one just off Via Nazionale on Via delle Quattro Fontane, both of which also have cafés.

Centro Macrobiotico Italiano Via della Vite 14 ☎06.679.2509. Mon–Fri noon–4pm and 7–11pm, Sat 7–11pm. If you love authentic Italian food but are also a devotee of natural foods, this is Rome's most central option for stocking up on wholegrain pastas and other such products from Italy's rich countryside.

Cinque Lune Corso Rinascimento 89 ☎06.6880.1005. Closed Mon. Great, easy-to-miss bakery that does the best pastries and cakes in the area around Piazza Navona.

Colapicchioni Via Tacito 76–78 ☎06.321.5405. Via Properzio 23–25 ☎06.6880.1310. Long-running Prati food store with two branches, the former mainly a baker's, the later incorporating a deli, but both selling the family's excellent *pangiallo* and other foodie goodies.

Comptoir de France Via Vitelleschi 20–24 ☎06.6830.1516. Mon 4–8pm, Tues–Sat 9.30am–1.30pm & 4–8pm. This slick and well-stocked store near Castel Sant'Angelo specializes in French wines, cheese and other Gallic goodies.

Costantini Piazza Cavour 16 ☎06.321.3210. Mon 4.30–8pm, Tues–Sat 9.30am–1pm & 4.30–8pm. Perhaps the city's best wine store, with a fantastic selection in its basement *enoteca*, with *grappas*, spirits and liqueurs upstairs. Next door is their elegant and expensive restaurant (see p.255).

Del Frate Via degli Scipioni 118–124 ☎06.321.1612. Mon–Sat 8am–8pm. This large wine and spirits shop is located on a quiet street near the Vatican, and has all the Barolos and Chiantis you could want, alongside shelves full of *grappa* in all shapes and sizes. See also p.255.

Dolceroma Via Portico d'Ottavia 20b ☎06.689.2196. Tues–Sat 8.30am–8pm, Sun 10am–1.30pm. First-class Austrian and American sweet classics – brownies, blueberry muffins and, best of all, white chocolate chip cookies.

Franchi Via Cola di Rienzo 200 ☎06.686.4576. Mon–Sat 8am–9pm. One of the best delis in Rome – a triumph of cheeses, sausages and an ample choice of cold or hot food to go, including delicious *torta rustica* and

roast chicken. They'll make up customized lunches for you, and they also have the wines to go with it.

Il Forno del Ghetto Via del Portico d'Ottavia 1 ☎06.687.8637. Sun–Thurs 8am–7.30pm, Fri 8am–3.30pm. This marvellous tiny kosher Jewish bakery, unmarked but in the heart of the Ghetto, has unforgettable ricotta pies and *pizza giudia* (a hard cake, crammed with dried and candied fruit) that draw quite a crowd.

Innocenti Via della Luce 21 ☎06.580.3926. Mon–Sat 9am–1pm & 4–7.30pm, Sun 9am–1pm; closed Aug 15–Sept 15. Trastevere's – and maybe Rome's – best *biscottificio*, a family operation for 100 years. Wonderful, chewy *croccantini* – half chocolate, half vanilla, plus *amaretti*, *brutti ma buoni* (hazelnut biscuits), *straccetti* (almond and hazelnut biscuits) and dozens more varieties.

Innocenzi Piazza San Cosimato 66 ☎06.581.2725. Mon–Wed, Fri & Sat 7.30am–1.30pm & 4.30–8pm, Thurs 7.30am–1.30pm. A great dry goods grocer, with all the usual rice and pasta and Italian goodies but also a great selection of stuff from around the world – tomato ketchup, teas, peanut butter, the works. A good option for homesick expats and foodies alike.

Moriondo & Gariglio Via del Pie' di Marmo 21–22 ☎06.699.0856. Mon–Sat 9.30am–1pm & 3.30–7.30pm. Just a short walk from the Pantheon, this is perhaps the city centre's most sumptuous and refined handmade chocolate shop – great for exquisitely wrapped gifts.

Panella Via Merulana 54 ☎06.487.2435. Mon–Fri 8am–1.30pm & 5–8pm, Sat 8am–1.30pm & 4.30–8pm, Sun 8.30am–1.30pm. The art of bread-making is the speciality here, as well as pasta, like colourful, hat-shaped *sombrerini*, packaged to take home.

Punturi Via Flavia 48 ☎06.481.8225. Mon–Fri 8am–8pm, Sat 8am–2pm. One of Rome's many great *gastronomie*, with a bakery, cheese and cold meat counter, and superb pizza by the slice – plus a couple of tables in the back to enjoy it.

Quetzalcoatl Via delle Carrozze 26 ☎06.6920.2191. Mon–Sat 10am–7.30pm. Some of Rome's most sublime chocolates, presented as if they were art; once you taste them, you'll probably feel that they are. All sizes of gift boxes available.

Roscioli Via dei Giubbonari 21–23
☎06.687.5287. Daily 8.30am–8pm. Cheeses,
salamis and a very good selection of wine.
Plus food is served at lunch and early
evening. Roscioli also has its own bakery
across the street at Via dei Chiavari 34
(☎06.686.4045).

Shaki Piazza di Spagna 65 ☎06.678.6605.
Mon–Sat 9am–8pm, Sun 10.30am–1.30pm &
2.30–7pm. Located right on Piazza di
Spagna to make it easy for visitors to stock
up on the entire range of canned sauces
and delectables Italy has to offer, plus
there's a unique selection of Italian pottery
and other handicrafts. See also p.259 for its
wine bar around the corner.

Trimani Via Goito 20–22 ☎06.446.9661.
Mon–Sat 9am–8.30pm. One of the city's
largest and best wine shops, and handily
close to Termini if you want to stock up
before heading off to the airport.

Valzani Via del Moro 37 ☎06.580.3792.
Wed–Sun 10am–8.30pm; closed June–Sept 15;
extended hours at Christmas and Easter. One
of the oldest of the city's confectioners, still
keeping up tradition with marvellous
mostaccioli and *pangiallo* (both are traditional dried fruit and nut honey bars, the
former chocolate-covered), *torrone*,
sachertorte and, at Easter, huge, gift-filled
chocolate eggs which you can have your
name etched on.

Volpetti Via Marmorata 47 ☎06.574.2352.
Mon–Sat 8am–2pm & 5–8pm. It's worth
seeking out this Testaccio deli, which is truly
one of Rome's very best. If you're lucky, one
of the staff will give you samples of their
truly incredible *mozzarella di bufala*. Volpetti
also has its own *tavola calda* round the
corner (see p.251).

▲ Volpetti

Home and design

Arcon Via della Scrofa 104 ☎06.683.3728. Mon
3.30–7.30pm, Tues–Sat 9am–1pm &
3.30–7.30pm. This slick store is a visual feast
for lovers of Italian contemporary furniture
design, with lots of easy-to-carry accessories as well as large pieces.

Art'e Piazza Rondanini 32 ☎06.683.3907. Mon
1–7.30pm, Tues–Sat 9.30am–7.30pm. Ultra-
modern kitchenware and home furnishings,
including lamps, clocks and kitchen utensils
and appliances in flashy neon colours and
shiny stainless steel. The perfect stylish gift
to yourself from Italy.

Azi Via Manara 7 ☎06.581.8699. Mon
3.30–7.30pm, Tues–Sat 9.30am–1.30pm &

City-centre supermarkets

Rome's food stores and delis are so good that you shouldn't need to use a **supermarket** too often, but for pasta and other basics the supermarkets in the city centre
can be useful, especially if you're self-catering or just want somewhere easy to pick
up a picnic. Some of the more conveniently located ones are below. For **food
markets**, see box, p.287.

GS/Dì per Dì Via del Gesù 58; Via Vittoria 22; Via del Governo Vecchio 119; Corso
Vittorio Emanuele 290; Via Monterone 5; Via Poli 47; Via SS. Quattro Coronati 53.

De Spar Corso V. Emanuele 42; Vicolo di Moretta 10 (off Via Giulia); Via del Pozzetto
123; Via San Bartolomeo de' Vaccinari 78 (Ghetto); Termini station.

Sma Via della Frezza 8; Piazza Santa Maria Maggiore.

Standa Via Cola di Rienzo 173; Viale Trastevere 60.

3.30–7.30pm. Anything curiously or cunningly designed for the home is likely to be found here. The owners comb the earth for trendy, generally high-tech treasures, and the result is a truly unique shop – in two locations, around the corner from each other in Trastevere.

C.U.C.I.N.A. Via Mario de' Fiori 65
Ⓣ06.679.1275. Mon 3.30–7.30pm, Tues–Sat 10am–7.30pm. A shop filled with modern kitchen appliances, including a large selection of Italian cafetieres.

De Sanctis Piazza di Pietra 24 Ⓣ06.6880.6850. Mon–Sat 10am–1.30pm & 3–7.30pm. This shop has been selling ceramics since 1890 and their city-centre store offers a slightly classier souvenir than you'll find anywhere else around here.

Frette Piazza di Spagna 11 Ⓣ06.679.0673. Mon 3.30–7.30pm, Tues–Sat 9.30am–1.30pm & 3.30–7.30pm. This famous luxury linen shop is happy to fill custom orders and will ship their products anywhere.

'Gusto Piazza Augusto Imperatore 7
Ⓣ06.323.6363. Daily 10.30am–2am.
Everything for the aspirant gourmet: wines, decanters, glasses, and all the top-of-the-line kitchen gadgets you could ever hope to find. Also a large selection of cookbooks in English.

Il Giardino di Domenico Persiani Via Torino 92 Ⓣ06.488.3886. Mon 3.30–7.30pm, Tues–Sat 9am–1pm and 3–6pm. An experience not to be missed – a quiet garden setting filled to the brim with all sorts of creations in ceramic: everything from glazed tiles to full-sized copies of famous statuary. Pieces made to order.

Spazio Sette Via dei Barbieri 7 Ⓣ06.686.9747. Mon 3.30–7pm, Tues–Sat 9.30am–1pm & 3.30–7.30pm. Designer housewares of all sorts are the speciality here, for decades the shop of choice for Romans who want something chic and stylish for their home or as a gift.

Music

Disfunzioni Musicali Via degli Etruschi 4 Ⓣ06.446.1984. Mon 3–8pm, Tues–Sat 10.30am–8pm. Supplying nearby college students with a huge collection of both new and used music. A large selection of underground, rare and bootlegged recordings.

Metropoli Rock Via Cavour 72 Ⓣ06.488.0443. Mon–Sat 9am–1pm & 4–8pm. The place to come if you are looking for old and out-of-print recordings, whether it's classical, rock or jazz. Two floors stocked floor-to-ceiling with vinyl, 33rpm and 45rpm, as well as new and used CDs.

Mondadori Via del Corso 472 Ⓣ06.684.401. Mon–Sat 10am–11pm, Sun 10am–8.30pm. One of the city's best mainstream collections of CDs, plus foreign magazines and books.

Ricordi Via del Corso 506 Ⓣ06.361.2370. Mon–Sat 9.30am–8pm, Sun 10am–1pm & 3–8pm. Rome's largest and most complete music store, with a good array of CDs, plus books on music, scores, musical instruments, DVDs, sound equipment and concert tickets.

Soul Food Via di San Giovanni in Laterano 192–194 Ⓣ06.7045.2025. Tues–Sat 10.30am–1.30pm & 3.30–8pm. This vinyl junkie's paradise is the city centre's only CD-free zone when it comes to music. Lots of stuff from the 1960s and 1970s, and genuinely enthusiastic staff too.

Perfumeries

Materozzoli Piazza San Lorenzo in Lucina 5 Ⓣ06.6889.2686. Mon 3–7.30pm, Tues–Sat 10am–1pm & 3–7.30pm. Ancient city-centre perfume store selling classic scents from all over the world, plus toiletries and shaving products.

Roma-Store Via della Lungaretta 63 Ⓣ06.581.8789. Mon 4–8pm Tues–Sat 9.30am–1.30pm & 4–8pm. Not a football merchandise store but in fact a shop selling classic perfumes – Acqua di Parma, Penhaligons and suchlike – scented soaps, lotions and candles. Only the very finest from Italy, France and England.

Stationery

Antica Cartotecnica Piazza dei Caprettari 61 Ⓣ06.687.5671. Mon–Sat 10am–1.30pm & 3–7.30pm. Long-running and beautiful pen store near the Pantheon, with lots of new as well as old and antique models.

Campo Marzio Via di Campo Marzio 41 Ⓣ06.6880.7877. Daily 10am–1pm & 2–7pm. Part of a small chain, this is dedicated to cool pens and writing accessories, briefcases and pencil cases.

Ditta G. Poggi Via del Gesù 74–75 Ⓣ06.678.4477. Mon–Sat 10am–1pm & 4–7.30pm. Fantastic, long-established art materials shop, with a huge range of specialist paints and accessories, as well as more mainstream pens, pencils and stationery.

Fabriano Via del Babuino 172 ☎ 06.3260.0361. Mon–Sat 10am–7.30pm. Fabriano paper from the Marche has been around for hundreds of years and is of the highest quality. This central Rome branch sells bright and contemporary stationery, wallets and briefcases.

Il Papiro Via del Pantheon 50 ☎ 06.679.5597. Daily 10am–8pm. The most central branch of this originally Tuscan chain stocks fine paper and notebooks, as well as the fancy pens to go with them.

Pineider Via dei Due Macelli 68 ☎ 06.239.344. Mon 3.30–7.30pm, Tues–Sat 10am–1.30pm & 3.30 7.30pm. This exclusive store has been crafting beautiful stationery items and handmade bags and wallets for Roman society since 1774. Another branch at Via della Fontanella di Borghese 22 (☎ 06.687.8369).

Stilo Fetti Via degli Orfani 82 ☎ 06.678.9662. Mon 3.30–7.30pm, Tues–Sat 9am–1pm & 3.30–7.30pm. Great city-centre pen shop, with lots to choose from and all the major brands – and elegant leather briefcases too.

Miscellaneous and gifts

Ai Monasteri Corso del Rinascimento 72 ☎ 06.6800.2783. Mon–Sat 10am–1pm & 3.30–7.30pm, closed Thurs afternoon. Cakes, spirits, toiletries and other items made by monks.

AS Roma Store Piazza Colonna 360 ☎ 06.6920.0642. Mon–Sat 10am–6pm. The best-stocked and most central location for AS Roma merchandise, with the usual shirts, leisurewear and babygros.

Decker & Musico Via San Vincenzo 29 ☎ 06.678.5435. This long-established store sells beautiful pipes, inlaid wooden boxes and other lovely handcrafted objects. If you

smoke a pipe, hours of fun can be had just lounging around chatting to the guys here about their favourite subject.

Carmignani Via della Colonna Antonina 42–43 ☎ 06.679.5449. Tues–Sat 10am–2pm and 3–7.30pm. Even if you don't smoke, you will appreciate the beauty of the handmade pipes, shiny silver cigar holders and cutters and poker sets, in this small shop a few minutes from the Pantheon.

Cesare Diomedi Via E. Orlando 96–97 ☎ 06.488.4822. Mon–Sat 9am–7.30pm. A few minutes' walk from Piazza della Repubblica, two floors filled with luxury leather goods, Versace clocks, Cartier wallets, and all sorts of other fancy gifts.

Ferrari Store Via Tomacelli 147–152 ☎ 06.689.2979. Daily 10am–7.30pm. What better souvenir to take back than an accessory from this Italian motor racing icon? It's not a cheap store, by any means, but there's a range of things to buy whatever your budget – from a €30 remote-control car to pricey Ferrari-themed jewellery.

Fratelli Alinari Via Alibert 16a ☎ 06.679.2923, ⓦ www.alinari.it. Mon–Sat 3.30–7.30pm. If you want to know what Rome's piazzas looked like before McDonald's came to town, come here for a fine selection of black-and-white photographs of Rome from over 100 years ago. Prices start at around €40.

La Bottega del Marmoraro Via Margutta 53b ☎ 06.320.7660. Mon–Sat 8.30am–7.30pm. Enrico and Sandro Fiorentini, a father-and-son team, are skilled artisans, creating personalized marble plaques for every occasion, as well as statuary, both ancient and modern reproductions.

Old Soccer Via di Ripetta 30 ☎ 06.321.9448. Daily 10am–8pm. Old-fashioned Italian football shirts from around €70 – ironically enough, made in England.

Food markets

Rome's **food markets** are a perfect place to stop to pick up a snack or picnic provisions. The one on Campo de' Fiori is the city's most famous and picturesque, and has been around for the last four hundred years. Other central options include: the market between the Termini railway tracks and Piazza Vittorio Emanuele, off Via Lamarmora; Piazza San Cosimato in Trastevere; Piazza dell'Unità in Prati; Piazza Alessandria east of Villa Borghese; Via Magnagrecia in San Giovanni; Piazza Testaccio in Testaccio. Most are **open** Mon–Sat 7am–2pm.

Polvere di Tempo Via del Moro 59
℡ 06.5880.0704. Mon 3.30–8pm, Tues–Sat
10am–1pm & 4–8pm. For that astrolabe
you've always dreamed of, as well as a
huge array of ancient and medieval devices
for telling time, stop by this arcane little
shop. They also have alchemists' rings that
double as sundials and loads more oddities
and curiosities.

Markets

Borghetto Flaminio Piazza della Marina 32.
Sept–July Sun 10am–8pm; entrance €2. A
partly covered flea market with plenty of
knick-knacks, designer clothing and
antiques. Rummage alongside Rome's well-
heeled shoppers and celebrities.
Fontanella Borghese Piazza della Fontanella di
Borghese. Mon–Sat 9am–7pm. A small print
and book market off Via del Corso, where
you can find expensive antique prints and
etchings along with inexpensive
reproductions.
Galleria delle Stimmate Largo delle Stimmate 1.
Sept–May last Sun of the month 10am–7pm.
Mostly household goods, and some
jewellery, with some great finds like antique
lace, silver serving dishes and old cutlery.
La Soffitta Sotto I Portici Piazza Augusto
Imperatore ℡ 06.3600.5345. **Sept–July first and
third Sun of the month 10am–7pm.** Flea market
selling a diverse mix of bric-a-brac, jewellery
and old records.
Piazzale Ankara Last Sun of the month
8am–8pm. Antiques, books and bric-a-brac
on this unprepossessing square next door
to the Stadio Flaminio.
Piazza Vittorio Emanuele Between Via
Lamarmora and Via Ricasoli. Mon–Sat 7am–1pm.
The market that used to take place in this
square is now over by the Termini railway
tracks. One building houses cheap clothes
and household goods, the other fresh fruit
and veg and other food stalls.
Porta Portese Sun 5am–2pm. Rome's most
famous and largest market by far, stretching
from Piazza di Porta Portese a mile or so
down Via Portuense and into the streets
around, with hundreds of stalls selling
myriad goods, including antiques, oriental
artefacts, clothing, carpets, art, tools, appliances, fake brand-name jeans, underwear,
linens, and even puppies. And the brand is
expanding: nowadays there's a second
Porta Portese market every Sunday
morning, in Pigneto between Via Togliatti
and Via Prenestina (same times).
Underground Via Francesco Crispi 96. Oct–June
first Sun of the month 10.30am–7.30pm.
Located in an underground parking garage
near Piazza di Spagna, and selling all the
usual flea market finds, but with a special
section for children's goods.
Via Sannio Mon–Fri 9am–1.30pm, Sat
9am–6pm. Near San Giovanni metro station,
this market sells mostly cheap clothing,
bags and trashy jewellery, including lots of
fake brand names, plus an extensive
secondhand section at the back.

21

Sports and outdoor activities

S pectator sports are popular in Italy; the hallowed *calcio*, or football, is far and away the most avidly followed, and tends to overshadow everything else. Rome, with two clubs in the top division (Serie A), is no exception. As for **participation** in sport, there isn't quite the same compulsion to hit the hell out of a squash ball or sweat your way through an aerobics class after work as there is, say, in Britain or the US. However, the notion of keeping fit is becoming as fashionable here as it is in most European countries – especially when it offers the opportunity to wear the latest designer gear.

Cycling

The month of May sees the *Giro d'Italia* (Italy's national race) spin through Rome's cobbled lanes, but for most visitors **cycling** is far too daunting to be enjoyable. However, the Appia Antica is ideal for a ride (see p 148), especially on Sundays when it's (theoretically) closed to automobile traffic and the cyclists almost outnumber the strollers. See p.27 for details on **renting bikes**.

▲ Cycling on Via Appia Antica

Football

Rome's two big **football** teams, AS Roma and SS Lazio, play on alternate Sundays between September and May at the Stadio Olimpico, northwest of the city centre. Unsurprisingly, feelings run extremely high between the two teams, and derby games are big – and sometimes violent – occasions. **Roma**, currently managed by ex-Chelsea boss Claudio Ranieri, and captained by the talismanic veteran (and local boy) Francesco Totti, are traditionally the team of the inner-city urban working class, and perennially the better of the two sides, while traditionally right-wing Lazio trail somewhat. However, after a lot of investment in the team **Lazio** won the championship in 2000, only to have Roma bounce back in 2001 to take their third *scudetto*. Needless to say, it's a breathless rivalry that can go either way when the two sides meet, despite Lazio's recent financial woes and lack of success on the pitch.

Ticket details are below, but bear in mind that the Stadio Olimpico is enormous, with a capacity of close to 80,000, and at most games, except perhaps Roma–Lazio clashes, you should be able to get a ticket for all but the cheapest seats. However, due to crowd trouble they are a bit harder to get hold of than they used to be, and you have to go through an online booking service – Ⓦ www.listicket.it.

To **get to the stadium** on public transport, you can take tram #2 from Piazzale Flaminio to Piazza Mancini or bus #910 from Termini and then walk across the river; alternatively, take bus #32 from Piazza Risorgimento or #271 from Piazza Venezia direct.

Lazio Ⓦ www.sslazio.it. Lazio supporters traditionally occupy the Curva Nord end of the ground (colours, blue and white; symbol, the eagle), where you can sometimes get seats for €15–25 (but the atmosphere can be intimidating and not altogether pleasant); seats in the *distinti*, or corners of the ground, or the *tribuna*, along the sides, are more expensive; you should reckon on paying around €60–150 for a reasonable *tribuna* ticket.

Roma Ⓦ www.asroma.it. Fans of Roma (colours, red and yellow; symbol, the wolf) occupy the Curva Sud, which is usually completely sold out to season-ticket holders, making a visit to a Roma game a slightly more expensive business, since the cheapest seat you'll find will be in the *distinti*, for €25–35. *Tribuna* seats go for €75–150.

Golf

If you simply can't go a week or two without hitting a ball, it's worth knowing that **golf** is slowly becoming a popular sport in Italy. Most clubs welcome non-members but you must be able to produce a membership card from your hometown club. For more information, call the *Federazione Italiana Golf*, Viale Tiziano 74 (Ⓣ06.323.1825, Ⓦ www.federgolf.it). All of the following offer an eighteen-hole course and a driving range:

> If you want more information about the **Italian football season** in general, the *Federazione Italiana Gioco Calcio* (Ⓦ www.figc.it) has all the season's fixtures. If your Italian is good enough get hold of one of the Italian sports newspapers, which are published daily and focus heavily on football. The Rome-based *Corriere dello Sport* will have details of any upcoming games, as will the other two papers: the pink *Gazzeto dello Sport* and *Tuttosport*.

Circolo del Golf di Roma Acquasanta **Via Appia Nuova 716a** ⊤06.7834.6819, ⓦwww.golfroma.it; closed Mon. Eighteen-hole course south of Rome. There's a bar and outdoor pool too, if you're bringing some non-golfing friends. Golf Club Parco de' Medici **Viale Salvatore Rebecchini 39** ⊤06.655.3477, ⓦwww.golfparcodemedici.com; closed Tues. Southwest of the centre, towards Fiumicino, with eighteen holes, plus a driving range. Country Club Castel Gandolfo **Via Santo Spirito 13, Castel Gandolfo** ⊤06.931.2301, ⓦwww.countryclubcastelgandolfo.it. In Castel Gandolfo (see p.215), down in the Castelli Romani, this is the pope's local course and has excellent facilities, including a restaurant and bar.

Gyms

If you're in the habit of a regular workout and want to keep it up even while you're checking Rome's sights off your list, here are a few handily located facilities:

Farnese Fitness **Vicolo delle Grotte 35** ⊤06.687.6931, ⓦwww.farnesefitness.com. Mon–Fri 9am–10pm, Sat 11am–6pm, Sun 10am–1pm; closed Aug. Decent gym right in the centre of town. Aerobics classes are included in the daily fee. €10 per day. Fitness First **Via Giolitti 44** ⊤06.4782.6300, ⓦwww.fitnessfirst.it. Mon–Fri 7.30am–11pm, Sat & Sun 9am–8pm. Right by Termini, this branch of the chain offers a variety of classes, such as yoga, spinning and Thai kickboxing, on offer in this spanking clean establishment. €16 per day.

Fitnext **Piazza Mignanelli 23** ⊤06.679.6003. Mon–Fri 8am–10pm, Sat 11am–7pm; closed Aug. One class included in the fee, including yoga and Pilates. €20 per day. Roman Sport Center **Viale del Galoppatoio 33** ⊤06.320.1667, ⓦwww.romansportcenter.com. Mon–Fri 7am–10.30pm, Sat 7am–8.30pm, Sun 9am–3pm. Rome's largest, oldest and most prestigious fitness centre, in Villa Borghese, has a host of offerings, including Olympic-sized pools, squash courts and hydromassage and saunas. €26 per day.

Riding

There are not very many options for those who are looking to go **horseriding** in Rome. The only real option is Il Galoppatoio at Via del Galoppatoio 23 (Tues–Sat 9am–7pm, Sun 9am–1pm; ⊤06.322.6797), a posh riding club that offers expensive lessons in an idyllic atmosphere in the heart of Villa Borghese. Lessons last an hour but you have to sign up for ten (around €150). More feasibly, there's the Maneggio Cavalieri dell'Appia Antica, Via dei Cerceni 15 (ⓦwww.cavalieriappia.altervista.org, ⊤06.780.1214; groups only), where you'll pay around €25 for a gentle one-hour trot.

Running

The **Rome Marathon** (ⓦwww.maratonadiroma.it) circles around the city's most famous monuments on the third Sunday in March, and is a nice opportunity to run through the city centre free of cars and crazy drivers. It starts and finishes on Via dei Fori Imperiali and the course follows the river, going as far north as the Ponte Milvio and as far south as the Basilica di San Paolo. If you're not up for a full marathon, or even anything like it, it's worth knowing that there's also a 4km fun run through the centro storico on the same day.

Other annual races you might want to take part include the **Rome–Ostia half-marathon** every February (ⓦwww.romaostia.it), and the **Roma–Appia 14k** each April, which takes you past all the sights of the Appian Way.

The rest of the time the traffic and congestion make it impossible, and sometimes even dangerous, to jog in Rome, but luckily there are plenty of **green spaces** to escape the traffic. The most popular is Villa Borghese, where there are plenty of places to jog, including the Piazza di Siena, a grass horsetrack in the centre of the park. Other good options include the Villa Ada, a lush and vast green space north of the city centre, which has a running track, and the Villa Doria Pamphilj above Trastevere, which offers nice paths with exercise stations along the way. For more central – and public – jogging, the Circus Maximus is the perfect size and shape, although it gets busy with tourists.

Swimming

If you feel like cooling off on a hot summer's day, a dip in a **swimming pool** may be the perfect cure. Unfortunately, most of Rome's pools are privately run and can

Splashing out: Rome's hotel pools

Hotel swimming pools are relatively rare in Rome, especially in the centre, and not surprisingly the hotels that have them are generally five-star. However if you're not willing – or able – to splash out on a fancy room you can still cool off in one of the hotel pools listed below, though facilities may only be available in restricted hours, and **entrance fees** to non-guests are fairly hefty. You should reckon on paying €20–25 for a half-day, €40–50 for a full day, and more if you opt for one of the spa treatments that are often available.

One of Rome's prettiest, most secluded pools is at the **Aldrovandi Palace** (see p.232) on the northern edge of Villa Borghese. Surrounded by lush foliage, it's large enough for a good swim. The hotel offers a package with a swim and gourmet lunch at its Michelin-starred restaurant, *baby*. Nearby is the **Parco dei Principi**, Via Frescobaldi 5 (℡06.854.421, Ⓦwww.parcodeiprincipi.com), whose 25-metre pool, set in a garden edged by umbrella pines, is close enough to the zoo to hear the lions roar at late-afternoon feeding time. More centrally, the **Radisson Blu Es** (see p.229) has a lovely rooftop pool that's open from noon until 8pm, and the **Exedra** (see p.229), nearby, stays true to the area's ancient function as the Baths of Diocletian, with an outdoor pool that's close to the bar and restaurant and has a view over the rooftops beyond the square, though it's really designed for a cooling soak rather than a vigorous swim; there's also a spa.

On Via Veneto, the **Westin Excelsior** (see p.228) has a small indoor pool, set among Neoclassical columns intended to suggest the baths of ancient Rome; spa treatments are available, as well as a jacuzzi, steam bath, sauna and gym. Near the Colosseum, the functional **Mercure Roma Delta Colosseo**, Via Labicana 144 (℡06.770.021) has uninspired decor and caters to tour groups, but its rooftop pool has a bar and good views of the ancient arena.

Across the Tiber, the **Rome Cavalieri Hilton** Via A Cadlolo 101 (℡06.350.91, Ⓦwww.romecavalieri.com/) has lovely gardens and three outdoor swimming pools that often serve as a venue for the wheeling and dealing of its guests. West of the Vatican, along Via Aurelia Antica, the **Crowne Plaza St Peter's** Via Aurelia Antica 415 (℡06.664.20, Ⓦwww.crowneplaza.com/) has a 25-metre outdoor pool and spa with a small indoor pool and gym, and is open fairly late in the evening. Deep enough for a good swim, the black-tiled pool at **Black Hotel** Via Raffaello Sardiello 18 (℡06.6641.0148, Ⓦwww.blackhotel.it) has free morning shuttles to and from Metro Ottaviano. North towards Trastevere, the **Grand Hotel del Gianicolo** (see p.231) recently added a curvaceous mosaic-tiled outdoor swimming pool to keep visitors from plunging into the nearby seventeenth-century fountain.

be quite expensive (see box opposite), though there are a couple of affordable public pools (see also "Gyms"). If you fancy a spot of real pampering it's worth booking a day at a hotel spa.

Oasi di Pace Via degli Eugenii 2 ⊤**06.718.4550,** ⓦ**www.ct-oasidipace.it. June–Sept daily 9.30am–6pm.** The "Oasis of Peace" is just off the Via Appia and has a lovely open-air pool that makes for a wonderfully atmospheric place to take a dip, as well as spa treatments.

Piscina delle Rose Viale America 20 ⊤**06.5422.0333,** ⓦ**www.piscinadellerose.it. Mon–Fri 10am–10pm, Sat & Sun 9am–7pm.** Down in EUR, and easily reachable on Metro line B, this is Rome's largest public pool, accessible for a rate of €13 a half-day, €16 a day.

Tennis

The massive **Foro Italico** sports complex (see p.178) hosts the Italian Open, or Rome Masters as it's now known, one of the city's biggest annual sporting events, held during the first two weeks of May. For more information contact the Federazione Italiana Tennis, Via Eustachio 9 (⊤06.855.894, ⓦwww.federtennis .it), or the Foro Italico itself (⊤06.3685.8218). If you want to hire a court, the Foro Italico also has public courts, or there's the Circolo della Stampa, Piazza Mancini 9 (⊤06.323.2454) and Tennis Belle Arte, Via Flaminia 158 (⊤06.323.3355). Courts cost €10–12 an hour.

Kids' Rome

talians love **children**. Don't be surprised by how much attention people pay yours here: peeking into buggies and cheek-pinching are quite normal, as is help lugging pushchairs up steps and giving up a seat for you and your child on public transport. That said, though there have been significant improvements of late, Rome has a surprisingly limited number of activities specifically geared towards children. Luckily, touring the sights of Rome is something that children can enjoy if it's approached in the right way – hopping on and off one of the several open-top bus tours (see p.39) is a great way of giving them a fun introduction to the city's highlights, while certain **sights** are especially interesting for kids – Castel Sant'Angelo with its park and playground, the Colosseum (where there are usually Roman soldiers dressed up in full costume), and of course throwing coins into the Trevi Fountain and sticking a hand in the Bocca della Verità and daring to tell a fib. There is also a handful of relatively new attractions aimed directly at children, notably the Time Elevator, Rewind and Explora. Among Rome's **parks**, the Villa Borghese is the most convenient, and has a lot to offer kids – rowboats, a little train, pony rides, bikes, and on its northeastern side the Bioparco or city zoo.

Eating out with kids in Rome is easy – the numerous pasta and pizza options ensure that there's something for even the fussiest of eaters (failing that the kitchen is almost always willing to rustle you up a plate of plain spaghetti with butter or parmesan), while the relaxed waiting staff go out of their way to charm and amuse the kids. And if you're on the go, you can always head to the nearest *gelateria*, or grab a slice of juicy pizza to keep them quiet. For more information, *Romac'è* (see p.35) often has details of what's on for children that week.

Day-trips

If it's hot and you're having a hellish time in the city, it might just be best to call it a day and get away, either for a picnic or an energy-releasing romp. Day-trips kids might enjoy include **Ostia Antica** (see p.208), **Tivoli** (see p.204), with its villas and Roman site, and, further afield, the charming town of **Bracciano** (see p.213) with its beautiful lake offering swimming and boating. Consider also the **Parco dei Mostri** (Park of Monsters) at Bomarzo (daily 8am–sunset; €9, 4–8yrs €7; ☎0761.924.029, ⊛www.bomarzo.net), 93km north of Rome – basically a garden, but with crazy sculptures, weird buildings and surreal conceits that make it one of Lazio's top tourist attractions. You can get to Bomarzo by bus from Viterbo, which in turn is easily reached by train from either Stazione San Pietro or the Laziale platform at Termini.

Finally, there are plenty of sandy **beaches** within easy reach of the city centre, most of them an hour or less away by train (see pp.216–217 for our favourites).

Babysitting

If you simply have to have a break from the kids for a day or an evening, English-speaking **babysitters** are available through Angels, Via dei Fienili 98 ☎06.678.2877 or 338.667.9718, ⓔaupairs65@hotmail.com.

Books and maps

Pick up the English version of *ConosciRoma*, available free from any tourist kiosk; it's a children's **map** of the centre with interesting facts about sights, daily life in ancient Rome, and stickers. While you're there also grab a copy of the free *Conosci-Roma* booklet (Italian only) *"La città per ogni età"*, which has details of what to do with your kids in Rome divided by age group. Look out also for the "then and now" books of ancient sites with overlay transparencies that are available in most tourist shops: they can work wonders to bring piles of weathered stones to life.

Parks and outdoor activities

Aquapiper Via Maremmana Inferiore 29.3km, Giudonia ☎0774.326538, ⓦwww.aquapiper.it. Daily 9am–9pm. Adults €13, Sun €18, children €5, 0–10yrs free. Metro B to Ponte Mammolo, then bus to the park, or train to Guidonia from Tiburtina station then by a shorter bus ride. This very well-equipped water park has loads of rides, including the biggest wave machine in Europe, and is perfect for restoring sight-fatigued families. But avoid summer weekends when it can get very busy.

Bioparco Via del Giardino Zoologico, Villa Borghese ☎06.360.8211, ⓦwww.bioparco.it. Daily: Jan–March & Nov–Dec 9.30am–5pm; April–Oct 9.30am–6pm, open till 7pm Sat & Sun April–Sept. Adults €10, children over 1m tall €8, kids under 1m go free. Rome's zoo, on the northern edge of Villa Borghese (see p.164) is a large, typical city-centre zoo, recently much improved and reinvented as the "Bioparco" and focusing on conservation and education yet still providing the usual animals kids are after – tigers, apes, giraffes, elephants, hippos and much more – though the separate *Rettilario* (Reptile house) costs an extra €2.50, a bit of a rip-off. The zoological museum next door (see p.297) has also been revamped.

Janiculum Hill High up on the Janiculum, this park is a good place to keep kids amused, with pony rides, carousels, balloon sellers and puppet shows, while adults enjoy a great view of the city below. The puppet shows (see box, p.297), are top-notch and kids can choose to take their favourite character home with them from the colourful selection on sale. You might want to time your visit to coincide with the daily firing of the cannon at noon. See also p.162.

Orto Botanico Via Corsini. Tues–Sat 9.30am–6.30pm. Adults €4, 6–11yrs €2, under-6s free. A peaceful oasis in the heart of Trastevere, the city's botanical gardens have palm-lined paths, fountains, a meandering rose garden, towering bamboo patches and lush greenhouses to keep the kids amused for a while. The benches and paths around the Fountain of Tritons, near the entrance, are a meeting place for local mothers, nannies and toddlers. See also p.161.

Villa Ada Beautiful grounds just north of the city with plenty to keep youngsters amused, including a roller-skating rink, bike paths, two playgrounds and ponds. See also p.176.

Villa Borghese As well as the Bioparco (see above), this huge park offers plenty of entertainment for young ones. Enter at the northern side, via the Viale delle Belle Arti entrance, to find pony rides, a children's train, swings and paddleboats on the lake complete with Greek temple. On the southern side of the park, the Pincio Gardens have a playground and carousels and places to hire bikes or a *risciò*, the latter particularly good fun for families (see p.164).

Villa Celimontana Up on the Celian Hill, these public gardens have nice views over the river, a playground and pony rides. See also p.129.

Piazzas, playgrounds and pussycats

Rome's abundant **piazzas** with their cobbled expanses, fountains and cafés are often just as much fun for kids to run around in as playgrounds – especially in the early evening when everyone's out for a stroll and the street sellers and buskers liven things up even more. Piazza Santa Maria in Trastevere is always a lively place, as is Piazza Navona (with the added attraction of two toy shops; see p.298) and Piazza di Spagna. Villa Borghese, Villa Sciarra, Villa Ada and Villa Celimontana all have **playgrounds**; there are also very good play areas in Piazza Vittorio Emanuele, at Piazza Santa Maria Liberatrice in Testaccio, and in Piazza San Cosimato in Trastevere.

The city's **cat colonies** are usually a big hit with kids – check out the one at Largo di Torre Argentina where cat-spotting among the ancient ruins is a popular pastime while, at the cat sanctuary alongside it, kids can get up close to some of the inhabitants that are up for adoption. The volunteers who look after the cats here are always happy to show you round, and they also take care of other colonies around the city – ones to visit are those at the Colosseum, at Piazza Vittorio Emanuele (see p.122) and around the Piramide Cestia in Testaccio (see p.144). You can find out more at Ⓦ www.romancats.com.

Villa Doria Pamphilj Main entrance on Via di San Pancrazio. A ten-minute walk east from the Janiculum Hill, Rome's largest park is a great place for kids to let off steam – more like real countryside in parts, it's the perfect walking, cycling or picnic spot and has a pretty lake filled with basking turtles and surrounded by woods. See also p.163.

Villa Sciarra Entrances on Via Calandrelli and Viale delle Mura Gianicolensi. A little way to the south of the Janiculum Hill, this small park is a bit out of the way but has a lovely little playground, though the adjacent aviary has seen better days and is now populated largely by pigeons.

Museums and attractions

Castel Sant'Angelo Lungotevere Castello 50. Tues–Sun 9am–7.30pm. Adults €8, children free; free guided tours in English Sat & Sun at 4.30pm. Along with the Colosseum this is one of the most exciting of the city's ancient monuments for kids. Hadrian's mausoleum has through the centuries served as a papal escape route in times of trouble and the city's prison, and has all the grisly, dungeon-like spookiness you'd expect from such a history – fortifications, drawbridges, lots of suits of armour and swords – and a wide, spiral ramp leading to the mausoleum itself adds to the atmosphere. There are also great views over the city from the top. See also p.182.

Colosseum Daily 8.30am to one hour before sunset; adults €12, children from EU countries under 18 free, non-EU countries €7.50. Loaded with atmosphere given its setting as the stage for many a grisly end for both humans and beasts, Rome's most famous ancient monument can't fail to capture kids' imaginations. For €5 they can have their picture taken with one of the gladiators outside. See also pp.89–91.

Explora – Museo dei Bambini di Roma Via Flaminia 82 ☎ 06.361.3776, Ⓦ www.mdbr.it. Timed entry for 1hr 45min slots: Tues–Sun at 10am, noon, 3pm & 5pm; Aug Tues–Sun at noon, 3pm & 5pm; advance booking recommended. Adults and children over 3 €7, 1–3yrs €3; 0–1yrs free. Geared towards kids under 12, this learn-as-you-play centre aims to

▲ Explora – Museo dei Bambini di Roma

teach children about themselves and the world they live in through hands-on activities. It's all laid out in the form of a small city – kids can shop in the mini-supermarket, pay cheques in at the bank, fill up their car at the garage and post mail in the post office. There's also plenty of purely fun stuff, such as a puppet theatre and a playground.

Museo della Civiltà Romana & Planetario Piazza Agnelli 10, EUR ☏ 06.592.6041. Tues–Sat 9am–2pm, Sun 9am–1.30pm; adults €6.50, €8.50 including planetarium, children free. This museum has lots of stuff that will interest ancient Rome-addicted kids, among them replicas of the city's famous statues and buildings as well as more everyday artefacts. But the real favourite is the museum's scale model of Rome in the time of Constantine, which takes up a whole room. On the same site, there's also a planetarium and astronomy exhibition, but it's not as thrilling as you'd expect and audio shows are only in Italian (Sept–June Tues–Fri 9am–2pm, Sat & Sun 9am–7pm; July & Aug Tues–Fri 8.30–11.30pm, Sat & Sun 4.30–11.30pm; call ☏ 06.06.08 to reserve a seat – advisable at weekends).

Museo di Zoologia Via Aldrovandi 18 ☏ 06.6710.9270, ⓦ www.museodizoologia.it. Tues–Sun 9am–7pm. Adults €6, under-18s free. Located next to the Bioparco, this museum has a permanent exhibit, Animals and their Habitats, in its new wing, while a variety of stuffed animals fill the older part

of the museum, though sadly labels are in Italian only.

Ostia Antica Viale dei Romagnoli, Ostia Antica. March 8.30am–5pm, April–Oct Tues–Sun 8.30am–6pm, Nov–Feb 8.30am–4pm; €6.50. Every bit as atmospheric and mesmerizing as Pompeii, the ruins of Rome's ancient port will give kids a great feel for what a Roman city was like. It's a must-see for any child who has read *The Thieves of Ostia*, the first in the Roman Mysteries series by Caroline Lawrence, in which a sea captain's daughter and her pals set about solving a mystery in 79 AD Ostia.

Rewind Via Capo d'Africa 5 ☏ 06.7707.6627, ⓦ www.3drewind.com. Daily 9am–7pm. Adults €15, kids aged 5–12 €8 April–Oct, free Nov–March. Shows here take you through a pseudo-archeological dig and then sit you down for a 3D film that has you pounding through the streets of the ancient city, taking in a debate in the Senate House and a spot of gladiatorial combat in the Colosseum. The effects aren't bad, and kids might prefer it to the virtual reality of the better-established Time Elevator.

Time Elevator Via dei SS. Apostoli 20 ☏ 06.9774.6243, ⓦ www.timeelevator.it. Daily 10.30am–7.30pm; shows every hour, lasting 45min. Adults €12, 5–12s €9; not suitable for children under 5. Flight-simulator seats and headphones (English audio available) set the stage for a virtual tour of three thousand years of Roman history; an excellent way to prime the kids (not to mention their parents) for the sights they will be seeing.

Puppetry and films

Puppetry has been delighting Italian children for hundreds of years, and Rome has a few venues for viewing puppeteers in action. Sometimes you can find a show in English, but the storyline is visually explanatory and kids don't seem to care whether they understand the words or not. The **outdoor theatres** on the Janiculum Hill (see p.162), and in EUR on Largo K. Ataturk, are said to be the only places to view the true puppeteers left in Rome. Both are free, although a small donation is expected. You can also see shows near the Janiculum at the Teatro Verde, Circonvallazione Gianicolense 10 (☏ 06.588.2034, ⓦ www.teatroverde.it), a children's theatre where they also put on musicals and marionette shows (Sat & Sun at 5pm; family tickets €9) and the newer Teatro San Carlino in the Pincio Gardens in Villa Borghese (☏ 06.6992.2117, ⓦ www.sancarlino.it; tickets €6), which puts on regular weekend shows in May, June and September.

Villa Borghese is also home to the diminutive **Cinema dei Piccoli**, almost opposite the Casa del Cinema at Viale Pineta 15 on the Via Veneto side of the park (☏ 06.855.3485), which is not only the smallest cinema in the world, with just 63 seats, but also one of the oldest, in business since 1934. There are showings Wed–Fri at 5pm & 6.30pm, and at weekends at 3.30pm, 5pm & 6.30pm.

La Befana

There are many stories about **La Befana**, always depicted as an ugly old woman who flies along on a broom draped in black. The most recognized version is that she was outside sweeping when the three kings walked by; she stopped them and asked where they were going. The kings responded that they were following a star, in search of a newborn baby. They invited her to come along, but she declined, saying she had too much sweeping and cleaning to do. When she found out who it was the kings were off to find, her regret for not having joined them was so great that she has spent eternity rewarding good children with presents and sweets and bad children with pieces of coal on the day of Epiphany, **January 6**. Each year, from early December until this day, Piazza Navona sets up the Befana toy fair, where endless stalls tempt children with every sort of sticky sweet and even chunks of black sugar made to look like coal. There are also toy stands and manger scenes where children leave letters for La Befana, asking her for specific presents and toys.

Shops: books, toys and clothing

Al Sogno Piazza Navona 53 ☎06.686.4198. Mon 3.30–7.30pm, Tues–Sat 9.30am–1pm & 3.30–7.30pm. Perfectly located at the north end of Piazza Navona, with two floors of stuffed animals, handmade dolls, board games and replicas of Roman soldiers.

Benetton Via Cesare Battisti 129–131 ☎06.6992.4010. Mon 3.30–7.30pm, Tues–Sat 9.30am–1pm & 3.30–7.30pm. Just one of several locations of this famous Italian chain that sells clothes for children and adults. This one conveniently has a children's hairdresser on the second floor.

Bertè Piazza Navona 108 ☎06.687.5011. Mon 3.30–7.30pm, Tues–Sat 9.30am–1pm & 3.30–7.30pm. One of Rome's oldest toy stores at the other end of the piazza from Al Sogno (see above), with toys for children of all ages.

La Cicogna Via Frattina 138 ☎06.679.1912; Via Cola di Rienzo 268 ☎06.689.6557. Mon–Sat 10.30am–7.30pm, Sun 11am–7pm. From newborns to adolescents, these outlets of the stylish national chain ("The Stork") carry designer everything for kids, and maternity wear too. Not cheap.

Città del Sole Via della Scrofa 66 ☎06.6880.3805. Mon 3.30–7.30pm, Tues–Sat 11am–1.30pm. Toys, games and books for kids in a great central location.

Giunti al Punto Piazza Santi Apostoli 59/62 ☎06.6994.1045. Tues–Sat 9.30am–7.30pm, Sun 10.30am–1pm & 4–7.30pm. Fantastic specialist kids bookstore, mainly Italian but with a small stock of books in foreign languages, as well as DVDs and puzzles and games too.

IANA Via Cola di Rienzo 182 ☎06.6889.2668. Mon 3.30–7.30pm, Tues–Sat 10am–1.30pm & 3.30–7.30pm. Popular Italian chain store offering moderately priced kids' clothes.

Marina Menasci Via del Lavatore 87 ☎06.678.1981. Mon 3.30–7.30pm, Tues–Sat 9.30am–1pm & 3.30–7.30pm. Toy store that sells exclusively wooden toys, in a great location a few steps from the Trevi Fountain.

Contexts

Contexts

History

T he history of Rome is almost the history of the western world, and as such is hard to encapsulate in a potted guidebook form. Inevitably the best we can do here is provide the basic framework. However, knowing at least some Roman history is crucial to an understanding of the city – its sights and monuments are often interconnected and will mean much more if you have a basic grasp of the continuum of events and their relationship to each other. We've tried to contextualize as much of the information in the guide as possible, but we recommend you take a look at some of the historical texts we list in "Books", pp.322–324.

Beginnings

No one knows precisely when Rome was founded, though excavations on the Palatine Hill have revealed the traces of an **Iron Age** village dating back to the ninth or eighth century BC. The **legends** relating to Rome's earliest history tell it slightly differently. Rea Silvia, a Vestal Virgin and daughter of a local king, Numitor, had twin sons – the product, she alleged, of a rape by Mars. They were supposed to be sacrificed to the gods but instead the two boys were abandoned and found by a wolf, which nursed them until their adoption by a shepherd, who named them **Romulus and Remus**. Later they laid out the boundaries of the city on the Palatine Hill (after arguing as to its exact location Remus chose the Aventine Hill and Romulus the Palatine Hill, and the latter won), but it soon became apparent that there was only room for one ruler, and, unable to agree on the signs given to them by the gods, they quarrelled, Romulus killing Remus and becoming the city's first ruler, in 753 BC.

Whatever the truth of this, there's no doubt that Rome was an obvious spot to build a city: the Palatine and Capitoline hills provided security, and there was, of course, the **River Tiber**, which could be easily crossed here by way of the Isola Tiberina, making this a key location on the trade routes between the neighbouring regions of Etruria and Campania.

The Etruscans

The **Etruscans** dominated Etruria – the area of Italy from the northern part of the peninsula as far south as Rome. Little of their history is known, their language was of non Indo-European origin, the architecture that survives is almost exclusively that of tombs, and their art has a particular and personal quality quite unlike that of the Romans or even the Greeks. Long before other Italic tribes, they took the important steps towards creating central urban nuclei, with twelve city-states, and at the height of their civilization in the sixth century BC one of their greatest cities, Cerveteri (or Caere) had a population of over 25,000. Rome may or may not have been an Etruscan town, but the Etruscans' influence on the kingdom of Rome was very strong, and three of its legendary seven kings were Etruscan, the first being **Tarquinius Priscus** (616–579 BC). Under his rule, Rome began to develop as a city: the first buildings of the Forum were raised, the rudiments of the city's sewage and water system – the Cloaca Maxima – were put in place, and the walls of the Capitoline Hill were built. Rich finds from this period include the contents of the Regolini-Calassi tomb, displayed in the Vatican museum, and there are numerous artefacts from all over northern Lazio in the city's marvellous Villa Giulia. Although the Romans finally overcame the Etruscans and obliterated much of their history, it is likely that the Etruscan influence on Rome continued long into the Republic – indeed it was an Etruscan soothsayer, Spurinna, who warned Julius Caesar about the ides of March.

The Roman Republic

Rome as a kingdom lasted until about 509 BC, when the people rose up against the last, tyrannical Etruscan monarch, **Tarquinius Superbus**. Tarquinius was a brutal, unpopular ruler, but the crunch came when his son, Sextus, raped a Roman noblewoman, Lucretia. She committed suicide shortly after, and her husband, along with one Lucius Junius Brutus, helped to lead an uprising that led eventually to the establishment of a **Republic** – a reaction, basically, against the autocratic rule of the Etruscan monarchs. The Roman Republic was to last nearly five hundred years, and was a surprisingly modern, and democratic, form of government, based on the acknowledged fact that the fate of the Roman people and its patrician classes were inextricably bound up together (the acronym SPQR, which you still see everywhere, stands for "Senatus Populusque Romanus" or "The Roman Senate and People" or as the French cartoon character Obelix would have it "Sono Pazzi Questi Romani" – "these Romans are crazy"). The **Senate** represented the patrician families, and elected two consuls from their number to lead Rome – in itself a forward-thinking act after years of absolute rule – while the people were allowed to elect two tribunes to represent their interests, even vetoing the appointment of senators they disagreed with. The city prospered under the Republic, growing greatly in size and subduing the various tribes of the surrounding areas – the Volsci and Etruscans to the north, the Sabines to the east, the Samnites to the south. The Etruscans were finally beaten in 474 BC, at the battle of Cumae, and the Volsci and Sabines soon after. Rome later drew up its first set of laws, in 451 BC, inscribing them on bronze tablets and displaying them prominently in the Forum – by now the city's most important central space.

Despite a heavy defeat by the **Gauls** in 390 BC, when they took the entire city except for the Capitoline Hill (a night assault was reputedly foiled by the cackling of sacred geese kept on the hill which woke the besieged soldiers), by the following century the city had begun to extend its influence beyond the boundaries of what is now mainland Italy, pushing south into Sicily and across the ocean to Africa and Carthage. In the meantime Rome was also trying to subdue the **Samnites**, who occupied most of the land in the southern part of what is now Italy, waging wars on and off between 343 BC and 290 BC that led eventually to the Romans occupying most of the region that is now Campania, south of Rome. Beyond mainland Italy, the next hundred years or so were taken up by the **Punic Wars**, against **Carthage**, the other dominant force in the Mediterranean at the time, and really the only thing standing between Rome and total dominance of the region. The First Punic War, fought over Sicily, began in 264 BC, and continued for around twenty years until Carthage surrendered all rights to the island, while the Second Punic War was famously started in 218 BC by Hannibal's march across the Alps by elephant, and ended, after years of skirmishes in southern Italy, in 202 BC. By the time Rome had fought and won the Third Punic War, in 146 BC, it had become the dominant power in the Mediterranean, subsequently taking control of present-day Greece and the Middle East, and expanding north, also, into what is now France, Germany and Britain.

Domestically, the Romans built **roads** – notably the Via Appia, which dates back to 312 BC and was built as a means of moving around troops during the Samnite wars – and developed their civic structure, with new laws and far-sighted political reforms, one of which cannily brought all of the Republic's vanquished enemies into the fold as **Roman citizens**. However, the history of the Republic was also one of internal strife, marked by factional fighting among the patrician ruling classes, as everyone tried to grab a slice of the riches that were pouring into the city from its plundering expeditions abroad – and the ordinary people, or plebeians, enjoying little more justice than they had under the Roman monarchs. In 87 BC, a power struggle between two consuls, Lucius Cornelius Sulla and Gaius Marius, led to a **civil war** in which Sulla, in 82 BC, eventually emerged as the sole leader of Rome. He initiated terrifying revenge against his opponents and introduced laws which greatly reduced the powers of the city's elected and appointed officials. Gaius Marius's nephew, **Julius Caesar**, later emerged as a powerful military leader and over the course of eight long years he conquered Gaul and Britain, and then returned to fight another civil war against his rival Pompey, which he won. Following this victory, he was proclaimed "dictator of Rome". It was the last straw for those eager to restore some semblance of the republican vision, and Caesar was murdered in the Theatre of Pompey on March 15, 44 BC, by conspirators concerned at the growing concentration of power into one man's hands.

However, rather than returning Rome to the glorious days of the Republic, the murder of Caesar in fact threw it back into turmoil. After his death, Julius Caesar's deputy, **Mark Antony**, briefly took control, joining forces with Lepidus and Caesar's adopted son, Octavian, in a **triumvirate**. Their armies fought against, and defeated those controlled by, Caesar's assassins, Brutus and Cassius, in a famous battle at Philippi, in modern-day Greece, in 42 BC. Their alliance was further cemented by Antony's marriage to Octavian's sister, Octavia, in 40 AD, but in spite of this things did not go well for the triumvirate. Lepidus was imprisoned and Antony, unable to put his political ambitions before his emotional bond with the queen of Egypt, Cleopatra, was defeated by Octavian at the battle of Actium in 31 BC. Antony escaped to Alexandria, where he committed suicide, with his lover, the queen, leaving Octavian in command.

The Imperial era

A triumph for the new democrats over the old guard, **Augustus** (27 BC–14 AD) – as Octavian became known – was the first true Roman emperor, in firm control of Rome and its dominions; indeed "Augustus" became the name by which all future Roman emperors were known. Responsible more than anyone for heaving Rome into the Imperial era, Augustus was determined to turn the city – as he claimed – from one of stone to one of marble, building arches, theatres and monuments of a magnificence suited to the capital of an expanding empire. Perhaps the best and certainly the most politically canny of Rome's many emperors, Augustus reigned for forty years.

Augustus was succeeded by his stepson, **Tiberius** (14–37 AD), who ruled from the island of Capri for the last years of his reign, and he in turn by **Caligula** (37–41 AD), a poor and possibly insane ruler who was assassinated after just four years in power. **Claudius** (41–54 AD), his uncle, followed, at first reluctantly, and proved to be a wise ruler, only to be succeeded by his stepson, **Nero** (54–68 AD), whose reign became more notorious for its excess than its prudence, and led to a brief period of warring and infighting after his murder in 68 AD, with Vitellius, Galba and Vespasian all vying for the position of emperor.

Vespasian (69–79 AD) was eventually proclaimed emperor, thus starting a dynasty – the **Flavian** – which was to restore some stability to Rome and its empire. Vespasian started as he meant to go on, doing his best to obliterate all traces of Nero, not least with an enormous amphitheatre in the grounds of Nero's palace, later known as the Colosseum. Vespasian was succeeded by his son, **Titus** (79–81 AD), and soon after by his other son – Titus's brother – **Domitian** (81–96 AD), who reverted to imperial type, becoming an ever more paranoid and despotic ruler until his murder in 96 AD, when all his decrees were declared void. **Nerva** was declared emperor (96–98 AD), thus beginning the rule of the "five good emperors" who were known for their moderate policies and for giving Rome

The Rulers of Rome

Roman Kings
Romulus (753–716 BC)
Numa Pompilius (715–674 BC)
Tullus Hostilius (673–642 BC)
Ancus Marcius (642–617 BC)
Lucius Tarquinius Priscus (616–579 BC)
Servius Tullius (578–535 BC)
Lucius Tarquinius Superbus (535–509 BC)

Roman Republic
c.509 BC–82 BC (death of Marius)

Roman Dictators and Triumvirs
Sulla (82–78 BC)
Triumvirate of Julius Caesar, **Pompey** and **Crassus** (60–53 BC)
Pompey (52–47 BC)
Julius Caesar (45–44 BC)
Triumvirate of Antony, **Octavian Caesar (Augustus)** and **Lepidus** (43–27 BC)

Roman Emperors
Augustus (27 BC–14 AD)
Tiberius (14–37)
Caligula (37–41)
Claudius (41–54)
Nero (54–68)
Galba (68–69)
Otho (69)
Vitellius (69)
Vespasian (69–79)
Titus (79–81)

Domitian (81–96)
Nerva (96–98)
Trajan (98–117)
Hadrian (117–138)
Antonius Pius (138–161)
Lucius Verus (161–169) co-emperor with **Marcus Aurelius** (161–180) co-emperor with **Commodus** (177–192)
Pertinax (192–193)
Didius Julianus (193)
Septimius Severus (193–211) co-emperor with **Geta** (209–211) co-emperor with **Caracalla** (211–217)
Macrinus (217–218)
Elagabalus (218–222)
Alexander Severus (222–235)
Maximinus Thrax (235–238)
Gordian III (238–244)
Marcus Philippus (244–249)
Decius (249–251)
Trebonianus Gallus (251–253)
Aemilianus (253)
Valerian (253–260) co-emperor with **Gallienus** (253–268)
Claudius II (268–270)
Quintillus (270)
Aurelian (270–275)
Marcus Claudius Tacitus (275–276)
Florianus (276)
Probus (276–282)
Carus (282–283)
Carinus (283–285) in competition with **Diocletian** (284–305)
Constantine I (306–337)

much-needed stability under the Pax Romana. He was succeeded by his adopted son (successors being chosen by merit), **Trajan** (98–117 AD), whose enlightened leadership once again allowed Rome and its colonies to settle to some sort of stability. Trajan also expanded the empire greatly, conquering the lands to the east – Turkey and modern-day Romania – and it was under his rule that the empire reached its maximum limits. Trajan died in 117 AD, giving way to his cousin, **Hadrian** (117–138 AD), who continued the grand and expansionist agenda of his predecessor, and arguably provided the empire's greatest years. The city swelled to a population of a million or more, its people housed in cramped apartment blocks or *insulae*; crime in the city was rife, and the traffic problem apparently on a par with today's, prompting one contemporary writer to complain that the din on the streets made it impossible to get a good night's sleep. But it was a time of peace and prosperity, the Roman upper classes living a life of indolent luxury, in sumptuous residences with proper plumbing and central heating such as Hadrian's own villa at Tivoli. Hadrian's successor, **Antoninus Pius** (138–161 AD), and then **Marcus Aurelius** (161–180 AD), ruled over a largely peaceful and economically successful empire, until 180 AD, when Marcus Aurelius's son, **Commodus** (180–192 AD), assumed the throne but wasn't up to the task, and Rome entered a more fragile phase. Predictably, Commodus was murdered, and eventually replaced by **Septimius Severus** (193–211 AD), thus initiating the Severan dynasty – again a time of relative calm, although the political and military skills of Severus unfortunately weren't matched by those of his sons, Geta and Caracalla. **Caracalla** (211–217 AD) murdered his brother before assuming power for himself in 211 AD.

The **decline of Rome** is hard to date precisely, but it could be said to have started with the Emperor **Diocletian** (284–305 AD), an army officer from present-day Croatia who assumed power in 284 AD and, in an attempt to consolidate the empire, divided it into two parts, east and west. Known also for his relentless persecution of Christians, Diocletian abdicated in 305 AD, retiring to the vast palace he had built for himself in what is now Split, on the Dalmatian coast, giving rise to a power struggle that concluded with the battle of the Ponte Milvio in Rome, in which Constantine defeated his rival, Maxentius, at the same time as converting to Christianity due to a vision of a cross in the sky he saw the evening before the battle. The first Christian emperor, **Constantine** (306–337 AD), ended Diocletian's persecution of the faith, and shifted the seat of power to Byzantium in 325 AD, renaming it Constantinople. Rome's heady period as capital of the world was over, and the wealthier members of the population moved east. A series of invasions by Goths in 410 AD and Vandals about forty years later only served to quicken the city's ruin. The imperial buildings decayed and became buried, the Roman Forum languishing beneath the Campo Vaccino or "cow pasture", and by the sixth century the city was a devastated and infection-ridden shadow of its former self, with a population of just twenty thousand.

The rise of the papacy

It was the **papacy**, under Pope **Gregory I** ("the Great"; 590–604) in 590, that rescued Rome from its demise. Thomas Hobbes described the papacy as none other than "the Ghost of the deceased Roman Empire, sitting crowned upon the grave" and in an eerie echo of the empire, Gregory sent missions all over Europe to spread the word of the Church. The missions publicized its holy relics, so drawing pilgrims, and their money, back to the city, and in time making the papacy the natural authority in Rome. The pope took the name "Pontifex

Maximus" after the title of the high priest of classical times (literally "the keeper of the bridges", which were vital to the city's well-being). Four of the city's great basilicas were built during this time, along with a great many other early Christian churches, underlining the city's phoenix-like resurrection under the popes, who as well as building their own new structures converted those Roman buildings that were still standing – for example fortifying the Castel Sant'Angelo to repel invaders and converting the Pantheon into a Christian church. The crowning a couple of centuries later of Charlemagne as **Holy Roman Emperor**, with dominions spread Europe-wide but answerable to the pope, intensified the city's revival, and the pope and city became recognized as head of the Christian world.

There were times over the next few hundred years when the power of Rome and the papacy was weakened. Conflict between the pope and the Holy Roman Emperor raged. While the Holy Roman Emperor could claim absolute power over the secular world, the pope claimed not only spiritual power but also the right to crown and therefore validate the emperor. At times popes excommunicated emperors, at other times emperors imprisoned popes. The Ghibellines (supporters of the emperor) and the Guelphs (supporters of the pope) ravaged many Italian cities and Rome was attacked on several occasions. Robert Guiscard, the Norman king, sacked the city in 1084; a century later, a dispute between the city and the papacy led to a series of popes relocating in Viterbo. Things became so unstable that in 1308 the French-born Pope **Clement V** (1305–14) transferred his court to Avignon. In the mid-fourteenth century, Cola di Rienzo, a self-styled "tribune" of Rome, seized power, setting himself up as the people's saviour from the decadent ways of the city's rulers and forming a new Roman republic. But the increasingly autocratic ways of the new ruler soon lost popularity; Cola di Rienzo was deposed, and in 1376 Pope **Gregory XI** (1370–78) returned to Rome. However, things got distinctly worse shortly after Gregory's death when a dispute over his successor's election led to the Great Schism and the unnerving proposition of two popes – one in Rome and the other in Avignon. This was finally resolved in 1417, with the election of the Colonna family pope, Martin V, but the battling popes had taken their toll on the fabric of Rome.

The Renaissance and Counter-Reformation

As time went on, power gradually became concentrated in a handful of wealthy Roman **families**, who swapped the top jobs, including the papacy itself, between them. Under the burgeoning power of these popes, the city began to take on a new aspect. The names of the families are etched on the city's buildings – Villa Borghese, Piazza Barberini, Palazzo Farnese. Churches were built, the city's pagan monuments rediscovered and preserved, and artists began to arrive in Rome to work on commissions for the latest pope, who would invariably try to outdo his predecessor's efforts with ever more glorious self-aggrandizing buildings and works of art.

This process reached a head during the **Renaissance**; Bramante, Raphael and Michelangelo all worked in the city, on and off, throughout their careers. The reigns of Pope **Julius II** (1503–13) and his successor, the Medici pope, **Leo X** (1513–21), were something of a golden age: the city was at the centre of Italian cultural and artistic life and site of the creation of great works of art like Michelangelo's frescoes in the Sistine Chapel, the Raphael Rooms in the Vatican Palace and fine buildings like the Villa Farnesina, Palazzo Farnese and Palazzo Spada, not to mention the commissioning of a new St Peter's as well as any number of other churches. Many of the capital's national art collections began life under these patrons of the arts. The city was once again at the centre of things, and its population had increased to a hundred thousand. However, in 1527 all this was brought abruptly to an end, when the armies of the Habsburg monarch and Holy Roman Emperor, **Charles V**, swept

Papal reigns

Celestine III (1191–1198)
Innocent III (1198–1216)
Honorius III (1216–1227)
Gregory IX (1227–1241)
Celestine IV (1241)
Innocent IV (1243–1254)
Alexander IV (1254–1261)
Urban IV (1261–1264)
Clement IV (1265–1268)
Gregory X (1271–1276)
Innocent V (1276)
Adrian V (1276)
John XXI (1276–1277)
Nicholas III (I277–1280)
Martin IV (1281–1285)
Honorlus IV (1285–1287)
Nicholas IV (1288–1292)
Celestine V (1294)
Boniface VIII (1294–1303)
Benedict XI (1303–1304)
Clement V (1305–1314)
John XXII (1316–1334)
Benedict XII (1334–1342)
Clement VI (1342–1352)
Innocent VI (1352–1362)
Urban V (1362–1370)
Gregory XI (1370–1378)
Urban VI (1378–1389)
Boniface IX (1389–1404)
Innocent VII (1404–1406)
Gregory XII (1406–1415)
Martin V (1417–1431)
Eugenius IV (1431–1447)
Nicholas V (1447–1455)
Callixtus III (1455-1458)
Pius II (1458–1464)
Paul II (1464–1467)
Sixtus IV (1471–1484)
Innocent VIII (1484–1492)
Alexander VI (1492–1503)
Pius III (1503)
Julius II (1503–1513)
Leo X (1513–1521)
Adrian VI (I522–1523)
Clement VII (1523–1534)
Paul III (1534–1549)

Julius III (1550–1555)
Marcellus II (1555)
Paul IV (1555-1559)
Pius IV (I559–1565)
Pius V (1566–1572)
Gregory XIII (1572–1585)
Sixtus V (1585–1590)
Urban VII (1590)
Gregory XIV (1590–1591)
Innocent IX (1591)
Clement VIII (1592–1605)
Leo XI (1605)
Paul V (1605–1621)
Gregory XV (1621–1623)
Urban VIII (1623–1644)
Innocent X (1644–1655)
Alexander VII (1655–1667)
Clement IX (1667–1669)
Clement X (1670–1676)
Innocent XI (1676–1689)
Alexander VIII (1689–1691)
Innocent XII (1691–1700)
Clement XI (I700–1721)
Innocent XIII (1721–1724)
Benedict XIII (1724–1730)
Clement XII (I730–1740)
Benedict XIV (I740–1758)
Clement XIII (1758–1769)
Clement XIV (1769–1774)
Pius VI (1775–1799)
Pius VII (1800–1823)
Leo XII (1823–1829)
Pius VIII (1829–1830)
Gregory XVI (I831–1846)
Pius IX (1846–1878)
Leo XIII (1878–1903)
Pius X (1903–1914)
Benedict XV (1914–1922)
Pius XI (1922–1939)
Pius XII (1939–1958)
John XXIII (1958–1963)
Paul VI (1963–1978)
John Paul I (1978)
John Paul II (1978–2005)
Benedict XVI (2005–)

C

CONTEXTS | History

into the city determined to avenge himself after having been excommunicated by Pope Clement VII (1523–34). He occupied the city and wreaked havoc for a year while the pope cowered in the Castel Sant'Angelo, witnessing the end to the splendours of Renaissance Rome.

The ensuing years were ones of yet more restoration, and perhaps because of this it's the **seventeenth century** that has left the most tangible impression on Rome today, the vigour of the **Counter-Reformation** throwing up huge, sensational monuments like the Gesù church that were designed to confound the scepticism of the new Protestant thinking, and again using pagan artefacts (like obelisks), not to mention the ready supply of building materials provided by the city's ruins, in ever more extravagant displays of wealth. The Farnese pope, **Paul III** (1534–49), was perhaps the most efficient at quashing anti-Catholic feeling, while, later, Pope **Sixtus V** (1585–90) was perhaps the most determined to mould the city in his own image, ploughing roads through the centre and laying out bold new squares at their intersections. This period also saw the completion of St Peter's under **Paul V** (1605–21), and the ascendancy of Gian Lorenzo Bernini as the city's principal architect and sculptor under the Barberini pope, **Urban VIII** (1623–44) – a patronage that was extended under the Pamphilj pope, **Innocent X** (1644–55).

The eighteenth and nineteenth centuries

The **eighteenth century** saw the decline of the papacy as a political force, a phenomenon marked by the occupation of the city in 1798 by Napoleon's forces; **Pius VI** (1775–1800) was unceremoniously sent off to France as a prisoner, and **Napoleon** declared another Roman republic, with himself at its head, which lasted until 1815, when papal rule was restored under **Pius VII** (1800–23). The years that followed were fairly quiet in Rome, if not in the rest of Italy, where the relatively despotic rules of the various city-states and fiefdoms that made up what we now know as Italy were at odds with the new ideas of centralization and modernization of the **reunification movement**, led by Giuseppe Mazzini. The revolutionary year of 1848, when popular revolts were sparked all over Europe, led to widespread unrest in Italy. In 1849 a pro-Unification caucus under **Mazzini** declared the city a republic and forced Pope Pius IX to leave Rome in disguise. However, Mazzini was chased out after a short four months by Napoleon III, who restored the papacy. There was further fighting all over Italy in 1859 and 1860 as forces for the Risorgimento or Unification of Italy gathered strength. Victor Emanuele of Savoy and his prime minster, Camillo Benso, Conte di Cavour, managed to bring the French on board against the Austrians who had control of the Lombardy–Venetia region. But, despite winning the second war of independence, they were betrayed by the French, who made a private settlement with the Austrians whereby the Austrians would hold on to Venetia while giving up Lombardy. This came to nothing, but growing anger at this outrage galvanized the movement still further and forces under Giuseppe **Garibaldi**, who had defended Rome with Mazzini in 1849, waged an effective guerrilla campaign in Sicily and southern Italy, which ceded the territories to King Victor Emmanuel. Eventually Florence became the capital of the new kingdom in 1864. Garibaldi made repeated attempts to capture Rome – occupied by Pope Pius IX and protected by the French – but he was arrested and sidelined by the new regime, embarrassed by his growing power and charisma. In 1870 French troops were withdrawn from Rome to fight the Franco–Prussian war, allowing Italian forces to storm the walls at Porta Pia and retake the city. Rome was declared the capital of the new Italy under Victor Emmanuel II (who moved into the Quirinale Palace), and the by now powerless pontiff, **Pius IX** (1846–78), was confined in the Vatican until agreement was reached on a way to coexist. The initial **Law of Guarantees** drawn up by the new government defined the relationship between the state and the papacy, and acknowledged the pope as sovereign within the Vatican but no further; it was rejected by the pope, leaving the status of the Vatican in limbo for years to come. In the meantime **Agostino Depretis** became the first prime minister of the new Italian state, and one of its greatest politicians, remaining in power until 1887, and seeing the new country through the difficult early years.

Modern times

As capital of a modern European country, Rome was (some would say still is) totally ill-equipped. The **Piemontese rulers**, from the region in northwest Italy, set about building a city fit to govern from, cutting new streets through Rome's central core (Via Nazionale and Via del Tritone) and constructing grandiose buildings like the Altar of the Nation. **Mussolini** took up residence in Rome in 1922, and in 1929 signed the **Lateran Pact** with Pope **Pius XI** (1922–39), a compromise which finally forced the Vatican to accept the new Italian state and in return recognized the Vatican City as sovereign territory, together with the key basilicas and papal palaces in Rome, which remain technically independent of Italy to this day. Mussolini had typically bombastic visions for the city, and not only constructed new buildings and neighbourhoods such as Foro Italico, the University, EUR and Cinecittà, but also new thoroughfares and views within the historic centre itself. He created grand avenues, the better to march his troops along, including Via della Conciliazione, which connected St Peter's to the river, a scheme going back to the times of Pope Nicholas V (1447–55). Mussolini also "liberated" the monuments of Imperial Rome from the surrounding mess of buildings – the Arch of Janus, the Temple of Vesta, the Theatre of Marcellus. But he also bulldozed his way through ancient sites such as the Roman Forum and medieval *borghi* of the city to achieve this, behaving not unlike the popes and families of old.

Rome was declared an "open city" during **World War II**, and as such emerged from the war relatively unscathed. However, after Mussolini's death, and the end of the war, the Italian king, Vittorio Emanuele III, was forced to abdicate and Italy was declared a republic – still, however, with its capital in Rome.

After the war Italy became renowned as a country which changes its government, if not its politicians, every few months, and for the rest of Italy Rome came to symbolize the inertia of their nation's government – at odds with both the slick, efficient north, and the poor, corrupt south. Despite this, the city's growth was phenomenal in the postwar years, its population soaring to close on four million and its centre becoming ever more choked by traffic. Rome was in the spotlight for fifteen minutes during the **Sixties**, when it was the (cinematic) home of Fellini's *Dolce Vita* and Italy's bright young things. However, in the **Seventies**, when the so-called Anni Piombi or "years of lead" arrived, Rome became a focus for the polarization and terrorism that was going on nationwide in Italian politics – a period when there were troops on the streets and the country often seemed on the brink of civil disruption. Since then, beginning with the "Mani Pulite" or "clean hands" enquiries of the **early 1990s**, the landscape of Italian politics has changed massively, and Rome in particular saw a period of stable government under mayor **Francesco Rutelli**, and a clean-up of the city for the **Millennium**, when buildings and monuments that had been closed for decades were restored and reopened. This process continued under the popular and urbane mayor, **Walter Veltroni**, who worked hard to improve cultural life and public services, launching Rome's first annual film festival, opening the Casa del Jazz and Casa del Cinema and building the new Auditorium on the north side of the city centre, which opened to great fanfare in 2006. Veltroni stepped down in 2008 to become leader of the new Italian Democratic Party, and the city's ambitions have stalled a little bit since. Work on the new metro line (metro C), continues but is not expected to be complete until 2015, and the current mayor, **Gianni Alemanno**, the city's first right-wing mayor for sixty years, has reversed many of Veltroni's initiatives, criticizing his predecessor's focus on the arts and picking up on popular concerns about immigration and public services. Among other things, he has pledged to pull down the controversial new Ara Pacis building, and has already downgraded the film festival and other cultural events. Whether he makes the city a better place to live, or to visit, remains to be seen. But change is coming, no question. Perhaps uniquely among European capitals, Rome retains a feel in its central districts that is still peculiarly local – and defiantly Roman. Visit now while it still exists.

Writing on Rome

There has been so much written about Rome over the years that picking out something that encapsulates the city in a few words is a hard if not impossible task. There's nothing, however, quite like the reaction that Rome induces in first-time visitors. However much they may have read, and no matter how well travelled they are, no one is ever quite prepared for the exuberant confusion of the city. The three pieces we have chosen are all about coming to Rome for the first or second time; all were written in the modern era, and as such are still highly relevant to what you see today; but they were written long enough ago to be also enjoyed as history.

Elizabeth Bowen

A novelist and travel writer, Elizabeth Bowen was born in Dublin in 1899. Her book, *A Time in Rome*, from which the following extract was taken, was first published in 1960.

The Confusion

Too much time in too little space, I thought, sitting on the edge of my bed at the end of the train journey from Paris. Never have I heard Rome so quiet before or since. I had asked for a quiet room, this was it. It was on the fourth floor, at the back. The bed was low, the window was set high up, one half of it framing neutral sky, the other a shabby projection of the building. Colour seemed, like sound, to be drained away. The hour was half-past four, the day Tuesday, the month February. I knew myself to be not far from the Spanish Steps, which had flashed past the taxi like a postcard. These anti-climactic first minutes became eternal. My bedroom's old-fashioned double room, with key in the lock and the tab dangling, had been shut behind him by the outgoing porter; stacked on trestles at the foot of the bed here was my luggage for three months. Through a smaller doorway showed the tiles of a bathroom wanly reflecting electric light. I was alone with my tired senses.

The hotel, from what I had seen of it, was estimable and dignified, nothing gimcrack. The corridor, dark and extremely long, had been lined with noble old-fashioned furniture, and in here was more of it, on top of me. Close to my pillows was the telephone, sharing the marble top of a commode with a lamp with the Campidoglio on its shade. After my one thought I felt unequal to any others and lay down flat. The bedhead was in a corner, so I switched on the lamp and tipped up the shade, to continue my reading of a detective story – interrupted just at the crucial point by my train's arrival at Rome station.

When I emerged from the story, darkness had fallen and I was hungry. Taking with me the *Walks of Rome* of Augustus Hare, I left the hotel to look for dinner. In these surrounding little streets, lit up like aquariums and tonight anonymous, saunterers passed me in vague shoals. Restaurant after restaurant was empty; blue-white electricity, hatless hatstands, as chalky and void as the tables' napery. Here and there a waiter posed like a waxwork. Spying through glass doors or over blinds, I began to fear something had gone wrong – actually all that had happened was, I was ahead of the Roman dinner-hour. So I ended in yellow-brocaded Ranieri's, where they showed a polished lack of surprise, among foreigners other than myself. Great gilt candelabra were on the chimney-piece, and for each of us a little vase of anemones. But here I was afflicted by something else: it seemed uncouth to read while dinner was served. Stealing a glance now and then at Augustus Hare, I never succeeded in getting further than Dr Arnold's 1840 letter to his wife: "Again this date of Rome; the most solemn and interesting that my hand can write, and even now more interesting than when I saw it last." This was not my first visit to Rome either.

Next day, I changed my room for an outside corner one, a floor higher. This, with the freshness following on what seemed more absolute than a mere night's sleep, altered the feeling of everything like magic. I found myself up in a universe, my own, of sun-coloured tiled floor, sunny starchy curtains. Noise, like the morning, rushed in at the open windows, to be contained by the room in its gay tranquillity. Roses, bleached by seasons of light, rambled over the cretonne coverings of the two beds. The idea of Rome, yesterday so like lead, this noonday lay on me lighter than a feather. Life at this level had a society of its own: windows across the way, their shutters clamped back, looked pensively, speakingly in at mine.

The quarter in which the Hotel Inghilterra stands is early nineteenth century. It fills the slight declivity, shallow as the hollow of a hand, between the Pincio and the Corso, and is bisected by the *de luxe* Via Condotti, apart from which the quarter is unassuming. It has acoustics of its own, echoes and refractions of steps and voices, now and then of the throb of a car in low gear nosing its way among the pedestrians. Every narrow street in this network is one-way; the system is dementing to motorists, who do not embroil themselves in it willingly. Radio jazz, a fervent young singer at her exercises, a sewing-machine tearing along, and the frenetic song of a small-caged bird, hooked to my sill, were my sound-neighbours. From top-but-one storey windows I beheld one crinkled continuous tawny roofline: all the buildings fitted into this quarter, like segments of a finally solved jigsaw, are one in height as they are in age. They are ochre, which was giving off a kind of August glow on to the mild spring-winter morning: on throughout the chilliest time of year smoulders the afterglow of Rome's summers. And my streets, on a grid plan, sunken deep between buildings, also are all alike: sunless, down there, for the greater part of the day, they stretch so far that they fade away at the ends. Small shops, workshops, bars and restaurants line them, with apartments or offices above. Banal, affable, ripe to become familiar, this was the ideal Rome to be installed in: everything seemed to brim with associations, if not (so far) any of my own. I began to attach myself by so much as looking. Here I was, centred. I dared to hope that all else might prove as simple. It did not.

One trouble is that Rome's north-south axis, Via del Corso, does not run due north, due south. It slants, thereby throwing one's sense of direction, insofar as one has one, out of the true. The Piazza Venezia, at one end, is east of Piazza del Popolo at the other. Then, there are the exaggerated S-curvings of the Tiber; one minute the river is at one's elbow, the next lost. A stroll along the embankment is one of the least enjoyable in Rome; the dustiest, baldest, most unrewarding. (To stand on a bridge is another thing.) The Tiber is not intended to be followed; only trams do so, and those in very great numbers. They grind by unceasingly, and one does well to take one.

Then again, there are far more than seven hills: how is one to be clear which the seven are? This seems to be one of the primal facts which guidebooks are obstinate in withholding. Viewed from above, from the Janiculum lighthouse or a terrace of the Pincio gardens, Rome as a whole appears absolutely flat, or, if anything, sunken in the middle like a golden-brown pudding or cake which has failed to rise. Down again in the city, you register gradients in aching foot muscles – this does establish that Rome is hilly. Knowledge of Rome must be physical, sweated into the system, worked up into the brain through the tinning shoe-leather. Substantiality comes through touch and smell, and taste, the tastes of different dusts. When it comes to knowing, the senses are more honest than the intelligence. Nothing is more real than the first wall you lean up against sobbing with exhaustion. Rome no more than beheld (that is, taken in through the eyes only) could still be a masterpiece in cardboard – the eye I suppose being of all the organs the most easily infatuated and then jaded and so tricked. Seeing is pleasure, but not knowledge.

In shape the Capitoline and the Palatine are hills unmistakably; so is the Aventine, at the other side of the trough of the Circo Massimo. But the Caelian, Esquiline, Viminal and Quirinal are ambiguously webbed together by ridges. On the whole I have come to suppose that these *are* the Seven – but if so, what of the Pincian, "hill of gardens" and Janiculum, bastion across the river? I asked a number of friends, but no two gave me the same answer; some did not want to be pinned down, others put forward their own candidates. That I should be set on compiling a definitive list of the Seven Hills, eager to check on all, to locate each, was, I can see, disillusioning to people who had hoped I might show more advanced tastes. So, given the equal unwillingness of guidebooks to disgorge anything like a list, I left Rome, when the end of my time came, no more certain as to the Seven Hills.

An excerpt from *A Time in Rome*, reprinted with the kind permission of Curtis Brown Group Ltd on behalf of the estate of Elizabeth Bowen. ©Elizabeth Bowen 1959

William Weaver

William Weaver served as an ambulance driver during World War II and first visited Rome a few years later. He became the most sought-after translator of Italian literature of the second half of the twentieth century, translating most of the modern Italian literary greats at one time or another. The following extract, part of his introduction to Steerforth Press's anthology of modern Roman literature, details his first impressions of the city, and his relationships with some of the writers he later came to work with.

Open City

It was raining when we arrived, and the rickety bus finally emptied us – me and my Neapolitan friend Raffaele – into a small, dark square near the Borsa. This was Rome? True, there were some scarred ancient columns along a street-front, but they were grimy with soot. I had imagined a city of snowy white, elegant classical forms, resembling perhaps the columned Citizens National Bank in Front Royal, Virginia, my childhood paragon of fine architecture. Rome, I saw, in shock, was different from the black-and-white Alinari photographs of art history courses; it was orange, yellow; rust-color; there were even a few neon signs blinking on baroque facades in the early winter dusk.

From the Piazza di Pietra we went to our pensione. Again, with reminiscences of E.M. Forster in my head, I imagined a place of relaxed conversation and, of course, a room with a view. The Pensione Sieben had once been a solid, spacious, middle-class apartment. Now the Siebens (he was an elderly German, a retired translator) lived in the kitchen and in a crammed bedroom next to it. An old lady, Herr Sieben's mother, occupied the next bedroom. In the front of the apartment, my friends Peppino and Mario shared the former salon, a once-splendid room now almost empty save for two cots, a desk, and a wood-burning stove, jutting from what was a formerly decorative fireplace.

Across the vestibule was a much smaller room, where I was to sleep. It also contained two cots, but the few square meters could not accommodate even a small desk. The cot farther from the door was occupied by Achille, another Neapolitan friend, an actor just getting his first small roles in a repertory company specializing in new Italian plays (they were not usually very good, so the bill changed often; Achille was building a large, useless repertory). Until the previous week, my cot had been occupied by yet another Neapolitan, Francesco Rosi, an aspiring film-maker; now he had landed an enviable job, as assistant to Luchino Visconti, and had just gone off to Sicily to join the director in working on what was to prove an enduring masterpiece, *La terra trema*. The room's single window gave on an air-shaft and a blank wall.

Achille was a trying roommate. Unless he had a rehearsal, he slept until midday (so I had to dress in the dark). Afternoons, he received his lovely and long-suffering girl-friend, and I was expected to go out for an extended walk – it was a rainy winter – and stay out until dark. He was a hypochondriac, and when he discovered my super-giant family-size bottle of aspirin – calculated to last me for my whole Italian stay – he began happily popping pills; the aspirin level in the big jar descended at an alarming rate. He was also fascinated by my clothes, ordinary as they were, and constantly borrowed them, with or without asking me first. He particularly liked to wear them on stage; so I became used to seeing my Princeton sweatshirt or my favorite striped pyjamas turn up on a set representing an Italian living room.

After a few days in Rome, I dutifully made my way to the University, planning to enroll in some courses, to justify and, presumably, enrich my Italian stay. My first real tangle with Italian bureaucracy ensued: a nightmare of waiting in the wrong line, lacking this or that document, failing to understand angry, shouted directions from the grouchy staff behind the windows or the confusing attempts at help from equally beleaguered Italian students.

I gave up (two years later, thanks to a Fulbright, I actually enrolled at the University and attended a few classes), and determined to dedicate myself to my other Roman project: the novel I expected to write. Having published two stories in national magazines (*Harper's Bazaar* and *Mademoiselle*, which had published stories of Truman Capote and other rising stars), I – and my friends – assumed that a novel was the next step. There was just one difficulty: I had nothing I particularly wanted to write about. But I didn't let that stop me. Mornings, when Peppino had gone off to his job at the Rai, the Italian State Radio, and Mario to his classes at the Accademia di Arte Drammatica, I moved into the former salon, sat at their desk, opened my copious notebooks (a Gide fan, I could not contemplate writing a novel without keeping journals, *cahiers*), and tried to work. I had never been successfully self-critical. But even permissive me soon had to concede that the novel was a dud.

If the rain let up, I soon found an excuse to go out. The excuse was always the same: my determination to get to know Rome. It was not a matter of visiting churches, studying frescoes, deciphering inscriptions. I wanted to gulp down real Roman coffee in the morning, eat real Roman pasta at lunch, drink all the real Roman wine I could afford. I wanted to read the newspapers, see the movies and the plays, hear the music.

I was perfectly situated. Dreary as the Pensione Sieben looked at first, it turned out to be a hive of cultural, and social activity; a center of fun. The big salon of Peppino and Mario served as a gathering-place for a host of young people from the Accademia, writers from the Rai, and other newly-arrived Neapolitans aiming to break into film or journalism.

And I had a trump-card of my own. I was an American, and to the Italians – whatever their ages or degree of fame – that nationality inspired endless curiosity.

For many I was the first American they had encountered, except perhaps for a stray GI a few years earlier. And so I was consulted as the expert on everything American: my opinion on William Wyler was seriously pondered. I was asked whether I would place Gershwin in the mainstream of white jazz or in the area of classical music (the question, for me, was unanswerable, as I knew far more about Puccini than about my popular compatriot). I was invited to contribute to nascent literary magazines, some of them born only to die after the first issue, which perhaps included my little piece on Karl Shapiro or John O'Hara.

Through a visiting American I met the Italian painter and writer Dario Cecchi, a few years my senior, scion of an Italian literary/artistic family with ramifications extending into every area of Italy's cultural life. Dario's father was the eminent and powerful critic Emilio Cecchi; his sister was Suso Cecchi d'Amico, the script-writer of Visconti and others, and her husband, Fedele d'Amico, was a brilliant, polemical music critic and polymath, eventually to become a treasured friend and colleague.

The chain of acquaintances grew, link by link, creating degrees not of separation but of connection. And some of these connections soon became hubs, branching off in one direction after another. It was Dario who took me first to meet Princess Marguerite Caetani. He told me little about her beyond the fact that she was American-born (a Chapin from Connecticut), a patron of the arts who had lived for many years in France, but had returned to Italy with her musician husband before the second world war and had remained in Rome. In Palazzo Caetani she edited an international literary review, *Botteghe Oscure*, after the name of the street where the Palazzo had stood for many centuries. The fact that Communist Party Headquarters now stood in that same street, making its name a synonym for the pci, was a minor nuisance that the Principessa airily dismissed.

We stepped into the dark courtyard of the great, grim palace, took an elevator to the piano nobile, and were shown into a huge, high-ceilinged hall, hung with dusty portraits (I looked around for Boniface VIII, the Caetani pope pilloried by Dante, but I couldn't identify him): then Dario, who knew his way around the palace, led me to a modern corkscrew staircase in a corner of the room. We climbed it and, passing through a plain little door at its top, stepped into a large, but cozy, New England living room: sofas covered in beige monkscloth, low tables, a fire in the fireplace, French windows revealing a broad terrace beyond. A large tea-pot stood on one table, and plates of sandwiches circulated.

The Principessa, in heather tweeds, only a few wisps of her gray hair out of place (to hint at her artistic side?), welcomed me warmly. And the welcome was equally warm from other guests, all clearly frequenters of the house. They were not many, and I remember almost all of them, as they all became friends of mine very soon: Elena Croce, the daughter of the philosopher but with a lively mind of her own; Umberto Morra, an aristocratic anti-Fascist and old friend of Bernard Berenson; Ignazio Silone – whose works I had read in translation – with his beautiful, ebullient Irish wife Darina, whom I had already met for a fleeting moment. And Giorgio Bassani, titular editor of *Botteghe Oscure*, though Marguerite clearly made all the operative decisions, while encouraging Bassani to propose new writers, especially for the Italian section of the magazine. At that time, Bassani was known, if he was known at all, as a poet; he had just published the first of what were to become the now classic *Five Stories of Ferrara*.

After that first visit, I returned to Palazzo Caetani countless times, and each visit was memorable, especially those when I was alone with Marguerite, who soon discovered – and exploited – my boarding-school experience as a proofreader. The Italian printers, excellent artisans, inevitably made gibberish of some of the magazine's English and French texts, and complaining authors drove Marguerite to despair ("Alfred Chester called me this morning from Paris, he cried all last night because of the mistakes in his story.") My work was unpaid – and I put in long hours – but I had ample occasion to appreciate Marguerite's real generosity. Not only did she soon publish my work: she also invited me to any number of meals. Food at the Caetani table was plain, but as I lived from day to day, a steak gained was a steak earned.

And the company! For foreign literary visitors of a certain level, Palazzo Caetani was an obligatory stop. One week there would be a tea-party for "Cousin Tom" (known to me as T.S. Eliot), in Rome to give a reading at the British Council, but also to enjoy a honeymoon with his new wife Valerie. The great poet's radiant happiness was evident, irrepressible. For much of the party he and his wife sat side-by-side on one of Marguerite's comfortable low sofas, and he could not refrain from touching her, patting her hand, pressing her arm, like an enamored schoolboy. Standing not far away, I pointed out Eliot's enraptured behavior to Alberto Moravia. "Senile sexuality," the novelist commented tartly. I remembered this remark some decades later when Moravia himself, by then close to eighty, married Carmen Llera, forty-odd years his junior.

Between the world wars, Marguerite had lived much of the time in Paris, where her house just outside the city was also an intellectual gathering place (Berenson's letters tell of visits there from the Armistice meetings, which he was attending). So the Palazzo in Rome welcomed many French visitors, among them René Char, Francis Ponge, Henri Sauguet. And there were also musicians, partly because of Prince Roffredo's background as a composer (he was Liszt's godson and had known the Wagners); in the Caetani salon I first heard Gian Carlo Menotti and Tommy Schippers discuss a festival they were beginning to think about, a place for young artists in some Umbrian town, perhaps Todi, or perhaps Spoleto.

Umberto Morra, a Piedmontese count, whose family had been close to the royal family (Umberto's father, a general, had served as the Savoys' ambassador to the court of the Czar), lived in a single room in Rome, in the apartment of some old friends. But he led an intense social life, and he particularly enjoyed entertaining new arrivals to Rome, arranging introductions. Often he would invite a new acquaintance, with perhaps one or at most two old friends, to tea at Babington's tea rooms in Piazza di Spagna. The atmosphere at Babington's certainly belonged to another world, but what world was it? I suppose the unpretentious setting was meant to evoke pre-war England (pre-first war, that is), and the motherly old ladies with their starched frilly caps who brought the tea and scones and cake looked like Margaret Rutherford stand-ins, imported directly from some Staffordshire village. But then you realized they spoke little English, and that smattering came out with a thick Italian accent.

In any case, the tea was authentic and delicious, the scones came with homemade jams; and the company was always stimulating. Whether at Babington or, for grander luncheons, at the Stanze dell'Eliseo, a quirkish private club, with Morra you were always sure to meet someone who was not just interesting but was actually a person you were eager to know: Jimmy Merrill was a Morra gift to me, and so – in Florence – was Bernard Berenson. Later, when Morra headed the Italian Institute in London, he introduced me to the great Maurice Bowra, to the equally legendary Judge Learned Hand. His was a mobile salon. When you came to know him really well, he would invite you for a weekend at his comfortable, slightly shabby villa in Tuscany (Moravia "stole" the villa to use as the setting of his novel *Conjugal Love*). Again the house party was always varied, relaxed, unexpected. Even the occasional bore – the garrulous widow of a distinguished anti-Fascist friend, for example – was, somehow, a bore you were glad to meet.

An excerpt from *Open City: Seven Writers in Postwar Rome*, edited by William Weaver, published by Steerforth Press of Hanover, NH. ©William Weaver 1999

William Murray

William Murray wrote regularly on Italy for the *New Yorker*. The following piece – one of many from his now out-of-print collection of Italian writings, *Italy: The Fatal Gift*, records his early years living in the city at the start of the 1950s, in particular a Campo de' Fiori that perhaps no longer exists but is still eminently recognizable today.

Voices

I don't think I began to understand Rome, and my own involvement in Italian life, until I moved to the apartment on the fourth floor of a run-down Renaissance palazzo at one end of a piazza called the Campo de' Fiori. The piazza is in the middle of the old papal city, surrounded by narrow, twisting little streets that thread their way among blocks of ancient houses dating back, many of them, to the fourteenth century. The rooms of my apartment were huge, with beamed and frescoed ceilings, thick walls, and tiled floors, and there was a terrace, awash in flowers and trellised ivy. I slept, or tried to, in a front room with a large window looking out over the piazza. At first, I was startled by the noise. There were lulls, but never long periods of uninterrupted silence. In the very early morning hours, I would sometimes be wakened by the explosive buzzing of a motor scooter, the rumbling of cart wheels over the cobblestones, the crash of some unbelievably heavy objects onto the pavement. Mostly, however, even at night, the sounds consisted of voices, individual and concerted, blending into and succeeding each other in a never ending choral composition of pure cacophony. It was astonishing.

Actually the sheer volume of sound at certain periods of the day didn't surprise me. I had known all along that the Campo de' Fiori was the site, six days a week, of a large open-air market. I would get up in the morning and open my shutters to look down over a sea of gray canvas umbrellas sheltering perhaps as many as two hundred stands. A great crowd of shoppers ambled and pushed down narrow aisles between rows of heaped edibles of all kinds. Directly beneath my window alone, at the northwestern end, of the piazza, I counted thirteen vendors of vegetables and several selling preserves, cheeses, and sausages. On my way across the piazza to a café where I often had breakfast and read the morning paper, I would pass pushcarts of fresh vegetables piled into great green mounds, tables buried under soft white and brown mushrooms, pyramids of cherries, apples, oranges sliced to reveal their dripping interiors, pears, apricots, bunches of white and green asparagus, enormous beets and onions, tiny round potatoes, huge heads of fresh lettuce, green and red peppers, artichokes, tomatoes, carrots and wild strawberries. Along one whole side of the piazza stretched a seemingly endless line of butcher stands, behind which the butchers themselves, in soiled white smocks, wielded their cleavers and large flat knives under the plucked bodies of chickens and the bloody carcasses of lambs and kids hanging in rows from steel hooks. There were also bunches of pigs' feet, chunks of tripe, chains of plump sausages. At the far end of the piazza, the fishmongers presided over damp boxes and baskets of the day's catch – fish of all shapes, flaming red, blue, and silver, soft masses of squid and small octopuses, mountains of white-and-gray minnows with tiny, dead bright-button eyes, dozens of small, dark-red clawless Mediterranean lobsters. And scattered along the periphery of these crowded rows of comestibles were still other stands, selling pots and pans, dishes, glassware, cheap toys, shoes, and clothing. The stone face of the piazza, roughly rectangular and roughly the same size as football field, disappeared every morning of the week but Sundays and holidays under umbrellas, the tons of merchandise, the shuffling feet of thousands of shoppers.

Many other voices besides those of the market invaded my room. The most insistent and violent one belonged, I guessed, to a woman in her thirties. She lived in one of the apartments near the corner of Via dei Cappellari, somewhere behind the lines of laundry that hung, dripping relentlessly, across the street. Her voice was shrill and hard and piercing: it would come soaring across the piazza from behind the wall of laundry like a battle cry from the ranks of an army advancing behind flapping pennants. "Ah Massimo-o-o" it would scream. "Massimo-o-o, where the hell are you, you dirty monkey? Get the hell up here right this minute! Massimo-o-o! If you aren't home in two minutes, you little bastard, I'll break your head! Massimo-o-o imbecile! You hear me? Get right up here now before I come down and break your arm! Ah Massimo-o-o! Massimo-o-o! Cretino! Imbecille! A' vie' qua-a-a!" These tirades often became so vituperative, menacing and foul-mouthed that I'd find myself wondering how the woman could keep it up. I'd go to the window and gaze down into the piazza, hoping to spot Massimo among the hordes of children swarming through the market or, on Sunday, around the base of Bruno's statue. The voice would scream on, threatening mayhem and the vengeance of heaven on the object of its wrath, but no little boy would separate himself from his fellows and go running across the cobblestones. At least, I never noticed him.

Massimo apparently did hear, however, and eventually he would come home. The voice would cease its screaming imprecations and remain silent for some time. After a while, though, I'd hear it again – usually around two o'clock in the afternoon, when the market had closed up and the commercial uproar had abated somewhat. The intensity and depth of emotion would still be evident in the voice, but the tone had altered dramatically. "Massimo! Massimo!" I would hear it shout. "Treasure of my heart, flower of my life, why don't you eat? Eat, eat! You want to die of hunger? You want your mother to perish of grief? You want your papa to die of shame, to tell me I don't cook like I used to? My love, my sweet, my angel, have another tomato, eat your bread, drink your milk. Eat, eat, love of my life! Here, Mama will give you a big hug and a kiss! You eat now! Massimo-o-o! Tesoro! Amore! Mangia, che ti fa bene! Cocco! Angelo!"

I tried often to imagine what Massimo looked like. I saw him as a small boy of seven or eight with dirty knees and scuffed shoes, black hair and red eyes, red cheeks, and sturdy shoulders, but too fat for his age. I'd see him climb the stairs to the sounds of threats and fury, bursting in to be met by a hug and a light cuff and a mound of steaming spaghetti. Who, anywhere around the Campo, would not have heard of him? At the newsstand, I once idly enquired about him, but the young man who sold me my newspaper couldn't identify him, either. "Ah, Signore, it could be any one of them," he said, indicating with a flick of his hand a crowd of urchins then engaged in kicking a soccer ball around the piazza. "Massimo? A common enough name. And here everyone shouts from the windows all the time. Do you not notice?"

This young man's name was Remo. He and his family had been tending their stand, on the corner of Via dei Baullari, for thirty-five years. They would take turns sitting like benevolent gnomes inside a very small wooden booth festooned with magazines and newspapers. Nothing escaped their vigilant attention. Remo rarely smiled, and he thought that life in the piazza had deteriorated a good deal since he first began to observe its goings-on. "Ah Signore," he said to me one day, "you like this market? It is not what it was. No indeed it isn't. On Saturdays you had to fight your way into the piazza, that's what I remember. Now – ". He shrugged. "Now, it's nothing. People are moving out. The ones who were brought up in this quarter, they do not like the old palazzi. When they have money, they move away. The rich and the foreigners are moving into the buildings now, but they don't buy in the market. They go to the supermarkets in the Parioli – drive all the way out there rather than buy in the piazza. No, it's not what it was." He was unhappy, too, about the crime in the area. "Dirty people," he said. "Gentaccia, that's what they are. The quarter is full of them. Every thief in town lives here. Do you have a car?" I told him I didn't.

"That's lucky for you," he said. "It would be stolen. Don't trust anyone you meet in the piazza. Anyone can see you're an American." At the time, I had seen no evidence of crime in the piazza, and I paid no attention to Remo's advice.

One night at about 2am I was awakened by the sound of loud masculine laughter and conversation outside my window. I looked down and saw a group of men directly below. They were talking and joking, making no effort to keep from disturbing the neighbourhood. I shouted down at them to keep quiet. One of them looked up briefly, but otherwise paid no attention. Their hoarse, merry voices continued to resound in the night air. After about ten minutes more of this, I went to the kitchen and came back with a large pot full of water. I asked them one more time to keep quiet, but I was ignored. I then leaned out of the window and poured cold water on their heads. Bellowing and cursing, they quickly scattered out and regrouped beyond the fountain, out in the piazza and well out of range. Through the slats in my shutters I saw them conferring angrily and occasionally pointing up toward my window. Slightly uneasy, I went back to bed.

The next morning, when I stepped out into the piazza, I was greeted by a young tough in wrinkled slacks and a torn jersey. He was unshaven, with close-set eyes and a snarl of oily-looking curls, and he had evidently been lounging against the wall of my building, waiting for me. "Hey you," he said hoarsely. "Hey, are you the one who threw water on us last night?"

The market was in full swing and the piazza crowded with people. I made up my mind not to be intimidated. "Yes," I said. "You woke me up." The youth shook his head gravely.

"That was a very stupid thing to do."

"Listen," I said. "I have some rights. I asked you twice to keep quiet and you paid no attention. You have no right to wake everybody up." "And you have no right to throw water on people."

This seemed a rather weak rejoinder to me, so I pressed my luck a little. "I could have called the police, you know."

The tough smiled, revealing a bright row of gold teeth. "No, no," he said, shaking his head. "You would not do that. No one in this quarter would do such a stupid thing. You have to live here – no?"

"I don't live here all the time," I said. "Besides, I don't like to be threatened."

The tough smiled again and spread his hands out wide. "Threatening you? Who is threatening you, Signore? I? I merely wish to protest against being doused with water in the middle of the night, that's all. That's not unreasonable, is it?"

"Mario, introduce me to the gentleman," I heard someone say.

I turned, and was confronted by a short, stocky, bald Roman in a rumpled but well-tailored brown suit. He had a round, affable face with large brown eyes and a strong, prominent, straight nose. He was smiling broadly. "Mario does not know my name," I said, and I introduced myself.

"Of course he does," the new arrival declared. "You are the American who lives on the fourth floor. Everyone knows who you are. I myself have often seen you in the piazza. Pleased to meet you. My name is Domenico. My friends call me Memmo."

"Were you also in the piazza last night?" I asked.

Memmo laughed. "Alas, yes," he admitted, "Luckily, you missed me. Mario, here, was soaked. That probably accounts for his sour face." He turned to Mario and clapped him roughly on the shoulder. "Hey Mario, cheer up! The bath did you good, eh? The first one you've had in weeks."

Mario made an effort to smile, but it did not seem entirely genuine. I concentrated on Memmo. "I'm sorry about it," I said. "But I was tired and wanted to get some sleep. You were directly under my window, and I asked you all several times to be quiet."

"Right," said Memmo. "Quite right. I think we will not chat there again. However, caro Signore" – he took my arm confidentially and pulled me a few feet off to one side – "don't do such a thing again. For your own good, Signore. No one would harm you, of course – Dio Mio, an American! But Mario and his friends can play such tricks, Signore! The apartment is so full of beautiful things. I have not seen it, but I know that it is. Apartments can be broken into, Signore, and even the most beautiful object can be made to disappear. What is the sense in playing tricks on people like Mario, eh?"

I looked back at Mario, who was still standing by the entrance to the building and regarding me sourly. "And you?" I asked. "What about you?"

"I?" he said. "Oh, I'm a friend of Mario's. He runs little errands for me. I have a shop here, just around the corner. You've passed it many times. Electrical equipment – radios, iceboxes, toasters, things like that. You've seen my shop, haven't you?"

I said that I had passed it often.

"Well, of course you have," Memmo said. "It's a very well-known store. Everyone in the neighbourhood knows me. Ask anyone."

"It's very kind of you to warn me," I said.

Memmo looked astonished. "Warn you?" he said. "Signore, I would not think of presuming to warn you. Still, it is important that you know how things are here on the piazza, eh?"

"Yes, I understand," I said. "Thanks very much."

"Forget it," Memmo said. "Forget the whole thing. And don't worry about Mario. Nothing will happen. Come and see me in the shop. Drop in any time – right there, just around the corner." He shook my hand and departed in the direction of his store. As he went, I saw him nod almost imperceptibly to Mario, who went off with him, not casting so much as a backward glance in my direction.

A couple of days later, I did drop in on Memmo. From the outside, the store looked like any other small shop dealing in electrical housewares, but since my encounter with Mario and Memmo and our oblique conversation, I had become curious about it. When I stepped inside the door, I discovered that the place was all but empty of merchandise. The window display featured a cheap washing machine and a secondhand refrigerator, but except for a couple of toasters and a small radio or two the store looked cleaned out. Mario and a couple of other shady-looking men lounged against the walls, smoking American cigarettes, while Memmo sat behind a small wooden desk. He had been talking into the telephone, but he hung up immediately when I came in. "Ah, buon giorno, buon giorno," he said, coming out from behind his desk and rubbing his hands briskly together. "How nice to see you! Thanks for dropping in."

"Business seems to be a little slow," I said.

"On the contrary," Memmo answered, smiling broadly. "Business could not be better."

"You've sold everything in the shop, then?"

"Well, not quite," Memmo said. "Come back here."

Memmo led me back to his desk, opened a top drawer, and pulled out a large, flat box full of Swiss wristwatches. "Look at this," he said, holding one up by the strap. "Fifty thousand lire, this watch costs. I sell it for thirty. Would you like it?"

I told Memmo that I already had a watch.

He put the watch back in the drawer and closed it. "Well, then, how about this?" he opened another drawer and showed me a pile of cigarette lighters. "Or these?" He produced boxes of cufflinks, tie clasps, studs, men's and women's bracelets, earrings, electric razors, razor blades, small bottles of cheap cologne, key rings, charms. Finally, with an elaborate little flourish of one hand, he opened still another drawer and took out a long, thin, expensive-looking case. "Perhaps there is a lady in your life?" He opened the box to reveal a handsome pearly necklace. "For you," he said, "for my friend the American, only a hundred thousand lire, eh?"

"No, thanks," I said. "I can't afford it."

Memmo sighed, cheerfully stuffed the box back into the drawer, and closed it.

"You seem to be selling everything here," I said.

Memmo smiled and shrugged. "Well, Signore, I believe in floating with the traffic, eh?" What you Americans call, I believe, the laws of supply and demand."

"How can you afford to sell these things so cheaply?" I asked.

"Signore, we have our own direct sources of supply," Memmo said. "We eliminate the middleman, as you would say. We import everything directly. You understand?"

"I think so," I said.

After that, I became increasingly aware of Memmo and his boys. Mario and half a dozen other young toughs strolled in and out of the shop, and several times I noticed them peddling objects through the marketplace. Once, I found Mario and a friend presiding at the corner of Via dei Baullari over a large stack of shoeboxes. They were selling sandals for five hundred lire a pair – a ridiculously low price. Occasionally, they would operate out of the back of a panel truck, selling everything from shirts to hardware. I never saw Memmo anywhere except inside his store, usually on the phone or in deep conversation with one of his young men.

One day, at the newsstand, I asked Remo about Memmo and his friends. Remo glanced sharply at me, then looked around to see if we were alone. "Stay away from them, Signore," he said in an undertone. "They are no good, that bunch. I let everything I hear go in one ear and out the other. It is better that way. But I tell you this Signore – the police drop in there from time to time, and it is not to pass the hours chatting, Memmo wasn't around for a long time last year, and that Mario – you know him?"

I said that I did.

"A bad one," Remo said. "He was a carpenter. Then he killed a man one day just because the fellow clapped him too hard on the back, or something. He did three and a half years. A hood, *un vero teppista*. Don't have anything to do with them."

"But who are they? Are they from around here?"

"All from this quarter, Signore, every one of them," Remo said sadly. "They give it a bad name. All over Rome, people say the Campo de' Fiori is a den of thieves. Memmo and his crowd – they're responsible for that. It's really too bad."

An excerpt from *Italy: The Fatal Gift*, reprinted with the kind permission of the author. ©William Murray

Books

There have been an enormous number of books published about Rome over the years, both in English, and of course in Italian, and the list below is inevitably extremely selective, concentrating on the odd travelogue, key texts on history and art, and on works of fiction that might be instructive – or fun – to read while you're in Rome.

History, art and architecture

Jonathan Boardman *Cities of the Imagination: Rome* (Signal). Like other books in the series, this is both a history of Rome and a celebration of the city and how it has featured in literature through the years.

Jerome Carcopino *Daily Life in Ancient Rome* (Penguin/Yale). Originally published in 1941, and consistently in print since, Carcopino's book is a classic, bringing to life the beliefs, social life and customs of ordinary Romans at the height of the empire.

Amanda Claridge *Oxford Archeological Guides: Rome* (OUP). Newly updated and expanded, this is an excellently written concise guide to the archeology of the ancient city – a good investment if this is your particular area of interest.

Christopher Duggan *A Concise History of Italy* (CUP). The best all-round history of the Italian nation that you can buy – concise and well written, covering everything from the fall of the Roman Empire to Unification and beyond.

Edward Gibbon *The History of the Decline and Fall of the Roman Empire* (Penguin). This abridged version is your best chance to read this classic text, conceived amid the ruins of the Roman Forum in the latter part of the eighteenth century and covering the period from the second century AD to the fall of Constantinople in 1453. If the short version isn't enough, Everyman publishes the whole thing in three volumes.

Christopher Hibbert *Rome: The Biography of a City* (Penguin). Simply put, the most entertaining and accessible historical introduction to Rome that you can buy – no less than you would expect from this most prolific of popular historians.

Tom Holland *Rubicon* (Abacus/ Anchor). Tom Holland's readable book pinpoints a specific but crucial period of Roman history, beginning with the Roman Republic at the height of its greatness and charting its decline up to the death of Augustus in AD 14. Good narrative history, documenting a fascinating era.

Keith Hopkins and Mary Beard *The Colosseum* (Profile). An extremely readable history of the famous monument, full of architectural, literary and often very funny anecdotes. Not only does it give you the background to its construction, demise and resurrection but also advice on site visits.

Philip Matyszak *Ancient Rome on Five Denarii a Day* (Thames & Hudson). A mock guide to the city for the Imperial-era visitor, with lots of entertaining advice along the lines of "there's no need to pack a toga", but it in fact provides a very detailed – and digestible – insight into the life, monuments and customs of the time.

Keith Miller *St Peter's* (Profile). Part of Profile's excellent series focusing on great monuments, this engaging and accessible book is the last word on St Peter's, covering both its long development and construction and its far-reaching influence.

Anthony Majanlahti *The Families Who Made Rome* (Pimlico). Part history and part on-the-ground itinerary, this book brings the buildings to life with "strange but true" histories of families such as the Borghese, Chighi and Farnese, whose stamp is all over Rome.

Charles L. Stinger *The Renaissance in Rome* (Indiana UP). The best book to focus exclusively on the Renaissance period in Rome, documenting the rehabilitation of the city under the papacy.

Giorgio Vasari *The Lives of the Artists* (OUP). There is no better background work on the artists of the Renaissance, written by a contemporary and correspondent of his subjects, who include Raphael, Michelangelo, and others less relevant to Rome. Available in a very readable English translation.

Margaret Visser *The Geometry of Love* (Penguin/North Point Press). Basically an extended tour of the church of Sant'Agnese fuori le Mura, and an absorbing study not just of the building and its history but also of the iconography and architecture of all Christian churches.

Travel and impressions

Elizabeth Bowen *A Time in Rome* (Vintage). Though written in the 1960s, Bowen's book endures because it is so engaging, and because it summarizes so well the longevity and continuity of Rome. See also p.311.

Tobias Jones *The Dark Heart of Italy* (Faber/North Point Press). Jones's book is immediately different from other books on Italy because it's about how Italians live now, and as such is a good book to take with you on any trip to Rome. A refreshing guide to the sleaze, corruption and dysfunctionality that make up the contemporary nation.

Carlo Levi *Fleeting Rome* (Wiley). Posthumously published in 2002, this collection of 33 essays, written over a decade spent in Rome in the Sixties and Seventies by the great

twentieth-century writer and politician, skilfully and evocatively encapsulate a city that no longer exists.

H.V. Morton *A Traveller in Rome* (Methuen). Like all Morton's books, this is a marvellously personal stroll around the sights, reflecting on history, architecture and culture.

William Murray *Italy: The Fatal Gift*. Out of print, but worth trying to get hold of for its perceptive essays on history and modern Italian life and culture, especially with regard to Rome, where Murray lived for many years, filing regular pieces for the *New Yorker*. Try also the in-print *City of the Soul* (Crown Journeys, US), Murray's latest slim volume of essays, walks and musings on the city. See also p.317.

Literature

Lyndsey Davies *Shadows in Bronze* (Arrow/Ballantine). Davies's second novel is perhaps the best introduction to the ancient Roman thrillers in which she specializes, following the doings of her sleuth, Marcus Didius Falco, during the period of the Emperor Vespasian. Like later

volumes, it has pace and humour, and is creditably well researched.

Robert Graves *I Claudius*; *Claudius the God* (Penguin/Vintage). Graves's two-volume pseudo-autobiography is perhaps the definitive dramatized account of Rome in the early years of its decline: both books are a thumping good read.

🏃 **Robert Harris** *Imperium*; *Lustrum* (Arrow). No one brings to life the Roman Republic quite as vividly as Harris, viewing the power struggles and intrigues of the main protagonists through the eyes of Cicero's faithful secretary, the freed slave Tiro. There are lots to choose from, but this is perhaps the best dramatization of the period you can read.

🏃 **David Hewson** *The Blue Demon* (Pan/Dell). The latest in Hewson's popular series of thrillers set in Rome, starring detective Nic Costa, and just as full of local colour as the rest. Good yarns, well told, and very Roman.

Conn Iggulden *The Gates of Rome*; *The Death of Kings*; *The Field of Swords*; *The Gods of War* (HarperCollins/ Dell). Iggulden's engaging four-book series, *Emperor*, is a historical romp documenting the rise and fall of Julius Caesar, from the rites of passage of the young man during the turmoil of the last decades of the Republic to his eventual murder in Pompey's theatre.

Allan Massie *Augustus*; *Tiberius*; *Caesar, Caligula* (Sceptre/Carroll & Graff). Massie's series of novels aspires to recreate the Roman Empire at its height through the imagined memoirs of its key figures, and does so with great success, in a series of novels that offers a well-researched but palatable way into the minutiae of the era.

Alberto Moravia *A Woman of Rome* (Steerforth Press, US). Probably the most pre-eminent postwar Roman novelist, Moravia uses the Rome of the Mussolini era as a delicate backdrop for this detached yet compassionate tale of a Roman model and prostitute. See also *Roman Tales* (OUP), a collection of short stories that has the lives of ordinary Romans as its thread.

Margaret Mazzantini *Don't Move* (Vintage). Intense psychological novel of midlife crisis, sex and obsession in Rome that was a massive bestseller in Italy and made into a movie directed by the author's husband. The city and its outskirts form a bleak, rain-soaked backdrop.

Iain Pears *The Raphael Affair* (Harper/ Berkeley). The first of Pears' successful series of thrillers with an art historical theme; all are set in Rome and make great holiday reading. Plenty of local settings and descriptions, not to mention fast-paced art-world intrigue, with robbery, forgery and general skullduggery.

🏃 **Glyn Pursglove** (ed) *Rome: a Collection of the Poetry of Place* (Eland). A wonderful little book, made up of a well-chosen selection of poems and extracts relating to all aspects and all eras of the city.

Stephen Saylor *Roma* (Robinson). Saylor is better known for his Giordanius detective yarns set in the days of the Roman Republic, but this epic novelization of the city's history up to the growth of the empire is maybe more appealing to the general reader.

William Weaver (ed) *Open City: Seven Writers in Postwar Rome* (Steerforth Press, US). An anthology of pieces by some of the best modern Italian novelists – Bassani, Silone, Moravia, Ginzburg, among others – selected and with an introduction by one of the most eminent postwar Italian translators. See also p.313.

Marguerite Yourcenar *Memoirs of Hadrian* (Penguin). Yourcenar's reflective narrative details the main events of the Emperor Hadrian's rule, most of it in the form of letters to his nephew, Marcus Aurelius, documenting at once the Roman Empire at its height and the very human anxieties of perhaps its wisest and most accomplished leader. See also Yourcenar's conceptual Roman novel, *A Coin in Nine Hands*.

Language

Language

Italian

T he ability to speak English confers prestige in Italy, and there's often no shortage of people willing to show off their knowledge, especially in Rome. But using at least some Italian, however tentatively, can mark you out from the masses in a city used to hordes of tourists, and having a little more can open up the city no end. The words and phrases below should help you master the basics. If you want a decent phrasebook, look no further than the *Rough Guide Italian Phrasebook*, which packs a huge amount of phrases and vocabulary into a handy dictionary format. There are lots of good pocket dictionaries – the Collins range represents probably the best all-round choice, with their Gem or Pocket formats perfect for travelling purposes.

Pronunciation

Italian is one of the easiest European languages to learn, especially if you already have a smattering of French or Spanish. Easiest of all is the **pronunciation**, since every word is spoken exactly as it's written, and usually enunciated with exaggerated, open-mouthed clarity. All Italian words are stressed on the penultimate syllable unless an accent (´ or `) denotes otherwise. The only difficulties you're likely to encounter are the few consonants that are different from English:

c before e or i is pronounced as in **ch**urch, while **ch** before the same vowels is hard, as in **c**at.

sci or sce are pronounced as in **sh**eet and **sh**elter respectively.

The same goes with g – soft before e or i, as in **g**eranium; hard before h, as in **g**arlic.

gn has the ni sound of o**ni**on.

gl in Italian is softened to something like li in English, as in sta**lli**on.

h is not aspirated, as in **h**onour.

When speaking to strangers, the third person is the polite form (ie *lei* instead of *tu* for "you"); using the second person is a mark of disrespect or stupidity. It's also worth remembering that Italians don't use "please" and "thank you" half as much as we do: it's all implied in the tone, but if in doubt, err on the polite side.

Words and phrases

Basics

Good morning	Buongiorno	Goodbye	Arrivederci
Good afternoon/ evening	Buonasera	Yes	Sì
		No	No
Good night	Buonanotte	Please	Per favore
Hello/goodbye	Ciao (informal; to strangers use phrases above)	Thank you (very much)	Grazie (molte/mille grazie)
		You're welcome	Prego

327

All right/that's OK	Va bene	Day after tomorrow	Dopodomani
How are you? (informal/formal)	Come stai/sta?	Yesterday	Ieri
		Now	Adesso
I'm fine	Bene	Later	Più tardi
Do you speak English?	Parla inglese?	Wait a minute!	Aspetta!
I don't understand	Non ho capito	Let's go!	Andiamo!
I don't know	Non lo so	In the morning	Di mattina
Excuse me	Mi scusi	In the afternoon	Nel pomeriggio
Excuse me (in a crowd)	Permesso	In the evening	Di sera
I'm sorry	Mi dispiace	Here/There	Qui/Là
I'm here on holiday	Sono qui in vacanza	Good/Bad	Buono/Cattivo
I'm English	Sono inglese	Big/Small	Grande/Piccolo
Scottish	scozzese	Cheap/Expensive	Economico/Caro
Welsh	gallese	Early/Late	Presto/Tardi
Irish	irlandese	Hot/Cold	Caldo/Freddo
American (masculine /feminine)	americano/a	Near/Far	Vicino/Lontano
Australian (masculine /feminine)	australiano/a	Quickly/Slowly	Velocemente/ Lentamente
a New Zealander	neozelandese	With/Without	Con/Senza
Today	Oggi	More/Less	Più/Meno
Tomorrow	Domani	Enough, no more	Basta

Signs

Entrance/Exit	Entrata/Uscita	Closed for restoration	Chiuso per restauro
Free entrance	Ingresso libero	Closed for holidays	Chiuso per ferie
Gentlemen/Ladies	Signori/Signore	Pull/Push	Tirare/Spingere
No smoking	Vietato fumare	Cash desk	Cassa
WC/Bathroom	Gabinetto/Bagno	Go, walk	Avanti
Open/Closed	Aperto/Chiuso	Stop, halt	Alt

Accommodation

Hotel	Albergo	hot/cold water	acqua calda/fredda
Is there a hotel nearby?	C'è un albergo qui vicino?	How much is it?	Quanto costa?
		It's expensive	È caro
Do you have a room…	Ha una cámera…	Is breakfast included?	È compresa la prima colazione?
for one/two/three person/people	per una/due/tre persona/e	Do you have anything cheaper?	Ha qualcosa che costa di meno?
for one/two/ three night/s	per una/due/tre notte/i	Full/half board	Pensione completa/ mezza pensione
for one/two week/s	per una/due settimana/e	Can I see the room?	Posso vedere la camera?
with a double bed	con un letto matrimoniale	I'll take it	La prendo
with a shower/bath	con una doccia/un bagno	I'd like to book a room	Vorrei prenotare una camera
with a balcony	con balcone	I have a booking	Ho una prenotazione

Questions and directions

Where?	Dove?	How do I get to...?	Per arrivare a...?
(Where is /where are...?)	(Dov'è/Dove sono...?)	How far is it to...?	Quant'è lontano...?
When?	Quando?	Can you tell me when to get off?	Mi può dire dove scendere?
What? (What is it?)	Cosa? (Cos'è?)	What time does it open/close?	A che ora apre/chiude?
How much/many?	Quanto/Quanti?		
Why?	Perché?	How much does it/ do they cost?	Quanto costa/costano?
It is/there is (Is it/is there...?)	C'e...?		
What time is it?	Che ore sono?	What's it called in Italian?	Come si chiama in italiano?

Numbers

1	uno	20	venti
2	due	21	ventuno
3	tre	22	ventidue
4	quattro	30	trenta
5	cinque	40	quaranta
6	sei	50	cinquanta
7	sette	60	sessanta
8	otto	70	settanta
9	nove	80	ottanta
10	dieci	90	novanta
11	undici	100	cento
12	dodici	101	centuno
13	tredici	110	centodieci
14	quattordici	200	duecento
15	quindici	500	cinquecento
16	sedici	1000	mille
17	diciassette	5000	cinquemila
18	diciotto	10,000	diecimila
19	diciannove	50,000	cinquantamila

Menu reader

Basics and snacks

Aceto	Vinegar	Olive	Olives
Aglio	Garlic	Pane	Bread
Biscotti	Biscuits	Pepe	Pepper
Burro	Butter	Riso	Rice
Caramelle	Sweets	Sale	Salt
Cioccolato	Chocolate	Uova	Eggs
Formaggio	Cheese	Yogurt	Yoghurt
Frittata	Omelette	Zucchero	Sugar
Marmellata	Jam	Zuppa	Soup
Olio	Oil		

The first course (*il primo*)

Bucatini	Thick, hollow spaghetti – classically Roman	Tortellini	Rings of pasta, stuffed with meat or cheese
Brodo	Clear broth	Vermicelli	Thin spaghetti ("little worms")
Farfalle	Butterfly-shaped pasta		
Fettuccine	Narrow pasta ribbons		

Pasta sauces (*salsa*)

Gnocchi	Small potato and dough dumplings	Amatriciana	Tomato sauce with diced guanciale or bacon (literally pig's cheek)
Maccheroni	Macaroni pasta		
Minestrina	Clear broth with small pasta shapes	Arrabbiata	Spicy tomato, with chillies ("Angry")
Minestrone	Thick vegetable soup	Carbonara	Bacon, pecorino cheese and beaten egg
Paccheri	Big hollow pasta tubes		
Pasta al forno	Pasta baked with minced meat, eggs, tomato and cheese	Cacio e Pepe	Pecorino cheese and freshly ground pepper
		Alla Gricia	Pecorino cheese and chunks of guanciale or bacon
Pasta e fagioli	Pasta with beans		
Pastina in brodo	Pasta pieces in clear broth	Alla Pajata	With calves' intestines
		Peperoncino	With olive oil, garlic and fresh chillies
Penne	Smaller version of rigatoni		
Rigatoni	Large, grooved tubular pasta	Pomodoro	Tomato
		Puttanesca	Tomato, anchovy, olive oil and oregano ("whorish")
Stracciatella	Broth with egg		
Tagliatelle	Pasta ribbons, another word for fettuccine		
		Al ragù	meat sauce
Tonnarelli	The same as bucatini, see above	Alle vongole	With baby clams

The second course (*il secondo*)

Meat (*carne*)

		Ossobuco	Shin of veal
		Pancetta	Bacon
Abbacchio	Young, roast lamb	Pollo	Chicken
Agnello	Lamb	Polpette	Meatballs
Bistecca	Steak	Porchetta	Roast suckling pig
Carpaccio	Slices of raw beef	Rognoni	Kidneys
Cervello	Brain, usually calves'	Salsiccia	Sausage
Cinghiale	Wild boar	Saltimbocca	Veal with ham and sage
Coda alla vaccinara	Stewed oxtail	Spezzatino	Stew
Coniglio	Rabbit	Trippa	Tripe
Coratella	Sweetmeats	Vitello	Veal
Costoletta	Cutlet, chop		

Fish (*pesce*) and shellfish (*crostacei*)

Fegato	Liver		
Lingua	Tongue		
Maiale	Pork	Acciughe	Anchovies
Manzo	Beef	Anguilla	Eel
Milza	Spleen	Aragosta	Lobster

Baccalà	Dried salted cod, usually served fried in batter	Ostriche	Oysters
		Pesce spada	Swordfish
Calamari	Squid	Polpo	Octopus
Cefalo	Grey mullet	Rospo	Monkfish
Cozze	Mussels	Sampiero	John Dory
Dentice	Sea bream	Sarde	Sardines
Gamberetti	Shrimps	Sogliola	Sole
Gamberi	Prawns	Tonno	Tuna
Granchio	Crab	Trota	Trout
Merluzzo	Cod	Vongole	Clams

Vegetables (*contorni*), herbs (*erbe aromatiche*) and salad (*insalata*)

Asparagi	Asparagus	Funghi	Mushrooms
Carciofi	Artichokes	Insalata verde/mista	Green/mixed salad
Carciofini	Artichoke hearts	Lenticchie	Lentils
Cavolfiore	Cauliflower	Melanzane	Aubergine
Cavolo	Cabbage	Patate	Potatoes
Cipolla	Onion	Peperoni	Peppers
Fagioli	Beans	Piselli	Peas
Fagiolini	Green beans	Pomodori	Tomatoes
Fiori di zucca	Courgette flowers, sometimes stuffed with anchovies	Puntarelle	A kind of chicory, very Roman
		Radicchio	Red salad leaves
Finocchio	Fennel	Spinaci	Spinach

Useful terms

Ai ferri	Grilled without oil	Arrosto	Roast
Al dente	Firm, not overcooked	Ben cotto	Well done
Al forno	Baked	Bollito/lesso	Boiled
Al sangue	Rare	Cotto	Cooked (not raw)
Alla brace	Barbecued	Crudo	Raw
Alla griglia	Grilled	Fritto	Fried
Alla milanese	Fried in egg and breadcrumbs	In umido	Stewed
		Ripieno	Stuffed
Alla pizzaiola	Cooked in tomato sauce	Stracotto	Braised, stewed
Allo spiedo	On the spit		

Cheese (*formaggi*)

Dolcelatte	Creamy blue cheese	Pecorino	Strong, hard sheep's cheese, used in Rome instead of Parmesan
Fontina	Northern Italian cheese, often used in cooking		
Gorgonzola	Soft, strong, blue-veined cheese		

| Provola/Provolone | Smooth, round mild cheese, made from buffalo or sheep's milk; sometimes smoked | Ricotta | Soft, white sheep's cheese |

Sweets (*dolci*), fruit (*frutta*) and nuts (*noci*)

Amaretti	Macaroons	Mandorle	Almonds
Ananas	Pineapple	Mele	Apples
Anguria/Coccomero	Watermelon	Melone	Melon
Arance	Oranges	Pangiallo	A heavy cake of fruit and nuts
Banane	Bananas		
Cacchi	Persimmons	Pere	Pears
Ciliegie	Cherries	Pesche	Peaches
Crostata	Pastry tart with a jam, chocolate or ricotta topping	Pinoli	Pine nuts
		Pistacchio	Pistachio nut
		Torta	Cake, tart
Fichi	Figs	Uva	Grapes
Fichi d'India	Prickly pears	Zabaglione	Dessert made with eggs, sugar and marsala wine
Fragole	Strawberries		
Gelato	Ice cream		
Limone	Lemon	Zuppa Inglese	Trifle
Macedonia	Fruit salad		

Drinks

Acqua minerale	Mineral water	Spumante	Sparkling wine
Aranciata	Orangeade	Succo	Concentrated fruit juice with sugar
Bicchiere	Glass		
Birra	Beer	Tè	Tea
Bottiglia	Bottle	Tonica	Tonic water
Caffè	Coffee	Vino	Wine
Cioccolato caldo	Hot chocolate	rosso/bianco/	red/white/
Ghiaccio	Ice	rosato/secco/dolce	rosé/dry/sweet
Granita	Crushed ice with coffee or fruit	Litro	Litre
		Mezzo	Half
Latte	Milk	Quarto	Quarter
Limonata	Lemonade	Caraffa	Carafe
Spremuta	Fresh fruit juice	Salute!	Cheers!

Travel
store

Travel

Andorra The Pyrenees,
Pyrenees & Andorra
Map, Spain
Antigua The Caribbean
Argentina Argentina,
Argentina Map,
Buenos Aires, South
America on a Budget
Aruba The Caribbean
Australia Australia,
Australia Map, East
Coast Australia,
Melbourne, Sydney,
Tasmania
Austria Austria,
Europe on a Budget,
Vienna
Bahamas The
Bahamas,
The Caribbean
Barbados Barbados
DIR, The Caribbean
Belgium Belgium &
Luxembourg, Bruges
DIR, Brussels,
Brussels Map,
Europe on a Budget
Belize Belize, Central
America on a Budget,
Guatemala & Belize
Map
Benin West Africa
Bolivia Bolivia, South
America on a Budget
Brazil Brazil, Rio,
South America on a
Budget
British Virgin Islands
The Caribbean
Brunei Malaysia,
Singapore & Brunei [1
title], Southeast Asia
on a Budget
Bulgaria Bulgaria,
Europe on a Budget
Burkina Faso West
Africa
Cambodia Cambodia,
Southeast Asia on
a Budget, Vietnam,
Laos & Cambodia
Map [1 Map]
Cameroon West Africa
Canada Canada,
Pacific Northwest,
Toronto, Toronto Map,
Vancouver
Cape Verde West
Africa
Cayman Islands The
Caribbean
Chile Chile, Chile Map,
South America on a
Budget
China Beijing, China,

Hong Kong & Macau,
Hong Kong & Macau
DIR, Shanghai
Colombia South
America on a Budget
Costa Rica Central
America on a Budget,
Costa Rica, Costa
Rica & Panama Map
Croatia Croatia,
Croatia Map, Europe
on a Budget
Cuba Cuba, Cuba
Map, The Caribbean,
Havana
Cyprus Cyprus, Cyprus
Map
Czech Republic The
Czech Republic,
Czech & Slovak
Republics, Europe
on a Budget, Prague,
Prague DIR, Prague
Map
Denmark Copenhagen,
Denmark, Europe on
a Budget, Scandinavia
Dominica The
Caribbean
Dominican Republic
Dominican Republic,
The Caribbean
Ecuador Ecuador,
South America on a
Budget
Egypt Egypt, Egypt Map
El Salvador Central
America on a Budget
England Britain,
Camping in Britain,
Devon & Cornwall,
Dorset, Hampshire
and The Isle of Wight
[1 title], England,
Europe on a Budget,
The Lake District,
London, London DIR,
London Map, London
Mini Guide, Walks In
London & Southeast
England
Estonia The Baltic
States, Europe on a
Budget
Fiji Fiji
Finland Europe on
a Budget, Finland,
Scandinavia
France Brittany &
Normandy, Corsica,
Corsica Map, The
Dordogne & the Lot,
Europe on a Budget,
France, France
Map, Languedoc &
Roussillon, The Loire,
Paris, Paris DIR,

Paris Map, Paris Mini
Guide, Provence &
the Côte d'Azur, The
Pyrenees, Pyrenees &
Andorra Map
French Guiana South
America on a Budget
Gambia The Gambia,
West Africa
Germany Berlin,
Berlin Map, Europe on
a Budget, Germany,
Germany Map
Ghana West Africa
Gibraltar Spain
Greece Athens Map,
Crete, Crete Map,
Europe on a Budget,
Greece, Greece Map,
Greek Islands, Ionian
Islands
Guadeloupe The
Caribbean
Guatemala Central
America on a
Budget, Guatemala,
Guatemala & Belize
Map
Guinea West Africa
Guinea-Bissau West
Africa
Guyana South America
on a Budget
Holland see
The Netherlands
Honduras Central
America on a Budget
Hungary Budapest,
Europe on a Budget,
Hungary
Iceland Iceland,
Iceland Map
India Goa, India,
India Map, Kerala,
Rajasthan, Delhi &
Agra [1 title], South
India, South India Map
Indonesia Bali &
Lombok, Southeast
Asia on a Budget
Ireland Dublin DIR,
Dublin Map, Europe
on a Budget, Ireland,
Ireland Map
Israel Jerusalem
Italy Europe on a
Budget, Florence DIR,
Florence & Siena
Map, Florence & the
best of Tuscany, Italy,
The Italian Lakes,
Naples & the Amalfi
Coast, Rome, Rome
DIR, Rome Map,
Sardinia, Sicily, Sicily
Map, Tuscany &
Umbria, Tuscany Map,

Venice, Venice DIR,
Venice Map
Jamaica Jamaica, The
Caribbean
Japan Japan, Tokyo
Jordan Jordan
Kenya Kenya, Kenya
Map
Korea Korea
Laos Laos, Southeast
Asia on a Budget,
Vietnam, Laos &
Cambodia Map [1
Map]
Latvia The Baltic
States, Europe on a
Budget
Lithuania The Baltic
States, Europe on a
Budget
Luxembourg Belgium
& Luxembourg,
Europe on a Budget
Malaysia Malaysia
Map, Malaysia,
Singapore & Brunei
[1 title], Southeast
Asia on a Budget
Mali West Africa
Malta Malta & Gozo
DIR
Martinique The
Caribbean
Mauritania West Africa
Mexico Baja California,
Baja California,
Cancún & Cozumel
DIR, Mexico, Mexico
Map, Yucatán, Yucatán
Peninsula Map
Monaco France,
Provence & the Côte
d'Azur
Montenegro
Montenegro
Morocco Europe on a
Budget, Marrakesh
DIR, Marrakesh Map,
Morocco, Morocco
Map,
Nepal Nepal
Netherlands
Amsterdam,
Amsterdam DIR,
Amsterdam Map,
Europe on a Budget,
The Netherlands
Netherlands Antilles
The Caribbean
New Zealand New
Zealand, New Zealand
Map

DIR: Rough Guide
DIRECTIONS for
short breaks

Nicaragua Central America on a Budget
Niger West Africa
Nigeria West Africa
Norway Europe on a Budget, Norway, Scandinavia
Panama Central America on a Budget, Costa Rica & Panama Map, Panama
Paraguay South America on a Budget
Peru Peru, Peru Map, South America on a Budget
Philippines The Philippines, Southeast Asia on a Budget,
Poland Europe on a Budget, Poland
Portugal Algarve DIR, The Algarve Map, Europe on a Budget, Lisbon DIR, Lisbon Map, Madeira DIR, Portugal, Portugal Map, Spain & Portugal Map
Puerto Rico The Caribbean, Puerto Rico
Romania Europe on a Budget, Romania
Russia Europe on a Budget, Moscow, St Petersburg
St Kitts & Nevis The Caribbean
St Lucia The Caribbean
St Vincent & the Grenadines The Caribbean
Scotland Britain, Camping in Britain, Edinburgh DIR, Europe on a Budget, Scotland, Scottish Highlands & Islands
Senegal West Africa
Serbia Montenegro Europe on a Budget
Sierra Leone West Africa
Singapore Malaysia, Singapore & Brunei [1 title], Singapore DIR, Southeast Asia on a Budget
Slovakia Czech & Slovak Republics, Europe on a Budget
Slovenia Europe on a Budget, Slovenia
South Africa Cape Town & the Garden

Route, South Africa, South Africa Map
Spain Andalucía, Andalucía Map, Barcelona, Barcelona DIR, Barcelona Map, Europe on a Budget, Ibiza & Formentera DIR, Gran Canaria DIR, Madrid DIR, Lanzarote & Fuerteventura DIR Madrid Map, Mallorca & Menorca, Mallorca DIR, Mallorca Map, The Pyrenees, Pyrenees & Andorra Map, Spain & Spain & Portugal Map, Tenerife & La Gomera DIR
Sri Lanka Sri Lanka, Sri Lanka Map
Suriname South America on a Budget
Sweden Europe on a Budget, Scandinavia, Sweden
Switzerland Europe on a Budget, Switzerland
Taiwan Taiwan
Tanzania Tanzania, Zanzibar
Thailand Bangkok, Southeast Asia on a Budget, Thailand, Thailand Map, Thailand Beaches & Islands
Togo West Africa
Trinidad & Tobago The Caribbean, Trinidad & Tobago
Tunisia Tunisia, Tunisia Map
Turkey Europe on a Budget, Istanbul, Turkey, Turkey Map
Turks and Caicos Islands The Bahamas, The Caribbean
United Arab Emirates Dubai DIR, Dubai & UAE Map [1 title]
United Kingdom Britain, Devon & Cornwall, Edinburgh DIR England, Europe on a Budget, The Lake District, London DIR, London Map, London Mini Guide, Scotland, Scottish Highlands

& Islands, Wales, Walks In London & Southeast England
United States Alaska, Boston, California, California Map, Chicago, Colorado, Florida, Florida Map, The Grand Canyon, Hawaii, Los Angeles, Los Angeles Map, Los Angeles and Southern California, Maui DIR, Miami & South Florida, New England, New England Map, New Orleans & Cajun Country, New Orleans DIR, New York City, NYC DIR, NYC Map, New York City Mini Guide, Oregon & Washington, Orlando & Walt Disney World® DIR, San Francisco, San Francisco DIR, San Francisco Map, Seattle, Southwest USA, USA, Washington DC, Yellowstone & the Grand Tetons National Park, Yosemite National Park
Uruguay South America on a Budget
US Virgin Islands The Bahamas, The Caribbean
Venezuela South America on a Budget
Vietnam Southeast Asia on a Budget, Vietnam, Vietnam, Laos & Cambodia Map [1 Map],
Wales Britain, Camping in Britain, Europe on a Budget, Wales
First-Time Series FT Africa, FT Around the World, FT Asia, FT Europe, FT Latin America
Inspirational guides Earthbound, Clean Breaks, Make the Most of Your Time on Earth, Ultimate Adventures, World Party
Travel Specials Camping in Britain, Travel with Babies & Young Children, Walks in London & SE England

For more information go to www.roughguides.com

"The most accurate maps in the world"

San Jose Mercury News

ROUGH GUIDE MAP

France

1:1,000,000 · 1 INCH: 15.8 MILES · 1CM: 10KM

CITY MAPS 24 titles
Amsterdam · Athens · Barcelona · Berlin
Boston · Brussels · Chicago · Dublin
Florence & Siena · Frankfurt · Lisbon
London · Los Angeles · Madrid · Marrakesh
Miami · New York City · Paris · Prague
Rome · San Francisco · Toronto · Venice
Washington DC
US$8.99 Can$13.99 £4.99

COUNTRY & REGIONAL MAPS 50 titles
Algarve · Andalucía · Argentina · Australia
Baja California · Brittany · Crete · Croatia
Cuba · Cyprus · Czech Republic · Dominican
Republic · Dubai · Egypt · Greece · Guatemala
& Belize · Iceland · Ireland · India · Kenya
Mexico · Morocco · New Zealand · Northern
Spain · Peru · Portugal · Sicily · South Africa
South India · Sri Lanka · Tenerife · Thailand
Trinidad & Tobago · Turkey · Tuscany
Yucatán Peninsula and more.
US$9.99 Can$13.99 £5.99

Plastic waterproof map
ideal for planning and touring

waterproof • rip-proof • amazing value
BROADEN YOUR HORIZONS

NOTES

Small print and
Index

A Rough Guide to Rough Guides

Published in 1982, the first Rough Guide – to Greece – was a student scheme that became a publishing phenomenon. Mark Ellingham, a recent graduate in English from Bristol University, had been travelling in Greece the previous summer and couldn't find the right guidebook. With a small group of friends he wrote his own guide, combining a highly contemporary, journalistic style with a thoroughly practical approach to travellers' needs.

The immediate success of the book spawned a series that rapidly covered dozens of destinations. And, in addition to impecunious backpackers, Rough Guides soon acquired a much broader and older readership that relished the guides' wit and inquisitiveness as much as their enthusiastic, critical approach and value-for-money ethos.

These days, Rough Guides include recommendations from shoestring to luxury and cover more than 200 destinations around the globe, including almost every country in the Americas and Europe, more than half of Africa and most of Asia and Australasia. Our ever-growing team of authors and photographers is spread all over the world, particularly in Europe, the US and Australia.

In the early 1990s, Rough Guides branched out of travel, with the publication of Rough Guides to World Music, Classical Music and the Internet. All three have become benchmark titles in their fields, spearheading the publication of a wide range of books under the Rough Guide name.

Including the travel series, Rough Guides now number more than 350 titles, covering: phrasebooks, waterproof maps, music guides from Opera to Heavy Metal, reference works as diverse as Conspiracy Theories and Shakespeare, and popular culture books from iPods to Poker. Rough Guides also produce a series of more than 120 World Music CDs in partnership with World Music Network.

Visit www.roughguides.com to see our latest publications.

Rough Guide credits

Text editor: Natasha Foges
Layout: Jessica Subramanian
Cartography: Karobi Gogoi
Picture editor: Ed Steer
Production: Rebecca Short
Proofreader: Karen Parker
Cover design: Dan May, Chloë Roberts
Photographers: Natascha Sturny and James McConnachie
Editorial: London Andy Turner, Keith Drew, Edward Aves, Alice Park, Lucy White, Jo Kirby, James Smart, Róisín Cameron, James Rice, Lara Kavanagh, Emma Traynor, Emma Gibbs, Kathryn Lane, Monica Woods, Mani Ramaswamy, Harry Wilson, Lucy Cowie, Alison Roberts, Joe Staines, Matthew Milton, Tracy Hopkins, Ruth Tidball; Delhi Madhavi Singh, Lubna Shaheen, Jalpreen Kaur Chhatwal
Design & Pictures: London Scott Stickland, Dan May, Diana Jarvis, Mark Thomas, Nicole Newman, Sarah Cummins, Emily Taylor, Delhi Umesh Aggarwal, Ajay Verma, Ankur Guha, Pradeep Thapliyal, Sachin Tanwar, Anita Singh, Nikhil Agarwal, Sachin Gupta

Production: Liz Cherry
Cartography: London Ed Wright, Katie Lloyd-Jones; Delhi Rajesh Chhibber, Ashutosh Bharti, Rajesh Mishra, Animesh Pathak, Jasbir Sandhu, Alakananda Roy, Swati Handoo, Deshpal Dabas
Online: London Faye Hellon, Jeanette Angell, Fergus Day, Justine Bright, Clare Bryson, Aine Fearon, Adrian Low, Ezgi Celebi; Delhi Amit Verma, Rahul Kumar, Narender Kumar, Ravi Yadav, Debojit Borah, Rakesh Kumar, Ganesh Sharma, Shisir Basumatari
Marketing & Publicity: London Liz Statham, Jess Carter, Vivienne Watton, Anna Paynton, Rachel Sprackett, Laura Vipond; New York Katy Ball, Judi Powers; Delhi Ragini Govind
Digital Travel Publisher: Peter Buckley
Reference Director: Andrew Lockett
Operations Assistant: Becky Doyle
Operations Manager: Helen Atkinson
Publishing Director (Travel): Clare Currie
Commercial Manager: Gino Magnotta
Managing Director: John Duhigg

Publishing information

This fourth edition published September 2010 by
Rough Guides Ltd,
80 Strand, London WC2R 0RL
Mindmill Corporate Tower, Plot No. 24A, Sector 16A, Film City, NOIDA 201301, India
Distributed by the Penguin Group
Penguin Books Ltd,
80 Strand, London WC2R 0RL
Penguin Group (USA)
375 Hudson Street, NY 10014, USA
Penguin Group (Australia)
250 Camberwell Road, Camberwell, Victoria 3124, Australia
Penguin Group (Canada)
195 Harry Walker Parkway N, Newmarket, ON, L3Y 7B3 Canada
Penguin Group (NZ)
67 Apollo Drive, Mairangi Bay, Auckland 1310, New Zealand
Cover concept by Peter Dyer.

Typeset in Bembo and Helvetica to an original design by Henry Iles.
Printed and bound in Singapore
© Martin Dunford 2010
Maps © Rough Guides
No part of this book may be reproduced in any form without permission from the publisher except for the quotation of brief passages in reviews.
352pp includes index
A catalogue record for this book is available from the British Library
ISBN: 978-1-84836-527-8
The publishers and authors have done their best to ensure the accuracy and currency of all the information in **The Rough Guide to Rome**, however, they can accept no responsibility for any loss, injury, or inconvenience sustained by any traveller as a result of information or advice contained in the guide.

1   3   5   7   9   8   6   4   2

Help us update

We've gone to a lot of effort to ensure that the fourth edition of **The Rough Guide to Rome** is accurate and up-to-date. However, things change – places get "discovered", opening hours are notoriously fickle, restaurants and rooms raise prices or lower standards. If you feel we've got it wrong or left something out, we'd like to know, and if you can remember the address, the price, the hours, the phone number, so much the better.

Please send your comments with the subject line "**Rough Guide Rome Update**" to ©mail @roughguides.com. We'll credit all contributions and send a copy of the next edition (or any other Rough Guide if you prefer) for the very best emails.

Have your questions answered and tell others about your trip at ®www.roughguides.com

Acknowledgements

Thanks as ever to Caroline, Daisy and Lucy, and also this time to Heather, for sampling vegan food, babysitting and all-round good company.

And of course to Natasha, who is a constant and well-informed editorial companion.

Readers' letters

Thanks to all the readers who have taken the time to write in with their comments and suggestions (and apologies if we've inadvertently omitted or misspelt anyone's name):

Julie Beckford, Hugo de Bondt, David Earley, Rebecca Harden, Brian Hutchin, Eefje van Ingen, Mr and Mrs T. Keegan, Sophia Lambert, Teresa Leese, Osmund Lind Iversen, Doreen Palmer, Gemma Rebello, Brian Shepherd and Pat Russell, Natalie Taylor.

Photo credits

SMALL PRINT

Index

Map entries are in colour.

INDEX

O

M

N

O

P

W

Map symbols

maps are listed in the full index using coloured text

– – –	Chapter boundary		⧫	Place of interest
═══	Major road		ⓘ	Information office
──	Minor road		⊠	Post office
▬	Pedestrianized road		⊞	Hospital
⊏ ⁼ ⁼ ⊐	Tunnel		🅿	Parking
⊓⊓⊓⊓	Steps		🚻	Toilets
- - - -	Path		▣	Restaurant
▬▬▬	Railway		◉	Hotel
──	River		⊼	Campsite
──	Wall		⊤	Fountain
)(	Bridge		✡	Synagogue
✈	Airport		⊞	Church
Ⓜ	Metro station		▬	Building
⊙	Memorial		⬭	Stadium
∴	Ruins		⁺⁺⁺	Christian cemetery
∩	Arch		▦	Park
⊠	Gate			

So now we've told you about the things not to miss, the best places to stay, the top restaurants, the liveliest bars and the most spectacular sights, it only seems fair to tell you about the best travel insurance around

WorldNomads.com

keep travelling safely

Recommended by Rough Guides

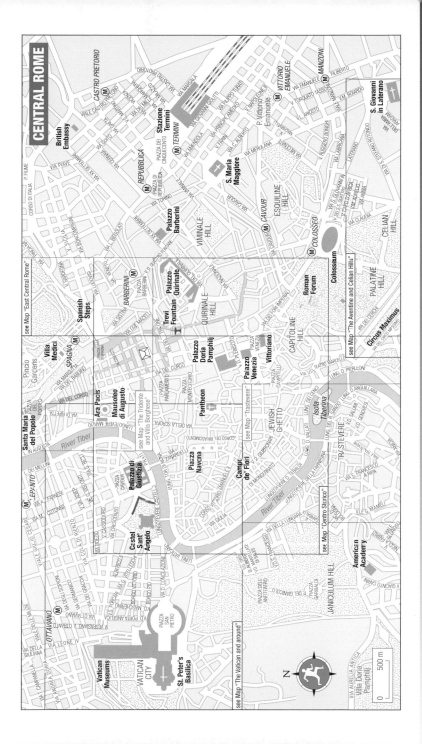

CENTRAL ROME

British Embassy

VIA PALESTRO

P. FIUME

VIA PIAVE

CORSO D'ITALIA

CASTRO PRETORIO

M

VIALE CASTRO PRETORIO

VICO. GIO. AMENDOLA

VIA VOLTURNO

VIA GAETA

VIA MONTEBELLO

VIA S. MARTINO D. BATT.

VIA VICENZA

VIA MILAZZO

VIA MARSALA

VIA CASTRO PRETORIO

VIA DEI MILLE

Stazione
Termini

VIA XX SETTEMBRE

VIA FLAVIA

VIA SERVIO TULLIO

VIA LUCANIA

VIA SICILIA

VIA CALABRIA

VIA SARDEGNA

VIA MARCHE

VIA PIEMONTE

VIA AURORA

VIA BASILICATA

VIA S. NICOLA DA TOLENTINO

VIA SAN BASILIO

VIA FRATTINA

Spanish
Steps

Villa
Medici

M
SPAGNA

Pincio
Gardens

PIAZZA DI SPAGNA

VIA MARGUTTA

VIA DEL BABUINO

Ara Pacis

Mausoleo
di Augusto

Santa Maria
del Popolo

PIAZZA
DEL
POPOLO

VIA DI RIPETTA

VIA DELLA SCROFA

VIA DEL CORSO

River Tiber

LUNGOTEVERE MARZIO

PIAZZA CAVOUR

VIA CRESCENZIO

Palazzo di
Giustizia

Castel
Sant'Angelo

LUNG.TEVERE CASTELLO

LUNGOTEVERE

VIA DELLA CONCILIAZIONE

M
LEPANTO

M
OTTAVIANO

VIA GIULIO CESARE

VIALE DELLE MILIZIE

VIALE GIULIO CESARE

VIA LEONE IV

V. VESPASIANO

V. GERMANICO

VIA COLA DI RIENZO

V.D. PORTA ANGELICA

VIA DI PORTA CAVALLEGGERI

Vatican
Museums

VATICAN
CITY

PIAZZA
SAN
PIETRO

St. Peter's
Basilica

see Map "The Vatican and around"

see Map "The Vatican and around"

REPUBBLICA

PIAZZA
DELLA
REPUBBLICA

M

VIA NAZIONALE

VIA TORINO

S. Maria
Maggiore

Palazzo
Barberini

VIMINALE
HILL

M
BARBERINI

PIAZZA
BARBERINI

Palazzo
Quirinale

Trevi
Fountain

Palazzo
Doria
Pamphilj

Pantheon

QUIRINALE
HILL

QUIRINALE
HILL

Palazzo
Venezia

Vittoriano

PIAZZA
VENEZIA

CAPITOLINE
HILL

Piazza
Navona

Campo
de' Fiori

JEWISH
GHETTO

Isola
Tiberina

TRASTEVERE

River Tiber

Roman
Forum

Colosseum

M
COLOSSEO

ESQUILINE
HILL

VIA CAVOUR

VIA NAPOLEONE III

VITTORIO
EMANUELE

M
MANZONI

VITTORIO
EMANUELE

M
MANZONI

S. Giovanni
in Laterano

CELIAN
HILL

PALATINE
HILL

Circus Maximus

AVENTINE
HILL

JANICULUM
HILL

American
Academy

VIA AURELIA ANTICA

Villa Doria
Pamphilj

see Map "East Central Rome"

see Map "The Trident and Villa Borghese"

see Map "The Aventine and Celian Hills"

see Map "Trastevere"

see Map "Centro Storico"

N

0   500 m

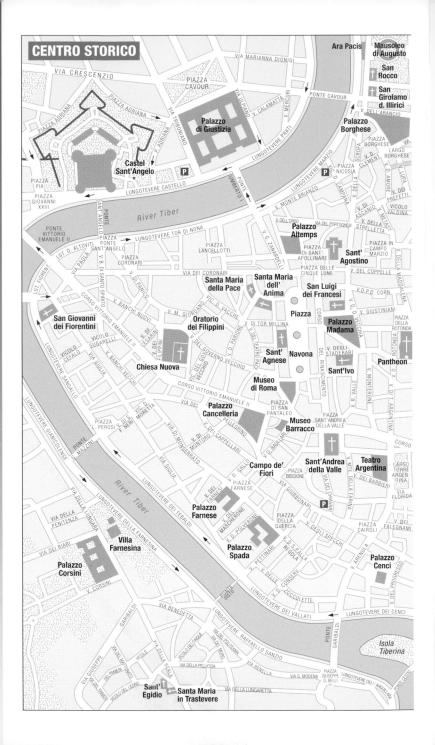

CENTRO STORICO

Ara Pacis

Mausoleo di Augusto

San Rocco

San Girolamo d. Illirici

VIA MARIANNA DIONIGI

VIA CRESCENZIO

PIAZZA CAVOUR

PONTE CAVOUR

Palazzo Borghese

PIAZZA ADRIANA

PIAZZA ADRIANA

Palazzo di Giustizia

PIAZZA BORGHESE

LARGO BORGHESE

V. D. CLEMENT

PIAZZA ADRIANA

V. DELL'ARANCIO

VIA DELLA SCROFA

Castel Sant'Angelo

PIAZZA PIA

PIAZZA GIOVANNI XXIII

LUNGOTEVERE CASTELLO

PIAZZA NICOSIA

V. DI CAMPANA

V. DELLA LUPA

V. DEI PREFETTI

VICOLO VALDINA

LUNGOTEVERE MARZIO

River Tiber

V. MONTE BRIANZO

V. DELL'ORSO

VIA DEL PORTOGHESI

V. DI ASCANIO

V. DELLA STRETTA

PONTE VITTORIO EMANUELE II

PONTE SANT'ANGELO

LUNGOTEVERE TOR DI NONA

PIAZZA LANCELLOTTI

Palazzo Altemps

PIAZZA DI SANT' APOLLINARE

PIAZZA DELLE CINQUE LUNE

Sant' Agostino

PIAZZA IN CAMPO MARZIO

V. DELLA MADDALENA

LGT. FIORENT

VIA PAOLA

V. B. DI SANTO SPIRITO

PIAZZA SANT'ANGELO

PIAZZA CORONARI

VIA DEI CORONARI

V. DI PANICO

Santa Maria della Pace

Santa Maria dell' Anima

V.D.P.D. CORN.

V. DEL COPPELLE

V. DI PANICO

CORSO VITTORIO EMANUELE II

V. BANCHI NUOVI

V. M. GIORDANO

San Luigi dei Francesi

V. GIUSTINIANI

San Giovanni dei Fiorentini

VICOLO CEFALO

VICOLO SUGARELLI

V. D. VACCHE

Oratorio dei Filippini

Piazza

PIAZZA DELLA ROTONDA

LUNGOTEVERE SANGALLO

V. BANCHI VECCHI

SS. CESARINI

DI TOR MILLINA

VIC. D. TEATRO PACE

Palazzo Madama

Pantheon

Chiesa Nuova

VIC. DEL GOVERNO VECCHIO

V. DI PARIONE

Sant' Agnese

Navona

V. DEGLI STADERARI

V. DEL RINASCIMENTO

Sant'Ivo

CORSO

V. DI ARGENTINA

CORSO VITTORIO EMANUELE II

Museo di Roma

PIAZZA DI SAN PANTALEO

V. R. VALLE

V. MONTERONE

PIAZZA L. PEROSI

V. DI MORETTA

VIA DEI BANCHI VECCHI

Palazzo Cancelleria

PELLEGRINO

PIAZZA SANT'ANDREA DELLA VALLE

Museo Barracco

CORSO

VIA GIULIA

VIA DEL MONSERRATO

V. DEI CAPPELLARI

Sant'Andrea della Valle

Teatro Argentina

LARGO TORRE ARGEN-TINA

V. DEI BARBIERI

LUNGOTEVERE DEI TEBALDI

V. DI GALLO

Campo de' Fiori

PIAZZA BISCIONE

V. DEI GIUBBONARI

VIA DEL MELONE

VIA FLORIDA

VIA DELLA PENITENZA

PIAZZA FARNESE

V. DEL MASCHERONE

Palazzo Farnese

V. DEL POLVERONE

PIAZZA DELLA QUERCIA

V. DEGLI SPECCHI

PIAZZA CAIROLI

V. DEL FALEGNAMI

VIA DELLA LUNGARA

VIA DELLA FARNESINA

Villa Farnesina

Palazzo Spada

V. PETTINARI

V. DELLE ZOCCOLETTE

V. DELLE CONSERV

REGOLA

V. DI S.PALLA

V. ARENULA

Palazzo Cenci

V. DEI RIARI

Palazzo Corsini

V. CORSINI

LUNGOTEVERE DELLA FARNESINA

PONTE MAZZINI

River Tiber

LUNGOTEVERE DEI VALLATI

LUNGOTEVERE DEI CENCI

V. DEL PROGRESSO

VIA BENEDETTA

LUNGOTEVERE RAFFAELLO SANZIO

PONTE GARIBALDI

Isola Tiberina

GARIBALDI

VIA GIUSEPPE

VICOLO

V. DELLA SCALA

V. DELLA PELLICCIA

VIA DEL CINQUE

VICOLO DEL CINQUE

VIALE DI TRASTEVERE

VIA G. MODENA

VIA RENELLA

PIAZZA GIUSEPPE G. BELLI

LUNGOTEVERE DEGLI ANGUILLARA

PONTE CESTIO

Sant' Egidio

Santa Maria in Trastevere

VIA DELLA LUNGARETTA

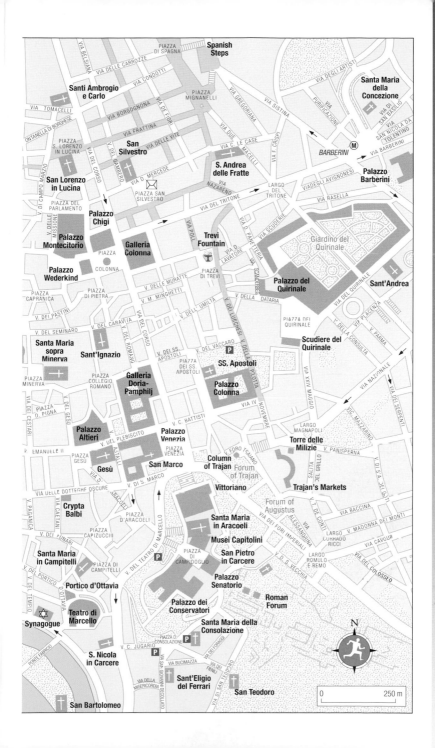

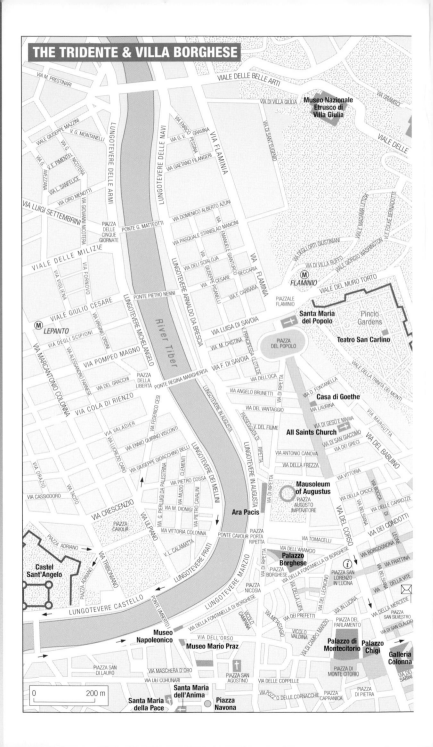

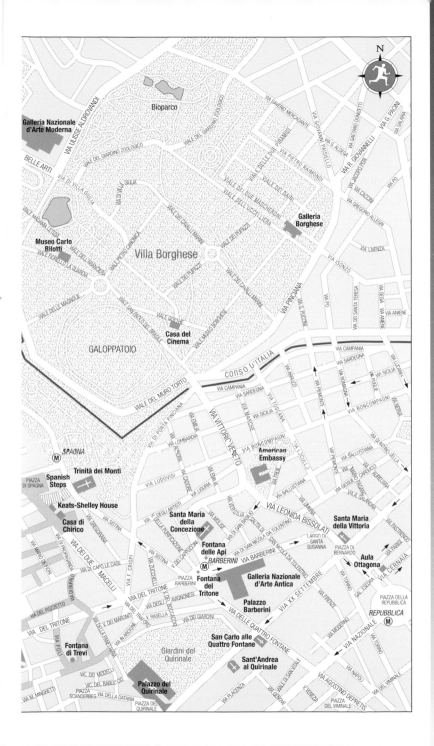

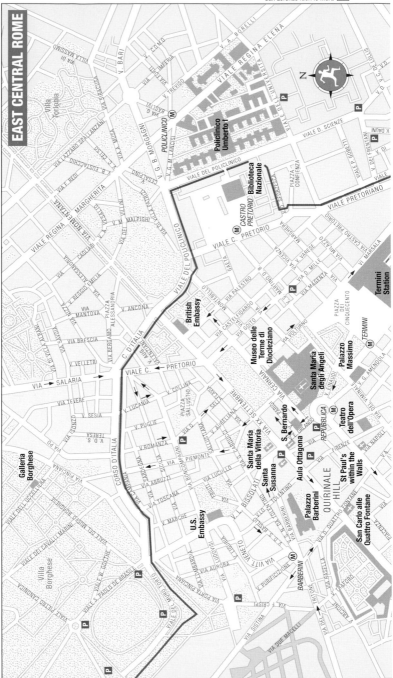

EAST CENTRAL ROME

N

Villa Torlonia

Villa Borghese

Galleria Borghese

Policlinico Umberto I

POLICLINICO M

Biblioteca Nazionale

CASTRO PRETORIO

CASTRO PRETORIO M

British Embassy

Museo delle Terme di Diocleziano

Santa Maria della Vittoria

Santa Susanna

S. Bernardo

Aula Ottagona

Santa Maria degli Angeli

Palazzo Massimo

Termini Station

TERMINI M

U.S. Embassy

Palazzo Barberini

St Paul's within the Walls

Teatro dell'Opera

REPUBBLICA M

QUIRINALE HILL

San Carlo alle Quattro Fontane

BARBERINI M

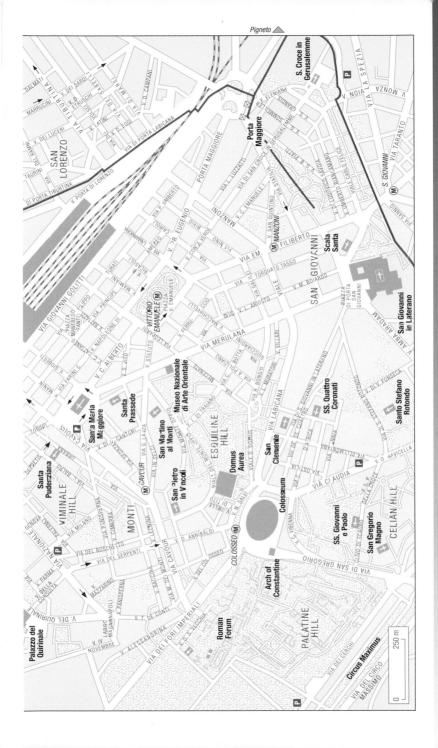

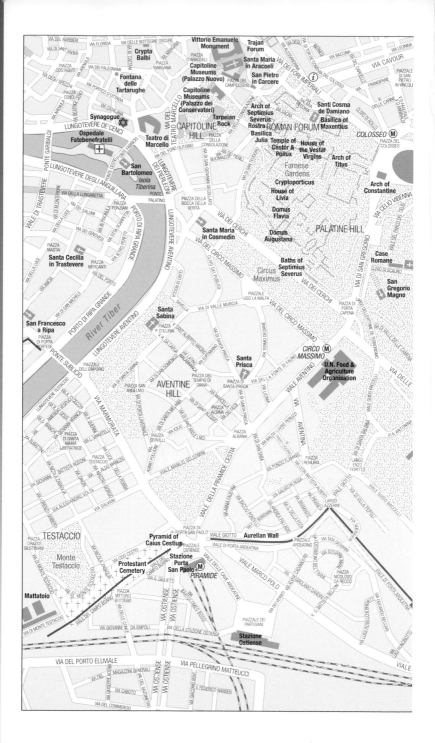

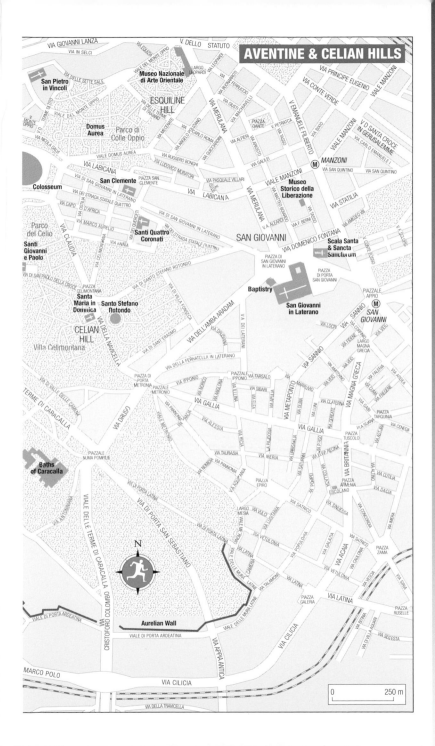

AVENTINE & CELIAN HILLS

VIA GIOVANNI LANZA
VIA IN SELCI
VIA DELLE SETTE SALE
V. DELLO STATUTO
VIA EQUIDIA
V. DI TITO
VIA GIOVANNI LANZA
LARGO LEOPARDI
VIA LEOPARDI
VIA PRINCIPE EUGENIO
VIALE MANZONI

San Pietro in Vincoli

Museo Nazionale di Arte Orientale

VIA CONTE VERDE

VIALE DEL MONTE OPPIO
VIALE DELLE TERME DI TRAIANO
VIA BUONARROTI
VIA FERRUCCI
VIA GIUSTI
VIA MACHIAVELLI
PIAZZA DANTE
V. PETRARCA

ESQUILINE HILL

V. EMANUELE FILIBERTO

V D SANTA CROCE IN GERUSALEMME
VIALE MANZONI
VIA CARLO EMANUELE I

Domus Aurea

Parco di Colle Oppio

VIA MERULANA
VIA MECENATE
VIA MICHELANGELO
VIA CARLO ROMA
VIA ALFIERI
VIA ARIOSTO
V. TASSO

VIALE DOMUS AUREA
VIA NICOLA SALVI
MONTE OPPIO
VIA GIACOMO BONI

VIA DOMUS AUREA
VIA RUGGERO BONGHI
VIA GALILEI

Ⓜ **MANZONI**
VIA SAN QUINTINO
VIA SAN QUINTINO

VIA LABICANA
VIA LUDOVICO MURATORI

Colosseum

San Clemente

PIAZZA SAN CLEMENTE
VIA DI SAN GIOVANNI IN LATERANO
VIA PASQUALE VILLARI
VIALE MANZONI

Museo Storico della Liberazione

VIA DEI STRADA STATALE QUATTRO
VIA CAPO D'AFRICA
VIA OSTILIA

VIA LABICANA
VIA MATTEO BOIARDO
VIA MERULANA
VIA F. BERNI
VIA ALBERTO

VIA STATILIA

VIA AMEDEO VIII
V. F. TASSO
V. S. CROCE

VIA MARCO AURELIO
VIA CELIMONTANA
VIA QUERCETI

Santi Quattro Coronati

VIA DI SAN GIOVANNI IN LATERANO
VIA DI STRADA STATALE QUATTRO

SAN GIOVANNI

VIA DOMENICO FONTANA

Scala Santa & Sancta Sanctorum

CONTE ROSSO

Parco del Celio

VIA CLAUDIA
VIA ANNIA

Santi Giovanni e Paolo

VIA DI SAN PAOLO DELLA CROCE
PIAZZA CELIMONTANA

PIAZZA DI SAN GIOVANNI IN LATERANO

PIAZZA DI PORTA SAN GIOVANNI

PIAZZALE APPIO

Santa Maria in Dominica

Santo Stefano Rotondo

Baptistry

Ⓜ **SAN GIOVANNI**

VIA SANNIO
VIA SANNIO
VIA COPPINO

CELIAN HILL

VIA DELLA NAVICELLA
VIA DI SANT'ERASMO

San Giovanni in Laterano

VIA DELL'AMBA ARADAM
V. DEI LATERANI
VIA DELLA FOSCA

VIA LOCRI
VIA FIDENE
VIA VEIO
VIA SATRICO

LARGO MAGNA GRECIA
VIA FALERIA
VIA AOSTA

Villa Celimontana

VIA DI VILLA FONSECA

VIA DELLA FERRATELLA IN LATERANO

PIAZZALE IPPONIO
VIA FARSALO

VIA METAPONTO
VIA MARRUVIO

VIA GABII
VIA CUMA
VIA TREBENE

MAGNA GRECIA

VIA DI VALLE DELLE CAMENE

PIAZZA DI PORTA METRONIA
VIA IPPONIO
PIAZZALE METRONIO
VIA NORICO
VIA ALESSINA

VIA SIBARI
VIA ELEA
VIA LUNI
VIA LUNI
VIA CELERE

PIAZZA TARQUINIA
VIA SUANA
VIA CENEDA

TERME DI CARACALLA

VIA DRUSO
VIALE METRONIO
VIA ALESSIA

VIA PADOSSA
VIA RIOIA
VIA LA PADOSSA

VIA GALLIA

VIA CLATERNA

PIAZZA TUSCOLO
VIA SUANA
VIA ASTURA

Baths of Caracalla

PIAZZALE NUMA POMPILIO

VIA TAURASIA
VIA IBERIA
VIA SATURNIA
VIA RUP PECINA

PIAZZA ARMENIA
VIA CONCORDIA

VIA CUTILIA
VIA DACIA

PIAZZA EPIRO

VIA AQUILANA
VIA PANNONIA
VIA NUMIDIA

VIA COLLATIA
VIA ERCOLANO

VIA BRITANNIA

LARGO MESIA
VIA VULCI
VIA SATRICO
VIA SINUESSA

VIALE DELLE MURA LATINE
VIA LUSITANIA
VIA POPULONIA
VIA GALATIA

PIAZZA ZAMA

VIA LATINA

PIAZZA GALERIA
VIA MESSA
VIA SIRA

PIAZZA RUSELLE

N

VIA DI PORTA LATINA
VIA DI PORTA LATINA
VIA VETULONIA
VIA LATINA
VIA TALAMONE
VIA VETULONIA

Aurelian Wall

VIALE DELLE MURA LATINE

VIALE DELL'ANTONINIANA
VIALE DELLE TERME DI CARACALLA
VIA CRISTOFORO COLOMBO

VIA DI PORTA ARDEATINA
VIALE DI PORTA ARDEATINA

APPIA ANTICA

MARCO POLO

VIA CILICIA

VIA CILICIA
VIA DI VILLA ADDARI
VIA SEG ESTA

VIA DELLA TRAVICELLA

| 0 | 250 m |

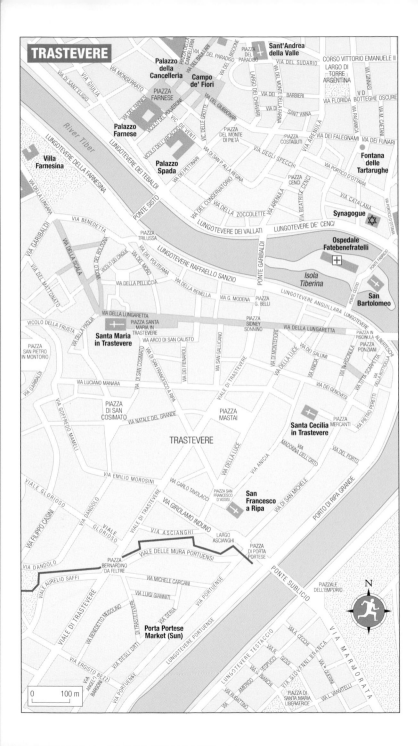

TRASTEVERE

Sant'Andrea della Valle

CORSO VITTORIO EMANUELE II

LARGO DI TORRE ARGENTINA

Palazzo della Cancelleria

Campo de' Fiori

PIAZZA FARNESE

Palazzo Farnese

Villa Farnesina

River Tiber

Palazzo Spada

Fontana delle Tartarughe

Synagogue

Ospedale Fatebenefratelli

Isola Tiberina

San Bartolomeo

Santa Maria in Trastevere

PIAZZA SIDNEY SONNINO

TRASTEVERE

PIAZZA DI SAN COSIMATO

PIAZZA MASTAI

Santa Cecilia in Trastevere

San Francesco a Ripa

Porta Portese Market (Sun)

N

0   100 m

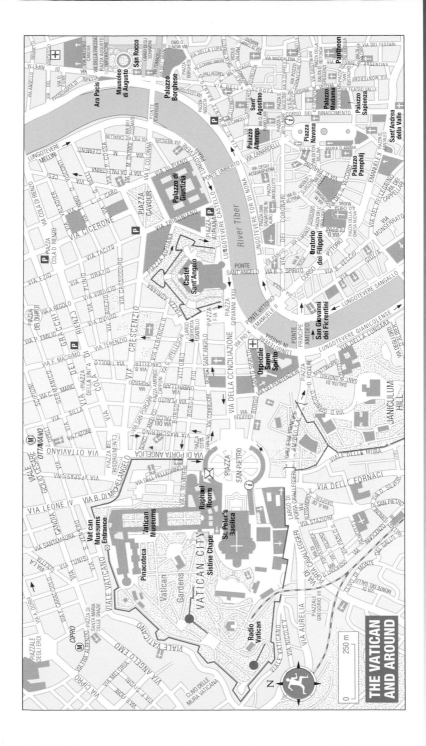

THE VATICAN
AND AROUND

0   250 m

N

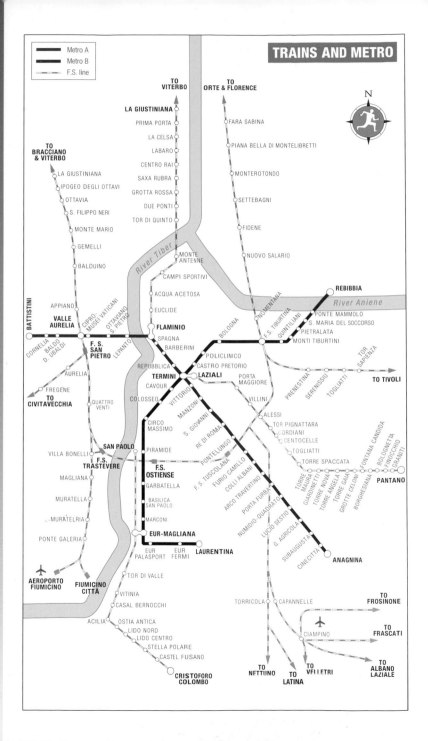